D1451952

Encyclopedia of Furnishing Textiles, Floorcoverings and Home Furnishing Practices, 1200–1950

Clive Edwards

Encyclopedia of Furnishing Textiles, Floorcoverings and Home Furnishing Practices, 1200–1950

LUND HUMPHRIES

Published in 2007 by
Lund Humphries
Gower House
Croft Road
Aldershot
Hampshire GU11 3HR

and

Lund Humphries
Suite 420
101 Cherry Street
Burlington
VT 05401–4405
USA

Lund Humphries is part of Ashgate Publishing

www.lundhumphries.com

British Library Cataloguing in Publication Data
Edwards, Clive, 1947–
Encyclopedia of furnishing textiles, floorcoverings and home furnishing practices, 1200–1950
1. Interior decoration – History – Encyclopedias
2. Furniture – Encyclopedias 3. Textile fabrics –
Encyclopedias 4. Floor coverings – Encyclopedias
I. Title
747'.03

ISBN: 978–0–75463–265–8

Library of Congress control number: 2007931459

Designed by Kevin Brown at park44.com
Edited by Linda Schofield and Howard Watson

Printed in United Kingdom

Contents

List of Figures and Plates

COLOUR PLATES

Guide to Use

The encyclopedia is planned with alphabetical entries A–Z. The topic titles are generally based on modern spelling. Generic topics, such as carpets, usually have a brief overview, then the reader is referred to detailed entries relating to specific or particular types. Some generic headings, such as protective furnishings, include case covers and loose covers as there are substantial overlaps that are easier to understand together. These individual entries direct the reader to the particular location. Many entries are cross-referenced in relation to their construction and/or fibre content. They are also referenced to associated topics. For example, curtain pole is also referenced to cornice pole, French rod and railway. Words that appear in bold in the text indicate their own individual entry. There are two bibliographical referencing systems: items cited in the entries are listed in the bibliography at the end of the encyclopedia. At the end of many entries, readers are referred to specialist reading and reference material as appropriate.

Introduction

The main aim of this book is to provide a comprehensive reference work of products and their uses in the area of furnishing textiles, interior furnishings and floorcoverings used in domestic interiors. The emphasis is on British and American domestic textiles and furnishings, and the consumption of them over the period 1200–1950, although references are made to European and other cultural influences, especially to India and the Far East.

The approach is based on the author's *Encyclopaedia of Furniture Materials, Trades and Techniques* (Ashgate, 2001) and therefore includes primary and secondary source material, patent information, contemporary descriptions of use, technical information, etc. It is intended to be of value to a wide range of readers including the casual visitor as well as the researcher.

Each entry gives a definition of the term, the etymology of the name and its origins, as appropriate. In the case of textiles, fibres and construction methods are noted. Most entries have examples of use taken from contemporary sources. The progress of a cloth through time and the change in yarns used are noted when possible.

The variable nature of spelling before the seventeenth century has meant that I have assumed responsibility for adjusting some of the variations that occur in early texts, as this ensures some degree of clarity, and thereby assists comprehension. In cases where the meaning is clear, I have left the original text.

It is important to point out what has been omitted. Any encyclopedia has to be selective to some degree. Technical construction details, descriptions and discussions of designs and designers are areas that are already well served. Particular specialist fields, such as Oriental carpets and rugs, lace, embroidery and needlework, are also generally beyond the scope of this work, although mention is made of some aspects of their use. As the book is a history rather than a guide to identification, the reader is referred to the many fully illustrated works that show images of textiles and their usage.

Finally, acknowledgement is made to the many scholars who have prepared the ground for this work through their own researches. Although the bibliography points to the works used, I should like to draw particular attention to earlier historians such as Percy Macquoid and Robert Symonds. More recently, the researches of Geoffrey Beard, Lesley Boynton, Christopher Gilbert, Peter Thornton and Annabel Westman have been invaluable to me, particularly in relation to historic upholstery and textile use. In terms of textiles themselves, the work of Pamela Clabburn, Donald King, Santina Levey, Florence Montgomery and Mary Schoeser has also been extremely helpful.

A – Z entries

Abaca
A fibre derived from the abaca plant (Manila hemp) that has been used for textiles, hats and matting, probably from the early eighteenth century. According to Caulfeild & Saward (1887), the fibre was introduced into France for dress, **tapestry** and **upholstery** work, and in India it was made into 'muslins and linen cloth' (p.1). In the 1950s, it was used as a **weft** in some upholstery fabrics (*The Mercury Dictionary of Textile Terms*, 1950).
See also **Hemp**, **Matting**, **Muslin**.

Abbot's cloth
Cotton, **linen** or **union** basket weave cloth used for hangings and **curtains**. Also known as **Monk's cloth** (USA).
See also **Weave: Basket**.

Abnakee rug
An American **hooked rug** made on a **jute**, **burlap/hessian** background. Twilled **wool flannel** is dyed and cut into strips and then hooked into the base. Bold designs are a feature of these rugs, which were popular in the early twentieth century. Many of the designs were developed from Native American imagery. A variation was discussed by Mabel Priestman who explained that 'the Abnakee rugs are made of all-wool unbleached flannel twill, which is afterwards dyed [to] the desired shade. These are among the most beautiful and durable of the rugs, their weight and beauty of colour making them a valued possession which will last a lifetime' (1910, p.161).
See also **Rag rug**.

FURTHER READING

Albee, H.R. (1901). *Abnakee Rugs*, Cambridge, Mass.: The Riverside Press.

Accordion pleat
An upholsterers' term for a **pleat** made by the application of heat and pressure to create an overlapping series. The knife-edge effects are used only in lightweight materials.

Accordion shade
Window **blinds** generally made of cloth that pulls up in narrow, sharply **pleated** folds. They hang flat when extended.
See also **Roman blind**.

Acetate
See **Art silk, Rayon**.

Acorn
A small wood or metal fitting fixed to the end of a **cord** to make the operation of a **blind** or similar contrivance easier. They are made in a similar shape and size to the oak tree acorn, hence the term.

Acrylic
A synthetic fibre made from acrylonitrile, which is derived from coal, petroleum and other materials. It is used in the manufacture of furnishing fabrics, **blankets** and **carpets**. It is warm, strong and crease resistant and is a popular **wool** substitute. It has relatively low abrasion resistance. Modacrylic (modified acrylic) is an **upholstery** yarn that is sometimes blended with other fibres. These yarns have been commercially available since the 1940s.
See also **Back-coated fabric**, **Foam-backed curtain**, **Pillow**, **Velvet**.

Adelaide mat
'This mat is made of a coarse twisted fringe of worsted threads, which is closely sewn upon a padded hempen back. This mat is always coloured and usually bordered, two colours being generally used in each mat.' (Brown & Gates, 1872, p.184.)

Adhesive
There are a number of applications for adhesives in the preparation of **drape** and **upholstery**. Firstly, they may be employed as a dressing on materials to dustproof or to stiffen them. Secondly, they are used to fix one material to a substrate, such as a fabric to a **cornice**, or a **skiver** to a desktop. Thirdly, they can act as a finish to a cut raw edge of a fabric (to stop the weave unravelling), or to set **embroidery** to prevent distortion caused by **stitch** tension, or to bond carpet **pile**. Fourthly, they might be used to fix one upholstery structure layer to another, such as **cushion foams**, or to attach **trimmings** and **passementerie**.

There are three main types of adhesive based on their origins. Firstly there are the proteins (animal glues) including gelatine, skin glue (rabbit, scotch), fish glues (isinglass) and casein. Secondly, the vegetable-based glues including polysaccharide gums, e.g. gum arabic or acacia gum, and vegetable mucilage such as starch. Thirdly, there are the newer synthetic glues including cellulose derivatives, hot melt polyamides and rubber cements.

These materials may be applied by brush, gun or spray and are often produced for specific roles.
See also **Bonded fabric**.

Afghan
See **Sofa rug**.

Agra cloth
A cloth that is as coarse as **burlap/hessian** (Hunter, 1918).

Aigrette
The feathers of birds, especially egret, osprey or ostrich, made into a tuft or plume shape to decorate the corners of four-poster beds. They spring out of the cups fitted on each corner of the bed. Aigrettes were most

popular in the seventeenth century.
See also **Bed furniture**, **Cup**, **Feather**.

Aiguillette
A pointed metal tag which is used to finish off a **cord**. The origin of the term reflects the French word for 'needle'. They are used extensively in military uniform work and therefore made a connection between decorative **needlework** and **passementerie**. In furnishing applications, they were used often in conjunction with other **trimmings** and decorative features.

Albatross
A lightweight, plain or **crêpe** weave textile usually of **wool** or blends with a napped surface. It was often used in the twentieth century for underwear and children's garments. It was also employed for **curtaining**: 'Albatross with taffeta bindings in various colors is an inexpensive and rather new winter hanging. Use a green albatross edged with black, a rose edged with a deeper tone, or a cream edged with blue, always taking care to bring out the warmest colors in the room.' (Foster, 1917, p.191.)

Allapeen (aka Alapeen)
A mixed cloth woven from **wool** and **silk**, or a **mohair** and **cotton** blend that was apparently similar to **poplin**. It was chiefly used for men's clothing but was also sold by upholsterers. References are found from the 1730s but appear to die out by the latter part of the century. In 1751, Thomas Baxter, an upholder (upholsterer) of Boston, Mass., held in his shop the following: '88yds of allepeen totalling £63.10.0' (Cummings, 1964, p.15).

Alentours
A **border** for tapestries differing from standard borders that often simulated picture frames. The alentours, first developed at the **Gobelins tapestry** factory *c.*1714, simulated a decorated panel with *trompe-l'oeil* figures and flowers. The alentours filled a large part of the work so that the central motif representing a framed picture was shown off against the alentours frame. The benefit of the process was to reduce the complexity of the design, allowing less experienced workers to produce this part and also enabling customers to specify sizes.
See also **Gobelins tapestry**, **Tapestry**.

Algerian (aka Algerienne)
A **woollen** fabric that originally came from Algiers. In the later nineteenth century the name referred to a striped **cotton** (or cotton and **silk**) cloth used for covering sofas, hangings and **curtains**.

Algerian appears to have been introduced into Europe in the mid-nineteenth century, when it received significant acclaim from design critics. Charles Eastlake commented that it was 'made chiefly of cotton and was also designed with horizontal stripes of colour on an unbleached white ground … and had the additional advantage of being washable' (1878, p.99).

Around the same time, the American critic, Clarence Cook, extolled its virtues: 'The stuffs called Algeriennes, made of silk and cotton, in gay but well-harmonized stripes are serviceable, and look well to the last' (1878, p.67). In the same year, the amateur decorator and author, Lady Barker, commented on the use of 'Algerine': 'the other [bed], of modern carved oak, had been copied from the pattern of an old settle. It was low and wide, with only one deep well-stuffed mattress, round which an Algerine striped blue and white cotton cloth had been wrapped.' (1878, p.43.) By 1887, its use seems to have gone beyond interiors. Caulfeild & Saward described it as having:

> Alternate stripes of rough knotted cotton web and one of a delicate gauze-like character, composed of silk. It is employed for the making of women's burnouses, in imitation of those worn by the Arabs. It used to be produced in scarlet and creamy-white, as well as in the latter only. (1887, p.4.)

Although used for dressmaking, it remained a favourite for furnishers of the period. The French historian Henri Havard (1887) explained that 'Algerienne' was particularly suitable for **portières**, curtains and **wall coverings**, as well as for covering sofas and divans. In the USA, it was specifically used for **awnings** and curtains. By 1950, it was defined as a French coating fabric made of alternate stripes (*The Mercury Dictionary of Textile Terms*, 1950).
See also **Timbuctoo**.

Algerian fibre
The shredded leaves of the North African palm grass *Chamareops humilus*, which are made to curl in a process similar to that used on animal **hair**. It is sometimes dyed black. The fibre was used in **upholstery** work as a first filling because it has good resilient properties over a long period. It was certainly known in the later nineteenth century and was used for upholstery work well into the twentieth century.

Alhambra quilt
A **jacquard** figured fabric with a plain ground **weft** and two **warps**. The cloth is woven by a combination of jacquard for the figure and healds

1. Alhambra quilt detail (E. Ostick, The Draper's Encyclopaedia, *1955)*

for the plain foundation, with a warp for each. The figuring warp is usually two-ply and coloured, while the ground warp is single and undyed. The figuring warps float on the back of the cloth when not required for the design. The figuring is often very large with only one repeat to a **quilt**. The Army & Navy Stores in London sold both blue-and-white and red-and-white Alhambra quilts from their 1907 catalogue.

Alhambra was also a generic name for low-priced bed quilts, which were heavy enough to provide some warmth. Many were woven with **borders** and a centred ornamental design (French, 1937, p.135). In 1950, the Alhambra was described as 'the cheapest quilt made and very popular' (*The Mercury Dictionary of Textile Terms*, 1950). In 1955, it was noted that the Alhambra quilts had recently reappeared. It was explained that Alhambra bedcovers were an example of the extra warp method of textile decoration (Ostick, 1955, pp 319 and 355).
See also **Bedspread**.

Alligator cloth
In 1950 this was described as 'a trade name for a coarse plain-weave cotton fabric coated with a varnish finish to imitate alligator skin that was used for upholstery'. (*The Mercury Dictionary of Textile Terms*, 1950.)

Alpaca
A woven fabric using yarns spun from the very fine **wool** of the alpaca, a Peruvian sheep species. It was first introduced in the 1830s and used occasionally on side chairs in the nineteenth century. The yarns were also used in **Utrecht velvet** production in the nineteenth century. In the mid-twentieth century, the yarns were sometimes combined with **cotton** and then roller-printed with small patterns for use as **casement curtains**.

Aluminium coated lining
A **curtain lining** material where the inside-face is coated with aluminium particles to exclude heat, light or cold. The visible side is usually cream-coloured, woven **cotton sateen**. It was introduced in the later twentieth century.
See also **Insulated lining**.

Alva marina (aka Ulva marina, Zostera)
A name for dried **seaweed** that was prepared and used as a coarse **upholstery** and bedding **stuffing**. It had very poor resistance and durability. Nevertheless, it was used for a range of upholstery tasks. Early in the nineteenth century, the Birmingham furnishing draper, Thomas Harris, advertised the sale of Alva marina amongst many other upholstery requisites (John Johnson Collection, Bodleian Library Oxford University). In 1844, Webster & Parkes talked of the upholstery use of seaweed as follows: 'Well spoken of as a stuffing for mattresses; does not harbour vermin ... is tolerably light and soft... If not sufficiently washed is said to attract moisture, owing to a little salt remaining in it' (p.297).

The 1853 bedding catalogue of the London firm, Heal, lists the following mattress types based on fillings: 'palliasse / Alva marina / bordered flock / coloured wool/white wool/ upper white wool (to use over feather beds) / Best French / Horse hair / spring mattresses' (Heal, 1972). This seems to show the lowly place Alva marina held in the pecking order. In 1866, Alva marina was defined as a pseudo-fibre in the *Treasury of Botany* and was described as follows:

> The common sea wrack has leaves varying from one to several feet in length, and rarely more than a quarter of an inch broad. These are commonly used for packing, and by upholsterers for stuffing mattresses and cushions, being sold for that purpose under the names of Ulva marina or Alva marina. (Lindley, 1866.)

It was later pointed out that 'alva marina has been objected to for stuffing mattresses as likely to absorb damp; the saline properties would, nevertheless, prevent its giving cold. Other weeds and mosses, the products of Italy and America, are used for the same purpose, and are cheaper than horse-hair and wool' (Bitmead, 1912, p.17). It was generally out of use by the early twentieth century.
See also **Grass: Sea wrack grass**, **Mattress**, **Moss**.

Amamee
Indian (Bengal) plain-weave **cotton** cloth used for clothing and furnishings. In 1924, it was defined as 'smooth, closely woven cotton cloth from Bengal. The coarser grades were called Tissuti and the finer ones Bissuti. Used for shirts, bedcovers, curtains and also for printing' (Harmuth, 1924, p.6).

Amens
A figured **worsted** cloth with a double or treble **warp**, often **brocaded** or figured. The name probably derived from Amiens where it was first made. It was occasionally used in the later eighteenth century for **upholstery**.

American cloth
See **Oilcloth**.

American Oriental
An American trade name for machine woven **carpets** and **rugs** that have been processed to imitate washed Oriental rugs.

> There are rugs made with an artificial sheen or lustre in imitation of genuine oriental [rugs]. They may be of Wilton, Axminster or velvet weaves. Some have the regular appearance of power-loom rugs on the back; others show the pattern clear through as do the genuine orientals. These rugs are the so-called 'American orientals'. They vary widely in their quality the finest being very beautiful and durable, with all the outward appearance of colour lustre and design of the genuine. The poorest being distinctly inferior... The most common method [of creating an artificial sheen] is the employment of the same chemical wash method used on true, modern orientals. (Bennett, 1937, p.111.)

American tapestry
A process of **tapestry** making, using a **silk warp** and needle-worked **embroidery** silks rather than a shuttle. This process was developed by Candace Wheeler in the latter part of the nineteenth century, and sold through the Associated Artists' atelier. They were sold as 'American tapestries made by embroidery alone' (Burke, 1986, p.98–102).

Anabasse
An eighteenth-century Lancashire **blanket** material that imitated a blue-and-white striped loincloth material from India. By the twentieth century, *The Mercury Dictionary* defined it as a striped blanket material that was made in France for use in her colonies (*The Mercury Dictionary of Textile Terms*, 1950).

Animal skin
Skins including furs, complete with **hair** or **wool**, are untanned hides

that are cleaned and dressed. The subcutaneous side is very thoroughly scraped and dried. After drying, the skin is manipulated to soften the handling. Sometimes the skins are oil or alum dressed on the flesh side to improve their qualities, and they are often lined.

For centuries animal skins have been used in furnishings, often for bedding and for floorcovers. Writing in the twelfth century, Alexander Neckam discussed the making of a bed: '...next, a coverlet of green cloth or of coarse wool, of which the fur lining is badger, cat, beaver or sable, should be put' (Holmes, 1952, pp 82–3). The 1386 inventory of Arnold Monteney listed: '1 covering of pure miniver [white fur] of 26 timbers [40 skins is 1 timber] and 38 skins, and 1 fur of martens of 60 skins and 1 fur of squirrel of 5 timbers and 15 skins and 1 covering of conies' (Steer, 1958, p.155).

Although used on the floors during the Middle Ages, they seem to have gone out of use by the seventeenth century, certainly in fashionable homes. One example that seems exceptional is 'one baire skin with the haire on' in the Great Closet of Kensington Palace in 1697 (Thornton, 1978, p.148).

By the nineteenth century, they appear to have been revived as interior furnishings. The use of small skins as floor **rugs** grew. In 1813, the Duke of Buccleuch's London house sported '2 white Sheep Skin door rugs' and 'a brown sheepskin rug for stairs' (Ellwood, 1995, p.197). In 1827, John Wilson, a cabinet-maker and upholsterer from Liverpool, offered for sale 'brown Lapland rugs, white sheepskin rugs' (*DEFM*, 1986, p.98). A little later, J.C. Loudon discussed the use of skins as mats:

> One of the best for a cottager's bedroom door is a black or grey sheepskin with all the wool on. A black or dark goatskin makes also a very handsome mat. Skins with white or other coloured hair or wool make very handsome mats but are hardly advisable for a cottage, as they require washing. (1839, p.347.)

Accent rugs made from natural shaped or formed animal skins were a feature of the later nineteenth-century interior, especially in the 1880s and 1890s. In 1884, the London retailers, Maple and Co, recommended sheepskins, goatskins and the skins of the wolf and the bear for use in the interior. They went on to say that 'a favourite arrangement of the bearskin is a black centre with a brown surround, or vice versa; or the complete skin of a "grizzly" mounted on black' (Maple and Co, 1884, p.36). The American authors, Williams & Jones, in their work, *Beautiful Homes,* suggested a range of animal skins including sheep or lamb as well as game animals, but also listed common skins, 'such as rabbit, squirrel, opossum, raccoon and even the domestic cat' (1878, p.306). They commented that, 'many may smile to see that pussy may be made into a thing of use and beauty but if the furrier will use her skin for muffs and tippets, surely we may for rugs etc' (1878, p.306). This type of practice was apparently also fashionable in England. Ward & Lock's *Home Book* (1880) recalled the use of 'the skin of a favourite brown setter of Irish breed [which] lay before the washstand in perfect harmony'. The skins of more exotic animals, such as leopards and tigers, were also featured in later nineteenth-century interiors, often being examples of trophies from hunting.

In the twentieth century, various sheepskins and goatskins have been popular as floor and bed rugs. Other animal skins (apart from those converted to leather) have also been used for **upholstery**, including zebra, pony and cow skins, which have all been used as seat coverings. See also **Leather**.

Antimacassar (aka 'Tidy' or Chair back)

A device to protect the upper back portions of upholstered chairs.

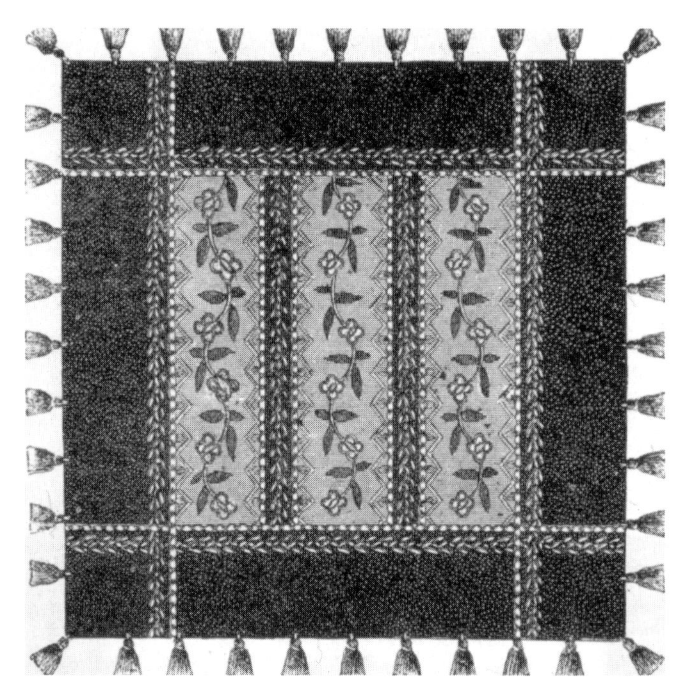

2. Antimacassar design (S. Caulfeild & B. Saward, The Dictionary of Needlework, *1887)*

Although strictly referring to the nineteenth century, these **protective furnishings** had their origins in the eighteenth century. During that period, **silk** flaps intended to match the main covering were fitted to **upholstery** to protect it from wig powder.

In the nineteenth century, antimacassars were a decorative flap of textile that did not match the upholstery but were designed to protect the fixed upholstery covers of furnishings from spoiling from the effects of macassar oil used by men as a hair dressing. The original antimacassar was almost invariably made of white crochet-work, very stiff, hard and quite uncomfortable. By the third quarter of the nineteenth century, they became less fussy and were made of soft coloured stuffs, usually worked with a simple pattern in tinted wools or silk. Robert Edis recommended that they should be 'of some good embroidered stuff or well-designed crewel work, fixed securely to the chair or sofa backs, so as not to be liable to be carried off as pendants to the fringe of a lady's dress or to the buttons of a gentleman's coat' (1881, p.193).

A more serviceable, though less attractive, alternative to the antimacassar was suggested in 1840. *The Workwoman's Guide* proposed 'a kind of case of Holland to fit half way down the [back] cushion which protects the cover from being soiled by the head on leaning back. Each arm chair should have two or three of these cases for wash and wear' (Hale, p.206). Antimacassars remained popular well into the twentieth century and were usually associated with the three-piece suite. See also **Antimacassar pin**, **Headrest**.

Antimacassar pin

U-shaped pin designed to hold **antimacassars** in place.

Antique satin

See **Satin**.

Antique taffeta

See **Taffeta**.

Antique textile

Although furnishing textiles have been recycled for centuries, it was during the second half of the nineteenth century that the use of antique textiles in furnishing schemes became a particular fashion. Unwanted shawls, **lace** and embroideries were all used to drape furniture or to be applied to **portières**, **curtains**, etc. Not everyone considered this to be appropriate. Writing in 1889, in her *Art of Decoration*, Mrs Haweis commented: 'the recent fashion of covering chair-seats with exquisite antique silks, old brocades and delicate feather-work is a waste of good things which were better applied elsewhere' (p.219). On the other hand, another female commentator, Mrs Watson, enthusiastically explained in her *The Art of the House* the attraction of old fabrics. Talking of **fireplace curtains**, she suggested that the 'things that are pre-eminently more excellent for this purpose are antique brocades or broderies whose dyes have been harmonized, whose designs are blurred by time, the master-decorator' (1897, p.487).

In the USA, a similar taste was evident. In *Our Homes and Their Adornments*, Almon Varney discussed the use of 'very old portieres ... brought home by travellers from the East, including Smyrna, and imported in great quantities'. He added that 'stripes of old woollen stuff, loosely caught together by coarse woollen cord, and embroidered evidently by hand [in] odd combinations of red, black and white, can be seen in fashionable houses' (1883, pp 262–3).

Old fabrics were again used in decorative interiors in the 1920s. The American *House Beautiful Furnishing Annual* of 1926 commented that antique fabrics were: 'procurable, in better or worse states of preservation, and in the case of those of the seventeenth and eighteenth centuries, in some numbers'. This taste encouraged manufacturers to produce imitations and copies using old designs as well as employing 'dusty' colours and shabby effects. In 1950, *The Mercury Dictionary of Textile Terms* commented on textiles woven with slub yarns as being interesting through the 'wonderful "shabby" effect that has been achieved. None of these looks in the least new ... and ... appear as having been mellowed by time' (Schoeser and Rufey, 1989, p.176).

The revival of a taste for Victorian interiors from the 1960s again encouraged a taste for 'antique' textiles, which have become collectables in their own right as well as providing decorative accessorisation. Reissues of woven or printed designs from the archives of manufacturers, collections or museums, sometimes called 'document fabrics', also found a niche in furnishing schemes of the second half of the twentieth century. The demand for accurate textiles to furnish historic interiors has, in part, prompted this, but commercial demand has also been a factor.

See also **Brocade**.

Appliqué (aka Laid-on work)

Appliqué is a method of **embroidery** decoration that is applied onto the base material rather than worked into it directly. Although it may refer to other materials, it usually suggests various textiles cut out in decorative shapes, which are then applied onto the surface of another fabric with an embroidery **stitch** or by **couching**. By using contrasting colours and fabric types often upon a plain ground, the result can create a three-dimensional effect. During the Elizabethan and early Stuart times, plant and animal motifs, worked on **canvas**, were often cut out and fixed to plain ground fabrics, frequently **velvet**, for use as **cushions** and hangings. The Spangled Bed at Knole, covered in red **satin** with applied **cloth of gold** and silver, made in the early seventeenth century, is a superb example of the process. Other fine examples are found in Hardwick Hall, Derbyshire.

3. Appliqué pattern designed for a cushion (S. Caulfeild & B. Saward, The Dictionary of Needlework, *1887)*

The practice never went away entirely and became fashionable again in the nineteenth century. Mrs Orrinsmith, writing in *The Drawing Room*, suggested that 'heavy patterns worked upon Holland, cut out and sewn on serge and cloth, with an edging of filoselle or twisted silk make decorations suitable for portières' (1877, p.73). In the following year, American author, Hudson Holly, favourably remarked on **curtains** made of 'unbleached linen, with stripes of blue and red flannel sewed upon its surface and [with] black lines of narrow velvet' (1878, p.213).

In the twentieth century, 'appliqué **borders** applied to ready-made curtains of **Bolton sheeting**, taffeta or satin rep' were offered for sale (Williamson & Cole Co, 1912). Appliqué was also recommended in the 1930s as a particularly suitable effect on **pelmets**, especially if it was carried out in a free manner and not as a set pattern.

Reverse appliqué (découpé) has a fabric sewn underneath the top cloth, which is cut away to reveal the under cloth.

See also **Bobbin net**, **Couching**, **Lace**, **Needlework**, **Needlework seating**, **Patchwork**, **Trimming**, **White-work**.

FURTHER READING

Nevinson, J.L. (1936). 'Late sixteenth century appliqué work in Scotland', *Burlington Magazine*, 68, April, pp 170–6.

Aquatic grass

Any grassy plant that grows in or near water is called an aquatic. It produces fibres that may be used in matting or **upholstery**.

See also **Grass**, **Matting**.

Arabian lace

See **Lace**.

Archway curtain

Curtains that are planned and cut to fit interior architectural features such as archways and curved detail, as opposed to a simple rectangular drape over the space. They were especially popular during the late

nineteenth century and early twentieth century as framing devices for internal doors, passages and openings.
See also **Portière**.

Argentine cloth
See **Tarlatan**.

Argyle gimp
See **Gimp**.

Armazine (aka Armozeen)
Armazine (*armoisin* in French) is a lightweight **silk taffeta**-like fabric, often black. Although used for clerics' gowns and mourning attire, it was also used for hangings and **curtains**.

By the eighteenth century, it was imported into England from Lyon in France, as well as from Italy and the East Indies. Postlethwayt identifies two varieties: *arains*, which was striped or **checked**, and *damaris*, which was flowered. He also described 'armozeen' in general terms as a 'silk stuff, or kind of taffety, of an indifferent goodness. It is made at Lyons and in several places in Italy'. East Indian armozeens were 'slightly inferior to those made in Europe and of an inferior quality. Their colours, and particularly the crimson and red, are commonly false, and they have but little gloss and no brightness at all' (Postlethwayt, 1751). The Chiswick House inventory of 1770 shows that there were 'three blue Armozeen festoon window curtains' (Rosoman, 1986, p.98). In 1752, Richard Carr, mercer, was paid £34.2s.0d. for 62 yards of Armurine, supplied to Lady Leicester at Holkham House (Beard, 1997, p.304).

In the nineteenth century, a heavier ribbed version of armazine was used for **portières**, curtains and covers. However, Caulfeild & Saward defined it as 'a strong make of thick plain black corded silk, a kind of taffeta, employed for scholastic gowns and for hatbands and scarves at funerals' (1887, p.14).

Armure
A broad class of fabrics with 'pebbled' surfaces that are produced by figures or textures woven on a **rep** base or a figured weave. The name may be derived from an original fabric, which was woven with a small-interlaced design of chain armour and used for military equipment during the Crusades, or alternatively from the French word *armoires* for coat-of-arms. Caulfeild & Saward suggested that it was derived from the French *armure*, where the name was applied to **silk** or **wool** and meant a small pattern. They also noted a satin armure and armure bosphore (1887, p.14). Originally, armure was a heavy silk fabric with this pebbly effect. It was later made from a range of fibres, but especially **cotton**, silk, wool, **rayon**, synthetics and blends. Woven in plain, twill or rib, the background often has a small pattern made with **warp** floats on the surface to give a raised effect. 'When a jacquard figure is introduced on a rep background, it is called armure.' (Denny, 1928, p.83)

In America during the early twentieth century, armure was recommended for **couch covers** and **portières** (Dyer, *c.*1923, p.202). It was also used for other furnishing purposes. Mrs Northend discussed a room where 'One ivory enamel dressing table has the fronts of drawers, sides and top of blue silk figured armure.' (1921, p.256.) In England, armure was particularly recommended for loose covers and portières (Smithells, 1950). In the 1950s, it was mainly used for seating materials and, on occasion, **bedspreads** and slipcovers.

Arras
A generic name used in England for **wall coverings** or hanging screens placed around the walls of a room. Arras was a recognised source of such materials. Tapestry factories were established in Arras during the late thirteenth century, and were so well known that the town gave its name to any wall covering used in the period. By the mid-fifteenth century, the factories had declined in popularity as **Tournai** overtook them, but they remained in business until early in the sixteenth century and the term has since referred to tapestry of any manufacture.

The difference between arras and tapestry appears to be one of quality, although the distinctions are blurred. By 1558, arras was defined as tapestry with gold [thread] called Arras and was therefore more valued than **hair** or **wool** tapestry work. Arras was used in a range of interior situations including hangings, **cupboard cloths**, **bed furniture**, **costers**, **dorcers** and **cushions**. An early reference is from 1397, where the will of John of Gaunt listed 'drapes d'Arras'. Henry VI had 'one tapite d'arras pur le cupbord' (*Rot. Parl.*, II, Henry VI), whilst Cecily, Duchess of York, owned 'a bed of arras', and Lord Richard Scrope of Bolton owned four 'costers de opera d'arras' (Leaf, p.6). A little later, the *Wardrobe Accounts of Edward IV* (1461–1483) listed an arras-mender who was 'hourly in the wardrobe for working upon arras and tapestry' (Nicholas, 1830). Over 100 years later, a different use was listed in the 1611 Hatfield inventory: 'three window Clothes of Arras worke wrought with silk and lyned with satten abridges' (Beard, 1997, p.286).

Counterfeit arras was a name given to a distinct material that was different from tapestry and also from **painted cloth** upon which the decorative scenes, familiar from tapestry work, were painted. It seems likely that counterfeit arras was a fine quality tapestry but without the metallic threads as in the authentic arras. In the will of Henry Sever, dated 1471, he wishes his '*banker de counterfeit arras dividanture inter servientes meos*' (*Testamenta Ebor.*, vol.III, p.189). In 1507, the Archbishop of York, being in debt to the King, surrendered his effects including 'all the Arras as well the fine arras as counterfeit Arras' (*Testamenta Ebor.*, vol.IV, p.311).

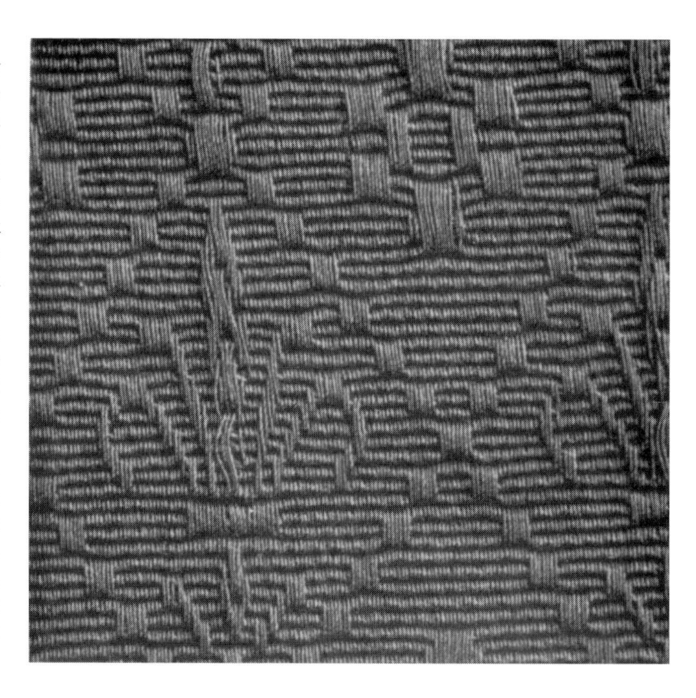

4. Example of armure weave showing the distinctive raised effects (G.L. Hunter, Decorative Textiles, Coverings for Furniture etc., *1918)*

See also **Arras cloth**, **Tapestry**, **Verdure**, **Window cloth**.

FURTHER READING

Campbell, T. (1995–6). 'Tapestry quality in Tudor England: problems of terminology', *Studies in the Decorative Arts*, 3, pp 29–50.

Arras cloth

A twentieth-century term for a loosely woven **jute** cloth produced in a range of widths and shades and used for **curtains**, and table and cushion covers (*The Mercury Dictionary of Textile Terms*, 1950). It appears that it was particularly popular in the USA. The American author, Mabel Priestman, extolled the virtues of arras cloth early in the twentieth century.

> Arras cloth, or craftsman's canvas, has been a joy to the privileged few who happened to know where and how it could be obtained. Happily, it can now be bought at one or more shops in every city. It is very like every-day burlap in weave, and is made of a mixture of linen and cotton. It possesses a slight variation in texture that is very desirable in draperies. It is made in Scotland in a wide range of colors, which fade so little with years of wear, that the effect is only a softening of tone. It is now obtainable in linen color as well as the art shades. People who have always appreciated linens enjoy those with a coarse mesh called 'bloom linens'. They are an inspiration for making appliqué upon Arras cloth or other shades of linen. (Priestman, 1910, p.119.)

Arras cloth was particularly associated with the American Mission style and oak furniture of the early twentieth century.
See also **Arras**.

Artificial horsehair

An imitation of horsehair made from viscose **rayon** of a heavy denier with either a round or flat filament. Another version was described in 1924: 'Certain grasses are treated for a brief period with concentrated sulphuric acid or chloride of zinc, rendering the fiber very strong, elastic and similar in appearance to real horsehair.' (Harmuth, 1924, p.9)
See also **Hair**, **Haircloth**.

Art canvas

See **Craftsman canvas**.

Art embroidery (aka Art needlework)

A category of secular needlework that developed out of ecclesiastical embroidery during the second half of the nineteenth century. The use of **silk**, **crewel** threads and **appliqué** techniques often distinguish it. The 'art' designation referred to the freedom of the embroiderer to select not only the design, but also the **stitch** type direction and colouring to be used. *The Dictionary of Needlework* published in 1887 explained that art needlework was a term 'recently introduced ... for all descriptions of needlework that spring from the application of a knowledge of design and colouring, with skill in fitting and executing' (Caulfeild & Saward, p.14). The art embroidery movement was an attempt to restore secular embroidery to its proper place in the arts. It was also partly a reaction by a small group to the excesses of the mid-nineteenth century **Berlin wool-work**, aniline **dyes** and unsophisticated patterns.

The Royal School of Needlework was the first to initiate such moves, and these were followed by regional British developments such as the Leek Embroidery Society. This movement also found followers in the USA where schools of needlework were established in Philadelphia, Boston, Chicago and elsewhere. The London-based School of Art Needlework (later the Royal School) promoted the serious study of old needlework and its adoption in the period from 1872 onwards. The revival of art needlework was a result of the developments of ecclesiastical embroidery, which itself paved the way for development in twentieth-century embroidery work.
See also **Embroidery**, **Needlework**.

FURTHER READING

Alford, Lady M. (1886). *Needlework as Art*, London: Sampson Low Marston.

Lambert, Miss (1842). *Handbook of Needlework*, London: John Murray.

Morris, B. (1962). *Victorian Embroidery*, London: Herbert Jenkins.

Schoeser, M. (1998). *The Watts Book of Embroidery, English Church Embroidery 1833–1953*, London: Watts and Co (especially ch.2, C. Weaver, 'My life is an embroidery').

Art linen

Plain-weave **linen** cloth, woven with even threads that are particularly suitable for **embroidery**, as they are easy to draw out. It is supplied either bleached or coloured, and is commonly used to produce embroidered **cushion** covers, **tablecloths** and centres. Art linen was especially popular in the early twentieth century.

Art muslin

A loose term for fine **cotton** dyed or printed fabrics with a glazed finish, used in the **upholstery** trade (*The Mercury Dictionary of Textile Terms*, 1950). In the 1908 novel, *Anne of Green Gables* by Lucy Maud Montgomery, a room was described as having 'the floor covered with a pretty matting, and the curtains that softened the high window and fluttered in the vagrant breezes were of pale-green art muslin' (ch.33).
See also **Muslin**.

Art serge

A heavy, coarse **woollen** fabric with a fibrous surface, usually twill woven and piece-dyed, often in a dark green colouring. T. French suggested that art serge was suitable for **table covers**, dress, draw and **portière** curtains (*Book of Soft Furnishing*, 1937, p.68).
See also **Serge**.

Art silk (aka Artificial silk)

A rayon acetate blended fabric that resembles **silk**. It was developed by Comte Hilaire de Chardonnet in 1884. The term was used in the 1920s as an abbreviation of artificial silk, and the material was used for furnishings by that time. Elizabeth Dyer explained that 'Art silk [is] like China silk but a little stiffer, and with dull luster. An inexpensive, soft texture used in **lining** curtains or lampshades, but too thin to use alone. The name is sometimes applied to casement cloth or to artificial silk fabrics used for glass curtains as well as draperies' (Dyer, *c.*1923, p.203). Commenting on the question of imitation in 1924, the French designer Bénédictus wrote in *Art et Décoration*, that:

> I am aware that [art silk] has found a use in furnishings. But it has been considered as a shameful substitute, a simple counterfeit of real silk, and to make the public buy, we ask [art silk] to supply at a cheaper rate the same sumptuous effects as real silk.

He went on to point out that these cloths had 'an aggressive shine, vulgar colours' and 'a glassy look' and realised that 'a new material needed a new aesthetic' (Schoeser & Dejardin, 1991, p.183).

In 1937, art silk, made up in plain or fancy weaves, was apparently used widely in British home furnishings: 'With the exception of plain artificial silks, (rayon) which are largely used for dress or drawer curtains, slub, fancy weaves and brocades are largely used for drawer curtains and valances. Plain taffetas are especially suitable for bedspreads and cushions' (French, 1937, p.67).

By the 1950s, the use of the term art silk was deemed misleading and was gradually discontinued.

See also **China silk**, **Rayon**.

FURTHER READING

Anon. (1967). 'From nitrate rayon to acetate rayon', *CIBA Review*, 2, pp 2–33.

Foltzer, J. (1921). *Artificial Silk and its Manufacture*, London: Sir I. Pitman.

Art square

A power-woven Kidderminster **ingrain carpet** (flat, non-pile reversible two- or three-ply carpets) produced in seamless 'squares', often finished with a **border** and a **fringe**. This nineteenth-century invention was an important product that widened the market for carpets. In 1885, *The Kidderminster Shuttle* explained its popularity:

> A handsome seamless 'square' with artistic border, leaving a margin of flooring all round, is more attractive and convenient. It is more easily and therefore more frequently taken up of cleaning operations; many of the patterns are reversible, as good one side as on the other; and though an honest, good carpet, it is cheap. (Bartlett, 1978, p.78.)

The American mail order company, Montgomery Ward, advertised 'Jute Art Squares' and 'Leicestershire Art Squares' in their 1895 catalogue. The jute squares were specified for use as 'crumb cloths, druggett or rugs to cover worn areas of carpet'. While in 1912, the English retailers, Williamson & Cole, advertised 'Reversible Art Squares'.

When laying the square of carpet in a room it was usual to leave an 18 inch (46 cm) border around it, which might be left plain or covered with **linoleum** or **felt**.

See also **Chlidema square**, **Habberley carpet**, **Ingrain carpet**, **Kidderminster carpet**, **Smyrna rug**.

Art ticking

A particular form of **mattress upholstery** material that was more decorative than the traditional striped tickings. It was 'distinguished from regular bed ticking by its printed design, usually in stripes of pink, green or blue combination, often with small floral pattern'. It was used for 'mattress and pillow covers and sometimes as cretonne' (Denny, 1923, p.17). This description was confirmed in the 1920s when art tickings were described as 'printed floral fabrics of ticking weave, employed to provide more decorative covers for mattresses, pillows etc; Now a material contemporaneous in purpose and appearance to cretonne' (Stephenson, 1926). This definition was still current in the 1950s (*The Mercury Dictionary of Textile Terms*, 1950).

See also **Mattress-making**, **Ticking**.

Asphalt tile

Hard surface floorcovering developed in the 1920s but not put into mainstream production until the 1940s. Interestingly, by the late 1940s there was no asphalt in the composition, it being made from synthetic resins with an asbestos binder. It was a major competitor to **linoleum**.

See also **Felt-base**.

Astrakan

A **pile** fabric using curled **mohair** yarns on a **cotton** or **woollen** base, woven to resemble the fur of the Astrakan sheep. It was 'occasionally used as a trimming for upholstery purposes in the West End trade' (French, 1947).

Atlas

A fabric that was certainly known in England by 1687 (*London Gazette*, no.2273/7). The name was originally derived from the Arabic *atlas*, meaning 'smooth silk' (**satin**). It was a rich **cotton warp** and **silk weft** fabric, woven with a satin surface in a striped or flowered pattern. It was most fashionable at the end of the seventeenth century and in the early eighteenth century. Daniel Defoe wrote *c.*1690 that at Windsor Castle, 'the late Queen Mary set up a rich Atlas and Chintz bed, which in those times was invaluable, the chintz being of Masulipatam on the coast of Coromandel' (*A Tour Through the Whole Island of Great Britian*, vol.1, letter 3). In the same year, John Hervey 'paid Mrs Cawne for a rich piece of India Atlas for dear wife £13.10.od' (Macquoid & Edwards, 1924, p.7). Its fashionable status meant that it was not long before imitations were made in England. In July 1702, the *London Gazette* published an advertisement for 'rich atlases in imitation of those made in India' (Edwards, 1964, p.22).

A decade later, atlas fabric was still seen as exotic. Pierre Motteux, who kept an 'India shop' in London, was, in 1712, offering 'rich brocades, Dutch atlases, with gold and silver or without, and other foreign silks of the newest modes' (*Spectator*, 30 January 1712). In another example, the material was not apparently highly valued. In the 1710 Dyrham inventory, there were 'a dozen of atlas cushions in a chest', located in the garret over the brew house lumber-room (Walton, 1986, p.66). On the other hand, Celia Fiennes praised the material on her visit to Fetcham Park in 1712, where she saw through a window 'one ground bedchamber which was an Indian attlass [sic] white very fine' (1995, p.240).

The Duke of Chandos at his house Canons, in 1747, had his dressing room **curtains**, hangings and chair covering of green and gold atlas. Contemporary compilers of encyclopedias were also aware of and impressed by its qualities. In 1751, *The Universal Dictionary* noted that:

> It must be owned that the manufacture of them [atlas] is wonderful and singular; and that especially in the flowered atlasses, the gold and silk are worked together after such a manner as no workman in Europe can imitate; but yet they are very far from having that finer gloss and lustre which the French know how to give their silk stuffs. (Postlethwayt, 1751.)

Ten years later, *A New Dictionary of Trade and Commerce* described atlas as 'A silk satin fabric, manufactured in the East Indies, whereof some are plain, striped, or flowered... It must be confessed that the manufacture is admirable particularly in the flowered atlasses the gold and silk being employed therein after a manner inimitably European' (Rolt, 1761).

By the later nineteenth century, 'atlas' was defined as the generic name for satin in many European languages (Beck, 1882), although it was still recognised as a rich Indian satin in the early twentieth century.

Attachment method

Drape, **upholstery** and soft furnishings require a wide range of attachment methods for the various parts of the work undertaken, whether for curtains and drapes, upholstery or floorcoverings.

See also **Adhesive**, **Buttoning**, **Carpet fitting and planning**, **Curtain pole and rod**, **Four-point platform**, **Hook and loop**, **Rubber webbing**, **Stair rod**, **Stitch**, **Tack**, **Webbing**.

Aubusson carpet
Smooth-faced tapestry woven **carpets** were produced at Aubusson in the later eighteenth and the nineteenth centuries. Carpets made with a knotted **pile** were also made at Aubusson from around 1742 as well as **Brussels carpets**. These carpets were produced in large volumes in the nineteenth century when wall hangings were less fashionable. Often they were designed in order to produce a particularly charming and delicate effect.
See also **Aubusson tapestry**, **Moquette carpet**.

FURTHER READING
Jarry, M. (1969). *The Carpets of Aubusson*, Leigh-on-Sea: F. Lewis.
Sherrill, S.B. (1996). *Carpets and Rugs of Europe and America*, New York: Abbeville, pp 96–108.

Aubusson tapestry
A group of workshops established by the early sixteenth century that operated in the workers' own homes around the villages of Aubusson and Felletin. The enterprise received an official charter in 1665 but, as most of the weavers were Huguenots, it suffered a decline after 1685. The business revived in the 1730s and during the nineteenth century made reproductions of earlier designs. In the twentieth century, Jean Lurcat and other modern artists such as Graham Sutherland and Raoul Dufy supplied cartoons.
See also **Aubusson carpet**, **Tapestry**.

FURTHER READING
Bertrand, P.-F., Chevalier, D. & Chevalier, P. (1988). *Les tapisseries d'Aubusson et de Felletin, 1457–1791*, Paris: Solange Thierry.
Weigert, R. (1962). *French Tapestry*, London: Faber and Faber.

Austrian blanket
See **Blanket**.

Austrian shade (aka Austrian blind)
Mid-nineteenth-century commentators noted that 'these are called by upholsterers festoon curtains and were very general before the French manner was introduced of making them slide on a rod' (Webster & Parkes, 1844, p.250). One commentator in the later nineteenth century referred to them as always being made of **silk** (Moreland, 1889, p.172). They were revived in the later twentieth century where the distinction between festoon and Austrian curtains was that the Austrian remained ruched at the bottom even when fully let down. (Festoon curtains were ruched along the whole length.) In the later twentieth century, Austrian **blinds** were also often made from '**net**' type materials.
See also **Austrian shade cloth**, **Balloon shade**, **Casement cloth**, **Festoon**, **Krinkle**, **Plissé**, **Ruche**, **Venetian curtain**.

Austrian shade cloth
A **seersucker** type of fabric woven from mercerised **cotton**, which was woven with wide stripes and used for bed furnishings and **curtains** and **awnings**. The description and use is explained in this passage from *Textile Fabrics*:

> Casement cloth and plisse are being used widely in the place of blinds. Plisse has alternate stripes of crêpe and plain surface. It is heavier than the plisse used for clothing, and is frequently called Austrian shade cloth. Plisse shades are finished with a braid or fringe and are so arranged that they pull up and down by means of cords with tassels. (Dyer, *c*.1923. p.206.)

See also **Austrian shade**, **Casement cloth**, **Plissé**.

Awning
Awnings, referred to in the Renaissance as *tende*, were initially a cloth draped on a frame and fixed to the wall, while a pole, supported on brackets, protruding from the wall, allowed it to cut out sun but permit air circulation. Awnings, often adapted from sails, were also used in hot climes as sun protection.
The Venetian fan **blind**, which has a Venetian blind and two side blinds that can be pulled up together on the outside of the window to regulate light and air, was a nineteenth-century version (Loudon, 1839, p.270).
In 1907, Hasluck showed how outside sun-blinds were used to screen painted front doors in the form of an awning. The term still refers to shades of various sorts, often for use outdoors.
See also **Bonnet blind**, **Duck**, **Venetian blind**.

Axminster carpet (Hand-knotted)
Hand-knotted **carpets** that were originally made in the English town of Axminster in Devon. Thomas Whitty started the manufacture of these carpets in Axminster in 1755. Whitty was encouraged by the Royal Society of Arts which, in 1756, offered premiums for the best carpets not measuring less than 15 by 12 feet (4½ by 3½ metres), made after the manner of Turkish carpets. Although Thomas Moore won the premium in 1757, and Claude Passavant won it in 1758, Whitty shared in both prizes, and in 1759 won outright in the third round.

5. Luxurious early twentieth-century Austrian shades (G.L. Hunter, Decorative Textiles, Coverings for Furniture etc., *1918)*

6. A hand-tufted Axminster carpet, probably eighteenth century (C. Faraday, European and American Carpets and Rugs, *1929)*

The Axminster factory was an attraction for visitors and it is thanks to them we have a view of the workings. Mrs Abigail Adams described the workshops in 1778 in a letter to an American correspondent:

> The manufactory of carpets is wholly performed by women and children. You would have been surprised to see in how ordinary a building this rich manufactory was carried on... They have but two prices for their carpets woven here; the one is eighteen shillings a yard, and the other twenty-four a square yard. They are woven of any dimensions you please, and without a seam. The colours are most beautiful, and the carpets very durable (Roth, 1967, p.41).

In 1777, Samuel Curwen visited the factory and wrote: 'here is also wrought, besides his own, of a peculiar construction, Turkey carpet. So very like in figure, colour and thickness as not to be distinguished from the genuine article' (ibid. p.42).

Whitty's factory was also visited in 1791 by E.D. Clarke in his *Tour through the South of England.* He described the weaving process, and in particular how:

> the work is chiefly done by women. We saw forty of these employed; the pattern lays before them and with their fingers they weave the whole. This they execute with great quickness, and it is amusing to observe how fast the most elegant designs are traced out by the fingers of old women and children. (Macquoid & Edwards, 1924, p.194.)

The products of the factory were highly esteemed. The Revd Thomas Moore wrote in his *History of Devonshire from Earliest Times to the Present* (1829–31) that the 'carpets [of Axminster] were never in higher repute than at present. His Majesty's Palaces at Brighton and Windsor are graced by the labours of the women of Axminster as are also the mansions and countryseats of the nobility.' Despite this endorsement, the factory closed in 1835. Moore's explanation of the work involved may explain the demise:

> The thickness of these fabrics being greater than any others of the kind, and the quantity of raw materials used in the manufacture of them being consequently large, – the labour, as the work is done by the fingers, being minute and tedious, – and considerable sums, occasionally thirty or forty pounds being spent on the pattern, the price of them is necessarily high.

In fact, production moved to the town of Wilton in 1835 and remained there until well into the twentieth century.

See also **Axminster carpet (Machine woven)**, **Chenille Axminster**, **Imperial Axminster**, **Kurastan**.

FURTHER READING

Hine, J. (1889). 'The origins of Axminster carpets', *Reports and Transactions of the Devonshire Association for the Advancement of Science Literature and Art*, 21, pp 331–7.

Jacobs, B. (1970). *Axminster Carpets 1755–1957*, Leigh-on-Sea: F. Lewis.

Rose, B. (2002). 'Early Axminster carpets', *Hali*, 129, pp 92–100.

Sherrill, S.B. (1996). *Carpets and Rugs of Europe and Amer a*, New York: Abbeville, pp 187–212.

White, G. (1895). 'The making of Axminster carpets', *Art Journal*, new series, pp 325–30.

Axminster carpet (Machine woven)

The machine process of weaving **carpets** is completely different to the hand-knotting method. There are three weaving methods: chenille, gripper and spool. Between 1876 and 1877, Americans Halycon Skinner and Alexander Smith developed technical improvements in mechanised **pile** carpet weaving. Manufacturers Tomkinson and Adam, in Kidderminster, soon introduced these techniques into England. The products were based on the concept of mechanically inserting tufts, from pre-wound spools of yarn prepared according to the design, into the **warp** threads initially, and later into the **weft** threads. The yarn for each weft row is wound on a separate spool in accordance with the pattern progression. The yarns are cut at the point of presentation to the warps and the tufts inserted. The benefits included an unlimited colour range. In 1884, the British company Brinton acquired the rights to develop the 'nipper' or 'gripper' mechanism, which was patented by

7. A machine-woven Axminster carpet, c.*1960 (Stoddard and Co)*

FAR LEFT
8. Spool Axminster machine-weaving techniques, c.1960 (Private Collection)

LEFT
9. Gripper Axminster machine-weaving techniques, c.1960 (Private Collection)

Brinton and Greenwood in 1890. The 'gripper Axminster' is a carpet woven in such a manner that mechanical grippers pull the yarn: it is then cut off and inserted at the point of weaving. The **jacquard** mechanism selects the coloured yarns and presents them as appropriate to the grippers, but is usually limited to eight colour frames. Later, the two techniques were combined in the spool-gripper process that enjoyed the benefits of both.

Looms up to 3 yards (2.74 metres) wide were developed in the late 1920s and a 10 ft 6 inches (3 metre 15 cm) wide loom was introduced in 1932. In the 1930s, **tapestry carpets** declined in favour of a huge increase in gripper Axminster, especially those woven as 'Seamless Squares'.

See also **American Oriental**, **Axminster carpet (Hand-knotted)**, **Chenille Axminster**, **Imperial Axminster**.

FURTHER READING

Bartlett, J.N. (1978). *Carpeting the Millions, The Growth of Britain's Carpet Industry*, Edinburgh: John Donald.

Robinson, G. (1966). *Carpets*, London: Pitman.

Axminster moquette

An American, machine-made **carpet** developed from the 1870s.

Back tacking

An **upholstery** technique that allows fabrics to be neatly secured to a frame by using hidden fixings. It involves cutting the materials to be used (i.e. there may be more than the **top cover**) to the size required. The top edge of the outside top fabric is placed face down on the top of the frame. A strip of starched **muslin** or card is placed to form an edge, which is then tacked or stapled through the fabric to the frame. The cloth is then pulled over the muslin or card to show the face side. The bottom of the fabric panel is then tacked in the usual way on the lower underside of the frame. The method also works for batch work and, since the latter part of the twentieth century, ready-made tacking strip has been used in factory upholstery work.

See also **Tacking**.

Back-coated fabric

A backing is sometimes added to a furnishing fabric to enhance its qualities. **Acrylic** or **latex** backing may be added to **upholstery** fabrics to give dimensional stability and ease of cutting and sewing. In fabrics that are applied directly to a wall or upholstery using gluing methods, the backing avoids seep-through of the **adhesive**.

In other cases, fabric may be bonded to a knitted or woven substrate. This is applied when lightweight fabrics are used for upholstery. Barrier materials such as **foams**, blackout or flame-resistant finishes can be applied as backing depending on the end use.

See also **Stretch cover**.

Bafta

A general term for plain **calico** made in various regions of India and exported to Europe since at least 1598. Sir Henry Yule (*Hobson-Jobson*, 1903, p.47) defined it as:

> a kind of calico, made especially at Baroch; from the Persian *bafta* [for] 'woven'. The old Baroch *baftas* seem to have been fine goods. Nothing is harder than to find intelligible explanations of the distinction between the numerous varieties of cotton stuffs formerly exported from India to Europe under a still greater variety of names; names and trade being generally alike obsolete.

The fabric was particularly used in the nineteenth century for furnishing purposes in France. By the early twentieth century, the name defined a **silk** fabric.

Bag strapping

An **upholstery** binding **tape** used to preserve selvedges. Caulfeild & Saward said it resembled a very broad stay-tape (1887, p.35).

See also **Binding**.

Baize

The name baize is actually derived from the plural form of bay (i.e. bayes). One of the New Draperies, bay was originally a fine lightweight **woollen** cloth that was woven with a **worsted warp** and woollen **weft** and was finished with a nap on one side. It was introduced into England from France and the Netherlands during the sixteenth century. Baize was originally a fabric used for garments, but the heavier versions were then used for stiffening and lining, coverings and **curtains**, and were widely used for billiard and card-table tops. It was sometimes combined with **damask leather** to make protective covers for pier tables etc., as well as for other protective duties.

In 1601, Lady Shrewsbury's bedchamber in Hardwick Hall had 'five curtains of purple bayes' (Boynton, 1971, p.31). In 1637, Queen Henrietta Maria was supplied by Ralph Grynder with '25 yards of fine broad bayse to case 2 chairs 6 folding stools and a couch being cased down to the ground' (Beard, 1997, p.289). In 1641, the Tart Hall inventory recorded 'A red bayes to go round about my Lords bed' (Cust, 1911), and in the 1659 inventory of Hampton Court there are 'three large curtains of scarlet bazes being a case about the bed'. An estimate from 1699 for beds at Hampton Court included 'Bays to line quilts and head board cloth' (Beard, 1997, p.299).

By 1698, Celia Fiennes had already commented on Colchester as a centre of the production of baize: 'the whole town is employed in spinning, weaving washing drying and dressing their Bayes, in which they seem very industrious' (1949, pp 131–2). In 1741, Chambers confirmed the pre-eminence of the Colchester area in his definition:

> a kind of coarse open woollen stuff, having a long nap; sometime friezed on one side, and sometimes not friezed, according to the uses it is intended for. The stuff is without wale, being wrought on a loom with two treadles, like flannel. The manufacture of bays is very considerable in England particularly about Colchester; and in Flanders about Lisle and Tournai, &c. (*Cyclopaedia*)

During the eighteenth century, it was used for protecting a range of furniture types, including covers for sideboards, and also for lining mirror glasses and cases. *A New Dictionary of Trade and Commerce* noted that 'the looking glass-makers likewise use [baize] behind their glasses to preserve the tin or quick-silver, and the case-makers to line their cases' (Rolt, 1756). It continued to be used as a playing table surface. In 1730, Hampton Court was supplied with 'one green cloth carpet for ye play table' (Beard, 1997, p.302).

Baize also protected clothes in cupboards. The material was intended to flap over the clothes that were placed on the shelves. In 1767, Chippendale invoiced Nostell Priory: 'To a very large mahogany clothes press ... sliding shelves, covered with marble paper and Bays aprons.' (Gilbert, 1978, p.186.)

The use of baize as a protective cover for carpets was also promoted in the eighteenth century. Sir Lawrence Dundas had 'A large carpet and a green baize cover to d[itt]o' (Coleridge, 1967, p.198). In 1768, Thomas Moore sold the Earl of Coventry 'a green baize cover to a carpet £2.5s.10d.', no doubt to protect one of his own creations (Gilbert, 1987, p.106). The practice continued into the early nineteenth century as Sheraton recorded that '[Baize] is much in use by cabinet-makers and upholsterers. By the latter, bays is issued to cover over carpets, and made to fit round the room, to save them. Bays is used by cabinet-makers to tack behind clothes press shelves to throw over the clothes' (1803, p.40).

The continuing use of baize as a furnishing material was recorded later in the nineteenth century. Caulfeild & Saward noted that 'It is used for linings, cuttings, floorcloths, bags etc and is made in various widths from one yard to two. A superior quality has latterly been made which is employed for tablecloths' (1887, p.18).

See also **Bocking**, **Carpet protection**, **Crumb cloth**, **Lamp rug**, **Oil-cloth**, **Protective furnishing**, **Rateen**, **Washstand mat**.

Baldachin

A **canopy** over a chair, that was often ceremonial in character and design. Mentioned in the seventeenth century by Evelyn. Sheraton described a baldachin as a canopy, either as an architectural feature or as a canopy for an important chair. He illustrated an example of a Masonic chair with baldachine (1803, p.28). *Baldequin* was the French name for a dome most often situated above the bed (Bimont, 1770). Baldachin was also a name for a **brocaded** cloth with rich yarns. Chambers in 1753 referred to 'Baldachin ... popularly baudekin ... a rich kind of cloth.' (Supplement to *Cyclopaedia*.)

See also **Baudekin**, **Crepine**, **Dome**, **Tester**.

Balin

A coarse plain-weave fabric made from **jute**, flax, etc. and used for **upholstery** coverings (*The Mercury Dictionary of Textile Terms*, 1950).

Ball fringe

See **Fringe: Ball**.

Balloon shades

Popular term for **curtains** raised or lowered by **cords** and rings, made in several variations and distinguished mainly by their bottom hem that, when the curtain is raised, billows in a series of graceful puffs suggesting balloons. They are more voluminous and casual than Austrian shades or blinds. They sometimes have the fullness in the width made into **inverted pleats**. They were also known as cloud or poufed shades.

See also **Austrian shade**.

Band

A device to hold back **curtains**, which was made from shaped fabric, stiffened with **canvas** and fitted with a ring at each end to fit over a hook screwed to the wall. Bands were often decorated with **fringes** or **embroidery** to match **valances**. They became popular around 1850 and have been in and out of fashion ever since. Brown & Gates explained that 'Gimp bands [are] used for looping curtains apart from the centre to the side of the window. They are not uniform in width, but are wider at the centre than at the ends' (1872, p.212).

Banker

A **cushion** or seat covering, often of **tapestry**, mainly used in the Middle Ages. The term is derived from the French *banquer* (bench). They were often used in conjunction with dorcers and costering. Early references confirm this. For example, in a 1395 will there was a 'Hall, with docere, costers and bankers' (*Early English Wills*, 1882, p.5), and in 1485 there was reference to 'the dorsers all of camaca, the bankers all of taffeta' (*EE Misc.*, 1856, p.4).

Nearly 100 years later they were still in use. A will of 1574 listed 'a hawlinge, a banker of wannes, and ij fox skynnes' (*Richmond Wills*, 1853, 248, *OED*). They appear to have still had commercial value for the next 100 years and continued to be made from tapestry. The *Tudor Book of Rates* for 1582 listed 'Bankers of verdure the dozen piece' (Willan, 1962, p.18) and this description was repeated in 1660 (1660, Act 12 Chas. II, iv. Schedule).

See also **Costering**, **Dorcer**.

Barbary matting
See **Matting: Barbary**.

Bargello (aka Flame stitch, Florentine stitch, Hungarian point, Irish stitch)
Needlepoint design that creates geometric patterns in diamonds, peaks and valleys. The stitches run parallel to the **canvas** grid, unlike traditional **needlework** where they slant. In bargello work, the stitches cover two or more meshes with each stitch so the work is speedier. The technique was particularly popular in the seventeenth and eighteenth centuries.
See also **Stitch: Flame**.

Bark cloth
Real bark cloth is a non-woven fabric made from the inner bark of certain South Sea Island trees found especially in Hawaii and Fiji etc., where it is beaten until thin and transparent like **muslin**.

Imitation bark cloth is a dobby woven **crêpe cloth** similar to **cretonne** that may be dyed or printed. It is made with a broken surface to imitate the look of bark. It was very popular in America in the first half of the twentieth century.
See also **Weave: Dobby**.

FURTHER READING

Fehling, L. (1999). *Fabulous Barkcloth: Home Decorating Textiles from the 30s, 40s and 50s*, Atglen, Pa: Schiffer.

Barnard Castle carpet
This **carpet** was a Kidderminster-type ingrain, woven in the locality of Barnard Castle, Durham, from around 1815 to the mid-nineteenth century. By 1836, seven firms in the area were operating more than 400 looms. By 1858, the trade had declined, and by the 1870s production had almost ceased.
See also **Ingrain carpet**, **Kendal carpet**, **Kidderminster carpet**.

FURTHER READING

Coggins, D. (1996). *People and Patterns: The Carpet Weaving Industry in 19th Century Barnard Castle*, Barnard Castle: Bowes Museum.
Hemingway, J. (1996). 'Jacob Allison (1795–1868), carpet manufacturer of Barnard Castle and Cotherstone', *Textile History*, 27, 2, pp 195–206.
Shea, W. (1984). *A History of Carpet Making in Co. Durham*, Durham: Durham County Council.

Barracan (aka Baracan)
A coarse goat **hair camlet** whose name is derived from the Persian *barak*, meaning a garment of camel hair. It also refers to a plain-weave **worsted** cloth like a camlet. The term 'barracan' appears to have been mainly used in the eighteenth century, while the name 'paragon' was more common in the seventeenth. The name also refers to a **blanket** used in Spain that was woven from coarse **wool** or goats' hair. Norwich weavers changed the type name to paragon. An early twentieth-century description noted that it was:

> [A] closely woven heavy cloth used for furniture covers or drapery, made of doubled and hard twist worsted yarn warp and three or six-ply, hard twist worsted filling and finished with moiré effect. It has warp ribs. Later also made with silk or wool warp and goat's hair filling, to form weft ribs. (Harmuth, 1924, p.14)

In the mid-twentieth century, the name referred to a heavy woollen fabric used for furniture covers and **drape** with a **moiré** finish (*The Mercury Dictionary of Textile Terms*, 1950).
See also **Paragon**.

Barrage
An inexpensive **linen** cloth, woven with **brocade**-like designs. Made in Northern France in the eighteenth century and still known in the nineteenth century.

Barras
A coarse **linen** fabric imported from Holland from the sixteenth century onwards. One hundred years later, the *Plain dealing Linen draper* (J.F., 1696) noted that barras when 'well whited' served as 'ordinary sheets for poor people'. The name was probably obsolete by the early eighteenth century.
See also **Canvas**, **Sheet**.

Base cloth
See **Bottom linen**.

Base strip
Slats of timber used to support **mattresses** and bedding. 'A set of tester laths and a set of base strips' were supplied by John Moreland of an unknown address in 1768 (*DEFM*, p.627).

Bases
The lower valance sections of bed 'furnitures' intended to hide the space below the frame. They are usually suspended from the **counterpane** or from the bedposts. Chippendale referred to bedpost designs as preferential to valances or bases: 'all designed with pedestals, which most certainly look better than bases of stuff around the bed' (*The Gentleman and Cabinet Maker's Director*, 1762, Plate XXXIV).
See also **Pante**, **Valance**.

Basil
See **Bazil**.

Batik
An ancient hot wax, resist-dyeing process (mentioned by Pliny) whereby the design is drawn with a *tjanting* (spouted bowl), or blocked onto cloth using wax and the *tjap* (block). When the fabric (generally **cotton**) is dyed, the wax protects the cloth and these sections remain undyed, although it sometimes cracks, giving a characteristic veined effect. After completion of the process, the wax is removed. Well known as a technique in Southeast Asia, especially in Java and Bali, it was known in Europe from the sixteenth century. From the nineteenth century, the batik process was extensively copied by machine printing, but was also encouraged as a handicraft. Batik was particularly recommended for use for **drape** and covers in the 1920s.

FURTHER READING

Buhler, A. (1972). *Ikat, Batik, Plangi*, Basel: Pharos Verlag.
Elliott, I.M. (1984). *Batik: Fabled Cloth of Java*, Harmondsworth: Viking.
Rouffaer, G.F. & Juynboll, H.H. (1899–1914). *Die Batjk-Kunst und ihre Geschichte*, 3 vols, Haarlem: Kleinmann.

Batiste
A sheer fine fabric that has been woven from most fibres at one time or another, but usually refers to fine **linen** used for dresses, linings and **trimmings**. Batiste is the French word for cambric. Simmonds suggests that it was named after M. Batiste who first produced it in Cambray (1858).

In her book on bedroom decoration, Lady Barker mentioned the use of batiste in conjunction with **muslin** as being appropriate for summer **quilts**, **toilette** and **screen** materials (1878, p.22).

Batiste was also specified in America for **comforts**. A guide to department stores noted that: 'the coverings for comfortables may be of Cheesecloth, Silkoline, Challis, Sateen, Chintz, Silk, Batiste' (Thompson, 1917, p.129).

See also **Cambric**.

Batten

A thin piece of timber that fits into the bottom hem of a **roller blind** or shade to give the blind rigidity and a point for the fixing of the pull **cord**. It also refers to the timber framing applied to a wall in preparation for walling fabrics.

Batting

American name for a fibre of **wool**, **kapok**, **cotton** or **polyester** fluffed up, made into sheets, or supplied loose in bags and used for padding and **quilting**. Batting has been used on occasions to make up compound materials or for **curtain** edges and **interlining** from the mid-nineteenth century.

See also **Bump**, **Comfort**.

Baudekin

Originally, it was an embroidered **silk** material woven with a gold thread **warp** and a silk **weft** (sometimes known as **Baldachin**). The name may derive from either Baldacus near Babylon or from Baldacco, the Italian name for Baghdad. It was introduced into Europe around the eleventh century and used for regal garments or church hangings. Later, it was an important furnishing fabric.

In the royal household of Henry VI (1422–61), baudekin featured extensively in the furnishings:

> 1 selour de drap baudekin d'or, 1 tent bed de drap de baudekin d'or avec tout l'aparaille, 2 chair cloths de baudekin blanc et vermaile broche de corones d'or, 1 celur, 1 tester de soy baudekin pale blue et vermaille, l'ouvrage de vert; 1 drap d'estate de baudekin rouge et blanc overt des corons d'or, and 2 long cushions the same. (*Rot. Parl.*, II, Henry VI.)

Later the term baudekin was applied to rich shot silks and even plain silks, which were used for bed hangings. In 1509, the inventory of Edmund Dudley records 'a testar of bawdiken embrodrid … a counterpoint of bawdekin' (Beard, 1997, p.282). Sir John Gage had 'an olde tester of tholde faction of clothe of bawdkyn and white damask paned' (ibid. p.283). *The Wardrobe Accounts of Edward VI* of *c.*1550 list 'Baldekyn of silk at xxxiiis iiiid the piece' (Edwards, 1964, p.29).

Bayadere

A nineteenth-century textile term referring to a plain-woven fabric designed with contrasting horizontal stripes. The name is derived from the Bajadere dancing girl of India, who wore striped garments. Now it refers to any horizontal stripe pattern. Mainly used as a dress material.

Bay

See **Baize**, **Bocking**.

Bazil (aka Basil)

Sheepskins that are tanned in bark are called bazil. Distinctive characteristics arise from the bark used, which is dependent upon location. For example, in England oak-bark, in Scotland larch and in Turkey oak-galls have been used (Waterer, 1968, p.158). An early reference to bazil is in the *Tudor Book of Rates* (1582) which noted the importation of 'Skinnes for leather … Basill, buffe for cushions, portingale [Portugal] red hides, roan, salt, Spanish, spruce and swan skinnes' (Willan, 1962, p.56).

This particular sheepskin leather, which was comparatively thin, was explicitly specified in the 1679 bylaws of the Upholders' Company to be used only for **upholstery** linings and not for **top covers** (Houston, 1993, p.58). However, in July 1668, it was used for loose covers for some **turkey work** chairs, when James Somerville supplied Holyroodhouse with 'red bazil skins with thongs' (Cooke (ed.), 1987, p.53).

In the eighteenth century, Samuel Norman's inventory included brown **damask** skins, white sheepskins, **roan** skins, bazil skins and gilt skins (Kirkham, 1969, p.509). Bazil was also used for covering inexpensive trunks in the later eighteenth century. As this material was relatively thin, the use of brass corners and studs helped to reduce premature wear. In 1801, W. Felton, regarded it as 'inferior leather … [that] tears almost like paper' (Legg, 1994, p.40, note 56). In the twentieth century, bazil was sometimes used for **upholstery**.

See also **Leather**.

Bead curtain

Curtains made with glass and wood beads, strung on separate threads to make a screen effect and hang in a doorway. The bead curtains represented a mid-nineteenth-century taste for an ersatz Turkish style. Design critics were often hostile. The journal *House Beautiful* commented in 1898 that 'if there be any practical or decorative use to which one may put portières of beads or coloured bamboo, it has never been discovered' (March 1898, p.120).

However, in the early twentieth century, they were again used as **portières** or dividers between rooms, and particularly recommended as a home handicraft:

> A new idea for curtains has just been developed by another clever craft-worker. Geometrical designs are drawn on the material, which may either be burlap, or monk's cloth, or any heavy **cotton** material. It fact, it is not necessary that it should be cotton, as this design would look especially well on inexpensive grey blankets. This kind of bead decoration is peculiarly well adapted for ornamenting a portière, but it is also very effective when it is employed for curtains. (Priestman, 1910, p.178.)

See also **Beadwork**.

Beaded fringe

See **Fringe: Beaded**.

Bead mosaic work

See **Beadwork**.

Beadwork

An **embroidery** process that used beading techniques to finish off or make accessories for the home. It was popular in Europe in the late sixteenth and early seventeenth centuries in England especially, and was applied to small furnishing items as an alternative or addition to **stumpwork** for mirrors, picture frames, boxes and **cushions**.

Glass bead embroidery was particularly used for hangings during the early eighteenth century. These hangings were mainly used as wall panels in exclusive houses. The practice appears to have originated in France as explained by Saint-Aubin in his *L'Art du Brodeur* (1770).

Beadwork was revived in the nineteenth century and used in conjunction with **Berlin wool-work**. Beads could be needled onto a **canvas** pattern or directly to the round work material already mounted. It was particularly used for prie-dieu chairs and stools, and for screens and **mantel drapery**, often in combination with Berlin wool-work. Caulfeild & Saward noted that bead mosaic work was used from 1855 for decorating hanging baskets, lampshades and dinner rings (1887, p.23). Beadwork was still used for making curtains in the home in the twentieth century.

See also **Bead curtain**.

FURTHER READING

Cassidy-Geiger, M. (2001). 'Glass bead embroidery for interior decoration' in Mertens, W. (ed.), *Transitory Splendour: Interior Textiles in Western Europe 1600–1900*, Antwerp: Hessenhuis Museum, Stadsbestuur, December 2001–March 2002, pp 307–12.

Priestman, M.T. (1910). *Handicrafts in the Home*, New York: J. Lane, pp 171–80.

Beauvais carpet

Tapestry floor **carpets** with a smooth face were woven at the Beauvais tapestry factory from *c.*1780–90 and from 1794–1814.

See also **Beauvais tapestry**, **Tapestry carpet**.

Beauvais tapestry

The Royal tapestry factory was founded in Beauvais, France during 1664 and closed in 1793, but re-opened as a state factory in 1794. Throughout the eighteenth century, furniture covers were woven there, often in sets to match wall hangings. In the nineteenth century, the manufacture of furniture covers en suite with wall hangings continued, as well as some floor **carpets**. The factory finally closed in 1940 and amalgamated with **Gobelins tapestry** factory. It is still in business today making commissions.

See also **Beauvais carpet**, **Tapestry carpet**, **Wall covering and hanging**.

FURTHER READING

Badin, J. (1909). *La Manufacture de Tapisserie de Beauvais*, Paris: Société de Propagation des Livres d'Art.

Coural, J. & Gastinel-Coural, C. (1992). *Beauvais: Manufacture Nationale de Tapisseries*, Paris: Centre Nationale des Arts Plastiques.

Weigert, R.A. (1962). *French Tapestry*, London: Faber and Faber.

Bed carpet

Although **rugs** were often used as bedside **carpets**, the term bed carpet refers to a specifically planned carpet of (usually) three narrow strips designed to fit around the bed in a U-shape.

An early example of rugs intended for bedside use is recorded in the Hardwick Hall inventory of 1601 that lists 'three foot turkey carpets the ground of them white to lay about the bed' (Boynton, 1971, p.25). The term may also refer to bedcovers. On 14 August 1683, an order from London to the East India Co was made for **bed furnitures** that included instructions that 'Each bed to have to it 2 small carpets, 1½ yards wide and 2 yards long' (Irwin & Schwartz, 1966, p.35).

By the eighteenth century, fitted bed carpets were fashionable and the type of carpet was varied. At one extreme was Mrs Delany who wrote to her sister in 1752: 'My candlelight work is finishing a carpet in double cross-stitch on very coarse canvas, to go round my bed' (1861, III, p.176). Turkey carpet was also used. The more exclusive hand-knotted works of **Axminster** or **Moorfields**, which were woven as a single piece,

10. Bed carpet around the State Bed at Blickling Hall (©NTPL/Angelo Hornak)

followed them. The best would be carpets designed for particular room schemes that were supplied to match the furnishings. Apart from these hand-worked carpets, Brussels and Wilton weaves were popular. In 1764, Sir Lawrence Dundas was supplied by William France with 'a Wilton Roman pavement carpitt to fit all-round the bed with a border on the outside' (Gilbert, 1967, p.57). A very particular example was the bed carpet of red cloth **brocaded** with gold, silver, red and blue **velvet** in the state bedroom listed in the Chandos inventory (Cornforth & Fowler, 1974, p.215).

In the nineteenth century, shaped bed carpets were clearly still available, but in one case at least were not considered best value. *Cassell's Household Guide*, 1870, referred to 'mitred carpets of Kidderminster may be joined at the corners, and placed round the bedstead in one piece. This plan entails the losing half a square of material at each corner, or nearly a yard of carpet; and besides a servant cannot so well shake carpets of such form' (vol.1, p.184).

See also **Brussels carpet**, **Wilton carpet**.

Bedcloth

A name for an extra broad **worsted** cloth like **say**, which was well established by the sixteenth century. Used specifically for bed **curtains** and hangings, it was woven from 2½ to 4 yards (2.29 to 3.66 metres) wide and in lengths of 10, 12 or 24 yards (9, 11 or 22 metres). Norwich weavers stated that 'The [materials called] say and piramides may also be affirmed to be that ancient cloth ... called a bed; the difference only consisting in the breadth and fineness'. John James in his history of worsteds suggests that bed cloth was the same as say, and was used for curtains, beds and **wall coverings** (1857, p.144 and Appendix). Bed cloth was also woven as a **serge** type with a **linen warp**. It was often embroidered with decoration.

See also **Bed furniture**.

Bedclothes

The essential materials for making a bed have remained remarkably consistent over many centuries, although the details have changed. An ensemble of sheets, **pillowcases**, blankets and padded covers have been the fundamental arrangement. In the twelfth century, Alexander Neckam described how:

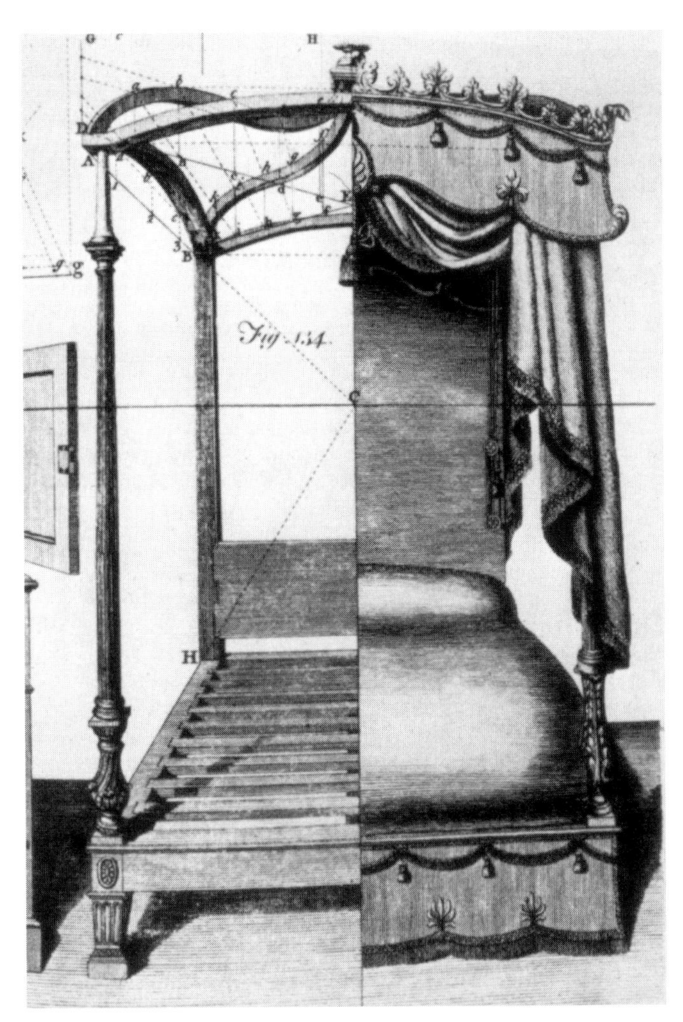

11. Bed frame and furnishings, 1778 (T. Malton, A Compleat Treatise on Perspective…*)*

> On the bed itself should be placed a feather mattress to which a bolster is attached. A quilted pad of striped cloth should cover this on which a cushion for the head can be placed. Then sheets of muslin, ordinary cotton or at least pure linen, should be laid. Next a coverlet of green cloth or of coarse wool, of which the fur lining is badger, cat, beaver or sable. (Holmes, 1952, pp 82–3.)

Eight hundred years later, it was explained that:

> The outfit for a bed consists of a lightweight cotton pad to lay over the mattress, pillows, sheets and pillow cases, blankets, comfortable and spread. Sheets and blankets should be of generous length to tuck in well at the bottom of the bed and at the sides. The comfortable may be folded and laid on the outside. (Kellogg, 1905, p.170.)

See also **Bed furniture**, **Blanket**, **Bolster**, **Counterpoint**, **Coverlet**, **Duvet**, **Eiderdown**, **Flock**, **Fustian**, **Mattress**, **Pillow**, **Quilt**, **Rugg**, **Sheet**.

Bed cord (aka Bed line)
Wooden bed frames required a suspension system to hold the bedding in place. Bed cords were ropes that were threaded through holes drilled in a bed frame to create a supporting web. They were clearly something that needed periodical replacement as 'bed lines and cord etc' were in the stock inventory of an Essex grocer in 1692 (Steer, 1969, p.213). The use of bed cords lasted well into the nineteenth century but, by this time, they were only a small part of the supporting system that was often either a **canvas** sheet laced to the bed frame, or wooden slats. In 1840, instructions in *The Workwoman's Guide* included the following information about assembling beds: 'The sacking is next tightly laced up with strong cord, and ought to be pulled together and knotted by a man as a woman is scarce strong enough to do it effectually' (Hale, 1840, p.191). With the advent of divan bases and metal bedsprings designed to fit onto bedsteads, bed cords became obsolete.
See also **Bed mat**, **Spring**.

Bed curtain
See **Bed furniture**.

Bedford cord
A nineteenth-century name for a fabric not widely used for furnishings but heavy enough for **upholstery**. It is woven from **wool** or **worsted** and has been made in **cotton**, **silk** and **rayon**. It has the cords running the length of the cloth and the cord effects can vary in size and colour. The **weft** yarns are woven alternately into one cord and then floated behind the next. The towns of Bedford, England and New Bedford, Mass. each claim the fabric. *How to Furnish and Decorate*, published in *c.*1897, noted that 'a material which looks much like the dress fabric called Bedford cord will be much used for inexpensive portieres' (Cooperative Building Plan Association, New York). Bedford cord was used for upholstery in the mid-twentieth century and beyond (Bendure & Pfieffer, 1947, p.611 and Smithells, 1950).
See also **Piqué**.

Bed furniture
Bed furniture is the name for the complete ensemble of bed hangings, either fixed or movable, that was suspended around and on a bed. The ensemble was comprised of curtains, testers, covers and **drapes** that decorate a bed frame. The practice of furnishing a bed was very ancient, but was developed in the early Middle Ages and eventually grew into the spectacular confections of the eighteenth century. The bed hangings usually comprised curtains ranging in number from two to six, depending on the splendour of the bed. They might be pull-up (in which case only three were required) or they would operate as **draw curtains**, which pulled on rods and rings. Bed curtains were used to enclose the bed. Initially, they simply curtained the bed for privacy and warmth, and were held by rods fixed across the room or from **cords** suspended from hooks mounted in the ceiling. Later they were part of the complete bed furniture scheme. The curtains (often two head and two **foot curtains**) would be supplemented by cantoons and bonegraces, which covered the corner meeting points. The ensemble would also have valances for inside and outside, as well as base valances. The tester and head cloth finished off the hangings. The **counterpane** was also considered part of the hangings. Finally, **finials**, **aigrettes** or **cups** completed the ensemble.

An early example from the will of the Countess of Gloucester of 1399 listed the following bed furniture: '*Item, un lit, over testers, coverlitz, curtyns, et tapitz, qe a eux appertient.*' (*OED*) A description from 1472 of a bed made up for the Lord of Gruthere, by the wife of Edward IV, gives a clear idea of the luxury possible:

> There was ordained a bed for himself of as good down as could be gotten, the sheets of raynes, also fine fustians, the counterpoint clothe of

gold, furred with ermine, the tester and the celer also shining cloth of gold, the curtains of white sarcenet, as for his head suite and pillows they were of the Queen's own ordinance… (Macquoid, 1904, p.67.)

The full effect was also shown in a later example. In the Ham House inventory of 1679, the Queen's Bedchamber was listed with a bed and its winter furniture:

Six curtains and four cantoones, valanes, and basis of cloth of gold with flowers of blew velvet lined with skie colour sateen with gould embroidered fringe, tester, head cloth and counterpane embroidered with gould, four cups covered with the same of ye curtain and white feathers on the top of them' (Thornton & Tomlin, 1980, p.144).

Apart from the luxurious examples that continued to be produced, there was a growing market for similar effects, though in **cotton**. This demand was met by imports of printed cloth. This very explicit order from London to the East India Co's operation in India, dated 14 August 1683, explains the demand for the ready-made bed furniture market:

100 suites of painted curtains and valances, ready made up of several sorts and prices, strong, but none too dear, nor any over mean in regard you know our poorest people in England lye without any curtains or valances and our richest in damask etc. The valances to be 1 foot deep and 6½ yards compass. Curtains to be from 8 to 9 foot deep, the two lesser curtains each 1½ yards wide, the two larger curtains to be 3½ yards wide and 2 yards long. The tester and head piece proportional. A counterpane of the same work to be 31½ yards long, half of them to be quilts and the other half not quilted. Each bed to have to it 2 small carpets, 1½ yards wide and 2 yards long. Each bed to have 12 cushions for chairs of the same. (Irwin & Schwartz, 1966, p.35.)

In 1704, an extraordinary bed was advertised in *The Postman* as a lottery prize that appeared to have exceptional furniture to it:

A rich bed seven foot broad, eight foot long and about fourteen foot high in which no less than two thousand ounces of gold and silver, wrought in it containing four curtains, embroidered on both sides alike on a white silk tabby; three villains [valances] with tassels, three basses, two bonegraces, and four cantoneers embroidered on gold tissue cloth cost £3000, put up at £21400. (Macquoid, 1905, p.175.)

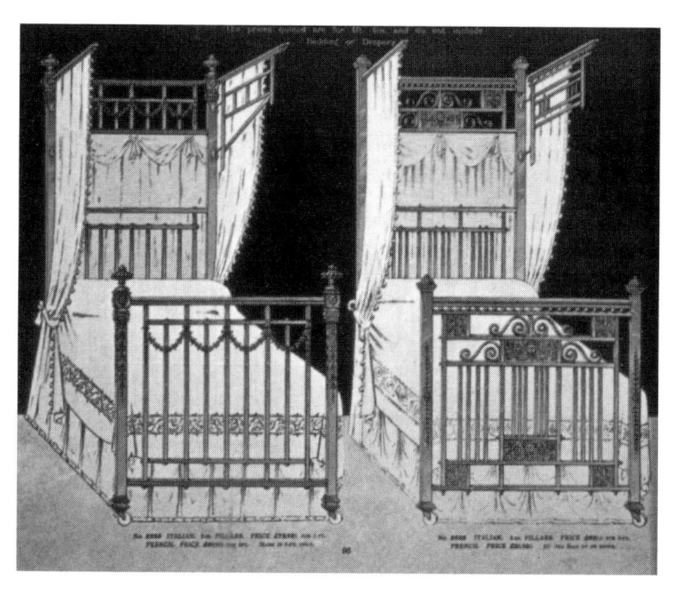

12. *Italian-style bed drapes, early twentieth century by H. Myers and Co*

The care and expense lavished on bed furniture is evident from Henry Purefoy's letter in 1735 to Anthony Baxter, an upholsterer: 'My mother intends to have the bed made up in the house by reason [if] the work must be cut it will require great care to have it fastened right again' (Eland, 1931, p.101).

Choice in the arrangement of the bed curtains was evident in the comment from Chippendale's *The Gentleman and Caginet Maker's Director*: 'The curtains are omitted [from the drawing] but may be made either to draw up in drapery, or to run on a Rod.' (1762, pl.41.) Choice was also important in the fabric selection. Hepplewhite in his *Cabinet Maker and Upholsterer's Guide* recommended the following fabrics to use for bed furniture:

They may be executed of almost every stuffs, which the loom produces. White dimity, plain or corded, is peculiarly applicable for the furniture, which, with a fringe with a gymp head, produced an effect of elegance and neatness truly agreeable. The Manchester stuffs have been wrought into Bed-furniture with good success. Printed cottons and linens are also very suitable; the elegance and variety of patterns of which, afford as much scope for taste, elegance and simplicity, as the most lively fancy can wish… In staterooms, where high degrees of elegance and grandeur are wanted, beds are frequently made of silk or satin, figured or plain, also of velvet, with gold fringe, etc. (1789, pp 17–18.)

Late eighteenth- and early nineteenth-century bed curtains were also fitted with cords and **pulleys** that allowed them to be pulled up to air the space and reveal the carving on bedsteads. This was sometimes referred to as festooning. In the example of Sheraton's Elliptic bed 'the curtains are drawn up by pulleys fixed in the under tester, and thus forms a drapery, by being tied to the pillars with cords' (*The Cabinet Maker's and Upholster's Drawing Book*, Appendix, 1802, p.6).

The choice of fabric for bed curtains was still important to Loudon. In 1839, he wrote that:

Moreen used to be employed for the hangings of best beds and bedroom windows … [but] is now considered as apt to harbour moths and other vermin; and therefore in these economical times, it is much less used than formerly. It has, however, the advantage of not taking fire so readily as chintz or dimity (1839, p.1080).

He noted that **chintz** was used for bed curtains and, in those cases, they were 'generally lined with cotton of a different colour, sometimes plain, and sometimes spotted' (ibid. p.1079). *The Workwoman's Guide* was also concerned with these aspects of bed curtain planning.

Beds that are furnished with thick drapery, such as stuff, moreen, damask or linens, seldom if ever, require linings, while chintzes and sometimes dimities are lined with glazed calico, in which case, care should be taken that the colour of the lining harmonizes not only with the bed furniture, but with the papering of the room. The fringe, tassels, ribbons, cord, and other decorations should match in colour with the lining. The pattern of the material should also be a consideration. Stripes or small patterns are suitable for small rooms, while large flowers or patterns best accord with large ones. (Hale, 1840, p.193.)

Apart from the considerations of fabric choice, the nineteenth-century housewife was conscious of the fine detail of bed furniture preparation. *The Workwoman's Guide* again:

> Bed furniture is composed of a top, a back, two head curtains, two foot curtains, one to outer and one to inner valance, one bottom valance and sometimes extra drapery laid on the back of the bed. When beds are lined, the lining is put inside the curtains, and within the top and back of the bed ... the curtains should just touch the ground, as also should the foot valance... The valances accord with the rest, having often fringes added to give greater finish. (ibid.)

At around the same time, the American author, Miss Leslie, gave a common sense reason for using bed curtains as more than simply decoration:

> The winter climate of most parts of America is such that as to render curtains highly desirable at that season, to all who can conveniently procure them. It is not necessary to draw them closely all round; but if the heads of the sleepers were always screened from the cold air of a cold room, there would perhaps be fewer toothaches, rheumatic pains, coughs and sore throats. (1841, pp 303–4.)

However, in the summer season the arrangement changed:

> In summer, after the curtains are taken down and put away, it is well, on a high post bedstead, to have a tester and top valance of dimity or white muslin; otherwise, the bare post and top rail will look naked and ungainly. There should also be a white foot-valance to correspond. (ibid. pp 307–8.).

By the 1870s, the taste for bed curtains was becoming an issue in relation to health and welfare. *Cassell's Household Guide* suggested a range of textiles for bed furniture. These included white **dimity** with deep white **bullion fringe** or netted **lace**; dimity with a chintz or coloured **cambric border** and chintz lined with a complementary colour or other combinations (1870, pp 241–2). However, they went on to say: 'Bed curtains are necessary or not according as a sleeping room is draughty or otherwise... Very often it is sufficient to drape the window and unless unmistakeably needed, the bed is better without' (ibid. p.372).

Even if they were used, advice as to how they should be fitted up, and what fabrics to use, continued to be offered. Charles Eastlake suggested that bed curtains should never be made longer than is necessary for actual use. 'If they hang within two or three inches of the floor it will be quite near enough'. The practice of looping voluminous curtains over cords when too long is 'a foolish and ugly fashion' (1878, p.212).

In an 1894 issue of *Household News*, concerns about bed curtains and the restriction of fresh air were again raised: 'if they [bed curtains] must be used, then make a valance fifteen inches deep about the canopy, and loop the long hangings clear back to the head post to admit air to the sleeper' (February, p.330).

In the twentieth century, bed hangings have fluctuated as fashions have changed, but in general have been abandoned for contemporary use.

See also **Bonegrace**, **Canopy**, **Cantoon**, **Curtain**, **Head cloth**, **Sparver**, **Tester**, **Train**, **Valance**.

FURTHER READING

Cummings, A.L. (1961). *Bed Hangings, A Treatise on Fabrics and Styles in the Curtaining of Beds 1650–1850*, Boston: SPNEA.

Gentle, N. (2001). 'A study of the late seventeenth century state bed from Melville House', *Furniture History*, 37, pp 1–16.

Hayward, M. (1998). 'Repositories of splendour Henry VIII's wardrobes of the robes and beds', *Textile History*, 29, 2, Autumn, pp 134–56.

Montgomery, F. (1979). 'Set of English crewel work bed hangings', *The Magazine Antiques*, 115, February, pp 330–42.

Bed head

See **Headboard**.

Bed lace

Bed lace was a decorative **binding** for use with **bed furniture** and **mattresses**. In the 1728 inventory of the shop of James Pilbeam, a mercer of Chiddingly, Sussex, there was listed 'Three groce of bed lace: £1 10s od' (http://www.chiddingly.gov.uk/History/James%20 Pilbeam.html).

In 1887, bed lace was defined as 'a description of binding of white cotton, twilled or figured and employed for binding dimities. It is likewise made in chintz colours, and in a diamond pattern for furniture prints, and striped with blue for bed ticking and palliasses' (Caulfeild & Saward, 1887, p.26). This definition was still acceptable in 1950 (*The Mercury Dictionary of Textile Terms*, 1950).

See also **Lace**.

Bed mat

A **straw** or woven **rush mat** used as a platform to lay onto the **bed cords** to give more comfort to the sleeper. Randle Holme mentions sack or mat bottoms to beds and distinctions are known between London and Cornish varieties (Thornton, 1984, p.370). Reference was made to itinerant sellers of bed mats in Fletcher & Shirley's comedy play *The Night Walker* of 1625: 'Buy a mat for your bed, buy a mat! A hassock for your feet' (*OED*). They were still in use in the early eighteenth century: Elizabeth Eve of Writtle had a Bedmatt and cords in her inventory in 1705 (Steer, 1969, p.232). Later, they were sometimes used as protection for carted furniture. Later still, bed mats made from fabric and padding were supplied to protect mattresses from the woven spring bases used in the nineteenth century and onward.

See also **Spring**.

Bed protection

Protective bed **curtains**, running on a separate outer rod, were designed to enclose beds and their more precious hangings to preserve them when not in use. From the mid-seventeenth century, prestige beds, especially, were supplied with a set of 'case curtains' and extra rods to keep the main fabrics clean and dust free.

In the 1659 inventory of Hampton Court, Charles I's bed had '3 large curtains of scarlet bazes being a case about the bed' (Macquoid & Edwards, 1924, p.35). In 1683, the Queen's Bedchamber in Ham House had 'a tower de leet [tour de lit] of white panches with a guilt rod' (Thornton & Tomlin, 1980, p.145). In the 1690s, Daniel Marot annotated one design for a bed with outer case curtains as necessary '*pour conserver le lit contre le poussière*' (to preserve the bed against dust) (Thornton, 1978, p.177). In 1703, the striped **velvet** and **silk** lined bed in Dyrham Park had case curtains of **worsted paragon** protecting it.

During 1786, Sir John Griffin Griffin was supplied with 'an outside polished curtain rod, made to fold on the Doom, with a set of Irish cloth curtains to draw round the bed' (Beard, 1997, p.310). These curtains, costing £1.15s.od., protected the state bed, which had cost him £398.os.od. in total.

Bed protection was not just reliant on case curtains. Around 1712, Celia Fiennes commented upon the arrangements in Ashtead Park: 'there are several bedchambers well furnish'd [with] good damask beds and hangings and window curtains of the same, and so neatly kept folded up in clean sheets pinn'd about the bed and hangings' (1995, p.232). While in the mid-nineteenth century, the ever-practical *Workwoman's Guide* explained the use of cloth or paper to protect fine

13. Bed protection for the State Bed (reconstruction), Dyrham Park (©NTPL/Andreas von Einsiedel)

furnishings on beds: 'Large sheets of coarse brown paper pasted together in lengths should be laid over the beds to catch dust. Some persons lay hurden or coarse linen between the head of the bed and these sheets of paper' (Hale, 1840, p.192).
See also **Bed cloth, Case rod, Compass rod**.

Bed rod
Rods intended to support bed **curtains** and **drapes**. Sheraton noted that they 'circumscribe the foot pillars, and the sides of the rod screw off about 8 inches from the pillars towards the head end, where the side rods slip onto a screw hook' (1803, p.298). He went on to say that **canopy** bed rods were 'made in two parts which lap past each other... These rods are made with a long plate at each end bent down about an inch, with two or three screw holes, with which to fix them to the underside of the rail' (ibid.).
See also **Bed protection**, **Case rod**, **Compass rod**.

Bed rug
See **Rugg**.

Bedspread
Bedspreads are a textile covering for a bed akin to a coverlet or counterpane. The term was introduced in America in the mid-nineteenth century. The names of bedspreads often reflect the type of fabric or the process from which they are produced. Elizabeth Dyer, writing in around 1923, noted the following types and commented upon them:

> Dimity bedspread. Not the same as dress dimity, but heavier. Resembles a lightweight, fine-wale pique. Because these spreads are lightweight, they wrinkle quickly, but they are easier to launder than some other kinds. They are the cheapest kind of regular spread, and come in several qualities.
>
> Ripplette. A trade name for a crinkled crêpe fabric, easily laundered, serviceable, lightweight, comes in various grades, but it is not considered very expensive.
>
> Satin Marseilles. A rich, lustrous, beautiful texture with woven figures, which stand out as in a brocade or damask. These spreads are expensive, and heavy to launder, but they wear well and are very good-looking.
>
> Lace (used over color). It is dainty, and elaborate, but often too ornate for the modest room.
>
> Unbleached muslin. In the last few years there has been a fad for embroidering unbleached muslin in gay colors and using it as a bedspread. It makes an inexpensive but often artistic and attractive covering, especially for simple bedrooms. It does seem, however, inconsistent to spend time embroidering such coarse, cheap material. It stays clean better than white, but owing to its embroidery it has to be washed carefully. For a change, unbleached muslin with cretonne appliquéd on it makes an inexpensive and attractive covering. These are fads. (pp 211–2.)

She went on to discuss the purchase of bedspreads:

> In buying a spread, decide what type you want. If a heavy, handsome one, you will probably choose a Satin Marseilles. If you want an expensive, handsome one and do not object to its wrinkling quickly, then hand-embroidered or Madeira linen would probably interest you. If you prefer a lightweight, easily laundered and inexpensive spread, then consider dimity, ripplette, or honeycomb. (ibid.)

Later twentieth-century cloths used for bedspreads have included **quilted**, stitched, tufted, sculptured deep **pile**, hobnail and honeycomb. The tufted bedspreads were popular for many years. The subtle distinctions between the different types of mid-twentieth-century tufted bedspreads were explained in *America's Fabrics*:

> Unclipped tufting is a continuous running stitch, which leaves uncut loops of tufting on the surface. The running stitch can be noted on the back of the fabric.
>
> Clipped tufting is made the same as unclipped tufting, except that as the decoration is stitched on, a knife cuts the loops. The back is the same as that of unclipped tufting. Clipped tufting is often wrongly called 'chenille tufting'. Any fabric or decoration called 'chenille' must employ chenille yarns.
>
> Candlewick or hobnail is made the same as tufting except that there is no continuous row of stitches in the back. The tufting is spaced, and the stitches on the front are cut, so that individual tufts of yarn are spaced throughout the face of the fabric.

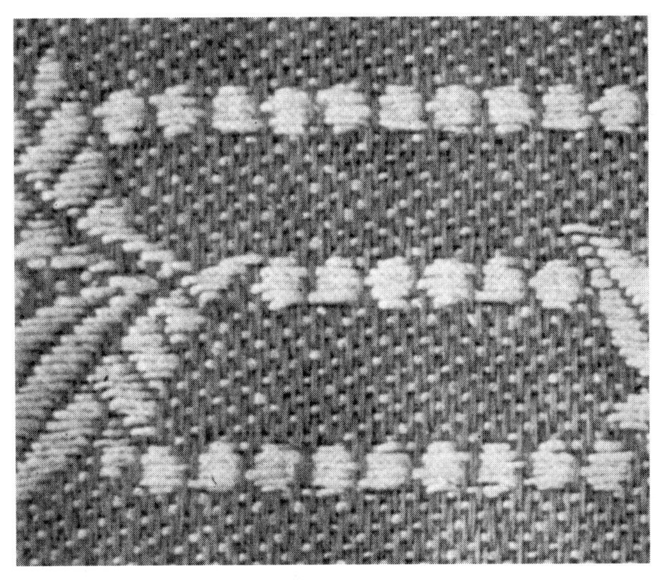

14. Detail of weave structure of a Grecian bedspread (E. Ostick, The Draper's Encyclopaedia, *1955)*

Unclipped punch work is accomplished differently from tufting. The low, uncut-pile is in a pattern. On the back of the fabric, the stitches are finer and more closely set than in tufting.

Clipped punch work is the same as unclipped punch work except that the loops are cut by hand to form a closely set, velvety pattern. (Bendure & Pfieffer, 1947, p.576.)

A little later, the British publication *The Draper's Encyclopaedia* recorded the following examples of bedspreads available:

Candlewick bedspread – tufted cloth that is easily adapted to changing designs and colours as it does not use a jacquard.

Linen bedspread – with an imbricate [scale-like] pattern called the shell design, often specified in 1950s for hospital use.

Grecian bedspread – made from one warp and one weft. It is sometimes mistaken for Alhambra. In the Grecian, all the binding is done by the jacquard. The warp is usually coloured and the weft a white condenser.

Honeycomb bedspread – uses the honeycomb weave for the ground part of the design. They are usually made all white.

Jaspé bedspread – is usually **stencil printed** on a grey (unbleached) cotton cloth. The cloth is woven with irregular coloured stripes to form a background for the printed design. The stripes are unequal in spacing and may be of a neutral colour, e.g. fawn or they may tone with the intended colour of the print, e.g. green stripes for a printed design with two or three tones of green.

Patent satin bedspread – the cloth consists of a raised figure on a plain ground, the figure being made with a coarse weft bound with a fine warp. They are usually woven white but may have a coloured weft. They were used widely for public services such as railways, ships and hospitals. (Ostick, 1955, p.355.)

See also **Alhambra quilt**, **Candlewick**, **Counterpane**, **Counterpoint**, **Coverlet**, **Cretonne**, **Dimity**, **Honeycomb**, **Jaspé**, **Mitcheline**, **Muslin**, **Satin**, **Stitch**, **Summer spread**, **Tufted carpet**.

Beere
See **Pillow bere**.

Belgian tapestry
A textile that was introduced *c.*1880. It was woven from **jute**, sometimes mixed with **linen**, and curiously was a speciality of Glasgow. It had coloured designs and was woven 52 inches (132 cm) wide. *The Dictionary of Needlework* explained that 'it is employed for covering furniture and making hangings of all kinds' (Caulfeild & Saward, 1887, p.26).
See also **Dundee tapestry**.

Belgian ticking
See **Ticking**.

Belladine fringe
See **Fringe: Belladine.**

Bellandine
A raw **silk** often used for **fringes**, **tassels** and the like. It was also used as sewing silk. Imported into Europe from the Near East, Postlethwayt described it as 'a kind of raw silk which the Levant or Turkey merchants call white silk and our workmen bellandine' (1751).

Belzamine (aka Belmozeen, Belzemine)
A type of watered and striped **silk** dress fabric that was sometimes used for furnishings. In the mid-eighteenth century, Sir Lawrence Dundas' 'Belzamine Bedchamber' at Moor Park had furnishings of 'crimson and yellow Belzamine' (Walton, 1980, p.396). It remained fashionable into the last quarter of that century at least. Arthur Young commented upon the Duke of Bedford's French bedchamber at Woburn, saying it was 'exceedingly elegant; the bed and hangings a very rich belmozeen silk' (Young, 1770, vol.1, p.24).

Benares
A furnishing fabric with a **cotton warp** and cotton/**rayon weft** in **brocade** designs (*The Mercury Dictionary of Textile Terms*, 1950).

Bengal
Piece goods exported from the Bengal region of India during the seventeenth century. Textiles were often striped and usually of a **silk/cotton** mix. A reference from a 1680 poem by Polexfen mentioned that: 'their Persian silks, Bengalls, Printed and Painted Calicoes are used for beds, hanging of rooms' (*OED*). 'Bengal Stripes' were striped **ginghams** brought originally from Bengal and first made in Great Britain at Paisley (*Draper's Dictionary*, Beck, 1882).
See also **Bengaline**, **Muslin**.

Bengaline
Heavy **poplin**-type woven cloth, with **warp** faced crosswise ribs that are round and raised like poplin. It was initially made of **silk** in Bengal, India and was first sold as **Bengal**. It often has **wool** or **cotton** filling in the ribs, which does not show. Petersham is bengaline woven to ribbon widths. The name bengaline appears to have been a later nineteenth-century introduction. In 1887, Caulfeild & Saward defined it as a

French textile, only 24 inches (61 cm) wide, woven from silk and wool, like poplin but with a larger cord (1887, p.27). It was later woven from **rayon** or cotton and recommended for **curtains**, covers and beds (French, 1947).
See also **Cotele**.

Berber

A name given to a style of **carpet** and the yarns used, and usually refers to cut-**pile** and loop-pile carpeting made from natural coloured 'berber' **wool** yarns. The speckled effect of the greys, browns and creams was attractive to consumers, particularly in the period following the 1970s.

Bergamot (aka Tapissèries de Bergame)

A woven fabric or **tapestry** composed of a coarse mixture of **flock** and **hair** mixed with **cotton** or **hemp warps**, apparently first produced at Bergamo in Italy. It was patterned with **wefts brocaded** in a mix of colours and designs. It was woven on a wide loom in panels that could then be stitched together. **Border** widths were also woven so that complete hangings of any size could be made up. They were particularly made in Rouen and were sometimes called *tapisseries de Rouen. The Universal Dictionary of Trade Commerce*, 1751 described them as:

> a coarse tapestry, which is manufactured with several sorts of spun thread [including] silk, wool cotton, hemp, ox, and cow or goat's hair. It is properly a weft of all those sorts of thread, the warp of which is commonly hemp. Formerly the French tried to send some bergamos into foreign countries. Particularly towards the north; but at present they are scarce used but anywhere in the kingdom, and chiefly at Paris, there being few tradesmen, or mean people, in that great city, who would not think it a disgrace, if when they set up they had not a bergamo tapestry in their rooms. (Postlethwayt.)

Postlethwayt then explains the patterns available:

> Some [patterns] are after the manner of the point of Hungary; other with broad stripes, worked with the figures of flowers, birds, or other animals, some with broad and narrow stripes, even, and without figures; others again which are called China's and Scale's, because they are worked so as to imitate the point of China, and the scales of fishes.

In 1786, Chambers referred to 'Bergamot' as a coarse tapestry. Nearly 100 years later, Beck still defined bergamot as 'a common tapestry, made of ox and goats' hair with cotton or hemp'. (1882)
See also **Dornix**.

FURTHER READING

Thornton, P. (1960). 'Tapissèries de Bergame', *Pantheon*, VI, XVIII, Jahrgang, March.

Berlin wool-work

A form of **needlework** that is particularly associated with mid-nineteenth-century upholstered chair or seat covers. It was the first type of needlework to be commercialised and practised widely by the middle classes as a form of homemade **upholstery** covering. Based on the ancient *opus pulvinarium*, it is usually worked in a cross-stitch. It was also known as **canvas work** and in this case worked with a tent stitch. It was mainly produced by amateurs using imported German **woollen** yarns, called zephyrs, which were worked into square meshed canvas using cross- or tent stitches. The novelty was the use of printed and coloured paper patterns, which showed a grid plan of the threads that could be counted out. The introduction of machine-made double thread canvas helped to ensure an exact correspondence between the

15. Berlin wool-work sewing pattern (S. Caulfeild & B. Saward, The Dictionary of Needlework, *1887)*

counted cross-stitches and the published paper patterns supplied on squared paper. Berlin was the centre of the production and sale of the yarns and patterns, with the earliest patterns being published in 1803–4. In 1810, Ludwig Wilhelm Wittich issued patterns with hand-coloured squares, which were exported widely and published in magazines such as the American *Godey's Lady's Book*.

However, it was not until 1831 that the first serious importation of patterns and yarns into England began, by a Mr Wilks of Regent Street, London. By the early 1840s, the method became highly fashionable so that by the mid-1840s designs were sometimes printed directly onto the canvas with instructions issued in letters and numbers. In 1846, Henry Wood published 50 designs suitable for furniture in his *A Useful and Modern Work on Cheval and Pole Screens, Ottomans, Chairs and Settees for Mounting Berlin Wool Work*, confirming that the work needed mounting professionally before it could be used.

The designs were often in the 'style troubadour' with elements of images from the works of Walter Scott, or popular Victorian artists. However, the most popular appear to have been floral designs of great variety. By the 1850s, restrained designs, often on a background of white, were giving way to black backgrounds with harsh-coloured woollen yarns (resulting from the development of coal-tar **dyes** in Germany) offering stained-glass brilliance. The resultant work was widely used for mounting into pole **screens** and **fire screens** and **upholstery**.

Berlin wool-work was not without its critics. Miss Lambert, writing in 1842, considered that some might think that 'needlework as practiced at the present time, is but a mechanical art; and the recent invention of Berlin patterns may somewhat favour the opinion. This we entirely disown… [it is] done for sale in Germany, where neither taste nor judgement are displayed' (Lambert, p.21).

By 1886, *The Magazine of Art* was vituperative in its comments: 'With such signs of improvement, we may feel sure that whatever betides, so disastrous a crisis as the Berlin wool epidemic is henceforth impossible. It has left in its wake vestiges not even now effaced.' The authors of *The Dictionary of Needlework* also expressed concerns about the design quality: 'The work itself is capable of good results, and is strong and lasting; but when it degenerates into the mere copying of patterns conceived in defiance of all true art principles, it helps to degrade and not elevate the mind' (Caulfeild & Saward, 1887, p.28).

In the 1840s, especially in the USA, a variation on Berlin work was introduced. It used the same method of stitching but the loops were trimmed to tufts and the whole design was made through a heavy ground fabric under a canvas. When finished, the canvas was removed, thread-by-thread, leaving the wool-work on the base cloth. The ubiquitousness of Berlin wool-work meant that it was regarded as synonymous with **embroidery** but, by 1912, it was apparently 'rarely employed except as a covering for footstools or chairs' (Bitmead, 1912, p.33).
See also **Art embroidery**, **Beadwork**, **Stitch: Cross**.

FURTHER READING

Hughes, T. (n.d.). *English Domestic Needlework, 1660–1860*, London: Abbey Fine Arts.
Karr, L. (1984). 'Berlin wool work' in Ring, Betty (ed.), *Needlework: An Historical Survey*, New York: Antiques Magazine Library, Main Street/Universe Books, pp 35–48.
Lambert, Miss (1842). *Handbook of Needlework*, London: John Murray.
Morris, B. (1962). *Victorian Embroidery*, London: Herbert Jenkins.
Proctor, M.G. (1972). *Victorian Canvas Work*, London: Batsford.
Vincent, M. (1988). *The Ladies' Worktable: Domestic Needlework in Nineteenth Century America*, Allentown, PA: Allentown Art Museum.
Warner, P. (1991). *Embroidery: A History*, London: Batsford.
Wood, H. (1846). *A Useful and Modern Work on Cheval and Pole Screens, Ottomans, Chairs and Settees, for Mounting Berlin Wool Work*, London: Ackermann.

Bias binding
A cloth strip cut at an angle of 45 degrees that makes the cloth stretch slightly. It is used as an edging or to wrap **piping** cord.
See also **Binding**.

Bible front
A sewing technique that is used to give sharp definition to the edges of upholstered work. It is made in conjunction with the first **stuffing**. A row of stitching is placed crosswise around the edge of the seat. The feather stitch is applied to the top to compress the edge into a sharp line of stuffing which then gives delineation to the finished seat.
See also **Stitch: Feather**.

Billiard cloth
A fine quality **woollen** cloth intended to cover the surface of billiard tables. It is finer, of a higher quality and with a better finish than the baize used in the eighteenth century for **table carpets** and desktops. In 1858, Simmonds' *Dictionary of Trade Products* defined it as 'Green woollen broadcloth manufactured to cover a billiard table which is piece-dyed and seventy-two inches to eighty-one inches wide'.
See also **Baize**.

Binder bar
Metal (brass, aluminium) bar devised to bind or hold the edges of **floorcloth**, **linoleum**, **matting** or **carpet** where they meet another surface or edge. Many varieties have been made including plain, corrugated and 'coiled on a roll' types. Specifically designated 'oilcloth plates' were being sold in the later nineteenth century for this purpose.

Binding
Bindings are a particular form of passementerie or **trimming** used in **upholstery** and furnishing work. For example, Bess of Hardwick in 1599 paid 22 shillings for 'three ounces of sylvar Lase for bynding lace for a bed' (Levey, 1998, p.31). According to Sheraton, binding was a term used by upholsterers to describe:

> The various kinds of narrow laces used to strengthen and ornament the edges of any sort of curtain, drapery or bed furniture. Bindings for ticking are about three fourths of an inch broad, of white and blue stripe of cotton and linen, others a little broader, of a diamond pattern of worsted and linen, the principle bindings are as follows: Bindings of silk ribbons, various. Silk and worsted ditto. Silk covered laces, of various colours, 1 inch and upward broad. Silk guard lace, and silk quality. (1803, p.51.)

A little later, specific bindings were referred to in *A Treatise on Haberdashery and Hosiery* where the following types were noted:

> Chintz binding used for binding white dimity and printed furnitures; and the following for binding bed ticks and mattresses viz blue striped binding.
>
> Diamond binding, otherwise None-so-Pretty.
>
> Common quality otherwise worsted binding.
>
> Venetian – is a fine kind of worsted binding used as the binders of Venetian blinds. (Perkins, 1833.)

Fifty years later *The Dictionary of Needlework* also recorded particular bindings for **upholstery** work that were very similar:

> Bag strapping [is] a binding employed by upholsterers, to preserve selvedges, and resembling a very broad stay-tape…
>
> Bed lace is a twilled or figured white cotton binding used for dimities. It is made in chintz colours for furniture, also in diamond patterns, and in blue stripes for bed tick and palliasses…
>
> Carpet bindings are made in plain and variegated colours to match the carpets. The best qualities are all worsted…
>
> Venetians are used for several purposes in upholstery. Their chief use, however, is at present for Venetian blinds … they are dyed ingrain, and are green, blue, yellow, white; they are now sometimes used for embroidery. (Caulfeild & Saward, 1887, p.35.)

See also **Bag strapping**, **Bed lace**, **Bias binding**, **Boot tape**, **Carpet binding**, **Ferret**, **Galloon**, **Guard lace**, **None-so-Pretty**, **Passementerie**, **Tapes**, **Venetian binding**, **Venetian blind**.

Bird's-eye
(a) A generic description for any material that is woven with a small figured design that resembles a bird's-eye. A true bird's-eye is woven with an appearance of a small diamond shape having a dot in its centre. It is often woven with loosely twisted yarns making a soft absorbent fabric. The term also refers to the woven pattern of a dot in a diamond shape in other materials.
(b) Bird's-eye is also a very soft, lightweight and absorbent fabric, usually of dobby weave with a loosely twisted filling to increase absorbency. It is made from **cotton** and **linen** or a blend of **rayon** staple and cotton

and is used as a **towelling** or napkin material. It is also called 'diaper cloth' and is used for that purpose as well.

Known as a dress and a furnishing fabric from at least the seventeenth century, it was also a type of **carpet**. An Act of 1678 regulating the London cloth market listed 'Bird's eye carpeting, Bristol carpet and all sorts of carpeting' (Thornton, 1978, p.353).

See also **Weave**.

Birom Banies
See **Calico**.

Black work (aka Spanish work)
An **embroidery** style worked in black **silk** on white **linen**, employed especially in Spain and England in the sixteenth century. Although used for apparel, it was also intended for decorating **cushions** and **pillowcases** etc. Katherine of Aragon may have introduced it into England, although it was probably known before. The 1537 inventory of her Wardrobe goods at Baynard Castle lists 'one pair of sheets of fine Holland cloth wrought with Spanish work of black silk upon the edges' (Camden Society, *Camden Miscellany*, 1855, vol.III). A similar reference is found 70 years later when the 1601 Hardwick Hall inventory listed '3 curtains wrought with black silk needlework upon fine holland cloth with button and loops of black silk' (Boynton, 1971, p.23).

See also **Needlework**.

Blanket
Both a term for a fabric and a covering for beds, originally of undyed **wool**. Mythically, the material is named in honour of Thomas Blanket (Blanquette), a Flemish weaver who lived in Bristol, England, in the fourteenth century, who was allegedly the first to use it for sleeping to keep warm. According to Henn Havard, the *blanchet* was a form of white **linen** bedding originating in medieval France.

An early English reference from 1392 is in *Piers Plowman*: 'nober blankets in hus bed'. The fact that they were used in pairs is noted in a will of 1444 that refers to 'a pair of blankettis' (Surtees Society, *Testamenta Eboracensia; or wills registered at York 1836–1902*, vol.II, 1855, p.111). In the sixteenth century and onward, they were often made from fustian with a fuzzy napped surface.

Superior, thicker blankets called 'Spanish blankets' were in use in Tudor times. Although introduced into Norwich by Flemings, they were later made in Oxfordshire. In 1578, a reference to 'Oxon blanckettes alias Spannyssche rugges' in an Exchequer account make a link between Witney and Spanish **rugs** or blankets (Kerridge, 1985, p.35). They continued to be judged highly (see below). The Hardwick Hall inventory of 1601 listed 'sixe spanish blanketes' (merino wool) in Bess's bedchamber (Boynton, 1971, p.31) and, in 1679, the Ham House inventory had Spanish blankets recorded as well as **silk** blankets.

Decoration was sometimes integral to the blanket. In his 1653 inventory, Cardinal Mazarin had 'fine woollen coverlets [or blankets] from England with four blue crowns in the four corners' (Thornton, 1978, p.113). This decoration was described 100 years later, when it was noted that:

> In order to adorn them, they work stripes of blue and red wool at each end, and a crown at each corner; with this difference however, that the stripes are worked in the loom; and the crowns are worked with a needle, after the blankets are finished, and before they are sent to the fuller. (Postlethwayt, 1751.)

Sheraton was quite specific about the types of wool that were used:

> The most famous place for [blanket] manufacture is Witney, in Oxfordshire. The wool of which blankets are made is called felt wool, or that which comes off sheepskins. Of the head wool and bay wool made blankets of 12, 11, 10, quarters broad; of the ordinary and middle sort, blankets of 8 and 7 quarters broad, of the best tail wool blankets of 6 quarters wide. (Sheraton, 1803, pp 55–6.)

The tradition established by the seventeenth century continued into the nineteenth century. In 1840, *The Workwoman's Guide* noted that 'rose' blankets:

> were generally sold in pairs, or two woven together. These, for beds must be cut, in which case, the edges are sewed over in a very wide kind of button hole stitch, with red or other coloured wools, also a kind of circle or star is often worked in the corner with various coloured wools. (Hale, p.200.)

By the latter half of the nineteenth century, *The Dictionary of Needlework* noted that blankets could be woven, knitted or made from needlefelt. Spanish blankets were the most expensive and still considered amongst the best as they were woven from Spanish **merino** wool. Other blanket varieties included Yorkshire blankets that were used by servants or for putting under **sheets**; Austrian blankets that had coloured stripes and were used as **portières**; as well as scarlet blankets and grey and brown charity blankets (Caulfeild & Saward, 1887, p.36). Similarly, *Cassell's Household Guide* recommended the 'brightly coloured Austrian blankets [that] many people use for travelling rugs as well as for bedding'. They also commended 'Aldershot blankets, made of dark wool, slate coloured or brown, [which] are useful for servants' blankets, and they are inexpensive' (1870, vol.1, pp 285 and 346).

One idea that links blankets to **coverlets** is mentioned in *Cassell's Household Guide*, where they discuss a method of putting 'six blankets quilted together like a coverlet and which can readily be taken apart, washed and put together again, [to use] as a topping for a spring mattress' (ibid. p.285).

Two blankets woven together, as mentioned above in 1840, were again discussed nearly 100 years later:

> Blankets often come double; i.e., two blankets are woven together at one end. This double kind is hard to handle, but it has this advantage when a pair folded regularly proves too short for the bed you can fold it with one layer shorter than the other, thus getting length enough to tuck in. You cannot do this with two cut blankets. (Dyer, *c*.1923, p.209.)

Acrylic, **cotton** and other fibres have been used in the second half of the twentieth century for marketing reasons.

See also **Barracan**, **Bedclothes**, **Caddow**, **Chalons**, **Fledge**, **Fustian**, **Hudson's Bay blanket**, **Lindsey-woolsey**, **Navajo rug**, **Rugg**, **Serge**, **Stitch**, **Swanskin**, **Trucking cloth**.

FURTHER READING

Plummer, A. & Early, R. (1969). *The Blanket Makers 1669–1969*, London: Routledge and Kegan Paul.

Blind
A generic name for a wide range of products mainly intended to keep the sun from penetrating interiors, but incidentally offering protection from dust, prying eyes and also acting as a decorative feature in their own right. Sheraton (1803) describes them as well as any: 'Amongst cabinet-makers, [blind] denotes some kind of opaque medium, placed

or fit into a window as a check, either to the sun's rays, or to the intruding eye of an overlooker. Of such mediums, there is a great variety, either placed internally or externally.' (For particular varieties see under individual entries below.)

During the later eighteenth and early nineteenth centuries, patent activity for the design and making of window blinds was extensive. In 1760, Gowin Knight patented a 'machine window blind' (Patent no.750) and, in 1768, Thomas Laycock devised 'window blinds for coaches and other carriages' (Patent no.891). In 1769, Edward Bevan patented improved 'Venetian window blinds', in 1812 Benjamin Cook devised a method of making window blinds (3609), and in 1821 Charles Tuely (4603) patented window blinds. In 1823, Barron and Wilson devised a new way of constructing and manufacturing window blinds and of converting Venetians into projecting blinds. Between 1826 and 1850, there were 14 patent applications for developments in blind design. According to Sheraton:

> The cheapest kind of blind is that of green canvas fixed to two sticks, either of mahogany or wainscot, hung by a couple of rings and hooks screwed to the lowermost sash frames. Those sort most commonly used are of mahogany, either to fold in two or in one leaf, with green stuff of some kind strained into a rabbet in the frame. These blinds are sometimes fixed with slip hinges, so that the frames may occasionally be taken off. When they are made to fold, they have a bolt on the left side, and a turnbuckle in the centre of the right to keep them to their place. (1803, p.57.)

In 1808, George Smith recommended that when **curtains** did not fully draw across, they 'require spring blinds of the same colour as the principal draperies to drop behind the muslins and the Drapery to remain fixed' (p.2).

Towards the end of the century, *Cassell's Household Guide* was explicit about blind choice:

> The front windows [of a house] may have Venetian blinds if it be a southern aspect, while if facing the north they may be made of buff union cloth, which produces a mellow warm tone when the light passes through it, or the newly-introduced red blinds, which are equally pretty and comfortable looking. (1870, vol.1, 19.)

The practical Mrs H.W. Beecher recommended that window blinds made from 'common burlaps, with a small outlay of money and a large outlay of ingenuity, may be made very charming in effect' (Beecher, 1879).

By the early twentieth century, it was suggested to American department store buyers that blinds were 'carried for accommodation' as 'there is little profit in them and a scale in this line is of no particular advantage'. They went on to describe the three main qualities: 'Opaque which was the cheapest shade; Cambric being the best wearing shade tested and adopted by the US for use in all government buildings; and the Holland as the dressiest and best appearing shade for residences' (O'Leary, 1916, p.100).

Cane

Cane blinds were fixed to the lower half of the window for screening purposes, but were open enough to allow some light. Two cane blinds were supplied for some windows at Hampton Court in 1730 (Beard, 1997, p.302).

In the later nineteenth century, *Ward & Lock's Home Book* (1880) pointed out that 'cane blinds are at present much in use for sitting rooms'. By 1881, Robert Edis was decrying 'the curious twisted cane inventions, which are bad in design, and infinitely too spotty and strong in colour to be pleasant accessories in any room in which artistic decoration is thought of' (1881, p.267).

16. Cane window blind (Anon., Artistic Homes or How to Furnish with Taste: a handbook for all housekeepers, *1880)*

Transparent/Painted

The idea of sun-blinds that let in light, but shield the interior from the rays, has a long history. Known during the Renaissance in Italy, the examples of oiled paper and cloth indicate an early interest in the possibilities of translucent materials. Early types of blind used a framework of sticks onto which was mounted paper or **linen** to make a 'window'. Examples of this are recorded from 1217. By 1594, Sir Hugh Platt recommended the use of parchment, which could be painted. In his work, *The Jewel House or Art and Nature*, he explained the process:

> Strain [the finest parchment] upon a frame ... and when it is dry oil it all over with a [brush] ... and when it is thorough dry, it will show very clear, and serve in windows instead of glass especially in such rooms as are subject to overseers. You may draw any personage, beast, tree, flower, or coat armour upon the parchment before it is oiled, and then cutting your parchment into square panes, and making, slight frames for them, they will make a pretty show in your windows, and keep the room very warm. This I commend before oiled paper, because it is more lasting, and will endure the blustering and stormy weather much better than paper. (Ayres, 1981, p.97.)

In 1687, John Smith, in his work *The Art of Painting in Oyl...*, described 'the manner of painting cloth or sarsnet sash-windows'. The material was wetted, strained onto the frame and, when dry, varnished. The fabric could be paper, **silk** or linen. This was fitted inside glazed sash windows and acted as a sun shield. When verdigris was mixed with the varnish, it created a green colour, which was 'very comfortable to the sight'. On the paper or silk fabric, you might 'paint upon them what fancy you please, but a landskip is most common and natural' (Smith, 1687).

In 1729, John Brown, a London upholsterer, advertised that he 'made and sold Window Blinds of all Sorts, Painted in Wire, Canvas, Cloth and Sassenet [Sarcenet], after the best and most lasting manner so that if ever so dull and dirty they will clean with sope and sand and be like new' (Heal, 1953, p.25). Chippendale supplied Lansdowne House in 1770 with 'A pair of folding window blinds of green painted canvas and mahogany frames' (Gilbert, 1978, p.256).

The nineteenth century saw a rise in the popularity of transparent blinds. In 1807, Edward Orme discussed how to decorate blinds of silk, linen or wire **gauze** in his *An Essay on Transparent Prints*. Orme's blinds pulled up out of a box near the windowsill. In a similar vein to John Smith's examples from the seventeenth century (see above), in 1814 John Dobson, a Newcastle upholsterer, advertised in the *Newcastle Courant* that he stocked transparent window blinds 'on which are painted gentlemen's seats, parks or pleasure gardens' (16 April, *DEFM*, p.247).

Twenty years later, Nathaniel Whittock, in his *Decorative Painters' and Glaziers' Guide*, published in 1827, described his method of making painted window blinds (ch.V, p.188). He particularly recommended fine Scotch **cambric** or **lawn** as the base fabric for transparent blinds.

The American authors Webster & Parkes also discussed blinds decorated with painted designs in transparent colours of various subjects, including landscapes, stained glass, arabesque patterns, etc. (1844) These were very popular in America. Writing in 1850, Andrew Downing suggested that the best arrangement was to have blinds:

> of plain brown or drab linen. Nothing can be more vulgar and tawdry for a country house than most of the transparencies and painted curtains… If they are badly painted, as is generally the case, they are an offence to cultivated taste, if they are well painted with copies of landscapes, etc. they are not good in the sense of pictures, while they only hide, nine times out of ten, a more interesting view of the real landscape without. (Thornton, 1984, p.225.)

About the same time, the American Great Western Oil Cloth and Window Shade Manufactory of Cincinnati advertised that:

> We now have a complete assortment of these tasteful and neat shades for parlors, chambers etc, both in plain borders and with neat centre pieces. In these goods, we keep none but the best, made on the finest cambric, and of pure gold leaf. Painted shades are particularly recommended – of every description, comprising Fancy borders, Landscapes, Gothics, and Imitation Venetians suitable for halls, dining rooms, chambers, etc. (Pettit, 1970, p.216.)

Miss Leslie, in *The Lady's House Book*, discusses the use of short window blinds made from fabric which was partially translucent: 'For sitting rooms, chambers, etc., the blinds generally in use are of white muslin. Those of plain unfigured Swiss or Scotch muslin look much the best, but are more easily seen through than when the muslin is striped or cross barred' (1854, pp 191–2). She went on to describe their making with a hem and a case at the top through which to run a long tape. The tape would suspend the 'blind' from a nail in each side of the window frame.

Similar arrangements were suggested in the British publication, *Artistic Homes*, where blinds were recommended for bedrooms and it was said that 'nothing was better than plain book muslin. Two slender canes or peeled willow wands make better rods for these than either tapes, wire, or in especial [sic] the ugly flat pieces of brass sometimes adopted' (Anon., 1880, p.35). An alternative was suggested: 'Dried ferns sometimes coloured, and fixed on the glass are occasionally used as low blinds but the practice has little to recommend it' (ibid. p.36).

In the twentieth century, this form of **muslin** was still recommended:

> Muslin and the finer cambric are the fabrics generally used for window shades. The finishes or coatings depend upon whether shade or blind is to be opaque or translucent. A pyroxylin shade cloth has a cellulose compound applied to an unfilled cambric fabric. Linseed oil is used for hand painted shades. (Bendure & Pfieffer, 1947, p.594.)

Wire

From the late seventeenth century, woven wire or gauze wire screens mounted into a wooden frame were made to fit windows. In 1695, the Earl of Dorset sent '2 wyre skreens' to Copt Hall (Beard, 1997, p.297). By 1730, John Brown (Heal, 1953, p.15) was advertising that he stocked 'Blinds for windows made and curiously painted on canvas, silk or wire'. Wire blinds were also noted in the contents of Robert Walpole's house in Chelsea. When it was sold in April 1747, it included a sale lot of '2 brass wire window blinds'.

Early nineteenth-century commentators still recommended the painted versions. Loudon, in his *Encyclopaedia*, suggested that the blinds be painted or 'ornamented with landscapes, figures or other objects; or in the case of a country tradesman, in a roadside cottage, they may exhibit the owner's name, or the implements or products of his trade' (1839, p.342). In the mid-nineteenth century, *Godey's Lady's Book* compared these wire or painted blinds to Venetians and noted that:

> They last a long time, and are free from the objections peculiar to the Venetian and muslin. But any attempt to disfigure them by absurd ornaments should be rigidly avoided. A plain band of one or two colours, running round, about an inch or two from the edge, is, in general, the suitable decoration for wire blinds. Beside the wire gauze made in England, there is a kind imported from China which has a very fanciful appearance, with its grotesque paintings, and which suits well with the style of certain old-fashioned rooms. (June 1860, p.508.)

In the 1880s, in America especially, wire screens manufactured in plain colours or decorated with patterns were popular. They were particularly intended as protection against the ingress of insects. Edis considered they had a 'general dirty and dingy look, and everlasting painted ornament of Greek fret or honeysuckle border' (1881, p.266).

Instructions for their manufacture were still being offered in 1907. Paul Hasluck discussed the manufacture of wire blinds from wire gauze or perforated zinc in his work on window blinds.

See also **Austrian shade**, **Blind holland**, **Bonnet blind**, **Bookcase blind**, **Canvas**, **Casement blind**, **Curtain paper**, **Diaphane**, **Festoon window curtain**, **Florentine blind**, **Helioscene blind**, **Jalousie**, **Mini blind**, **Oriental blind**, **Pinoleum**, **Roller blind**, **Roman blind**, **Short blind**, **Shutter blind**, **Spanish blind**, **Union**, **Venetian blind**.

FURTHER READING

Brightman, A. (1972). *Window Treatments for Historic Houses, 1700–1850*, Washington, DC: National Trust for Historic Preservation.

Cornforth, J. & Fowler, J. (1974). *English Decoration in the Eighteenth Century*, London: Barrie and Jenkins.

Garrett, E.D. (1990). *At Home: The American Family, 1750–1870*, New York: Abrams.

Hasluck, P. (1907). *Window Blinds*, London: Cassell.

Huls, M.E. (1986). *Window Treatments: A Bibliography of Current Literature*, Monticello: Vance.

Kron, J. & Slesin, S. (1978). *High-Tech: The Industrial Style Source Book for the Home*, New York: Potter.

Macfarlane, J. (1959). 'Shades of our forefathers', *Antiques*, 96, August, pp 122–5.

Mayhew, E. & Myers Jr, M. (1980). *A Documentary History of American Interiors from the Colonial Era to 1915*, New York: Scribner.

Nielson, K.J. (1990). *Window Treatments*, New York: Van Nostrand Reinhold.

Orme, E. (1807). *An Essay on Transparent Prints and on Transparencies in General*, London: The Author.

Parrissien, S. (1992). *Curtains and Blinds*, London: The Georgian Group.
Rees, Y. (1990). *Window Style*, New York: Van Nostrand Reinhold.
Thornton, P. (1978), *Seventeenth-Century Interior Decoration England, France, and Holland*, New Haven and London: Yale University Press.
Thornton, P. (1991). *The Italian Renaissance Interior, 1400–1600*, London: Weidenfeld and Nicolson.
Westman, A. (1997). 'Eighteenth century window blinds at Audley End: a recent discovery', *Furniture History*, 33, pp 157–62.
Winkler, G.C. & Moss, R. (1986). *Victorian Interior Decoration; American Interiors, 1830–1900*, New York: Holt.

Blind chintz
A nineteenth-century **printed cotton** cloth made in widths from 36 to 100 inches (91 to 254 cm) in increments of 2 inches (5 cm). The designs were principally stripes that were printed to resemble **Venetian blinds**. The enormous selection of widths confirms its use as a substitute for blinds (Caulfeild & Saward, 1887, p.36). In 1950, *The Mercury Dictionary of Textile Terms* mentioned that blind chintz had a glazed finish and was usually green, blue, brown or grey.
See also **Chintz**, **Printed blind**.

Blind cord
The **cords** that are intended to raise or lower window **blinds**. 'These are made of linen or cotton thread and of flax covered with worsted. In amber, blue, crimson, green and scarlet' (Caulfeild & Saward, 1887, p.36). *The Mercury Dictionary of Textile Terms* (1950) concurred.

Blind frame
A frame designed for a sash window upon which is fixed a blind or other cover. John Smith (1687) referred to them concerning his arrangement for fitting stretched paper or **silk** to act as a transparent blind in a window.
See also **Blind**.

Blind holland
A **cotton** or **linen** fabric that was intended especially for making window blinds. Caulfeild & Saward explained:

> A description of Holland is employed for window roller blinds, and in cotton as well as linen. They are highly glazed and sized, so as to be less influenced by dust, and are made in white, blue, buff green and in stripes of different colours. The widths begin at 28 inches and increase by 2 inches up to 100. (1887, p.253.)

See also **Holland**, **Silesia**.

Blister cloth
A fabric with a pebbled surface that may be produced in the loom by varying tension, by chemical means or by using various yarns that shrink at differing rates.

Block fringe
See **Fringe: Block**.

Block-printed
See **Pintado**, **Printed textiles**.

Bobbin lace
See **Lace**.

Bobbin net (aka Brussels net)
Bobbin net was the first machine-made netted fabric (usually **cotton**), imitating bobbin lace. A fine or coarse hexagonal mesh was obtained by twisting the **wefts**. The multi-thread machine was invented in 1808 by John Heathcoat and then later adapted to power working and the **jacquard**. Heavier weights were used for **curtaining**. In 1836, it was noted as being a recent invention (Taylor, 1836, p.217). Plain bobbin nets were used as a base for **embroidery** or **appliqué** during the nineteenth century.

In 1905, Alice Kellogg noted that: 'The least expensive lace curtain is one of plain bobbinet which may be bought by the yard and finished with an edge or insertion.' (Kellogg, 1905, p.153.)

Bobbin net was still recommended for curtains in the 1950s, especially in conjunction with **ruffles** and **tiebacks** rather than just straight hangings. It was also recommended for dressing tables, lampshades and **pillows** fitted over a lining (Taylor, 1951). It has also been made in **silk**, **rayon** and **nylon**.

A variety of bobbin net with small dots scattered over the surface was called point d'esprit.

Bobble fringe
See **Fringe: Ball**.

Bocasine
The name appears to come from the Spanish *bocaci*, and the French *boucassin*, meaning 'cotton stuff', and it was used for linings and **upholstery** work in the medieval period.

In 1434, Lady Elizabeth de Hay owned '*unum materas de bokasyn*' (Leaf, 1934, p.21). Cotgrave in 1611 suggested that it was: 'a kind of fine buckeram that hath a resemblance to taffeta, and is much used for lining' (ibid. p.2). Henry VI's inventory listed '1 cushion de bokasyn', (ibid. p.21) while 'Bugasines or Calico Buckrams' were listed in the Massachusetts *Book of Rates* for 1660 (Montgomery, 1984, p.171).

Bocking
The name of a town in Essex, where weavers produced a baize cloth. Bocking is close to Braintree and Colchester, the centres of the manufacture of baize. Bocking is a particular type of baize. In 1783, Beawes noted that 'Bocking baise is sold by measure and are only fit for the Portugal market, whilst the Colchester Baise are solely vendible in Spain'. It was probably also used as a protective material. In 1840, Theodore Baker advertised in the *Boston Almanac* (p.126) that he 'has for sale Quilts, Counterpanes, Comforters, Bockings, Crumb Cloths'.
See also **Baize**.

Body Brussels
A term originating in America, to describe narrow-woven body Brussels **carpet**, where the face yarns run in the body of the cloth when not required for the pattern (i.e. uncut Wilton weave). It is identified as body Brussels to differentiate it from tapestry Brussels (see **Tapestry carpet**). One early twentieth-century American commentator extolled its virtues:

> Body Brussels is perhaps the favorite carpet, and dealers tell us they sell more of it than of any of the others. It is made in several qualities, the best being $1.75. This grade is really the cheapest in the long run, as it is extra heavy and will wear much longer than the $1.40 quality. It is made in exclusive designs, and only the best dyes are used. Body Brussels can be bought at the following prices $1.75, $1.50, $1.40, and $1.25, but these prices are subject to change. The $1.25 carpet is the

> same quality as the $1.40, but the designs are usually old, and are not exclusive to any one firm. Sometimes an unpopular design is really good, but has not been found by people of good taste, and so has been overlooked. (Priestman, 1910, p 52.)

See also **Brussels carpet**, **Wilton carpet**.

Body carpet
Body **carpet** is a term denoting the width of carpeting as being either 27 inches (69 cm) or three-quarters of a yard. Before the advent of **broadlooms**, carpeting was woven at this width due to loom restrictions. It may also refer to four-quarter or 36 inch wide (91 cm) cloth.
See also **Carpet fitting and planning**, **Chlidema square**, **Underfelt**.

Bohemian tick
See **Ticking: Bohemian**.

Bolster
A cylindrical stuffed **pillow**, often used in conjunction with beds or sofas, in use since ancient times. In around 1000 AD, 'Beddum and bolstrum' were mentioned in *Beowulf* (line 2,484). Bolsters fitted the width of the bed, and the pillows were often laid against them. Bolsters were later used as under-pillows. Frequent references in sixteenth- and seventeenth-century inventories attest to their widespread use. In the early nineteenth century, Sheraton explained:

> Bolster, among upholsterers, is that part of bedding used to rest the head upon, and serves as a foundation for the pillows. Bolsters stuffed with hair is, in my opinion, the best. The bolsters of sofas and couches are generally covered with the kind of stuff with which the seats are covered. (1803, p.64.)

In the later nineteenth century, it was noted that the 'round bolster is now generally made of pasteboards or hoop or ticking goods stuffed with excelsior' (Moreland, 1889, p.264).
See also **Bolster case**, **Chair-bolster**, **Cushion**, **Millpuff**.

Bolster case
A removable and washable bag-like case intended for a **bolster**. They were often designed to match bedding or **upholstery** as appropriate.
See also **Pillow (Fustian)**.

Bolting cloth (aka Miller's gauze)
A material originally used for 'bolting' meal or flour through a sieve or bolter, hence the alternative name of Miller's gauze. It was described by Denny as: 'A thin, stiff, transparent fabric made of silk in the gum. Closer and stiffer than voile. Woven in Switzer-land. There are four grades denoting coarseness of mesh. Used chiefly for fine sifting in flour mills. Other uses: stencils, making foundation for wigs and toupees, dress trimmings' (1923, p.22).
Although it had this specific use, it was also adopted for furnishing use. In the medieval period, it was known as 'bultecloth' from the Latin *bultare* – 'to sieve'. A bed was partly furnished with 'iii curtains of bultell tapet' and in another example there were '*tres curtinae rubiae de bultyn*' (*Testamenta Ebor.*, vol.I, p.208 and vol.III, p.4).
By the later nineteenth century, bolting cloth was woven mainly from **wool** and employed for use in samplers. It was also woven with **silk**, woollen or **hair** yarns. Later it was defined as an uncoloured open-weave material made of silk or **rayon** used for screen printing fabrics. In 1950, Smithells said it could be used in place of **net** for small **curtains**.

Bolton coverlet (aka Bolton work)
Bolton work is an all-white material that is woven with **weft**-figured geometric designs in a looped **pile** and used especially for bed coverlets. **Fringes** are sometimes added on **borders**, and initials and weaving dates may also be included. They were known early in the seventeenth century, as the 1610 Cockesden inventory lists 'a Bolton coverlid' (Halliwell, 1854).
In 1767, the American traveller, Samuel Rowland Fisher, recorded in his journal how 'at Bolton about 12 miles from Manchester are woven cotton quilts, the same as those done with a needle, and very neat' (Montgomery, 1984, p.172).
Robert Southey railed against the designs of some coverlets (probably of the Bolton variety). In 1807, he wrote that the counterpane is 'of all English manufacturers the least tasteful; it is of white cotton, ornamented with cotton knots, in shapes as graceless as the cut box in a garden' (1807, vol.1. pp 160–1). The Bolton region continued weaving these products until the 1950s.
See also **Caddis**, **Caddow**, **Counterpane**, **Coverlet**, **Whitework**.

FURTHER READING
Burnham, H.B. (1971). 'Bolton quilts or caddows: a nineteenth century cottage industry', *Bulletin de Liaison du CIETA*, 34, pp 22–9.

Bolton sheeting
Cotton cloth with 2/2 twill weave, a fine **warp** and a condenser **weft**. It has a smooth non-rub surface, was often piece-dyed but was also printed, and has been known as **workhouse sheeting** or Bolton twill. In 1880, it was explained that 'Bolton, or workhouse sheeting, is a coarse twilled cotton fabric, seventy-two inches wide, of a beautiful soft creamy colour' (Higgin, 1880, ch.II., p.12).
Other than for bed use, Bolton sheeting was also utilised for soft furnishings and for **embroidery**. Mrs Orrinsmith in *The Drawing Room* recommended it as a base for embroidering lighter **curtains** (1877, p.73). Alternatively, Caulfeild & Saward thought it was suitable for curtains and other room hangings (1887, p.37).
In the twentieth century, 'appliqué borders applied to ready-made curtains of Bolton sheeting' were offered for sale in a catalogue of a British retailer (Williamson & Cole, 1912). An American author later defined Bolton sheeting as: 'English thick, coarse, twilled and unbleached cotton sometimes dyed cream color and woven originally 72 inches wide; used for crewel embroidery, for dresses, aprons, hangings' (Harmuth, 1924, p.22).
The sheeting was also used to line interior walls, a practice that continued well into the twentieth century. In 1938, it was recorded that in T.E. Lawrence's study: 'He hung the walls of his study with green Bolton sheeting which made it very quiet' (D. Garnett, *Letters*, 40, *OED*). Smithells recommended Bolton sheeting for plain fitted chair covers. (1950)
See also **Appliqué**, **Sheet**, **Wall covering and hanging**.

Bolzas
A **cotton drill** type of fabric. In 1761, it was described as 'a sort of ticking, which comes from the East Indies. Some are quite white and others with yellow stripes, the stripes are made with raw cotton thread' (Postlethwayt, 1751).

Bombazet
A twill or plain-weave **worsted** cloth used for **curtains** that bears a resemblance to **bombasine**. An American fabric dictionary described bombazet: 'In France a smooth, plain-woven or twilled cloth of hard-spun

English worsted yarn, with single warp, finished without a glaze.' (Harmuth, 1924, p.23.)

Woven in England since the eighteenth century, it was also known as a furnishing fabric in America. An example from an August 1819 newspaper advertisement listed 'Blue, Chintz, Bombazet and Dimity Curtains' that were being sold at the auction of the stock in trade of Baltimore upholsterer John Hoburg (Montgomery, 1984, p.172).

Bombasine (aka Bombazine)
Originally, the name was derived from the late Latin *bombasinum*, meaning 'a silk texture', but the name 'bombasin' was also applied to **cotton** fabrics.
(a) A twilled or corded dress material, composed of **silk warp** and **worsted weft**; sometimes also of cotton and worsted, or of worsted alone. In black, the material was much used in mourning. Developed in Bruges, it was a form of dimity that was introduced into England in the late 1560s–70s, and was woven in Canterbury, Norwich and later in London. In 1582, the *Tudor Book of Rates* listed it by 'the piece containing twenty yards' (Willan, 1962). In 1831, *The Cabinet Cyclopedia* noted that 'their manufacture, which once employed a vast number of looms in Spitalfields, has for some time been almost wholly confined to the city of Norwich. Bombasins are all woven grey, that is with silk of the natural colour and they are dyed in the piece' (Lardner, 1831, p.299).
(b) Although a dress material, bombasine was also used for furnishings. The well-known 1677 inventory reference to 'two curtains of white bumbasine' in the wardrobe room of Ham House refers to bombasine (Thornton & Tomlin, 1980, p.164).
See also **Crêpe cloth**, **Dimity**.

Bomber cloth
A term for broken twill weave cloths, usually of **cotton**, with twice as many **warp** as **weft** yarns. The warp yarns are usually fine and woven in groups of two. The cloth was usually printed and used for **drapes** in the mid-twentieth century (Bendure & Pfieffer, 1947, p.612).

Bonded fabric
Two layers of cloth permanently joined with resin or **adhesive**. For furnishing purposes, these are often a face cloth and a backing with a particular feature, which may be related to performance or decorative finish. **Warp** laminated fabric uses various warp yarns laminated or bonded onto a substrate that can then be used as a **wall covering**, for example.
See also **Stitch bonded fabric**.

Bonegrace
Narrow **curtains** used in the seventeenth and eighteenth centuries that were hung at the corners of beds. In conjunction with the larger side curtains, they completely enclosed the occupant and avoided draughts. They usually hung at the back corners of a bed.
See also **Bed furniture**, **Cantoon**.

Bone lace
See **Lace (Bobbin).**

Bonne femme
An American term for a decorative **lace curtain**. According to an early twentieth-century publication on tasteful interiors:

> The average window needs two sets of curtains and a shade. Sometimes a thin net or lace curtain, a 'bonne femme' is hung close to the glass, but this is usual only in cities where privacy has to be maintained by main force, or where the curtains of a floor differ greatly. Thin curtains in combination with side curtains of some thicker material are most often used. (Throop, 1912, p.182.)

A little later, a workshop manual explained that 'Bonne femmes' were a 'form of sash curtain with a frilled lower edge said to have been originated from the temporary employment of a frilled dancing skirt as a window shade in a dancer's bedroom' (Stephenson, 1926).

Bonnet blind
A form of **awning** used for exterior shading of windows with a curved profile like a bonnet. Loudon referred to an improved method of fitting bonnet blinds as being patented in 1826 (1839, p.270). The blinds were lowered from a **cornice** box, which kept them tidy when not being used. Iron stays held them tight and at an angle to the window so they looked like a contemporary bonnet-hood. The blind frames were covered 'in strong linen, of the kind called gingham, and is generally striped with blue and white colours, which harmonise remarkably well with the sky and clouds' (ibid.).
See also **Blind**.

17. Bookcase curtain, c.1889 (J. Reed & E. Lavin, Needle-craft Artistic and Practical, *1889)*

Bonnet cotton
Nineteenth-century sewing **cotton** that was employed for **calico** bonnets (hence the name) but was also used in **upholstery** work.

Bookcase blind
The interiors of bookcases were sometimes fitted with **blinds** to protect the contents. In 1813, Rudolph Ackermann described in his *Repository of Arts* a blind that replaced bookcase doors:

> A drapery of silk, suspended within side and at the top of the case by a spring roller, in the manner of a blind, and is made to draw to the bottom of the case, where spring locks are placed to receive the means for confining it; they are connected at the side by grooves, and thus become as protecting as doors would be, without the weight or inconvenience. (vol. X, July 1813, p.42.)

See also **Bookcase curtain**, **Fluted silk**.

Bookcase curtain
The use of **curtains** acted as both a functional and decorative accessory to bookcases. Initially books had been kept on shelves that had a curtain drawn over them. Later in the seventeenth century, glazed bookcases were introduced. The curtains were then put on the inside of the case. By providing a discreet covering, they protected the books from the light and from prying eyes. The practice was common by the mid-eighteenth century. In 1760, Chippendale charged Sir William Robinson for 'sewing silk brass pins and making 4 silk curtains for your bookcase [using] 7 yards of green lustring' (Gilbert, 1978, p.143). In some examples, the material was tacked to bookcase doors.

By the early nineteenth century, Rudolph Ackermann had suggested 'curtains of cloth or silk, or of other coloured materials' for a study bookcase, as they were 'more ornamental, and more readily made to harmonise with the woodwork' (vol. III, 3rd series, 1824, plate 3).

Mrs Spofford recommended dyed green **leather** curtains for bookcase shelves (1878), and in the same year Charles Eastlake simply suggested 'stamped scalloped leather valances along the tops of shelves as a dust preventer, which adds to the effect of the bookcase' (1878, p.129). A little later, Mrs Haweis in the *Art of Decoration* suggested that bookcase curtains 'should be in a thin material such as cretonne or coloured Corah silk, and should slip to and fro on smooth and silent rings' (1889, p.307).
See also **Persian**.

Book muslin
See **Muslin: Book**.

Book pillow
A **pillow** support designed to prop up books whilst being read on a table. They were made from padded cloth often with embroidered features.

FURTHER READING
Wingfield Digby, G. (1963). *Elizabethan Embroidery*, London: Faber and Faber, pp 107–8.

Boot tape
An eighteenth-century **linen binding** tape used to finish off edges and seams of **carpets**. George Bowes was supplied with a 'Bed-carpet, being bordered the seams, mitres and edges boot-taped containing 12 yards' in 1743 (Medlam, 1990, p.146). It was also used to support tapestries and hangings.

Bordecloth
In the medieval period, this term referred to a cloth used to cover boards (tables). The word later referred to the yarns from which such covers were woven, usually **linen**. In 1376, the Corpus Christi College inventory listed '8 pannus lineus est unus pannus albus vocatur bordecloth' (Leaf, 1934, p.23). In the 1603 inventory of Hengrave, the Great Chamber had 'one large bord clothe or grene clothe, to laye over ye carpets of ye long borde' (Clabburn, 1988, p.167).
See also **Cupboard cloth**, **Denant**, **Runner**.

Border
The need either to finish off a textile furnishing with a decoration or to disguise fixings was an essential part of the upholsterer's trade. The role of **passementerie** was important for bordering **curtains** and **upholstery**, whilst borders were also used to finish off **wall coverings** and **carpets**. In 1803, the *Cabinet Dictionary* explained that borders were 'general terms, both amongst cabinet-makers and upholsterers, but chiefly the latter, who are concerned with a boundless variety, both of carpet and paper hangings' (Sheraton, p.74).

Designs for borders seem to have been interchangeable. George Smith, in his 1812 publication *Collection of Ornamental Designs*, noted that he offered designs for borders that were 'capable of being executed in carpeting, paper or silk; they might also be cast in ormolu or bronze'.

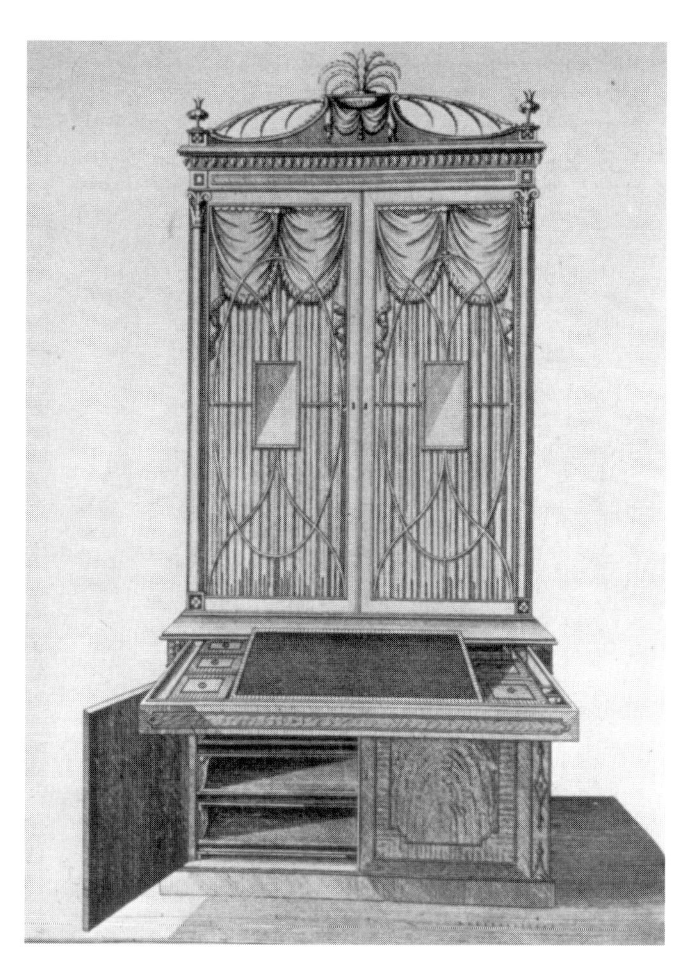

18. Bookcase with silk curtain and drapery (T. Sheraton, The Cabinet Maker and Upholsterer's Drawing Book, *1793)*

Carpet borders
Woven strips of carpeting designed to complement the main pattern were sold as borders. In the mid-eighteenth century, Benjamin Franklin wrote to his wife after having purchased carpeting: 'There is enough for one large and two small ones, – it is to be sewed together, the edges being first pull'd down, and care must be taken to make the figures meet exactly, there is bordering of the same' (Cornforth & Fowler, 1974, p.213). *The Workwoman's Guide* recommended a worked border, with **drugget** in between for stair carpet, either made at home or ready-purchased (Hale, 1840, p.202).

Carpet borders were used in **Chlidema squares** and, in the twentieth century, found a niche in bordering rooms or stairs with fitted carpets.

Curtain and cover borders
In some cases, particular borders were sold to complement hangings. In Cronström's correspondence of 1695, he notes half-width brocatelle borders available to match *brocatelle de Venise* (Thornton, 1978, p.360).

Sophie von la Roche recorded seeing a bedroom at St Leonard's Hill in 1786: 'It is hung with a delicate monotone pale-blue chintz, with a border of the sweetest garlands embroidered in blue of the same shade on a white ground, similarly the curtains, quilts on both beds, and chair covers' (Cornforth & Fowler, 1974, p.139).

In 1818, Ackermann described how 'the curtains are edged by a border… The material with which they are composed is an exquisitely fine woollen cloth, on which the border is painted by hand, as is frequently done on velvet' (*The Repository of Arts etc.*, December 1818, Plate 100). Andrew Downing explained the use of curtains and borders to his American readers:

> For the plainest cottages, therefore, one would use chintz, which may be had for a few cents a yard, and which, if selected with regard to harmonizing in color with the carpet and walls, will always produce a pretty effect, at very little cost. Printed **cotton**s are also manufactured for this purpose, with separate borders that may be sewed on, to heighten the effect. (Downing, 1850, p.374.)

In the twentieth century, fashions sometimes called for borders to be sewn on the leading edges of curtains, **pelmets** and other decorations.

Wall and hanging borders
Fringes and **braid** were used in the seventeenth century but, in the eighteenth century, wood, papier-mâché, composition etc. were employed to finish off the exposed edges of wall coverings. In the mid-eighteenth century, the use of textile panels and borders was developed as a wall treatment, deriving from the pilaster strip used in France.

See also **Alentours**, **Chintz**, **Couching**, **Flounce**, **Gallon**, **Gilt leather**, **Lace**, **Needlework carpet**, **Purl**, **Shawl bordering**, **Trimming**, **Valence**.

Bottom linen
A coarsely woven **linen sackcloth** or **canvas** that is used to cover the **webbing** in upholstered work. It is a support for the filling and may be cut so that the edges can be turned in over a roll of filling material to create a 'French edge'.

Bouclé
A French term for looped. *Bouclé* fabrics have loops occurring at intervals on the woven surface or are knitted from *bouclé* yarns. These were used in the 1940s for **drape** in the USA (Bendure & Pfieffer, 1947, p.612).
See also **Carpet**, **Fringe**, **Thread**.

Boudoir carpet
In 1950, *The Mercury Dictionary of Textile Terms* defined this as a reversible **carpet**, woven in plain-weave of **worsted** and **cotton** yarns. It was heavy and firmly constructed.

Bourette
Striped and **checked** fabrics woven from a **weft** of *filoselle*, spun from **silk** waste (or the outer fibres of cocoons carded and spun but not reeled). It has a characteristic knotty slub effect and a rough surface. It was popular through the second half of the eighteenth century, and well into the nineteenth century.

Bourré
A French term that refers to **quilted**, padded or stuffed articles. The name translates as the verb 'to stuff'.

Bow and band
A form of passementerie used in the eighteenth century, in conjunction with **French curtains**, to hold them back when open.

Bows were also used to disguise hooks for picture hanging and mirrors. In the 1684 inventory of Kilkenny, there were 'three knots of ribbon to the looking glass', in Her Grace's bedchamber (Thornton, 1978, p.384). These traditions continue.
See also **Passementerie**.

Box pleat
A box pleat is a decorative **pleat** that uses a greater width of fabric than a standard pleat. It is sewn into 'box' shapes by creasing and pleating the fabric. The name may derive from the 'box-iron' used for pressing it out or from the finished shape. Eastlake favoured box pleats for bed canopies and stipulated that they 'should never be less than four or five inches in width at intervals of about eight to ten. They should be pressed down as flat as possible and when necessary maybe kept in shape by a stitch on either side' (1878, p.210).

Box spring
See **Mattress: Box spring**.

Braid
A woven or printed **trimming** that is made in the form of a band, which is used to give a decorative finish to furnishings. Braid is used for bed hangings, window **curtains** and seating, as well as to emphasise shapes or to cover seams. Now generic, it was originally a narrow **woollen** tape used for **binding** or as the base for a more complicated trim.

In the seventeenth and eighteenth centuries, references to 'lace' often really referred to braid, as early examples were plaited on **cushions** in the manner of bobbin lace, with threads pinned on and weight attached to them. This caused confusion in naming as this braid was sometimes called 'lace'. Braid may be machine woven or hand-made using crochet, tatting or **macramé** methods.
See also **Braided rug**, **Fringe**, **Galloon**, **Gimp**, **Guard lace**, **Lace**, **None-so-Pretty**, **Orris**, **Passementerie**, **Purl**.

Braid (weighted)
Lead shot inserted into a tape tube. It is used for weighting **curtains** in their lower hem for better draping qualities.

Braided rug
A floorcovering made from strips of cloth, which are braided and then sewn together in rug shapes. They have a particular association with North America and the early European settlers. Braided rugs were often a home craft but also became available commercially in the USA by the early twentieth century. A textbook on household arts explained that care needed to be taken in designing them:

> The old-fashioned braided rug and the rag rug are useful for certain kinds of furnishings. The old-fashioned patterns of 'hit and miss' are sometimes distracting, because of the way in which the white is introduced, but when woven with a plan so that the spacing, line, light, and dark have been kept in mind, they are quite pleasing. (Kinne, *c*.1913, p.72.)

Braided rugs were still offered in the USA as a commercial proposition in the later twentieth century, and they also remain a craft product.
See also **Braid**, **List**, **Rag rug**, **Rug**.

Brass rod
Brass cased rod was often recommended for the suspension of **net**, panel and **casement curtains**, the rod being supported by brass barrel brackets.
See also **Case rod**.

Bridges satin
See **Satin: Satin de Bridges (Bruges)**.

Brindley valance
A Brindley valance is one that is integrally fitted to the top of the **curtain**. In the 1880s, when curtains and **portières** were often made to a standard drop, the turning over of the top to create a valance to fit the window or door was common practice. In 1883, Varney reported that **lambrequins** had been 'superseded by a valance which will shove aside with the curtains' (p.277). By the mid-twentieth century, it was usually used with **dress curtains** (French, 1947). It is also useful for **portières** or windows that are so near the ceiling that a **pelmet** cannot be hung satisfactorily.
See also **Valance**.

Brioche cushion
Cushions made up from multi-coloured stripes in such a way so they resembled oranges or sea urchins. Knitted panels were fitted together in the manner of orange segments, and fitted over **stuffing** to make a floor cushion or footstool.

Brise-bise (aka Brisby)
Lace curtaining intended for hanging across the lower part of a window horizontally by means of a rod or wires, manufactured from 15 to 27 inches (38 to 145 cm) and sold by length. The narrow widths were sometimes used at the top of the window to form a **valance**. They were woven with a slot in one selvedge and often a scalloped edge if required. The term is derived from the French for 'wind-breaker'. They were used from the early twentieth century.
See also **Curtain ring**.

Bristol carpet
A flat woven **carpet** probably of the **Kidderminster** or **Scotch** type. It was most likely thinner as it was used for **curtains** and **valances** as well as for floors. Kerridge suggests that 'carpetine' was made in Bristol from around 1600 to 1680. It seems to have been made from **linen** or **hemp warps** and either **cotton** or **union wefts**, on both broad and narrow looms (Kerridge, 1985, p.124).

In March 1637, Christian Bruce purchased for Hardwick Hall some 'Bristowe stuff'. The first Earl also had some Bristol carpeting in his London house, which he used at the windows (Levey, 1998, p.80). In 1657, the Revd Giles Moore of Horsted Keynes noted that: 'I payd to William Clowson, itinerant upholsterer, for 6 yds and 3 qrs of Bristol carpetting at 3s. a yd' (Moore, 1847, *Diary*, 16 April 1657). An Act of 1678 regulating the London cloth market listed 'Bird's eye carpeting, Bristol carpet and all sorts of carpeting' (Thornton, 1978, p.353).
See also **List**.

Broadcloth
A fine quality plain carded **woollen** cloth (originally the opposite of narrow cloth) of double width exceeding 29 inches (74 cm), usually between 54 and 63 inches (137 cm and 160 cm), fulled after weaving. It was used not only for garments, but also for bed hangings and **tablecloths**. It was usually dyed black or indigo, and was once considered the best of all woollen materials. The *OED* records its first use in 1420.

A bed was also furnished with broadcloth in 1609, when the inventories listed '3 beds of Broadcloth vidz one purple, one carnation, one green' (Cust, 1918, p.40). A different use for it was found in 1600 in the

19. Brise-bise net curtain with slot for rod (E. Ostick, The Draper's Encyclopaedia, *1955)*

Ingatestone 'Dining Chamber', where there was 'a long [table] carpet of green broad cloth fringed upon the sides with narrow green silk fringe' (Macquoid & Edwards, 1954, p.71). It was still being used for bed hangings at the end of the seventeenth century in America. The 1693 inventory of Margaret Thatcher of Boston, Mass., included '1 red broad cloth suit of curtains and valaines' (Montgomery, 1984, p.179). During the twentieth century, in the USA, **cotton** or **rayon** broadcloth, with fine crosswise ribs, was being made from high-quality mercerised cotton to produce a soft lustrous fabric that was used for **bedspreads**, **drape** and tablecloths (Bendure & Pfieffer, 1947, p.613). In Britain, in the 1950s, it was suggested that broadcloth could be used for home furnishings (Smithells, 1950).
See also **Kersey**, **Penistone**, **Table cover**.

Broadloom

A generic term to define **carpeting** that is woven more than 72 inches (1.83 metres) in width. Erastus Bigelow probably introduced the first broadloom carpet in 1877. In 1905, the English company, Brintons, produced carpet from the first power-driven wide loom, which was 15 feet (4.57 metres) wide. The benefits of broadloom as a response to the demand for fitted room carpets were obvious, as they alleviated the need for seams and joins.
See also **Carpet fitting and planning**, **Saxony**.

Brocade

A compound fabric that uses supplementary **weft** yarns to create figured or embroidered effects. Strictly speaking the term should be linked to the name of the ground cloth it is worked upon, e.g. brocaded **satin**.

In continuous brocades, the additional yarns float behind the base cloth when not required; in discontinuous brocades, the supplementary weft yarns are only woven in the patterned areas. The figures in brocade are rather loose, while in **damask** the figure threads are actually bound into the material.

While probably of ancient Chinese and Indian origin, brocades were certainly woven in Italy (Lucca) in the thirteenth century. By the seventeenth century, it was noticed that 'clothe of silke, brocado and divers sorts of merchandise came out of Persia' (Hakluyt, *Voyages, OED*). In the seventeenth century, **upholstery** covers were sometimes brocaded with gold or silver threads and this practice continued into the eighteenth century.

Chambers' *Cyclopaedia*, noted that:

> Formerly the term was restrained to cloths wove either of gold, both woof and warp, or of silver, or of both together but by degrees, it came likewise to pass for such as had silk intermixed to fill up, and terminate the flowers off gold or silver… At present, any stuff of silk, satin, or even simple taffeta, when wrought and enriched with flowers &c. obtains the denomination of brocade. (1741–3)

By the mid-eighteenth century, brocade was defined as 'a stuff of gold, silver or silk, raised and enriched with flowers, foliages, or other ornament according to the fancy of the merchant, or manufacturer, who invents new fashions' (Postlethwayt, 1751).

Over 100 years later, imitations often took the place of metals. In 1872, it was noted that coloured yarns were used to imitate the gold or silver threads (Brown & Gates, 1872). The strict definition and associated quality was losing its place to a more inclusive definition by the early twentieth century.

> The word brocade cannot be restricted to fabrics of this class [high quality period designs based on jacquard], and in modern usage it is applied to all fabrics figured in the jacquard. These can be single textures in cotton, wool, linen, silk and rayon or any combination of both. The figuring may optionally be weft only, warp only or a combination of both… Brocades may be woven with the colour of the warp differing from that of the weft. Large quantities of brocades are woven grey and piece-dyed in self colours. They may also be woven from two materials such as cotton or viscose rayon warp and acetate rayon weft or acetate combined with some other yarn, Such goods can be piece-dyed in two colours at one operation. (French, 1937, pp 127–8.)

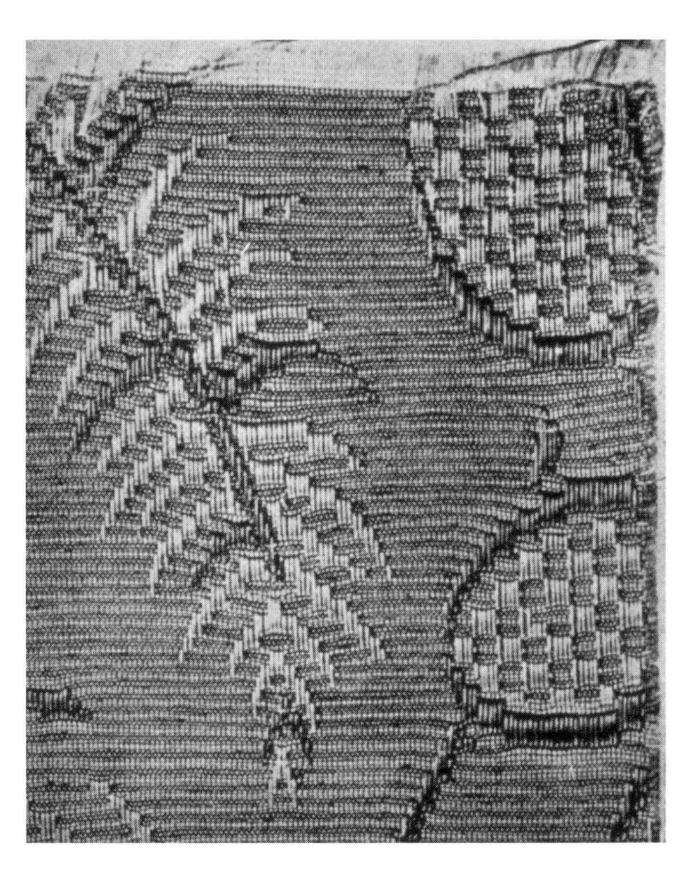

20. Detail of brocade weave (T. French and Co, The Book of Soft Furnishing, *1937)*

Brocade now refers to multi-coloured fabrics that create a brocaded effect but have various coloured yarns woven right across the weft of the fabric. In both, the background is often a satin weave.

Cotton

This often has the ground of **cotton** with the pattern of **rayon** and **silk**. The pattern is usually in low relief.

End and end

Alternate **warps** of differing colours are brought up as required to give the design, usually with a single coloured weft.

Four-ply

A napery fabric using two warps and one set of wefts in which four colours are used.

Jacquard and dobby
Rich, heavy, elaborate design-effect brocade. Sometimes woven with coloured or metallic threads making the design stand out against a satin-weave background. The pattern may be satin on a twill ground or twill on a satin ground and is often reversible.

Warp
A brocade with vertical patterning yarns in place of the more usual weft yarns.
See also **Antique textile**, **Baldachin**, **Bergamo**, **Brocart**, **Brocatelle**, **Casement cloth**, **Damassin**, **Lampas broché**, **Leno brocade**, **Liseré**, **Leno brocade**, **Paduasoy**, **Tabaret**, **Tissue**, **Weave**.

Brocart
A French term referring to (often) **silk brocades** embroidered or embellished with gold or silver thread.

Brocatelle
True brocatelle is a **lampas** weave made of **silk** warps and **linen wefts**, with a smooth raised figure of binder warps usually in a **satin** weave construction. Present-day materials may have changed from the thirteenth and fourteenth-century fabrics, but they still have the embossed figure in the tight, compact woven warp-effect. While brocatelle is sometimes classed as a flat fabric, it is distinct from **brocade** in that it has a pattern in high relief in a sort of blistered effect. Brocatelle was apparently woven in imitation of Italian tooled **leather**, and was therefore patterned similarly to **damasks** and **velvets**.

Brocatelle first appeared in England in Norwich *c.*1590, and has since then been used for hangings as well as **upholstery**. It was important for **wall coverings** as its stiffer yarns made it hang flat: this feature made brocatelle less useful as a **drape** material. However, there are many examples of its use as a **curtain** or **upholstery** material. In a 1680 French dictionary, its use was defined as: *étoffe de fil et de laine don't on fait des houses [dust covers] de lit, don't on couvre des chaises et tapisse [mats] des cabinets*' (Braun-Ronsdorf, 1960, p.23). In 1669, John Evelyn recorded seeing 'a chair and desk covered with brocatelle … and cloth of gold' (*Diary of John Evelyn,* 9 July 1669). Whilst in 1695 it was recorded that in the Royal Wardrobe at Windsor there was a 'large old eating room in the low lodgings [that] was hung with yellow, white and crimson brocatella' (Macquoid & Edwards, 1924, I, p.104). In some cases, particular **borders** were sold to complement the brocatelle hangings. In Cronström's correspondence of 1695, he notes half-width brocatelle borders available to match *brocatelle de Venise* (Thornton, 1978, p.360). In an upholstery example from 1715, France Lapière's inventory recorded 'one brocadelloe easy chair' (*Furniture History*, 30, 1994, p.8).

By the mid-eighteenth century, definitions seem to imply that it had lost something of its former glory. Postlethwayt defined it as:

> A kind of stuff proper to make hangings and other furniture. A slight stuff made with cotton, or coarse silk, in imitation of brocadoes. There are some all silk and others all of wool. They also give the name brocatelle to another sort of slight stuff called ligature or mezeline. (1751–5)

Ten years later, Rolt agreed with Postlethwayt's definition of brocatelle but added that: 'the Venetian brocatelle has always been in most esteem' (1761). That it was still used for walls is confirmed by the Earl of Bristol's accounts, which note £11.10s. was paid to Mr John Watson, upholsterer, for 'ye Brokadel hangings in my wife's anti-chamber' (Macquoid & Edwards, 1924, p.104).

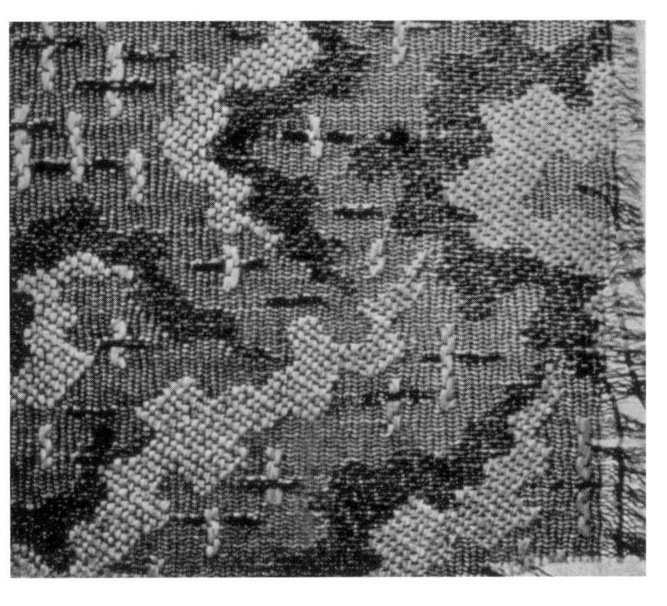

21. Detail of brocatelle cloth (T. French and Co, The Book of Soft Furnishing, *1937)*

In the nineteenth century, brocatelle was still an important furnishing fabric. According to an American definition of 1872, brocatelle had changed from a silk or **cotton** fabric and was:

> A fabric composed of a fine linen warp and a coarse woollen woof. It is woven in damask patterns, stripes etc. either plain or colored. The surface of the figure or stripe is twilled. This figure is formed by the warp, which in the cheapest grades is usually black. A superior quality is composed entirely of wool and called 'wool damask'. (Brown & Gates, 1872.)

A British authority defined brocatelle as 'a French term for linsey-woolsey. A silk material for drapery, the linings of carriages and the like. It is also made of silk and cotton mixed, or of cotton only, after the manner of brocade' (Caulfeild & Saward 1887, p.48).

By 1892, brocatelle was unsympathetically compared to brocade and described as 'a coarse or inferior brocade or figured fabric commonly

22. Brocatelle silk c.*1845, modern copy (Classic Revivals)*

made of silk or cotton but having a more of less silky surface used chiefly for curtains, furniture coverings, tapestry linings and linings for carriages' (Cole, 1892).

In 1937, it was again defined as 'a heavy cloth used for furnishings and drapery made with a brocade figure woven by a jacquard with a silk warp. The jacquard figuring is developed in the satin weave, and the ground has crosswise ribs. The picks that are hidden may be cotton or wool' (French, 1937, p.129). Nowadays, any woven fabric with a plain ground and a raised woven design is called a brocatelle.
See also **Coteline**, **Weave**.

FURTHER READING

Braun-Ronsdorf, M. (1960). 'Mixed fabrics of later times', *CIBA Review*, 12, pp 16–28.

Broché

Broché is figured by weaving in additional threads by way of swivel weaving. The term originates from the French *brocher*, meaning 'to stitch'. In 1877, Knight simply defined broché-goods, as 'goods embroidered or embossed'. Another authority defines broché as 'a French term denoting a velvet or silk textile, with a satin figure thrown up on the face' (Caulfeild & Saward, 1887, p.48). In the twentieth century, broché was an inexpensive figured fabric usually with **rayon warps** and **cotton wefts**, not to be classed as **damask**.
See also **Broché carpet**, **Broché quilt**, **Lampas broché**.

Broché carpet

A Brussels-ground loop-**pile** weave **carpet**, with a figure formed by cut-pile.
See also **Broché**, **Brussels carpet**.

*23. Brussels carpet design by Bright and Co Macclesfield (*The Art Journal Illustrated Catalogue of the Great Exhibition – London 1851*)*

Broché quilt

Broché in this context refers to **quilts** that have been embroidered or embossed.

Brown holland

See **Holland**, **Linen**.

Bruges satin (aka Bridges satin)

See **Satin: Satin de Bridges (Bruges).**

Brusselette carpet

A **carpet** woven with a ribbed effect that is created from the use of a loosely tensioned coarse **warp** in the weaving process.

Brussels carpet

A **carpet**-type that is woven on a 'Brussels' loom that allows a loop-**pile** carpet to be produced. It employs an extra **worsted warp** woven over rods so that it forms loops for a pile. Three sets of warps are used: a chain warp which combines with a **weft** of fine **linen** or **hemp** to make the base; a stuffer warp to give body; and the pile warp which may be available in up to five or six colours. Brussels carpets have a smooth, slightly ribbed close pile surface and a well-defined pattern that contribute to their appearance, although they are often considered less luxurious than **velvet** cut-pile carpeting. Wires were passed over the yarns, which created loops, but if the wires had blades inserted, they cut the loop into pile and made a velvet pile carpet.

Various origins have been cited for the introduction of Brussels carpet weaving into England, but they appear to have been woven in England since the later seventeenth century. In 1720, the Earl of Pembroke persuaded weavers from the French **Savonnerie** factory to work in Wilton and teach local weavers how to make Brussels carpet. Some credit goes to John Broom as the person who established the manufacture of Brussels carpeting in the town of Wilton in 1740. Others say a weaver from **Tournai** was invited to establish the first Brussels (**mockado**) loom in 1749 (Burton, 1890, pp 182–3). In any event, an early reference from 21 April 1730 to Brussels carpet is in the accounts of Benjamin Mildmay, Earl Fitzwalter, who had 'a little Brussels carpet' (Hefford, 1987, p.8). It was certainly known in the USA by the 1790s at least, if not earlier. Newspaper advertisement lists included 'Carpets and Carpeting of the very best Brussels quality, to the newest landscape and other elegant patterns' (1798 advertisement, Roth, 1967, p.35).

The carpet was first woven on draw looms, and then, in 1825, the **jacquard** mechanism was adapted to the products made in Kidderminster. In 1846–8, the American, Erastus Bigelow, produced Brussels carpets mechanically on a power loom. In 1851, Skinner introduced a steam-powered Brussels loom at the Great Exhibition and demonstrated it in Kidderminster. This process was developed further by G. Collier of Halifax in 1851 and was in wide use by the 1860s.

Initially, Brussels carpets were used in fashionable interiors. Thomas Moore supplied Lord Coventry with 'A fine carpet Brussels flower'd pattern crimson ornament' in April 1765 (Gilbert, Lomax & Wells-Cole, 1987, p.62). The narrow width also made Brussels carpeting suitable for stairs and passages. Indeed, the *New York Gazette and General Advertiser* listed in May 1799 a sale of 'striped Brussels carpeting for Stairs and Entries' (Roth, 1967, p.36).

The problem brought about by the expense of the pile yarns running below the surface until required for the pattern was overcome by the development of the tapestry or printed Brussels carpet. Here the warp yarns were dyed in strips as the design dictated before weaving; it could then be woven without the jacquard.

Writing in 1838, in the *British Cyclopaedia of the Arts*, Charles Partington noted that the 'Brussels carpets are not made in large squares, but in pieces about seven eighths wide [i.e. 27 inches]... When well made they are very durable, and being at the same time elegant, they are at present much in request for the good apartments' (Montgomery, 1984, p.181). The qualities of Brussels carpet were extolled again by Harriet Spofford. Writing in 1878, she considered that there were 'no prettier carpets than the Brussels, although others may be more luxurious to the foot ... with the proper padding they may be made equally luxurious, and more durable than any' (p.174).

As with many carpets, there were particular trade names applied. Examples include the 'Leicestershire three-thread Brussels' carpet that was advertised in Montgomery Ward's catalogue of 1895, and the Imperial Brussels where 'the figure is raised above the ground, and its pile is cut, but the ground is uncut' (Ure, 1875).

See also **Bed carpet**, **Body Brussels**, **Brussels Tapestry**, **Hair cord**, **Jute carpet**, **Moquette carpet**, **Wilton carpet**.

FURTHER READING

Bartlett, J.N. (1978). *Carpeting the Millions, The Growth of Britain's Carpet Industry*, Edinburgh: John Donald.

Robinson, G. (1966). *Carpets*, London: Pitman.

Brussels coverlet

A Brussels **coverlet** was probably a bed **counterpane** that may have been woven with a looped pile. Sheraton refers to them as part of a long list: 'Also Diamond or Brussels coverlets' (1803, pp 182–3). James Newton supplied '3 stout Brussels coverlets' to Earl of Breadalbane in 1811 (Ellwood, 1995, p.187).

Brussels curtain

A later nineteenth-century **curtain** fabric made in St Gall, Switzerland, which employs Bonnaz machine-embroidered chain **stitch** upon plain net. It may be made in one layer or two.

See also **Lace**.

Brussels tapestry

An important set of tapestry factories, using high and **low warp** looms, were established in Brussels. Although founded in the thirteenth century, they first rose to importance in the later fifteenth century, mainly due to their fine technical abilities. Their fortunes revived in the early seventeenth century due, in part, to the influence of Rubens who produced many cartoons for the factories to work with, although the main centre for tapestries moved to Paris at this time. The factory continued in business until the end of the eighteenth century, closing in 1794. The Brussels tapestry tradition was revived in the second half of the nineteenth century.

See also **Brussels carpet**, **Tapestry**, **Tapestry carpet**.

FURTHER READING

D'Hulst, R.A. (1967). *Flemish Tapestries from the Fifteenth to the Eighteenth Century*, New York: Universe Books.

Duverger, E. Van (1985). *Tapisseries et arts textiles, l'art flamand des origens à nos jours*, Antwerp: Stadsbestuur, pp 189–204, 311–21.

Duverger, J. Van & Duverger, E. Van (1953–86). *Artes Textiles*, 11 volumes, Ghent: Centrum voor de Geschiedenis van de Textiele Kunsten.

Buckram

A term that is common, in various early forms, to many European languages, as in the French *bouqueran* or Italian *bucherame*, the derivation of which is unknown although the *OED* gives 1222 as a date of first use.

In the early fourteenth century, buckram was a loosely woven cloth made from **hemp**, **cotton** or **linen** that was used as a material for **bed furniture**. This use is referred to in an inventory entry of 1488 that listed a 'selur and testur and v costrynges [hangings] of bokeram' (R. Morton, *Archaeological Journal*, XXXIII, 327, *OED*). In 1586, Sir Edward Littleton owned '2 bedsteads with a branch buckram canopy and gilt belles with curtains' (West, 1962, p.111).

Buckram appeared to have been used as a case covering material as well as for beds. In 1588, Robert Dudley had a carved and embroidered walnut chair that was sufficiently important to have 'a case of buckerom to the same' (Beard, 1997, p.284). A little later, in 1603, the Great Chamber at Hengrave had a set of high-joined stools 'covered with carpet work like the carpets, fringed with crewell' which were covered with 'yellow buckrams', as were two great chairs covered in crimson figured **satin** but fitted with the same yellow buckram covers (Clabburn, 1988, p.167). The use of buckram as a covering was also exemplified in the 1604 Tart Hall inventory that lists a 'long shovel board table with cover of old yellow buckram' (Cust, 1911, p.99). It was also used as a **curtain** material at this time. For example, Ingatestone had 'two old window curtaines-lyned with blew buckeram' in 1600.

It appears that buckram was imported in the early sixteenth century. The *Tudor Book of Rates* for 1582 listed buckram as being of 'French making for hangings the dozen pieces' (Willan, 1962, p.11) and, in 1622, Malynes noted 'the commodities which are not made at all or but in small quantity in England, and may be practised are many [including] Buckrams, Tapistrie, Bustians, Cambrickes' (p.229).

One hundred years later, its use had changed. Its use as a lining material was specifically noted in the Byelaws of the Upholsterers' Company (1679) which state that they will not allow 'any tester or valance of silk, camlet, cloth, kersey, serge, or of any other stuff but such as they shall lyne with buckram, calico or canvas' (Houston, 1993, p.58).

Since the fifteenth century, it has also been stiffened with gums, flour paste or china clay (about 45 per cent of weight) and used for reinforcement work in the making of **valances** etc. By 1742, a standard definition of it was as 'a strong, coarse linen cloth stiffened' (Bailey).

Modern buckram is woven from **cotton**, sometimes in **linen** or synthetics, in a plain-weave. It is cheap, low-textured, loose weave, very heavily sized and stiff, but can be softened with heat and then shaped while warm. It is particularly used for **pelmet** shapes, etc.

See also **Bocasine**, **Buckram (fusible)**, **Dornix**, **Protective furnishing**, **Trellis cloth**.

Buckram (fusible)

A twentieth-century white **cotton**, glue-impregnated strip used for hand-pleated **curtain headings**. It avoids the visible **stitches** by being fused to the cloth with heat.

See also **Buckram**.

Bullion fringe

See **Fringe: Bullion**.

Bulrush

See **Grass**.

Bulteclothe
See **Bolting cloth**.

Bumbasine
See **Bombasine**.

Bump
Cotton waste made into a **blanket**-like fabric as **interlining**. It is used to improve **drape** and add insulation to **curtains**.
See also **Batting**, **Interlining**.

Bunting
A plain-weave **cotton** or **wool** fabric usually used for flags and banners. The distance between the threads and picks is roughly the same as the yarn diameter. This enables the cloth to blow in the lightest of winds and assists in drying out after wetting. Better quality **worsted** bunting has been used for **curtains** etc. in the USA (Bendure & Pfieffer, 1947, p.614).
See also **Say**, **Tammy**.

Burlap
A name of uncertain etymology for a coarse **canvas** made of **jute** and **hemp**. It is often used for wrapping-bags for transport or, especially in the USA, for **upholstery spring** covering and other tasks.

At one time, it appears to have been made from **linen**. In 1695, there was a reference to 'Course Linnens commonly called Borelapps' (6 Act 7 & 8 Will. III, x, 16). A year later, the *Merchant's Warehouse* commented on its use for dress: 'I shall begin with Bore-laps; because that for Shifts or Shirts is counted and is known to be a very strong Cloth' (J.F., 1695).

By the later part of the nineteenth century, burlap was sometimes painted or stencilled to imitate **carpet** designs such as Turkey patterns. It was also suggested for window **blinds**. The American author, Mrs H.W. Beecher, recommended that window blinds made from 'common burlaps, with a small outlay of money and a large outlay of ingenuity, may be made very charming in effect' (Beecher, 1879). A fine variety was also used for **curtains** in the late nineteenth and early twentieth centuries, and was recommended for wall decoration, plain, painted or stencilled.

In the twentieth century, American authors again recommended burlap for furnishing applications including walls, upholstery and **drapes**. Dyer mentioned burlap as a 'coarse, heavy, durable material used for wall coverings, and for upholstery that will have hard wear' (*c.*1923, p.204). In 1936, Denny suggested its use for **wall coverings** or drapery purposes and as a foundation for **hooked rugs** (1936, p.10).
See also **Abnakee rug**, **Hessian**, **Stencil printing**.

Burn-out
A pattern-making process that uses caustic alkalis to remove protein fibres, and acids to remove cellulosic fibres, from the cloth. This partial destruction or devouring of the fibres in a fabric creates the pattern, e.g. voided **velvet** (also known as devoré).

Button and loop
A seventeenth-century method of joining bed **valances**, **curtains** and covers 'sides to edges' with a **braid** loop fixed over a toggle or button. In 1601, Hardwick Hall had '3 curtains wrought with black silk needlework upon fine holland cloth with button and loops of black silk on the sides' (Boynton, 1971, p.23), while in the 1641 Tart Hall inventory 'the curtains are lined with network and edged about with a silk and gold fringe, bottones and loopes' (Cust, 1911). By the eighteenth century, these had become decorative, in order to disguise the hooks and eyes that were then used beneath the loops.
See also **Hook and loop**.

Buttoning
A method of fixing **upholstery fillings** that follows tufting, which has been used at least from the late eighteenth century. The **silk** or **wool** tufts used in the seventeenth and eighteenth centuries were, to some extent, replaced in the late eighteenth century by buttons or rings.

Loudon noticed that 'small rings are used covered with the same leather as the chair; these rings being found to look as well as, and wear better than, tufts of silk; at the same time they do not harbour dust' (1839, p.1049). By the middle of the nineteenth century, as designs demanded more **stuffing** and more cover, deep buttoning, as opposed to float buttoning, was developed. This ties the buttons through the stuffing to the foundation **canvas**. The buttoning was a technical imperative to hold the stuffing in place, but it soon became a distinct aspect of upholstered furniture. The crapaud, sofa, confidante and chesterfield are all nineteenth-century examples of upholstery that relied on buttoning, usually in conjunction with **spring** suspensions for this effect.

As buttoned or tufted upholstery was a major feature of the later nineteenth century, it is not surprising that attempts were made to try to simplify the process by mechanised means. However, it was not until the end of the century that a satisfactory method was marketed, mainly in the USA. The tufting machine produced a 'quilt' of backing, stuffing and material **top cover** buttoned together, which could then be applied to a sprung frame with much more speed and ease than the traditional built-up process. Naturally, this encouraged the division of labour and a consequent reduction in the skill required for the upholstering of chairs and sofas.
See also **Capitonné**, **Tufting**, **Van dyke**.

Caddis
(a) A cheap **worsted tape** or ribbon that was known well into the eighteenth century. The 1580 *Book of Rates* listed 'Cadas or cruel ribbon'.
(b) **Cotton wool** or **silk** floss that was used as padding. This definition dates from *c.*1400.
(c) A French worsted material similar to **serge**. The *OED* records a reference from 1536 for 'One carpet of cadys for the table xij d'. '220 ells caddis tapestry' valued at £22 was landed in London in May 1568 (Dietz, 1972, p.82)
See also **Caddow**.

Caddow (aka Cadow)
(a) Coarse **woollen rugs** or coverlets, especially those made in Ireland, that were used for bedding. In 1579, 'ij fledge blankets vs. ij caddow blankets ij s. iiij d' were listed in a will (*Richmond Wills*, 1853). In 1595, the yeoman of the wardrobe in the Montague household had to ensure that in guests' rooms the following rule was observed 'to remove the quilts at night and to have yrishe rugges lay'd in their places' (Thornton, 1978, p.355). In 1610, it was recorded that Ireland produced coarse 'wool caddowes … or coverlets' (*OED*). Cotgrave defines caddow as a 'couverture velouté [coverlet with a **pile**], an Irish Rug, Mantle or Cadowe'. It was still referred to in 1688 by Randle Holme who defined it as a coverlet or **blanket**.

(b) A decorative form of quilting that was once a speciality of the Bolton district of northwest England and often given as wedding presents. The caddow is a **weft**-figured handloom process with a plain-weave ground, with the figured decoration created by uncut loops of weft pile. J.H. Nodal noted that the name 'Caddies is still used in Bolton for a special make of sheets and quilts' (*Let*, 1887, *OED*).

By the early twentieth century, caddows seem to have been in decline, and by the 1930s were obsolete. A trade publication fondly referred to them:

> [Caddow] is a little known but exceedingly interesting type of quilt that is not now met with commercially, although formerly it was a trade of fair dimensions in the Bolton district. The caddow is a handloom product, and is one of the few fabrics it has not been found feasible to produce on power looms. The fabrics have a plain-weave ground, tightly woven with strong, coarse yarns, and has outstanding distinguishing feature of figured ornamentation formed by uncut loops of weft pile. The designs were of a highly conventionalised character, and many were highly prized. Caddow quilts have great strength and durability, and at one time, it was a practice to include among wedding presents a caddow with the names of the happy couple and date of marriage woven in, and this was expected to last their married life. (French, 1937, p.129.)

See also **Bolton coverlet**, **Coverlet**, **Quilt**, **Quilting**, **Rugg**.

FURTHER READING

Burnham, H.B. (1971). 'Bolton quilts or caddows: a nineteenth century cottage industry', *Bulletin de Liaison du CIETA*, 34, pp 22–9.

Café curtain

In the 1950s, café curtains were introduced as part of a fascination for the culture of Paris and as a change from cross-over or full length **nets**. They were short straight-hanging **curtains**, often in tiers, used to cover the lower and sometimes upper portions of a window or door. They hung on wood or metal poles, which were placed across the top and centre of the window. They were often finished with a scalloped top edge and sometimes hung by tabs of cloth.
See also **Cottage curtain**, **Grommet**, **Scalloped heading**.

Café rod

A slim brass rod used to hang **café curtains** or scalloped **curtains**.

Caffa

(a) A rich **silk** cloth, apparently similar to **damask**, that was much used in the sixteenth century. Its name may derive from Caffa, a Crimean town in which it was supposed to have been first woven. In 1531, Henry VIII possessed 'white caffa for the Kinges grace' (*Wardrobe Accounts of Henry VIII*, 18, *OED*), while in 1552 it was noted that: 'The said bedmaker received twenty-two yards and three quarters of crimson capha for a damask to the same bed' (Strype, *Ecclesiastical Memorials*, II. ii. ii. xiv. 359, *OED*).
(b) A kind of **cotton** cloth, painted with several designs and colours, made in India, which occurred in commerce in the eighteenth century. In 1752, Beawes mentions 'some others [i.e. places] dependent on Caffa, which serves them for an Almagazen' (Beawes, p.780). By 1810, caffa was defined as 'painted cotton cloth, manufactured in the East Indies, and sold at Bengal' (*Encyclopaedia Britannica*, vol.49).

Caffar damask (aka caffart, caffard)

The name 'caffard' appears to originate from the French for counterfeit. In this sense, it is an inferior damask of **silk warp** and **linen**, or **wool** and linen, or other combinations for the **weft**. The *Tudor Book of Rates* for 1582 mentions 'Damask and carfar damask the yard' (Willan, 1962, p.21). During the eighteenth and nineteenth centuries, they had a **satin** ground and the patterns were often in Oriental designs. Postlethwayt, writing in 1751, declared:

> they have a stuff in France which they call cassart damask made in imitation of the true damask, but they have the woof of hair, coarse silk, thread, wool or cotton. Some have the warp of silk and the woof of thread; others are all thread, both warp and woof and others again all of wool.

Sheraton (taking a definition given by Postlethwayt in 1751) noted that caffart damask was 'made in imitation of the real thing, having woof of hair, coarse silk, wool or cotton. Some have the warp of silk and woof of thread' (1803, p.191).

Caffoy

Caffoy was referred to as a cloth woven with a **woollen pile** on a **satin** ground that was produced in imitation of **silk velvets** and **damasks**. It was probably first imported into England from Abbeville, France, in the sixteenth century. Indeed, in 1752 Beawes listed the products of Abbeville, as 'Plush, Caffoy, Ticking, etc' (p.686). It was woven from *c.*1577 by immigrant Flemings, largely in the Norwich area of East Anglia, and was popular in the seventeenth and early eighteenth centuries for **upholstery**, bed hangings and **wall coverings**.

An early reference from 1590 to caffoy is in the **bed furniture** of Lady Morison at Cassiobury (Beard, 1997, p.31). It also appears in the Ingatestone inventory of 1600 that refers to a 'blue Caffoy canopy and valance with birds and beasts in white silk and gold upon it' (Emmison, 1954, p.12). Caffoy appears to have remained a fashionable furnishing fabric as, in the 1726 Erthig inventory, there are references to caffoy upholstery covers and, in 1731, John Loveday saw the Houghton salon hung with scarlet caffoy (Clabburn, 1988, p.241), while the family drawing room had a yellow caffoy used as a wall covering. A little later, in 1744, Mrs Delany used crimson caffoy in her drawing room and, in 1765, the saloon furniture at Stowe was also upholstered in caffoy (Cornforth & Fowler), 1974, p.132).

It would seem to have been less popular by the latter end of the eighteenth century.

Calamanco

See **Calimanco**.

Calencas

A printed toile produced in France (Alsace and Nantes) in the later eighteenth century. It was exemplified by the use of a range of red shades with a black outline to the designs, which invariably had a leafy floral design. Another version appears in the City of Nantes archives: '*des mi-calencas et calencas ou toiles fines et superfines, peintes à l'anglaise jusqu' 8 et 18 couleurs*' (Ville de Nantes, HH34).
See also **Toile**.

Calico

Originating in Calicut, on the southwest Indian coast (hence the name), calico is one of the oldest **cotton**s. It is generally rather coarse and light in weight, although heavier than **muslin**. The patterns were printed by either discharge or resist printing on one side only. It is not always fast in colour and is often sized for crispness, although this washes out. Whilst it may be similar to **percale**, the range of textiles listed under the generic name of calico is wide, and includes plain, printed, stained and dyed versions as well as chintz and muslins. Imported from India in the late sixteenth century onward, it was later manufactured in Europe. It was certainly used as a furnishing fabric in Europe from the sixteenth century. In 1559, 'calico curtains' were listed in the inventory of Southampton resident Margaret Pyd, whilst another resident, John Smith, had a 'cubborde cloth of callycowe' (Lemire, 2003, p.67).

By the seventeenth century, the demand for painted calicos had increased enormously, so much so that designs produced in England were sent out to India to be made up by local calico painters. In 1634, Sir Thomas Herbert noted that 'The Bannyans sell Callicoes, Cheney Sattins, Cheney ware' (*Some Years Travels*..., p.41), and it appears to have been popular through the seventeenth century. In 1698, John Fryer noted that 'staple commodities [of India] are calicuts white and painted, palempores, carpets, [and] tea' (p.34). Many examples demonstrate this taste for calico in domestic furnishings. The Montacute House inventory of 1651 listed '2 callico window curtains' (Beard, 1997, p.291). In 1675, the upholsterer Pat Barrett supplied Edward Sackville with 'watered callicoe' and 'stained callicoe' for hangings (ibid. p.294), whilst in 1688, there was a 'calleco chamber' at Cowdray where the wall hangings, window curtains, bed hangings and **table covers** were all of painted calico (Thornton, 1978, p.116).

Known in North America by the later seventeenth century, a Boston inventory of 1684 records '2 pr. white calico curtains, valients, tester cloths and 6 covers for chairs', as well as 2 calico sideboard cloths, a calico cuberd cloth and 1 quilt of calico colerd and flowerd' (Montgomery, 1984, p.185). A little later, in 1691, John Bowles of Roxbury, had 'painted calico curtains and vallaines' (Cummings, 1961, p.16). By 1695, Margarita van Varick in New York listed '2 stript callico curtains, cullerd calico curtains, valances, napkins, pillow beers, bibs and children's beds' among her possessions (Montgomery, 1984, p.185).

Some authors saw pitfalls in particular varieties. In 1696, *The Merchant's Warehouse Laid Open* mentioned a variety called Birom Banies (striped brown and white calico), which was widely used for the lining of beds. He pointed out that, as it was 'naturally a rotten sort of wear, for that reason [it] is fit only to hang up for curtains either for beds or windows' (J.F., 1696).

An important outlet for printed calico was in bed quilt-making. In 1697, professional quilt-makers petitioned the Government against import restrictions on their calicoes. Their petition stated amongst other points:

> That depriving the quilt-makers of the liberty of using printed callicoe carpets will be a detriment to the Government, as to the customs and duties, and also the woollen manufacturers; there being great quantities of Norwich, Kidderminster, Kendal and other stuffs, used for the backsides of quilts...
>
> That the calicoes used in making quilts, are cut into square pieces and printed in form of a carpet which renders them unfit for cloaths or garments of any kind: Neither can they be used in household furniture any otherways but in quilts, being only fit for that purpose. (Osler, 1987, p.88)

During the eighteenth century, calico remained popular as a furnishing fabric. In 1701, an invoice to the Duchess of Norfolk included a charge for 'making and putting up 2 Indian Callico window curtains...' (Beard, 1997, p.299). The Dyrham Park inventory of 1710 records a fully co-ordinated use of calico in the Terras Bed Chamber. This had 'an Indian Callico Bed; a counterpane and 4 pieces of hangings Indian callico; 2 window curtains and vallains of callico; 4 elbow chairs Irish stitch with white painted callico covers' (Walton, 1986, p.59). In 1727, Daniel Defoe wrote explaining the apparent need to restrict imports:

> The Queen [Mary] brought in the love of fine East-India Callicoes such as were then called Masslapatan, Chintes, Atlasses and fine painted calicoes, which afterwards descended into the humour of the common peoples so much as to make them grievous to our trade, and ruining to our manufacture, so that parliament were obliged to make two Acts at several times to restrain, and at last, prohibit the use of them. (*Complete English Tradesman*, 1727, p.266)

Mr Purefoy corresponded with his upholsterer, Anthony Baxter, in 1735, regarding '2 pieces of sprigged callicoe [which] are of different patterns so would not do for our other parlour' (Eland, 1931, p.171).

By the mid-eighteenth century, Chambers described calicoes with a catch-all definition: 'divers kinds, plain, printed, painted, stained, dyed, chints, muslins and the like' (*Cyclopaedia*, 1753). Three years later, Rolt explained that calico was 'now prohibited to be worn, printed or coloured, otherwise than by needlework, upon account of its prejudicing the woollen and **linen** manufacturers of Great Britain and Ireland' (1756).

Thomas Sheraton observed the wide range of calicoes available:

> Calicoes are of different kinds, plain, printed. Stained, dyed, chintz, muslins and the like... Some of them are painted with various flowers of different colours; others are not stained, but have a stripe of gold and silver quite through the piece, and at each end is fixed a tissue of gold, silver and silk intermixed with flowers. The printing of calicoes was first set on foot in London about 1676, and has long been a most important article of commerce. (1804–7, p.235.)

Although George Smith noted that calico should 'where good drapery is required, be glazed mellow; the small chintz patterns holding a preference in point of effect, especially for draperies', he added that for eating rooms and libraries 'calico when used, should be of one colour; in shades of moreen or scarlet' (1808, p.xii). Calico was also highly praised by Ackermann in his *Repository of Arts*, especially during the period 1809–10.

By the early nineteenth century, calico had two definitions. According to the 1828 edition of Webster's *American Dictionary*, 'In England, white or unprinted **cotton** cloth is called calico. In the United States, calico is painted cotton cloth, having not more than two colours'.

Calico remained a useful furnishing fabric. In 1839, Loudon suggested that simple **curtains** for cottages might be made:

> From calico, dyed crimson, blue or any other ingrain colour that will wash. They may also be made from dimity with a strip of glazed calico, about an inch and a half wide, of any colour suitable sewn on about two inches from the margin... Coloured calico cut in van dykes or in any other pattern, and sewed on close to the edge, may be substituted for the plain strip if preferred. (1839, p.341.)

From the late eighteenth century to the mid-twentieth century, commercial fabric printing was often called calico printing even if the base cloth was not cotton. In North America calico still refers to a patterned cloth, often with small all-over designs.

See also **Bafta**, **Calico (Down-proof)**, **Chintz**, **Counterpane**, **Decca work**, **Dowlas**, **Fly**, **Indienne**, **Madapolam**, **Mercoolees**, **Mober banies**, **Moree**, **Provençal print**, **Quilt**.

FURTHER READING
Irwin, J. & Hall, M. (1971). *Indian Painted and Printed Fabrics*, Ahmedabad: Calico Museum of Textiles.
Lemire, B. (2003). 'Domesticating the exotic: floral culture and the East India calico trade with England *c.*1600–1800', *Textile: Journal of Cloth and Culture*, 1, March, pp 64–85.
Rothstein, N. (1969). 'The calico campaign of 1719–1721', *East London Papers*, 7, 1, July, pp 3–21.

Calico (Down-proof)
Down-proof **calico** is a tightly woven cloth finished by **waxing** and often used as a 'feather-proof' **cushion** case. In an unbleached version it is used as a final covering before a **top cover** (often hide) is fitted in **upholstery** work. Calico has also been used to encase pocket springs in **mattresses**.
See also **Spring: Pockets**.

Calimanco (aka Calamanco) (Fr. *Calmande*)
A **worsted** material related to **satin** with a high gloss, hot-pressed effect, glazed with a coating of beeswax, often twilled and chequered in the **warp** so that the **checks** show on one side only. Originally from Flanders, the term was first recorded in England in 1592 (*OED*). Calimanco production was particularly associated with Norwich, Norfolk, which remained the centre of the trade in the early nineteenth century. These glazed worsted fabrics were used for hangings and **upholstery** as well as for dress materials.

Calimanco was particularly well known in the eighteenth century. In 1723, Savary des Bruslons wrote:

> Calamande, called in Holland, particularly at Amsterdam, calaminque. A stuff similar to that formerly called Ras d'Utrecht, which is made in the Brabant and in Flanders… The stuff is very glossy and is made twilled in the warp; thus the twill appears only on one side, the right. It is ordinarily made all of wool. But there are some in which the warp is mixed with silk, and others in which some goat's hair is used. There are calamandes of all colours and styles; some plain and solid; others with bands of flowers; other stripes; and others watered. A great many are used throughout Flanders and the Brabant, and in France… Calamande is appropriate for clothing, night robes, petticoats, upholstery and is very generally in use. (Cummin, 1941, p.183.)

In the 1728 inventory of the shop of James Pilbeam, a mercer of Chiddingly, Sussex, there was listed 'Two hundred yards of callimenco at 10d per yard £8 3s 8d' (http://www.chiddingly.gov.uk/History/James%20Pilbeam.html) It was also used in America by the early eighteenth century. In 1726, the Boston upholsterer, Thomas Fitch, wrote to a client:

> I concluded it would be difficult to get such a Calliminco as you propos'd to cover the ease chair, and having a very strong thick Harratine, which is vastly more fashionable and handsome than a Calliminco. I have sent you an ease chair cover'd with sd Harrateen which I hope will sute you. (Montgomery, 1984, p.256.)

Despite these remarks, in Boston during 1729 there was advertised for sale 'a handsome bedstead with calaminco curtains, vallens, tester and window curtains' (ibid. p.185).

In the 1771 inventory of Felbrigg Hall, there was some 'Green calamanco in a trunk for window curtains' (Clabburn, 1998, p.241). At the beginning of the nineteenth century, Sheraton (following des Bruslons) recorded that calamanco was 'A sort of woollen stuff manufactured in England and Brabant, and is chequered [twilled] in the warp, whence the checks only appear on the right side. Some calamancos are quite plain, others have broad stripes adorned with flowers, some with broad stripes quite plain and others watered.' (1803, p.121.)

By 1887, Caulfeild & Saward noted it was 'highly glazed, plain or twilled raised in stripes or brocaded' and 'resembles Tammies and Durants'. It was then used for women's petticoats (p.58).
See also **Everlasting**, **Lasting**, **Russell**.

FURTHER READING
Cummin, H. (1941). 'Calamanco', *Antiques*, 39, April, pp 182–4.

Camaca
A **tabby lampas** weave cloth often woven of **silk** and used for furnishings in the fourteenth and fifteenth centuries. Camaca was particularly associated with Lucca, an Italian weaving town. The 1375 will of Edward Lord Despencer bequeathed 'my great bed of blue camaca, with griffins, also another bed of camaca, striped with white and black' (*OED*). In 1485, there was reference to 'the dorsers all of camaca, the bankers all of taffeta' (*EE Misc.*, 1856, p.4). Camaca very seldom appears after this date.
See also **Weave: Lampas**.

Cambric (Fr. *Batiste*)
A fine plain-weave **linen** (and later **cotton**) textile, which is either bleached or piece-dyed. It is similar to batiste but is stiffer and has fewer slubs. Originally made in Cambrai, France, of linen yarns, it was initially imported for use in church **embroidery**, sheeting and **table linens**. An early domestic use is recorded in the 1535 inventory of Katherine of Aragon who had **sheets** made of 'camerycke cloth' (Clabburn, 1988, p.117). The *Tudor Book of Rates* for 1582 listed 'Camarick the piece, containing thirteen ells English' (Willan, 1962, p.12).

In 1622, it was noted that 'the commodities which are not made at all or but in small quantity in England, and may be practised are many as Buckrams, Tapistrie, Bustians, Cambrickes' (Malynes, 1622, p.229). In the 1728 inventory of the shop of James Pilbeam, a mercer of Chiddingly, Sussex, there was listed 'Tenn yards and a half of cambrick at ls 6d per yard, £0 15s 9d' (http://www.chiddingly.gov.uk/History/James%20Pilbeam.html). Cambric was sometimes used for **drape** in the early nineteenth century. *The Palladium* (Boston) in 1810 noted a suite of **curtains** for sale. They were advertised as 'consisting of 168 yards cambric chintz, 168 ditto light blue cambrick, for lining ditto with pendant fringe, binding etc; gilt pins, suitable for a drawing room or best chamber-all new and of the most modern patterns' (Montgomery, 1984, p.187).

In the early twentieth century, cambric was highly recommended for window blinds, being specified for USA Government offices in 1916 (see **Blind**), while in 1947, it was noted that glazed cambric was suitable for **linings** and curtains (Bendure & Pfieffer, p.615).
See also **Batiste**, **Muslin**.

Camlet (aka Camblet)
A plain-weave cloth, woven in a wide range of widths and yarns, used for dress and furnishings. Any cross rib textile was called *camelоté* and a waved design was 'chambletted' in England. Coarse camlets were *grosgrains* or *grosgrams* in Europe. The spelling with cham- was the prevalent one in English until after the Restoration. The ultimate origin is obscure. At the earliest known date, the word was associated (by Europeans) with camel **hair** materials; but it may be derived from the Arabic *khamlat*, which is the nap or **pile** on the surface of cloth. Khamlat was defined by Dr Johnson as: 'camelot, silk and camels hair, also, all silk or velvet, especially pily and plushy' (1773).

According to Hazel Cummin (1942, p.310), there are three major versions of camlets, which refer to particular fabrics:

(a) A fine closely woven stuff of combed and twisted yarns both warp and weft. Originally, of goats' hair, it was later made in Europe of wool usually mixed with silk in the effort to produce a harder grain and to imitate the sheen of mohair.
(b) A stuff of simple weave, in which a grain or ribbing in the weft was obtained by special management in the loom, usually by the heavier or harder yarns for weft than for warp.
(c) Characteristically a plain cloth the beauty of which depended upon fineness of materials, close expert weaving, and beautiful colour effects dyed in the yarns. Changeable and jaspered effect obtained by the use of different coloured threads for warp and weft ever much in favour. (*Antiques*, 70, December 1942, p.310.)

Originating in the thirteenth century, English camlets were made from Norwich **worsted**, whilst the Low Countries made camlets from goats' hair or a hair and **silk** mix, with 'Brussels camlets' apparently being the benchmark. The production of camlet was noted by Camden who explained that the wealth of Coventry 'arose in the last age from its woollen and camblet manufacture' (Camden, *Britannia* 1610, cited in Edwards, 1964, p.110).

The 1537 accounts of Katherine of Aragon's Wardrobe Stuff included 'two curteynes of silke chamlette, paned red, grene, russette, yalowe, and tawneye, cont; viij bredis of the saide stuff unlyned' (Beard, 1997, p.282).

The decorative effects made by the application of heat and water were clearly a feature of camlets. Distinctions were referred to in the 1582 *Book of Rates* that listed: 'Chamlets watered and unwatered the peece/ the double peece containing twenty yards' (Willan, 1962, p.16).

In 1620, Sharpe and Wilton took out a patent (Patent no.17) for a new method of making camlets 'in the Turkish manner', achieved by cold rather than hot pressing. John Evelyn also recorded that he 'went to see ... the pressing and watering ... [of] grosgrans and chamblettes with weights of an extraordinary poyse put into a rolling machine' in Tours (*Diary of John Evelyn*, 8 May 1644). Camlet was clearly an esteemed cloth for furnishings in the seventeenth century. The walls of the Ham House 'bedchamber within' were furnished with 'four pieces of gray hayre camolet, with scarlet fringe' (Thornton & Tomlin, 1980, p.109). The specific reference to hair is interesting. In 1698, Celia Fiennes saw 'camlet and mohair beds' in the Cupola House at Bury St Edmunds (1995, p.139). A year later, an estimate for beds to be supplied to Hampton Court included '50 yards camblet to make the bed' (Beard, 1997, p.299).

The demand for camlet continued into the eighteenth century. Striped camlet was listed for window **curtains** and window seats in the 1715 inventory of upholsterer, Francis Lapiere (Westman, 1994, p.8). In the 1728 inventory of the shop of James Pilbeam, a mercer of Chiddingly, Sussex, there was listed 'Ten peeces of camblet at £1 per peece £10 0s 0d; One hundred fifty and four yards of camblet at 1s 4d per yard, £10 5s 4d; One hundred and two yards of camblet at 1s per yard, £5 2s 0d' (http://www.chiddingly.gov.uk/History/James%20Pilbeam.html). In 1730, Hampton Court was billed for 'two pr of camblet window curt[ain]s to match ye yellow camblet bed', to be used in the grooms' bedchamber' (Beard, 1997, p.302). By 1736, camlet was described as a 'sort of stuff made of camels hair, silk etc., mixed' (Bailey). Postlethwayt probably has the best definitions of the various finishes:

Figured camlets are those of a single colour, on which have been stamped, or imprinted, various figures, flowers, foliages, &c. This is performed with hot irons, which are a kind of moulds that are passed under a press at the same time with the stuff. The figured camlets only come from Amiens and Flanders. The trade of them was formerly pretty considerable; at present there are but few of them sold, which serve commonly for church ornaments, or for making some household furniture... Wave camlets are those on which a kind of waves have been impressed, as on tabbies, by making them pass several times under the calendar... Water camlets are such, which being taken from the loom, undergo a certain preparation with water, after which they are put into the hot press, that renders them smooth and glossy. (1751–7.)

By 1774, another definition explained that: 'Stuffs made from the hair of [the Angora goat] are well known among us by the name of camlet' (Goldsmith, vol.II. p.35). Later still, Sheraton described camlet as 'a stuff sometimes of wool, silk and sometimes of hair especially that of goats, with wool and silk' (1803, p.122).

American consumers also appreciated camlet. Boston citizen, Samuel Sewall, wrote in 1719: 'to be bought. Curtains and Vallens for a bed, with Counter-pane, Head-Cloth and Tester, of good yellow watered worsted camlet, with Trimming, well made, and Bases, if it be the fashion. Send also of the same Camlet and Trimming, as may be enough to make Cushions for the Chamber Chairs' (Montgomery in Cooke (ed.), 1987, p.166). In 1725, fellow American, Thomas Fitch, wrote to John East, a London upholsterer, requesting bed hangings to be made from 'very good broad scarlet in grain double worsted camlet' (Jobe, 1974, p.28).

By the later nineteenth century, the various natures of camlet were explained by the American author, Beck:

In [the] production [of camlets], the changes have been rung with all materials in nearly every possible combination; sometimes of wool, sometimes of silk, sometimes of hair, sometimes of hair with wool or silk, at others of silk and wool warp and hair woof. Those of our day have had cotton and linen introduced into their composition. They have been made plain and twilled, of single warp and weft, of double warp, and sometimes with double weft also' (1882).

See also **Barracan**, **Camleteen**, **Cheney**, **Grosgrain**, **Harrateen**, **Mohair**, **Moreen**, **Paragon**, **Poplin**, **Siamoise**, **Stuff**, **Tammy**.

FURTHER READING

Cummin, H. (1942). 'Camlet', *Antiques*, 92, December, pp 309–12.

Camleteen

Bailey defined it as 'a sort of fine worsted camlet' (1730–55). Postlethwayt gave a different definition in that camleteen was a stuff of 'mixed wool and goat's hair, thread or cotton' (1751–55). By the early twentieth century, camleteen was simply an inferior or imitation camlet-type fabric.
See also **Camlet**.

Campaign fringe

See **Fringe: Campaign**.

Candlewick

Candlewick was an unbleached **muslin** bed **sheeting** (also called Kraft muslin) used as a base for the application of **weft**-figured candlewick tufting. The candlewick itself is made from heavy plied looped yarns, which are needled into the base cloth and then cut to give the fuzzy effect and the cut yarn look of chenille. The candlewick bedspread has

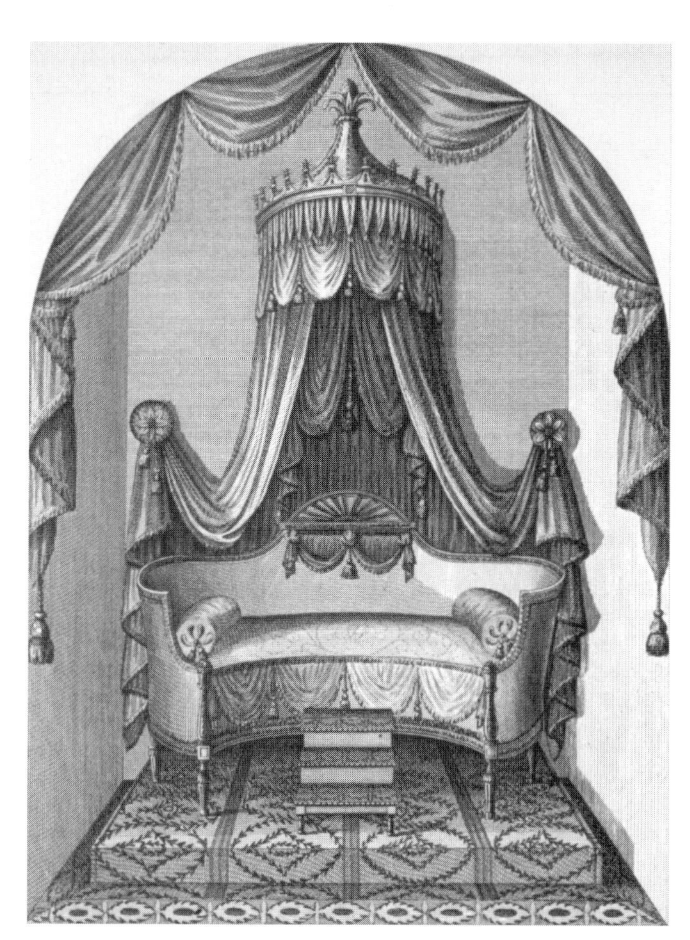

24. Design for a canopy for a French or sofa bed (T. Sheraton, The Cabinet Maker and Upholsterer's Drawing Book, *1793)*

variegated lines of tufts that form the pattern, whereas the chenille has continuous lines. Leaving the **pile** uncut may alter the effect (see also **Chenille**). In the twentieth century, candlewick was used for bedspreads, **drapes**, housecoats and beachwear.

The candlewicking process was explained in 1947: 'candlewick or hobnail is made the same as tufting except that there is no continuous row of stitches in the back. The tufting is spaced, and the stitches on the front are cut, so that individual tufts of yarn are spaced throughout the face of the fabric' (Bendure & Pfieffer, 1947, p.576). *The Draper's Encyclopaedia* also noted that tufts of pile yarns were needled into a crinkly sheeting cloth with the **embroidery** machine: 'They use single needles for intricate work and multiple needles for simple lines and borders. Candlewick bedspreads are made from tufted cloth that is easily adapted to changing designs and colours, as it does not use a jacquard' (Ostick, 1955, p.356).
See also **Bedspread**.

Candlewicking
An embroidering technique that loops yarns into an unbleached cloth. The yarns are cut to create a tufted effect. It is used for **bedspreads**. The method is also the origin of the basic **tufted carpet** process.
See **Candlewick**.

Cannellé (aka Cannetillé)
A French term for a tightly woven cloth, textured to resemble a brick wall. An extra **warp** floats on the surface and is bound in steps to form a brick-like effect.
See also **Tobine**.

Cannelle rep
A **silk** rep made with two **warps**. A single warp forms the ground while two-fold yarns float to create the distinctive ribs.
See **Rep**.

Canopy
An early name for a textile covering that was used for both beds and chairs of estate. The name comes from the Latin *conopeum*, meaning a 'net or pavilion over a bed', or from *konops* – Greek for 'gnat'. The term has connections with both utilitarian and impressive uses. For example, canvas was used for a canopy at Tart Hall in 1641 'for two beds to keep the gnats away' (Cust, 1911), while the Easton inventory of 1637 listed 'one crimson velvet canapie ... with two rich taffeta changeable trayned curtaynes to it' (Thornton, 1978, p.367).

An important use of canopies was to furnish beds. Suspended cone-shaped or dome-shaped canopies, often fitted with curtains that reached and encompassed the head and foot of the bed (trains), were in fact both useful and decorative.

In addition to their use over beds, they were often part of the ensemble of chairs of state where the canopies might be called 'cloths of estate'. These were suspended on chains from the ceiling with fixed side curtains, **valances** and a head cloth. All were designed en suite with the other furnishings, especially with the seat of honour or chair of estate. Other examples of their use include canopies over busts, portraits and looking glasses. In 1606, Jane Ward of Ipswich had 'a looking glass with an old green say canepe' (Reed, 1981, p.101).

By the eighteenth century, Bailey simply defines a canopy as 'a tester and curtains for a bed' (1753), although 'a canopy of state of crimson silk damask wrought and fringed with gold' appears to have still been on show in Knole in 1799. For eighteenth-century funerals, black **velvet** canopies were used or hired.

The original use returned to fashion early in the nineteenth century. Sheraton explains that: 'Canopies, amongst us, are generally used as a covering or tester, for French or sofa beds and are often of a spherical figure, or otherwise of a bell shape. They are certainly a handsome ornament when they are executed in a tastey manner' (1803, p.127).

As tastes changed, and the matter of bed furnishings became a major issue for the Victorians, Moreland wrote in 1889 saying 'the full canopy covering the entire bed is seldom used... The usual method is to use the half canopy ... attached to the wall ... kept in place by an iron rod or chain with a turn buckle'.
See also **Celure**, **Cloth of estate**, **Lawn**, **Pavilion**, **Sparver**, **Tester**, **Train**.

FURTHER READING

Thornton, P. (1974). 'Canopies, couches and chairs of estate', *Apollo*, 100, October, pp 292–99.

Cantaloon
A cantaloon is a fine quality Catalonian **woollen** bedcover. The term was later employed to describe **worsted** materials produced in France and England during the seventeenth and eighteenth centuries. Lewis Holland of York County, Virginia, had 16 pieces (939 yards) of cantaloon stuff at 4d per yard in his inventory dated September 1731 (Colonial Williamsburg, www.pastportal.com). Postlethwayt said that Bristol had 'some considerable manufactures of woollen stuffs,

particularly cantaloons, which are carried on chiefly by French refugees' (1751–5).

Canton flannel
Twilled soft **cotton** fabric with a long nap. An American definition explains:

> This is so called from Canton, China, because it was first imported into England from China. It is also called cotton flannel. It is made of soft twisted yarns woven with a twill weave and has a nap raised on one side. It is finished as unbleached or bleached canton flannel and is dyed in plain colors. It may be used for winter undergarments white or unbleached. When dyed it may be used for interlinings or draperies. (Thompson, 1917, p.62)

The southern Chinese city of Canton exported a range of textiles from the 1860s onward, hence the name.
See also **Flannel**.

Canton linen
See **Grass cloth**, **Ramie cloth**.

Canton matting
See **Matting: China**.

Cantonnière
A decoration for a window or door, which is an inverted U-shape, like a fixed **lambrequin** that extends to the floor. Designed to hide the window or doorframe completely, it may be made from **tapestry** or other suitable material.
See also **Cantoon**.

Cantoon
(a) A strong kind of **fustian**, with diagonal twill, that showed a fine cording on one side and a smooth bright surface on the other. Although mainly used for apparel, there are references to furnishing applications. In 1688, the *London Gazette* (No.2328/4) advertised 'A Cantoon grey cloth Bed and tester'.
(b) A narrow **curtain** from the French **cantonnière**, which fitted around the front posts of a four-poster bed, intended to close the gap between the side and end curtains.
See also **Bed furniture**, **Bonegrace**, **Cantonnière**.

Canvas
A plain material, woven from fibres such as **hemp**, **linen** or **cotton** that could be made in a variety of textures and weights from *c.*200 to 2000 g/m^2 (7 to 70 oz per 1.2 square yards). It has been used unbleached as the base for various needleworks and for the undersides of chairs, and dyed for seating, such as stools, deck chairs and tubular steel stacking chairs. In medieval times, it was widely used for utilitarian purposes such as sails and tents, but it was also used as a base for painted work that was to be mounted on chests or hung on walls. Henry Shaw (1856) recorded a medieval chest with wrought-iron works 'the spaces between covered with canvas, on which are painted imitations of fruit and flowers' (Kirk, 1981, p.186).

Although it was most well known as a base for needlework, it did have other applications. For example, canvas was used at Tart Hall in 1641 'for two beds to keep the gnats away' (Cust, 1911).

In the eighteenth century, Postlethwayt described the various canvases available including: 'A very clear unbleached cloth of hemp or flax wove very regular in little squares. It is used for working tapestry with the needle, by passing the threads through the intervals of squares. There is coarse, middling and fine canvas' (1751). Fenning noted its use for window blinds as well as for other applications: '[Canvas is] very clear unbleached cloth of hemp or flax, wove in little squares, used for working tapestry by the needle, for blinds of windows, towels, and to cover stays &c' (1768). Chippendale supplied Nostell Priory with '2 pair of mahogany folding window blinds with painted green canvas in ditto' (Gilbert, 1978, p.184). Canvas was also used to protect expensive wall hangings. Harewood had canvas and paper hangings over the yellow **damask** in the sitting room (ibid. p.210).

In the nineteenth century, green-coloured canvas or **bolting** was still being used for window blinds and, at the end of the century, canvas, **denim** etc. was recommended for wall coverings which might be lightly painted over to give a textured effect. It was also used in handicrafts. **Rug** canvas was used 'as a ground for the working of fancy worsted or yarns, for the various ornamental squares, circles, &c. intended to be placed upon tables and sideboards &c., to prevent their being scratched, or damaged' (Perkins, 1833).

In the 1950s, deck chair canvas was suggested for fitted chair covers (Smithells, 1950).
See also **Blind**, **Burlap**, **Canvas work**, **Craftsman canvas**, **Duck**, **Needlework**, **Painted cloth**, **Ticking**, **Wall coverings and hangings**.

Canvas work
A term used to define **embroidery** worked by counting the threads of the base cloth. It was used for **upholstery** and applied to decorate **cushions** from the early seventeenth century. The use of tent, cross or Irish **stitch** worked on **canvas** was often the basis for the making.
See also **Bargello**, **Berlin wool-work**, **Needlework**, **Stitch: Cross**.

Cape
A slip of fabric fitted to the top of a chair back that hangs down to protect **upholstery** covers from hair powder, etc.
See also **Antimacassar**, **Scarf**.

Capitonné
A nineteenth-century French buttoning technique for **upholstery** that is often regularly spaced in a pattern resembling a chequerboard.
See also **Buttoning**, **Tufting**.

Capping
A decorative treatment for the top of the wall under the architrave. It was fashionable around the end of the seventeenth and beginning of the eighteenth centuries. The cappings were often made of **festoon**-shaped cloth, **fringes** or **braids**.

Caranday fibre
A fibre produced in the mid-twentieth century in Argentina, produced from the leaves of the palm *Copernica cerifera*. It is used for cheap **upholstery** and **mattress stuffings**.

Carde
A (possibly **linen**) fabric used in the medieval period for **canopies**, **curtains** and **linings**. *The Draper's Dictionary* lists Carda, or Carduus, as 'an inferior silk, supposed to have been made of the coarse outer filaments of cocoons, probably used for linings'. Four pence an **ell** was paid in 1278 for '119 ells of carda, for thirty-four surcoats to be used in a tournament' (Beck, 1882). A furnishing reference from a will of 1426

recorded 'a blewe bedde of Tapecery & a selour with curteyns of carde' (*Early English Wills*, 1882, p.76).

Carpet

The name given to various textiles used to cover beds, furniture, walls and floors. It has also been used in **upholstery** and sometimes for **wall coverings** or **curtains**. From the sixteenth century, however, carpet also meant a plain or patterned fabric woven with a raised surface of tufts (either cut or looped), and used as a floorcovering. Other floorcoverings have been made without a tufted surface, and of these some are simple shuttle-woven materials, plain or enriched with needlework or printed with patterns; others are woven after the manner of tapestry weaving or in imitation of it, and a further class of carpets is made of felt. Although carpet weaving by hand is, and for centuries has been, an Oriental industry, it has also been, and is still, pursued in many European countries both by hand and machine.

The products of carpet manufacture can be placed into six main divisions: (a) woven **pile** carpets (*tapis moquettes*) which are either looped (**bouclé**) or cut (*velouté*); (b) flat surface carpets (*tapis ras*) as in hand tapestry-woven material; (c) printed carpeting; (d) tufted carpets; (e) non-woven carpets; and (f) knotted pile.

See also **Art square**, **Aubusson carpet**, **Axminster carpet**, **Barnard Castle carpet**, **Beauvais carpet**, **Berber**, **Body carpet**, **Border, Broché**, **Brussels carpet**, **Brusselette**, **Cinema pile carpet**, **Chenille Axminster**, **Chlidema square**, **Cord carpet**, **Cotton carpet**, **Cotton chain carpet**, **Damask carpet**, **Dhurrie, Donegal carpet**, **Double cloth carpet**, **Dutch carpet**, **Exeter carpet**, **Felt carpet**, **Fulham carpet**, **Habberley carpet**, **Hair carpet**, **Hemp carpet**, **Imperial, Ingrain carpet**, **Jaspé carpet**, **Jute carpet**, **Kalmuc, Karastan, Karvel**, **Kendal carpet**, **Kidderminster carpet**, **Knitted carpet**, **Lea carpeting**, **Leather carpet**, **List carpet**, **Matting, Moorfields carpet**, **Moquette carpet**, **Mosaic carpet**, **Mottled tapestry**, **Muskuetta**, **Needleloom carpet**, **Needlework carpet**, **Paper carpet**, **Patchwork carpet**, **Patent-back carpet**, **Pile**, **Rag carpet**, **Romsley carpet**, **Rubber-backed carpet**, **Savonnerie**, **Saxony**, **Scotch carpeting**, **Smyrna rug**, **Strip carpeting**, **Table carpet**, **Tapestry carpet**, **Terry carpet**, **Tournai carpet**, **Tufted carpet**, **Turkey work, Velvet carpet**, **Venetian carpet**, **Wilton carpet**, **Worcester carpet**, **Yorkshire carpeting**.

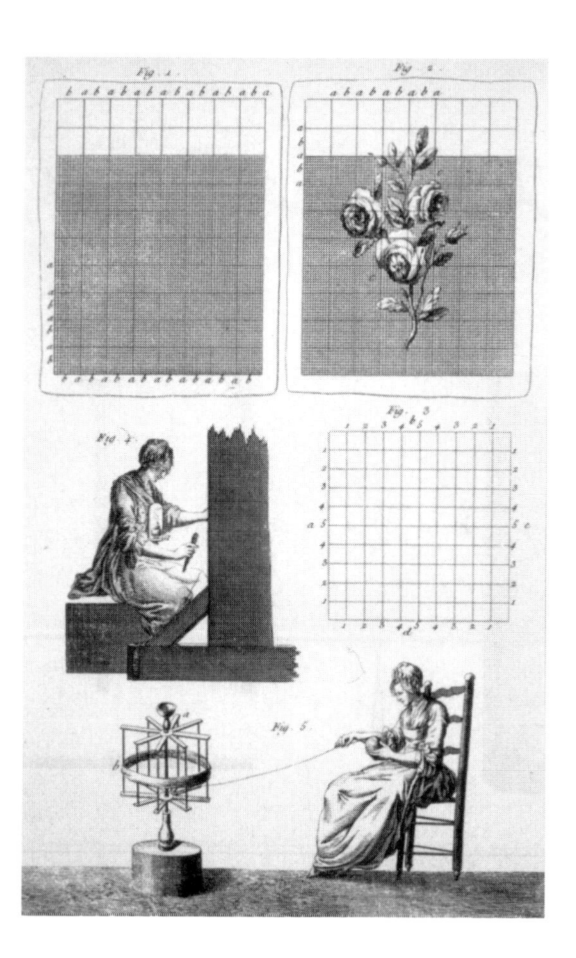

25. *Carpet weaving: detail of design transfer, weaving and winding operations (D. Diderot,* Encyclopédie, *1751 72)*

FURTHER READING

Bartlett, J.N. (1978). *Carpeting the Millions, The Growth of Britain's Carpet Industry*, Edinburgh: John Donald.
Bevan, G.P. (ed.) (1876). *British Manufacturing Industries*, 'Carpets', by Christopher Dresser, London: Edward Stanford.
Bigelow-Hartford Carpet Co (*c.*1925). *A Century of Carpet and Rug Making in America*, New York: The Company.
Board of Trade (1947). *Working Party Report, Carpet*, London: HMSO.
Brinton, R.S. (1919). *Carpets*, London: Pitman.
Faraday, C. (1929). *European and American Carpets and Rugs*, Grand Rapids: Dean-Hicks, reprinted 1990, Woodbridge: Antique Collectors' Club.
Kidderminster Library (n.d.). *Hand List of the Special Collection of Works on Carpets and Textiles,* Kidderminster: Kidderminster Library.
Robinson, G. (1966). *Carpets*, London: Pitman.
Smith, L.D. (1984). 'Industrial organisation in the Kidderminster carpet trade 1780–1850', *Textile History*, 15, 1, pp 75–100.
Tattershall, C. & Reed, S. (1934, 1966). *A History of British Carpets*, Benfleet: F. Lewis.
Taylor, A. (1874). *History of Carpet Trades*, Heckmondwike: J. Ellis.
Von Rosentiel, H. (1978). *American Rugs and Carpets, Seventeenth Century to Modern Times*, New York: William Morrow and Co.
Wyatt, M.D. (1868). *Reports on the Paris Universal Exhibition of 1867*, vol.xi, containing 'Report on carpets, tapestry and other stuffs for furniture', London: private circulation.

Carpet backing

A term referring to the material that is fixed to the back of a **carpet**, usually tufted, to increase its handle and support. The primary backing is the base into which the pile is needled or otherwise fixed. The secondary backing (or double backing) is applied as a separate process after tufting. This is often a **jute**-based fabric, but may be **polypropylene**. In some cases, a foam rubber backing or sprayed textured rubber is applied.
See also **Foam-backed cloth**, **Tufted carpet**.

Carpet binding

A decorative edging applied to cut **carpet** to avoid fraying. In 1887, the best were made with all-**worsted** yarns, while inferior ones were woven with worsted and **cotton**. They were apparently available in plain or **chintz** designs (Caulfeild & Saward, p.61).

Carpet binding as an alternative to back strapping has been used to finish off edges, especially for non-**pile** carpets. Webbing is sewn to the edge of the carpet with buttonhole **stitches** and the other edge of the webbing is hemmed to the **carpet backing**.
See also **Binding**.

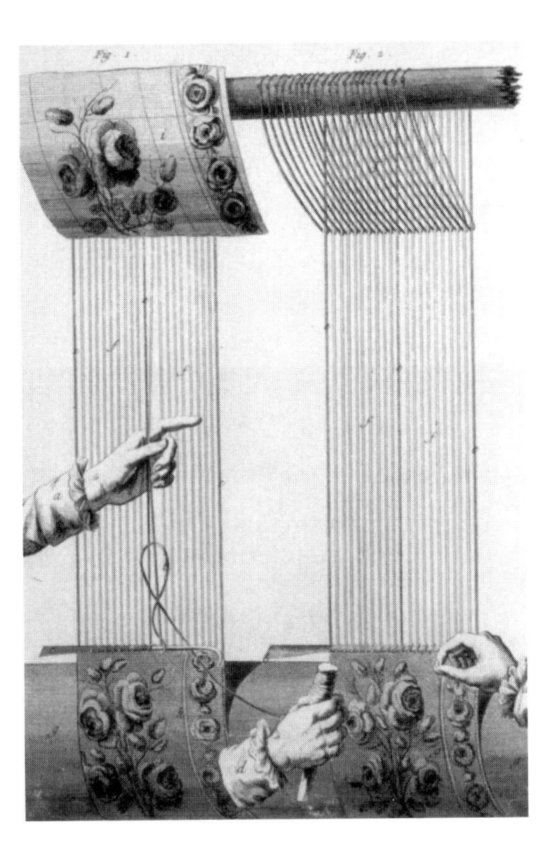

26. Carpet weaving: knotting operation (D. Diderot, Encyclopédie, *1751–72)*

Carpet cover and protection

The need to protect valuable **carpets** from everyday wear and tear was a sensible precaution that was commonplace by the seventeenth century in homes with carpets. The carpets in question were both **table carpets** and floor carpets. The 1603 inventory of Hengrave, the Great Chamber listed 'one large bord clothe or grene clothe, to laye over ye carpets of ye long borde' (Clabburn, 1988, p.167). **Baize** or serge was commonly employed to make up these carpet covers.

The use of baize as a protective cover for carpets was also promoted in the eighteenth century. In 1768–9, Thomas Moore sold the Earl of Coventry a 'green baize cover to a carpet for £2.5s 10d' (Gilbert, Lomax and Wells-Cole, 1987, p.106). In 1771, William France supplied **linen** protection for carpets: 'For 125½ yds of green glazed linen to line your green Bay for a carpet to cover the Axminster ditto' (Walton, 1980, p.103). Writing to a customer in 1772, Edward Elwick suggested that 'to cover the carpet a common green frize is the best' (Gilbert, 1976, p.47). In January 1778, the Chippendale firm charged £31.2s. for 'Thread and piecing out the Serge Carpet in Breakfast room to fit the floor, making eyelet holes in d[itt]o. And laying down with studs compleat' (Gilbert, 1978, p.251). Carpet protection was also supplied to stairs. In the accounts of Harewood House there is a payment to Reid the upholsterer 'after he had laid the carpet on the great staircase, covered it with oilcloth and serge…' (Clabburn, 1988, p.173).

In 1789, fashion considerations affected the choice of protection. Ninian Home wrote to Chippendale '…there must be a covering for it [a new carpet] of green serge. Perhaps that may not be fit for a drawing room, or that now some other sort of stuff is used for carpets. Make them of what you think is right' (Gilbert, 1978, p.51). The protective practices continued into the early nineteenth century. Sheraton recorded that: '[Baize] is much in use by cabinet-makers and upholsterers. By the latter, bays is issued to cover over carpets, and made to fit round the room, to save them' (1803, p.40).

Drugget was an important carpet protecting material by the end of the eighteenth century and since. *The Workwoman's Guide* noted that druggets are 'chiefly employed to lay over another carpet, to preserve it when the room is in daily use, and only removed for company. Sometimes druggets alone are laid and when of handsome brown or marone colour look extremely well' (Hale, 1840, p.202).

See also **Crumb cloth**, **Drugget**, **Frieze**, **Serge**.

Carpet fastener

A number of methods have been used to 'fit' **carpet**. The choice is often dependent upon the end use of the floor. If the carpet was to be permanently fixed, the method called 'turn and tack' was often employed. The edges of the carpet were turned under and nailed through around the skirting. Tackless gripper rods have superseded this method of fixing. These are plywood bars with many small pins fitted to them that are nailed to the floor. The carpet is then stretched on to them and held taut.

If the carpet needs to be removed periodically, i.e. for a dance floor, other methods are employed. The ring and pin, or pin and socket systems use pins fixed to the floor and either the carpet is sewn with rings that fix onto the pins or has pins pushed through it into sockets in the floor. In January 1778, the Chippendale firm charged £31. 2s. for 'thread and piecing out the Serge Carpet in Breakfast room to fit the floor, making eyelet holes in d[itt]o. And laying down with studs compleat' (Gilbert, 1978, p.251).

If the floor is too hard to be nailed directly, drilled lead plugs may be used. These require a hole to be cut into the hard floor that is then plugged with lead; these can then accommodate the nailing. For fastening on the stairs, carpet rods, clips and eyes have all been used. These have been made from a variety of materials including brass, steel, iron, lead, wood and bakelite. In the *Servants' Directory* of 1760, Hannah Glasse suggested: 'If you lay a stair cloth on, let it be a hair-cloth, fastened on with hook and long wires. The Turners can supply you; they will never move till wore into holes' (Gilbert, Lomax & Wells-Cole, 1987, p.95). Five years later, an account for work at The Vyne was submitted for '54 wires, 108 staples run with lead for carpets' (Gilbert, 1987, p.95). In 1778, Methley Park had a new staircase covered with 'haircloth for top to bottom [fitted] with lead bars' (ibid.). In 1805, Stourhead had 'brass wires fitted into brass eyes'. Variations on these methods continued into the twentieth century.

See also **Carpet fitting and planning**, **Carpet fastener**, **Smoothedge**.

Carpet fitting and planning

The idea of close covered or 'fitted' **carpet** was well known by the mid-eighteenth century. Isaac Ware commented in 1756 that 'the use of carpeting at this time has set aside the ornamenting of floors in a great measure; it is the custom almost universally to cover a room entirely so that there is no necessity of any beauty or workmanship underneath' (*Complete Body of Architecture*, Book II, p.123). The fact that the cut-**pile** surfaced carpets, both **Brussels** and **Wilton**, were only woven in narrow widths, and then seamed up with **borders**, meant that there was an amount of preparatory work including accurate measuring, cutting and sewing before the final fitting.

According to Sheraton, carpet fitting first started with the laying out of the borders and mitres around corners, fireplaces, etc. The mitres where then cut and the **body carpet** matched to them by being tacked down, using a **carpet strainer**. The cuts were then tacked together with sealing thread and taken back to the shop for completion. It was then sewn, returned to the room and tacked, and finally strained down (1803, pp 132–3).

In the 1840s, it was recommended that small pieces of **leather** be fitted on the tacks to prevent them penetrating the carpet completely. Webster & Parkes suggested sewing loops of tape or cases of strong **linen** to the under edge of fitted carpet and then threading them over a brass rod which was hooked or held by rings against the skirting (1844, p.255). *The Workwoman's Guide* explained how this process went:

> The rod should be a little longer than the breadth of the carpet, and a Holland or linen case sewed very firmly underneath the carpet so as just to come to the edge of it, or even strong tape loops would answer as well. Run the rod along them, and let it pass each end into two or more brass rings or hooks fastened to the floor. (Hale, 1840, p.202.)

In the twentieth century, whilst the principles remained the same for sewing and fitting body carpet, the advent of **broadloom** and **tufted carpets** made it far easier to have fitted carpets in most rooms. In addition, the use of sewing machines for seaming widths of carpet, specially developed tools for stretching, **adhesives**, and proprietary fixings have made the job more straightforward, although careful planning of the cuts, as well as pattern matching, is still often necessary in big spaces.
See also **Carpet fastener**, **Smoothedge**, **Tacks**.

Carpet fork
A (USA) term for a **carpet** stretcher designed to fit carpets in the mid-nineteenth century.

Carpet lining
The Mercury Dictionary of Textile Terms (1950) defined this as 'a thin padding of carded cotton laid between strips of cheap cotton cloth or paper, and pasted down or stitched together'.
See also **Underlay**.

Carpet rod
See **Carpet fastener**.

Carpet strainer (Stretcher)
A tool for stretching fitted **carpets**. James Newton charged Matthew Boulton four shillings for a carpet strainer in August 1798 (Ellwood, 1995, p.177).

Carpet thread
Defined in 1887 as a 'three cord sewing thread with a soft satin-like finish (Caulfeild & Saward, p.61). It was used to sew strips of **carpet** together to make up as required to fit a particular space.

Carpet upholstery (aka Saddlebags)
In the nineteenth century, ranges of **carpets** were used as **upholstery** cloth. They included authentic hand-woven Oriental **rugs** as well as machine-made carpets. The latter category included **velvet**, Brussels, Tapestry Brussels, Wilton and **Axminster** weaves. The London upholsterer, Thomas Dowbiggen, supplied Drummond Castle in 1829 with '3 ottomans … stuffed in the best manner and covered with your Persian carpet' (*DEFM*, p.253).

Particularly popular from the 1880s, carpet remained a fashionable choice for inexpensive suites and folding chairs until the early part of the twentieth century. Folding chairs in the USA and Europe used specially designed and woven widths of carpet for folding chair seats and backs. Carpet upholstery was particularly associated with what was known as Turkish upholstery. Carpet pieces, saddlebags, etc. were also used as panels on seats and backs, or as **cushions**. Not surprisingly, Liberty of London sold such items and described the coverings as 'fine old Persian rugs … very choice in texture and colour … there are never two alike' (*Liberty Handbook*, Roth, 2004, p.48).

Carpet upholstery was revived in the later twentieth century as 'Kelim' upholstery.
See also **Brussels carpet**, **Kelim**, **Moquette**, **Tapestry**, **Wilton carpet**.

FURTHER READING

Lownds, G. (1980). 'The Turkoman carpet as a furnishing fabric' in, Pinner, R. & Franses, M. (eds), *Turkoman Studies*, I, London: Oguz, pp 96–101 and 270.
Roth, R. (2004). 'Oriental carpet furniture: a furnishing fashion in the West in the late nineteenth century', *Studies in the Decorative Arts*, 11, Spring/Summer, pp 25–58.

Carpet worsted
Worsted yarns used for **carpet** work. In 1887, this was defined as 'coarse sewing thread or worsted yarns in bright colours made up in balls. Sold in paper bags of 3lb or 6lb and used for darning or renewing carpets' (Caulfeild & Saward, p.61).

Carsey
See **Kersey**.

Cascade
A **pleated** fabric feature that hangs either side of a swag. It has the top and one edge cut straight, the other edge is cut at an angle so that when hung the contrasting lining is on show.
See also **Swag**, **Tail**.

Case cover
See **Protective furnishing**.

Case curtain
See **Bed protection**.

Case rod
The iron, steel or brass rod supplied from which to hang bed case **curtains**. They were often polished brightly and were usually fixed to the **tester** itself so the protective case curtains could hang freely over the actual bed curtains. In 1688, Jean Poictevin supplied 'a bernished case rod for the bed' to the Duke of Hamilton (Beard, 1997, p.291). An expensive example is from 1714, when Queen Anne's bed had 'a very large burnisht case Rodd double gilt with gold for £15.0.0d'. The upholsterer Hamden Reeve supplied this (ibid. p.300).

A hundred years later, Sheraton noted how they were fitted: 'rods for beds, are made to circumscribe the foot pillars, and the sides of the rod screw off about eight inches from the pillars towards the head end, where the side rods slip on to a screw hook' (1803, p.298).
See also **Bed protection**, **Compass rod**, **Curtain pole and rod**.

Cased heading
A simple hemmed heading that creates a case, which allows a rod or pole to be inserted.

Casement blind

In the early twentieth century, an alternative window blind was made from casement cloth, **silk** or **taffeta**, which was seen as an improvement on **holland roller blinds**. They were intended for the top lights of a window only. 'Short casement blinds should always be provided for these upper windows, to be drawn whenever it is necessary to keep out the strong sunlight.' (*Cassell's Household Guide*, 1912, II, p.290.)
See also **Blind**, **Casement cloth**.

Casement cloth

A general term defining many lightweight furnishing fabrics that have a sheer quality. Commonly, it refers to a plain weave, somewhat heavier than average **calico**, but more loosely woven. Casement cloth (in shades of white, cream, ecru and other light tints) often supplanted **lace** for use as window **curtains** in the early twentieth century and is sometimes described as **sun curtain** material. It was also used as a base for **stencil printing**. An early twentieth-century American definition explained:

> This fabric has been woven in England and France for a century or so, and we are just beginning to import it in large quantities. It is made of a soft wool challie, which, when made with a wide hem, hangs in soft, clinging folds and can be easily drawn to one side with rings and cords. An interesting variation of the wool challie is to have the warp of silk and the weft of wool. The silk gives rather more resilience to the fabric and preserves the softness after it is cleansed. There are some casement cloths made of mercerized cotton and **linen**. They are not entirely satisfactory, however, for when hung after being cleaned they assume a certain stiffness, which the wool, or the silk and wool, never acquires. (Robertson, 1917, p.123.)

Elizabeth Dyer concurred and explained that 'Casement cloth [is] a lightweight, soft, attractive material that can be purchased in wool, mohair, linen, cotton, silk and mixtures. [It] resists sun and dust, washes well, [and is] easy to take care of. Similar to pongee and in the pongee color' (*c.*1923, p.205). She went on to discuss its particular uses:

> Casement cloth and plissé are being used widely in the place of blinds. Plissé has alternate stripes of crêpe and plain surface. It is heavier than the plissé used for clothing, and is frequently called Austrian shade cloth. Plissé shades are finished with a braid or fringe and are so arranged that they pull up and down by means of cords with tassels. Casement cloth, when used in place of curtains or shades, is usually hung on small rings, which are slipped over a brass rod. (ibid. p.206.)

Some years later, Denny noted that casement cloth was a 'lightweight curtain fabric in a variety of weaves and textures of mercerised cotton, rayon, mohair, silk and combinations' (1936, p.13).

The Draper's Encyclopaedia later suggested that the name casement should be used for lightweight curtain materials. 'They are lighter in weight than cretonnes and are to be used where light is to show through the drapes. They are usually woven with plain-weave but small dobby or jacquard motifs are introduced. These are called figured casements. They should be vat dyed in fawn or other light tints.' (Ostick, 1955, p.371.)

End and end jacquard casement

A medium-weight casement cloth that was popular in the 1950s; also called 'cotton and rayon brocade'. The **warp** has alternate ends of **cotton** and **rayon**. The cotton warp and **weft** weave a plain cloth in which the rayon warp forms a design. The figuring of the cloth is on the extra warp principle and often the jacquard design is overprinted with a floral design. The coloured woven **brocades** of the British Utility period (1940–50) used dyed yarns with an all rayon warp and a cotton condenser weft.
See also **Austrian shade cloth**, **Jacquard**, **Plissé**.

Casement curtains

Two pairs of **curtains** hung together, with a short one for the top window and a longer one for the main window.
See also **Net**.

Casement rep

Casement **rep** has been used to refer to a medium-weight **curtain** fabric heavier and more opaque than true casement, produced in a rep weave often in combination with **satin** stripes or a rep ground (French, 1937, p.131). According to *The Mercury Dictionary of Textile Terms* (1950), casement rep was 'a heavy repp used for curtains, hangings etc. in plain dyed, striped or jacquard effects'.

Cashmere

Although usually referred to as a dress or shawl fabric woven from the **hair** of the Kashmir goat, cashmere has been known as a furniture material. It was also a **woollen** material woven in imitation of true cashmere both in England and in France. In October 1840, 'Cashmeres' were advertised in a list of **upholstery** fabrics sold by Richard Munn, an upholsterer of Oxford Street, London (*DEFM*, p.636). In the 1853 New York Industrial Exhibition, there was 'a specimen of cashmere furniture [cloth], printed with copper rollers, in the chintz style, in ten colours' which was noted as being 'admirable, in the clearness and distinctness of the large masses of colour. The design is of the floral type usually adopted for furnitures' (Wallis, 1854, p.30).
See also **Cassimere**.

Cassimere (aka Kerseymere)

A twilled soft **woollen** cloth of medium weight, patented in England in 1766 by Francis Yerbury (Patent no.858). The name seems to be a corruption of **cashmere**. Described as a thin superfine cloth, it was woven in plain and fancy types, which was widely used for clothing, but it was also employed as a furnishing fabric. Upholsterer, James Newton, supplied Viscount Villiers in 1804 with '8 large hassocks richly trimmed in superfine herseymere [sic] cases with printed borders' (Ellwood, 1995, p.179). In 1808, George Smith suggested that drawing room **drape** should have 'under curtains of muslin or superfine cassimere' (1808, p.1). For eating rooms, he went on to say 'a material of more substance is requisite than for rooms of a lighter cast' and 'for such purposes superfine cloth or cassimere will ever be the best; the colours as fancy or taste may direct; yet scarlet and crimson will ever hold the preference' (ibid. p.xii). Rudolph Ackermann also referred to Kerseymere as a suitable cloth for window **curtains** (*Repository of Arts*, August, 1811).

Cat's-tail

See **Grass**.

Cedar bark

The name of a **woollen crêpe** cloth used for furniture covers in the London 'West End' trade (French, 1947).

Celure (aka Celour)

A celure was a canopy covering a bed, dais, altar, etc. or a portable canopy that was carried above the host of the proceedings during a procession. It was also a medieval name for the **tapestry** of a wall, or a screen of **drapes**, often embroidered with the coat-of-arms of the owner. The *Boke of Curtasye, c.*1460 (http://www.archive.org/details/bokeofcurtasyeen00halluoft, lines 442-5), describes the bed:

> ...For lordys two beddys shalle be made
> Both outer and inner...
> That henget shale be with hole sylour.
> With crochettis and loupys sert on lyour...

The distinction between a whole celure and half celure was important in designating rank in the medieval times. In 1418, a will bequeathed 'A bed of Lyn with a hool silour and Coverlet also a bed of red and grene dimi Selour' (*Early English Wills*, p.36). By 1553, the celure was still part of the ensemble of a bed: 'One seller & tester of reede and greene seye with curtens of the same' (*Lancashire Wills*, vol.I, p.105, *OED*). The celure remained a part of the ceremonial bed for some time after. Charles I's inventory of 1659 records a bed in the Rich Bedchamber that had the 'ceeler and headcloth ... of rich cloth of gold with inward vallens' (Macquoid & Edwards, 1924, I, p.35).
See also **Canopy**, **Sparver**, **Tester**.

FURTHER READING

Eames, P. (1971). 'Documentary evidence concerning the character and use of domestic furnishings in the fourteenth and fifteenth centuries', *Furniture History*, 7, pp 41–60.
Eames, P. (1997). 'The making of a hung celour', *Furniture History*, 33, pp 34–42.

Cendal
See **Sendal**.

Chain
Brass drapery chains were popular in the late nineteenth century for restraining hangings and holding in place **curtains**, **portières**, etc. The 1895 Montgomery Ward retail catalogue (p.351) listed 'Brass drapery chains for looping back and holding in place curtains, portières, etc'.

Chair bolster
A later nineteenth-century head rest in the form of a **bolster** but intended to be used in conjunction with a chair. They were often embroidered and fitted with a **cord** to hang over the back of the chair.

Chair screen (aka Chair back screen)
Chair screens are objects intended to protect the chair and the sitter from the heat of an open fire. In the closet adjoining the dining room of Harewood House in 1795 there were '4 Chairback Fire Screens' (http://www.harewood.org/chippendale/archives/inventory.htm). In *c.*1813, '2 chair back screens covered with scarlet tammy' were supplied to the Duke of Buccleuch's London house (Ellwood, 1995, p.198). The ever-practical Loudon illustrated a detachable **straw** back screen in his *Encyclopaedia* (1833, p.350). By the mid-nineteenth century, Miss Leslie described how to make back screens at home:

> Get a large sheet of the thick stiff pasteboards used by bookbinders and trunk makers, with a knife pare off the edges, and trim to the required size... Make a double case (like a pillow case) of dark chintz or moreen, open at one end, to slip over the pasteboard. You may also have slighter chair screens by simply making cases of thick moreen, without pasteboard; leaving the lower end opened to slip down over the chair back. (*Lady's House Book*, 1854, pp 153–4.)

In England, woven cane chair screens were probably introduced *c.*1860.
See also **Screen**.

Chair webbing
See **Webbing**.

Challis
A fine **silk** and **worsted** fabric introduced from Norwich *c.*1832 and used for dressmaking as well as for **casement curtains**. Challis was made on a similar principle to the Norwich **crape**, only thinner and softer, composed of much finer materials. Instead of a shiny surface, as in Norwich crapes, it was produced without gloss, and with a very pliable handle. It was also printed. Caulfeild & Saward noted it 'was printed in coloured flowers on a white ground, which has the effect of velvet painting' (1887, p.64).

In the early twentieth century, it had clearly changed from a superior cloth to a more mundane material that was used for window **blinds** (Maple and Co, 1900). A little later, an American author recommended cheaper grades for a range of uses: 'Challis is an inexpensive cotton fabric of plain-weave and printed pattern. It varies considerably in quality and price. A cheap, rather coarse grade is used for covers for comfortables, kimonos, etc., while the better qualities are used for dresses and dressing sacques' (Thompson, 1917, p.62).

The American authority, Denny, writing in 1936, confirmed that challis was a 'lightweight soft printed material similar to voile but coarser. It is used for comforters, linings and draperies' (p.13). In the 1940s, challis was described as 'an extremely soft, lightweight, well draping fabric, firmly but not too loosely woven with fine [wool rayon or cotton yarns]. Usually it is printed with a small floral design, but may be bleached or dyed a plain colour'. It was used for **comfort** covers, **drapes**, **linings**, etc. (Bendure & Pfieffer, 1947, p.617.)

In the late twentieth century, it was still regarded as a sheer, lightly napped, plain-woven fabric of fine **wool** or **rayon**.

Chalons
An **upholstery** textile that is related to **dornix**. Its name may derive from its place of manufacture, Châlons-sur-Marne, in France. Chalons is also a medieval and Italian Renaissance term (*celone*) for a **tapestry** and a bedcover. Chalons are also defined as **blankets**. Double chalons were cloths woven full width, doubled over and then quilted through and used for beds. Chaucer, in 'The Reeve's Tale', writes:

> and in his own chamber hem made a bed
> With shetes and with chalons fair y-spread.
> (*Canterbury Tales, c.*1387, lines 4139–40.)

Another literary reference is in 1480, when Caxton wrote 'His bedde was cover'd with a chalon' (*OED*). The term appears to have become obsolete by the early seventeenth century.
See also **Serge**, **Shalloon**.

Chambray
A type of **gingham** fabric that is often woven with a coloured **warp** and white **weft** but any two different yarns may be employed. Chambray was utilised in America as a furnishing fabric. In the mid-nineteenth century, the Beecher sisters recommended using it as a decorative addition to the hem of **muslin curtains**. In the early nineteenth century, it was used as a bed tick in the USA and, in 1947, it was again noted that it was used in heavier qualities for **tickings** (Bendure & Pfieffer, 1947, p.617). In 1951, Taylor recommended chambray be used

Checks for the Kitchen

If careful thought is given to planning a kitchen and a cheerful scheme of colour chosen, the housewife's tasks will seem so much lighter.

In a kitchen arranged like this there will be no tiresome running about for this and for that. All the necessary equipment is at hand.

You couldn't find a handier placing of sink, dresser and draining board.

The curtains are of Surregina Loom Cotton and the paintwork is painted orange yellow, while the walls and ceiling are enamelled a lighter hue.

Surregina Loom Cotton, Gold (guaranteed unfadable), 2/11½ per yard, 31 inches wide, from Messrs. Williamson & Cole, Ltd.

27. Check fabric in a kitchen setting, room set, c.1935 (Private Collection)

for curtains either in straight folds or in tieback treatments. It was also recommended for **bedspreads**. It is now usually used as a dress material and is considered similar to gingham and **madras muslin**.

Chamblet
See **Camlet**.

Chandin
A lightweight **cotton** fabric used for ceiling **drapes** that was originally from India. It was mentioned in *The Mercury Dictionary of Textile Terms* (1950).

Changeable
An early term for **tabby**-weave textiles using **warps** and **wefts** in various colours or shots, intended to allow light reflection to reveal the changeable colouring in differing aspects. An early example that mentions changeable is from 1480 in the *Wardrobe Accounts of Edward IV*, which listed 'green changeable velvet' (*OED*).

Later, in the sixteenth century, it is clear that this fabric was used for **curtains**. In the 1601 Hardwick Hall inventory, 'curtains of Chaungeable taffety' were recorded, and in another room 'a quilt of chaungeable taffetie sarcenet' as well as 'five curtains of chaungeable damask' were listed (Boynton, 1971, pp 24–6).
See also **Camlet**, **Sarcenet**, **Taffeta**.

Channelling
A decorative feature used in **upholstery** whereby fabric is pulled through the seat backs and held in place with **stitching** to create a channelled effect on the surface.

Check
Plain-weave **cotton**, **linen** or **wool** fabric with differing **warp** and **weft** colours that creates a chequered effect in the cloth. The chequered effect can also be printed. Although initially used for a number of purposes, e.g. an American inventory of 1644 records '2 checker blankets' (Cummings, 1961, p.20), checks were especially popular from the mid-eighteenth century for bed hangings and slipcovers. 'Furniture checks' were specially designed for **curtains** and chair coverings. An advertisement in the *Boston Gazette*, 1 September 1760, noted: 'Scarlet and crimson check for bed curtains' (ibid.). Bed hangings also took the eye of James Boswell, the diarist, who recorded his 'handsome tent bed with green and white check curtains [which] gave a snug yet genteel look to my room, and had a military air which amused my fancy and made me happy' (Montgomery, 1970, p.52). In 1764 William France supplied Sir Lawrence Dundas with 'a blue and white inch and inch check furniture to a 4 post bedstead and tester cloth and all bound, a paper cover to Do, with 4 olives to tye back the curtains' (Beard, 1997, p.307).

Checks were commonly used for loose or **case covers**. In 1756, Boston upholsterer, Samuel Grant, supplied 'six walnut chairs with crimson harrateen' and making '6 check covers for ditto' (Jobe, 1974, p.69). In 1766, Mary Reynoldson invoiced Lord Fairfax for '44 yards blew and white check used for 2 armchairs and 8 small chairs and large sofa' (Beard, 1997, p.308). In a description of **Manchester** and its surroundings in 1795, John Aikin noted that 'an application of the lighter open striped checks to bed hangings and window curtains forty years since, introduced the making of furniture checks, which have almost set aside the use of stuffs in upholstery' (Montgomery, 1984, p.197).

By the nineteenth century, checks seem to have descended the social scale. *The Workwoman's Guide* said that 'Beds for common use are hung with linen or cotton check, or stripe, print or stuff' (Hale, 1840, p.192).
See also **Crankey**, **Decca work**, **Gingham**, **Plaid**.

Cheese cloth
A loose plain-weave cloth that has had spates of fashion as a translucent **curtain** material. Its main attraction at one time appeared to be its cheapness. An American guide to drapers' goods noted that: '[Cheesecloth] was originally used for covering cheese. It is a cheap, thin fabric, either bleached or unbleached. It is used for cheap, fancy dresses when a draped effect is wanted; it dyes easily, drapes nicely for decorations, and is unsurpassed for cheapness and pleasing effect.' (Thompson, 1917, p.63.) The author also pointed out that 'the coverings for comfortables may be of Cheese-cloth, Silkoline, Challis, Sateen, Chintz, Silk, Batiste' (ibid. p.129).

It was used in the 1940s in America as a curtain material (Bendure & Pfieffer, 1947, p.617), whilst in Britain it was particularly suggested for use as curtaining for small windows in the 1950s (Smithells, 1950).
See also **Comfort**.

Cheney
Cheney is a **worsted** furnishing material that is related to **harrateen** and **moreen**. Broad or narrow, cheney was woven using bright colours

that were sometimes watered, embossed or striped. Commonly known as 'China' or other similar corruption, it may derive from the French *chaine*, meaning **warp**. It was sometimes called 'Philip and Cheney'. It was introduced into England by the Walloons and was being made in Norwich by at least 1608. By the mid-seventeenth century, it was also known in America. In a Cambridge, Mass. inventory of *c.*1640–50, there were 'Philop and Cheny curtains in graine with a deep silk fringe on the valance, and a smaller on the curtains, and a coverlet suitable to it, made of Red Kersie, and laced with a green lace, round [the sides and down] the middle' (Cummings, 1961, p.21).

The eighteenth century saw cheney still being employed for furnishings. In 1701, the *London Gazette* advertised that 'All sorts of Mercery Goods, viz. Bristol Stuffs, Toys, Shalloons, Silk Shags, Chenies will be sold by Auction' (No.3701/4). In 1710, the library of Dyrham Park was furnished with 'five pieces of scarlet and green cheny hangings, and six window curtains and valances of the same' (Walton, 1986, p.61). A little later, John Wood, in his *Description of Bath*, criticised its use: 'about the year 1727', houses were furnished 'with Kidderminster stuff, or at best with Cheyne, the woollen furniture of the principal rooms was made' (Ayres, 1981, p.24).

An American reference from 1746 explains its use in Boston, where it appears to be rather less important than the **damask** covers: 'Eight walnut tree chairs stuft back and seats covered with the same damask, eight crimson china cases for ditto, one easy chair and cushion, same damask, and case for ditto.' (Montgomery, 1984, p.199.) It seems to have gone out of fashion by the mid- to late eighteenth century.
See also **Moreen**.

Chenille

Chenille is the name for a double-sided fabric and a yarn. The prepared yarn resembles a caterpillar (the French *chenille* means hairy caterpillar). As a fabric, it is described as an ornamental corded fabric made from very short lengths of thick twisted **wool** or soft thick **silk** that are attached to an inner cord to surround it.

Chenille yarn is produced on a purpose built **leno** loom. Two pairs of fine leno threads are arranged in one dent of the reed, a distance apart equal to the thickness of the chenille required. After weaving, the cloth is cut up the centre of the division between two groups of leno, thus forming long strips to create the chenille yarn. This is then used as a **weft** in making **table covers**, hangings, **carpets**, etc. It has excellent draping qualities. When designed for hangings it is woven so that the chenille **pile** shows equally on both sides of the fabric so that it is reversible.

Denny (1928) offered three differing definitions of chenille. Firstly, it was a yarn that may be spun from silk, wool, mercerised **cotton** or **rayon**. Secondly, it was a cloth made with chenille yarns for filling, which was used for hangings and **couch covers**. Thirdly, it was a kind of carpet or reversible faced rug (**Smyrna** type).

Chenille fabric was popular in the mid-nineteenth century, especially for **portière** curtains. It was still used for these purposes in the early twentieth century. According to Dyer: 'Chenille [was] a fabric with a nap, used for draperies and portières; shows dust, but gives a rich, luxurious-effect' (Dyer, *c.*1923, p.202). In the 1930s, chenille fabric was also produced complete with a 'figured dado' for curtains and portières that simply required a **curtain** tape to be ready for hanging (French, 1937, pp 131–2).

By 1951, it was noted that chenille was 'originally used in decorating only in the cheaper grades for portières and couch covers, which in the search for new texture ideas both as adjunct for modern furniture and as replacement of the expensive imports during the depression, has reappeared in new forms and with new uses' (Taylor, 1951, pp 84–5).

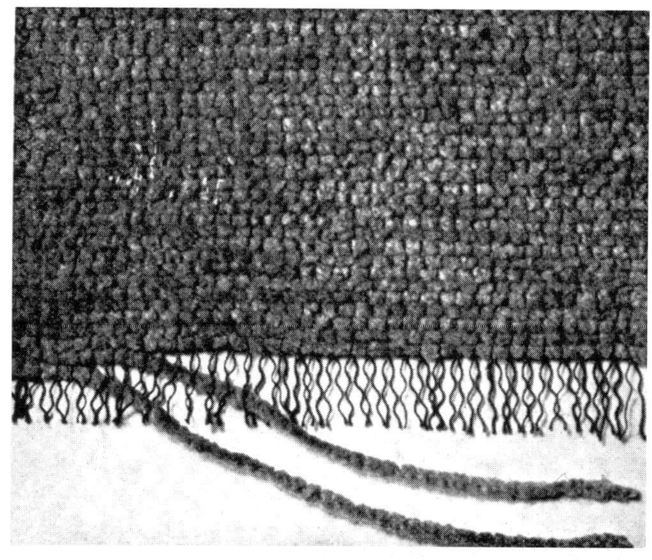

LEFT
28. Detail of chenille cloth showing 'fur' strips (E. Ostick, The Draper's Encyclopaedia, *1955)*

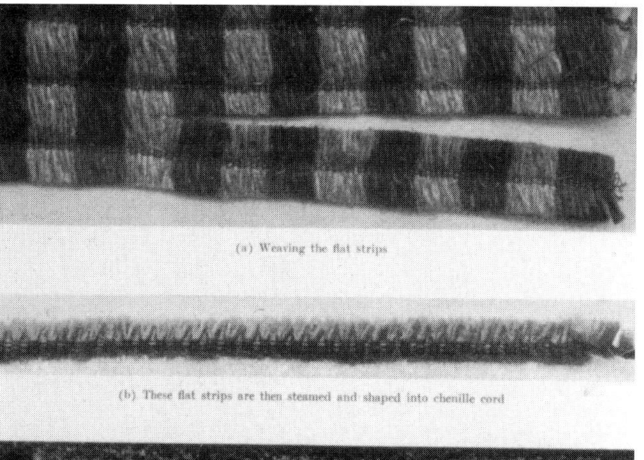

(a) Weaving the flat strips

(b) These flat strips are then steamed and shaped into chenille cord

(c) This cord is then itself used as weft, and locked with linen warps into the solid back

BELOW LEFT
29. The chenille making process (G.L. Hunter, Decorative Textiles, Coverings for Furniture etc., *1918)*

The Draper's Encyclopaedia described chenilles as 'Curtains and table covers made with single colour yarns. For a coloured chenille design, a complicated double weaving process is used for the multi-coloured designs on the ends, borders or dados of curtains' (Ostick, 1955, p.377).
See also **Chenille Axminster**, **Rug: Chenille**.

FURTHER READING

Greason, J.A. & Skinner, T. (2001). *Chenille, A Collector's Guide*, Exton: Schiffer.

Chenille Axminster
A machine-woven imitation of the hand-knotted **Axminster carpet**. The application of the chenille principle to carpets is credited to James Templeton of Glasgow who patented the idea (No.8169, 25 July 1839). The technique allows cut-**pile** carpets to be woven in an unlimited number of coloured yarns. The carpet has its pattern woven **weft**-wise across the fabric so resembling hand-knotted work to a degree. The making of chenille carpets comprises two processes. First, the chenille fur is woven and then the fur is used as a weft to form the pile in the carpet. The chenille fur strips were woven as supplementary wefts. These carpets were hand-woven until the introduction of power looms between 1871 and 1879.

The carpet manufacturer, Brinton, explained the advantages and disadvantages early in the twentieth century:

> The cheap Chenille fabric possesses several marked advantages over Brussels and Wilton, Tapestry, and even over tufted Axminster breadth squares. It is without seam; it gives a comparatively luxurious surface with the absolute minimum of wool; and it is practically unlimited in colour. Further, the looms are not expensive to erect and run, and in this respect, the Chenille square has an initial advantage over the seamless Wilton or tufted Axminster carpets, which necessitate costly and complicated machinery. On the other hand, it has its disadvantages. It is not made in a fineness of pitch which admits of effects of design obtainable readily in Wilton or even in tufted Axminster, while, however skilful the setting may be, there is an inherent tendency to irregularity in the pattern, which is apt to offend the critical eye. Further, in the cheaper qualities, which form the great bulk of the sale, the wearing qualities do not compare favourably with those of, say, Imperial Axminster. These disadvantages, however, do not deter that numerous class of consumers which demands an attractive carpet at a moderate price. (Brinton, 1919, p.70.)

Chenille was also used in America for carpet weaving. According to Leland Hunter, 'the most aristocratic of the shuttle-made carpets and rugs is the chenille Axminster, sometime called Scotch Axminster' (1918, p.158). In comparison to Brinton (above), Elizabeth Dyer considered American-made chenille as one of the better floorcoverings to buy:

> Chenille [is] made of soft, tufted or fluffy yarn which gives it a rich velvety appearance. It is probably the most luxurious and expensive domestic rug or carpet made, its cost being dependent upon the stock, the yarn, the width of the carpet, and the length of nap. It always comes in plain colors, so it is likely to show soil and dust badly. A gray with a faint reddish tinge called rose taupe shows soil less than most of the other colors and makes a delightful background for a room. It is often used in combination with Oriental rugs. (Dyer, *c.*1923, p.194.)

By the mid-twentieth century, the process had become uneconomical and it was widely superseded by the **broadloom** gripper Axminster process.
See also **Chenille**, **Imperial Axminster**, **Smyrna rug**, **Tuften carpet**.

FURTHER READING

Bartlett, J.N. (1978). *Carpeting the Millions, The Growth of Britain's Carpet Industry*, Edinburgh: John Donald.
Robinson, G. (1966). *Carpets*, London: Pitman.
Young, F.H. (1944). *A Century of Carpet Making 1839–1939*, Glasgow: James Templeton and Co.

Chenille rug
See **Rug**.

Chercanneys (aka Charconnae)
A name derived from the Hindi *charkhana*, meaning 'chequered'. It was a mixed **silk** and **cotton** cloth, mainly woven in the Orissa district. *The Merchant's Warehouse* explained that this was a 'checked cloth used for lining bed or window curtains' (J.F., 1696).

Chiffon
A sheer plain-woven fabric of fine hard twisted yarn (originally **silk**) often associated with a very lightweight fabric. It was introduced in the late nineteenth century.
See also **Glass curtain**, **Sheer curtain**, **Velvet: Transparent (Chiffon)**.

Chimney cloth
A strip of fabric stretched across the top of a fireplace to alleviate smoking fires. These were also known as *tours de cheminées* in France and were probably fitted with a detachable lining. There are references in England that mention chimney-cases or chimneypieces, which may be the same (Thornton, 1978, p.265). Charles I's inventories list 'chimney pieces' probably of **gilt leather** or **tapestry** (Jervis, 1989, p.297).

The American Van Varick inventory taken in 1695–6 included '2 chimnie cloths of Crimson ga[u]ze; 6 window curtains ditto –£6.10' (Montgomery, 1984, p.246). Later, they were sometimes made of leather or stretched on a frame (Edwards, 1870, pp 15, 219).
See also **Mantel drapery**, **Tour de cheminée**.

China matting
See **Matting: China**.

China silk
A plain-weave, lightweight fabric made with irregular **silk** yarns. Also refers to the machine-made silk, which resembles the hand-woven versions.
See also **Hobutai**.

Chiné
A term to describe the yarns of a cloth (**warp** and **weft** or both) that are dyed or printed to create clouded or flame effects. In addition, it refers to a printed cloth using these pre-printed warps that was often employed for French floral designs.
See also **Clouded**, **Ikat**, **Lustring**, **Sarcenet**.

Chintz
Originally, a name for the painted or stained **cotton** cloths imported from India; now, a name for a glazed plain-weave cotton cloth with a hard-spun fine **warp** and coarser slack twist **weft**, fast-printed with designs in a number of colours (generally not less than five), or dyed in plain colours. Chemical glazes withstand washing and the technique of resin schreinering creates a near permanent finish. It is also available semi-glazed. Semi-glazed refers to fabric that has been stiffened by friction – calendering starch or wax that washes out. Unglazed chintz may be called cretonne.

The name was originally 'chints', the plural of chint, itself derived from the Hindi *chint* or *chitta*, meaning 'spotted cloth'. It has also been found as chite. The original chintz was not glazed, and the word referred to any Indian printed cloth (see **Masulipatam**, **Palampore**, **Pintado**). Based on evidence from wills in Marseilles, chintz was first introduced to Europe from India via France in the 1570s. Chintz was soon brought into England and it became hugely fashionable for both dress and furnishings. The furnishing uses included **upholstery**, bed and **wall coverings**. A letter of 1619 to the East India Co from their agents discussed chintz for wall hangings: 'chintes for hangings in England ... 100 piece of the strongest sorts with different workes, viz. a corge [i.e. a score] of each sort answerable in cullers which will sufficiently serve for a suite of hangings of one room' (Irwin & Brett, 1970, p.24).

As early as 1626, specific bed hangings were occasionally imported and, in 1631, the East India Co established a large business in imported ready-made bed **drapes**. Samuel Pepys later recorded the fashionable use of chintz for both dress and furnishings. He wrote in his diary: 'bought my wife a chint that is a painted East Indian Calico for her to line her new study' (*Diary*, 5 September 1663).

Imitations of the original soon developed. In 1648, Benoit Ganteume and Jacques Bavilles set up a cotton-printing establishment in France and, by 1669, **Provençal prints** were being produced in Marseilles. In the same year, patterns were sent out from England rather than using local Indian designs. In 1676, a patent (Patent no.190) was granted to William Sherwin for a 'new way of printing and stayning calico' with a double-necked rolling press.

Its use and popularity were noted by Daniel Defoe who wrote that at Windsor Castle, 'the late Queen Mary set up a rich Atlas and Chintz bed, which in those times was invaluable, the chintz being of Masulipatam on the coast of Coromandel' (*A Tour Through the Whole Island of Great Britain*, vol.1, letter 3). At the beginning of the eighteenth century, he again commented upon chintz and noted that they had:

> crept into our houses; our closets and bedchambers, curtains, cushions, chairs, and at last beds themselves were nothing but calicoes and Indian stuffs, and in short almost everything that used to be made of wool or silk, relating to the dress of the women or the furniture of our house, was supplied by the Indian trade. (*Weekly Review*, 31 January 1708.)

Defoe's comments reflected disquiet in the **wool** trades. The taste for these sorts of material created unrest within weaving communities and, in 1701, following a 15 per cent duty imposition, all printed, stained or dyed calicoes were banned from use. This Act was amended in 1720 in an attempt to stop abuses, especially that of re-exporting. In 1736, the so-called Manchester Act was passed that allowed **linen** warp and **cotton** weft **fustian** to be printed, but it was not until 1774 that the restrictions were fully lifted. The French bans on chintz cloth types, in these cases to help the **silk** industry, were imposed in 1686 and were not lifted until 1759.

Nevertheless, the taste for chintz was difficult to prevent. Chintz 'carpets' were usually furniture covers for table stools and cupboards, but also referred to **bedspreads**. Celia Fiennes visited Mr Rooth in Epsom around 1712 and saw in Mrs Rooth's bedroom, 'a plad bed lined with Indian calico and an India carpet on the bed' (1995, p.235).

A small insight into the relationship of supplier and consumer can be seen in this passage of letters regarding an order for chintz. On 21 May 1738, Mrs Purefoy wrote to her supplier: 'I did write to you once before to know if you could get me 18 yards of chintz to make window curtains for a drawing room, or something that would suit workt chairs, workt in shades of white, but I have had no answer from you.' The upholsterer, Anthony Baxter, clearly soon wrote back, as by 4 June Purefoy wrote again:

> I rec'd Mr Baxter's letter of the 23rd of the last month. I cannot but think it must be the best chintz must do for our window curtains. You say the pattern is three yards long and our window curtains must be three yards and a quarter long and for the vaillangs [valance] and curtains we shall want eighteen yards of the best sort, if you will send it down with the lowest price. (Eland, 1931, pp 168–9.)

30. Chintz, late eighteenth century, cotton (M. Percival, The Chintz Book, *1923)*

After import restrictions were lifted, chintz remained just as popular. For example, Chippendale supplied Ninian Home with 'Extra superfine Chints callico galz'd and lined with calico' (Gilbert, 1978, p.273). By 1789, Hepplewhite was still able to recommend the use of printed cotton fabrics for bed hangings (1789, p.18).

In the early nineteenth century, chintzes designed specifically for chairs had their patterns printed so that they were centred on the seats and were supplied with a matching border. Sheraton noted that chintz 'may now be had of various patterns on purpose for chair seats, together with borders to suit them' (1793, p.374). These were often intended to match the **curtains** and other hangings of a room, with the designs based on the furniture print for curtains, a filler with a small overall print and the chair seat with the design (usually flowers) centred.

By the early 1800s, it appears that chintz was no longer highly fashionable: George Smith deprecatingly recorded how 'printed calicos may answer extremely well for secondary apartments, or for those in houses of persons of small fortune; but they are not at all suitable for persons of rank and splendid income' (1808, p. xii–xiii). More practically, in 1829, Mrs Parkes noted that 'every time ... a chintz bed has to be washed, the expense [of calendering and relining] is equal to that of buying a new one' (1829, pp 182–3). Despite this apparent problem, the ever-realistic Loudon noted that chintz was excellent for 'French beds' in cottages and for the modern villa 'chintz is generally preferred for bed curtains as it admits of being washed' (1839, p.337 and p.1079).

In America, Miss Leslie confirmed this usage in *The House Book*: 'Chintz curtains are now seldom seen in America except for bedrooms.' (1841, p.188.) This may also reflect the problem of cleaning. Nevertheless, for some commentators chintz could be used anywhere in the house because of its low price. Andrew Downing said:

> For the plainest cottages, therefore, one would use chintz, which may be had for a few cents a yard, and which, if selected with regard to harmonizing in color with the carpet and walls, will always produce a pretty effect, at very little cost. Printed cottons are also manufactured for this purpose, with separate borders that may be sewed on, to heighten the effect. (Downing, 1850, p.374.)

Later in the century, for some commentators, the bedroom remained the best place for chintz. Lady Barker wrote: 'chintz is what naturally suggests itself to the inquirer's mind as most suitable for the drapery of a bedroom, and there is a great deal to be said in its favour' (1878, p.21).

31. Chintz furnishing border, England, late eighteenth century (M. Percival, The Chintz Book, *1923)*

For others, chintz was an old-fashioned furniture covering and was outmoded in modern city homes at least. The American author, Cole commented that:

> Chintz is also known under the name of furniture print from its extensive use in covering furniture. About 1850, glazed chintz was greatly used for furniture, and some of the patterns, which have survived, are quite surprisingly bad. For this reason, and the fact that chair covers have gone out of fashion, the majority of the world got tired of Chintzes, when some enterprising manufacturer saw the beauty which might lie in a fabric called cretonne, which is simply a chintz without the glaze. It is a question whether Chintz is ever either suitable or saleable in a town. Its extreme daintiness seems as out of place in the grime and grind of a city as the innocent chat of a country cousin seems almost like a reproach to the short-haired advocate of 'women's rights'. (1892.)

Even in the early twentieth century, Americans were still apparently having problems with the need to re-glaze chintz every so often. According to Hunter, 'The chintzes used in England are often glazed, but the difficulty of having them freshened by re-glazing in America, has prevented chintzes from becoming popular here' (Hunter, 1918, p.322).

Despite all these remarks, at the beginning of the twentieth century the British still seemed to enjoy them. Chintzes were recognised to be 'so advantageous in price, durability and appearance, that they are often employed instead of silk fabrics' (Bitmead, 1912, p.35). This is confirmed by the remarks of the German architect and author, Hermann Muthesius, who wrote in his *The English House* about the revival of chintz for **upholstery** and the addition of matching curtains:

> The covers of upholstered furniture are no longer made of velvet or plush but at best of a patterned woollen material. But chintz covers have recently become even commoner than wool. Chintz was originally used only for loose covers during the period the house was uninhabited. Such covers are particularly necessary in London where the smoke from coal with which the air is perpetually laden quickly begrimes unwashable materials. As a result of conditions in London, it soon became customary to keep the chintz covers on for daily use... Once upholstered furniture had been covered with chintz, the same material began to be chosen for curtains. Thus, the whole drawing room has gradually been transformed into a room decorated in chintz... The clean chintz covers and matching curtains give the room an air of freshness, healthfulness and fragrance. One feels the same confidence in it as in a freshly made bed. (1904, p.213.)

Hugh Phillips, writing in 1912, captured the romance of chintz: 'So delectable are their soft, faded colours, so fascinating are the designs, and ... so enchanting is the old-world musty scent which always clings to them, that it would be hard indeed to withhold one's affection' (Hayden, 1912, p.341). Elsie de Wolfe, writing in her book *The House in Good Taste*, also sold the idea of chintz: 'It seems to me that there are no more charming stuffs for bedroom hangings than these simple fabrics with their enchantingly fanciful designs... How amusing it would be in our own modern houses to change the bed coverings, window curtains and so forth twice or three times a year.' (1913, p.197.) Dyer brought the bedroom theme to the fore when she pointed out that: 'Glazed chintz is quite stiff and is used for fancy window shades, especially in children's rooms and bedrooms.' (*c*.1923, p.202.) Frank Lewis, writing in 1935 about the history of chintz, was also caught up in a wave of nostalgia like Phillips above:

> What a pleasant sounding name – What pleasant thoughts it brings to the mind – the old country cottage with its grandfather clock, the burnished copper warming pan, and those gaily coloured chintz curtains. The country house with its bright chintz covers, so reminiscent of the home and all it means. Truly chintz may be said to represent the feeling of the Englishman, and his home, as it really is. (1935, p.13.)

Two years later, chintz was again commented upon, less fancifully than by Lewis, but nonetheless still using the language of delicacy and delight, as well as suggesting chintz for many locations:

> Chintz is usually lined when used for curtains, but charming effects may be obtained with an unlined chintz, which allows the sun to filter through and illumine the design. Walls may be covered with chintz instead of paper, and in that case, the curtains may be made in the same chintz, edged with the plain colour that predominates. It also makes pretty sun blinds. There is a vogue for quilted chintz for bedspreads. It costs rather more than double the price of the plain chintz. (French, 1937, pp 132–3.)

The Draper's Encyclopaedia was much more prosaic and defined chintzes by their finish:

> In the past the gloss was obtained by starch and calendaring. Now the fabric can be given a permanent finish by using synthetic resins. This type of finish is covered by patents and is guaranteed under the names of Calpreta and Everglaze. Typical chintz designs have white or light coloured grounds, sometimes relieved by fine pin dots. The motifs are usually small natural flowers. Other designs have bright coloured flowers on fine foliate structures. (Ostick, 1955, p.373.)

A mid- to later twentieth-century taste for a country house style, established by decorators such as Colefax and Fowler, has been maintained in more mainstream outlets in France, UK and the USA.

Quilted chintz
'A recent development in furnishing fabrics is the quilted chintz in which the pattern is emphasised by neat stitching and a slight padding, popular with the [London] West End trade.' (French, 1947.)
See also **Blind chintz**, **Border**, **Calico**, **Cretonne**, **Furniture print**, **Indienne**, **Mercoolees**, **Patch**, **Plastic chintz**, **Printed cotton**, **Quilt**, **Toile de Jouy**, **Washing furniture**.

FURTHER READING

Beer, A.B. (1970). *Trade Goods. A Study of Indian Chintz in the Collection of the Cooper-Hewitt Museum of Decorative Arts and Design*, Washington, DC: Smithsonian Institution Press.
Bredif, J. (1989). *Classic Printed Textiles from France 1760–1843, Toiles de Jouy*, London: Thames and Hudson.
Bunt, C. & Rose, E. (1957). *Two Centuries of English Chintz 1750–1950*, Leigh-on-Sea: F. Lewis.
Hayden, C. (1912). *Chats on Cottage and Farmhouse Furniture, with a Chapter on Old English Chintzes by Hugh Phillips*, London: Fisher Unwin.
Irwin, J. (1959). 'The etymology of chintz and pintado', *Journal of Indian Textile History*, 4, IV, p.77.
Irwin, J. & Brett, K.B. (1970). *Origins of Chintz*, London: Victoria and Albert Museum.
Irwin, J. & Hall, M. (1971). *Indian Painted and Printed Fabrics*, Ahmedabad: Calico Museum of Textiles.
Lewis, F. (1935). *English Chintz from the Earliest Times to the Present Day*, Benfleet: F. Lewis.
Percival, MacIver (1923). *The Chintz Book*, London: Heinemann.

Chitte
See **Toile peinte**.

Chlidema square
Before the advent of **broadloom** carpet weaving, large carpets were made up from narrow woven **body carpet**. The Chlidema square was developed to avoid the shading problems that occurred with the made-up squares when **borders** and centre strips were sewn together at angles. The Chlidema was a carpet 'square' made up from sections of 27 inches (69 cm) of body carpet but which had a border and corner design built in. This avoided the variations in **pile** shading when squares were made up from body and border separately. The process made the squares more expensive. Also known as Cairo square.
See also **Art square**.

Choux
A **curtain** or other furnishing detail of circular gathered fabric that is lightly stitched together to give an illusion of being caught up in a design that resembles a cabbage effect. The fabric is mounted on a stiff backing and then attached to a **valance** or other part of the decorative scheme. If lighter materials are used, they are sometimes stuffed with lamb's wool to give shape.
See also **Rosette**.

Cinema pile carpet
A mid-twentieth century British name for a heavy-duty **Wilton carpet** with an extra thick **pile** to withstand heavy wear in public spaces. It has around 18 tufts per square inch (6.5 cm^2).

Ciré
A finish applied to fabrics, especially **satin**, to give a glossy effect or to keep out moisture. The finish is based on applications of wax or similar material that are applied in conjunction with heat or calendering.

Cisèle velvet
See **Velvet: Cisèle**.

Cleat hook
A double hook intended to hold the draw lines of **curtains**, wound in a figure of eight round the two hooks to secure them at a particular point. Loudon pointed out that in his opinion:

> Knobs of iron, brass or wood for the purpose of fastening line round, are far preferable to the hooks of different kinds in common use; because they have a more solid and architectural look; are far removed from the common nail; and not so apt to catch the corners of the laths of Venetian blinds, or to tear cloth blinds or curtains. (1839, p.342.)

Clipped
A term that refers to the cutting away or clipping of floating supplementary yarns in a cloth, so that decorative motifs can be isolated on the ground fabric.
See also **Dotted Swiss**.

Cloak pin
A brass peg fitting designed to hold the draw lines of window **curtains**.

They are made from cast and pressed brass, using designs such as paterae or rosettes, or they may be finished with enamel. The pins may also be of turned wood. In some cases, long shanks supported the pulled back curtain. In 1736, William Bradshaw invoiced the Earl of Stanhope for '6 cloak pins total 3s.od' (Beard, 1997, p.303). They were popular in the early nineteenth century for curtain supports, as well as to fasten **cords**. Paterae or rosettes were amongst the most fashionable designs. They were revived in the later nineteenth century and again in the twentieth century.
See also **Curtain pin**.

Cloth

A generic term that may refer to any material or fabric regardless of type. It is also a name for a closely woven **woollen** fabric fulled after weaving, with a shorn nap, making a velvety **felt** surface. This cloth, which was usually green, was used especially to line billiard, card and writing tables. It can be confused with **baize**.
See also **Billiard cloth**.

Cloth of estate

An ensemble of materials, including a **celure** (roof), a **tester** (back piece) and a **valance**, that makes up the whole cloth of estate. Sometimes the addition of a matching chair of estate, stool and **cushions** completed the grouping. This arrangement 'framed' the sitter and emphasised their position in society. An early reference to this is found in 1494 when a domestic etiquette book explained: 'the ninth question; whether in the same feast, the Queen's cloth of Estate shall hang as high as the Kings or not? Answer thereunto; the Queen's shall hang lower by the vallance' (*Household Ordinances*, Society of Antiquaries, 1790). The luxurious nature of the fabrics and their decoration is shown in this example: '1 cloth of estate of red and white baudekin covered witrh gold crowns, and 2 long cushions the same' (*Rot. Parl.*, II, Henry VI).

The cloth of estate played an important part in the ritual and ceremony of life in medieval times. A fifteenth-century courtesy book gives the following instructions: 'First the Usher must see that the Hall be trimmed in every point, and the cloth of estate be hanged in the Hall and that four cushions of estate be set in order upon the bench, being of silk or cloth of gold' (Eames, 1971, p.50). In 1540, Henry VIII decreed that 'no person except only the Kings children shall presume to sit or have place at any side of the cloth of estate in the Parliamentary chamber' (Macquoid & Edwards, 1924, II, p.126).

Although they lost some of their powerful associations, cloths of estate were used until the eighteenth century.
See also **Baldachin**, **Canopy**.

FURTHER READING

Hayward, M. (2005). 'Symbols of Majesty: Cloths of Estate at the Court of Henry VIII', *Furniture History*, XLI, 2005, pp 1–12

Jervis, S. (1989) 'Cloths of estate…', in McGregor, A. (ed.), *The Late King's Goods, Collections, Possessions, and Patronage of Charles I in the Light of the Commonwealth Sale Inventories*, London: A. McAlpine, Oxford: Oxford University Press, pp 292–5.

Thornton, P. (1974). 'Canopies, couches and chairs of estate', *Apollo*, 100, October, pp 292–9.

Cloth of gold or silver

A textile that used metal threads, either woven into the cloth on the loom or used in narrow weaves, such as **orrise** work. Probably originating in the thirteenth century, it was introduced into England in the early fourteenth century from Spain and Italy. The best varieties were made only from the metal 'yarn', whilst others were worked in a **silk** foundation. The gold threads were made in a variety of ways. The Venetians gilded vellum, cut it into strips and wrapped it around yarns. In Germany, especially Augsburg and Nuremberg, gold-plated silver bars were drawn out into wires that were flattened and wound round thread. Straight metal thread was called *filé*, whilst the spiralling version was *frisé*.

Cloth of gold or silver has been used for both **upholstery** and bed hangings. In a description of a bedroom made up for Lord of Gruthere by the wife of Edward IV in 1472: 'There was ordained a bed for himself the counterpoint clothe of gold, furred with ermine, the tester and the celer also shining cloth of gold.' (Macquoid, 1904, p.67.) Another bedroom with a splendid effect was found in the 1526 inventory of the Duke of Richmond that listed 'a testour, payned with clothe of gold, grene tynsell, and crymsen velvet' (Camden Society, *Camden Miscellany*, 1855, vol.III, p.18).

In the *Tudor Book of Rates* for 1582, a distinction was drawn between plain and wrought cloths: 'Cloth of gold, plain, the yard/ditto wrought/cloth of silver plain/ditto wrought' (Willan, 1962, p.16). Clearly it was a useful material for showing off wrought work or **embroidery**. In 1582, Edward Baker supplied '30 cushions of similar cloth of gold tissue, cloth of gold and velvet and satin of diverse colours, part embroidered with cloth of gold cloth of silver and satin of diverse colours, venice gold and silver…' (Beard, 1997, p.284). The Hardwick Hall inventory of 1601 listed 'seven pieces of embroidered cloth of gold and silver cloth of tissue' (Boynton, 1971, p.28). Charles I's inventory of 1659 records a bed in the Rich Bedchamber that had the 'ceeler and headcloth … of rich cloth of gold with inward vallens' (Macquoid & Edwards, 1924, I, p.35). Cloth of gold was still used later in the seventeenth century. For example, in the 1679 Ham House inventory of the Queen's Bedchamber there were:

> Six curtains and four cantoones, valances, and bases of cloth of gold with flowers of blew velvet lined with skie colour sateen with gould embroidered fringe, tester, head cloth and counterpane embroidered with gould, four cups covered with the same of ye curtain and white feathers on the top of them. (Thornton & Tomlin, 1980, p.144.)

See also **Arras**, **Baudekin**, **Filé**, **Frisé**, **Tinsell**, **Tissue**.

FURTHER READING

Arnold, J. (1988). *Queen Elizabeth's Wardrobe Unlock'd*, Leeds: Maney.

Braun-Ronsdorf, M. (1961). 'Gold and silver fabrics from medieval to modern times', *CIBA Review*, 3, pp 2–12.

Clouded (aka Chiné)

A term that refers to the smudged effect of a printed design that is not crisp and definite. This smudgy effect could be achieved by printing **warp** threads before weaving. The process could be applied to many yarns including **silks** and **woollens**. The resulting fabric was at one time particularly popular for **bed furniture**. In 1710, Mr Blathwayt's bedchamber in Dyrham Park, called the Clouded Room, was furnished with '6 pieces of clouded silk hangings, a clouded silk be lined with yellows striped persian, a counter pane of the same' (Walton, 1986, p.62). In 1738, Mary Blair of Boston had a 'clouded stuff bed with a chince quilt lin'd with silk' (Montgomery, 1984, p.200). The clouded effect was also found in **calimancoes** in the eighteenth century and later in **cretonnes**. In the late twentieth century, heat transfer techniques for printing the warp have been used in modern warp printing. Printing the finished cloth with an appropriate design can also simulate the general effect.
See also **Chiné**, **Silk: Clouded**.

Cluny tapestry
See **Tapestry: Cluny**.

Cluster fringe
See **Fringe: Cluster**.

Coated fabric
Coated fabrics, based on a pliant top layer applied to a fabric base, have a long history of use in furnishings. Waxes, rubber, gums, oils and plastic materials have all been used as a surface covering, usually over a woven substrate. For **upholstery** use, coated fabrics were usually intended to be an imitation of **leather**. These originated in the fourteenth century. They were developed in the nineteenth century and were improved upon in the early twentieth century, resulting in a wide range of coated fabrics.
See also **Lancaster cloth**, **Oilcloth**, **Polyurethene coated fabric**, **PVC**, **Rubber cloth**.

FURTHER READING

Blank, S. (1990). 'An Introduction to plastics and rubbers in collections', in *Studies in Conservation*, 35, 2, May, 53–63.
Brunn, M. (1990). 'Treatment of cellulose nitrate coated upholstery' in, Williams, M.A. (ed.), *Upholstery Conservation*, preprints of a symposium held at Colonial Williamsburg, 2–4 February 1990, American Conservation Consortium, East Kingston, NH, pp 449–55.
Buttery, D.N. (1976). *Plastics in Furniture*, London: Applied Science Publishers Ltd.
Christie, G. (1964). *Storeys of Lancaster, 1848–1964*, London: Collins.
Gooderson, P.J. (1996). *Lord Linoleum, Lord Ashton and the Rise of the British Oilcloth and Linoleum Industry*, Keele: Keele University Press.
Kovaly, K.A. (1970). *Handbook of Plastic Furniture Manufacturing*, Stanford, Conn.: Technomic.
McDonald, R.J. (1981). *Modern Upholstering Techniques*, New York: Charles Scribner's Sons.
Meikle, J.L. (1995). 'Presenting a new material: from imitation to innovation with Fabrikoid', *Decorative Arts Society Journal*, 19, pp 8–15.
Mossman, S. (1988). 'Simple methods of identifying plastics', *Modern Organic Materials*, Glasgow: Scottish Society for Conservation and Restoration, pp 41–5.
Neuberger, R. (1934). 'History and development of the leather cloth industry', *Upholstery*, 1, 4, July.
Seymour, R.B. & Mark, H.F. (eds) (1989). *Organic Coatings: Their Origin and Development*, Proceedings of the International Symposium on the History of Organic Coatings, 11–15 September 1989, Miami Beach, Florida, New York: Elsevier.
Stephenson, J. (1941). *Practical Upholstering*, New York: Clifford Lawton.
Thorp, V. (1990). 'Imitation leather; structure composition and conservation', *Leather Conservation News*, 6, 2, Spring, pp 7–15.
Wilson, L. & Balfour, D. (1990). 'Developments in upholstery construction in Britain during the first half of the twentieth century' in Williams, M.A. (ed.), *Upholstery Conservation*, preprints of a symposium held at Colonial Williamsburg, 2–4 February, American Conservation Consortium, East Kingston, NH.

Coburg cloth
Thin **worsted/cotton** or worsted/**silk** fabric twilled on one side that was introduced in 1843. Although used for women's dresses 'by the lower orders, who always employ them for mourning' (Caulfeild & Saward, p.85), it was in *Cassell's Household Guide* that Coburg cloth was recommended for **upholstery**: 'a good dark green Coburg cloth; it wears well, and can be replaced when shabby at small expense' (1870, vol.1, p.127).

Cocoa mat
Particular matting that is made from coir fibre. Large quantities of coconut fibre are woven in heavy looms, then cut up into various sizes, and finally bound round the edges by a kind of rope made from the same material. The mats may be of one colour only, or they may be made of different colours and in different designs. Sometimes the names of institutions, messages or mottoes are introduced into the mats. Another type of mat is made exclusively from the above-mentioned rope by arranging alternate layers in sinuous and straight paths, and then stitching the parts together.

According to the American journal *The Carpet Trade* in 1877, 'The first time coir matting was ever used as a floorcovering in any quantity was about twenty-six years ago [i.e. 1851] in St. George's Hall at Windsor, England, on the occasion of the christening of the Prince of Wales' (Rosentiel, 1978, p.23). It was certainly used in 1866 when 'a cocoa mat for the front door' and 14 yards (12.8 metres) of 4/4 cocoa matting were supplied to Sir Titus Salt for the harness room in his Yorkshire home (Boynton, 1967, p.84).

By 1872, cocoa mats were defined as coarse mats made of the bark fibres of the Cocoa palm. 'The outside of the mat is covered with a coarse **pile**. Coloured fibres are often used to produce borders, figures, etc.' (Brown & Gates, p.184.) This was confirmed by the retailers, Maple and Co, who sold cocoa matting by the yard (90 cm) from 18 to 72 inches (46 to 183 cm) wide, and offered it in 'olive, peacock and several other art shades' (1884, p.65).

In the 1950s, coir matting was sold in a range of qualities, including Angengo, Quilandy or Alapat, names that were based on the districts of southeast India or Sri Lanka, from where the fibres originated (Sheridan, 1955, p.347).
See also **Coir fibre**, **Mat**, **Matting**.

Coir fibre
A fibrous material derived from the husks of the coconut palm. The fibres are first processed by splitting the husks and then retting them in water. The result is beaten to loosen the fibres, which are then dried for use. The best coir is made from long fibres and is artificially curled, like **hair**. Long known as a cordage or **matting** material (see **Cocoa mat**), it seems to have been introduced around the 1840s (Webster & Parker, 1844, p.297) as an intermediate filling in **upholstery**, and has been widely used as such since then. In 1844, John Barsham patented a method of manufacturing matting for **cushions** and **mattresses** from coir fibres and the like (Patent no.10884). In addition, coir fibre was used to make coir mats. It works best when needled onto **hessian** to form pads that are fitted over **spring** upholstery. In the 1950s, it was recorded as the most widely used upholstery fibre filling in England. Also known as coco or ginger fibre.
See also **Cocoa mat**.

FURTHER READING

Bally, W. (1956). 'Coir', *CIBA Review*, 116, pp 2–32.

Coir mat
See **Cocoa mat**.

Comfort (aka Comforter, Comfortable)
American bedcovers comprising a warm, wadded layering of three fabrics (top, filling and backing), which are often tufted or tied rather than quilted. They were used as a substitute for **blankets** and used under a **bedspread**. Comforters are distinct from quilts or counterpanes, being usually warmer, more heavily wadded and less elaborate in decoration. This distinction is evident from the 1840 advertisement of Theodore Baker in the *Boston Almanac* (p.126) where he 'has for sale Quilts, Counterpanes, Comforters…'. Miss Leslie recommended that for a large double bed a comforter could be made from coloured **muslin** or from furniture **chintz** or cheap **calico**, where the lining and the outside are of the same material (1841, p.314). Cole said that they were originally made at home, but in 1892 they were so cheaply made by machine that home production had all but ceased. He estimated 3,000,000 were manufactured yearly in a range of fillings from **cotton** and **shoddy** to best eider (1892). Cole's comments were reiterated in 1917 in a treatise on the cotton and **linen** department of retail stores:

> [Comforters] are bed coverings similar to quilts, but with a thicker layer of wadding in them. Sometimes the words are used interchangeably. The coverings for comfortables may be of Cheese-cloth, Silkoline, Challis, Sateen, Chintz, Silk, Batiste. The wadding for the better grades may be of cotton batting or carded wool. Low-priced comfortables may be filled with coarse shoddy or flocks, short refuse wool. Down comfortables or puffs are filled with fine down feathers. These comfortables are exceptionally light and warm. Comfortables have been factory-made since 1875. Previous to that time, they were always made at home. Now factory-made ones are so inexpensive that it is scarcely worthwhile to make them by hand. They come in but one size, 72 x 78 inches, except the down puffs, which are made in several sizes. (Thompson, 1917, p.129.)

Comforters were described in detail in Dyer's work, *Textile Fabrics*. Firstly she described the various fillings:

> Comforts are made of cotton or wool wadding or down covered with some fabric, and tied or quilted. There are several grades. The cheaper ones are filled with wool and cotton wastes, the next with cotton batting, and the better grades with wool sheeting or fine down feathers. The last named are called down puffs. They are delightfully warm, soft, very light in weight, and can be laundered satisfactorily if care is taken not to wring them and to shake them frequently while they are drying. The cotton-filled are heavy, do not have so much warmth, and lose their softness when washed. Wool is very warm and lightweight, and can be washed if this is done with care. It is more satisfactorily dry-cleaned, and makes the most practical comfort, if one can afford it.

She then went on and discussed the coverings available along with their relative merits:

> The coverings for comforts should be chosen with respect to appearance and durability. Silkatine, challis, satin, China silk, sateen, cambric, silk and cotton mull, foundation silk, or silk brilliant, cotton challis, chintz, and lightweight cretonne are all used. Satin, of course, is used wholly for beauty. It soon becomes soiled, is difficult to clean, and altogether is very expensive. Sateen, cambric, cotton or wool challis, and chintz make serviceable coverings that furnish additional warmth. Comforts covered with these may be bought in attractive colors, giving beauty as well as serviceability. Silkatine, silk mull, and silk brilliant, although thin and lightweight, are serviceable, making soft, beautiful, silky, inexpensive coverings that can be easily washed or cleaned.

Finally she considered the merits or otherwise of making comforters at home:

> People who want an inexpensive and serviceable comfort, and do not care for beauty, buy wadding and cover it with two or three layers of cheesecloth, or any other inexpensive material. Cotton batting or wool wadding can be bought already quilted. This enables one to make a comfort easily and insures an equal distribution of the wool. It is as cheap to buy comforts ready-made as to make them. Some prefer to make them in order to have large sizes. Wool comforts come in two sizes, one for double and one for single beds. Cotton ones can be obtained in varying sizes. In order to keep the ready-made comforts from pulling out at the foot of the bed, some housewives take a piece of cheesecloth the same length as the width of the comfort, fold it and sew it to the lower end. This makes an extension of about sixteen or eighteen inches that can be tucked under the mattress so that the comfort does not pull out. (Dyer, *c.*1923, p.213.)

In the mid-twentieth century, American authors noted that 'the cotton fabrics most commonly used [for comforters] are heavy muslin, chintz and sateen. These fabrics may be plain, colored or painted. Soft cotton or **rayon** velveteen and rayon velvet make luxurious comfortables as do lustrous rayon satins and crisp taffetas' (Bendure & Pfieffer, 1947, p.581).
See also **Challis**, **Cheesecloth**, **Down**, **Counterpane**, **Quilt**, **Tufting**, **Wadding**.

Compass rod
A continuous one-piece **curtain pole** fitted around a four-poster bed designed to support case curtains. A 'strong compass rod and hooks' was supplied by William Bradshaw to Earl of Stanhope in 1736 (Beard, 1997, p.303).
See also **Bed protection**, **Case rod**.

Congoleum rug
See **Felt-base**.

Control rod
Short rods designed to hang on the leading runner of a **curtain track**. They allowed curtains to be drawn without handling the fabric itself. Similar devices may be fitted to **Venetian blinds**.

Copperplate print
See **Printed textile: Copperplate printing**.

Cord (line, bullion, rope, upholstery, welting)
Cord serves both a utilitarian and a decorative purpose. Decoratively, it is one of the simplest of **trimmings** and is often combined with **tassels** or other **passementerie**. It is stitched on edges to accentuate shapes or as a finish, or as an edging for **appliqué**. It is often used in conjunction with tassels for hangings and **tiebacks**. As a practical furnishing apparatus, it may be used to tie up **bed curtains**, draw window **curtains**, control blinds, suspend canopies and testers, support **mattresses** and hang pictures. Cords are made from twisted **cotton** or a worsted core, often with a **silk** wrapping. Various diameters of cord are used; the narrowest to cover seams and the thickest as tiebacks or **swags** for **drapery**.

One extravagant example of its use is from the 1661 inventory of Cardinal Mazarin, which noted 43 curtains, 'each curtain has fastened to it cords of white silk … with a tassel of gold and silk, at the end of the said cords serving to draw the curtains' (Thornton, 1978, p.140). Heavier varieties of cord or rope to hold back curtains and **portières**

were used in the later nineteenth century and onward.
See also **Bed cord**, **Blind**, **Canopy**, **Piping**, **Tester**.

Cord carpet

A general name for a range of carpets including Brussels, hair, sisal, etc., which had a corded surface effect.
See also **Brussels carpet**, **Hair carpet**, **Sisal carpet**.

Cord seat

Cordage has been used to produce seating and bedding since ancient times. More recently, a form of interwoven cord, sometimes called Danish cord, made from twisted, treated, brown kraft paper, has been used to make seats. Cord was widely used for bottoming chairs in the second part of the twentieth century, and was especially associated with Danish dining chairs. Other varieties of cord seating have included **grasses**, reeds, and extruded cellophane and plastic tube, which is often associated with exterior or patio furniture, originally in the 'contemporary' style of the 1950s.

Cord tidy

A simple gadget that allows the excess strings of drawn-up heading tapes to be wound up and kept safely hidden. This allows the heading tape to be opened out for cleaning of the **curtains**.
See also **Curtain tape**.

Cording set

A system of combined **curtain rail** and integral cords that allow the hung curtains to be opened by cords that run in the rail itself. The system may be fitted into cornice poles, or onto laths, or in a metal or plastic rail. It originated in the French rod system.
See also **French rod**.

Corduroy

A fabric woven from **cotton**, **rayon** or other fibres, made with a supplementary **weft** to produce a **pile** where the fibres of the weft form the surface to create cords or ribs in the **warp** direction i.e. lengthwise along the fabric. Corduroy can be produced with narrow, medium and wide **wales** (ribs), as well as chequerboard patterns. In the twentieth century, it has been used for **bedspreads**, **drapes** and **upholstery** (Denny, 1936, p.18; Taylor, 1951, p.37).
See also **Fustian**.

Cork carpet

A product with similarities to linoleum but the basic ingredient is ground cork pieces (not cork dust or wood flour), which are mixed with oxidised linseed oil and then calendered upon a **jute** backing, and rolled and finished as linoleum. Two versions were sold and known in the trade as either Taylor or Walton, depending on the binder process used. It is generally more resilient, warmer and quiet to the tread than linoleum and was recommended for living rooms, bedrooms, halls and passages. It was not, however, as effective in 'wet' areas.

> Cork carpet, glued directly upon the finished cement face of the concrete covering the site, has been successfully used, thus saving all the cost of flooring. It is absolutely necessary, however, that the concrete should be thoroughly dry and the cork carpet seasoned and guaranteed by the maker. This form of covering makes an excellent finish, for it is warm to the feet and, if properly laid, takes the place of the ordinary carpet, except perhaps that a few rugs can be added if desired. It looks best when of a plain colour without any attempt at patterns, and may be cleansed either by washing or by polishing with the beeswax mixture already referred to. (Fletcher, 1910, p.93.)

Cork **carpet** has enjoyed periods of popularity, especially in the twentieth century as it was a useful background to 'modern' interiors.
See also **Kamptulion**, **Linoleum**.

Cornice

A term used since the seventeenth century for the decorative treatments given to the tops of window arrangements or beds. They also refer to the wooden boxes from which **valances** and **curtains** were hung and operated. Cornish is an alternative spelling.

Chippendale advised that the 'cornice must rise as high as it can to hide the top of the tester' (*The Gentleman and Cabinet Maker's Director*, Plate XXXVIII). This plate shows a 'design of bed with carved cornices gilt or covered with the same stuff as the curtains' (ibid.). Chippendale supplied Ninian Home with '27 yards Chintz **cotton** to match, 2 neat Carved cornices to ditto covered with superfine cotton to match compleat' for Paxton House, in 1774 (Gilbert, 1978, p.274).

Cornices could be finished in a number of ways. Sheraton recommended japanning, carving or gilding. In addition, they could be

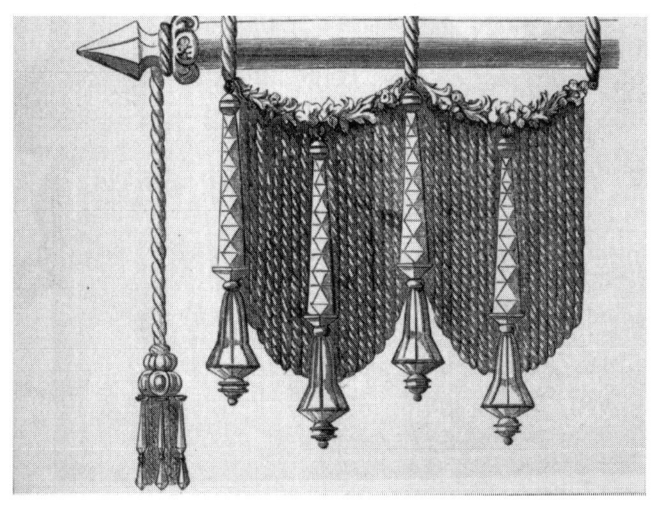

ABOVE LEFT
32. Examples of fashionable window cornices (T. Sheraton, The Cabinet Maker and Upholsterer's Drawing Book, *1793)*

LEFT
*33. Cornice and curtain ornament by Simcox and Pemberton (*The Art Journal Illustrated Catalogue of the Great Exhibition – London 1851*)*

painted, covered in fabric (matching or contrasting), or made from metal.

After becoming outmoded in the early nineteenth century, they had a revival from around 1820 onward. Rudolph Ackermann pointed out that cornices 'are now adopted in a great variety and will probably very soon supersede the late fashion of suspending draperies by poles and detached ornaments' (*The Repository of Arts*, 1820).

The newly introduced stamped metal cornices did not receive universal admiration. In America, Sloan noted in his *Homestead Architecture* that 'pressed brass cornices are not in such good taste as are wooden ones corresponding with the furniture' (1861, p.323). Eastlake considered them 'contemptible in design and worse than useless for not only does it afford, from the nature of its construction, no protection against the draught behind, but being made of thin, sharp-edged metal liable to cut and fray the curtain which it crowns' (1878, p.96). Fashionable cornices often reflected the woodwork of the room or the prevailing furnishing style. They were easily removed by the use of cornice slides or staples attached above the rod.
See also **Cornice pole**.

Cornice pole
A method of suspending **curtains** by hanging them from rings running on a wood or metal rod. They were also used to suspend **drapes** in fixed **swags**, etc. Brackets fixed to the architrave of the window supported the rod itself. Although rods have been used for centuries to hold curtains, the cornice pole is commonly associated with an early nineteenth-century origin. Loudon explained their operation:

> A round pole of wood is supported at each end by a bracket ... which is fixed by screw nails to the architrave of the window. The pole is kept securely in place by the screw-pin, which passes through the bracket, and is screwed into the pole so as to keep it quite firm. (1839, p.338.)

Not surprisingly, the design reformer, Charles Eastlake, criticised excessive poles, particularly singling out the metal types:

> The useful convenient little rod has grown into a lumbering pole ... [which] is not only hollow but constructed of metal far too thin in proportion to its diameter. Then in place of the little finials, which used to be fixed at each end of the rod to prevent the rings slipping off, our modern upholsterer has substituted gigantic fuchsias or other flowers made of brass, gilt bronze, and even china sprawling downwards in a design of execrable taste. Sometimes this pole being too weak for actual use is fixed up simply for ornament while the curtain slides on an iron rod behind it. (1878, pp 95–6.)

In his *Practical Decorative Upholstery*, Moreland recommended wooden poles that matched the joinery and deplored those fitted with brass **trimmings**. He recommended poles of brass tubing, which might be bronzed as well as 'real bamboo poles with ends and rings made in imitation'. He also encouraged poles that were covered with textiles especially when used in combination with **plush** fabrics (1889, pp 33–6).

Cornice poles have been made in a range of materials subsequently, including extruded aluminium and plastics. They have also been corded, fitted around bay windows and used in conjunction with **portières**. They remain part of the window furnisher's repertoire.
See also **Cornice**.

Cornish matting
See **Matting: Cornish**.

Corona
Originally, a hanging metal circle designed to hold candles in front of the rood-screen of a church. Later, it was employed as a circular or semi-circular metal ring supporting bed **drapes**, centrally mounted on the wall above the bed.

Coronation gimp
See **Gimp**.

Costering (aka Costers)
An ancient term for hangings or **curtains** derived from the French term *costier*, meaning 'hanging for walls'. They were often listed in inventories along with matching bankers and dorcers. Not surprisingly, **tapestry** or **arras** was an appropriate material for costerings. Lord Richard Scrope of Bolton owned four '*costers de opera d'arras*' (*Testamenta Ebor.*, vol.I).

In 1379, Elizabeth of York purchased 'best dorser, four costers and one banker' (*Privy Purse Expenses*, 1830, 242/2, *OED*). In 1463, John Baret of Bury bequeathed 'a tester with II costers small palyd of buckram blew' (Edwards, 1964, p.263). A blurring of distinctions is noted in 1480, when 'Tapettes otherwise called costerings' were listed in the *Wardrobe Accounts of Edward IV* (1830, 144). In addition, there were 'iiij costerings of wool paned red and blue with roses, sonnes and crowns in every pane', in the same accounts. In 1528, Sir William Compton's inventory listed 'in the parlour-item a costring of tapestry, lined with canvas containing one hundred and forty sticks square' (Edwards, 1964, p.263).
See also **Banker**, **Dorcer**, **Tapestry**.

Cotele
Bengaline cloth made from a **silk** or **rayon warp** and a **worsted weft** that is given a hard twist. The name is of French origin.
See also **Bengaline**.

Coteline
A rep-type furnishing fabric used in the nineteenth century. Sloan gives an American definition: 'The style of reps called cotelaine is very pretty, and no doubt will be a great favourite, as it has all the beauty of brocatelle with the advantage of novelty and a greater durability' (1861, p.323). Cotelan, according to Charles Eastlake, was a **silk**, **wool** and **cotton** mixture originating from Germany, which was often woven with a **diaper** work pattern (1878, p.99). In their 1900 catalogue, the furnishing store, Maple and Co, advertised 'coteline' for 'inexpensive drawing room curtains and covers where a rich effect can be ensured at little cost' (Maple and Co, 1900).
See also **Brocatelle**, **Rep**.

Cottage curtain
A combination of **café curtains** across the lower part of an opening and **tieback** curtains, usually **ruffled**, across the top of the window.
See also **Café curtain**.

Cotton
(a) Firstly, the term has been used for certain **woollen** cloths, like **frieze** (maybe founded on the nap or down), intended for furnishing purposes since the fifteenth century at least. These were particularly associated with Lancashire, Westmoreland and Wales, and included **fustians** especially. During the sixteenth century, imported cotton fibres were spun in these locations and gradually took the place of the wool.
(b) Secondly, it is the fibre of the cotton plant *Gossypium* and fabrics

made from yarns spun from this fibre. Cotton grows in staple form and can vary greatly in quality. The finishing processes also enhance the end product. Short staple cotton is carded then spun into yarn. Long staple cotton may be carded or combed. Both methods create a lustrous yarn. Combed cotton is always a two-ply yarn. The mercerising process invented in 1844 by John Mercer impregnates cotton with a caustic soda solution. This process enhances the yarns and the finished cloth so the best examples can rival **silk** in colour, intensity and feel.

Cotton yarns were used very early in textile history, especially in India *c.*3000BC. The industry was later established in the Mediterranean region and gradually spread through Spain (Spanish Arab word is *kutun*) to Italy and France by the twelfth century, and then to England by the fifteenth century. Imports of painted cottons (see **Calico** and **Chintz**) from India were made from the sixteenth century and these were later imitated in European factories. Printing processes continued to be developed using cotton cloth as a base (see **Printed cotton**).
See also **Austrian shade cloth**, **Bafta**, **Benares**, **Blind chintz**, **Bocasine**, **Bolton sheeting**, **Bomber cloth**, **Cambric**, **Chandin**, **Check**, **Damask**, **Dimity**, **Drill**, **Jaconet**, **Longee**, **Madapolam**, **Manchester**, **Marquisette**, **Masulipatam**, **Moree**, **Muslin**, **Nainsook**, **Percale**, **Purdah**, **Radnor**, **Sateen**, **Satin**, **Scotch cloth**, **Silkoline**, **Stafford cloth**, **Scrim**, **Ticking**, **Terry**, **Velour**, **Vermilion**, **Voile**.

FURTHER READING

Baines, E. (1835). *History of the Cotton Manufacture in Great Britain*, London: H. Fisher and Co, reprinted 1966, London: Frank Cass.

Hough, W. (1948). *Encyclopaedia of Cotton Fabrics*, Altrincham: Sherratt.

Mann, J. (1860). *The Cotton Trade of Great Britain: Its Rise, Progress and Present Extent*, London: Simpkin Marshall, reprinted 1968, London: Frank Cass.

Montgomery, F.M. (1970). *Printed Textiles: English and American Cottons and Linens 1700–1850*, London: Thames and Hudson.

Turnbull, G. (1951). *A History of the Calico Printing Industry of Great Britain*, Altrincham: Sherratt.

Wadsworth, A.P. & Mann, J. (1931). *The Cotton Trade and Industrial Lancashire 1600–1780*, Manchester: Manchester University Press, reprinted 1965, Manchester: Manchester University Press.

Cotton carpet

Cotton carpet with a shag-**pile** was developed in the second half of the twentieth century for bedroom and bathroom use.
See also **Dhurrie**.

Cotton chain carpet

'Scotch, Kidderminster and Cotton Chain are other names for ingrain rugs. Cotton Chain is a cheap, low grade of cotton ingrain.' (Dyer, *c.*1923, p.194.)
See also **Ingrain carpet**.

Cotton damask

See **Damask**.

Cotton flock

Natural fibre derived from the **cotton** plant. Cotton flock was used extensively as a yarn in textile manufacture as well as for **upholstery** filling. Short cotton fibres or linters are made into loose cotton **felt** for application as **wadding** in upholstery processes. Cotton fills are by-products of the manufacturing process of separating cotton seeds from cotton fibre. The short cotton linters, still attached to the seeds, are removed and formed into cotton **felt**. The earliest date for cotton wadding observed in upholstered furniture is *c.*1850. It is sometimes known as linter felt or cotton felt. As wadding, it has been used in the twentieth century to give a smooth feel over **hair** and eliminate the noise factor from the rustle of hair (Sheridan, 1955, p.86).

Cotton rep

A 35 inch (89 cm) wide cloth employed for the **lining** of **cretonne curtains** in the later nineteenth century.
See also **Rep**.

Cotton rug

See **Rug**.

Cotton velvet

See **Manchester velvet**.

Couch cover

Early twentieth-century cloth, often 60 inches by 3 yards (152 by 274 cm), woven as a panel to overlay couches.
See also **Throw**.

Couching

A term for an **embroidery** technique that produces a pattern by sewing lengths of thread or **cord** to the support fabric by way of small over and over couching **stitches**. Couching is used for gold, silver, **wool** or **silk** cords that are too large for **needlework**. It is often employed in conjunction with other techniques such as appliqué, **border** or scrollwork. In Italian **quilting**, the technique may be used to contrast and enrich the raised pattern of this type of quilting. In 1887, Caulfeild & Saward noted that 'ancient church needlework was profusely decorated with couchings' (p.90).
See also **Appliqué**, **Trapunto**.

Counterpane

The outermost cover of a set of bed furnishings that conceals other covering materials. The word appears to derive from *contrepoint*, itself from the Latin *culcita puncta*, i.e. **stitched** or quilted **cushion**. This was corrupted to contre-pointe, the English counterpoint, which in turn was changed to 'counterpane'. It has been suggested that the name may also come from the method of quilting (Thornton, 1978, p.179). Thus 'counterpane' and 'quilt' are, by origin, the same word. The term was formerly used for a variety of bedcovers, especially those woven of **cotton** or **wool**, but from the mid-nineteenth century onwards, it was generally replaced by the term 'bedspread'.

An early reference from 1440 is in the *Boke of Curtasye*, which required the groom of the chamber to 'lay the counterpane … on beddes fete' (Edwards, 1964, p.272). The complete bedding arrangement is identified in 1459, which had a bedchamber described with 'j fedder bed, ij blankettys, j pair of shchettys, j rede pane furryds with connyngs' (pane referring to counterpane) (*Paston Letters*, 336, I. 484, *OED*).

Over 200 years later, the term was still in use. In 1679, the *London Gazette* publicised (using both names) 'An Indian counter-pane or coverlid with silk and silver' (1434/4) and, in 1682, the Cowdray inventory listed 'painted quilted calico … counterpanes' on three beds (Thornton, 1978, p.370).

The taste for painted **calico** (**chintz**) bedcovers was also noted in the later eighteenth century when, in 1771, Mrs Lybbe Powys noted that Lady Blount of Mawley, Shropshire, 'has more chintz counterpanes

34. Counterpane crochet work (Private Collection)

than in one house I ever saw, not one bed without very fine ones' (King, D., 1958, p.919).

The interest in counterpanes was also found in America where they had alternate uses. Writing in 1783, Mary Hill Lamar explained that 'The Indian counterpanes make very pretty curtains for a back room or best bed room; as one counterpane of the largest size makes a window curtain, they come much cheaper than good English cotton ... they make beautiful beds lined with white, and with clothes and testers' (Montgomery, 1970, p.52).

At the beginning of the nineteenth century, Sheraton described coverlid, coverlet and counterpane together as:

> The utmost of the bedclothes that under which all the rest are concealed. The counterpane is a coverlet woven in squares, according to this derivation; of which there are many made of cotton. White cotton counterpanes of different qualities measuring from 7 to 16 quarters. Coverlets, more vulgarly coverlids, are of the following description, measuring from 5 to 9 quarters, various stripes. From 6 to 10 quarters black weft diapers, Worsted red weft ditto of the same size... Also, there are silk coverlets, bordered and fringed. [Also] Diamond or Brussels coverlets. (1803, pp 182–3.)

Robert Southey was clearly complaining about similar products (probably Bolton coverlets) when he described his counterpane which was 'of all English manufactures the least tasteful; it is of white cotton, ornamented with cotton knots, in shapes as graceless as the cut box in a garden' (1807, vol.1, pp 160–1).

Although in 1840 *The Workwoman's Guide* identified servants' counterpanes as being of 'dark brown, violet or grey colour, whilst cottagers are often of patchwork' (Hale, p.200), the white geometrics remained popular. Webster & Parkes' *Encyclopaedia* defined counterpanes as having 'little protuberances on the surface, dispersed after a certain pattern' (1844). These may have been similar in concept to the one shown in the Great Exhibition:

> [This] exhibits considerable improvement over the ordinary style adopted with so monotonous an effect in articles of this kind... The peculiar description of bed-cover, called counterpane (from counterpoint) is not now made extensively except of a very low quality; it is of the most durable kind but has been supplanted by quilts, on which the pattern is produced by the Jacquard loom. The knots or loops which forms the pattern [shown] are pulled up by the hand with a small steel instrument similar to a shoemaker's awl. This operation had been performed on this counterpane no fewer than 844,800 times. (*The Art Journal Illustrated Catalogue of the Great Exhibition*, p.85.)

By the early twentieth century, the manufacture of counterpanes was undertaken on a large scale. This account of American products explains the processes in detail:

> Counterpane is the outside cover of the bed. It is made of cotton and woven with a raised pattern, and may be either crochet or marseilles. The crochet counterpane is made of coarse, bleached cotton, woven in conventional patterns by means of a Jacquard attachment to the loom. The term crochet is used because of its resemblance to the old-fashioned 'crochet' spreads made by hand. The marseilles counterpane, so called because first made in Marseilles, has a compound weave but the embossed pattern, usually a large design, appears on one side only. The yarn for the face is much finer than that used for the back and has twice the number of threads. Both of these are woven in continuous strips into from five hundred to one thousand counterpanes in a piece. After leaving the loom, the counterpanes are inspected. Knots and ends are removed and then they are passed over rollers into the bleaching vat, where they remain for about two hours in a solution of chlorine. After being rinsed, boiled and blued the long strip is dried over smooth, heated rollers. The counterpanes are then cut apart with sharp knives, hemmed, folded, ticketed and shipped. (Thompson, 1917, p.131.)

The term was generally replaced by 'bedspread' or 'quilt' from the later nineteenth century.

See also **Bedspread**, **Bolton coverlet**, **Counterpoint**, **Coverlet**, **Coverlid**, **Marseilles**, **Quilt**.

Counterpoint

An outer bedcover usually of rich material, the name is synonymous with counterpanes and was used from the fourteenth to the mid-seventeenth century. The choice of material to cover the counterpoint was quite varied. In 1472, in a description of a bedroom made up for Lord of Gruthere by the wife of Edward IV, a luxurious counterpoint was listed: 'There was ordained a bed for himself ... the counterpoint clothe of gold, furred with ermine, the tester' (Macquoid, 1904, p.67). In 1509, Edmund Dudley had a range of different counterpoints in his Great Chamber to include a 'counterpoynt of verders, one of blew sarsenett lined with blew buckram, a counterpoint of popynjaye, a counterpoint of bawdekin' (Beard, 1997, p.282). In a 1533 inventory, Katherine of Aragon had 'a counterpoint of scarlet and in length III yards – sore perished with moths' (Edwards, 1964, p.272). Whereas in another reference there was 'a featherbed, a bolster, a counterpoint of tapestry work with beasts and fowls, lined with canvas' which furnished the Steward's chamber in Sir Henry Parker's Norwich house in the 1550s (Gloag, 1990, p.543). The use of tapestry for making counterpoints was also found in a 1588 will, which featured 'a feather bed, a bolster and a counter-point of tapestry' (*Lancashire Wills*, vol.III. p.13, *OED*).

Distinctions between bedcoverings were also important. The inventory of Mrs Elizabeth Hutton of Hunwick, taken in 1567, listed 'twelve pairs of blankets, and six happings, twenty coverlets, three coverings for beds of tapestry, and two of dornix' (Gloag, 1990, p.268).

Counterpoints were also made and decorated with **embroidery**. The 1601 Hardwick Hall inventory noted a 'counterpoint of black velvet

stript with silver, embroidered with pearls and purl', a counterpoint of embroidery and **needlework** 'with cloth of gold and divers other stuffes and with a gold fringes, a counterpoint of red cloth with yellow silk fringe' (Boynton, 1971, pp 24 and 29). In 1638, Anne, Viscountess of Dorchester owned '1 large counterpoint for a bed, of Holland wrought in colours of needle work of weaving work of worstead' (Clabburn, 1988, p.124). The term was superseded by counterpane by the end of the seventeenth century.
See also **Counterpane**, **Coverlet**.

Cover (Tight fitting)
Detachable but tight-fitted covers have been used on occasion for **upholstery**. They are particularly useful for chairs made '*a chassis*', where the covers may be changed according to season by removing the upholstered backs or seats. Compared to 'loose covers', which were slack in appearance, these tight covers generally gave a tailored appearance and finish to the upholstery on which they were used. Developed in the late seventeenth century, they were initially rather sloppy in production and finish, the covers being held on the chair with **hooks and eyes** and maybe tie-tapes. By the early eighteenth century, the upholsterers had developed sophisticated methods of attachment, which included metal or wood pegs fitted to the frame rails onto which the fabric was fixed sometimes with the use of **flies**. The **top cover** could be stretched and held through eyelets, either as metal rings or as buttonholes sewn in **linen** flaps.
See also **Protective furnishing**, **Seasonal furnishing**.

FURTHER READING

Balfour, D. & Gentle, N. (2001). 'A study of loose textile covers for seat furniture in England between 1670 and 1731' in Mertens, W. (ed.), *Transitory Splendour: Interior Textiles in Western Europe 1600–1900*, Antwerp: Hessenhuis Museum, Stadsbestuur, pp 295–9.
Cornforth, J. (2005). *Early Georgian Interiors*, London: Yale, pp 105–6.
Gill, K. (2001). 'Eighteenth century close fitting detachable covers preserved at Houghton Hall: a technical study' in Gill, K. & Eastop, D. (eds), *Upholstery Conservation: Principles and Practice*, Oxford: Butterworth-Heinemann, pp 133–44.

Coverlet
A term that is related to **counterpane**, which usually refers to the uppermost covering of a bed. The derivation appears to be from its early form *coverlite*, which seems to be derived from the French *couvre-lit* (*couvrir*, to cover and *lit*, bed). It was sometimes the case that beds had a coverlid and a counterpane, or a **counterpoint** and a coverlet. In the 1381 will of the Countess of March there was '*Un coverlet de worsted pur mesme le lit, un coverture de bleu, etc*' (Nicholls, *Royal Wills*, 1780, 100). In some cases they were embroidered. A will of 1395 included 'A keuerlet of red sendel ypouthered with Cheuerons' (*Early English Wills*, 1882, 4).

In the inventory dated October 1566 of Christopher Yarworthe of Easthorpe, near Southwell, Nottingham, there was 'In the parlour 2 mattresses, 2 coverlettes, 2 bolsters, two pillows, 3 pairs of sheets and 2 towells, 10s.0d' (*Kennedy*, vol.XXII, p.108).

Embroidery continued to feature on coverlets. In the 1600 Ingatestone inventory, a coverlet of 'taffeta sarcenet … embroidered all over with yellow twist, and lined with fine crimson woollen' was listed (Thornton, 1978, p.370). Hardwick Hall also had coverlets of fine **tapestry**, but interestingly also had 'three coverlets to hang before a window. A coverlet to hang before a door, [and] a counterpoint of tapestry before another door' (Boynton, 1971, pp 31–2). The distinction is not clear.

In other cases, coverlets appear to have been made like **rugs**. In 1611, Cotgrave defined 'Couverture veloute' (coverlet with a **pile**) as an 'Irish Rug, Mantle, or Cadowe'. Coverlets as quilts were also filled with **feathers**, certainly by the eighteenth century. In 1768, it was noted of the eider duck that its 'remarkably light, elastic, warm qualities, make it [eider down] highly esteemed, as a stuffing for coverlets' (Pennant).

Not surprisingly, critic Charles Eastlake had something to say about coverlets (and counterpanes):

> From an artistic point of view the counterpanes now manufactured for servant bedrooms, in which coloured thread is introduced for the knotted pattern on a grey or white ground are very suggestive in colour but I fear that any approach to this style of coverlet would be considered objectionable in 'best' bedrooms. (1878, p.214.)

Boutonné
French-Canadian type of coverlets using coloured **wools** in a **weft** loop weave patterning.

Jaquard
A generic name for coverlets woven in one piece with designs produced with the jacquard.

Rag
A coverlet made up with a weft of strips of rag or cloth.
See also **Bolton coverlet**, **Brussels coverlet**, **Caddow**, **Coverlid**, **Dornix**, **Jacquard coverlet**.

FURTHER READING

Ayres, J. (1968–70). 'American coverlets', *Textile History*, 1, p.92.
Davison, M. & Mayer-Thurman, C. (1973). *Coverlets: A Handbook on the Collection of Woven Coverlets in the Art Institute of Chicago*, Chicago: Art Institute of Chicago.
Pettit, F. (1970). 'Counterpanes and coverlets' in Pettit, F., *America's Printed and Painted Fabrics, 1600–1900*, New York: Hastings House.
Safford, C. & Bishop, R. (1972). *America's Quilts and Coverlets*, New York: E.P. Dutton.

Coverlid
A spelling variation of coverlet. In 1765, the *London Chronicle* recorded that 'Blankets and coverlids were distributed to the necessitous poor' (3 January). According to Sheraton (1803, p.182), coverlid was a common term for coverlets: 'Coverlets, more vulgarly coverlids, are of the following description…'.
See also **Coverlet**.

Coverpane
A particular cloth made from **damask**, **holland** or **diaper**, which may have been embroidered and edged with gold **lace**. The coverpanes were intended to cover the most important place setting at a dining table, especially so in the fifteenth century. One example was described as 'A rich scaffe cutt through with gold, silver and silk with a curious peece of cutworke to cover the bread and salt wrought with gould and silver' (Mitchell, 1998, p.87). They fell out of use towards the end of the sixteenth century.

FURTHER READING

Mitchell, D.M. (1998). 'Coverpanes: Their Nature and Use in Tudor England', *Bulletin de CIETA*, 75, pp 81–96.

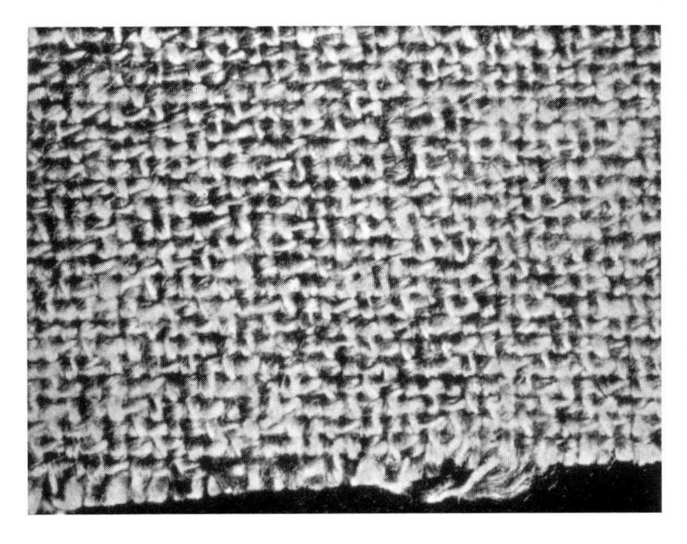

35. Detail of crash cloth (T. French and Co, The Book of Soft Furnishing, *1937)*

Covert
Twill weave medium- to heavyweight cloth, distinguished by a mottled appearance that was created by dark filling yarns and white/coloured **warp** yarns. **Cotton** versions were used for **bedspreads** and **drapes** in the USA in the 1940s (Bendure & Pfieffer, 1947, p.620).

Craftsman canvas (aka Art canvas)
A mixed flax and **jute canvas** cloth intended to reflect the Arts and Crafts movement's desire for honest truthfulness in materials. Gustav Stickley encouraged its use and had it produced in Scotland during the first decades of the twentieth century.

Crankey
A checked **linen** ticking material mainly intended for covering **mattresses**. Crankey is a northern English dialect word meaning 'checkered'. Thomas Chippendale supplied George Wyndham with 'a thick border'd crankey hair mattrass' in 1777 (Gilbert, 1978, p.286). In 1786, T.T. Byrd of Virginia was supplied with a 'wool cranky mattrass' (Montgomery, 1984, p.207). The term was still current in the 1880s where it was defined as linen and **cotton** ticking with an irregular zigzag pattern, giving its name (Caulfeild & Saward, 1887, p.92).

In the mid-twentieth century, *The Mercury Dictionary of Textile Terms* (1950) described crankey as **tabling** material and noted wider widths; it was still used for ticking.
See also **Check**, **Ticking**.

Crape
An anglicised version of the French word *crêpe*. It is a **silk** fabric of a gauzy texture, having a particularly crisp or crimpy appearance. It is woven of hard-spun silk yarn 'in the gum' or in a natural condition. There are two distinct varieties of the textile – Canton or Oriental crape, and hard or 'crisped' crape. The wavy appearance of Canton crape results from the particular way in which the **weft** is prepared, the yarn from two bobbins being twisted together in the reverse way. The fabric when woven is smooth and even, having no crêpe appearance. When the gum is subsequently extracted by boiling, it immediately becomes soft, and the weft, losing its twist, gives the fabric the waved structure, which constitutes its distinguishing feature.

The crisp and elastic structure of hard crape is not produced either in the spinning or in the weaving, but is due to processes through which the **gauze** passes after it is woven. Commercially, they are distinguished as single, double, three-ply and four-ply crapes, according to the nature of the yarn used in their manufacture. In Great Britain, hard crapes were made at Braintree (Essex), Norwich, Yarmouth, **Manchester** and Glasgow. In 1685, the *London Gazette* (no.2001/5) advertised '2 Pieces of Stript Silk Norwich Crape, and two Pieces of mixt Norwich Silk Crape not Stript'. The crape formerly made at Norwich was made with a silk **warp** and **worsted** weft, and later became bombasine. A very successful imitation of real crape was made in Manchester of **cotton** yarn, and sold under the name of Victoria crape.
See also **Austrian shade cloth**, **Bombasine**, **Crêpe cloth**, **Crêpe de Chine**, **Plissé**, **Seersucker**.

Crash
(a) Unbleached **linen** used as a basis for **embroidery**, especially in the mid-nineteenth century. According to Caulfeild & Saward, only Russia and Barnsley crash are correct (1887, p.93).
(b) A rather coarse heavy fabric made from irregular **tow** yarns in the **weft** of a plain-weave. The name is probably of Russian origin, the simplest and coarsest type of the cloth being known as 'Russia crash'. The Russian *krashenina* means dyed coarse linen. Crash is made from grey flax or tow yarns, and sometimes from boiled yarns. The terms grey, boiled, bleached, plain, twilled and fancy crash designate qualities. A range of crashes has been woven with and without fancy **borders**, whilst at the beginning of the twentieth century, **cotton** was introduced as **warp**, as well as mixed and **jute** yarns for **weft**. Some versions have the yarns beetled to flatten the fibres thus providing a more lustrous surface. A cotton crash version, in imitation of the linen, was made but was easily distinguishable, as after first washing it lost its linen appearance and did not possess the unevenness of yarns characteristic of linen crash. Printed effects were often applied, especially when the crash was designed for hangings. In 1936, crash was used as a **drapery** fabric, made in natural or coloured finishes from jute or spun **rayon** that could be combined with linen or cotton. It was deemed suitable for hangings, **upholstery**, **pillows** and table **runners** (Denny, 1936, p.19). In the 1950s, crash was sold for **curtains** and fitted chair covers, but unsuitable for loose covers, due to its loose weave (Smithells, 1950).
(c) Crash was also a technical textile term applied to a species of narrow **towels**, from 14 to 20 inches (36 to 51 cm) wide, and now used for towels in a width of *c.*25 inches (*c.*63 cm). After the cloth has passed through all the finishing operations, it is cut up into lengths of about 3 yards (2.7 metres); the two ends are sewn together and it is then ready to be placed over a suspended roller. For this reason, it is often termed 'roller towelling'.
See also **Crash (Russian)**

Crash (Russian) (aka Russia crash)
A particular crash type of textile that was exported from Russia. In 1812, 'Russia crash' was defined as 'a coarse sort of narrow Russia Linen commonly called Crash, and generally used as Towelling' (Smyth, 1812, p.125). Writing in the 1880s, Caulfeild & Saward went further:

> Russia crash was a coarse linen or hempen textile derived from Russia or made of Russian hemp. The widths vary between 16 and 22 inches. It is very durable the threads being rough and coarse in quality. It is sometimes employed as a foundation for Crewel embroidery, and

36. Cretonne design by the Silver Studio, 1925 (Silver Studio Collection, Middlesex University)

> much for jack (roller) towels. It is sold unbleached and is of a greyish-brown colour. (1887, p.439.)

See also **Crash**, **Hemp**, **Linen**, **Osnaburg**.

Crêpe cloth
A fabric made of various types of fibres (especially **worsteds**, **silks** and man-made fibres), with an irregular and crinkly surface. It is obtained by a variety of methods, including hard twisted threads or yarns; S and Z high twist yarns; by embossing processes; by printing with caustic soda; or by weaving with varied tensions. Although best known as a dress fabric, it was also used in furnishings. In the 1709 inventory of Samuel Codrington, there was 'one standing bedstead with japanned Cornish and feet, brown cloth curtains, and vallens with silk gimp fringe lined with stripe crepe, tester head piece and bases of the same' (Walton, 1980, p.407). It was occasionally used in America during the late nineteenth century as an **upholstery** fabric (Adrosko, 1990, p.108). In the mid-twentieth century, it was noted that 'One time confined to dress materials, but recently utilised in certain fabrics for the West End furnishing trade' (French, 1947).
See also **Cedar bark**, **Crape**, **Cretonne**.

Crêpe de Chine
A crinkled-effect fabric created by raw **silk** yarns that were swapped in their twist alternately. This gave a smooth lustrous surface that was soft to handle and draped well. Bendure & Pfieffer (1947, p.623) noted that it was used for **curtains** as well as dressmaking.
See also **Crêpe cloth**.

Crêpe moirette
A furnishing fabric with a hard-spun **cotton warp** and coarse **woollen weft** (*The Mercury Dictionary of Textile Terms*, 1950).
See also **Crêpe cloth**.

Crepine
A net or caul (of gold or silver thread, **silk lace**, etc.) for the hair, formerly worn by ladies. In **upholstery** terms it refers to deep **fringes** with a netted top band or header, used for locations where it would hang vertically without obstruction. It was particularly used for a dais, **baldachin**, or for finishing off bed **drapes**. It was used in the seventeenth century for **trimming** bed hangings. In 1721, Charles King noted that 'Beds, Matrasses, hangings, coverlids, quilts, crespins, fringes, and molets of silk' were for sale (*British Merchant*, II, p.230).
See also **Net**.

Crepoline
Cotton sateen embossed to increase lustre and give a **crêpe cloth** effect (Hunter, 1918, p.357).

Crete
A lightweight muslin-type **curtain** material that is generally heavier than madras muslin and on a plain ground. A drawing room furnished by the London firm, Collinson and Lock, had 'the windows hung with light curtains of Crete muslin printed in light shades of yellow pink' (Edis, 1881, p.211).
See also **Muslin**.

Cretonne
Cretonne was originally a French term for a strong fabric, woven with a **hemp warp** and **linen weft**. The name may derive from either the town of Creton in Normandy or more fancifully from a M. Cretonne of Paris. The name applied in England to an unglazed **printed cotton** or linen cloth. Known in the eighteenth century for **curtains** and linen, it has been particularly popular since the later nineteenth century for loose covers and **upholstery** work. It is now a **cotton** fabric with a thicker warp and a thinner, more loosely spun weft, having a lightly ribbed effect. It is finished in widths from 25 to 54 inches (64 to 137 cm). Printed cretonne often has very bright colours and patterns. The fabric has no lustre (when glazed, it is called **chintz**). Some cretonnes are warp printed in which case, they are usually completely reversible. It is used for bedspreads, chairs, **drapes**, **pillows**, slipcovers and coverings of all kinds.

'New' cretonnes, woven from a mix of hemp, **jute** or linen with cotton, were produced in the 1860s. They were printed with delicate patterns and, to some extent, they superseded chintz. Eastlake noted that 'The new cretonne now used for bed furniture, &c., is a good substitute for chintz, in so far as it will wash, and does not depend for effect upon a high glaze' (1878, p.100). A year later, the American author, Mrs H.W. Beecher, considered that 'The softness of the cloth, the delicacy of the colour … make it one of the most desirable and attractive materials for furnishing a country, or summer home' (Beecher, 1879, p.51). In 1887, it was recorded that cretonne was:

> A French name for a cotton fabric, which has latterly superseded, to a considerable extent, the use of chintz for upholstery work. It is to be had in every colour, both of ground and floral design; it is twilled, but unglazed (or calendered), and is made from 30 inches to a yard wide. (Caulfeild & Saward, 1887, p.95.)

Cretonne was recommended for bedroom furnishings including dressing tables and bed drapery. Particular printed effects could be achieved which had a different print on either side to make the fabric reversible, or using imitation **tapestry** designs printed in pigments that soaked into the soft, but twisted, yarns, thus giving a slightly worn effect. *A Complete Dictionary of Dry Goods* comments that:

> Forty years ago [i.e. 1852] when chintzes went out of fashion an enterprising Philadelphia manufacturer saw the beauty which might lie in printing the white cretonne with delicate patterns and finishing with glaze, and forthwith placed his inspiration upon the market. The fabric came into immediate and permanent popularity. It is used for many household purposes, chiefly however, for curtains, chairs and sofa coverings. (Cole, 1892.)

It went on to say, 'The soft tints and darker shades of Cretonne [as opposed to chintz] are always harmonious, and it is asserted by artists there is no fabric with the exception of brocade which looks so well for upholstery purposes' (ibid.).

Moreland, in his *Practical Decorative Upholstery*, considered four-poster beds: 'Cretonnes seem specially adapted to these old fashioned bedsteads, using ruffled trimming instead of fringe' (1889, pp 252–6).

In the early twentieth century, the name was applied to a strong, printed cotton cloth, stouter than chintz but used for very much the same purposes. It was usually unglazed and could be printed on both sides and even with different patterns. The cretonne often had a woven fancy pattern of some kind, which was modified by the printed design. It was sometimes made with a weft of cotton waste. In America, cretonne continued in popularity into the twentieth century:

> Cretonne a cotton fabric in plain or corded construction. Comes in many different weights and always has a printed pattern in gay colors. Cheerful, bright, easily washed, fades in the sun, resists the dust, comparatively inexpensive. Used for hangings, and (in heavier weights) for upholstery for wicker furniture, summer covers for chairs, and pillow covers. Especially suitable for summer. (Dyer, *c*.1923, p.206.)

Dyer also referred to cretonnes specifically intended for bedspreads:

> In [bed-] rooms that are simply done, cretonne is often used for the spread to introduce an element of color, or to match the hangings of a room. It gives a gay and attractive note, especially suitable for a child's or young girl's room or for summer use, although many people prefer white covers for their beds. A bed-spread may be hemmed or embroidered, or finished with a gimp or braid. Fringe is practically never used any more, because it is not serviceable. (ibid. pp 211–2.)

Similar practices were being undertaken in England. An English commentator writing in 1927 said that:

> Crêpe fabrics are also sometimes printed with decorative designs, and sold as a light and cheap material known as 'cretonne', which is employed extensively as loose coverings for furniture; also antimacassars, covers, curtains, hangings, and for many similar household articles. Cretonnes are usually printed on both sides of the fabric, with a design and colour scheme of a different character on each side, to make them quite reversible. (Nisbet, 1927, p.103.)

Another comment, from 1937, discussed English designs. 'Most cretonnes are printed on fabrics in the plain-weave, but in some widely spaced designs that have considerable masses of ground unoccupied by pattern, figured weaves of the oatmeal or crêpe type are sometimes used' (French, 1937, p.135). By 1955, cretonne referred to a wide range of furnishing fabrics. The weave was usually plain, but other weaves such as twill, hopsack, crêpe weaves and other small dobby effects were used. The weight varied from 4 to 8 ounces per square yard (142 to 284 grams per square metre) and the widths were 32, 36 and 48/50 inches (81, 91 and 122/127 cm). They were usually printed with vat dyes in bright colours, floral effects being particularly popular (Ostick, 1955, p.370).

Linen
In 1955, linen cretonnes were considered ideal for loose covers, woven with combed **tow** flax yarns that used neutral background for bright coloured patterns. Usually a plain-weave, with 6 to 8 ounces per square yard (212 to 284 grams per square metre) (Ostick, 1955, p.370).

Reversible
In 1955, reversible cretonne was particularly advised for unlined curtains. The duplex or push-through printing (limited to fairly open and light textured cloths) method was used (Ostick, 1955, p.370). Also known as **drapery print** (USA).

Warp-printed
Cretonnes woven with a white or plain weft over the printed warp create a softly outlined pattern. Warp-printed cretonnes are reversible, as the pattern shows equally on both sides. The warp is printed before weaving so when woven with a white or neutral weft the printed warp colours are reduced to delicate half tones. Warp-printed cretonnes are called 'shadow cretonnes or shadow tissues'. 'The warp is printed before weaving and when woven with a white or neutral coloured weft the printed warp colours are reduced to delicate half tones.' (Ostick, 1955, p.370.)
See also **Art ticking**, **Bedspread**, **Crêpe cloth**, **Shadow cretonne**.

Crewel and crewelwork
Crewels were originally the two-ply fine **worsted** yarns derived from **warp** ends and used for **embroidery**. Crewelwork now refers to embroidery (often using a stem **stitch**) of fine two-ply worsted **woollen** yarns on twilled **union** fabric, with a **cotton** warp and **linen weft**. It was used in the late sixteenth and seventeenth centuries to decorate hangings, **bed furniture** and **upholstery**.

An inventory dated 1551–60, of Sir Henry Parker of Norwich, included a 'stoole covered with needle work checkered with white, blue and tawney cruell' (Gloag, 1990, p.274). In 1601, Hardwick Hall had 'a carpet of yellow silk and purple cruell', a 'little carpet of cruell checkered red and yellow' and 'eight square cushions of needlework wrought with coloured cruells' (Boynton, 1971, p.25).

English work was made on **fustian** or occasionally **dimity**. Up to the 1750s, **satin**, long and short stem stitch (or crewel stitch), knot and other stitches were used and, in later pieces, so much yarn was employed that the design appeared in low relief. The designs were often drawn (stamped) on **base cloth** ready for the embroidery to be worked. For example, Lady Forbes (1683) left 'a web of green stamped cloth for bed hangings' (Rowe, 1973, p.106).

In the latter half of the nineteenth century, the fashion for crewelwork was revived as an antidote to **Berlin wool-work**. *The Young Ladies' Treasure Book* writes about crewelwork:

> The stitch used in crewel work is very old and very simple; but it is the least mechanical of all stitches used in fancywork, and much discretion in its practice is left to the worker; it is like hatching in chalk and water colour drawing so that the effect be good, it signifies but little what means the artist takes to produce it. This freedom gives a peculiar charm and fascination to working in long-stitch, which indeed has not inaptly been called painting with the needle. (1884, p.752.)

It has been suggested that the demise of crewelwork might have been influenced by the change in composition of jean fustian from a linen/cotton mix to an all cotton cloth that was far less suitable for embroidery work (Schoeser, 2003, p.169).

37. Crewelwork bed hanging, c.1690 (Private Collection)

A sidelight on the furnishing business in America is seen in this claim just post-war that: 'most decorators send to England to have the embroidery done by hand ... it looks well on some of the big club chairs that can be used in rooms where heavier furniture styles set the key' (Taylor, 1951, p.89).

See also **Crash (Russian)**, **Needlework**.

FURTHER READING

Baker, M.L. (1966). *A Handbook of American Crewel Embroidery*, Rutland, Vt.: Chas Tuttle.

Cummings, A.L. (1961). *Bed Hangings, A Treatise on Fabrics and Styles in the Curtaining of Beds 1650–1850*, Boston: SPNEA.

Davis, M.J. (1962). *The Art of Crewel Embroidery*, London: Vista.

Edwards, J. (1975). *Crewel Embroidery in England*, London: Batsford.

Montgomery, F. (1979). 'A set of English crewel work hangings', *Antiques*, 115, 2, February, pp 330–41.

Rowe, A.P. (1973). 'Crewel embroidered bed hangings in Old and New England', *Bulletin*, Museum of Fine Arts, Boston, 71, pp 102–66.

Crex fibre rug

See **Grass: Sedge**, **Matting**, **Rug**.

Cross-barred or checked muslin (aka Scotch check)

See **Muslin: Checked**.

Cross-over curtain

A variant of **glass curtains** whereby the inner edge of each curtain is fitted with a gathered frill. The curtains are hung on rods, one in front of the other, so that the curtains cross each other and can then be looped back in with a tie to make an X-shape.

See also **Priscilla curtain**.

Crumb cloth

A 'cloth' of various materials and sizes for use under a dining table. It was intended to catch crumbs and other debris from the dining table to protect the finer floorcovering underneath. Crumb cloths were made from a variety of fabrics including drugget, **baize**, **linen** or oilcloth. In 1728, the Governor of New York had 'Two old checkered canvas to lay under a table', presumably as crumb cloths (Little, 1975).

By 1854, three textiles were described in the *Lady's House Book* that were particularly suitable for crumb cloths, either 'of drugget, finished round the edge with carpet-binding, of thick green baize, or very strong stout linen' (Miss Leslie, pp 176–7).

In 1884, the London furnishers, Maple and Co, noted that:

> Linen damasks or drills are known under the term crumb cloths. They are made especially for covering carpets, and are largely sold for summer wear. They are also used as dancing carpets. The damasks are made in slate-grey colour and what is known in the trade as grey, which is really a sort of whitey-brown, with a diamond or other pattern'. (*Concerning Carpets*, p.90.)

In the same year (1884), an American publication entitled *Household Conveniences* advocated that 'eating should be done in rooms easily cleaned, with carpets of oilcloth, or similar material, or with bare floors, or with a linen crumb-cloth spread upon the carpet underneath the table' (pp 181–2). Soon after this, Caulfeild & Saward explained that crumb cloths were made from:

> heavy damask made in grey or slate colouring squares and widths the latter varying from 14 to 36 inches. The designs on these cloths are adopted for the purpose of embroidery being worked over in outline with coloured wools, silks, and crewels. For stair coverings, they can be had in grey and slate colour, and also with borders, varying from 18 inches to two yards in width. (1887, p.132.)

Crumb cloths remained important in the first half of the twentieth century. Maple and Co again advertised 'linen druggets or crumb cloths' in 1926. In 1950, *The Mercury Dictionary of Textile Terms* defined crumb cloths as 'Heavy coloured damask made in Ireland of flax yarns. They are both grey and slate and usually hand-embroidered round the pattern edges'. The reference to embroidered edges reflects the Victorian practice.

See also **Art square**, **Drugget**, **Dutch carpet**, **Oilcloth**.

Crush pile

Pile fabrics that have been exposed to heat, moisture, crushing, etc. to flatten parts of the pile in an irregular manner. The result reflects light at different angles.

Cuir-bouilli

A leather-working technique that uses the properties of **leather** which, when wet, can be manipulated into shapes, and, when dry, will retain these new shapes. Immersing the leather in boiling water (hence the

French name *cuir-bouilli*) can speed up the process. Once moulded, the leather was often treated with an oil or wax finish to ensure flexibility and waterproofing for covering furniture chests, trunks and boxes. An early example is recorded in 1337, when the Lord of Naste had '*1 coffre de cuir bouillit*' (Eames, 1971, p.135).

Although cuir-bouilli was widely used during the sixteenth century, it had a renaissance in the 1840s and 1850s – leather was reduced to a pap by shredding and boiling, then pressed into moulds to make embossed work, which was used on mirrored frames and chairs. In the 1851 Great Exhibition, the firm Leake of London exhibited a chair upholstered with embossed cuir-bouilli.

FURTHER READING

Waterer, J. (1948). 'The art of cuir-bouilli', *Country Life*, 5 November, pp 934–5.

Cup

Vase-shaped **finials** holding plumes intended to sit on each corner of a bed **tester**. The idea dates back to the mid-sixteenth century. The Ingatestone inventory of 1600 lists 'four gilt topps for the iiii corners of ye bed tester' (Emmison, 1954, p15). In the 1679 Ham House inventory of the Queen's Bedchamber, there were 'four cups covered with the same of ye curtain and white feathers on the top of them' (Thornton & Tomlin, 1980, p.144). In the inventories of Charles I there was 'One large box for cupps and feathers' (Jervis, 1989, p.296).
See also **Feather**.

Cupboard cloth

Cloths intended to cover the tops of cupboards or dressers had been in use from the Middle Ages. In 1440, John Russell, in his *Booke of Nurture*, noted 'the butler should cover thy cupboard … with the towel of diapery' (Edwards, 1964, p.277). The choice of fabric varied, although **linen** appears to have been a standard. In some cases, luxury prevailed. In the 1535 inventory of the possessions of Katherine of Aragon, there was 'a cupboard cloth of crimson velvet upon velvet bordered with cloth of tissue having III buttons and tassels of red silk and Venice gold, and lined with buckram, cont' in length III yards' (ibid.), whilst a John Smith from Southampton simply had a 'cubborde cloth of callycowe' (Lemire, 2003, p.67). In 1594, the inventory of Gilling Castle listed some 'new cubberede clothes' amongst the linen, whilst the Cockesden inventory showed 'a cupboard cloth of Indian stuff ' (Thornton, 1978, p.382). Cupboard cloths were also made from **Turkey work** and sometimes had **lace** edges that hung down over the side of the shelf.

In the seventeenth century, a cupboard cloth was used to cover at least the top stage and, in many cases, the whole edifice of a cupboard or dresser, especially when 'dressed' with plate. In 1601, Hardwick Hall had 'a cubbord [and] a turkey carpet for it…', as well as a magnificent 'court cupboard inlaide, a carpet for it of cloth of tissue and black wrought velvet with red and white silk fringe, lyned with crimson sarcenet' (Boynton, 1971, p.24).

One hundred years later, in the Dyrham inventory taken in 1703, there are still listed 'diaper sideboard cloths' demonstrating a continuity of use (Thornton, 1978, p.382). Also known as **frieze** cloth.

Curtain

A piece of cloth or similar material that is usually suspended over an opening to allow it to be drawn sideways. The word is derived from the old French *cortine* or *courtine*, itself from the Latin *cortina*, a diminutive of *cortis*, an enclosed space or court. In the Vulgate Bible, cortina is used to refer to the curtains of the tabernacle (Exodus, xxvi). A curtain may serve as a screen or hanging for either use or ornament, e.g. to enclose a bed (the earliest English use); to separate one part of a room from another; to regulate the admission of light at a window; or to prevent a draught at a door or other opening (see **Portière**). Curtains are now used chiefly to cover windows and doors, but for many centuries they surrounded every bed of importance, and sometimes, as in France, the space thus screened off was much larger than the actual bed and was called the 'ruelle'.

Medieval references to curtains show their early use. In 1320, Sir Beues refers to 'a couertine on raile tre, for noman scholde on his bed ise.' (*OED*.) In 1340 there is mention that, 'her beddyng was noble, of cortynes of clene sylk, wyth cler golde hemmez.' (*Sir Gawain & the Green Knight*, line 854.) An early reference to window curtains is from 1380, when Charles V of France had 'a small bedroom of vermilion serge … with a blue cloth curtain to be drawn before the window'. Later, an inventory of Anne of Brittany, drawn up in 1498, lists among other

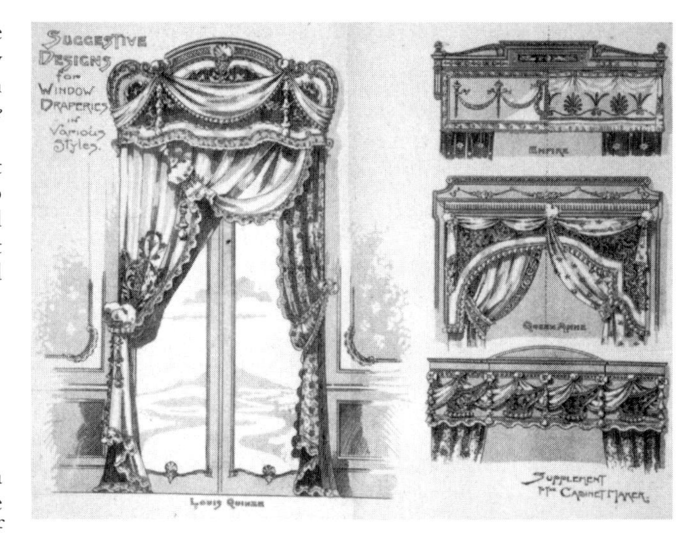

*38. Fashionable window draperies related to particular period styles, 1893 (*Cabinet Maker*)*

39. Arrowsmith patent curtain that applied designs to net, moreen or velvets grounds (The Art Journal Illustrated Catalogue of the Great Exhibition – London 1851)

items 'three crimson damask curtains trimmed with ribbon and rings' (see Braun-Ronsdorf, 1958, p.26).

By the sixteenth century, there is evidence of wider use of curtains for windows. Examples such as Edmund Dudley's inventory of 1509, which lists 'ij courteyns of grene say hanging in the Wynddowys' (Beard, 1997, p.282), and the 1590 Lumley inventory, which shows 21 'Traverses of silk for windows' (Cust, 1918, p.29), give a flavour. Originally, single curtains were used at windows. It seems that it was not until the seventeenth century that they were widely employed in pairs.

The 1600 Ingatestone inventory lists 'three curtaines of grene saye to the wyndowes' in the Garden Chamber with 'three curtain rodds to them' (Thornton, 1978, p.363). While the Hardwick inventory of 1601 shows 'Too curtains of red cloth for the windows' (Boynton, 1971, p.31). Ten years later, the 1611 Hatfield inventory indicates a range of textiles being employed for curtains (and in pairs). In the Great Chamber, there were 'eight window curtains of grene taffata lined with grene bayes, and four curtain rods' (Beard, 1997, p.285).

The range of textiles used was quite wide. The six examples below, from the 1611 inventory of Hatfield House, Hertfordshire, indicate something of this eclectic mix:

> 'Fower longe windowe Clothes of blacke and grene fugeured Satten with blacke and grene fringe'.
> 'Three window Clothes of Arras worke wrought with silke and lyned with sateen abridges'.
> 'One window Curtine of grene taffata lined with grene saye'.
> 'Eight window Curtins of blew Cloth'.
> 'Fowerten shallow Curtins of sackcloth'.
> 'Fower olde curtins of redd cloth'.
> (ibid. pp 286–7.)

By 1654, the Ham House inventories directly refer to 'a pair of deep window curtains of red cloth bordered with gilded leather and the curtain rod' (Thornton & Tomlin, 1980, p.10). In 1673, the French journal, the *Mercure Galant*, noted how curtains 'are now split down the middle instead of being drawn to one side; they are drawn apart to the two sides, this method has been introduced because it is more convenient and also because the curtains look handsomer like this' (III, 1673, p.203). By the mid-seventeenth century, curtains had certainly assumed a decorative importance over utility. **Valances** were added and divided curtains gave symmetry.

From the 1690s onward, the pull-up type was developed. Often called a festoon, these were raised by **lines** running through small rings sewn down the length of the curtain back (see **Festoon**). The other form of pull-up was with a **cord** running through rings sewn diagonally on the back of the curtain so that when drawn up they hung in a draped fashion, either side of the window.

During the eighteenth century, curtains became more important in overall schemes but were still often subordinate to the bed hangings in those rooms. From 1720, divided curtains were less fashionable and the pull-up types became more so. Festoon, **drapery** or reefed and French draw curtains were the main types used and by the 1750s were widespread. From the middle of the century, the draped or festoon curtain became popular in England and America, whilst the festoon was popular on the Continent.

By the last quarter of the eighteenth century, drapery and upholstered effects at windows grew in fashion. Window curtains often formed part of a scheme that included draped **wall hangings**, **swags** and **tails**, divided **pelmets** and so on.

The nineteenth century saw this taste develop further, although divided curtains seem to take over from festoons as the popular choice,

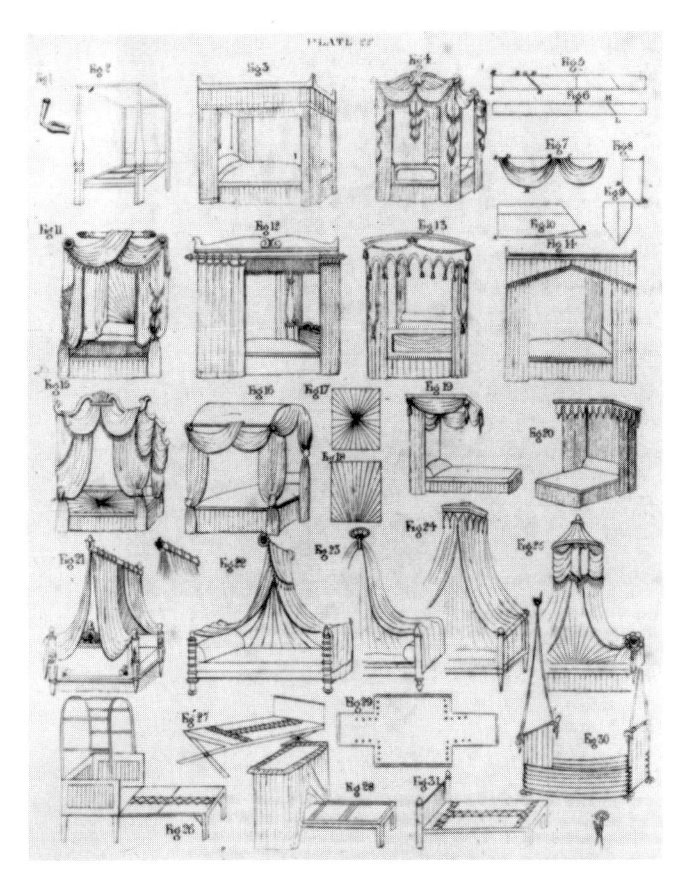

40. Curtain and bedding styles (S. Hale, The Workwoman's Guide, *1840)*

along with continuous drapery. These linked a number of windows, and were often used in conjunction with **blinds** that protected the drapes from the light. Sheraton explained the operation of **French curtains**:

> A cloth contracted or expanded at leisure … by means of rings fastened to the curtain and passing along a rod … [or being] fixed to the lath at times whether for windows or beds, and drawn up by pullies or otherwise tied up with tassels and lines. At present the most approved way of managing window curtains is to make them draw from the centre to each side of the window, by drawing a line which is fixed to a pulley rack, and communicates to the rod fixed to the underside of the window lath with hooks; and that the curtains may overlap each other in the centre, the rod is made in two parts shooting past each about two or three inches. (1803, p.185.)

George Smith, writing about interiors, explained the importance of curtains and drapes:

> The curtains with their draperies are supposed to be made up, either in plain satin or damask, of which there are two kinds, one being composed of silk altogether the other being a mixture of silk and worsted which last, though it may happen to be cheaper than the other, it will when cleansed or dyed, shrink considerably more… Drapery will ever give consequence to an apartment, and although it may for a time be in disuse from the caprice of fashion, it will always be adopted wherever good tastes prevails; economy may render the plain valance necessary, but it never can be introduced with a view of

producing a better effect and withal when the brass rods and large rings etc are added, the savings becomes very doubtful. In almost every design ... there arises a necessity for using a variety of colours, inasmuch as a gay and more lively effect is produced by the contrast but if we refer to a more chaste style of colouring ... it will be found in the use of one colour alone, such tint predominating throughout the whole two other tints may be used, but the three must be of one stock, each varying from the other by a darker or lighter graduation of the same tint. (1826, pp 175–6.)

The desire for curtaining went across the spectrum. In 1844, *An Encyclopaedia of Domestic Economy* suggested that:

the simplest kind of window curtain which may be used in the bedrooms of small houses or cottages consists merely of two pieces of dimity, printed calico muslin or other material of the proper length and width, nailed to the top of the architrave ... and kept back in the day by being looped up on each side by a cord fixed on the sides of the window. (Webster & Parkes, 1844, p.250.)

As with many other aspects of interior design, reformers railed against over-elaborate window dressing. Eastlake complained that curtains 'in heavy and artificial folds such as one sees depicted sometimes at one corner of a theatrical drop-scene ... is one out of many instances, which might be quoted to illustrate the perversion of modern taste in such matters' (1878, p.210). There was also a conscious move away from the idea of the unity of decoration to one where the curtains and other furnishings were a diverse choice of pattern and usage.

The twentieth century has seen a wide range of styles and new techniques develop, along with periodic revivals of interest in historic styles, country house styles, etc.

See also particular curtain types: **Bed -, Café -, Case -, Cottage -, Divided -, Drape, Draw -, Dress -, Glass -, Muslin, Priscilla -, Pull-up -, Rod -, Sheer -, Sun -, Under -, Venetian -.**

FURTHER READING

Agius, P. (1984). *Ackermann's Regency Furniture and Interiors*, Marlborough: Crowood Press.

Brightman, A. (1972). *Window Treatments for Historic Houses 1700–1850*, Washington, DC: National Trust for Historic Preservation.

Dornsnife, S. (1975). 'Design sources for nineteenth century window hangings', *Winterthur Portfolio*, 10, pp 69–99.

Dubois, M.J. (1967). *Curtains and Draperies. A Survey of the Classic Periods*, New York: Viking.

Gibbs, J. (1994). *Curtains and Drapes: History, Design, Inspiration*, London: Cassell.

Glaister, E. (1880). *Needlework*, London: Macmillan, pp 33–60.

Grier, K. (1988). *Culture and Comfort, People, Parlours and Upholstery 1850–1930*, Rochester, NY: Strong Museum.

Jameson, C. (1987). *Pictorial Treasury of Curtains and Drapery Design 1750–1950*, Thirsk: Potterton Books.

Lenoir, G.F. (1890). *Practical and Theoretical Treatise on Decorative Hangings or Guide to Upholstery*, London: Lyon-Claesen.

Moreland, G. (1889). *Practical Decorative Upholstery*, Boston: Lee and Shepherd, reprinted 1979, New York: E.P. Dutton.

Parissien, S. (1992). *Curtains and Blinds*, London: The Georgian Group.

Thornton, P. (1984). *Authentic Décor. The Domestic Interior 1620–1920*, London: Weidenfeld and Nicolson.

Verdellet, J. (1864). *Manuel géométrique du Tapissier*, Paris: Morel et Cie.

Westman, A. (1990). 'English window curtains in the eighteenth century', *The Magazine Antiques*, CXXXVII, 6, June, pp 1406–17.

Winkler, G.C. & Moss, R. (1986). *Victorian Interior Decoration; American Interiors, 1830–1900*, New York: Holt.

Curtain band

Cast or pressed gilt brass **curtain** bands superseded curtain or **cloak pins** from the second quarter of the nineteenth century. These were fixed into sliding sockets mounted on the architrave. They might sit vertically or horizontally and could range from simple cast-brass hooks to complex bouquet designs incorporating glass and brass decoration.

See also **Chain**, **Curtain pin**, **Tieback**.

Curtain lace

A generic name for machine-made, lace-style fabric for window **curtains**, such as Nottingham or **leno gauze**.

See **Lace**.

Curtain paper

A substitute in nineteenth-century American interiors for painted fabric **roller blinds**. Papers were manufactured approximately 35 inches (89 cm) wide and 1½ yards (1.37 metres) long and were intended to fit to roller mechanisms. They could also be made from wallpapers as a home craft. The practice was known since at least 1810.

In 1841, Miss Leslie recommended that **curtain** papers for blinds be 'lined with thick domestic muslin and bound with worsted ferret'. She restricted their use to 'common bedrooms, attics and for kitchens' (1841, pp 190–1), although this was not a universal disavowal. Indeed, in 1853, the British Commissioners' Report on the New York Industrial Exhibition gave them a specific mention:

A peculiar article in paper-hangings is largely manufactured for the Western States. This is about thirty-five inches wide, and is known as 'curtain paper'. An ornament, within a panel, is printed, extending the length of about 1½ yards and those are cut off and used as substitutes for roller blinds, by a large class of people in the West. (Lynn, 1980, p.366.)

In 1858, the *Dictionary of Trade Products*, borrowing from the report mentioned above, defined curtain paper, as 'a peculiar kind of paper-hanging made in the western states of America used as substitutes for roller blinds by a large class of people' (Simmonds, 1858). There were some examples of paper curtains with the pliancy and texture of paper **towelling** that allowed them to drape. In 1874, *The Practical Dictionary of Mechanics* still referred to curtain paper as 'a heavy paper, printed and otherwise ornamented, for window-shades' (Knight, 1877).

See also **Blind**.

Curtain pin

A nineteenth-century device designed for holding back **curtains** from a window. They were described as 'handsome rosettes of wood or metal' or in some cases made of 'Bohemian glass, mounted on rich gilt foliage tulips, lilies and fuchsia being among the favorites, given in different tints of glass to correspond with the curtains – as dead white, pale emerald green etc.' (*Godey's Lady's Book*, 47, August 1853, p.176.)

See also **Cloak pin**, **Curtain band**.

Curtain pole and rod

The simplest method of fixing a **curtain** over a window or door is to use a rod. They appear in early references. For example, in 1470, Rauf Underwood, a wire drawer, was paid 'for iij and a quarter of wire for to hang verdures against the grete window in the Queens old chamber' (Beck, 1882). The 1600 Ingatestone inventory listed the Garden chamber as having 'three curtains of green say to the windows [with] three curtain rods to them' (Thornton, 1968, p.363). The rods might be made into a feature by being gilded, tinned or japanned. Ralph Grynder supplied the Queen in 1637 with 'I large payre of Cortinge rodds being Tynned, with 4 lardg staples' (Beard, 1997, p.289).

Rods were used for bed curtains and protective outer curtains (see **Compass rod**), as well as to support protective curtains for **wall hangings** and pictures. The latter is evidenced in the Ham House Green Closet inventory of 1679, which has 'guilt curtain rods round the room' (Thornton & Tomlin, 1980, p.128).

The development of the French rod system improved the drawing of curtains, but in the later eighteenth century there began a flurry of inventive activity around the topic. In 1777, James Small, an upholsterer of St James's, London, patented a 'window lath for curtains: also for blinds' (Patent no.1164, 1 August). In 1783, William Playfair was granted a patent for 'making curtain rods' (Patent no.1373, 24 May). Various improvements were patented to window **blind** operation in the period 1790 to 1840. In 1849, Robert Harcourt received a patent for 'curtain and other rods' (Patent no.12898, 15 December), while a year later, Francis Papp's patent for 'curtain rods' was granted (Patent no.13390, 7 December). Sheraton's *Cabinet Dictionary* explains the nature of rods in the early nineteenth century and emphasises the French rod:

> The common rod is a piece of straight worked iron, with a hole at each end to slip onto screw hooks made for the purpose. The French window rod is made of brass, about three quarters of an inch diameter, having a pulley at the left end, and two at the right, one of which is fixed in a pin perpendicular to the rod. At present, they frequently make the French rods of satin wood, two to a window, to lap past each other about 3 inches in the centre. These rods have the same pulleys as those made in brass, which are mortised through satin wood rod, and are fixed with wire, and the hanging pulley at the right hand is all of brass and screwed into the rod. To keep the ends of the rod secure they are hooped with brass, let on to the ends, which are filed level with the wood. (1803, pp 297–8.)

Basic nineteenth-century curtain rods were still of iron with flattened ends. These ends were drilled with a hole to slip onto a hook or pin fitted to the head of the window or other appropriate place, including a bed frame. In the case of bed curtains, in place of iron rods or poles, Cassell's suggested 'handsome looking rods or poles of the same wood as the bedstead' (*Cassell's Household Guide*, 1870, vol.1, p.246).

When curtains were not held up by **cotton tape**, they were fixed on thin section **brass rods** that were fitted to brass sockets, which were in turn fitted to the window frame. The anonymous author of *Artistic Homes* suggested that:

> the apparatus used for suspending curtains is frequently of far too cumbrous and heavy a description. Poles and rings stout enough to hold up sail cloth, and occasionally a deep gilt cornice are adjuncts to the curtains quite out of character. Some people even commit the absurdity of actually hanging the curtains on a light iron rod close to the window and placing a great lacquered brass pole with ornamental ends and rings, along the inside of the window, with nothing to support and simply as an ornament. It is well to select the lightest and plainest of poles and rings. (1880, p.36.)

In 1877, Mrs Orrinsmith stated that 'Curtains should draw and withdraw easily. The usual elaborate arrangement of hidden strings and rings is troublesome and needless. It requires violently energetic labour on the part of the upholsterer to fit and keep it fitted and in working order' (1877, p.68).

During the twentieth century, the range of poles and rods increased with the use of new materials, such as aluminium, and new designs of suspension systems, such as railways. Traditional rods and poles continued to be used and were particularly revived from the 1970s onwards. See also **Cornice pole**, **French rod**, **Pulley rod**, **Railway**.

Curtain rail
See **Curtain pole and rod**.

Curtain ring
To facilitate the drawing of **curtains**, rings were used in conjunction with rods. The rings have been made from many differing materials, including iron, horn, brass, gutta-percha and wood. Curtain rings were initially fixed to the top of a curtain, but sometimes loops were sewn through the ring so that the curtain would hang 4 to 6 inches (10 to 15 cm) below the rod.

References to curtain rings occur in the fifteenth century. The London Port books noted the import of 48 lbs (22 kg) of curtain rings, in December 1567 (*London Port Books*, London Record Society, p.211). In 1633, Lord Howard of Naworth bought '100 courtinge ringes for 2s 4d' (Clabburn, 1988, p.133). In 1637, Ralph Grynder sold 'lardg burnish ringes for the cortinges' for the Greenwich home of Queen Henrietta Maria (Beard, 1997, p.289).

Brass (or pewter) rings appear to be an eighteenth-century introduction. They were cast in moulds or cut from a seamed pipe. They were then used in conjunction with bed and window curtains. By the early nineteenth century, hooks were recommended for bed curtains as they were easily removed for cleaning, although rings were often sewn directly to the header of curtains. In January 1829, James and Thomas Deakin received a patent for 'Making curtain rings and bell-pulls from horns and hoofs of animals' (Patent no.5753). Loudon recommended that a **curtain pole** should have 'fourteen rings, generally of brass'. For a common cottage, 'they might be made of iron bronzed and in the lower part of each ring, there is a small eye … in which is inserted the end of a wire hook … that is sewed along the inside of the upper margin of the curtain' (1839, p.338). The issue of noisy rings running on poles was a matter of concern to Victorians:

> One great disadvantage of these wooden rings is that with a slight motion even that caused by a person walking overhead, the [wooden] rings, if close together, rattle, which is an annoyance even to an ordinary sleeper and is wearisome to an invalid. (*Cassell's Household Guide*, 1870, vol.1, p.246.)

India rubber or gutta-percha rings were the response to this demand, as metal rings were not recommended at all. Nevertheless, smaller iron or brass rings were used for smaller rods, whilst turned wooden or hollow section brass rings were used on larger work.

Patented curtain rings with clips or safety pins were developed in the late nineteenth century onward and patented **pleat** makers allowed for attachment of the curtain. Specifically designed red, black or white bone rings for use on **brise-bise** curtains were used in the early twentieth century.
See also **Hook (curtain)**.

Curtain rod
See **Curtain pole and rod**.

Curtain serge

Caulfeild & Saward describe 'curtain serge' as a 'new material produced in several art colours. It is a stout all-wool stuff employed for **portières** and other hangings. It is 54 inches in width and is a handsome-looking fabric' (1887, p.132).

See also **Serge**.

Curtain tape

A woven **tape** with two lines of **cord** embedded in it, so designed that, when pulled, the cords will draw or **ruffle** the cloth to which it has been sewn. These tapes provide a simple method of creating a **heading** for a **curtain**.

In 1922, narrow fabric weavers, Thomas French and Co of Manchester, devised a tape based on the woven pocket machine gun belts; this was called Rufflette tape. The search for ever-better effects in curtain headings went on, and Thomas French was the first company to overcome drooping headings, with the launch of 'Giraffe' tapes, the first deep heading tape, patented by Roger French. Since then there have been many versions and varieties to create different heading effects. In the 1930s, there were a variety of types in addition to the woven pocket type. 'Draw-well' was a patented gathering tape woven with eyelets at intervals for hooks or rings. 'Pleateesi' was a reversible pleating tape, which created regular pleats. 'Hook pocket' heading tape did not pull up but was woven with hook pockets, and was mainly used for heavier fabrics. A plain heading tape resembling webbing was used for **box-pleated** curtains and very heavy **drapery**. Again, it did not pull up and had to have special hooks sewn on to it.

See also **Pleat**.

Curtain wire

L.H. French, in her *Homes and Their Decoration*, noted that 'some persons content themselves with using picture wire which often serves a most excellent purpose [for suspending curtains] for housekeepers cramped for means' (1903, p.281). In the same year:

> An admirable way of fastening a curtain intended to be serviceable as a screen from observation, is to string it top and bottom on copper wires. The annoyance of a blowing curtain is thus done away with. Though this method is hardly suitable for heavy materials such as duck, the idea of securing both ends of a curtain when used on a porch is obviously an advantage. Copper will not rust and streak the curtain as iron will. (W.M. Johnson, 1903. *Home building and furnishing*, New York: Doubleday, Page & Co, p.138.)

Expanding **curtain** wire was widely used for **net** curtains from the early twentieth century. It was later available covered in plastic sheathing. It is a simple and economic solution to fixing up lightweight curtains.

Cushion cloth

There is a reference in the *Tudor Book of Rates* for 1582 to 'cushen cloth of Holland making, per doz' (Willan, 1962).

Cushion

A bag or case made from various materials in which are enclosed fillings, designed to soften hard seats or to be sat upon at floor level. They also serve a decorative purpose. This simple definition belies the enormous range of cushion shapes, styles, fabric types and various fillings that have been employed in their making. Cushions have at various times been used in conjunction with upholstered chairs and sofas, used on the floor, on beds or chairs as bolsters, with stools or side chairs, and as a support or simply as a decorative addition.

Ancient Egyptian examples survive which are made from **linen** covers filled with waterfowl **feathers**. During the medieval period, cushions were important as portable decorative accessories. By the sixteenth century, cushions were made from sheepskin, stuffed with feathers and finally covered with cloth, **tapestry** or embroidered and decorated with passementerie. They were often made from two pieces of cloth sewn round the inner bag. In 1509, the Dudley inventory included 'A cussion of purpull velvett, ij cussions, the one side of crymson damask and the oder side black satin' (Beard, 1997, p.282).

An interesting example of recycling is in the 1588 inventory of Leicester House, where there were '4 square cushions all of black and purples figured satin and made of an old gowne of my ladye's' (Edwards, 1964, p.299). **Cloth of gold**, **satin damask** and **velvet silk** were used as covering for cushions at this time, while applied **embroidery** became a common decorative method for cushions well into the seventeenth century. The techniques included fine tent **stitch**, cross, or Irish stitch, and **stumpwork**.

The inventory of Hardwick Hall, although exceptional, does give an indication of the wide range of materials and techniques used for cushions in the early seventeenth century. In the seventeenth century, the carreaux, or **squab** cushions, were introduced. These were based on **leather**-lined floor cushions, a Moorish tradition introduced via Spain. A porte-carreaux was a cane frame designed to support the squab cushion, which was sometimes tufted, often in a fabric that was 'en suite' with a bed and its hangings. Bordered squab cushions were made for use with cane-seated chairs and were usually fixed with **tasselled cords** to the chair back. Squabs were firmer and made like a **mattress** with boxed sides, whilst the underside of the cushion was often lined or bottomed with an inferior material. In the seventeenth century, references to 'baggs filled with down' are found, although the fillings would be **down** and lamb's **wool** or white **horsehair**/wool mix for the best quality.

During the eighteenth century, Chippendale suggested that a sofa 'when made large ... [should] have a bolster and pillow at each end, and cushions at the back, which may be laid down occasionally and form a mattress' (1762, Plate XXIX). In this period, some squab cushions were supplied with **valances** and loose covers. Sheraton recorded that 'cushions are stuffed with hair in a canvas case and are then quilted or tied down and have loose cases into which they slip' (1803, p.186). Their popularity increased through the century.

In 1821, Maria Edgeworth wrote: 'I am now writing in a delightful armchair-high backed antiquity-modern cushion with moveable side cushions with cushion elbows lying on the lowest of low arms, so that there is just comfortable room to sit down in a place between cushions' ('Letters from England 1813–44', Clabburn, 1988, p.161).

In the twentieth century, the term cushion comprised a wide variety of loose **upholstery**. They refer both to the interiors, such as **latex** cushion or **spring**-filled cushion, as well as to the use or style. Floor cushions, beanbags, scatter cushions, pillow cushions, as well as the traditional models, have supplemented the standard cushion.

Foot

Miss Leslie recommended that 'A large, heavy, square foot-cushion of coarse linen stuffed hard and firmly with hair or with upholsterers' moss, and covered with carpeting, is a very usual and excellent accompaniment to a rocking chair' (*The Lady's House Book*, 1854, p.177).

See also **Bolster**, **Moss**, **Needlework**, **Passementerie**, **Pillow**.

Cuttance
In the twentieth century, cuttance was defined as a 'fine, heavy and stout silk satin of East India, with bright coloured woven stripes and cotton back; used for upholstery' (Harmuth, 1924, p.48).
See **Cuttanee**.

Cuttanee
During the seventeenth century, cuttanee was 'an important Gujarati export cloth of mixed silk and cotton in a satin weave, usually striped and sometimes interspersed with flowers. The name is derived from the Urdu kattani meaning "linen". Cuttance was much in demand for the making of **quilts**, which were popular in England' (Irwin & Schwartz, 1966, p.63). The early use of cuttanee was recorded in 1614: 'Cuttenees, a kind of satten, half cotton half silke' (ibid.). Imports of East Indian cuttanee were prohibited by 1719.
See **Cuttance**, **Silk**.

Cut velvet
See **Velvet**.

Cutwork
An openworked fabric made from **linen** in which sections are cut away. The spaces left are then filled with worked ornament, often in a geometric style. It was a precursor of true **lace** and originated in Italy in the fifteenth century. A **coverpane** using cutwork was described as 'a rich scaffe cutt through with gold, silver, and silke with a curious peece of cutworke to cover the bread and salt wrought with gould and silver' (Mitchell, 1998, p.87).

Cylinder printing
See **Printed textile**.

Dagswain
A rough coarse cloth used for **coverlets** from the fifteenth century. In 1519, it was said that 'My bedde is covered with a daggeswayne and a quylte. Some dagswaynys have longe thrummys [tufts, tassels or fringes] and iaggz [?] on both sides some but on one' (Horman, *Vulgaria*, p.167b). Harrison's *Description of England* records how 'we ourselves have lain full oft upon straw pallets, covered only with a sheet, under coverlets made of dagswain or hopharlots' (1577, p.201). In the *Tudor Book of Rates* for 1582, 'dagswaines the peece' were listed (Willan, 1962, p.21).

Dais
A tuft of cut **woollen** yarn used as a button in **upholstery** and **mattress-making**, particularly intended to stop the tensioned threads from cutting the top cloth.

Damasclene
A 1950s' trade name for an American cloth-type fabric used for **table covers**. It was finished in white, and 'linen **damask**' designs were stamped upon it (*The Mercury Dictionary of Textile Terms*, 1950).

Damas caffart
See **Caffar damask**.

Damas de laine
Damask with **worsted warp** and **weft**, used for **upholstery** in early nineteenth century.

Damas de Naples
Large floral-effect **damask** used for **upholstery**.

Damas des Indes
French **damask** woven from boiled-off **silk warps** and **silk wefts**. It was treated on the back with a gum and passed between heated rollers. It was used for hangings and **drapery** (*The Mercury Dictionary of Textile Terms*, 1950).

Damas économique
A particular **damask** intended for Imperial commissions in early eighteenth-century France. The cloth was specifically designed and woven to save money. This was achieved by weaving yarns of a mix of **cotton** and **silk**, and by avoiding expensive dyestuffs such as cochineal.

Damask
Essentially damask is both a weave and a generic textile name. It usually refers to figured materials woven in a compound weave of **silk** and **wool**, silk and **cotton**, or **worsted**, or cotton only, used for furniture covering, **curtains**, etc. The effect is achieved by a **warp**-faced **satin** weave for the ground, which is reversed for the pattern. In a single damask, the satin weave is tied every fifth **weft**; in a double it is at every eighth weft. It may be woven with elaborate designs and figures, often in a variety of colours, but it may also be self-coloured or white. According to Beck, 'True damasks are wholly of silk, but the term is now applied to any fabric of wool, linen or cotton, woven in the manner of the first damasks' (1882). Damasks are usually divided between multi-coloured patterned fabrics, or 'table' damasks that are self-coloured, relying on the reflection of light upon the woven pattern for effect.

Its name probably comes from Damascus, the city where, allegedly, it was initially manufactured. Later, it became a speciality of Italy, especially of Venice and Genoa. These centres remained the chief European suppliers until the seventeenth century. However, in the sixteenth century other centres of supply began to develop, especially in Norwich and later in Spitalfields (*c.*1570) in London.

Although particularly used for bed hangings, it was also common practice to use damask for **upholstery**. The *Tudor Book of Rates* for 1582 mentions a range of products including:

> Damask and carfar damask the yard
> Crimson or purple in grain the yard
> Damask napkins the dozen
> Damask towelling
> Damask tablecloth 22 yards or by yard
> Damask leather the dozen tawed.
> (Willan, 1962, p.21)

Early references to its use as a furnishing cloth are sporadic. In 1537, the Wardrobe of Katherine of Aragon lists among a range of furnishings 'two curteynes of damaske paned white and purple' (Beard, 1997, p.282).

An inventory of 1609 recorded 'two damask chaires, three low stools of damask and two long quishions of damask' (Cust, 1918, p.41). By the mid-seventeenth century, silk weaving was a flourishing industry in England, and damask was constantly in demand for furnishing. There are numerous references to its use. Nevertheless, damasks of 'foreign' origin were the most esteemed. In 1689, the *London Gazette* listed '3 Pieces of Crimson Missena Damasks, of a large Flower, commonly used for Beds, and Hangings of Rooms' (No.2425/4). *The Merchant's Warehouse Laid Open* pointed to the emphasis on beds in 1696, when damask was defined as being 'from [the] Indies made of silk which [is] commonly used for fine beds' (J.F., 1696). Celia Fiennes confirmed the taste for damask furnishings, often woven from worsted, when she visited Windsor in 1702 and recorded 'damask chairs and window curtains' (1995, p.232) in the large dining room, and in 1710 she noted 'a half tester bedstead hung with crimson and green damask' inside Ashtead Park 'of fine damask made of worsted. It looks pretty and with a gloss like camlett' (1995, p.339). Again, Defoe confirms this change from silk to worsted 'all the bed and hangings are of fine damask made of worsted' (Defoe, 1725, *A New Voyage Round the World* (1840 reprint, p.21). Early references in American inventories also note worsted, linen and silk damask for bed curtains, from 1720s onward.

Postlethwayt defined damask as 'a silk stuff, with a raised pattern, so as that which hath the right side of the damask, is that which hath the flowers raised and satinned. Damasks should be of dressed silk, both in warp and in woof' (1751–7).

41. Design for damask hanging (The Art Journal Illustrated Catalogue of the Great Exhibition – London 1851)

In the eighteenth century, damask was so highly regarded as a furnishing textile that made-up work was often supplied with protective covers. Bimont recognised the reasons for this popularity:

> The material which is most used for all sorts of furniture is damask. It has a brilliance that other sorts of materials do not have ... when it is strong, it has two advantages: the first is that it is better suited for use on seats; the second is that the flowers show up better. (Bimont, 1770, p.209.)

Damask still held an important position in the nineteenth century. George Smith noted that in 'elegant Drawing rooms plain coloured satin or figured damask assumes the first rank, as well as for use as richness' (1808, p.xii–xiii). During the nineteenth century, substitute yarns were used to lower the price of silk damasks. Worsted yarns, silk warps and cotton wefts, and wool and cotton mixes produced the damask effect at a cheaper price. Mixed damasks (linen warps and **jersey** or silk wefts) and worsteds were being especially used in upholstery.

In fact, damask was so popular that Rudolph Ackermann noted the printing of damask effects on cotton cloth in 1809. He wrote that they were 'equal to silk ... [and] if silk becomes objectionable from its expense, we strongly recommend the use of these new patterns. They need only be seen to become approved, and are particularly calculated for candle-light effect' (March, 1809, pp 188–9).

In 1812, Ackermann's *Repository* published patterns of:

> an entirely new article (white cotton damask with a traditional pattern of formalized leaves and flowers) for white beds and other furniture. It has a beautiful effect in the piece and produces a rich appearance when made up. This handsome manufacture will be found desirable to persons who have large establishments to furnish, for it wants no lining (November 1812).

The February 1821 edition of Ackermann's *Repository* stated that the 'loom of our country is now in that state of advanced perfection that damask of the most magnificent kind in point of intensity of colour and richness of pattern are manufactured at prices that permit their free use in well-furnished apartments'.

Satin damask was 'approved' for use in mid-nineteenth century American parlours and for plainer rooms worsted damask and damask laine were recommended. *Cassell's Household Guide* (1870) also recommended woollen damask for window curtains: 'the best material is good woollen damask; it wears well and keeps its colour, and may be after four years are re-dipped and calendered, and will look like new' (Vol.1, p.126). In the late nineteenth century, Cole described two distinct versions:

> Curtain damask of silk and wool or silk and cotton used chiefly for curtains, portières and furniture covering and table damask, which is fine twilled linen fabric, used solely for table linen. It is with a few exceptions ornamented with a pattern that is shown by the opposite reflections of light from its surface, without contrast of colour. (1892)

By the twentieth century, damask was still considered a most suitable furnishing fabric. However, the introduction of new yarns was significant. *The Book of Soft Furnishing* discussed contemporary trends in the fabrics of the later 1930s:

> The most noticeable innovation in damask in modern days [1937–8] is the introduction of rayon. With linen warp and rayon weft, beautiful table-cloths are being made, the lustre of the rayon adding just that

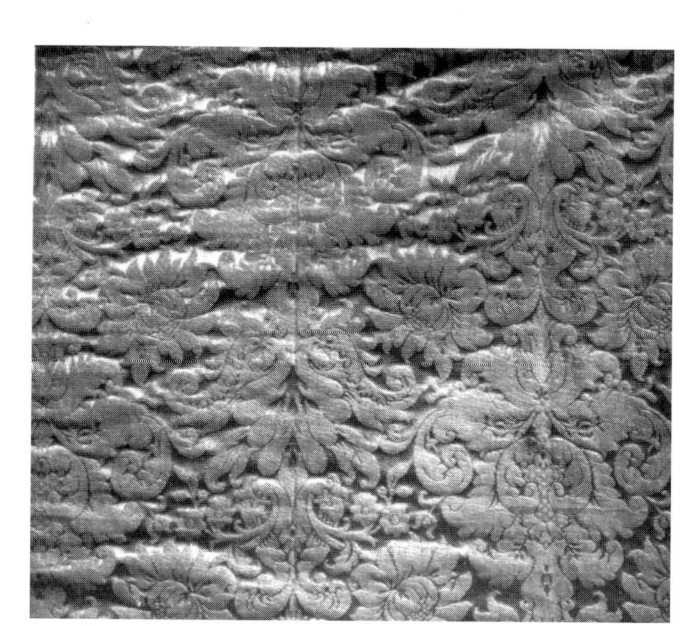

42. *Damask showing distinctive effects*

extra touch of seeming richness that the all-linen cloths lacked. (French, 1937, p.137.)

It then went on to discuss furnishing damasks in particular:

> Another development in damask fabrics is also due to the introduction of rayon, namely, the reproduction of old period designs or new designs of a similar character, for use as hangings and curtains as well as upholstery. Such fabrics can be produced at a much lower price than a similar weight of fabric in silk, and thus have a much wider appeal. Such fabrics may be all rayon, of one kind or of two kinds e.g. viscose and acetate dyed different colours; or half cotton and half rayon. The comparative dullness of the cotton is an admirable foil against the lustre of the rayon, which is depended on to enhance the general attractiveness of the fabric. (ibid.)

In the mid-twentieth century, damasks were also woven with a cotton warp and rayon weft, and have been widely used as a **ticking** on **mattresses** and divans.

Cotton
A cotton textile that is woven in imitation of linen damask. Cotton damask with a linen face has often been used for **table linen** and **tablecloths**.

> Cotton damask is also the name given to a material woven in a range of colours for curtains and other upholstery purposes. It is 54 inches in width, and varies in price; it is most durable, and bears almost endless cleaning. It has however, been much superseded by Cretonne. (Caulfeild & Saward, 1887, p.89.)

Double
The terms double damask and single damask are based on the ground weaves used in the **jacquard** and usually refer to quality distinctions, particularly in table linen. The single damask has a five-end satin **binding** and the double damask has an eight-end satin binding. The term double damask therefore usually implies a much finer setting of the threads. Double damask often has many more picks than ends, thus causing the weft figure to stand out more prominently in the finished cloth.

Linen
A reversible twilled linen fabric figured in the weaving with designs, which show up by opposite reflections of light from the surface; used mainly for table linen. Although well known for table use, linen damask was also employed for **crumb cloth** purposes. Made in a slate colour or grey with a diamond or other pattern, linen damask was also recommended for stair coverings.

From the late fifteenth century, the practice of weaving linen damask began in the Netherlands and it was widely used to make napkins and tablecloths as luxury items of domestic use. In 1624, a will bequeathed 'one suite of damask for his table' (*OED*). Its use as table linen was clearly explained in 1696 by *The Merchant's Warehouse Laid Open*: 'Damask is a very fine sort of Linnen, and is wrought into several sorts of fine Imagery, and Figures it is for few uses except for Table-Linnen' (J.F.).

Over a hundred years later, Sheraton described linen damask as follows:

> Damask is also a kind of wrought linen, made in Flanders and in some parts in England: so-called because of its large flowers, which resemble those of real damask. This kind is chiefly used for table service; but the Syrian damask, for all kinds of dress, and various hangings. (1803, p.191.)

43. *Damask woven in cotton and silk, c.1960 (Private Collection)*

44. Detail of a damask furnishing cloth (E. Ostick, The Draper's Encyclopaedia, *1955)*

In 1884, the London furnishers, Maple and Co, noted that:

> Linen damasks or drills are known under the term crumb cloths. They are made especially for covering carpets, and are large sold for summer wear. They are also used as dancing carpets. The damasks are made in slate-grey colour and what is known in the trade as grey, which is really a sort of whitey-brown, with a diamond or other pattern (*Concerning Carpets*, p.90).

Again, Cole defined linen damask as 'one that is a fine twilled linen fabric, used solely for table linen. It is with a few exceptions ornamented with a pattern that is shown by the opposite reflections of light from its surface, without contrast of colour' (1892).
See also **Linen**, **Rayon**, **Tablecloth**.

FURTHER READING

Bonneville, F. (1994). *The Book of Fine Linen*, Paris: Flammarion.
Burgers, C.A. (1987). 'Some notes on western European table linen from the 16th to the 18th centuries' in Cooke E.S. (ed.), *Upholstery in America and Europe From the Seventeenth Century to World War I*, London and New York: Norton, pp 149–62.
Mitchell, D.M. (1989). 'By your leave my masters; British taste in table linen in the fifteenth and sixteenth centuries', *Textile History*, 20, 1, pp 49–77.
Mitchell, D.M. (2001). 'Table linen in western Europe 1600–1900' in Mertens, W. (ed.), *Transitory Splendour: Interior Textiles in Western Europe 1600–1900*, Antwerp: Hessenhuis Museum, Stadsbestuur, December 2001–March 2002, pp 278–84.
Moore, A.S. (1914). *Linen from Raw Material to the Finished Product*, London: Pitman.
Prinet, M. (1982). *Le Damas de Lin: Histoire du XVIe au XIXe Siècle*, Bern: Fondation Abegg.
Swain, M. (1982). 'The linen supply of a Scottish household 1770–1810', *Textile History*, 13, 1, pp 77–89.
Warden, A. (1864). *The Linen Trade, Ancient and Modern*, London and Dundee, reprinted 1967, London: Frank Cass.

Merino
A damask cloth woven with **merino** wool yarns. George Smith noted that 'there is another material greatly in use, called Merino Damask, much of which is manufactured at Norwich, and makes up very beautifully, not requiring a lining' (1826).

Mixed (half)
A cloth woven from a silk and worsted mix, less expensive than silk. It was used in place of pure silk damask. Chippendale supplied it for Dumfries House, Mersham, and also to William Constable.

Nassau
Probably refers to the design of damask first woven by Passchier Lammertin (1563–1621). He sold two damask napkins to Prince Maurice, Count of Nassau, and then obtained a 12-year patent for the napkin design, which featured the Prince's arms, elaborate floral **borders**, and some text. Lady Kildare referred to 'Nassau damask' in her correspondence (Cornforth & Fowler, 1974, p.133). In 1773, Messrs Hill and Birchill publicised an auction that included 'genteel Cabriole Chairs finished in Nassau Damask' (*Bath Journal*, 29 March 1773).

Silk
Damask woven from silk yarns. Sheraton says of silk damask that 'It is a sort of silken stuff, having some parts raised above the ground, representing flowers or other figures. Damask should be made of dressed silks, both in warp and woof' (1803, p.191). Caulfeild & Saward defined silk damask as 'a material for purposes of upholstery, hangings, curtains, furniture coverings, etc., silk damask is as much employed as ever. It is very thick and rich in appearance and is the costliest of all stuffs for these purposes' (1887, p.449).

Worsted
A damask fabric woven from worsted yarns and widely used for upholstery work. It was fashionable from the late seventeenth century. Celia Fiennes commented upon fine damask made of worsted: 'It looks pretty and with a gloss like camlett' (1995, p.339). A particular mention of a 'yellow worsted damask bed' was made in the accounts of Jean Poictevin in January 1710 (Beard, 1997, p.300).

In the 1760s, the American, Samuel Moffat of Portsmouth, New Haven, decorated his 'Yellow chamber with bed hangings and window curtains of silk and worsted damask' (Cummings, 1961, pp 23–4).

According to Miss Leslie, writing in 1854, silk or worsted damasks were most usual for fashionable American houses. Caulfeild & Saward describe worsted damasks as 'thick cloths, to be had in many varieties of excellence, for the purposes of upholstery. They are produced in all colours, and the widths are suitable for curtains etc' (1887, p.524).
See also **Caffar damask**, **Caffoy**, **Calimanco**, **Damassin**, **Harrateen**, **Imberline**, **Lampas**, **Weave**.

FURTHER READING

Braun-Ronsdorf, M. (1955). 'Damasks', *CIBA Review*, June, 110, pp 3966–94.
Cornforth, J. (1989). 'A Georgian patchwork' in Jackson Stops, G.J., Schochet, L., Orlin, C. & MacDougall, E.B. (eds), *The Fashioning and Functioning of the British Country House*, Washington, DC: National Gallery of Art, pp 155–74.
Rothstein, N. (1990). *Silk Designs of the Eighteenth Century in the*

Collection of the Victoria and Albert Museum, London: Victoria and Albert Museum.
Stroheim & Romann (1969). *Damasks, Their Origin and Ornamentation*, New York: Stroheim and Romann.
Thornton, P. (1965). *Baroque and Rococo Silks*, London: Faber and Faber.
Ysselsteyn, G.T. (1962). *White Figure Linen Damask*, The Hague: Van Goor Zonen.

Damask carpet
A flat-weave single-ply **carpet**, similar in appearance to Venetian carpet. In 1827, Thomas Clarke patented the application of the **jacquard** to improve the manufacture of figured Venetian carpet woven in **warp** twill. He called the product Royal Damask Carpet (Patent no.5501). A variety of Venetian, sometimes named as Damask Venetian, was recommended for stairs and sitting rooms (*The Workwoman's Guide*, Hale, 1840, p.201). In 1866, Tomlinson described a variety of carpet called British or Damask Venetian 'as a kind of mixture of Venetian and Kidderminster' (*Cyclopaedia of Useful Arts*). By 1867, Ure explained in his *Dictionary of Arts and Manufactures* how 'figured Venetian carpets are woven in the two-ply Kidderminster looms'.
See also **Venetian carpet**.

Damask leather
The name damask **leather** refers to a seventeenth- and eighteenth-century method of processing leather by embossing with heat to imitate the patterns of damask material. The treated leather was most often used for protective coverings or cases for furniture, e.g. library tables and sideboard tops. An early reference in the 1582 *Tudor Book of Rates* is to 'Damask leather the dozen tawed' (Willan, 1962, p.22).

John Cobb provided 'candle spots of brown damask leather' to Croome Court in 1769 (Beard, 1993, p.103), and Chippendale supplied damask leather covers for fine furniture, for example. The Diana and Minerva commode at Harewood House had 'a damask leather cover the top', while at Paxton two pier tables had '2 damask leather covers lined and bound with gild leather' (Gilbert, 1978, p.57).

In 1803, Sheraton mentioned damask leather under the heading of **case covers** in his *Cabinet Dictionary*, explaining that they were 'covers for pier tables, made of stamped leather and glazed, lined with flannel to save the varnish of such table tops' (p.33). Siddons, writing in 1830, gave full instructions to show cabinet-makers how to prepare damask leather:

> Produce blocks of wood 2'6" x 2' wide, [then] draw patterns and carve out so it matches sides to sides and end to end. Strain the leather dry on the block with tacks and then with a glass-ball rubber of about four lbs. in weight pass it to and fro over the leather rubbing hard till you produce the pattern perfectly glazed on the leather. (p.185.)

See also **Gilt leather**, **Protective furnishing**, **Scorched leather**.

Damasquette
A damask woven with more than one **weft** to provide extra colour.
See also **Damassin**.

Damassin
A damask-type material woven with metallic wires or yarns that often feature in the floral designs. Rolt describes damassin as 'damask with gold and silver flowers' (1761).

It appears to have been well known in the nineteenth century as, in 1839, Ure defined it (following Rolt) as: 'a kind of damask, with gold and silver flowers, woven in the warp and woof; or occasionally with silk organzine', while in 1842, damassin was defined as 'a species of woven damask with gold and silver flowers' (Brande, 1842). A more complex definition is found published in *The Draper's Dictionary*:

> Damassin, Damasquitte, an ingenious modification of brocade invented by the Venetians in the 17th century, which by being subjected after being woven to great pressure between rollers, caused the metal wires which formed part of the fabric to appear in one unbroken and brilliant plate of gold or silver. (Beck, 1882.)

See also **Brocade**, **Damask**, **Damasquette**.

Darnix
See **Dornix**.

Decca work (aka Decker work)
Decca work was a **cotton** fabric from Dacca, India that was often made with floral motifs. Chippendale supplied 12 yards (11 metres) of 'fine decker work printed calico for chair covers' to Ninian Home at Paxton House in 1774 (Gilbert, 1978, p.274). In 1782, the inventory of Osterley noted that Mr and Mrs Child's bedchamber was fitted with 'Two Decca work Festoon window Curtains lined with green Silk Lathes Silk lines Tassels and Pins compleat' (Westman, 1993, p.80).

Denant
A fine **linen** material that possibly originated from Dinat in Belgium. It was used for a variety of household needs including **bordecloths** and napery. Isabella Wyleby owned '1 bordecloth et unum towel de Denant', in 1415 (Leaf, 1934), and in Henry VI's household there was '*ii pec de naperies Dynand*' (ibid.).

Denim
A **serge**-type cloth called *serge de Nîmes* in France and serge denim or denim in the English corruption. The *OED* gives a reference from 1695 for an early use of serge denim. At the beginning of the eighteenth century, they were both **worsted** cloths, but they gradually changed into an all-**cotton** cloth. It is now a strong 3/1 **warp**-faced twill weave cotton fabric, using a yarn-dyed warp and undyed **weft** yarns and is usually plain coloured. It originally had a dark blue, brown or dark grey warp with a white or grey filling, which gave a stippled effect. This cloth was used mainly for work clothes. It is now woven in bright and pastel colours with stripes as well as plain.

Denim was fashionable in the late nineteenth century for furnishings, and was recommended by commentators. The American decorators, Codman and Wharton, for example, suggested 'willow armchairs with denim cushions' (*The Decoration of Houses*, 1897, p.29). In 1898, *House Beautiful* magazine was recommending coloured denim as a **wall covering** (Vol.3, p.149). In 1903, it was even suggested as a floorcovering (French, 1903, p.143).

The first quarter of the twentieth century again saw denim being recommended by a range of interior decorating pundits. Firstly, Eliza Thompson, the author of an American trade publication, explained the two sorts available and distinguished between ordinary and 'art' denim:

> Denim is a heavy material with a twill weave, dyed in plain colors or with stripes and checks. It is used for men's overalls, jumpers and blouses. Art denim, a finer and better quality, is used for petticoats, furniture coverings, sofa cushions, draperies, and decorative purposes. (1917, p.65.)

Secondly, Mary Northend suggested schemes in her book, *The Art of Home Decoration*, which used denim as the basis of the planning:

> Denim in any one of a dozen shades procurable makes an excellent curtain. It should be scantly made and perhaps bound with satin, velvet or taffeta, or patched with a vivid bird whose plumage colorfully sings even though he cannot. A bright south room utilized as a study may have curtains of warm brown denim bound with exuberant little puffings of burnt orange taffeta, or a narrow strip of King blue satin appliqued with long-and-short stitches of amber yarn. (1921, p.84.)

Thirdly, Elizabeth Dyer noted that denim was particularly appropriate for slipcovers:

> Denim, a heavy, strong cotton fabric used to cover furniture. This comparatively inexpensive material is often put on furniture as a temporary protective covering until the customer decides upon the permanent one which will best match her furnishings. (c.1923, p.203.)

In the next decade, Denny explained that **drapery** denim (as opposed to the clothing version) had a finer and softer finish with the warp and filler either of the same colour or contrasting (1936, p.23). It was later used for upholstering under-seat **cushions** (**platforms**) in mid-twentieth-century American **upholstery** work. Figured denim has also been used for upholstery work. 'Art denim', woven in plain colours or in small figures, was used for upholstery in the 1940s and has periodically been used for draperies and upholstery since.

Devoré

See **Burn-out**.

Dhurrie

A type of **cotton carpet**-like cloth made in India. The name is a corruption of the Hindi *dari*. It is usually made in rectangular forms with **fringed** ends and has been used since the later nineteenth century for sofa covers, **curtains**, floorcoverings and **portières**. In 1880, Eliot James reported that '[Indian] dhurries are made in squares, and the ends often finished off with fringe; the colours are not bright, but appear durable' (*Indian Industries*, ch.IV. p.19).

In 1877, Mrs Orrinsmith, discussing door curtains, suggested that 'Dhurries which are also of cotton, and have richly striped patterns, might avail [as portières] in certain positions' (p.77). The London furnishing retailers, Maple and Co, seemed to concur with this advice and sold striped blue, white, red and green versions of dhurries in the 1880s, recommending them to be arranged on a **felt** floor or used for panels of **screens**, portières, curtains and **wall hangings** (*Concerning Carpets*, 1884, p.56).

A little later, Caulfeild & Saward defined a dhurrie as having:

> a pattern consisting of very broad stripes of equal width in blue and red or two shades of blue running across the cloth and has a deep striped border. It somewhat resembles a repp in its style of manufacture and measures about 1½ yards in width. Used for hangings, curtains and other articles of furniture (1887, p.268).

Dhurries were also used in the United Sates. Discussing the furnishing of the 'den', early in the twentieth century, Alice Kellogg suggested that: 'Over a yellow floorcovering of wool filling some Indian dhurrie rugs in colours repeating the blue of the pottery and the white of the wood-work, with an assertive little touch of red, were laid'. She went on to explain that:

> the imported dhurrie rugs are striking in design and colour, but not lasting. Their designs bear a close resemblance to the Navajos. The Indian dhurrie rugs resemble the Navajo in design and in brilliancy of colour, but their colour effect is too highly keyed for city homes. This make is a favourite on yachts and in camp interiors. (1905, pp 55 and 135.)

By 1955, a dhurrie was described as 'a flat pile-less type [of carpet] woven rather like a thick tweed. It is made at Agra, Lucknow and Delhi, and usually has a striped design' (Ostick, p.342). In recent times, it refers to a carpet woven without **pile** from heavy cotton yarns where patterns are formed by using coloured filling yarns.

FURTHER READING

Ajuja, S. (1999). *Dhurries: Flat Woven Rugs of India*, Woodbridge: Antique Collectors' Club.

Chaldecott, N. (2003). *Dhurries: History, Techniques, Patterns*, London: Thames and Hudson.

Chattopadhyaya, K. (1969). *Carpets and Floorcoverings of India*, Bombay: D.B.Taraporevala Sons and Co..

Cohen, S. (1982). *The Unappreciated Dhurrie*, exh. cat., London: David Black Oriental Carpets.

Francis, M. & Pinner, R. (1982). 'Dhurries, the traditional tapestries of India', *Hali Magazine*, 3, 4, March, pp 239–51.

Diaper

Since the fifteenth century, the name has been applied to a **linen** cloth woven on the damask principle, often with a diamond shape or bird's-eye design and mainly used for **towels** and tablecloths. In earlier times, diaper was a richer and more costly fabric, apparently of **silk**, woven or flowered over the surface with gold thread. The etymology of the word is popularly given as being from 'd'Ipre' (Ypres), a Belgian weaving town, but Rolt (1760) says it was a Venetian invention. Early French references mention '*diaspre que fu fais en Costantinoble*' and '*dyaspre d'Antioch*', and associate it with other fabrics of Byzantine or Levantine origin. Dr Johnson simply defined diaper as 'linen cloth woven in flowers and other figures; the finest species of figured linen after damask' (1756).

Diaper cloth has long been associated with bed furnishings. The 1601 Hardwick Hall inventory listed 'Too quiltes, whereof one lynnen the other diaper' in the bedchamber of Lady Shrewsbury (Boynton, 1971, p.31). Later on, *The Merchant's Warehouse Laid Open* suggested that 'Brown flower designs and white background from Holland [make] extraordinarily pretty for beds or hangings for rooms' (J.F., 1696). Dyrham House in 1710 owned '3 silk diaper window curtains and vallans' (Walton, 1986, p.61). In the inventory of Joseph Brown of Providence, Rhode Island, drawn up in 1786, there was '1 set Diaper bed curtains, old' in a small bedroom (Montgomery, 1984, p.218).

The important role diaper has played in domestic textiles has been generally associated with table furnishings. Early references discuss tablecloths, towels and cupboard cloths. In the 1480 *Wardrobe Accounts of Edward IV* there were 'Tableclothes of dyaper werk ij' (Nicholas, 1830, p.131) and some years later, in 1502, Richard Arnolde's *Chronicle* listed 'A borde cloth of dyaper, a towell of dyaper' (1811, p.244). The *Tudor Book of Rates* for 1582 listed 'diaper tableclothes the peece containing twenty yards/tablecloth the yard/towelling the peece/diaper napkins the dozen' (Willan, 1962, p.22). In 1676, the *London Gazette* advertised 'One Damask and two Diaper Table Cloaths, three dozen of Diaper Napkins' (No.1124/4). The Dutch connection continued into the nineteenth century: 'Diaper Tabling, of the manufacture of the kingdom of the United Netherlands' (J. Smyth, 1812, p.130).

Distinctions between Irish (damask linen), **union** (**cotton** and linen) and Russian (cotton) diaper were apparent by the early eighteenth century. See **Bird's-eye**, **Cupboard cloth**, **Damask: linen**, **Tablecloth**.

Diaphane (aka Diaphance)
White shiny **taffeta** fabrics with a painted or printed design upon them. They were used for window blinds and screens in the mid- to late nineteenth century and were sometimes referred to as diaphance. The term clearly derives from the word diaphanous (permitting light). Originally a French craft process for imitating stained glass, diaphanie was also a home craft undertaken by women to decorate windows or blinds with transfer patterns. In 1865, Alfred Standage published illustrations of window blinds in his *Practical Illustrations of Upholstery Work*, and called them diaphane blinds. In 1869, the French author, Garnier-Audiger, noted that diaphane was a shiny white taffeta suitable for blinds and screens, which could be painted or have designs printed upon it (*Nouveau Manuel Complet du Tapissier…*, 1869).

The material was also employed in the making of homemade decorations. Charles Eastlake condemned such crafts as do-it-yourself diaphanie as being 'utterly opposed to the principles of taste' (1872, p.194). It is not surprising then that *The Dictionary of Needlework* later described it as 'a woven silk stuff, having transparent coloured figures, and for some years past out of use, and scarcely to be procured' (Caulfeild & Saward, 1887, p.153).

Nevertheless, in the work *Artistic Homes*, the anonymous author suggests that for the so-called Gothic style, 'diaphanous curtains with patterns borrowed from old tapestries are best' (1880, p.35). It was obsolete by the 1920s.
See also **Blind: Transparent/Painted**.

Diaphanous tabby
Some sheer fabrics are sometimes classified under this title in the USA. See **Marquisette**, **Ninon**, **Tulle**, **Voile**.

Dimity (Fr. *Basin*)
Dimity is a stout **cotton** fabric, whose name was derived from the Greek meaning 'double thread', by way of the Italian *dimito*. It was woven in a plain-weave with a **warp** or **weft** rib effect, with raised stripes or small fancy figures. The twill band and the plain band form a contrast in the fabric that produces channels in the twill part and a relief effect in the plain. It was usually undyed, though sometimes a pattern was printed on it in colours. In other cases, it was used undyed for beds and bedroom hangings, and occasionally for garments. *The Mercury Dictionary of Textile Terms* noted that 'the term was given by Indian traders to a cotton cloth of the fustian character, and usually figured with raised stripes, giving the appearance of embossing due to thick weft floats' (1950, p.177).

Originally made in Italy as a kind of coarse cotton or **flannel**, it was first produced in England during the seventeenth century; it was later woven as a cotton and **linen** fabric, usually in opaque white or light shades, with a corded and slightly striped effect, achieved by alternating warp and weft faced stripes. According to Birdwood, 'Fustians, dimities and vermilions from cotton wool had been made in London and in Manchester from 1641' (1880, II, p.76).

In 1611, it was defined as 'a kind of coarse linzie-wolzie' (Florio, 1611), while in 1696, the varieties were briefly explained in *The Merchant's Warehouse Laid Open*: 'Dimetty … which is called Pillis Fustian is of great use to put feathers in for pillows'. Another was 'a sort of Calico-Dimetty wove with a wale like a plain Dimetty'. Thirdly, there was 'a finer kind of plain dimity "single wove" [which] was made in two varieties, with and without a nap; the latter kind, which was the finest "is used only for to work beds on"' (p.13). An example of use is the '4 Dimethy window curtains with vallence' in the Damask room at Shardeloes in 1698 (Eland, 1947, p.16).

The 1728 inventory of the shop of James Pilbeam, a mercer of Chiddingly, Sussex, distinguished between 'One peece of white dimmity £0 17s 0d; Fifty four yards and a half of striped dimmity at ls 2d per yard' (www.chiddingly.gov.uk/History/James%20Pilbeam.html).

Echoing Birdwood's observation above, Mrs Delany commented: 'I have been at as great a loss to get you a few yards of true Indian dimity. Your neighbour, Manchester, has brought the manufacture to so great a perfection that it is difficult to know which is the right'. Savary des Bruslons later described dimity in 1760:

> A twilled cloth, which must be manufactured entirely of cotton thread… There are dimities of different qualities and styles; wide, narrow, fine, medium, coarse, plain with a nap on one side; others with small imperceptible stripes without nap; and others with large stripes or bars, also without nap. They were used for underwear, counterpanes and summer bed hangings for the country window curtains etc. and those of India (white without nap) are the most appropriate for curtains. (Cummin, 1940, pp 24–5.)

During the eighteenth century, dimity was used for **curtains**, **bolsters**, **mattresses** and for bed furnishings. The inventory of the business of the Bastards of Blandford included 'one bedstead, feather bed, blankets, bolster, pillows, quilts, Ruggs, dimity wrought curtains' (Legg, 1994, p.29). In 1768, William France made hangings for Lord Mansfield's field bedstead 'out of his own Dimotty … to take off and on with the greatest ease for the sake of washing every curtain and tester' (Macquoid & Edwards, 1924, p.220). Dimity was again referred to by Parson Woodforde who 'had the two best chambers to sleep in and very handsome they were both very fine white dimity furniture very full and fringed', when he stayed at an inn in Norwich (*Diary*, 2 May 1792). Towards the end of the century, Hepplewhite found that 'white dimity, plain or corded, is peculiarly applicable for the [bed] furniture, which with a fringe of gymp head, produces an effect of elegance and neatness truly agreeable' (1794, p.18).

In the early nineteenth century, Abraham Rees, writing in his *Cyclopedia*, explained that dimity was similar to fustian but 'is ornamented in the loom, either with stripes or fanciful figures, and when woven is seldom dyed, but commonly bleached of a pure white'. A version was also mentioned by Rudolph Ackermann who discussed stamped dimity and described it as 'an entirely new article for white beds and other furniture… This handsome manufacture will be found desirable to persons who have large establishments to furnish for, as it wants no lining, and is sold by the piece at a very reasonable price' (*The Repository of Arts etc.*, November 1812, p.304).

Dimity remained popular, as Loudon, echoing William France's comments of 70 years earlier, noted that 'the usual material for hangings of cottage beds, especially for tent beds is dimity which has the advantage of being easily washed, and may thus be always contrived to have a clean appearance' (1839, p.337). In the case of 'modern villas', he added, 'dimity curtains, for both beds and windows, are considered in good taste, especially in the country where they keep long clean' (ibid. p.1080). According to *The Workwoman's Guide*, white dimity was 'sometimes lined with coloured calico with turned up hems, sometimes merely coloured hems, at others finished with white fringe, or frill with white cord and tassels' (Hale, 1840, p.193). The same work suggested that dimity could also be used to make a cover for a press bed.

White dimity maintained its position as a bed furnishing fabric well into the nineteenth century. In Volume 1 of *Cassell's Household Guide*, a range of textiles for **bed furniture** is suggested. These included white dimity with deep white **bullion fringe** or netted **lace**; dimity with a **chintz** or coloured **cambric border**; and chintz lined with a complementary colour or other combinations (1870, pp 241–2). Caulfeild & Saward described dimity and confirmed that:

> It is made both striped and cross-barred, plain and twilled, and is stout in texture, being made of double thread, with the pattern raised. The designs are various, and some are not only embossed, but printed. This fabric is employed for bedroom hangings and furniture… It is made in two widths 27 and 32 inches wide. (1887, p.154.)

Dimity was also used throughout the nineteenth century for slipcovers, particularly in the USA. In the 1880s, it was still used for bedroom hangings and furniture. Eastlake recommended it for bed curtains, especially in an otherwise colourful room. He added that a **braid** or trim in matching colour to paper or **carpets** would create an excellent effect (1878, p.209).

Dimity remained a useful furnishing fabric well into the twentieth century, although modern dimity does not directly resemble the older version, which was always considered 'stout'. Dimity was still particularly associated with bed furniture. In 1936, Denny discussed the 'Bedspread called dimity [which] are like seersucker with puckered stripes. Light in weight [they] wash well [and are] used in hospitals and other institutions. Also called Crinkle spreads.' (p.24.) A workshop manual published in 1947 stated that dimity was 'a strong cotton fabric, popular in country districts and on the Continent for bed hangings and bedroom furnishings. Satin and twill weaves are employed to produce contrasting stripes' (French, 1947). In the same year, dimity was defined as 'a sheer crisp corded fabric woven from cotton or linen yarns with cords running lengthwise to form stripes, or both ways to make checks. Cords may be single, double or triple grouped. Used for curtains, table runners, table scarves, bedspreads, lampshades, etc.' (Bendure & Pfieffer, 1947, p.625).

By 1951, Taylor commented that 'Dimity is one of the standard materials for ruffles on four-post beds. It also makes attractive simple dressing tables and summer spreads' (p.22). Smithells noted that 'its thin sheer crisp texture makes it admirable for small curtains' (1950). Nowadays, dimity is a cotton fabric with **check** or stripe corded effects produced by weaving two or more threads as one.

See also **Bed furniture**, **Bedspread**, **Bombasine**, **Fustian**, **Manchester**.

FURTHER READING

Cummin, H. (1940). 'What was dimity in 1790', *Antiques*, 38, July, pp 23–5, September, 111–12.

Discharge printing
See **Printed textile**.

Divided curtain
A symmetrical pair of curtains divided vertically.
See also **Curtain**.

Doily (aka D'Oyley)
A small ornamental **linen** napkin or mat, later made of paper, etc., used at the dessert serving of a meal. It is also used to decorate a plate beneath sandwiches, cakes, etc. According to one source, the origin is from the name of a mercer whose name was Doily or Doyley: 'the famous Doily is still fresh in every one's Memory, who raised a Fortune by finding out Materials for such Stuffs as might at once be cheap and genteel' (*Spectator*, no.283, 1712, p.18). Mr Doily kept a linen-draper's shop in the Strand, a little west of Catherine Street where he mainly sold dress materials.

Although some confusion exists as to the exact nature of the fabric, it is clear that it soon took on its well-known appellation and use. In 1711, Swift mentions their connection with table napkins: 'After dinner we had coarse Doiley-napkins, fringed at each end, upon the table to drink with' (*Journal to Stella*, 23 April, *OED*). In the 1790 Stow Hall inventory, there is listed '10 hand towels, 2 round ditto, 2 toilet covers and 28 doyleys' (Clabburn, 1988, p.244), and at the end of the century, in 1798, the *Gentleman's Magazine* referred to 'the small table napkin called a D'Oyley' (LXVIII. ii. 755/2).

Although associated with genteel behaviour, one example throws some doubt on this. In 1802, Rogers wrote that 'after dinner [in Paris] she threw about her some ugly and dirty English doyleys, which she also explained as the English fashion, and of which I felt quite ashamed' (Clayden, *Early Life*, 1887, 437, *OED*). Despite this attitude, they were seen as an important part of the nineteenth-century dining ritual. The American commentator, Miss Leslie, described doilies as:

> small napkins intended for wiping the fingers after fruit, and are placed round the table for that purpose. They are very generally of coloured cotton, with a **border**. We think it best to have white ones as they are much nicer, and the stains can be easily removed from them. Doilies are always fringed (1854, p.256).

Caulfeild & Saward suggested it was once a **woollen** stuff with a derivation from *dwaele*, the Dutch for **towel**, rather than the older attribution to a Mr Doily (1887, p.157).

Dome
In furnishing terms, a dome is associated with bed **upholstery**, and usually refers to a particular type of tester top in a domed shape. The upholsterers, France and Bradburn, made a domed bed top for the Earl of Coventry in 1764 for use in Croome Court. This particular dome was a complicated affair:

> [It was] made to take in part with a cove at the bottom in the inside and a Vitruvian scrole all round the top of the cove and a carv'd ornament in the centre of the inside, the outside of the bottom part work'd in fluted shapes to fit over the opening of the ornaments in the cornice, & the bottom part divided from the top by a molding carv'd with a Ovilo round where it is worked hollow in the bottom part below the molding, the whole outside a dome finished with a large centre vauze. (Beard, 1997, p.306.)

Sheraton simply describes a dome as an upholsterers' term for 'a spherical roof'. He goes on to mention a range of shapes and their particular terminology: 'These can be distinguished by the plan as a hip-dome which is raised from a square tester lath; an octagon dome from a tester lath of that shape; a polygonal dome base on a choice of shapes and a spherical dome based on a circle.' (1803, p.198.)

See also **Baldachin**, **Tester**.

Donegal carpet
A hand-knotted **carpet** woven on an upright loom in the Donegal area of Ireland. These carpets use the Ghiordes knot and are finished with a low **pile** height. Developed since 1878, the company has a reputation for making work for specific installations.

Dorcer (aka Dorsor, Dosser or Dorsal)
Originally, a term for the hangings fitted behind or on the backs of

either seats or altars. In some cases, the name refers to the **curtain** of a chair of state. It was probably intended to protect the user from the bare walls and also to emphasise the user's status. The name seems to be ultimately derived from the French *dos*, meaning 'back'. Today, it is still a specific term referring to curtains behind or on the back of an altar.

Early references include the note from *c.*1430–1440 in the *Book of Curtasy* that refers to 'the dosser cortines to hang in halle' (Edwards, 1964, p.306). A similar etiquette book, *c.*1450, suggests that the dorcer 'should be as wide as three widths of cloth of gold, and made just like the canopy of a bed' (ibid.).

The dorcer was often part of a set, along with costerings, bankers and **cushions**. The 1379 *Privy Purse Expenses* of Elizabeth of York lists 'Best dorser, four costers and one banker' (242/2, 1830, *OED*). In the hall of the cleric William Duffield (*d.*1452), the walls were covered in 'blue say halling cloth, which was complemented by a matching dorser thirteen yards long by four yards deep, two costers nine yards long by two and a half yards deep each one; a banker eight yards long and twenty-seven inches deep' (Kightly, 2001, p.3). The size is impressive.

The term generally died out after the fifteenth century when furnishing habits changed.

See also **Banker**, **Costering**, **Dorsour**.

Dornix (Darnix, Dornick or Domeck)

(a) A **linen warp** and **wool weft** fabric that was used for **upholstery**, **curtains** and **table covers** but especially associated with bedcovers. The name probably derives from Doornick, the Dutch name for **Tournai** (Flanders) where it was originally made. Flemish weavers introduced it into England (Norwich) in the fifteenth century, and it remained popular into the seventeenth century. In 1552, it was stated that 'The making of Hats, Dornecks and Coverlets of late begun within the City of Norwich' (1552 Act 5 & 6, Edward VI, *c.*24, *OED*). Dornix is distinguished by its relatively coarse texture and it is likely that it was akin to the Tapisséries de Bergame, the so-called 'poor man's tapestry'. Dornix was woven on large looms, often with repeat patterns in widely varying scales, but when used for upholstery the chosen patterns were comparatively large. As with many textiles, there were varieties. The *Book of Rates* for 1582 lists five varieties of imported dornix: 'dornix with caddas the peece contains fifteen yards/dornix with silk/dornix with wool/ dornix with thred. Dornix called French dornix the ell and the yard' (Willan, 1962, p.23). It was used for **cushions**, bed- and **wall hangings**.

An early reference from 1489 notes 'xij cuschingis and xij seruiotis of dornewick' (*OED*). The 1527 inventory of the goods of Thomas Cromwell includes 'ij olde qwyshyns of whyte and rede dornix, a hangyng of dornyxe' (Public Records Office). In 1601, Hardwick Hall had an embroidered bed with 'a curtain of darnix and a piece of buckerom about the bed to cover it' (Boynton, 1971, p.23). It was also used in the same house for window curtains in unspecified colours.

Hangings of striped dornix and a dornix **table carpet** of 'blue and white birdwork' are found in the Cockesden inventory of 1626 (Thornton, 1978, p.353). In a less fashionable Essex inventory of 1672, there was '1 Livory board and Darnix Cloth, I standing joined bed with Darnix curtains and vallents' (Steer, 1969, p.125).

Dornix was also used in America from early days for hangings and beds. The 1638 disposition of Mistress Glover noted '3 sorts of hangings, one of tapestry and striped hangings, and green darnicke' (Montgomery, 1984, p.215). In 1646, John Fairfield of Wenham, Mass., had 'Green lincye woolsie curtaynes and a darnick vallience' on his bed (Cummings, 1961, p.24). The 1696 dictionary, *New World of Words*, still defined it as 'a kind of stuff used for curtains, carpets and hangings, so called from Dornick' (Phillips).

It was rarely used after the beginning of the eighteenth century, although in the 1851 Great Exhibition there is a reference to 'pattern-weaving the twills and all its varieties … as dimities, dornocks &c' (*Art Journal Illustrated Catalogue of the Great Exhibition*, p.viii).

(b) Dr Johnson defined 'dornick' as 'A variety of linen cloth used in Scotland for the table' (1756). In this sense, it is often spelt 'dornock', and erroneously referred to the town of Dornoch in Scotland. Bailey defines it as 'a sort of stuff of which table linen is made' (1772).

In 1887, Caulfeild & Saward still defined dornick as 'a coarse linen cloth closely resembling diaper, decorated with a pattern of checkers in the weaving. It is made for household purposes, and chiefly for tablecloths' (1887, p.154).

See **Bergamo**, **Dorrock**.

Dorrock

Webster defined dorrock as 'a coarse linen fabric used for common household wear, nearly resembling diaper, and ornamented with squares. It derives its name from the town of Dorrock, in Scotland, where it was manufactured for tablecloths' (Webster & Parkes, 1844, p.951).

Dorsour

According to Caulfeild & Saward, dorsour is 'a species of cloth, made in Scotland, expressly for the wall-hangings of halls or chapels, to supply the place of tapestry' (1887, p.154).

See also **Dorcer**.

Dotted Swiss (aka Swiss muslin)

A **cotton** fabric, usually **voile** or a **lawn** in a plain-weave ground, woven with a swivel, **lappet** or flocked dot decoration. The dots could be placed regularly or irregularly and made in a single colour or multi-coloured. These fabrics were first made on handlooms in Switzerland and some still are. It is made 32 inches (81 cm) wide. The lappet version is the most permanent. When hand-woven with a swivel attachment, the dots are tied in by hand on the back of the cloth. The beauty and benefits of dotted Swiss were extolled by American author, Mary Northend:

> Here I want to say just a word on behalf of dotted Swiss. It seems to me that every year the dots grow more vari-colored, and they are scattered on backgrounds of colors ranging from somber black to orchid and heliotrope. Pale yellow besprinkled with blue dots would charmingly garb the windows of a springlike bedroom with buttercup yellow furniture, green rug and screen of black, blue and gold. Rose on blue would lend itself to the draperies in another room; scarlet dots on a black ground would flirt about the casements of an adorable scarlet, black and white breakfast room. And so on, ad infinitum. That one material alone might curtain your whole home without the slightest hint of monotony creeping in. (1921, p.87.)

Dotted Swiss has been used in the USA for **curtains**, **bedspreads** and dressing table skirts (Bendure & Pfieffer, 1947, p.626).

See also **Muslin: Swiss**

Double cloth

A fabric with two separate sets of **warps** and **wefts** that interchange at particular points so they are connected together. This technique creates a reversible patterned cloth with 'pockets'.

Double cloth carpet

One of the earliest types of machine-made **carpet**: it is made from two sets of **worsted warps** and two sets of **woollen wefts**. Woven on a draw loom, the pattern is found on both sides of the cloth in reversed colours. Double cloth carpet is also a name for 'tapestry-ingrain' carpet, which resembles the more costly three-ply carpets that were produced in England from 1841, but especially developed in the USA after 1850.

Double cloth is often called Kidderminster carpet generically. It should not be confused with face-to-face weaving, which produces two separate cloths from one loom.

See also **Barnard Castle carpet**, **Damask**, **Kendal carpet**, **Kidderminster carpet**, **Scotch carpeting**.

Dowlas

(a) A plain-woven coarse **linen** fabric made for clothing but also used for **sheeting**. The name probably originates from Doulas, a town in Brittany. In the 1582 *Book of Rates*, it is listed as 'Dowlas or lockram the peece' (Willan, 1962). In the 1688 Tredegar inventory, 'Dowels and Kenting' sheets are listed separately from those of **holland** cloth (Thornton, 1978, p.358).

In the 1728 inventory of the shop of James Pilbeam, a mercer of Chiddingly, Sussex, there was listed 'One double dowlass £3 10s od; Fforty ells of dowlass at ls 5d per ell £2 16s 8d; Seventeen peeces of dowlass at £1 2s per peece £18 14s od' (http://www.chiddingly.gov.uk/History/James%20Pilbeam.html). It was superseded by **calico** in the late nineteenth century. In 1882, *The Draper's Dictionary* noted that 'The name is still perpetuated in a strong calico made in imitation of the linen fabric'.

(b) A low-quality **cotton calico** fabric made to imitate true linen.

See also **Lockram**.

Down

The soft feathered undercoating of waterfowl consisting of the light down clusters without any quill shaft. Down has been known since ancient times as a luxurious **cushion** or **mattress** filling. Pure down is the most luxurious but it is often mixed with feathers (feather and down). This has been a favoured cushion filling for loose cushions on **upholstery** to the present time.

Chaucer recorded the use of down for mattress fillings in the mid-fourteenth century in his *Book of the Duchesse:* 'of downe of pure doves white, I will give him a feather bed' (1369/70). In December 1676, Fell noted 'by mo pd for 5 stone of downe to putt in a bedd for sister Lower at 2s 6d p stone' (Fell, 1920, entry for 07/12/1676).

In the early eighteenth century, Queen Anne was supplied by Hamden Reeve with 'a large fine dimity bed tick and bolster covered with white satin and filled with seasoned swans' down containing ninety pounds of down in them' (Heal, 1953, p.149). In 1768, Thomas Pennant wrote that the eider duck 'has remarkably light, elastic, warm qualities, make it [eider down] highly esteemed, as a stuffing for coverlets' (*British Zoology*).

Eiderdown has become a generic name for all types of **quilt**. However, real eider duck down is very exclusive and most quilts etc. have white to grey goose down or half-down fillings.

See also **Feather**, **Rabbit down**.

Drapery print

See **Cretonne**, **Drape and drapery**.

45. Drawing room drapery drawn with French rods (T. Sheraton, The Cabinet Maker and Upholsterer's Drawing Book, *1793)*

Drape and drapery

Drapery is a chiefly North American term (although used elsewhere) to refer to all the window treatments, hangings and the loose fabric furnishings of a room. The term covers swags and tails; French drapery; irregular drapery (where festoons are wider on one side than the other and the festoon appears to be a continuation of the curtain); raised drapery (used to treat a wide space or for uniting a series of windows, by relieving monotonous lines or creating an illusion of height); narrow festoons (for economy or limited space); looped-up drapery (fixed festoon often used in hallways or archways); flat or shaped **valances**; **portières**; **mantel drapes** and scarves.

Drapery as signified by Sheraton was:

> applied to the dressy parts of beds and window curtains, and is suspended to the tester of the former and the lath of the latter. In the art of painting, good drapery is of great consequence, and such it is in upholstery work; as there seems to be no article in that branch more eagerly sought after (1803, p.200).

Drapery was a major feature of early nineteenth-century interiors, and was a speciality of French designers. Although there were a great many individual styles, they generally followed a scheme that had upper drapery or a **pelmet** at the top; floor length curtains fitted behind this; and finally **glass curtains** against the window itself. For more than one window, the use of 'continuous drapery' was a feature of the period.

Mid-nineteenth century design reformers showed disapproval of drapery, especially used in excess. A.W.N. Pugin wrote in his work, *The True Principles of Pointed or Christian Architecture*:

> All the modern plans of suspending enormous folds of stuff over poles, as if for the purpose of sale or of being dried is quite contrary to the use and intentions of curtains and abominable in taste; and the only object that these endless festoons and bunchy tassels can answer is to swell the bills and profits of the upholsterers who are the inventors of these extravagant and ugly draperies, which are not only useless in protecting the chamber from cold, but are depositories of thick layers of dust, and in London, not infrequently become the strongholds of vermin. (1841, p.25)

Despite these critics, in the later nineteenth century draped textiles further reflected the softening of the home and were more than a stylis-

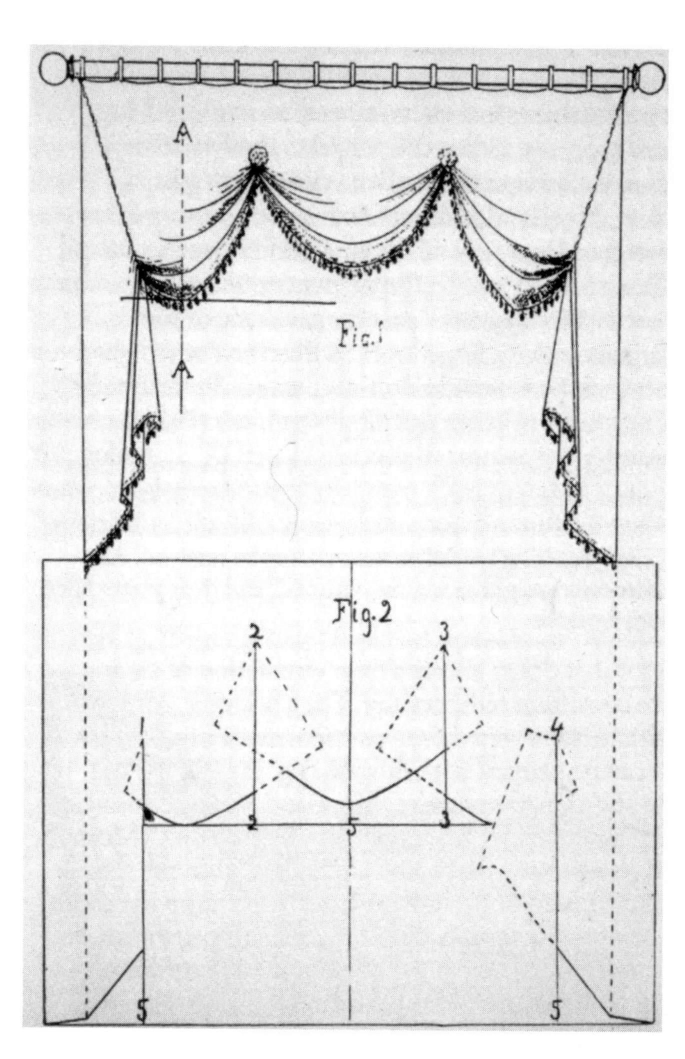

46. Drapery cutting plans (F.A. Moreland, Practical Decorative Upholstery, *1889)*

tic matter. A light-hearted comment from Mrs Haweis, in her *Art of Decoration*, which discussed drapery, explains:

> Draperies about a room always add to the home-like feeling of it. They not only exclude draughts, but they conceal the sharp edges and angles of woodwork, which uncovered always seems unhappy. I like curtains at every window and over every door. I like pretty stuffs, furs, embroideries, and mats, flung loose over couches and pianos. They fall then at every corner and every wrinkle into nice natural folds, so much pleasanter than tightly fitting cases, further tightened by buttons. (1889, p.303.)

The revival of a taste for fully draped schemes was a problem: 'When the French style of drapery came back [into fashion], there were comparatively few men in the trade who could originate or adapt designs' (Jacobs, 1890, p.17). Perhaps not surprisingly, the revival was considerably simpler, with shawls draped over poles allowing an end or both ends to hang down as a swag. Not all welcomed its return to fashion. In 1889, Moreland complained that French drapery had 'recovered its prestige to such an extent that in some cases it descends to actual slovenliness by overcrowding with material; whereas the object should be to decorate and not encumber the spaces' (1889, p.12).

The term drapery has also been used in conjunction with other words to explain usage. The 1895 Montgomery Ward retail catalogue (p.13) listed Drapery Silk, 'suitable for throws, sash curtains, mantel drapes, etc', as well as 'Drapery prints for furniture coverings or draperies', and 'Brass drapery chains for looping back and holding in place curtains, portières, etc'. Reference to curtains as drapes was common. In 1908, the Sears Roebuck catalogue listed 'A strong, well-made Nottingham Lace Curtain, one of the most stylish and attractive drapes one could possibly desire for the parlor window' (p.889).

See also **Bed furniture**, **Cornice**, **Curtain**, **Festoon**, **French drapery**, **Roman drapery**, **Scarf**, **Swag**, **Trail Tenting**, **Toilette**, **Wall covering and hanging**.

Draught work

Closely woven **worsted** used for window hangings in the late sixteenth and early seventeenth centuries. The household of Bess of Hardwick purchased some draught work 'to serve for wyndoe pieces to hang at Chelsey' in the late sixteenth century (Levey, 1998, p.30).

Draw curtain

A general term for **curtains** that may be drawn to the side of an opening. It specifically refers to those that move back and forth on a rod or **track** through a system of **cords** and **pulleys**, which is operated either electrically or by hand.

Draw rod

A rod fitted to the front leading edge of a curtain runner to assist with opening and closing and to avoid handling the edges of the curtain. They may be decorative **cords** or metal rods.

Draw-up curtains

Curtains that pull straight up to the **pelmet** or **cornice** by means of rings and cords attached to the back of the cloth. In 1743, George Bowes purchased, '187¼ yards of the best yellow silk and worstead damask to make hangings for the drawing room: a large draw-up window curtain and cover 12 chairs at 5s 9d per yard' (Medlam, 1990, p.144).

See **Austrian shade**, **Festoon**.

Dress curtain

Narrow **curtains** fixed at the side of an opening. They are used purely for decoration, as they do not have enough width or fullness in them to be drawn across to cover the intervening space.

Dressing table drapery

See **Toilette**.

Drill (aka Drilling)

A coarse twill weave, **cotton** cloth often associated with uniforms and work wear. The name appears to derive from the German *drillich* and Latin *trilix*, meaning 'three threads'. In the later nineteenth century, drill was made up into crumb cloths or dancing **carpets**. Maple and Co's retail catalogue noted 'the drills have a drab ground with coloured bars or stripes. These materials are used as well for covering stair carpets and for this purpose are woven with borders' (Maple and Co, 1884). In 1947, Bendure & Pfieffer recommended drill for **upholstery** and **curtains** and, in 1950, it was suggested for making up fitted chair covers (Smithells, 1950, p.221).

See also **Crumb cloth**.

Drugget

Originally, drugget was a cloth made of all **wool**, or a mix of wool and **silk**, or wool and **linen**, that was used for clothing. It has been suggested that it is a corruption of the French *droguet*, but the latter term refers to eighteenth-century silk cloth with a small pattern repeat. Drugget was later used for furnishing purposes including **curtains** and hangings. An early reference from 1580 to this usage mentions 'One pair of courtingis of b[l]ew & quhytt droggitt' (*OED*).

Eighteenth-century references also show that drugget was still occasionally used for curtains and **linings**. Samuel Shrimpton of Boston, Mass., in 1704 had a suit of drugget curtains in his inventory (Cummings, 1964, p.25). In 1710, the old nursery in Dyrham Park was recorded as having 'three pieces of grey druggett hangings' (Walton, 1986, p.63). In the 1728 inventory of the shop of James Pilbeam, a mercer of Chiddingly, Sussex, there was listed 'One hundred twenty and eight yards of druggett at ls 8d per yard: £10 13s 4d' (http://www.chiddingly.gov.uk/History/James%20Pilbeam.html). It was later defined by Chambers as 'a sort of stuff, very thin, and narrow, usually all wool, and sometimes half wool and half silk having sometimes the whale, but more usually without; and woven on a worsted chain' (*Cyclopedia*, 1751).

The German traveller, Johanna Schopenhauer, noted in the 1790s that 'In many [English] houses warm winter carpets are changed in the summer to cooler coverings, druggets of painted or waxed linen, made especially for the purpose and quite heavy.' (Schopenhauer, 1988.)

During the nineteenth century, its use changed, as did its make-up. It was increasingly utilised for camouflaging unsightly floorboards, or as an **underlay** for **rugs**. In addition, drugget soon became a universal name for any protective cloth. In 1810, Carlton House received '60 yards of Drugget to cover the whole of the West Ante room' and in 1813 'Two yellow drugget carpets planned to room for the additional library and Gothic bedroom' (Gilbert, Lomax & Wells-Cole, 1987, p.108). In 1810, James Newton charged Earl Breadalbane for 'Covering 4 doors with stout green druggett with black velvet round do' (Ellwood, 1995, p.185).

47. Drugget woven from linen in a damask design, c.1900 (National Trust for Scotland)

Decorating the edges or **borders** of drugget with **needlework** seems to have been common practice in the early nineteenth century. In 1808, the Picture Gallery and Library at Temple Newsam sported a 'green serge carpet with a needlework border' and in 1821, the sale catalogue of The Parsonage House at Oldbury, Salop, listed 'Eighteen yards and a quarter drugget stair carpeting with handsome needlework border, new' (Gilbert, Lomax & Wells-Cole, 1987, p.107).

Loudon made various points about flooring and the edge treatment of rooms: 'When a parlour carpet does not cover the whole floor, there are various ways of disposing of the margin between it and the wall. Some recommend oilcloth, other baize, drugget, coarse broadcloth, or brown linen … for our part we prefer painting the boards of the floor' (1839, p.344.)

Loudon went further by saying that:

> Green baize and drugget are often used as substitutes for carpets, and are not only cheap, but in many cases look remarkably well. When a drab drugget is used, a border of black or any dark coloured cloth, laid on about two inches from the margin, has a very good effect' (p.345).

Loudon also suggested that housewives might make druggets from 'remnants of cloth bought from the woollen draper, or tailor, and cut into any kind of geometrical shapes … sewed together, so as to form circles, stars or any other regular figures that may be desired'. When 'arranged with taste, [these would] produce a very handsome and durable carpet, at a very trifling expense' (ibid. p.345). A few years later, druggets were:

> Chiefly employed to lay over another carpet, to preserve it when the room is in daily use, and openly removed for company. Sometimes druggets alone are laid, and when of a handsome brown or marone colour looks exceedingly well. They should be very tightly stretched on the floor, so as not to present a wrinkle to view … (Hale, *The Workwoman's Guide*, 1840, p.202.)

Printed druggets were often referred to in the lists of stock in early to mid-nineteenth century trade cards. American authors, Webster & Parkes, recommended that for economy, homemakers might use drugget. They could have:

> a border only of carpet round the room, and the middle part may be covered with a drugget, painted or not, which will look as if the latter covered the middle of a large carpet; and this has the advantage particularly of bedrooms, that it is easily taken up to be shaken and dusted. (1844, p.256.)

By the mid-nineteenth century, it was a more coarsely woven fabric, in widths of up to four yards (3.6 metres), used as a protective cloth for tables, **carpets** and floors. It sometimes covered the whole carpet and later just areas prone to wear.

In the same way as it was used for floors, drugget was also employed on stairs as a protection. However, American authoress, Miss Leslie, disliked the practice of laying a strip of drugget on stair carpeting as not only was it unsightly but it also seemed that from 'the pains … taken by many persons … one might suppose that a stair-carpet was of all articles of furniture the most costly' (1854, pp 175–9).

Commentators continued to suggest drugget for a range of situations. In 1878, Harriett Spofford recommended drugget as a floorcovering and described it as 'coarsely woven flannel stamped in a brilliant pattern' or **burlap**, painted to imitate a turkey carpet (1878, p.173). By the later nineteenth century, the term had a number of meanings. In 1882, Beck's *Draper's Dictionary* described two sorts of druggett: 'Twilled druggets were known in trade as corded druggets, but when of linen warp and woollen weft, as threaded druggets'. While in 1884, Maple and Co of London sold drugget for covering carpets in two kinds. One was a 'stout worsted fabric of grey or brownish ground with a pattern in bars or stripes, [woven] nine feet wide with little claim to beauty but most durable'. The other was 'similar to baize with red or green ground and small printed pattern about four feet wide'. Stair widths were also available (Maple and Co, 1884). A third version was noted in *The Dictionary of Needlework*, where drugget was described as:

> a coarse cloth made of felt, and printed in various patterns and colours. [It was] not only employed as a carpet and to underlie carpets to preserve them from being cut and worn and to render them softer to the tread, but also employed as a lining for rugs made of skins. (Caulfeild & Saward, 1887, p.166.)

By 1900, drugget referred to glazed linen **damask sheets**, which were laid over carpets to protect them when families were not entertaining. In the 1910 Maple and Co house furnishing catalogue 'Linen Druggets or crumb cloths in every size from 2 yards square up to 8 x 5 yards' were listed.
See also **Carpet cover and protection**, **Crumb cloth**.

Drugget pin
Metal hooks let into the floor that were designed to have **druggets** fastened to them but were intended to allow for easy removal (Spofford, 1878, p.193).

Drugget rug
Drugget rug is a name for a non-pile type of **rug** produced in India from mixes of goat **hair**, **wool**, **cotton** and **jute**. Drugget rugs can have patterns woven into the fabric, either in stripes, in simple repeating diamond designs, or in patterns that are more elaborate. In America, Gustav Stickley and his 'Craftsman-style' circle in the late nineteenth century used versions of drugget rugs in their interiors. By the 1930s, an American definition described the drugget rug as 'heavy coarse durable rug woven in India with cotton warp and filling of jute and camel hair. Usually dark greyish brown with bright designs woven in, suitable for rustic interiors' (Denny, 1936, p.24).
See also **Dhurrie**.

Druid's cloth
An American fabric of loosely twisted **cotton** yarns or cotton mixed with **jute**, in a basket weave. It is akin to monk's cloth, but not so rough in texture. It has been used in the early twentieth century for furniture covers and drapes.
See also **Monk's cloth**, **Weave: Basket**.

Ducape
A plain-woven robust **silk poplin** (i.e. slightly corded) fabric, sometimes watered. It was known since the seventeenth century and used mainly as a dress textile. Its origin is not clear but, in 1678, Phillips described ducape, as 'a certain kind of silk used for women's garments' (*New World of Words*). It is a form of **grosgrain** but is softer in texture. There is a reference to ducape in a bill of 1687 submitted to Thomas Alchorne (Beard, 1997, p.321). Further reference is found in the 1842 *Penny Cyclopaedia*, which noted 'Persian, sarsenet, gros-de-Naples, ducapes, satin and levantines are plain silks, which vary from one another only in texture, quality or softness' (XXII. 12/1).

Duchesse toilet cover
A lady's dressing table cover set that included a long **runner**, a smaller runner and two small mats, often made of **lace** or **macramé** work.
See also **Toilette**.

Duck
A twill woven fabric originally produced with **linen** yarns, which has also been called canvas. The name is an Anglicisation of the Dutch *doek*, meaning 'linen cloth', and dates from the later seventeenth century. It is very closely woven and heavy, and is very durable. It may be unbleached, or finished in white, or dyed, printed or painted. Duck is made in various weights and has been used in furnishings for folding chairs in the later nineteenth century, as well as for slipcovers, **drapes**, sportswear, tents and many industrial uses.

Awning duck
A heavy, closely woven, striped duck material that is usually prepared from dyed yarns but may also be printed or painted. It was intended for exterior use as an **awning** and for summer furniture covers (Bendure & Pfieffer, 1947, p.609).

Russia duck
A version of duck, originally imported from Russia and used for jobs requiring strength. For example, it was specified for use as a floor protector. The Lord Chamberlain's Accounts note a charge in 1781 to a Mr J. Gilroy:

For 11 yds of strong Russia Duck 2s	£1 2s
For making above into a powdering carpet, with lead weights to the corners.	4s 6d

(Walton, 1980, p.279.)

In one case at least, it was used for **upholstery** work. A bill from 1794–5 included 'A cot ... the bottom strained with fine girth webb, cover'd with superfine Russia duck' (ibid. p.56).
See also **Canvas**.

Dundee tapestry
A textile woven from jute fibres, obtaining its name by association with Dundee, once one of the great jute processing cities of the world. In the USA, it appears to refer to a floorcovering: 'This carpet [Dundee tapestry] is made of jute, plain-woven. The patterns, which are electrotyped and printed, are intended to imitate Brussels 36 inch wide.' (Brown & Gates, 1872, p.175.) In England during 1925, the retail furnishers, Maple and Co of London, were offering jute tapestry for sale.
See also **Belgian tapestry**, **Jute**.

Dupion (aka Doupion)
A plain-weave **silk** fabric using yarns spun from raw rough silk taken from double cocoons (i.e. two silk worms that have nested together). The anglicised name reflects this origin: *doppione* being Italian for double. In spinning, the double strand is not separated so the yarn is uneven and irregular with a large diameter in places. The resulting fabric has a very irregular surface and shows many slubs. Imitations may be made from synthetic fibre yarns such as acetate or viscose. Dupion

yarns are also used in the weaving of shantung and pongee.
See also **Shantung**, **Pongee**.

Duplex

A fabric printed on both sides so that the design coincides, giving a completely reversible effect. Also known as a register print.
See also **Cretonne**.

Durance (aka Durant)

Originally, a material made from silk that was imported into England by the late sixteenth century.

By the eighteenth century it referred to a plain-weave, glazed **worsted** variety of **tammy** or everlasting, but finer than either. It was mainly used as a **lining** material, and was often dyed green. Chippendale supplied 'durant' as a **curtain** lining for the Dumfries House furnishing commission (Gilbert, 1978, p.138). In 1796, the furnishings of the Comte D'Artois' apartments in Holyroodhouse included window **blinds** of blue and of green durant (Swain, 1992, p.111).

In the later nineteenth century, durance was recommended as suitable for window blinds (Caulfeild & Saward, 1887, p.167).

In the twentieth century, its definition was different again. It was recorded as a heavy **felt**, woven to imitate **leather**, in a buff colour, with a smooth finish similar to a **billiard cloth**. Durance was also a name given to buff leather, hence the cross-over of name (*The Mercury Dictionary of Textile Terms*, 1950, p.194).
See also **Everlasting**, **Russell**.

FURTHER READING

Cummin, H. (1941). 'Tammies and durants', *Antiques*, 40, September, pp 153–4.

Duree quilt

According to *The Mercury Dictionary of Textile Terms* (1950) this is 'a bed quilt made with large patterns formed by coarse thread on a plain-weave background fabric either bleached or in colours'.
See also **Quilt**.

Dust ruffle

The **valance** of a bedcover that is fitted around the base and hangs to the floor to disguise the divan or bed base.
See **Base**, **Flounce**.

Duster

The traditional yellow household 'duster' that probably based its colour on the chamois **leather** is not, in fact, a true duster. In 1955, a distinction between polishing cloth and dusters was made. Dusters are usually made in:

> a traditional check pattern [red and blue checks on white ground] whereas polishing cloths are plain yellow. Polishing cloths have a raised fleecy nap; dusters generally have a plain unraised surface. Often customers only buy polishing cloths which are used for both dusting and polishing, but this is extravagant and not to be recommended (Ostick, 1955, p.300).

Dutch carpet

A plain-weave fabric with a **warp** face made from **jute** or other yarns with a ribbed surface. It was used as stair **carpeting**, especially in the nineteenth century. Webster suggested that it was like a thick **woollen** cloth, and then describes it as 'very strong and cheap carpeting, lately introduced. It is a yard wide, about three shillings a yard, all wool, and superior in wear to Kidderminster, but only woven yet in stripes and checkers' (Webster & Parkes, 1844).

In February 1856, Alexander Whytock confirmed the status and designs, noting that Dutch carpeting was 'originally a cow hair texture … now made of the lower qualities of wool; it is also a single web, and admits of nothing beyond stripes and chequers in its design' (*Journal of the Society of Arts*, February 1856).

Two years later, the *Dictionary of Trade Products* reported that Dutch carpet was now 'a mixed material of cotton and wool, used for floor-coverings' (Simmonds, 1858). Hair was an ingredient in Chamber's *Cyclopaedia* definition that stated that Dutch carpet was 'a coarser and cheaper version of the Venetian woven entirely of flax or a mixture of coarse wool and cow hair'.

It was still in use at the end of the nineteenth century, although with some reservations. *Cassell's Household Guide* was blunt: 'The hard Dutch carpets wear out directly' (1870, vol.1, 125). *Ward & Lock's Home Book* was more guarded but could still consider that hemp Dutch carpet was the 'cheapest carpet made and was not suitable for sitting rooms but may act as a crumb cloth in these situations' (1880–1). During 1884, retailers, Maple and Co of London, sold Dutch carpet. Their catalogue explained that 'though [it was] not perhaps very pretty', it was exceedingly durable and went on to describe it as having either 'a plain crimson, oak or green and on a mottled ground with bars or stripes of colour'. An all-wool Dutch carpet with **border** was sold especially for stairs in the same colourings. The hemp variety was commended as being particularly suitable for servants' rooms (Maple and Co, 1884).

As late as 1950, *The Mercury Dictionary of Textile Terms* described Dutch carpet and noted that 'Yarns are coloured to form stripes in the warp and black weft is always used. They are printed on floral or geometric designs in colours to blend with the woven stripes'.
See also **Crumb cloth**, **Hemp**, **Venetian carpet**.

Dutch matting

See **Matting: Dutch**.

Duvet

A **quilt** that is stuffed with **down** or other fibre, and is often sewn in channels to prevent movement of the filling. The name is derived from the French word for down. It is probably a duvet or similar that Samuel Pepys described when he recorded how he 'lay the softest I ever did in my life with a down bed after the Danish manner, upon me' (*The Diary*, 9 September 1665). Duvets were certainly known in the eighteenth century. Dr Johnson noted that in 1758 'there are now to be sold some duvets for bed coverings' (*Idler*, 1758, no.40).

The 1853 catalogue of the bedding business of Heal in London listed duvets and described them carefully: 'loose cases filled with down, similar to those used on the Continent, they are mostly used to lay across the foot of the bed, but as they have a larger proportion of down … than quilts they are applicable wherever extreme warmth is required' (Heal Ltd, 1972, p.5). Duvets survived or were revived in the later twentieth century, when a more casual attitude to bed-making was encouraged by the production of attractive duvet covers that allowed a bed to be made by covering the duvet, and then loosely throwing the complete set over the whole bed. Also known as a Continental quilt.

Dye

Fibres or yarns can be used in natural colours or be given colour by staining or dyeing with substances/pigments called dyes. Dyes may be

categorised as vegetable, mineral or synthetic. Dye categories include Acid (usually used on proteins and synthetics); Azioic (usually on celluloses); Basic/Cationic (usually on **acrylics**); Direct (usually on celluloses and ester celluloses); Disperse (usually on synthetics, especially **polyester**); Mordant/Pre-metalised (usually on proteins); Reactive (a chemical link used on most fibre types); Sulphur (usually on celluloses or ester celluloses); Vat (usually on cellulose); Optical brighteners (for most fibres; includes 'blueing' and fluorescent brighteners).
See also **Printed textile**.

FURTHER READING

Adrosko, R. (1968). *Natural Dyes in the United States*, Washington, DC: Smithsonian Institution Press.
Fairile, S. (1965). 'Dyestuffs in the eighteenth century', *Economic History Review*, 2nd series, XVII, pp.488–510.
Partridge, W. (1823). *A Practical Treatise on Dying* [sic] *of Woollen, Cotton, and Skein Silk*, New York; reissued and edited, with technical notes by J. de L. Mann & K.G. Ponting, Pasold Research Fund, Wilts., 1973.
Schweppe, H. (1979). 'Identification of dyes on old textiles' in *Journal of American Institute for Conservation*, 19, 1, pp 14–23.

Edge roll
This is a roll of fabric stuffed with a filling and then fixed to the edges of upholstered seats to give shape and durability.

Edge treatment
The completion of edges in **upholstery** work, both internally and externally, is an important part of the process. Edges give definition to the required shape or outline of an upholstered seat.

The earliest method seems to have been a simple braid or piping that defined the shape. By the early eighteenth century, squared edges were being fabricated, echoing the square frames of easy chairs. Fixing **webbing** along the side and front edges so that it stood proud of the frame formed these built-up edges. The **hair stuffing** was pulled to the side by **stitches** sewn through the side web so as to build up a firm edge.

By the later eighteenth century, the so-called French edge was introduced. This was made from a rolled pad of hair or **grass** that was inserted into an overlapping flap of **linen** extending from the first covering. This sewn-in edge 'former' gave a crisp shape to the neo-classical styles that were fashionable at the time.
See also **Bible front**, **Passementerie**, **Piping**, **Rolled edge**, **Trimming**.

Egyptian cloth
An open plain-weave cotton **cloth** made with long staple fibres.

Eiderdown
A cloth bag filled with the down of the eider duck. The true eider down has no quill so it is lighter and softer than **feather**. It is often considered the best quality filling for **quilts**. In 1768, the eider duck down was praised as it had 'remarkably light, elastic, warm qualities, [which] make it highly esteemed, as a stuffing for coverlets' (Pennant, *British Zoology*, p.243). By the mid-twentieth century, 'eider duck down' was hardly available in commercial quantities. Eiderdown is now a generic name for any bed quilt.
See also **Comfort**, **Down**, **Duvet**.

Ell
An ancient term defining cloth width:

2¼ inches = 1 nail
4 nails = 1 Quarter (23 cm)
3 Quarters = 1 Flemish ell (68.6 cm)
4 Quarters = 1 yard (92 cm)
5 Quarters = 1 English ell (114.3 cm)
6 Quarters = 1 French ell (138 cm)

The Scottish ell was 37 inches (94 cm). Harrison wrote that we measure 'by the yard, our woollen cloth, tapestry, arras, silks and laces, but our linen by the elne' (1577, p.455).

Embroidered carpets
See **Needlework carpet**.

Embroidered coverlet/quilt
As early as 1516, the traveller, Duaret Barbosa, wrote of India that 'they also make here very beautiful quilts and testers of beds finely worked and painted' (Clabburn, 1976, p.219). Gujarat embroidered **quilts** and **coverlets** were certainly imported by 1614 into England. They were often either a **calico** or **satin** base cloth embroidered with **silks**. Bengal (northeast India) embroidered work included quilted **bedspreads** worked with pictorial designs in yellow silk and also embroidered **muslin** piece goods. Bengal quilts were on sale in London by 1618: 'then was put on sale a Bengalla quilt of 3¼ yards along and 3 yards broad to be paid for in ready money, embroidered all over with pictures of men and crafts in yellow silk, Mr. Henry Garway bidding £20 for it' (Irwin & Schwartz, 1966, p.48).

The trade declined and, by 1724, Alexander Hamilton wrote that 'They [the people of Cambay] embroider the best of any people in India, and perhaps the world. Their fine quilts were formerly carried to Europe' (ibid. 1966, p.190).
See also **Embroidery**.

FURTHER READING

Irwin, J.C. & Hall, M. (1973). *Indian Embroideries*, Ahmedabad: Calico Museum of Textiles.

48. Embroidery chair, folding example, 1880s (Die Modenwelt)

Embroidery
The four basic techniques of embroidery are laid or couched work, raised work, flat running and filling **stitches**, and counted thread work.
See also **Appliqué**, **Art embroidery**, **Beadwork**, **Berlin wool-work**, **Black work**, **Canvas work**, **Couching**, **Crewel and crewelwork**, **Cut work**, **Fire screen**, **Fustian**, **Knotted work**, **Lace**, **Mantel drapery**, **Needlework**, **Patchwork**, **Petit-point**, **Quilting**, **Stumpwork**, **Tapestry embroidery work**.

FURTHER READING

Gostelow, M. (1979). *Art of Embroidery*, London: Weidenfeld and Nicolson.

English carpet
A later eighteenth-century American name for ingrain or Kidderminster **pile**-less, two-ply carpet.
See also **Ingrain carpet**, **Kidderminster carpet**.

Engraved roller
See **Printed textile**.

Entrefenêtre
Narrow **tapestries** especially designed to be installed in the blank space between two windows or doors.

Epingle
A name for a short, uncut looped **pile** fabric. The name has been used to refer to **moquettes** but without the associations of railway carriages.

Eponge
Eponge is French for sponge. In 1947, Bendure & Pfieffer described éponge as 'a loosely woven spongy fabric woven with soft ply yarns (cotton, wool or silk,), unevenly twisted. It has an irregular surface due to the distinctive knot-like irregularities in the ratiné yarns used in the filling [weft]' (p.628).
See **Ratiné**.

Everlasting
A **satin** weave (**worsted**) textile, often figured or **brocaded**, that was mainly used for coat linings and shoe tops but is now occasionally found in **upholstery** work. It has been used since the mid-seventeenth century. As 'lasting', it was used in the USA in the later nineteenth century as a substitute for **haircloth**.
See also **Durance**, **Lasting.**

Excelsior
A trade name for **upholstery** filllings used in the later nineteenth century, especially in the USA. It is composed of shredded timber shavings and has also been called 'pine state hair' or 'wood wool'. In the later nineteenth century, it was noted that the 'round bolster is now generally made of pasteboards or hoop or ticking goods stuffed with excelsior' (Moreland, 1889, p.264).

Exeter carpet
Hand-knotted Exeter **carpets** were made from 1756 by Swiss weaver, Claude Passavant, who ran the business for six years and produced some fine carpets. Extant examples include the inscription EXON and the date. In 1758, Passavant was joint winner of the Society of Arts' premium 'for the best carpet in one breadth after the manner of Turky carpets'. He shared this reward with Thomas Whitty of Axminster. Closure of the factory followed bankruptcy in 1761.
See also **Fulham carpet**.

FURTHER READING

Sherrill, S.B. (1996). *Carpets and Rugs of Europe and America*, New York: Abbeville, pp 152–71.

Eyelet
An American fabric made from white **cotton**, embroidered with open designs and used for lightweight **curtains** and unlined shades.

Faille
An **upholstery** cloth made from un-degummed **silk warp** and strong two-ply **cotton weft** yarns, in a plain-weave but showing a ribbed effect along the weft. It was introduced in the mid-nineteenth century.

According to Denny, it was made from a **rayon** warp and a cotton weft and used for **curtains** and slipcovers, either plain or printed (Denny, 1942, p.36). In 1951, Taylor described it as a 'horizontal rib fabric usually only applied to silk or synthetic yarns. Used for curtains and upholstery and dressing room requisites.' (Taylor, 1951.)

Fastening tape
See **Curtain tape**.

Feather
The plumage from a wide variety of birds has been used for practical and decorative purposes in furnishings since early times. The range used includes chicken, swan, goose, eider (Hudson's Bay feathers), egret, heron and ostrich feathers. Feathers are of three types: contour feathers that are the outer covering with stiff shafts and vanes; semi-plumes, such as ostrich, which have floppy vanes; and down feathers with no shaft and soft barbs in place of vanes. The feathers are further distinguished between live, i.e. plucked from a living bird, and those removed from dead birds. The former, being considerably more elastic, are the most sought after. A difference is also made between scalded feathers and dry pulled feathers. Scalded feathers refer to soiled feathers that had to be washed and cleaned; dry pulled feathers were simply plucked and dried in an oven. The qualities that should be used for **upholstery** include duck and goose feathers – particularly goose as they have a natural curl, because the central shaft is slightly curved instead of straight. Poultry feathers have a straight central shaft, which must be artificially curled to make them resilient. Chopped feathers are the cheapest of all.

High-quality feathers were much sought after and it is not surprising to find dishonest practices associated with their supply. The need to scrutinise the trade was recognised early on. In 1495, an 'Act against Upholsterers' was passed that remarked upon 'corrupte stuffes that is to say of scalded feders and drie pulled feather together and of flokks and feders together, which is contagious for man's body to lye on' (Houston, 1993, p.9). However, when used properly, feathers made luxurious beds. In 1539, Giles Corrozet honoured the

> Delicate soft and luxurious bed,
> Bed of tenderest down,
> Bed of good and fine feathers…
> (Jervis, 1989, p.20.)

Most of the sixteenth and seventeenth-century feathers imported into England came from Antwerp, although other centres did supply them, e.g. Bordeaux, Burgos and Denmark. For example, in 1637, Ralph Grynder supplied Queen Henrietta Maria with '46 pounds of fine Burgis feathers to fill the seat and winges [of a chair]' (Beard, 1997, p.289). The use of feather and down for upholstery fillings (as well as for bedding) was common practice by the latter part of the seventeenth century. In a further attempt at quality control in 1679, the London Upholders' Company maintained that no upholsterer should:

> Mingle … any flocks and feathers together to put on sale or shall put to sale … any corrupt or stinking feathers in any bedd bolster pillow cushion or in any cowches squabbs chairs or stooles and that every person using the said art or mystery shall cause his or her feathers to be cleansed of dust and quill before the same be put on sale… (Houston, 1993, p.57.)

Feathers remained important to the eighteenth-century upholsterer. For example, Chippendale maintained two feather rooms at his London premises, and another upholsterer, Paul Sanders, had listed in his inventory 46 lb of seasoned down, 480 lb of feathers, feather bags, as well as beating frames and poles for feathers (Beard, 1997, p.13). The beating frames and poles indicate that proper handling, i.e. drying and cleaning, was an important part of good practice then, as now. Feathers were 'dressed' by airing, or driven, by being beaten in a bag to loosen the dirt. John Fawkes, an upholsterer of Guildford (1754–7), had for sale: 'a large quantity of goose, duck and hen featherbeds, ready made and filled with the best dried feathers to lay on immediately … and feathers of every sort by the pound' (*DEFM*, p.293).

The quality of feathers varied greatly. Chippendale supplied the state bed at Harewood with 'finest and best-seasoned Hudson's Bay feathers' whereas Dantzig feathers were half the price (Gilbert, 1978, p.54). A little later, Sheraton commented on 'dress' feathers that 'make a considerable article of commerce particularly those of the ostrich, heron, swan, peacock, goose &c. for plumes, ornaments for the head and for beds'. He goes on to note (rather matter-of-factly) that in some parts of Britain geese are plucked five times in a year, 'which in the cold season sometimes proves fatal to them' (1803, p.207). In a reiteration of the advice given 200 years earlier, Sheraton had to warn against a clearly continuing problem of quality control: 'Several very imposing arts are practised by brokers and dealers in feathers which the strangers and fair traders ought to be aware of.' (ibid. p.208.)

The international nature of the feather trade continued into the nineteenth century with eider down still being imported from Denmark, using Hudson's Bay suppliers, while swans' down was still being imported from Dantzig. By the end of the century, British feather imports concentrated on German and Russian sources, along with a continuing home supply.

During the nineteenth century (the 1830s onward), the method of cleaning and purifying was often by steaming. In the twentieth century, feathers remained as upholstery filling as well as being used for **quilts**, eiderdowns and **duvets**. Feather beds were still being produced in the mid-century. In 1955, it was noted that 'there is a small but constant demand for feather filled mattresses' (Sheridan, p.128).

See also **Aigrette**, **Cup**, **Down**, **Eiderdown**, **Feather work**.

Feather bed

See **Mattress**.

Feather work

Apart from feathers for utilitarian purposes such as **cushion** and bed **stuffings**, there was a specific trade in exotic feathers imported into Europe. The trade of the plumassier specialised in this work for costumes, but also for decorative screens, panels and occasionally furniture and furnishings. Amongst the most well known were ostrich and egret feathers. The use of feathers for decorative work has been part of furnishing for well over 300 years. In rare cases, feathers were used to make complete ensembles comprising **testers**, bedcovers, and matching **upholstery** and wall decoration.

The first significant use was for the crestings of beds. These feathers were often mounted in vases on the corners of bed testers. Randle Holme recorded their use: 'The tester adorned with plumbes according to the colours of the bed' (1688, Book III, xiv, p.16). The decorations were often made from egret (Fr. *aigrette*) feathers but, more usually, they were made from white, occasionally coloured, ostrich feathers. In 1622, Drayton described 'the rich and sumptuous Beds, with Tester-covering plumes' (Poly-olb. xxvi. 85, *OED*). The accounts of the Royal Palace for both Charles II and William III show payments to Richard Chase and Robert Croft, feather dressers, for 'scouring a set of bed plumes for his majesty' (Edwards, 1964, p.37).

By the nineteenth century, feather work was used to describe a decorative technique often employed by amateurs, which consisted of covering **buckram** or other foundation, with a design made from birds' feathers and sewn onto the base. Used for **valances**, picture frames, chairs, brackets, **fire screens** and clothing, the range of feathers was limited only by the imagination.

See also **Feather**.

FURTHER READING

Cassidy-Geiger, M. (1999). 'The Federzimmer from the Japanisches Palais in Dresden', *Furniture History*, 35, pp 87–111.

Felt

A fabric produced by the matting or felting together of fibrous materials such as **wools**, **hairs** and fur. There are two separate types of felts: the first is a woven web that is later felted, the second is the true felt that is matted from the beginning. The lightweight 'woven felts' may be made up as a single cloth only, but for the heavier types, two or more cloths are woven together to become one finished heavyweight cloth. In true felt, the greatest disadvantage of wool, that it shrinks, is exploited in the processing so that individual fibres become interlocked under the influence of warmth and pressure. Various felts have been used for furnishing requirements, including **table covers**, linings, floorcoverings, **upholstery fillings**, **drapes** and accessories.

The London furnishers, Maple and Co, recommended plain felt for covering and protecting stair carpeting in 1884. Woollen felts have also been used for upholstery and **curtains**. During World War II, they enjoyed some popularity, as they were amongst the few unrationed textiles. They subsequently fell from favour.

See also **Felt carpet**, **Underfelt**.

FURTHER READING

Anon. (1958). 'Felt', *CIBA Review*, 129, pp 2–25.

Felt-base

Hard surface floorcoverings introduced *c.*1910, in competition with linoleum. The American United Roofing and Manufacturing Co, who manufactured 'Congo' asphalt roofing tiles, developed a range of asphalt and felt-based enamel printed **rugs**. Congoleum Co Inc of Philadelphia developed this new version of **floorcloth** or linoleum, known as Congoleum, or felt-base in the USA. The name derives from the Congo region of Africa, which was the source of the asphalt used in manufacture. The name Congoleum was a trade name, but other manufacturers made this form of flooring.

This material was made from paper or rag felt which was saturated with bituminous composition to harden and waterproof it. When dry, the surface was coated with a seal coat and then a wearing coat using a linseed oil composition. When this had set, rotary machines printed it with designs similar to the higher-priced linoleum. The finished merchandise was produced in yardage of up to 9-feet (2.7 metres)-wide, or the well-known, so-called 'carpet squares'. Under the trade name of Congoleum, they soon found a ready market for an imitation **carpet** that was both stainproof and waterproof. Felt-base was made in competition with linoleum but tended to have a different market as it was cheaper, less durable, and was more often sold as a 'rug' rather than a completely fitted floor. Competition between linoleum and the felt-base market grew and, in 1916, the Armstrong Cork Co of Lancaster, Pennsylvania, marketed a felt-based product called Fiberlin. They dropped the range in 1920, only to re-enter the market in 1925 with another felt-base product sold under the trade name of 'Quaker rugs'. No doubt, they considered that the name made a connection with 'old-fashioned' ideas of homeliness, thrift and value, as opposed to the more exotic-sounding Congoleum.
See also **Felt-base linoleum**, **Linoleum**.

FURTHER READING
Mehler, W.A. (1987). *Let the Buyer Have Faith: The Story of Armstrong*, Lancaster, PA: Armstrong World Industries.

Felt-base linoleum
A development by American company, Armstrong, was the introduction of Linoflor, a product that used both linoleum and felt-base technology to produce another cheaper product line. The product was a linoleum mixture applied to a felt-base and then printed with appropriate designs. In 1930, the British linoleum manufacturers, Williamson, entered into agreements with Armstrong to produce the material for the English and European markets. Their product was called Lancastreum.

In England, felt-base floorcoverings were made when there was a shortage of **jute** backing for linoleum, especially during wartime. The technique of manufacture used a paper felt impregnated with asphaltic bitumen. The back was painted but the surfacing material was the same as for linoleum. It was less thick than standard fabric-backed linoleum and was therefore inferior as regards wearing properties.
See also **Felt-base**, **Linoleum**.

49. *Congoleum felt base flooring advertisement* (Ladies' Home Journal, *1923*)

Felt carpet
A thick, felted fabric used as a surround for **carpets** or as a floorcovering in its own right, felt carpet has been available either plain or printed, according to fashion. The manufacture of the printed version was described in 1872: 'This is made by placing thin layers of felt across each other and beating them into a thick firm fabric, upon which the patterns are printed as upon calico.' It was made 27 inches (69 cm) wide (Brown & Gates, p.176).

Felt carpet was apparently also practical and economic. In 1870, *Cassell's Household Guide* pointed out that:

> Felt carpet is to be had in suitable tints; it is not expensive, and is easily made, and when good, will wear tolerably well. There are many advantages in a felt carpet; not among the least is that when it is worn out in the centre, the sides which are good can be cut off, bound, and arranged for bedside carpets (vol. 1, p.125).

In a similar guidebook, 'Patent Victoria Felt' carpets were suggested for bedrooms, but readers were warned against the printed pattern wearing off (Ward & Lock's *Home Book*, 1880).

In 1884, London retailers, Maple and Co, suggested felt was used for carpet surrounds, and as a base on which to lay **rugs**. They also sold 'printed felt carpet for secondary or upper bedroom floors. The material is 50 inches wide and can now be had in some exceedingly pretty designs', and they suggested that 'plain felts are now the most fashionable covering for stair carpets' (1884, p.91). Design commentators praised the plain versions. Hermann Muthesius remarked in 1904: 'From the purely artistic point of view, felt which is available in all colours and is of excellent quality (we are here thinking only of the plain makes, not of the hideous felt with printed patterns) makes an excellent floor' (p.180).

Murphy, a textile authority, who nevertheless suggested it still had a place in the early twentieth-century furnisher's repertoire, commented upon its decline:

> For many years, the felted carpet was a very popular floorcovering competing chiefly with the Scotch carpet. At present [1910] it doesn't hold a large place on the market, being opposed on the one hand by the more durable linoleums, and on the other hand, by the more pretentious tapestry carpets... For temporary decorative purposes and wide enclosed spaces felt carpets are still considered best by competent judges, being softer and more artistic than linoleum and practically quite as durable for underfoot wear. (1910, vol.6, p.140.)

See also **Felt**.

Felted rug
See **Rug**.

Ferret

A robust **tape** most commonly made of **cotton**, but also of **silk** and **worsted**. The silk ones are known as Italian ferret, probably because the Italian word *fioretti* means 'floss-silk'. Ferret is used for binding and is usually narrower than ordinary bindings. An early reference to silk ferret is in 1576 'when perchmentiers [i.e. passementiers] put in no ferret Silke' (*OED*). By the eighteenth century, it was defined as 'a kind of narrow ribband made of a meaner sort of silk, with a mixture of cotton, or thread' (Fenning, 1768). In the nineteenth century, it acquired a connection with **Venetian blinds**. In 1791, Mrs Papendiek commented upon 'the Venetian blinds I had new strung at home with silk ferret' (*OED*).

See also **Binding**.

Festoon

In terms of **drapery**, festoons are an important component of a scheme. They were particularly important in the early nineteenth century when expansive drapery schemes were fashionable. The skill in producing them lay in the cutting out and this was clearly explained by George Smith:

> We often see silk and calico tormented into every other form than agreeable, natural drapery. The mystery and difficulty of cutting out would vanish, did the artist but apply his mind with resolution to conquer his prejudices; to the workman very little knowledge is requisite beyond cutting out what is usually called a festoon, the arrangement, whether for continued drapery or for a single window, well and properly cut out, will answer for the whole. (1808, pp xi–xii.)

Festoons were still important at the end of the century. Moreland, in his *Practical Decorative Upholstery* (1889), distinguishes various types. He mentions regular festoons; **French drapery** festoons (where the fabric is intended to look as one piece with the swag hanging below the pole in the middle); irregular swags, which appear as a continuation of the **curtain** and raised drapery for uniting several windows or a wide space whereby a separate pole is higher in the centre; narrow festoons; and looped-up drapery. Festoon effects have continued as fashion dictates.

See also **Festoon window curtain**, **Swag**.

Festoon window curtains

Curtains characterised by soft, billowing, crescent-shaped folds produced either by pulling a single curtain straight up, or by pulling a single or divided curtain diagonally up and to the side, and secured in place by means of rings and **cords** attached to the back.

(a) Curtains with two straight pieces of cloth hanging to the sill, with **tapes** and rings sewn diagonally on the back, from bottom centre to outer top. When cords pull the fabric, the curtain gathers up in festoons with the **tails** or point hanging to the side of the window frame. They may be called **drapery** curtains.

(b) A flat curtain designed to pull up in one piece; drawn so as to form **swags** all the way down, using a system of cords running through rings sewn on the back, middle and sides. Also known as a Venetian curtain (especially in the USA).

They were fashionable in the eighteenth century. In June 1727, Thomas Phill was contracted for work at Kensington Palace, adapting existing curtains to the new fashion. He charged for 'taking down the window curtains in the Council Chamber and altering them from draw-back curtains to festoons and for putting them up again with sewing silk and nails used' (Westman, 1990, p.1410). The drapery version was made up by William France who supplied Sir Lawrence Dundas in 1764 with a bill for 'Making your own lustring curtains to 2 large windows in the blue damask bed chamber to open the middles and form a drapery on each side.' (ibid. p.1412.) In 1777, Israel Lewis, an upholsterer of Fleet Street, London, was granted a patent for 'festoon window curtains with springs' (Patent no.1162, 14 July). By the early nineteenth century, Sheraton described festoons as:

> Those [curtains], which draw up by pullies, and hang down in a swag. These curtains are still in use in bedrooms, notwithstanding the general introduction of the French rod curtains in most genteel houses. A festoon window curtain consists generally of three pulls, but when a window is extensive, they may have four or five. According to the number of pulls so must the window lath be pullied. (1803, p.208.)

Rather more simply, Loudon described festoons as follows:

> a piece of dimity, or other material … nailed to a flat piece of wood, in one end of which are inserted two pullies, whilst two others are let into it, one in the middle and the other at the opposite extremity. Three pieces of tape are sewn down the curtains, one on each side, and one in the middle. To each are affixed small rings at regular intervals. (1839, p.341.)

Early in the twentieth century, Hasluck described festoon blinds where he noted that: 'Much of the effect of the blind will depend upon the arrangement and skill of the needle worker, and the housewife's help will be invaluable. In many masculine hands the festoon-blind degenerates into mere bagginess' (1907, p.126). In 1937, festoon curtains were recommended, as 'there has been a steadily increasing demand on festoon blinds for the windows of high-class shops and in hotels and large private houses. They are particularly suitable where windows are circular, as the blind will conform to the curves of the window perfectly.' (French, 1937, p.61.)

See also **Austrian shade**, **Draw-up curtain**, **Festoon, Venetian curtain**.

FURTHER READING

Westman, A. (1990). 'English window curtains in the eighteenth century', *The Magazine Antiques*, CXXXVII, 6, June, pp 1406–17.

Westman, A. (1993). 'Festoon window curtains in neo-classical England: an analysis and comparison', *Furniture History*, 29, pp 80–7.

Fibrefill

A late twentieth-century **upholstery filling** made from crimped **polyester** fibres matted together to make a thick wrap, usually in conjunction with **polyurethane foam** interiors or as **wadding**.

Fibreglass

See **Glass fibre**.

Fibre

Fibres may be categorised simply into three groups:

Cellulosic or ester cellulosic group

This group includes cotton (genus *Gossypium*), which is ginned to remove plant waste before it is usable. The fibre length (staple) varies between a ½ and 2 inches (1.2 and 5.5 cm); linen (genus *Linum*), obtained from the bast stems of the plant that have an average length of 6 to 39 inches (15 to 100 cm). Bast fibres have to be retted (loosening stems by soaking) and then scoured (scotched) to remove the outer cover. Other bast fibres include jute (genus *Corchorus*) and hemp (genus *Cannabis sativa*), which

are treated in a similar way. The cellulosic properties of some plants allow for the production of regenerated cellulose, which lets them be dissolved, reformed and then extruded to make filaments.
See also **Abaca**, **Cotton**, **Hemp**, **Linen**, **Jute**.

Proteinaceous group
This group includes wool, silk and hair. Wool is the body hair of a range of animals including sheep, goat and camel. The fibres range from a ½ to 10 inches (1.25 to 25 cm) in length. Silk is a continuous filament extruded from the silk worm to create a protective cocoon. The cocoons are degummed and cleaned to loosen the filament, which is then processed. Hair is the hair of horses (mane and tails) and of other suitable animals.
See also **Alpaca**, **Hair**, **Mohair**, **Silk**, **Wool**, **Worsted**.

Synthetic group
This group includes rayon, nylon, polyester, and polypropylene.
See **Acrylic**, **Nylon**, **Polyester**, **Polypropylene**, **Rayon**.

Fibres may be used alone or may be combined/blended in a spun thread or in a textile structure. Fibres can be identified simply by burning tests, wet chemical tests (solubility or staining) or by microscopic identification of both longitudinal and cross-sections.

FURTHER READING

Appleyard, H.M. (1978). *Guide to the Identification of Animal Fibres*, 2nd edition, Leeds: WIRA.
Catling, D. & Grayson, G. (1982). *Identification of Vegetable Fibres*, London: Chapman and Hall.
Coleman, D. (2003). 'Man made fibre before 1945' in Jenkins, D. (ed.), *The Cambridge History of Western Textiles*, Cambridge: Cambridge University Press, pp 933–47.
Gohl, E.P.G. & Vilensky, L.D. (1983). *Textile Science – An Explanation of Fibre Properties*, Melbourne: Longman, Cheshire.
Harrop, J. (2003). 'Man made fibres since 1945' in Jenkins, D. (ed.), op.cit., pp 948–71.

Fibre rug
See **Kraft fibre rug**, **Rug**.

Figured casement
See **Casement cloth**.

Filé
Strips of gold or silver-gilt wound around a straight yarn to create 'gold' or 'silver' threads.
See also **Cloth of Gold**, **Frisé**, **Lamé**.

Filet net
Lace or darned netting based on a net fabric into which a pattern or design is darned. Although intended for **curtains**, it is possible to use it over another material for beds and dressing tables. Taylor (1951) recommended its use in conjunction with heavier **linens**, **brocatelles** and **damask** when these are used as over-draperies.
See also **Net**.

Fillet
A decorative finish to a **wall covering** that is intended to cover the tacks and fixings that secure fabrics on to the wall. They have been made from metal, composition (papier-mâché) or **passementeries** such as **braid**. They might be finished naturally, gilded or painted as required by the scheme.

Filling
See **Down**, **Eiderdown**, **Feather**, **Fibrefill**, **Kapok**, **Latex**.

Filoselle (aka Bourre de soie)
Yarns made from waste **silk**, the refuse of good silk reels. It was used for **needlework** and for inferior furnishing fabrics in eighteenth-century France, and it is still used as a needlework thread.
See also **Bourette**, **Ferret**.

Finial
Fittings designed to finish off cornice poles. These were popular through the nineteenth century and for the subsequent revivals of cornice pole use. Although they had a practical purpose of keeping the **curtain rings** on the pole, their designs followed the vagaries of fashion, changing from neo-classical through Gothic to rococo and exotic, as well as the naturalistic. In extreme examples, they might have the addition of red or white pressed glass 'flowers' in the form of lilies or convolvuluses. Eastlake decried the changes in finials brought about by fashion: 'in place of the little finials which used to be fixed at each end of the rod to prevent the rings slipping off, our modern upholsterer had substituted gigantic fuchsias, or other flowers, made of brass, gilt, bronze, and even china, sprawling downwards in a design of execrable taste' (1878, pp 95–6).
See also **Cornice pole**.

Fireplace curtain
A later nineteenth-century arrangement that covered an unused fireplace (in summer time, for example) with a **curtain** or **drapes** to decorate it. They seem to have replaced **fire screens**. In one case, a **lace** and **tarlatan** fabric curtain was recommended for a fireplace curtain: 'On each side [of the fireplace] hung curtains of fine lace, lined with

50. Fireplace curtains and valance (Cassell's Household Guide, *1870*)

coloured tarlatan or thin silk' (Cassell, 1870). In 1879, *The Art Amateur*, an American journal, published a small article on the subject, suggesting that the curtains could be made from 'cloth of gold, satin, velvet, brocade and painted or embroidered Indian muslin. The oriental style being now so popular, Persian needlework harmonizes perfectly with the quaint chimneypiece decoration, and utilizes to advantage any carefully stored specimens too short for window curtains…' (Burke, p.136). The English architect, R.E. Edis, when designing his own dining room in 1881, explained that under the lower shelf of the mantelpiece, 'I have arranged a light rod on which are hung russet-brown Utrecht velvet curtains to hide the modern mantelpiece, and to shut in the whole space when a fire in not required.' (1881, p.129.) The American author, Clarence Cook, in his *House Beautiful* (1878, p.126), recommended drapery that hung from the mantelshelf and hid the fireplace. In England, Mrs Watson explained that 'the [fireplace] curtains, drawn closely together, and hanging in simple folds, veil the disused altar with grace and discretion… The things that are pre-eminently more excellent for this purpose are antique brocades or broderies whose dyes have been harmonized, whose designs are blurred by time, the master-decorator' (Watson, 1897, p.487).
See also **Brocade**, **Mantel drapery**.

Fire screen
Screens designed to protect people from the direct heat of the open fire were used from at least medieval times to the twentieth century. There are two main types: the pole and the banner screen. The early ones were made of basketwork and were often circular. In 1603 Hengrave Hall had 'one little fine wicker screen sett in a frame of walnut tree' (Gloag, 1990, p.589). The decoration of fire screens began in earnest in the late seventeenth and early eighteenth centuries. **Tapestry** woven cloths or domestic **embroidery** were used as a filling for the panels, which were, by then, shaped with a sliding leaf and often looked like a cheval.
See also **Fluted silk**.

Flag
See **Grass**.

Flannel
A woollen cloth introduced in the sixteenth century. The name may derive from *gwlan*, the Welsh word for **wool**. It was originally similar to **baize** with a finer hand-spun **warp** and a loosely spun **weft**, but with a smooth soft surface. It was usually without a nap, of loose texture, and sometimes used for hangings as well as for protective covers. In the mid-eighteenth century, Chambers (1741–3) defined it as 'a kind of slight, loose, woollen stuff, not quilted, but very warm; composed of a woof, and a warp and woven on a loom, with two treadles, after the manner of bayes &c.'.

Its use for hangings is evident in the 1603 inventory of Hengrave, where there were 'wall hangings of grey flannel complete, with a valance indented, with lace and bells' (Clabburn, 1988, p.245). Whilst in the 1710 Dyrham Park inventory there was recorded a 'great cedar chest' in which were 'several large parcels of flannel for covering the furniture' (Walton, 1986, p.67).

During the eighteenth century, thick flannel material was recommended for the inside backs of large mirrors, to provide a soft bed for the silvered glass. It was also used to line **leather** chair covers, and there are occasional references to its use as **interlining**.

The upholsterer, George Smith, noted in 1808 that 'Salisbury flannel has been much used [for drapery]' (1808, p.xii). According to Beck, by the end of the nineteenth century, 'flannel was usually sold white' (1882).
See also **Canton flannel**.

Flat woven carpet
See **Barnard Castle**, **Bristol carpet**, **Ingrain carpet**, **Kidderminster carpet**, **Navajo rug**, **Scotch carpeting**, **Venetian carpet**.

Flax
See **Linen**.

Fledge
A sixteenth-century textile designation of a coarse **woollen** cloth, used to make **blankets**. In a 1579 will, there were recorded 'ij fledge blankets vs. ij caddow blankets ij s. iiij d' (*Richmond Wills*, Surtees, 1853), while in 1582 an inventory of the stores at Sheffield Castle included 'whole clothes of fledges to make fledges of' (Thornton, 1978, p.356). The 1601 Hardwick inventory included 'a white fledge' in Lady Arabella's chamber, and 'eight fledges about the bed' in Lady Shrewsbury's chamber (Boynton, 1971, p.32). It was not common after the beginning of the seventeenth century.

Flock
A general term for the tufts, particles and refuse of fibres or cloth weaving processes that can be bulked up and used as a filling. Usually these have been **cotton**, **silk** or **wool**. The wool or cotton versions were often used for **quilts** and **upholstery** work. G. Watson, a Liverpool cabinet-maker and upholsterer, advertised in March 1826 that he sold 'silk flocks for beds and mattresses at 6d pound and floss equal to hair or feathers and far more essential to health' (*DEFM*, p.949).
See also **Cotton flock**, **Mattress**, **Woollen flock**.

Floorcloth
A wax cloth was first described in 1578 by G. Fallopius, the recipe for which suggested treating **linen** cloth with a mixture of gum arabic, white lead, water and tallow wax, all applied to the **canvas**. By 1627, an English inventor, I. Wolfen, had obtained a patent for oilcloth. Nine years later, a patent was granted to Richard and Edward Greenbury for 'Painting with oyle cullors upon wollen cloath, kersey and stuffs being proper for hanging.' (Patent no.99/1636.) By the 1660s, a tradesman, Richard Bailey of Ludgate Hill, was recorded as 'maketh oylcloth the German way'. The end of the seventeenth century (1694) saw Simon Thenneman taking out a patent which described a method of printing figures and flowers on waxed cloth 'so they last as long as the stuffe itself' (Patent no.336/1694).

Although it is unclear when the first waxcloth was adopted as a floorcloth, references have been found to this use by 1722 and it is evident that English floorcloth was imported into America by at least 1736.

The trade in floorcloth was important enough for Robert Campbell to remark on it in his *The London Tradesman* (1747, p.245): 'In the Turner's shop we generally meet with Floor cloths, painted in oil colours which is performed by a class of painters who do little else. It requires no great ingenuity, and the wages of journeymen is the same as in other branches of painting.' An example of mixed goods selling was the business of Alex Wetherstone (*c*.1760), who traded as 'a Carpenter, Joyner and Turner' who 'sells all sorts of Floor cloths, Hair cloth, List carpets, Royal and other matting' (Heal, 1933, p.192).

Nathan Smith established the first recorded floorcloth manufactory in 1754 in the Knightsbridge area of London. In 1763, Smith applied for a patent that laid a mixture of rosin tar, Spanish brown, beeswax and linseed oil as an overlay onto a woven fabric (Patent no.787/1763). This seems to be the first mention of linseed oil – later to be the key ingredient and the basis of the linoleum manufacturing process. The same area in London attracted other firms and, in 1769, Crompton and Spinnage advertised 'Painted Floorcloths of all sorts and sizes painted in the summer at their Manufactory in Knightsbridge, dry and fit for immediate use' (Heal Collection, British Museum). The reference to summer was a selling point that referred to the need to cure the floorcloth in dry, warm conditions before use.

Floorcloth was used as a protection as well as a decorative flooring feature. In the accounts of Harewood House, there is a payment to Reid the upholsterer for 'laying down the carpet on the Great Stairs, oil cloth and serge covers to Do' (Gilbert, 1978, p.219).

The manufacturing process was complex. The **base cloth**, which might be as much as 8 yards wide and 25 yards long (7.3 metres by 22.8 metres), was nailed to an enormous frame of the same size that stretched it taut. The material was then sized back and front to lay the fibres and give a base upon which to paint. When this operation was done and dry, the painting could begin. The paint was so thick that it had to be trowelled onto the surface. Once the paint was dry, the surface was rubbed with pumice stones to remove any roughness. Another coat was applied until the required 'depth of body' was acquired. The process was time-consuming due to the need to allow each coat to dry. The next procedure was to print the design onto the cloth. This was originally done by brush but, as demand increased, a **stencil printing** process was introduced. This was still not efficient enough and eventually the use of engraved blocks was found to be the best mode of printing.

52. Floorcloth design, c.1895 (Private Collection)

51. Trade card of floorcloth makers Biggerstaff and Walsh (Courtesy of the Trustees of the British Museum)

Homemade and amateur versions were quite common. The following description explains:

> Canvas or common tow cloth is sewed with a flat seam, of the dimensions required; and nailed upon a floor; then wet with water even and thoroughly; and before dry is primed with any common colour. After two more coats of paint, and the filling any cracks with putty, the cloth is divided into squares or diamonds of which one-half are painted white; and the other half black. (Reynolds, 1812.)

In addition, Loudon, who, conceding that floorcloths were the most suitable kind of flooring for cottages, also warned that:

> Painted floorcloths may sometimes be used in lobbies and the passages of cottages, but they are not economical articles where there is much going out and coming in of persons generally employed in the open air, and of course wearing strong shoes with nails in the soles. When

> they are used in cottages the most appropriate materials usually employed for floors such as tessellated pavements, different coloured stones, wainscot etc. but for the better description of dwellings, where oilcloths are considered chiefly ornamental coverings, there seems to be no reason why the patterns should not be as various as those of carpets. (1839, p.346.)

Sporadic references in country-house muniment rooms provide evidence of floorcloth use throughout the eighteenth century. The earliest references so far located for floorcloth date from 1708, when Sir Thomas Dickens of Westminster had 'some canvas floor and stair cloths' (Sarin, p.137). A little later there is a payment to a Benjamin Powell in 1722 for a 'Bed tent and Markee £38.8s.0d and for a floor oyled cloth to lye in the tent 19s.0.d'. In 1728, another invoice shows payment for '20 yards of painted floorcloth at 2s 2d per yard and for a pole to roll it on' (Gilbert, Lomax & Wells-Cole, 1987, pp 5–6). In 1736, Denham Hall had 'a large floorcloth in the dining room' and in 1772 Nathan Smith supplied Sir John Griffin Griffin with a 'painted cloth for the chapple at Audley End in squares to imitate Portland and Breming stone pavement £2 4s a yard'. In 1780, the Great Hall at Appledurcombe had 'a floor cloth painted in imitation of India Matt' and a 'plain red floorcloth' for the Housekeeper's room. In 1789, Gillows supplied H. John Curwen of Workington Hall with 'an elegant patent painted floorcloth for the Hall containing 157 square yards the colours made to suit yr. furniture and a handsome border' (Gilbert, Lomax & Wells-Cole, 1987, pp 101–2). This fitted floorcloth idea was also found in an 1800 Chippendale account to Lady Heathcote, which was for '37 square yards plaited matt pattern oilcloth made to cover Hall compleat' (ibid. p.101).

In the nineteenth century, the more practical values of floorcloth were especially esteemed. In 1827, Attingham House had pieces of floorcloth painted to match the Turkey design **carpet**, which were placed under sideboards, either end of the fireplace and in the window embrasures. In the Grand Dining Room, there was 'a superior Turkey carpet, a piece of Turkey pattern floorcovering under the sideboard size 8½ yards by 2 yards wide. Ditto under a sideboard at the other end in the next hall and two piece ditto each side of the fireplace and 4 pieces ditto 32 inches wide under the windows.' (Gilbert, Lomax & Wells-Cole, 1987, p.101.) All of these were no doubt to save the carpet from spills.

In the USA, floorcloth use followed a similar pattern. The early existence of floorcloth is confirmed by the will of William Burnett, Governor of New York and New Jersey, who died in 1729 leaving 'two old chequered canvases to lay under the table' and a 'large painted canvas square as the room'.

Reynolds (1812) recommended diamond or square patterns for formal spaces, whereas Webster & Parkes (1844) suggested designs borrowed from Oriental **rugs**. However, narrow floorcloths for both passages and stairs were produced in widths of 18, 24 or 36 inches (46, 61 or 91 cm), and were often printed with a large pattern in the middle and a **border** of a smaller design. Miss Leslie, in the *Lady's House Book*, recommended floorcloths as:

> They save the trouble of scrubbing the floor, it being only necessary to wash them off with a wet cloth; and as they are so impervious to damp or to cold from open cracks between the boards, they make the kitchen as dry and warm as could be rendered by a woollen carpet; and they have the advantage of collecting and retaining no dust or grease. (1854, pp 183–4.)

The Beecher sisters gave full instructions as to the home production of floorcloth, in their *American Woman's Home*. It was inevitably a time-consuming process but the end result was considered worth the wait (1869, p.371).

The issue of 'curing' floorcloth was important, as the paint hardens with time. The age of a floorcloth then became a selling feature. Miss Leslie explains in her *Lady's House Book:*

> We have seen an English oilcloth that, not having been put down till five years after it was imported, looked fresh and new, though it had been ten years in constant use on an entry floor. An oilcloth that has been made within the year is scarcely worth buying as the paint will be defaced in a very little time, it requiring a long while to season. (1854, p.183.)

In the twentieth century, two qualities of floorcloth were made: heavy or hand-printed, and light or machine-printed, the latter still being made post-1918.
See also **Linoleum**, **Oilcloth**, **Paper carpet**, **Sailcloth**.

FURTHER READING

Edwards, C. (1996). 'Floorcloth and linoleum: aspects of the history of oil-coated materials for floors', *Textile History*, 27, 2, Autumn, pp 148–71.
Gooderson, P.J. (1996). *Lord Linoleum, Lord Ashton and the Rise of the British Oilcloth and Linoleum Industry*, Keele: Keele University Press.
Mehler, W.A. (1987). *Let the Buyer Have Faith: The Story of Armstrong*, Lancaster, PA: Armstrong World Industries.
Muir, A. (1956). *Nairn's of Kirkcaldy: A Short History of the Company 1847–1956*, Cambridge: Heffer.
Sarin, S. (2005). 'The floorcloth and other floorcoverings in the London domestic interior 1700–1800', *Journal of Design History*, 18, 2, pp 133–46.
Walton, F. (1925). *The Infancy and Development of Linoleum Floorcloth*, London: Simpkins and Marshall.

Florentine blind
An exterior window **blind**, made from **linen** cloth or similar, which filled the whole window. Popular in the later nineteenth century, it was fixed upon a spring roller to pull down and then the base was extended with two rods to open up the side wings. The whole blind could be drawn up into a box or behind a front board (Hasluck, 1907, pp 103–12).

Florentine stitch
See **Bargello**, **Stitch: Flame**.

Floss
Flat untwisted **silk** threads used for **embroidery**.

Flounce
Gathered or cased and corded **borders** fitted with **tapes**, which were then tied to rails of beds or chairs to cover the space between the rails and the floor. Developed in the later eighteenth century, they became common in the nineteenth and twentieth centuries.
See also **Base**, **Dust ruffle**, **Ruffle**.

Fluted silk
Fluted or ribbed **silk** materials, applied to prepared wall or furniture frames, were particularly fashionable in the early nineteenth century. Sheraton discusses the use of wire doors in cabinets and goes on to suggest that 'When wire-worked doors are introduced, they have generally green, white or pink silk fluted behind it' (1803, p.332). Sheraton's *The*

53. *Florentine blind* (*P. Hasluck,* Window Blinds, *1907*)

Cabinet Marker and Upholsterer's Drawing Book discussed a sofa bed design:

> It must also be observed, that the best kinds of these beds have behind what the upholsterer's call a fluting, which is done by a slight frame of wood fastened to the wall, on which is strained, in straight puckers, some of the same stuff of which the curtains are made (1793, p.379).

It became commonplace a little later, being used for covering **fire screens** and the bag frames of worktables (Loudon, 1839, p.1078). In 1864, an American company described fluted **tabbinet** fabric for wall decoration: '[Fabric is used] instead of paper, paint or tapestry, and when used for this purpose it is not put on tight and flat like paper or tapestry but fluted and has a magnificent appearance.' (Howe & Stevens in Montgomery, 1984, p.356.)

Fly

Flies are extension pieces sewn to the sides of top outer coverings of **upholstery** work to faciliate fixing. They are not seen, but are needed to complete the tight covering of chairs, etc. Flies are usually of **hessian** or **calico**, thus saving on the cost of the main cover.

Foam

The use of foamed materials in the twentieth century, either synthetic or natural (latex), revolutionised the **upholstery** industry. In traditional upholstery, the choice of filling materials has been led by considerations of cost, durability and the availability of skilled upholsterers. The introduction of regularised sheet or slab materials such as foam has meant that semi-skilled labour can build upholstery, parts can be pre-formed, and various types and densities can easily be used and fitted to make a satisfactory batch-produced manufactured article.

Synthetic foam

A cushioning product used widely in the later twentieth-century upholstery industry. Its manufacture is based on the interaction of a polyol and an isocyanate with water, in which a reaction is created so that polymers form and gas generation causes expansion. The introduction of plastic (polyether) foam as an upholstery material broadened the range of possibilities for upholsterers, especially in the finished profiles of their products. Initially introduced as a substitute for latex, it would also soon offer its own possibilities.

Although first noticed in 1848, its significance as a material was not recognised until 1937 when Dr Otto Bayer discovered the polymerisation process from a family of organic chemicals, known as **polyurethane**. Wartime encouraged experimentation so that, by 1952, Farben Fabriken Bayer had developed flexible polyurethane foams and, in 1953, the Du Pont Corporation also announced their process. The products were mainly used in the textile industry until the 1960s when polyether upholstery foams developed, which encouraged their use in seating applications.

The more recent developments in plastic foam technology have resulted in a range which offers a wide choice of densities and hardness factors, special features like fire retardancy, and ancillary developments to include **polyester** wraps (**fibrefill**) which give a softer feel and look to **cushions**.

Synthetic foam has also been used as loose filling for cushions, etc. in the form of crumb, spaghetti and chip cut. Other synthetics such as curled **nylon** monofilament and polystyrene beads have also been used. In some cases, reconstituted foam off-cuts are crumbed and reconstructed to form a new foam mix of very high density for heavy use.
See also **Latex**.

Foam-backed carpet

See **Tufted carpet**.

Foam-backed curtain

Crushed **acrylic** foam was used in the 1970s to self-line curtain fabrics and act as insulation.

Folkweave

Folkweaves are figured fabrics made with coarse yarns, usually produced in multi-colours. They have been used for **curtains**, fitted chair covers and **bedspreads**. *The Draper's Encyclopaedia* says of folkweave bedspreads: 'Folk weave is a very wide term and covers many types of cloths. They are machine-made by tappets, dobbies or jacquards and are generally loosely woven with coarse yarns. They are usually very colourful and in cross-over yarns.' (Ostick, 1955, p.357.) Also known as village, peasant or cottage weave.
See also **Homespun**.

Footboard

A footboard is a component of a bed frame that is often an upholstered and framed panel, fitted to the end of a bed. It may rise above the **mattress**.

Foot curtains

Bed **curtains** hung at the lower side ends of the bed that could be

drawn to cover the lower portion of each side.
See also **Bed furniture**, **Head curtain**.

Forfar

Unbleached **linen sheeting** that has been used mainly for wrapping and **towelling**. 'Hessian and Forfar are very coarse linens used for various purposes, as straining [i.e. webbing] on sofas etc.' (Webster & Parkes, 1844, p.951.)

Fortuny print

Mariano Fortuny (1871–1949), a Spanish artist who settled in Venice, developed techniques for dyeing and **stencil printing** fabrics, often with metallic pigments. The effects created were intentionally 'antiqued'. In 1909–10, he patented a technique for polychrome printing using wood block and stencils on **cotton** or **silk velvet**. Screen-printed fabric was sometimes stamped with gold or silver to add to the pattern. Twill or **satin** weaves were used as well as velvet and **velveteen** for the best qualities. The fabric has been used for **runners**, **upholstery** and **wall hangings**. Denny explained that these were:

> exclusive art fabrics made by Mariano Fortuny of Venice by a secret printing process. Rich Renaissance patterns were printed with lighter colour on dark background or stamped with gold or silver. May be on cotton sateen or twill or on velvet of cotton or silk. Used for [dress fabrics and for] ... wall hangings, runners, upholstery. (1936, p.29.)

Fortuny fabrics were described in 1947 as 'inexpensive printed fabrics reproducing richness of old Venetian cloth. They were imported into Britain prior to 1939' (French, 1947).
See also **Printed textile**, **Venetian cloth**.

FURTHER READING
De Omsa, G. (1999). *Fortuny: The Life and Work of Mariano Fortuny*, London: Aurum Press.
Deschodt, A.M. & Poli, D. (2001). *Fortuny*, New York: Abrams.

Four-point platform

A mid-twentieth century **upholstery** suspension method that used rectangular rubber sheets fitted with triangular fixing points in each corner, which were anchored to hooks in the corner of seat frames. Often used for show-wood upholstery frames that did not support full springing, the diaphragm effect spread loads evenly and allowed for thinner **cushions**. Originally developed for the motor industry, it was a simple and effective upholstery support for both show-wood and metal-framed upholstery.
See also **Platform**.

French curtain

A later eighteenth-century design term that refers to **curtains** intended to be drawn across a window by using **cords** and pulleys to operate them. Sheraton's *The Cabinet Marker and Upholsterer's Drawing Book* noted that:

> When the cords are drawn, the curtains meet in the centre at the same time, but are no way raised from the floor. When the same cord is drawn the reverse way, each curtain flies open, and comes to their place on each side... The cord passes on a side pulley fixed on the right hand. To effect this, the rod is made in a particular manner, having two pulleys at one end and a single one at the other. (1793, pp 408–9.)

See also **French rod**.

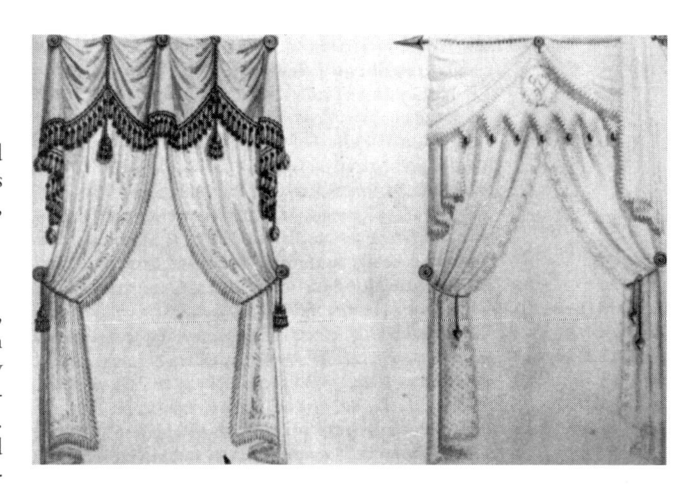

54. French drapery example (R. Ackermann, The Repository of Arts etc., *1810)*

French drapery

A term for swagged drapery that is arranged in layered fashion with **valances** and fittings. Webster & Parkes explained their use in the mid-nineteenth century:

> Valances are sometimes made in the form of festoons, and are then, by upholsterers, termed draperies; the festoon itself is called a swag, and the end that hangs down is termed the tail... These are frequently ornamented with fringes, tassels and cords in various ways. This, which is the former French style, was introduced some years ago, as being richer and more elegant than ours, at present [1844] it is less used. (1844, p.251.)

Webster & Parkes continue: 'One inconvenience in the elegant French draperies was the great skill and taste required to put them up well, and it is said the cutting out of this part of the upholsterer's work was kept as much as possible a secret, and seldom taught, even to their apprentices.' (ibid.)

This matter of skill would become an issue later in the century, 'when the French style of drapery came back [into fashion], there were comparatively few men in the trade who could originate or adapt designs' (Jacobs, 1890, p.17). The revival was considerably simpler, with shawls draped over poles, allowing an end or both ends to hang down as a swag. Not all welcomed its return to fashion. In 1889, Moreland complained that French drapery had: 'recovered its prestige to such an extent that in some cases it descends to actual slovenliness by overcrowding with material; whereas the object should be to decorate and not encumber the spaces' (p.12).
See also **Drape and drapery**, **Festoon**.

French mattress

See **Mattress: French**.

French overlay

A thin upholstered pallet or **mattress** that is often made without a **border**. True French overlays have a layer of **wool** topped with a layer of **hair**, finished with another layer of wool. They are used in conjunction with a full sprung mattress.

French pleat

Hand-sewn triple **pleats** used for **curtain** headings.
See also **Pinch pleat**.

French quilting
See **Marseilles**.

French rod
French rods refer to a **curtain** suspension system that appears to have been developed at the end of the eighteenth century. It had been developed to draw a pair of curtains by using two pulleys at one end of the rod and one pulley at the other so the curtains could be drawn using the **cord** rather than touching the fabric itself. Sheraton describes French rods:

> At present the most approved way of managing window curtains is to make them draw from the centre to each side of the window by drawing a line which is fixed to a pulley rack and communicates to a rod fixed to the underside of the window lath with hooks; and that the curtains may overlap each other in the centre, the rod is made in two parts, shooting past each other about two or three inches. These rods are frequently made of satin wood, and secured with brass hoops at each end having in each rod three pullies. (1803, p.185.)

The French rod was specifically described as being 'made of brass, about three quarters of an inch diameter, having a pulley at the left end, and two at the right, one of which is fixed in a pin perpendicular to the rod' (1803, p.298). The system, in a range of variations, remains in use.
See also **Curtain pole and rod**, **French curtain**, **Pulley rod**.

French shawl drapery
See **French drapery**.

Frieze
A **woollen** fabric with a napped finish (**frisé**) designed for warmth and comfort and was, therefore, often used for clothes. Certainly known since the fifteenth century, it was also used for **wall hangings** and **bed curtains** from the seventeenth century. The inventory of Tart Hall (1641) records amongst many entries for freize, 'for this room [Great Chamber] there is a suit of freeze hangings in the Wardrobe', and in Mr Thomas Howard's chamber 'also belongeth Hangings and Chayres of freeze now in the Wardrobe' (Cust, 1911).

In the eighteenth century, frieze was also used for carpet protection. Leeds retailers, Wright and Elwick, wrote in 1772 to their customer John Grimston: 'The green frieze is a strong coarse article made in this neighbourhood very suitable for the purpose [of carpet covering] and cheap.' (Gilbert, 1976, p.47.)

In some cases, it appears that 'freeze' was intended as a winter hanging cloth, which was replaced yearly by summer hangings. By the end of the eighteenth century, it was mainly used for clothing. Sheraton defined it as 'woollen cloth or stuff for winter wear, being friezed or knapt on one side; where probably it derived its name' (1803, p.215).

Writing in 1931, Midgley noted that frieze was a 'heavy rough tweed fabric produced from a coarse wool fibre: also in lower qualities from a mixture of shoddy or mungo. Made in coloured mixtures chiefly of a grey character'.
See also **Carpet cover and protection**, **Frisé**, **Rugg**, **Tweed**.

Fringe
Fringe is defined as a decorative arrangement of hanging threads, widely used on a range of interior furnishings including hangings, **curtains**, bed furniture, **throws**, **cushions** and seat **upholstery**. Not only do they decorate the textiles, but also in many cases they add weight to assist draping (see examples below).

Early fringes appear to be have been simple forms hanging directly from a netted heading: later **tasselled** or tufted fringes were made from **floss silk**. Tudor inventories list many fringed items including **sparvers**, celours, **testers** and **canopies**. One example relates to the cushions supplied in 1582 by Edward Baker to the Queen Elizabeth. These were:

> part embroidered with cloth of gold, cloth of silver, and satin of diverse colours, Venice gold and silver, silver and silk spangles in colour lined with satin of diverse colours, lined with lace on the seams with gold and silver lace, fringed, buttoned and tasselled with Venice gold, silver and silk… (Beard, 1997, p.284).

Randle Holme made an early indication of the wide range of fringes available. In referring to bed valances, he listed bed fringes as 'Inch fringe, caul fringe, tufted fringe, snailing fringe, gimpe fringe with tufts and buttons and vellum fringe' (1688, III, XIV, p.16).

Fringes were clearly an important component of upholstery in the later seventeenth century. The petition by the **woollen** manufacturers against the cane chair makers noted that: 'To perfect these [chairs] for use there was expended above twenty thousand pounds sterling of silk fringe, which silk is the product of our cloth from Turkey' (1689).

Fringe use continued to be based on fashion. One hundred and fifty years later, Sheraton recorded that 'The French have now begun to use fringe at the bottom of their chair backs.' (1803, pp 214–15.) The fashionable furnishings described by Ackermann often refer to the use of fringes in the commentary to the illustrative plates in his *Repository*, but they are not consistent. Parisian fringe, for example, consisted of hangers of three ball shapes of increasing size, followed by a smaller one falling from the points of a **border**. Persian fringes had hangers consisting of a tiny ball, a teardrop and a large ball suspended from the point of a zigzag edging.

By the later nineteenth century, extravagant fringe work was being criticised by reformers. Eastlake was particularly scathing about the use of fringe:

> Now manufacturers, have not only lost sight of the original motive of fringes, but they make it of fantastically turned pieces of wood, twisted round indiscriminately with silk and woollen thread; and these are often attached to a valance scarcely deeper than the fringe itself. One may even see cord fringe sewn on stools, fire screens etc. where it is utterly inappropriate, and where in short, no one but a modern upholsterer would ever think of putting it. (1878, p.96.)

The parts of a fringe are referred to as the header, the hangers and the skirt, which is the decorative part, usually below the header.

Ball
Made with a variety of sizes and details, but always including bobbles or balls. It is used for curtain and **blind** edges.

Beaded
A fringe where beads are suspended on the skirt cords.

Belladine
Made from raw Levant silk. In 1735, Stephen Langley supplied to Chiswick House '170 ounces of the best fine green Baladine silk fringe cut, made wt a broad head to be used to ye 10 chairs, 2 Saffoys and hangings' (Beard, 1997, p.303).

Block
A plain fringe overlaid by small hangers or loops.

55. Fringe examples (G.L. Hunter, Decorative Textiles, Coverings for Furniture etc., *1918)*

Bouclé
A fringe where the skirt has a twisted yarn.

Bullion
This fringe is usually recognised by a thick twisted wool or silk cord or rope-like feature of between 3 and 12 inches (7.6 and 30.5 cm) in thickness. Sometimes incorporating gold and silver thread, **cotton** bullion fringe was chiefly used for bedroom furniture in the later nineteenth century. **Twine** fringe may refer to very fine bullion. Scallop is a bullion-type with a scalloped edged skirt. Ackermann, in March 1815, refers to 'a bullion fringe or one of those excellent imitations of which so readily deceive the eye even of the connoisseur'.

56. Ornamental fringe for window (The Art Journal Illustrated Catalogue of the Great Exhibition – London 1851)

Campaign
This fringe has small bell-like tufts. Derived from the French word *campane*, meaning 'bell', this fringe was a form of passementerie popular between 1680 and 1710. It had hangers shaped as bells spaced along the fringe. The Duchess' chamber in the Ham House inventory of 1679 had hangings of crimson and gold **damask** with a campaign fringe (Thornton & Tomlin, 1980, p.54).

Cluster
A fringe where the skirt edge is graded to give a saw-tooth effect.

German
A fringe made from white cotton of 1½–3 inches (3.8–7.6 cm) in width, used for trimming **blinds** and bed furniture.

Knotted
A fringe where the skirt cords are knotted together.

Moss
A fringe with a fine, compact and soft-edged skirt.

Moulded or pendant
A fringe with small pendant droops of turned wood wrapped in silk, etc.

Mullet
In 1721, reference was made to 'Beds, Mattresses, hangings, coverlids, quilts, crespins, fringes and molets of silk' (King, *Brit. Merchant*, II, 230).

Tassel
A fringe with the skirt made with silk cord tassels.

Thread
A fringe made from unspun line **warps**.

Toilet
Fringes made in white cotton and between ¾ of an inch and 2 inches (2 and 5 cm) wide.

Trellis
A term to describe elaborate fringe constructions using plain and netted fringes together and in various colours that reflect the trellis arrangement. Trellis is often knotted in macramé fashion, and may be homemade on a small frame.

Worsted fringe
A furnishing fringe made from **worsted** wool yarns that were available from 2½ to 4 inches (6 to 10 cm) in depth and in a wide range of styles. *The Dictionary of Needlework* defined three main types of worsted fringe: 'Plain-head, Plain-head and Bullion, and Gimp head. Tassels were also made to match' (Caulfeild & Saward, 1887, p.534).
See also **Bed furniture**, **Belladine**, **Crepine**, **Knotted work**, **Macramé**, **Net**, **Passementerie**, **Ruche**, **Trimming**, **Valance**.

Frisé
(a) A **pile** fabric, usually **mohair** (though many other fibres have been employed), of uncut loops used for **upholstery**. Introduced in the late nineteenth century (*OED*, 1884): 'Frisé materials are everywhere, frisé

meaning a raised design … in silk, looking as if it had been woven over pins and the pins withdrawn'. Designs may be made by contrasting the height of loops, using cut and uncut loops, various coloured yarns or by surface printing. It is made usually with uncut loops in an all-over pattern. Shearing the loops at different lengths sometimes patterns it. Some are made both with cut and uncut loops in the form of a pattern so that extra **warp** pile yarns woven over wires may cut or leave the pile to produce loops. In the twentieth century, **rayon** was the most popular yarn for frisé, but mohair, **silk** and synthetics were also used. The ground or backing yarns were usually made of **cotton**. Sometimes **jute** or **hemp** was combined with the cotton.
(b) Flat strips of gold or silver-gilt wrapped on a spiral thread, producing a wrinkled effect that sparkles in the light.

Fulham carpet
A **carpet** and **tapestry** factory was established in Fulham (London) in 1753 by émigré Pierre Parisot. He employed **ex-Savonnerie** workers but extreme prices meant that the business never fully developed itself. Parisot discussed how:

> the manufacture of Chaillot [carpets] is altogether of wool, and worked in the manner of Velvet. All sorts of Figures of Men and Animals may be imitated in this work; but Fruits and Flowers answer better; and the properest employment for this Art is to make Carpets and all sorts of Skreens. (Parisot, 1753)

The factory closed in 1755, but Claude Passavant bought it and moved the business to Exeter.

FURTHER READING

Parisot, Peter (1753). *An Account of the New Manufactory of Tapestry After the Manner of That at the Gobelins; and of Carpets After the Manner of That at Chaillot, &c., Now Undertaken at Fulham*, London: Dodsley.
Sherrill, S.B. (1996). *Carpets and Rugs of Europe and America*, New York: Abbeville.

Fur
See **Animal skin**.

Furnishing serge
Twill woven **wool** or wool/**cotton** mixture of coarse texture and fairly heavy weight. It was used for **curtains**, **bedspreads** and fitted covers in the 1950s.
See also **Serge**.

Furnishing tweed
Tweeds were usually woven with coarse yarns and plain or small designs, often with a textured effect. It was used in the 1950s and 1960s for 'contemporary' furniture **upholstery**. Harris and other island tweeds were popular accompaniments to open-sided teak-framed sofas and chairs.
See also **Harris tweed**, **Tweed**.

Furniture cover
See **Protective furnishing**.

Furniture print
Furniture print became an alternative name for chintz due to its extensive use in the covering of furniture, especially in the second half of the nineteenth century.
See also **Chintz**.

Fustian
A class of fabrics that have changed their meaning over time. Initially it appears to have been a **linen warp**, **worsted weft** cloth. From *c.*1600, the worsted was gradually replaced by a **cotton** weft and, by the early nineteenth century, the linen warp was replaced with a cotton one. The name is possibly derived from El-Fustat, a suburb of Cairo, Egypt, where it may have been first made, and a kind of cloth has certainly long been known under that name. It probably entered England from Spain (Spanish *fuste*, meaning 'substance') and was used from the Middle Ages for clothes and bed hangings. In some cases, fustian has been a synonym for the blanket itself.

Its use for bedding was evident early on. A reference from *c.*1440 in John Russell's *Book of Nurture* instructed the Chamberlayne to ensure that once his master had gone to church the 'fustian and shetis be clene' (Edwards, 1964, p.319). A description of a bedroom from 1472, for the Lord of Gruthere, a guest of Edward IV, explains one use: 'There was ordained a bed for himself of as good down as could be gotten, the sheets of raynes, also fine fustians' (Macquoid, 1904, p.67). The 1480 *Wardrobe Accounts of Edward IV* noted 'Pillow beres off fustian unstuffed iiij' (Nicholas, 1830, p.131), and the *Household Ordinances* of Henry VII *c.*1490 showed that the King had a fustian and **sheet** under his feather bed and then over the bed was a sheet, with another fustian over it (Edwards, 1964, p.319). A reference from 1558 refers to 'ij blanketts of fustheyn' (*Wills & Inventories, illustrative of the history, manners, language, etc. of the northern counties of England,* Surtees Society, 1835, p.162).

Fustian was imported into England from a range of European cities including Milan, Naples, Augsburg, Ulm and Genoa. The *Tudor Book of Rates* for 1582 listed: 'fustian the bale containing twenty-two peeces and a half /fustian the half peece/ fustian the whole peece/fustian of Naples the peece/Fustian called Jean fustian the whole peece/Fustian called Millan fustian the whole peece' (Willan, 1962, p.27). Fustian of Naples was used as an **upholstery** material in the Tudor court. For example, 'William Grene the King's coffer-maker charged for making a coffer covered with fustian of Naples and being full of drawe boxes, to put in stones of divers sortes' (Leaf, 1934)'. An example of the use of Holmes (Ulm) fustian is found in 1611, when Robert Cecil was charged for '5 yards of holmes fustian for 3 pillowes at 1s 4d per yard' (Beard, 1997, p.285).

The Royal patronage of fustian continued in the seventeenth century. In 1637, Ralph Grynder supplied Queen Henrietta Maria with '20 yards of fine fustian for an Upper quilt' for her use (ibid. p.289).

In a 1604 Act of Parliament, it was noted that in Norwich 'time out of mind there had been a certain craft called Shearman, for sheering as well worsteds, stamins and fustians as also all other wool cloths' (Thornton, 1978, p.356). The supremacy of fustians as **woollen** cloth was being challenged by the growth of cotton fustians. In 1621, the London fustian dealers made a petition complaining that:

> About twenty years past [*c.*1601] diverse people in this Kingdom, but chiefly in the Countie of Lancaster, have found out the trade of making of other fustians, made of a kind of Bombast or Downe … commonly called Cotton Wool; and also of linen yarn most part brought out of Scotland, and othersome made in England, and no part of the same fustians of any wooll at all. (Wadsworth & Mann, p.15.)

This change was confirmed in a 1641 pamphlet entitled *Treasure of Traffic*, where it was explained that Manchester bought in London cotton wool 'and perfects it into fustians, vermilions, dimities and other stuffs' (Roberts).

The linen fustian was also used as a base for **embroidery**. In 1687, Samuel Sewall wrote to his English supplier: 'my wife would entreat your good lady to pleasure her so far as to buy for her, white fustian drawn, enough for curtains, wallen, counterpaine for a bed, and half duz chairs, with four threeded green worsted to work it' (Cummings, 1961, p.25).

In *c.*1727, John Wood described how 'such [furnishings] as was of linen, consisted either of corded Dimaty or coarse Fustian; the matrons of the city, their daughters and their maids flowering the latter with worsted, during the intervals between seasons to give the beds a gaudy look' (Ayres, 1981, p.24). A similar example is found in America. An advertisement in the *Boston Gazette*, May 1736, listed a 'fine fustian suit of curtains, with a Cornish and base mouldings of a beautiful figure drawn in London, on frame full already worked…' (Cummings, 1961, p.25).

Fustian remained popular into the eighteenth century. The *Merchant's Warehouse* described 'Dimetty, which is called Pillus Fustian, is of great use to put Feathers in for Pillows' (J.F., 1696, p.8). In 1710, the Terras Bed Chamber of Dyrham Park was furnished with 'a white fustian covering quilt' (Walton, 1986, p.59). In the 1728 inventory of the shop of James Pilbeam, a mercer of Chiddingly, Sussex, there was listed 'Six peeces of coloured fustian at £l 8s per peece £8 8s od; Sixty yards ditto at ls per yard; £3 os od' (http://www.chiddingly.gov.uk/History/James%20Pilbeam.html).

Chambers points out that:

> right fustians should be made of cotton yarn both woof and warp but a great many are made, the warp of which is flax, or even hemp. There are fustian made of several kinds, wide, narrow, fine, coarse; with shag or knap, or without it. There are also a great many made whereof the warp is flax or even hemp (1751).

Chambers' comments were insightful as, by 1772, Bailey could note that fustian had changed and was 'a sort of nappy cotton cloth now made of cotton only. Formerly of linen and cotton together' (Bailey, 1772). This change meant that the older fustian types were known by alternative names such as **corduroy**, **velvet** and velveteen. Fustian was also known in the late eighteenth century as Manchester velvet, then **velour**. Hepplewhite commented that 'the Manchester stuffs have been wrought into bed-furniture with good success' (1789, p.18). Fustian continued to be used through to the early nineteenth century.

The terminology was still an issue for twentieth-century authors. Midgley noted 'these [fustians] include a great variety of structures. Some merchants apply this term to all heavily wefted cotton cord fabrics; others include weft pile fabrics. Cut corduroys are sometimes designated fustians.' (1931.)

See also **Blanket**, **Cantoon**, **Dimity**, **Manchester velvet**, **Moleskin**, **Pillow (fustian)**, **Quilt**, **Russell**, **Velveteen**.

FURTHER READING

Anon. (1885). *The Complete Guide to Fustian Manufacturing…, By a practical man*, Bury: Trimble and Burton.

Wadsworth, A.P. & Mann, J. (1931). *The Cotton Trade and Industrial Lancashire 1600–1780*, Manchester: Manchester University Press.

Gabardine

Twilled cloth, on occasion used for **drapes** when in a heavier weight than dress material (Bendure & Pfieffer, 1946, p.591).

Galloon

A narrow, closely woven embroidered decorative **braid**, **tape** or ribbon, made from **wool**, **silk** or **cotton**, often combined with silk or **worsted** yarns as well as metal 'yarns'. Also a narrow **lace** of gold or silver (also known as orris) produced in a wide range of widths, weights, textures etc, for decoration and **binding**. It was used in the seventeenth century to create a **border** for fabrics that were particularly used on chair backs. Galloon was also used to cover edges and seams. Caulfeild & Saward explained:

> There are two descriptions of this article. One is a strong, thick gold lace with an even selvedge at each side. It is woven with a pattern in thread of gold and silver, on silk or worsted both plain and watered, and is employed in uniforms and on servants' livery hats. The other is of wool, silk, or cotton combined with silk or worsted, and is used for trimming, and binding articles of dress, hats, shoes and furniture. (1887, p.219.)

In the twentieth century, the term was still used as a **trimming**: 'A modern draped dressing table in the style of the eighteenth century is draped in green and silver shot taffeta and old galloon. The small bench before it is of wood, painted pale green with silver' (Northend, 1921, p.253). Galloon also refers to the outer border of a **tapestry** panel that resembles a ribbon. It sometimes has the factory or weaver's mark.

See also **Pane**.

Garlick (aka Gulix, Gulick)

A **linen** material of various finishes imported from Goerlitz, a town in Silesia, or from the town of Juliers (Dutch: *Gulik*) near Aachen. Seemingly widely used for household requirements, 'Gulix' was described in *The Merchant's Warehouse Laid Open* as 'being the most proper of any for fine shifts or sheets' (J.F., 1696).

Gathering tape

See **Curtain tape**.

Gauffrage (aka *Gaufré*)

A French term for blind embossed or relief effects applied with heated rollers or impressed with a patterning tool, often used on materials intended for **upholstery**. The technique was patented in France in 1838 and has been used to create waffle, blistering or **honeycomb** effects.

Gauze

A general term applied to woven fabrics in which some of the **warp** threads cross and re-cross with others, besides interlacing with the **weft**. It is a light, transparent fabric; originally of silk, and now made of **linen** or **cotton**, woven in an open manner with very fine yarn. The origin of the name is disputed (see Emery, 1980, p.191). In the weaving of gauze, the warp threads, in addition to being crossed as in plain weaving, are twisted in pairs from left to right and from right to left alternately, after each shot of weft, thereby keeping the weft threads at equal distances apart, and retaining them in their parallel position. The textures are woven plain, striped or figured, and the material has had many designations, according to its appearance and the purposes to which it is devoted. The term 'gauze' is often applied generally to transparent fabrics whichever fibre is used, and also to the fine woven wire-cloth used in window **blinds**, etc.

In 1688, Randle Holme referred to 'Housewife's cloth made of hemp or flax, Holland, tiffany, gawse' (III, p.349/1). In America, gauze was soon adopted for furnishing uses. The van Varick inventory taken in

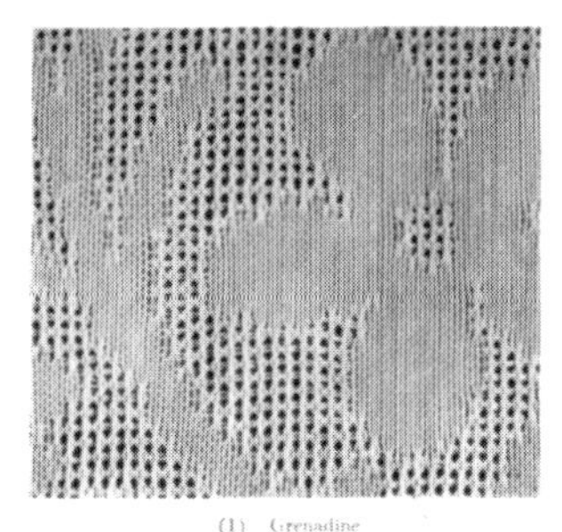
(1) Grenadine

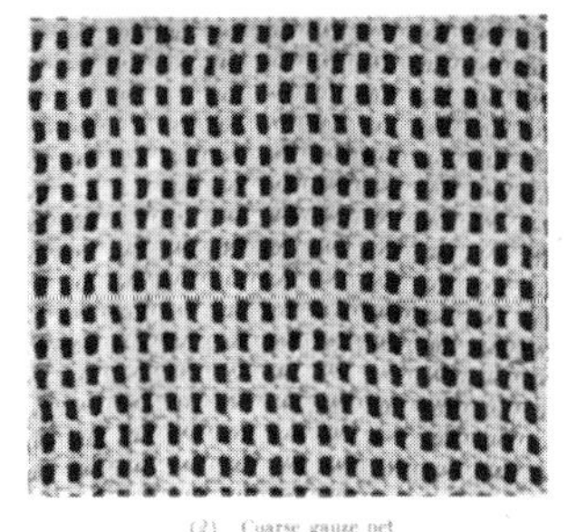
(2) Coarse gauze net

(3) Striped gauze

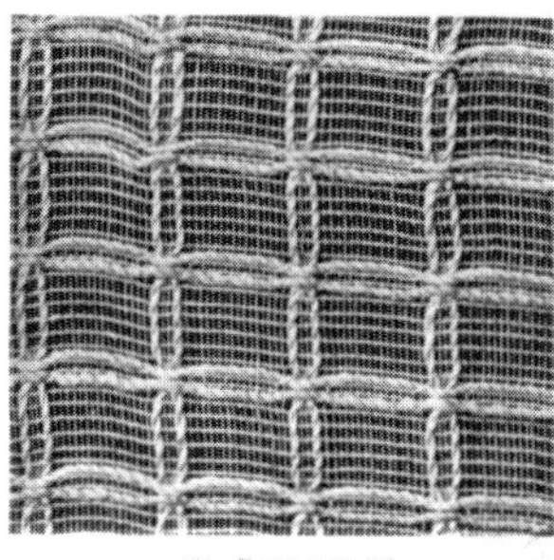
(4) Fancy gauze net

57. Gauze and net weave examples (G.L. Hunter, Decorative Textiles, Coverings for Furniture etc., *1918)*

1695–6 included '2 chimnie cloths of Crimson gaze; 6 window curtains ditto – £6:10s.0d.' (Montgomery, 1984, p.246).

In the eighteenth century, Chambers defined gauze as 'a very thin, slight, transparent kind of stuff, wove sometimes of silk, and sometimes only of thread… There are figured gawzes; some with flowers of gold and silver, on a silk ground; these last are chiefly brought from China' (1741–3). Silk gauze was a prominent and extensive industry in the west of Scotland during the second half of the eighteenth century, but on the introduction of cotton weaving, it greatly declined.

Gauze was used in the eighteenth century for window blinds and **toilette** covers. In 1791, '1 deal dressing table covered with orange coloured silk and a spotted gauze cover' was noted (Walton, 1980, p.414).

Gauze seems to have fallen out of favour as a furnishing fabric in the nineteenth century. In 1947, it was defined as a 'cotton, rayon or silk cloth similar to cheesecloth but with more tightly twisted yarns and used for trimmings and curtains' (Bendure & Pfieffer, p.631). Gauze is still manufactured.

See also **Bolting Cloth**, **Leno**, **Marquisette**, **Short blind**, **Silk**, **Tarlatan**, **Tiffany, Weave: Gauze**.

Genoa damask
See **Damask**.

Genoa silk
See **Silk**.

Genoa velvet
See **Velvet: Genoa**.

Georgette crêpe
A sheer, loosely woven fabric made from high twist yarns alternating in the direction of the twist in both **warp** and **weft**. It was used for **curtains**, **bedspreads**, lampshades, etc (Bendure & Pfieffer, 1947, p.631). See also **Crêpe cloth**.

German fringe
See **Fringe: German**.

Gilt leather
An Islamic technique that was often called 'Spanish leather' on account of its origin. It was usually made from calves' skins faced with silver or tin foil. The panels were embossed or punched with patterns that were then painted in colours. The foil ground was glazed with a yellowish varnish that gave the 'gold look' to the foil. Gilded and tooled **leathers** were also produced in a similar manner.

The manufacture of gilt leather reached Spain by the thirteenth century and grew in importance until around 1600 after which time it declined and the techniques were dispersed. Venice was an important centre and other Italian cities employed gilt leather workers in the sixteenth century. Gilt leather work was also undertaken in the Netherlands, England and France. English workshops were known for their Chinoiserie-style designs used on hangings and **screens**, but the Netherlands was the most well-known centre. In the early seventeenth century, a technique was devised that used wooden printing moulds to emboss the surface. This created repeat pattern leather that, when gilded and painted, reflected light most successfully.

Extensively used for wall hangings, gilt leather was also used for **upholstery** coverings up to the latter part of the seventeenth century, and was made particularly in Flanders and the Netherlands. The panels had to be made up by being sewn together and then mounted on **battens** fixed to the wall. In 1583, Kenilworth Castle had 16 pieces of gilt leather; some paned gilt and blue etc., while in 1601, Hardwick Hall's stair chamber had 'six pieces of gilt leather hangings twelve feet deep' (Boynton, 1971, p.23). In other cases, it seems that it was combined with cloth hangings. In 1639, Anne Viscountess Dorchester had '1 sute of gilt leather and grene cloth hangings for my Ladies closet.' (Clabburn, 1988, p.91.) This combination was fashionable as Pepys explains later. In 1660, he recorded how: 'this morning my dining room was finished with grene serge hangings and gilt leather which is very handsome' (*The Diary of Samuel Pepys*, I, p.269). The upholstery sometimes matched wall hangings as an ensemble. In 1637, Easton Lodge listed 'one high chair, one low chair, and three low stools all of gilt leather suitable to the hangings in the closet of the Chapel' (Thornton, 1978, pp 104–5).

Some leather hangings were embroidered. For example, Sir Henry of Scrivener had in his lodging chamber 'calfe skins silvered and wrought

58. Leather hangings, seveteenth century, Ham House (©NTPL/John Bethell)

upon with a large flower in blew worsted; they come short of the ground having the breadth of a panel of wainscot below them, and a frieze and a cornish above them' (Macquoid & Edwards, 1924, p.257). The 1658 Verney Papers mention negotiations around the supply of gilt leather: 'Rather than go to a much higher price for hangings etc. I would gladly bestow a matter of £88 in wainscot for my parlour, then, I should like very well this painted leather for a suit of chairs and stools.' (Macquoid, 1904, p.177.) On occasion, gilt leather was used for other furnishing items such as **table carpets** and screens. At Kilkenny in 1684, the Great Dining Room had 'three French gilt-leather carpets fitted to the tables' (Thornton, 1978, p.242). In 1681, Sir Alexander Brand petitioned for a monopoly to manufacture Spanish leather. He certainly supplied Kinross House and Dalkieth with gilt leather panels.

The taste continued into the eighteenth century. In 1702, Mr Blathwayt arranged for his gilt leather hangings to be fitted in the vestibule of Dyrham Park: 'As soon as Mr Skelton's man comes he shall take the first opportunity of Moist Weather for putting up the gilt leather which is thought most proper for this work' (Walton, 1986, p.34). The reason for this was explained when Blathwayt complained that, 'The gilt leather in the great parlor very ill put up and must be stretcht which can be done only in wett weather.' (ibid. p.41.) John Hutton, a London gilt leather worker, supplied Earl Fitzwalter in February 1735 with a 'set of gilt leather hangings blewe and gold, with a damask figure and mosaic border' (*DEFM*, p.469).

Although out of fashion by the mid-eighteenth century, it was used in a small way as a **border** for wall coverings. It was still being used in the Governor's palace in Williamsburg in 1771 (Thornton, 1984, p.100). It was later revived in the 1840s when a taste for antique styles was prevalent.
See also **Spanish leather**, **Wall covering and hanging**.

FURTHER READING

Huth, H. (1937). 'English chinoiserie gilt leather', *Burlington Magazine*, 71, 412, July, pp 25–7, 30–33, 35.
Koldeweij, E. (2000). 'Gilt leather hangings in chinoiserie and other styles: an English speciality', *Furniture History*, 36, pp 61–101.
Waterer, J. (1971). *Spanish Leather: History of its Use from 800 to 1800 for Mural Hangings, Screens, Upholstery, Altar Frontals, Ecclesiastical Vestments, Footwear, Gloves, Pouches and Caskets,* London: Faber and Faber.

Gimp

A hard-spun **silk**, **worsted** or **cotton cord**, wrapped with other yarns to form an openwork **braid**. Widely used as an edge decoration, it is also employed to cover **tacks** on the edge of **upholstery** work. The word nearly corresponds in meaning to the French *guipure*, from *guiper*, 'to whip' or wrap (a cord, etc.) with thread or silk. Now chiefly applied to a kind of **trimming** made of this. Caulfeild & Saward defined gimp as:

> An open work trimming used on both dress and furniture, and in coach lace making. It is made of silk, worsted, or cotton twist, having a cord, or a wire running through it. The strands are plaited or twisted, so as to form a pattern. The French word passementerie has much superseded that of gimp, in reference to the finer sorts for dress. (1887, p.222.)

Now it is an openwork trimming, made from silk, **wool** or cotton, often twisted with a cord or wire running through it. The strands are looped, plaited or twisted to make a pattern similar to wickerwork. More complex gimps include 'embassy', which is stiff and symmetrical, for use in straight work, and 'shell', which is flexible and looser.

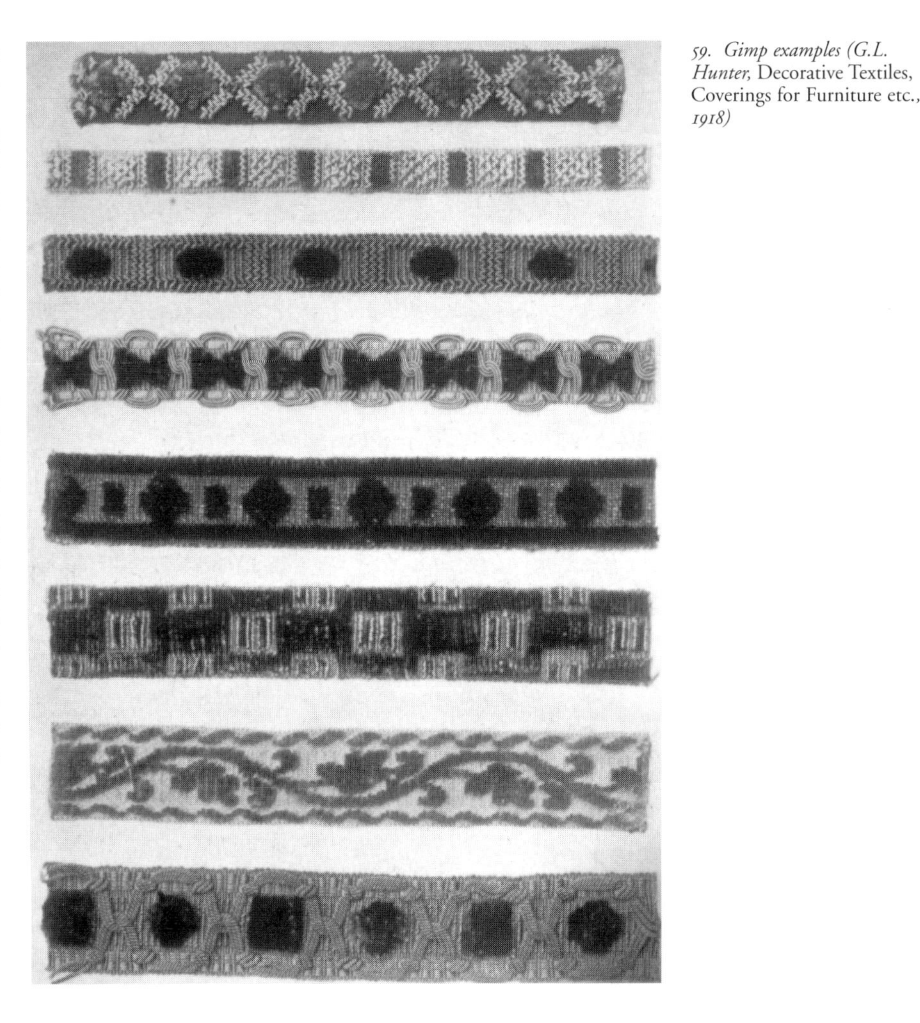

59. Gimp examples (G.L. Hunter, Decorative Textiles, Coverings for Furniture etc., *1918)*

Argyle
A woven figured narrow fabric approximately 6¼ inches (16 cm) wide, with a double wave raised pattern on a flat ground. It is widely used on upholstery trimming, especially on the edges of wooden-frame chairs.

Coronation
An upholstery trimming which has a 'grain of wheat' design woven into it. It is about ½ an inch (1.25 cm) wide.

Gymp-head
Narrow openworked braid for finishing upholstery work to conceal the turnings on edges. It is nailed on or sewn over seams (Caulfeild & Saward, 1887, p.248).
See also **Passementerie**.

Gimp pin

Gimp pins are small thin nails, enamelled or lacquered, available in a range of colours. They are used to attach gimp **braid**, **fringes** and exposed backs of outer covers. Known in the late eighteenth century as 'copper pin nails'. Today, they are generally of fine cut steel. (Small wire nails have been used for the same purpose.)
See also **Gimp**.

60. Gingham cloth (M. Sheridan, The Furnisher's Encyclopaedia, *1955)*

Gingham

A cloth originally of **cotton** and **tussah silk**, from northeast India and Malaya. It was imitated in the West in all-cotton. A nineteenth-century version was made from **linen**. The name probably comes from the Dutch *gingang*, itself being derived from the Malay *ginggang*. It is now a plain-weave cotton fabric made with dyed yarns, often in stripes and **checks** with multiple-stranded **warps** and **wefts**. Medium or fine yarns of varying quality are used to obtain the checks, **plaids**, stripes and plain effects. **Tissue** or zephyr ginghams are sheer, being woven with finer yarns and a higher thread count.

Early references are found in the East India Co's Letter Book of 1670, which records an order from Bengal: '2,000 pieces of striped Ginghams, according to pattern now sent, 10,000 coloured ginghams, 10 yards long, full yard wide, most graies, even colours, free from rowes, and of best sorts' (Irwin & Schwartz, 1966, p.65).

Gingham was widely used in the eighteenth century for **case covers** and **upholstery** and was often referred to as 'check'. For example, in 1742, the Westminster upholsterer, William Greer, supplied case covers of 'fine cotton cheque' for chairs in the drawing room at Gibside (Cornforth, 2005, p.105).

The nineteenth-century writer, J.C. Loudon, referred to bonnet blinds, noting that the frames were covered 'in strong linen, of the kind called gingham, and is generally striped with blue and white colours, which harmonise remarkably well with the sky and clouds' (1839, p.270). Although gingham was made in plain white, full colour or plaid, it was the balanced check that became a furnishing favourite.

In the twentieth century, gingham was considered economical and pretty for window treatments. One American author wrote:

> If you want the least expensive of all hangings for windows, ginghams can be so used as to look charming. Try the small pink and white checks or green and white or blue and white. You can use this gingham for covering beds, dressing-tables, a bureau, tables and to hang at closet doors. (Burbank, 1922, p.153.)

Gingham remained popular after World War II:

> If woven with white and coloured cotton yarns they are usually the same number of white and coloured yarns in the same sequence in the warp as in the filling [weft]… Ginghams are mercerised and thus have a soft lustrous appearance. Used for curtains, draperies, spreads, and dressing table skirts. (Bendure & Pfieffer, 1947, p.632.)

See also **Bonnet blind**, **Chambray**.

Girth web

See **Webbing**.

Glass bead embroidery

See **Beadwork**.

Glass cloth

An ancient process of drawing glass into fibres was revived in the eighteenth century. Glass fibres for ecclesiastical fabrics were produced in Austria, France and Italy. In 1713, the Paris Academy received a glass fibre cloth woven by the Venetian, Carlo Riva. In the later nineteenth century, Caulfeild & Saward recorded a cloth made from glass: 'A glass tablecloth shines with a satiny opalescent lustre by day and under gas light shows remarkable beauty.' (1887, p.223.) Spun glass cloth was first patented in the USA in 1880 by Hermann Hammesfahr of Pittsburgh, Pennsylvania. The cloth made entirely or mostly of spun glass was a novel invention. Traditionally, the glass fibres were peeled off a solid glass rod that was heated and came into contact with a large spinning metal wheel. The results were like thin strands of glass wire. Although the fabric was often woven entirely of spun glass, sometimes silver, **silk** or fine wire were used for the **weft**. In 1950, *The Mercury Dictionary of Textile Terms* concurred and found it mostly used for church decoration. Glass cloth is also a term for glass towelling.

See also **Glass fibre**, **Glass towelling**.

Glass curtain

Thin, flat-hanging **curtains** that are hung against the window glass and cover the entire window, or directly over a window shade: they are intended to filter the light and offer privacy. For these reasons, they are usually kept drawn.

In the later nineteenth century, they were made from **silk**, muslin or madras, and trimmed with soft **fringes**, usually being hung from a small rod. They were often supplied in pairs, in lace patterns such as Brussels, Swiss, Irish point or Nottingham. Glass curtains could be hung to the sill or a little lower when they might be tied back with ribbon or small loops of silk.

In 1947, the following cloths were recommended for making up into glass curtains: **organd**, **dotted Swiss**, **chiffon**, **ninon**, **voile** and **scrim**. Also recommended were **grenadine**, marquisette and madras gauze. If opacity was required, **pongee**, **casement cloth** and muslin were selected (Bendure & Pfieffer, 1947, p.586).

See also **Gauze**, **Lace**, **Muslin**, **Sheer curtain**, **Under curtain**.

Glass fibre

Continuous filaments drawn from molten glass have been used in the production of textiles. Commercial success occurred particularly after World War II, although attempts were made prior to this. Glass fibre cloth was printed, textured or plain, and being fire, water and pet proof,

was seen as a miracle fibre. Its low abrasion resistance meant that it was difficult to handle. Domestic furnishings made from this fibre fell from favour by the 1970s.
See also **Glass cloth**.

FURTHER READING

Anon. (1963). 'Glass fibres', *CIBA Review*, 5, pp 1–52.

Glass towelling

Cloth made from **linen**, **cotton** or **rayon**, although linen is best, as it does not shed lint. It is a rather loosely woven fabric of high twist yarns, often in blue or red stripes or **checks**, though other colours have been used. Glass towelling has also been produced in white with a coloured **border**, and has been used for **towels**, kitchen **curtains**, **table covers**, etc.

Gobelins tapestry

A French tapestry workshop that arguably produced the most technically proficient tapestries ever made. Established as tapestry workshops around 1607, it was in 1662 that they were taken over by the Crown to produce tapestries for the King. Charles Le Brun was appointed artistic director in 1663. The Gobelins workshop executed tapestry on a high **warp** loom with thick warp yarns and soft **wool wefts** that were beaten up to completely hide the warp, thus creating a horizontal ribbed effect. Towards the end of the century, the subject matter changed from historical and political imagery to more entertaining and amusing designs based on fables and themes. In the eighteenth century, the alentours borders took on some greater importance in the design of the tapestry.

By the 1770s, the factory was producing **upholstery** covers in competition with Beauvais. Gobelins tapestry work was particularly associated with a taste where chair covers were also woven en suite with wall tapestries. Osterley Park has a fine set. A furniture example is from *c.*1780 when Sir Richard Worsley ordered that his drawing room be supplied with '8 cabriole elbow chairs carved and gilt in burnished gold and covered with Gobelin Tapestry. A sofa to match covered with ditto' (Boynton, 1965, p.44).

Through the nineteenth century, the factory produced tapestries that were copies of well-known paintings. This was achieved by the development of an enormous range of yarn shades. By the 1930s, the Gobelins and Beauvais workshops merged and worked exclusively for the French government.

62. Gobelins loom showing tapestry weaver manipulating the warps for bobbin insertion (D. Diderot, Encyclopédie, *1751–72)*

Confusion over names occurred when an elongated tent **stitch** called Gobelin stitch was introduced to needleworkers in the 1840s to imitate woven tapestry. This was subsequently called tapestry work and caused misunderstanding with the woven techniques. Another more general use of the name was mentioned in 1872, when Gobelins tapestry was defined as a 'fine, figured worsted fabric' which 'is principally used for curtains, hangings etc.' (Brown & Gates, 1872).
See also **Alentours**, **Beauvois tapestry**, **Tapestry**.

FURTHER READING

Fenaille, M. (1903–23). *Etat Général des Tapisseries de la Manufacture des Gobelins depuis son Originé jusqu' à nos jours, 1600–1900*, 6 vols, Paris: Hatchette.

Weigert, R. (1962). *French Tapestry*, London: Faber and Faber.

61. Gobelins tapestry after a cartoon by Charles Le Brun (1619–90), woven by Etienne Claude Le Blond (c.1700–51) and Jean de La Croix (active 1662–1712) at the Manufacture Royale des Gobelins, Paris, France. Hanging entitled 'Autumn', c.1710, wool and silk, slit and double interlocking tapestry weave. (Gift of the Hearst Foundation in memory of William Randolph Hearst, 1954.260, The Art Institute of Chicago. Photography ©The Art Institute of Chicago)

Goblet pleat

Pinch-pleated curtain heading with the top edge pushed out to form a goblet shape. The effect can be achieved by using a variety of implements. These **pleats** became fashionable in the later nineteenth century and onward. A simple device to create goblet effects was marketed by the Gobelin Co of Washington that used a cup-shaped device and a spring clip to hold the fabric around the cup shape (Winkler & Moss, 1986, p.213).

Godet

A piece of wedge-shaped fabric (a gore) that tapers from wide to narrow, and is intended for insertion into seams for added fullness. It is used for slipcovers, bedcovers, etc.

Gorgoran

An East Indian **silk** cloth that is woven with alternating plain and patterned stripes. It was used for **curtains** in the eighteenth century. According to Antonio de Morga (1559–1639), in his *History of the Philippine Islands*, Chinese merchants sold 'damasks, satins, taffetans, gorvaranes, picots, and other cloths of all colors, some finer and better than others' to the inhabitants of the Philippines (www.gutenberg.org/etext/7001).

Grass

Any plant of the *Gramineae* family, which includes cereals, reeds and bamboos. Many varieties have been used in furniture-making since ancient Egyptian times, especially for bottoming chairs and **stuffing upholstery** work.

Bulrush (Scirpus lacustris)

Growing up to 10 feet (3 metres) high in wet marshy areas, it has a smooth stem completely free of leaves and nodules, making it an ideal bottoming material. It is a member of the sedge family and although called 'rush' is not botanically of that family.

Cat's-tail (Typha latifolia)

A common term that refers to reedy marsh plants with brown furry flower spikes resembling that specific part of a cat. Cat's-tail grass has been used at various times as an upholstery filling. As early as 1474 these fillings were referred to in England (in conjunction with thistle down) as an inferior and unsatisfactory material: 'feather beds and bolster stuffed with thistle down and cats' tails … [have] been deceivably made to the hurt of the King's liege people' (Houston, 1993, p.5).

Over 300 years later, in 1803, Richard Wevill's inventory of his Philadelphia upholstery business included: 'a small cattail mattrass' valued at $2.50 and 'a lot of cattail' valued at $1.00 (Cooke [ed.], 1987, p.117).

Cat's-tail was still used in the early twentieth century for a range of tasks: 'The leaves have been used by coopers for inserting between the staves of their casks. They have also been used for making chair bottoms, thatching huts and making baskets. The seeds are finely composed, and when ripe the down easily separates; it has been used for stuffing pillows.' (Hannan, 1902, p.2.)

Cotton grass

A general name for the genus *Eriophorum*. Cotton grass has been used for **pillow** stuffing.

Flag

The common name for the wild iris, sweet sedge or sweet flag, although the term can refer to a range of grass or water plant species. Flags were used for bottoming chairs in New England during the seventeenth century.

Marsh grass (Juncus effusus)

Any grass that grows in marshy ground especially *G. spartina.* It was used as a stuffing material in seventeenth-century upholstery in America and England. Initially, bunches of grass were arranged to cover the seat and back, with the protruding ends packed over the frame to protect the **leather** covers from chaffing. In more sophisticated work, grass was prepared in rolls, which delineated an outline that would then be filled with **hair**.

Prairie grass

A wiregrass from the prairies of North West America, which, in the later nineteenth century, was converted into a pliable twine and used in the manufacture of woven 'wicker' style furniture.

See **Grass: Marsh grass**.

Reed (Typha)

Reed mace has long sharp leaves growing round the base and has the easily recognised brown furry sausage-shaped flower. Reed is called cat's-tail in the USA and, mistakenly, bulrush in England. Also known as fen down.

Seagrass

In its natural state, seagrass is a coarse grass or sedge. It belongs to the *Cyperus* family that is a native of Bengal, though may be found in China and Malaya where it is used for basket making. The natural colour of seagrass is somewhat like rush and is used for seating, stools and chairs. It is, however, much easier to use than rush since it is available in long lengths, does not require damping, and it allows for a greater variety of patterns.

Sea wrack grass (Zostera marina)

A dried **seaweed** upholstery filling material, described as being:

> found on the coast of Norfolk; abundantly in the Orkneys and Hebrides; and on the northern shores of the German ocean. When gathered it is repeatedly washed in fresh water, to deprive it of all its saline particles; and being dried in the sun it is twisted into thick ropes and in that state sent to the manufacturer who has it untwisted and cut into short lengths for use. (Loudon, 1839, p.325.)

Also known as **eel grass** and **Alva marina**.

Sedge

A grass-like flowering plant that grows in marshy areas. Sedges are generally distinguished from grasses by their triangular stems and by leaves with closed sheaths. William Nicholls of Bedwardine in Worcestershire had 'one segg chair and one segg stool' (West, 1962, p.117). In a different context entirely, a variety of sedge (*Carex stricta*) was used to weave into furniture. It was used in the manufacture of Prairie Grass furniture from 1900 by a subsidiary of the American Grass Twine Co. The range was available in 'Natural Green' or 'Baronial Brown' and was sold under the trade name of Crex. The taste for this range lasted until World War I after which time woven paper substitutes took over much of the trade.

Wiregrass

See **Grass: Marsh grass**, **Grass rug**, **Matting: Rush**.

FURTHER READING

Howlett, C. (1990). 'The identification of grasses and other plant materials used in historic upholstery' in Williams, M.A. (ed.), *Upholstery Conservation*, preprints of a symposium held at Colonial Williamsburg, 2–4 February, American Conservation Consortium, East Kingston, NH, pp 66–91.

Grass cloth (aka Canton linen)

Woven from the inner bark of the *Boehmeria nivea.* It resembles **linen** and is a fine light cloth. It has been used for **table covers** (*The Mercury Dictionary of Textile Terms*, 1950).

See also **Ramie cloth**.

Grass rug
See **Rug**.

'Gravy-proof' cloth
An American **tablecloth** material that is treated with a very fine stain-resistant plastic coating. This makes the cloth almost indistinguishable from an untreated version.

Grecian bedspread
See **Bedspread**.

Grenadine
A **silk** or **wool** textile used for dresses in the nineteenth century. It is also a fine **cotton** material that was used for **under curtains** in the USA from the later nineteenth century. It was also used for **mosquito netting**: 'In some houses belonging to wealthy Cubans, the mosquito nettings are made of fine pineapple cloth, while in Spain a silk grenadine with a narrow stripe of blue is often used.' (French, 1903, p.110.)

By the early twentieth century it was defined as:

> A cloth of very open texture constructed in the gauze weave, usually made of silk and worsted. Often has a fancy stripe of different weaves. It has not been used much in recent years. The term 'grenadine' weave, is however, often applied to openwork fabrics with fancy stripes. (Dyer, *c.*1923, p.291.)

Grenadine was also popular as a curtain fabric from the 1930s to the 1950s. Bendure & Pfieffer define it as 'a loosely woven fabric with hard twisted yarns that are dyed before weaving, producing check or stripes. Curtain grenadine often has a clipped swivel dot or dobby pattern.' (1947, p.632.) Smithells (1950) refers to it as 'an open leno weave cotton curtain fabric'.
See also **Muslin: Madras**, **Marquisette**, **Weave: gauze**.

Grenfell cloth.
Defined in 1936 as a 'closely woven water-repellent windproof fabric of Egyptian cotton. Originally, a cloth designed for garments in the Grenfell Mission, Labrador. Now sold as yardage. Used for sports clothes, shower curtains, upholstery, drapery.' (Denny, 1936, p.34.)

Grille
A later nineteenth-century decorative pierced wooden panel in a variety of patterns used to fit the top part of a sash window with **curtains** below. Moreland, in 1889, recommended that either they were painted to match the interior woodwork with the curtains drawing behind them, or they were lined or backed with matching material to the curtains (1889, pp 19–20). They were also used internally in doorways to support **portières**, or simply as dividers. Grilles were widely sold in the decades either side of 1900, in some cases by mail order.

Grommet
A metal ring punched through fabric to create a secure hole into which poles, wire or rods can be safely inserted. They are used in conjunction with **café curtains** on occasion.

Gros
A French term for fabrics with a cross rib. It also refers to thick, chunky fabrics.

Gros de Londres
A closely woven fabric with a crosswise ribbed effect having alternate heavy and light ribs. The effects are achieved by weaving groups of **weft** yarns as one. Used for **curtains** and dresses (Bendure & Pfieffer, 1947, p.632).

Gros de Naples
Plain-woven **silk** textiles produced with a corded effect. In 1830, Stafford House, London, was supplied with '2 furniture doors with semicircular trellis work finished in bronze green and lined at back with grey Gros-de-Naples' (Yorke, 1996, p.74). In 1831, Dionysus Lardner wrote in his *Cabinet Cyclopedia*: 'Gros de Naples is made of stouter and harder thrown organzine silk and is put together with more care and labour, containing a greater number of threads, both warp and shoot in a given surface. Ducapes are likewise plain-wove stout silks, but of softer texture than the last.' (1831, p.296.) The *Penny Cyclopaedia* (1842) explained that 'Persian, sarsenet, gros-de-Naples, ducapes, satin and levantines are plain silks, which vary from one another only in texture, quality or softness' (XXII. 12/1).
See also **Ducape**.

Grosgrain
A term for any plain-weave textile that has a corded effect created by heavier **weft** yarns. In particular, it refers to **silk** or silk mixture cloths made from grosgrain yarns (large, rounded twists) that produced a thick corded-effect fabric, suitable for **upholstery**. The name derives from the French **gros**, meaning 'thick'.

The *Book of Rates* for 1582 mentions both 'Grograin silk the yarde' and 'Grograin chamlets' (Willan, 1962, p.30). One of the New Draperies, its use was recorded in 1643 as an upholstery cover in Worcester House: '1 elbow chair and 8 stools of silver figured grograine' (Clabburn, 1988, p.246). In 1651, the Montacute sale inventory listed '4 blew grosgraine curtaines with vallins' (Beard, 1997, p.291). A year later, John Evelyn noted a visit 'to see the manner of chambletting silk and grosgrains at Monsieur La Doree's in Morefields' (*Diary of John Evelyn*, 30 May 1652).

In the eighteenth century, it was used in America. For example, John Williams of Boston, in his 1734 inventory had 'a bedstead and silk grogrun furniture' (Cummings, 1961, p.37).

By the mid-twentieth century, Smithells recorded that it was 'a firm close corded silk, or silk and cotton fabric, used for curtain ties, lampshades and various other trimmings' (Smithells, 1950).
See also **Bengaline**, **Camlet**, **Ducape**, **Tabby**.

Gros point
See **Stitch: Cross**.

Guard lace
A thin figured **tape** or **braid** originally for garments in the seventeenth century, but later used for **binding** the edges of **curtains**. The word guarding meant being edged with **lace** or other trim in fifteenth and sixteenth-century inventories.

Gunny
A coarse **jute** cloth made in India and sent to the West since the early eighteenth century. The Sanskrit name for a sack is *goni*. Gunny is particularly associated with **sackcloth** and bale wrapping, although it has been used for **curtains** and flooring in meagre interiors.
See also **Hessian**.

Habberley carpet
Defined by *The Mercury Dictionary of Textile Terms* (1950) as 'a cheap carpet produced in art squares from 2½ to 4 yards wide and length. Woven with cotton warp and different coloured wefts of wool and cotton mixtures'.
See also **Art Square**.

Habutai (aka China silk)
A soft, pure **silk** plain-weave fabric of close, firm, but uneven texture of low-quality unthrown raw silk in the gum. In the nineteenth century, it was used for clothes. In the twentieth century, it was employed in making up and lining lampshades, **cushion** covers and accessories.

Hair
Animal hair has been used extensively in the furnishing trades both as **upholstery filling** and for weaving into cloth (see **Haircloth**). Curled horsehair is considered to be one of the best traditional upholstery fillings for both mattresses and seating as its resilience remains for long periods. A spring is permanently set in the hair by boiling or steaming tightly-twisted ropes of prepared carded hair, which give the effect of many resilient individual fibres. Horsehair was most favoured, but hair from other animals was also employed from at least the fifteenth century.

The early use of animal hair in upholstery is evident from the plea made by the Upholders' Company in 1495. They complained of persons who used very poor quality hair and brought the craft into disrepute. Therefore, in 1495, an 'Act against Upholsterers' was passed which forbade the use of 'horse hair, fen downe [reed mace], neetis [oxen] hair, deer's hair, and goat's hair which is wrought in lyme fattes [grease], and by the heat of a man's body, the savour and taste is so abominable and contagious that many of the King's subjects [have] thereby been destroyed…' (Houston, 1993, p.9).

Horsehair became more valued as upholstery methods developed. Between 1660 and 1661, Charles II had John Caspert supply him with chairs that specified 'curled hair to fill the chair back' (Thornton, 1978, p.225). By 1679, its value was so widely recognised that attempts began to imitate and substitute it in upholstery work. By this time, it was also used as a mattress filling.

In the eighteenth century, it appears that it was common practice to re-use old hair by teasing it out and adding new when needed. In 1819, it was commented that:

> The best picked hair is made of horse or bullock tails, and should not be mixed with short hair. This is the case however with common hair, and the quality of the article is known by the greater or lesser quantity of the short kind that is introduced. (Martin, 1813, p.115.)

In America, Sloan's *Homestead Architecture* noted that the best horsehair is brought from South America, however 'an inferior quality of domestic cattle hair is used in cheap upholstery, but it always retains the odor [sic] of the barn-yard and in damp weather it is offensive when used to stuff sofas, chairs or mattresses' (Sloan, 1861, p.321). Sloan went on to mention another odd mix of hog hairs and horsehair, which was a cheap substitute for the real thing. He commented that it was 'a dangerous article for housekeepers as it generates moths and is the prolific cause of great increase of this domestic pest' (ibid. p.322).

By the twentieth century, hair had also been rubberised and formed into pads, but loose curled hair remains part of the traditional upholsterers' repertoire, whether for mattresses or upholstery.
See also **Hair carpet**, **Haircord**, **Mattress**, **Mohair**, **Rubberised hair**.

Hair carpet (aka Haircloth)
A twilled material with a **weft** of spun hair (often goat) and **cotton linen** or **wool warps**. It seems to have been a speciality, sold by turners in the mid-eighteenth century, for carpeting stairs.

In the *Servants' Directory* of 1760, Hannah Glass suggested 'If you lay a stair cloth on, let it be a hair-cloth, fastened on with hook and long wires. The Turners can supply you; they will never move till wore into holes…' (Gilbert, Lomax & Wells-Cole, 1987, p.95). A year later, a New York business was offering 'English and Scot's carpets and Hair cloth for Stairs' (Roth, 1967, p.32). Other examples demonstrate the utilitarian nature of the cloth. The 1763 inventory of John Linnell's London house listed haircloth in a number or rooms, with the parlour having 'a Wilton carpet made of old pieces, a list carpet and a piece of hair cloth' (Hayward & Kirkham, 1980, p.178). Whilst in 1778, Methley Hall, Yorkshire, had the new staircase laid with 'Hair cloth from top to bottom with lead bars' (Gilbert, Lomax & Wells-Cole, 1987, p.95).

In 1910, London retailer, Gillows, advertised 'Best Horsehair Carpet- this is specially manufactured to stand rough wear; grey centre, red border 22½; 27; 36 in' (Gillow Co Records, Westminster Library, London). Hair carpets remain available.
See also **Hair**, **Haircloth**.

Haircloth (aka horsehair material)
An **upholstery** textile that is woven mainly from horsehair, although it has also been made from camel, goat or even dog hair. It is woven at an average 27 inches (68 cm) width (varying between 14 and 40 inches [35 and 101 cm], depending on the hair length) in **sateen**, twill and rep weaves, as well as plain, striped, chequered or **damask** effects. The fabric had a **linen** or **cotton warp** with a hair **weft**, thus giving a glossy surface appearance. Dark horsehair is usually dyed black, whilst the lighter hairs are reserved for dyeing into other colourways.

It appeared in the fifteenth and sixteenth centuries where it was used as a backing cloth for the 'holes' in aumbrys. In the later seventeenth century, Randle Holme referred to haircloth as a 'covering material for arks' (1688).

The cloth was particularly used for covering chairs, especially dining chairs, from the mid-eighteenth century. James Barber of Newark advertised in 1778 that 'the trade may be supplied with any quantity of the new fashioned hair covering for chairs' (*DEFM*, p.38). By the end of the century, Hepplewhite's *The Cabinet Maker and Upholsterer's Guide* still recommended that 'mahogany chairs should have the seats of horsehair, plain, striped, chequered, &c. at pleasure' (1789, p.2).

Haircloth was also popular in the nineteenth century due to its strength, imperviousness and cleanability. In the mid-nineteenth century, its **silk** effect gave it the name of 'satin hair' in the USA. However, Christopher Dresser pronounced it 'inartistic in its effect' (1873, p.72), so it is not surprising to find that during the 1876 Centennial Exhibition it was noted that 'modern fashion has driven this material from fashionable drawing rooms; but its durability still causes it to be retained in unambitious apartments' (Adrosko, 1990, p.108).

Caulfeild & Saward confirmed that traditional techniques continued in the later nineteenth century. It is 'dyed crimson, claret, green and scarlet, and is largely manufactured at Sheffield and Worcester and is partially hand-made in a loom, owing to there being no continuous thread of hair to render machinery available' (1887, p.248).

Artificial horsehair made from thick filament viscose **rayon** was used to replace horsehair in the 1920s, due to shortages of the real product.
See also **Hair**, **Seating**.

FURTHER READING

Congram, M. (1980). 'Haircloth upholstery', *Nineteenth Century*, 6, 4, pp 48–50.

Hair cord

A mid-twentieth century **Brussels** type loop-**pile carpet** often woven with a coarse yarn of a goat **hair** and synthetic fibre mixture, usually limited to plain colours. The foundation yarns are sometimes dyed to prevent the grinning (the opening of pile) being too obvious since they generally have a short pile height.

Half curtain

See **Café curtain**, **Sash curtain**.

Half damask

See **Damask: Mixed (half)**.

Half-silk

Specialities of Venetian **silk** factories, half-silks were woven textiles with a main **warp** of **linen**, though having a binding warp of silk and a **weft** of silk.

Halling

See **Dorcer**, **Wall covering and hanging**.

Hangings

See **Wall covering and hanging**.

Happing

An early name for a **coverlet**, **quilt** or **rug**. It is derived from the verb 'to hap', meaning 'to cover over' or 'layover'. In 1556, a Durham merchant, William Dalton, had 'a feather bed, a twilt, a happing [coverlet] and a bolster' (Wright, 1871, p.480). The inventory of Mrs Elizabeth Hutton of Hunwick, taken in 1567, listed quantities of bedding including: 'twelve pairs of blankets, and six happings, twenty coverlets, three coverings for beds of tapestry, and two of dornix' (Gloag, 1990, p.268).
See also **Counterpane**.

Harden (aka Hurden)

A coarse fabric made from 'hards' or 'hurds', which are the coarser parts of flax or **hemp**. It was made from the fifteenth century and used for **sheets**, **towels** and **tablecloths**. In 1570, a will included 'One payer of sheets of hurden' (*Bury Wills*, Camden Society, p.156), and in 1668, Markham explained that 'that which comes from the flax being a little towed again in a pair of Wool Cards, will make a course harding' (Markham, II. V., 1668, 134, *OED*).

It was still in use in the nineteenth century. *The Workwoman's Guide* explained one of its roles: 'large sheets of coarse brown paper pasted together in lengths should be laid over the beds to catch dust. Some persons lay hurden or coarse linen between the head of the bed and these sheets of paper' (Hale, 1840, p.192).
See also **Linen**, **Sameron**.

Harrateen (aka Harratine)

A (moiré) **worsted** fabric with a worsted **warp** and a thicker worsted **weft** giving a ribbed effect. It was finished by watering and stamping. A speciality of Norwich, England, it was an important **woollen** furnishing fabric that often had a hot-pressed design applied, imitating **damask**. It was also used unwatered.

The 1750 Holker manuscript describes harrateen as 'A kind of woollen mohair [moiré] of which the warp as well as the weft is of wool and manufactured in Norwich. The wavy pattern is made by means of a hot press, the use of which is little understood in France. This kind of material is used for furnishing' (Montgomery, 1960, p.241).

It was used in the eighteenth century for a range of furnishings. On 26 September 1711, the Duke of Newcastle wrote to the Duke of Montagu concerning 'Six field Bedsteads with Crimson harateen furnitures' (*New English Dictionary on Historical Principles*, 1888). It was also used in America. In 1726, the Boston upholsterer, Thomas Fitch, wrote to a client of this material:

> I concluded it would be difficult to get such a Calliminco as you propos'd to cover the ease chair, and having a very strong thick Harratine which is vastly more fashionable and handsome than a Calliminco. I have sent you an ease chair cover'd with sd Harrateen which I hope will sute you. (Montgomery, 1984, p.256.)

During 1731, 'one new harrateen bed, bedstead and Cornish all compleat never used' was listed in the inventory of the business of the Bastards of Blandford (Legg, 1994, p.29). In 1735, 'a field bedstead and bed, the covering blew harrateen' was sold in Boston. In 1748, the English newspaper, the *General Advertiser*, published an advertisement for 'Ready-Made Furnitures either of Harrateen, Cheney, Flower'd Cotton, Checks' (No. 4440). Harrateen remained popular until the 1750s, when it tended to be replaced by textiles that were more washable.

However, it did not completely lose favour. Examples of its use can be found in 1811, when the Hardwick Hall dining room was fitted out with 'a very large green haraton festoon window curtain' (Levey, 1998, p.91). In the USA, Esther Hewlett (1825) suggested that 'If you have curtains … the best are linen check harrateen' (Cummings, 1961, p.26). By 1882, it was defined rather dismissively as 'an imitation of Moiré in commoner material for purposes of upholstery' (Beck).
See also **Moiré**, **Moreen**.

Harris tweed

All Harris tweeds are hand-woven on the islands off the northern coast of Scotland (Outer Hebrides). There are two types: one in which the fabric is woven from hand-spun yarn, and the other where the fabric is woven from machine-spun yarn. Today, very few are woven from hand-spun yarns as it takes too much time and labour. The textile is always stamped in addition to having an identification label, which any Harris tweed always bears. Much is woven in 27 and 28 inch (68 and 71 cm) widths; some also in 54 inch (137 cm). It was popular in the 1950s and 1960s as **upholstery** covering for open wooden-framed seating.
See also **Furniture tweed**, **Tweed**.

FURTHER READING

Thompson, F. (1969). *Harris Tweed: The Story of a Hebridean Industry*, Newton Abbot: David and Charles.

Hassock

A thick firm floor **cushion**, often stuffed with rushes or **straw**, used to rest the feet on. In domestic use, they were covered with fabric or **carpet** and used as footstools or small seats. They were referred to in 1625: 'Buy a mat for your bed, buy a mat! A hassock for your feet' (John Fletcher & James Shirley, *The Night Walker*, vol.I, *OED*). Loudon said:

> A footstool either plain or covered with carpeting is an article of essential utility in every cottage where there is a mother; and it also forms

a seat for a child. In England, they are very commonly formed by covering a bundle of bulrushes with rush matting, and they are then called hassocks. (1839, pp 315–6.)

The Workwoman's Guide explained that: 'these may be got up very cheaply at home. The most simple and prettiest for a bed-room or even a sitting room is a cloth or velvet hassock braided over, or otherwise ornamented' (Hale, 1840, p.207).
See also **Brioche cushion**, **Humpty**.

Headboard
A shaped board designed to be placed or fitted on the head of the bed as a decorative feature and also to retain the **pillows**. It was located in front of any **head cloth**. Spectacular designs were used in the later seventeenth century for state beds and this practice continued into the eighteenth century. Hepplewhite's *The Cabinet Marker and Upholsterer's Guide*, explained about the role of headboards:

> To this bed is added a stuffed headboard, with ornament and drapery over it. The drapery may be the same as the furniture or the lining; the ornaments gilt; the headboard is stuffed, and projects like as the back of a sofa. The addition of stuffed headboards gives an elegant and high finish to the appearance of beds. (1789, Plate 97.)

Headboards in the later part of the twentieth century may simply hold pillows on the bed. They may be covered in a fabric to match **curtains** or other **drapes** in a bedroom, or a variety of other finishes and effects may be applied. They remain part of the furnishings of a bed.
See also **Bed furniture**.

Head cloth
A single stationary hanging that was fixed at the head of a bed, which often matches the **bed curtains**. The head cloth extended from the **canopy** to just below the **headboard**, and it was usually lined. State beds often had an embroidered cipher centred on them. In the seventeenth century, the technique was often to make up a head cloth in panels of curtain fabric and of **festooned** plain fabric. The fixing of the head cloth was mentioned in 1730: 'The Tester-Cloth, to which the Head-cloth and inside and outside Vallens are to be fixed.' (Southall, *A Treatise of Buggs*, p.40.)
See also **Tester**.

Head curtain
Bed curtains hung at the upper side ends of the bed that could be drawn to cover the upper portion of each side.
See also **Bed furniture**.

Headings
See **Accordion pleat**, **Box pleat**, **Curtain tape**, **French pleat**, **Goblet pleat**, **Inverted pleat**, **Pelmet**, **Pencil pleat**, **Pinch Pleat**, **Pleater hook**, **Pleat**, **Ruffling**, **Scalloped heading**, **Smocked**, **Valance.**

Heading tape
See **Curtain tape**.

Head rest
An early twentieth-century cloth used for chair backs. They were large squares of cloth laid over the head of a chair. These are not the same as antimacassars.
See also **Antimacassar**.

Hearth rug
Small rugs placed in front of the fire probably have a long and undocumented history. They were certainly sold specifically from the early eighteenth century. An advertisement in the *Daily Courant* in November 1711 mentioned 'Turkey carpets ... of small size to put ... by the chimneys to sit on' (Gilbert, Lomax & Wells-Cole, 1987, p.59).

In the nineteenth century, Loudon discusses hearth rugs and mentions how 'a cheap rug may be formed of a piece of drab drugget bound with black, or any other colour to suit the paper and curtains, and fringed either with or without a strip of cloth of the same colour as the binding, laid on about two inches from the margin' (Loudon, 1839, p.346). Hearth rugs woven in a **Brussels** weave, and later still in **Axminster** weave, were popular later in the nineteenth century. Hermann Muthesius noted that the hearth rug 'is a small rug of the exact width of the fender, or a little wider; it is of special quality and may be called the show-piece of the floor' (Muthesius, 1904, p.181).
See **Mohair rug**, **Rug**.

Helioscene blind
A blind arrangement for exteriors of windows with a series of small hoods fixed upon a set of frames made of light iron (Julius Jeffreys, Patent no.1551, 11 July 1851).
See also **Blind**.

Hemp (*Cannabis sativa*)
A fibrous stem of the Indian hemp plant which has been used for hessian, huckabuck, buckram, scrim, canvas and sackcloth, though it has been replaced in recent times by **jute**. Hemp is more durable than jute and coarser and stronger than **linen**. Discarded hemp fibres known as tow have also been used as **upholstery filling**.

In 1696 a linen called hemp-roles was described as 'A strong coarse Linnen and when whited, very good for sheets for poor people.' (J.F., *The Merchant's Warehouse Laid Open.*) It was also used as basis for painted canvas.

In the nineteenth century, hemp was used to manufacture carpeting (see **Hemp carpet**) and, in the early twentieth century, Manila hemp was widely used in various forms for doormat production.
See also **Abaca**, **Bergamo**, **Brussels carpet**, **Buckram**, **Burlap**, **Canvas**, **Crash (Russian)**, **Cretonne**, **Dutch carpet**, **Frisé**, **Fustian**, **Harden**, **Hessian**, **Huckabuck**, **Monk's cloth**, **Moquette**, **Painted cloth**, **Russia tapestry**, **Scrim**, **Tapestry**, **Tow**, **Towel**.

FURTHER READING
Castellini, L. (1961–2). 'The hemp plant', *CIBA Review*, 5, pp 2–31.

Hemp carpet
A nineteenth-century **carpet** woven from hempen yarns. On 11 April 1807, Thomas Paty was granted a patent for 'Weaving and manufacturing East India sun-hemp into carpets and carpet-rug mats' (Patent no.3031). It was a utilitarian flooring which, according to Brown & Gates, had little durability or colour permanence (1872, p.175). It seems that *Ward & Lock's Home Book* confirmed that description, as they noted that hemp carpet was the cheapest carpet made and was not suitable for sitting rooms, but 'may act as a crumb cloth in these situations'. Although it seems to have been particularly popular in the USA, it was also sold in England. During December 1878, Charles Smith of Liverpool advertised that he stocked 'East India carpeting', apparently made 'from a vegetable production of the East Indies particularly adapted from its cheapness and durability for stair cases, halls, common sitting rooms etc.' (*DEFM*, p.825). In the same year, Thomas Wilson, an upholsterer of Exeter, adver-

63. *Helioscene window blind (P. Hasluck,* Window Blinds, *1907)*

tised 'East India hemp carpeting' (*DEFM*, p.989). In 1884, the furnishers, Maple and Co of London, sold 36 inch (91 cm) wide hempen **Dutch carpet** for servants' rooms (1884, p.78). In 1892, Cole noted that carpets made entirely of hemp, were first imported from Russia, but were now made in the USA in considerable quantities:

> They are extremely cheap and durable, but are chiefly used in offices, passages and places where a cheap carpet is required to deaden the sound. An excellent floorcovering for offices and business rooms is also made of cocoa fibre. It is woven open to let the dust pass through, and is extremely durable and cheap. (p.64.)

A year later, mail order retailers, Montgomery Ward, were selling 'printed hemp carpet' in imitation of **Brussels carpet** and, in 1907, their competitors, Sears Roebuck, were offering '18 inch hemp stair carpet at 11 cents per yard' (**ingrain carpet** was 36 cents and **matting** 27 cents per yard). Soon afterwards, it was being praised, although the price seems to have gone up: 'There is a kind of hemp carpet that is very durable and only costs about 35 cents a yard, which would make either a good rug or mat.' (Wilson, 1911, p.39.)

By 1950, the English *Mercury Dictionary of Textile Terms* still suggested that hemp carpet was largely used in the USA for offices, public halls and passageways.
See also **Dutch carpet**, **Hemp**.

Hessian
A woven cloth made from **linen** or **jute** fibres sometimes called **canvas**; it is often woven 72 inches (183 cm) wide specifically for **upholstery** purposes. The name is probably of German origin (*hessen*) as the 1660 *London Book of Rates* refers to 'Dutch barras and Hessen canvas' (Beck, 1882). Hessian has been made in a range of qualities including the tightly woven **spring** canvas (used for upholstery work relating to springing) which is woven with flat threads, and the **scrim** version woven with rounded threads, which is used as a covering of the first **stuffing** that is stitched into place. Hessian has also been used for lining the interiors of upholstery frames. It is available in various weights from 7½ to 16 ounces (212 to 454 grams).

Hessian has been used to line walls for hanging fabrics. In 1743, George Bowes was charged for '55¾ yards of yellow ell wide hessian to line the said hangings at 12d.' (Medlam, 1990, p.144).

During the later nineteenth and early twentieth century, hessian-type materials were sometimes recommended for **curtains** and **wall coverings** especially for the do-it-yourself market. In the 1960s, there was a fashion for paper-backed hessian wall coverings and fabrics.
See also **Burlap**, **Gunny**, **Jute**.

High warp tapestry
See **Tapestry**.

Hilling
Hilling is the name for a particular textile covering for a bed. There are references to hilling in the fourteenth century, but a clear description is found in a will of 1520 that bequeaths 'my best bed hillinge of tapstre werke' (*Lancashire Wills*, 1857, vol.II, p.9).

It was still defined as 'Hilling, the quilt of a bed, a bed rug' in an 1888 Sheffield glossary (*OED*).
See also **Rugg**.

Holdback
A piece of **curtain** hardware designed to hold back the curtain or **drape**.
See also **Tieback**.

Holland
A plain **linen** cloth imported from Holland since the early fifteenth century that was used for **sheets**, **pillowcases**, case covers, **blinds**, etc. The name holland later became a generic title for linen cloth usually of the better qualities.

When holland was imported unbleached it was called brown holland (see below). Holland was also sometimes linked with 'whited canvas, a standard sheeting, whereas sleazy holland (see **Silesia**) was associated with **Scotch cloth**. During the seventeenth century, holland became the accepted name of the highest quality of plain-woven linen suitable for napery, bed linen and shirting.

It was most widely used for sheeting and was often used as a quality designation. Katherine of Aragon's 1537 inventory of her Wardrobe goods at Baynard Castle lists 'one pair of sheets of fine Holland cloth wrought with Spanish work of black silk upon the edges' (Camden Society, *Camden Miscellany*, 1855, vol.III). Henry VII had 'lxxix ells iii quarts of Holland linen cloth for the making of fifteen pillow beeres,

Holland cloth for the same beds and beryngshetes of Holland cloth.' (Leaf, 1934.) In 1553, a Bury will included 'one pair of Holland Sheets.' (*Bury Wills,* Camden Society) These traditions continued. The 1601 Hardwick Hall inventory listed '3 curtains wrought with black silk needlework upon fine holland cloth with button and loops of black silk.' (Boynton, 1971, p.23.) Over 100 years later, in the *Boston Gazette* (29 May–5 June 1727), there were advertised 'linen cloth, diapers, kentines, chequered linen and Holland', which were 'lately imported from Glasgow'. The Felbrigg inventory of 1771 listed 'Blue and white striped Holland for a bed' (Clabburn, 1988, p.247).

It was not only employed for sheeting, but was also used for blinds. In addition, it was particularly recommended for removable covers and for chair back **cushion** 'caps' in the mid-nineteenth century. *The Workwoman's Guide* explained that 'Holland [removable] covers are the most durable but look cold.' (Hale, 1840, p.206.) A little later, Mrs Orrinsmith in her book, *The Drawing Room,* recommended 'fine Holland [as it] makes very pretty curtains, and offers fair opportunity for effective embroidery.' (1877, p.67.) From the eighteenth century, when finished with either a glaze or beetled effect, it was used for roller and spring blinds. Caulfeild & Saward observed that holland was:

> Unbleached and made in two descriptions – the glazed and unglazed. The former is employed for carriage or chair covers and trunk linings; the latter for articles of dress-men's blouses, women's and children's dresses, and many other purposes. A description of Holland is employed for window roller blinds, and in cotton as well as linen. They are highly glazed and sized, so as to be less influenced by dust, and are made in white, blue, buff green and in stripes of different colours. (1887, p.253.)

By the 1890s, Cole noted that holland was either glazed or opaque. The opaque was woven with both **linen** and **cotton** and finished with a sizing of oil and starch (*A Complete Dictionary of Dry Goods*).

Brown holland

A partially bleached or unbleached holland linen cloth. In 1763, William France charged for '3 rowler curtains of brown Holland … for the 3 windows in the bedchamber and dressing room of Croome Court.' (Beard, 1997, p.306.) It was also used for protective coverings. When glazed, it may be used for covering furniture (Caulfeild & Saward, 1887, p.49). The 1885 inventory of Brodsworth Hall listed 'Brown Holland bags for curtains/loose cases for furniture and chandeliers' (Stevens in Gill & Eastop (eds), 2001, p.144).

See also **Blind holland**, **Garlick**, **Protective furnishing**.

Homespun

Homespun is a coarse hand- or machine-woven fabric, originally plain-woven with hand-spun home-grown **wools** that created a **tweed** look. It was originally woven in the homes of peasants, hence the name. It was very serviceable and was used for a range of purposes. Genuine homespun is produced in very limited quantities and, more recently, it has been woven on power looms. It was particularly used for **upholstery** and **drapes** in the USA in the 1940s (Bendure & Pfieffer, 1947, p.633).

See also **Wadmal**.

Honeycomb (aka Waffle weave)

A weave effect, which creates textures that have been widely used for **towels** and bed **quilts**. The quilts are woven with one **warp** and one **weft** of good quality yarns and are **jacquard** figured in bold geometrical designs, developed by honeycomb weaves. One authority discussed honeycomb bedspreads: 'Honeycomb or crochet. These are heavier spreads. They stay clean longer and are very durable, but heavy to launder. They, too, come in various grades, and are not considered expensive' (Dyer, *c.*1923, pp 211–2).

The 1955 *Draper's Encyclopaedia* (p.355) lists 'Honeycomb Bedspreads' as a separate type that uses the honeycomb weave for the ground part of the design. In this case, they were usually made all white (Ostick).

See also **Bedspreads**.

Hook

The use of hooks, enabling curtains to be hung onto rails or the eyes of rings, meant that **curtains** could be removed at will. Hooks might be sewn onto **tapes**, or they might be the pin type (like a safety pin), or designed to fit into woven pocket tapes of various types. Their origin is difficult to trace although the earliest date in the *OED* is 1505.

Loudon recommended that a **curtain pole** should have 'fourteen rings, generally of brass'. For a common cottage, he suggested that the rings 'might be made of iron bronzed: and in the lower part of each ring there is a small eye … in which is inserted the end of a wire hook … that is sewed along the inside of the upper margin of the curtain' (Loudon, 1839, p.338). Hooks were recommended for bed curtains for easy removal for cleaning, although rings were often sewn directly to the header of curtains. Mrs Peel suggested that 'Curtain-hooks should be button-holed on with waxed thread.' (1898, XIV, p.237.)

Later, a range of hooks was devised to suit various **headings** and weights of cloth, including proprietary brands designed for particular heading and rail types. The traditional hooks were later made from plastic and **nylon**, as well as brass, aluminium and zinc-plated metal.

See also **Curtain ring**, **O**.

Hook and eye

A fastening system that uses small metal hooks and small ring-shaped 'eyes' that were sewn to each side of the opening respectively. It was used in the seventeenth century to fix hangings on to walls (Thornton, 1978, p.134), and also to link **valances** at the corners of beds underneath a decorative loop and toggle.

The system was also used as a method of fitting loose covers around chair frames. In 1686, Jean Poictevin invoiced work for the Queen's bedchamber including 'false covers for the chairs and stools, silk, tape, rings, hooks and eyes [value] £20' (Beard, 1997, p.292). In July 1771, Chippendale charged the Harewood account with 'setting on hooks and eyes on the bases to the beds on the attic floor' (Gilbert, 1978, p.214).

They remained in favour until the introduction of zips, in the early twentieth century.

See also **Button and loop**, **Coated fabric**.

Hook and loop

A fixing technique, similar to **hooks and eyes**, that linked **valances** at the corners of beds, underneath a decorative loop and toggle.

Hook-and-loop tape

Velcro® is the trade name given to a fixing system for fabrics using hook-and-loop fasteners. Velcro was invented in 1948 by George de Mestral, a Swiss engineer. De Mestral named his invention after the first syllables of the words *velours*, for the **pile**, and *crochet*, for the hooks. Velcro consists of two layers: a 'hook' side, which is a section of fabric covered with miniature plastic hooks, and a 'loop' side, which is covered in equally

small plastic loops. When the two sides are pressed together, the hooks catch in the loops and hold the pieces together. This sort of fixing is used to attach **pelmets**, etc. for subsequent easy removal if required.
See also **Velour**.

Hooked rug

Floor- and bedcoverings developed in the mid-nineteenth century in America and England. They were made with **homespun linen**, or later, machine-woven **cotton** or **burlap** base into which the pile was formed by strips of rags brought through the base in loops (sometimes cut). Different effects could be achieved by the use of various coloured rags, varied loop heights and differing designs, from simple geometric ones to complex landscapes.

Writing in the first quarter of the twentieth century, Seal discussed their use:

> There is to be noticed a great revival of the hooked rug, that rug of later colonial days, and many amusing and rather decorative rugs have been found among the flood of antique hooked rugs that has lately deluged our country. A rug of this sort should be used as an accent on a plain carpet, or in connection with a plain room-sized rug. Or hooked rugs may claim a very rightful place in the quaint bedroom with decorative painted floor. (1924, p.38.)

The term also refers to two-ply yarns sewn through linen ground and to patched rugs which have scraps of fabric sewn to an under cloth.
See also **Abnakee rug**, **Rag rug**, **Rug**, **Rugg**, **Sabatos rug**.

FURTHER READING

Beitler, E.J. (1973). *Hooked and Knotted Rugs*, New York: Sterling.
Difranza, H. & Franco, B. (1990). 'American hooked rugs', *The Magazine Antiques*, 143, October, pp 788–97.
Kopp, J. & K. (1985). *American Hooked and Sewn Rugs: Folk Art Underfoot*, New York: E.P. Dutton.
Turbayune, J.A. (1991). *Hooked Rugs: History and the Continuing Tradition*, West Chester, PA: Schiffer.

Hopsack

A fabric made in a basket weave with coarse yarns, from a range of fibres including **cotton**, **wool**, **linen**, **rayon**, **silk**, **hemp** and **jute**. It has a rather rough texture and is fairly durable. It is often quite bulky but is woven in various weights dependent upon end use. Probably introduced in the late nineteenth century, it was used for **drapes** in the USA (Bendure & Pfieffer, 1947, p.633). Meanwhile, in England, Smithells commented that hopsack was 'a hardwearing woollen fabric coarse and hard, of an open basket weave. Suitable for curtains, also made from linen and cotton' (1950, p.227).
See also **Weave: Basket**.

Horsehair

See **Hair**, **Haircloth**.

Hourglass curtain

A **glass curtain** fixed on rods or wires at the top and bottom, then gently tied with ribbon or similar at the centre to make a waisted effect. They were used on windows and glass doors.

Huckabuck

A stout **linen** or **cotton-union** cloth, with the **weft** threads thrown alternately up, so as to form a rough surface creating a 'huck' or 'eye' pattern. The dobby or basket **weave** creates a bumpy effect making it very suitable for towelling use. Most huckabucks have small squares on the surface that stand out from the background, and are woven in white, or in colours, or with coloured **borders** or stripes. The motif is made from a series of floats, some of them rather long, which gives a loose effect in certain areas.

Originally, all these cloths were woven with linen yarns. According to Cole (1892), the name is (fancifully?) derived from a corruption of 'huckster-back', which was any sort of pedlars' ware that might be carried on the back.

An early mention of huckabuck is in *The Merchant's Warehouse Laid Open,* where it is described as 'a sort of Diaper made in England, and is very strong, called Huckaback' (J.F. 1696). The diaper refers to its use as a **tablecloth** as well as towelling. Indeed, in 1707, the *London Gazette* referred to 'One Huckaback Tablecloth.' (No.4379/4).

The town of Darlington in County Durham was famous for huckabuck manufacture in the eighteenth century. In 1721, the *New General Atlas* noted that Darlington 'has a considerable Manufacture in Linen and the best Hugabacks'. While in 1727, Daniel Defoe noted that 'Darlington particularly excels in Huckabacks of ten Quarters wide, which are made no-where else in England.' (*A Tour Through the Whole Island of Great Britain*, vol.III. p.162.) Daniel Defoe again mentions huckabuck when he is describing the linen sold at Warrington near Liverpool, which 'is generally speaking a sort of table linen, called huk-a-back or huk-a-buk; tis well known among the good housewives so I need not describe it' (vol.III, p.10). In 1778, the *English Gazetteer* (2nd edition) repeated this comment and recorded that 'Warrington has a particular market every week for the linen called huckaback, the manufacture of its neighbourhood'.

It remained important into the nineteenth century. The 1851 Exhibition showed 'Tape and damask-bordered huckaback towels.' (*The Art Journal Illustrated Catalogue of the Great Exhibition*, p.512.)

By 1947, huckabuck was still being used for towels, **quilting** covers, **drapes**, etc. (Bendure & Pfieffer, p.634).
See also **Diaper**, **Macramé**, **Towel**.

Hudson's Bay blanket

A heavyweight **blanket** milled and raised from long staple wool, originally woven for the Hudson's Bay Co, *c.*1780. They were made with a solid ground and a coloured **border**, striped all over, or solid colour with darker end borders. A number of short stripes about 4 inches (11 cm) long, called 'points', were woven into the edge at right angles to the selvedge. The points once represented a barter value of one beaver skin.

Humpty

A round or oval cloth-covered pouffe or low, padded **cushion** or seat, also known as a dumpty. They were commonly made at home. In 1926, the *British Weekly* recorded how 'The ladies of the village are busy making humpties, soft cushion seats to pull up on the rug before the peat fire.' (18 March, 600/2.)

Ikat

An Indonesian and Malayan word for a widely known technique of dyeing yarns through a resist agent. The **warp** is made into a rope and sections are tied as tightly as the design demands. When the warp is opened, the pattern is shown on the yarn and comes through into the cloth. Similar effects can be made with **weft**-dyed yarns and sometimes both techniques are used together in double ikats.
See also **Chiné**.

FURTHER READING

Buhler, A. (1972). *Ikat, Batik, Plangi*, Basle: Pharos Verlag.

Imberline
Damask with a multi-coloured effect, produced by 'laying in' the **warp** in colours, giving a variegated striped effect. Developed in France from the eighteenth century onward.

Imitation leather
See **Coated fabric**.

Imperial
A three-ply ingrain or Scotch carpet developed by Thomas Morton in 1824, and used in the USA by 1833. It had the thickness of a triple cloth and more variety of colouring. In 1892, Cole described the three-ply carpet:

> Ingrain carpet consists of a cotton or wool warp with a wool filling, and is woven in strips one yard wide. It is composed of two distinct webs interwoven together at one operation, and is therefore a double or two-ply carpet. Three-ply carpet is composed of three distinct webs, which by interlacing and interchanging their threads produce a different pattern on each side, and at the same time permitting much greater variety of color, with a corresponding increase of thickness and durability in the texture.' (p.59.)

See also **Double cloth carpet**, **Dutch carpet**, **Ingrain carpet**, **Kidderminster carpet**, **Scotch carpeting**.

Imperial Axminster
A quality designation for woven **Axminster carpets**. The manufacturer and author Brinton explained:

> As in other carpet fabrics, there are in Axminster plenty of varieties of qualities; but there are comparatively few differences in structure, such differences as exist being mainly matters of pitch, tuft, or method of tufting and binding. The original Axminster quality was called the Royal. This is about 5 per inch in the pitch, and 6 in the beat-up, with a tuft of about ⅞ in. This held the field until 1893, when a strong invasion of the British market by American Axminster, offered at a considerably lower price, caused the Axminster makers of this country to bestir themselves to meet this competition. They did so strenuously; and the result was the production of the quality known as the Imperial Axminster, which had an instant and a lasting success. This was made in a pitch of 7 to the inch, and a beat-up of about 6 and ½, and was put on the market at a moderate price. For many years it held the position of being the critical quality of the whole trade; the standard by which the value of other qualities was measured, and, as has been intimated, it is only of recent years that its position has been challenged by the Chenille Axminster. (Brinton, 1919, p.50.)

See also **Chenille Axminster**.

Imperling
Probably a coarse German **linen**, which may be a misspelling of inderkin. The *Tudor Book of Rates* for 1582 included 'Imperlings the dozen.' (Willan, 1962, p.34)
See also **Inderkin**.

Inderkin
In 1696, it was defined as 'a sort of Cloth of no great use … only proper for towels, it is a coarse narrow cloth which comes from Hamborough … it is made in the worst of hemp' (J.F., *The Merchant's Warehouse Laid Open*).
See also **Imperling**, **Towel**.

Indian goods
A general term used in the seventeenth and eighteenth centuries to describe any imported fabric from India or the Far East.
See for example **Bafta**, **Chintz**, **Embroidered coverlet/quilt**, **Gingham**, **Gunny**, **Indienne**, **Indian stuff**, **Jaconet**, **Madapolam**, **Masulipatam**, **Mercoolees**, **Muslin**, **Palampore**, **Patch**, **Pintado**.

FURTHER READING

Irwin J. & Schwartz, P.R. (1966). *Studies in Indo-European Textile History*, Ahmedabad: Calico Museum of Textiles.
Lemire, B. (2003). 'Domesticating the exotic: floral culture and the East India calico trade with England *c.*1600–1800', *Textiles: The Journal of Cloth and Culture*, 1, March, pp 64–85.

Indian head
An American trade name used by the J.L. Stifel Co for plain **cotton** fabric that is woven with uneven yarns, thus giving the cloth a textured finish. It is similar to **gingham** or **chambray** and has been used for **drapes** and **table linen**.

Indian matting
See **Matting: India**.

Indian stuff
A term referring to a woven material imported into England from India. **Stuff** was a general term for any woven cloth. The Cockesden inventory of 1610 listed a 'cubberd cloth of Indian stuff', and 'four new curtains, never used, of Indian stuff'. There was also a 'bedstead corded with the testor, vallens and curtains of streaked Indian stuffe silke' (Thornton, 1978, p.242). Hardwick Hall had 'a quilt of yellow India stuffe imbroidered with birds and beasts and [with] white silk fringe and tassels' (Boynton, 1971, p.25).
See also **Indian goods**.

Indienne
The French name for imported '**chintz**' fabrics and a common term for any printed **linen/cotton** cloth. These textiles were in use in Marseilles by 1580. By 1648, French printers in Marseilles were imitating the imported Indian printed **calicos**. Bimont suggested their use for **bed furniture**: 'two different sorts of indiennes or other stuff, or two different designs; the inside of the bed is in one colour and the outside in the other, as are the bed curtains, which are not seamed together' (Bimont, 1770, p.34). Indiennes printed in black, red, or black and red in combination, were referred to as *les indiennes ordinaires*.
See also **Patena**, **Provençal print**.

Ingrain carpet
A flat woven **carpet** made in a compound structure (double or triple cloth) with the **wefts** dominant, as opposed to the **Venetian carpet** that has the **warp** dominant. The process of intersecting webs makes a **pile**-less, double construction, loom-woven carpet. The double construction made the carpet reversible with the colours swapped over on each side. Ingrain carpets may be simple (commonly two threads), though may also be woven on a multiple-harness jacquard loom that may have up to six coloured weft threads. The term ingrain is mainly used in the USA. The two-ply version is often called Kidderminster carpet and the three-ply is often called Scotch carpet. The cloth was woven in narrow strips up to about a yard (91 cm) wide, the Scottish ell (37 inches, or 94 cm) being popular in that country.

64. Ingrain carpet samples, Danvers Carpet Co, USA, c.1870 (Photograph courtesy of Peabody Essex Museum)

In America these ingrain sorts of carpets were known as **English carpets** during the second half of the eighteenth century and, by the end of the century, were being advertised as 'English ingrained' (Roth, 1967, p.30). They were simultaneously designated as Scotch ingrain, so the location of the production influenced the name.

Ingrain was the principle carpet woven in the USA through the nineteenth century. The similarity of the weaving process with **double cloth coverlets** is seen in the many advertisements of weavers who produced carpets, and double and single **coverlids**. Later in the nineteenth century, Montgomery Ward offered a choice of two-ply ingrain, two-ply extra heavy, half-**wool** or all-wool ingrain carpeting. Sears Roebuck advertised Ingrain Art Squares in 1897 and offered two- and three-ply ingrain carpeting by the yard (91 cm) in 36 inch (91 cm) widths (*Sears Catalogue*, 1897, Dry Goods section).

In the early twentieth century, Elizabeth Dyer made the point that ingrain carpet was of variable quality but could be tolerable:

> Ingrain is an inexpensive, reversible carpet, sometimes called flat-surfaced because it has no pile. The better qualities are all-wool. This carpet does not compare in beauty with the pile carpets, and in the cheaper qualities is not worth buying. But in the best grades, ingrain carpet will give satisfactory service where thickness or softness is not required. Scotch, Kidderminster, and Cotton Chain are other names for ingrain rugs. Cotton Chain is a cheap, low grade of cotton ingrain. (*c.*1923, p.194.)

In 1950, the British *Mercury Dictionary of Textile Terms* noted that ingrain was usually 36 inches (91 cm) wide, used two- or three-fold yarns, and commented that 'they are very expensive but very enduring'. By 1960, they were still mentioned as an alternative with the appearance similar to a hand-made **tapestry**. Although clean in use and dirt resistant, the carpet has a hard, resilient quality and uninteresting texture (Wilson, 1960, p.183).

See also **Barnard Castle carpet**, **Dutch carpet**, **Imperial**, **Kendal carpet**, **Kidderminster carpet**, **Scotch carpeting**.

FURTHER READING

Habib, V. (1997). 'Scotch carpets in the eighteenth and early nineteenth centuries', *Textile History*, 28, p.161.

Kraak, D.E. (1996). 'Ingrain carpets', *The Magazine Antiques*, 149, January, pp 182–91.

Roth, R. (1967). *Floorcoverings in 18th-Century America*, Smithsonian Papers, Washington, DC: Smithsonian Institution, pp 29–35.

Swain, M. (1978). 'A note on Scotch carpets', *Furniture History*, 14, pp 61–2.

Inner curtain

See **Under curtain**.

Insulated lining

Lining materials that have been treated with a coating to reflect **heat** back into a room. Milium used **aluminium coated lining** on **sateen** to achieve this effect in the later twentieth century.

Interlining

The practice of interlining **curtains** or hangings to assist drape, and provide warmth is called interlining. Various materials appear to have been used, including **linen**, **flannel** and **silesia**.

In 1735, the Countess of Burlington was charged £3.17s.6d. 'for being supplied with 64 yards of strong linen to line' and for 'sewing the same together to interline the damask hangs in the room at Chiswick' (Beard, 1997, p.303). While in 1798, Matthew Boulton was charged for '9 yards of Flannel to interline draperies' by James Newton (Ellwood, 1995, p.176).

Moreland's *Practical Decorative Upholstery* still advised the use of **cotton** flannel for interlining purposes, but when required for room darkening he suggested the use of silesia cloth (Moreland, 1889). In 1906, Noetzli recommended bump for particular work but it seems that many cheap soft materials were used, if considered necessary. In the later twentieth century, bump or wadding was regularly used for curtain work.

See also **Batting**, **Bump**, **Wadding**.

Inverted pleat

The decorative **pleats** at the top of **curtains**, which meet in the middle like a reverse **box pleat**.

Irish cloth

The Mercury Dictionary of Textile Terms (1950) defines Irish cloth as 'a medieval English woollen cloth, made in red and white for linings'. In 1768, John Morland supplied to an unknown client 'Irish cloth for head and tester cloths and inside valance' (*DEFM*, p.627). In 1786, Sir John Griffin Griffin was supplied with 'a set of Irish cloth curtains to draw round the bed' (Beard, 1997, p.310).

Irish rug

See **Caddow**.

Irish stitch

See **Bargello**, **Stitch: Flame**.

Irish terry
See **Terry**.

Italian quilting
See **Couching**, **Quilting**, **Trapunto**.

Italian stringing
This technique allows **curtains** to join at the centre, whilst the **heading** remains fixed. The curtains are drawn back and forth by diagonal cords placed one-third down the curtain, thus creating a reefed effect.
See also **Festoon window curtain**.

Jabot
Originally a frill or **ruffle** used in combination with a shirt. In furnishing use, it was a window feature made from a vertically hanging fabric cut to make a point. It was used with **swags**. Jabot is also the name of a ruffled **drapery** heading.

Jaconet
A firm but thin, closely woven **cotton** cloth, which was originally imported from India. It was woven with a small all-over pattern and was popular in the eighteenth century, mainly for dress applications. The name is probably derived from a corruption of the Urdu Jagannathpur in Cuttack, where the cloth was originally manufactured.

In 1769, the *Public Advertiser* listed 'Dozen Book and Jaconot Muslins and clear Lawns.' (14 November, 3/3, 260) and, nearly 100 years later, *The Art Journal Illustrated Catalogue of the Great Exhibition* showed 'India jaconets. Cambric of various qualities.' (p.482.)
See also **Muslin.**

Jacquard
One of the most important developments in weaving technology, the jacquard was invented by Joseph Marie Jacquard about 1801 as an improvement to the draw loom. It was an apparatus that manipulated the **warp** threads by raising them in accordance with a programmed series of punched cards attached to wires, linked to the warps. By raising or lowering as required, the weaver could produce patterns in fabrics ranging from the very simple to highly complex. It was applicable to anything from **nets** to **carpet**. Its role in developing the furnishing market was important especially when powered versions were patented in the 1840s.
See also **Alhambra quilt**, **Armure**, **Axminster carpet**, **Brocade**, **Brussels carpet**, **Casement cloth**, **Counterpane**, **Coverlet**, **Damask**, **Honeycomb**, **Kraft fibre rug**, **Lace**, **Moquette**, **Rep**, **Rug**, **Satin**, **Tapestry**, **Ticking**, **Tissue**, **Towel**, **Velvet**, **Wilton carpet**.

Jacquard coverlet
A term of convenience given to large, typically unseamed coverlets with intricate patterns and elaborate **borders** that were woven with a special mechanised loom attachment.
See also **Jacquard**.

Jalousie
Shutters or **blinds** with fixed or adjustable slats that exclude rain and provide ventilation, shade and visual privacy. The name appears to be derived from the Spanish *gelosia*, meaning 'jealousy', and its first recorded use as a window reference is from 1591 (*OED*). In 1877, Mrs Orrinsmith noted in *The Drawing Room* that nothing is so effectual to give shade as jalousies, 'such as one sees continually in France and Italy, and they are most furnishing [sic] in their outside effect upon a new and bare-looking house' (p.66).

Japanese matting
See **Matting: Japan**.

Jardinière curtain
A name for a **curtain** design that has a shaped finish to the hem to reveal some of the window. It works well with sheer fabrics.

Jaspé
A fabric with a shaded appearance, produced with **warp** threads of uneven colour or pattern, combined with single colour **weft** yarns. It has been used for **bedspreads** and **curtains**. In 1937, it was noted that 'a typical modern jasper is made with a free use of variously coloured slub yarns in the warp, and gaily-coloured lustrous rayon weft, producing striking designs that were in every way suitable for window draping and hangings' (French, 1937, p.139).

By 1950, Smithells defined jaspé as 'a plain-weave ridge cotton fabric woven in random colour schemes with distinctive dots and stripes on the surface, Suitable for loose covers, curtains and bedspreads.' (p.228.) Jaspé bedspreads were particularly highlighted in *The Draper's Encyclopaedia*:

> The jaspé spread is usually stencil printed on a grey (unbleached) cotton cloth. The cloth is woven with irregular coloured stripes to form a background for the printed design. The stripes are unequal in spacing and may be of a neutral colour, e.g. fawn or they may tone with the intended colour of the print, e.g. green stripes for a printed design with two or three tones of green. (Ostick, 1955, p.357.)

See also **Damask**, **Satin**, **Taffeta**.

Jaspé carpet
A **carpet** with a regular flame-like pattern, traditionally made by using **pile** yarn, dip-dyed in hanks to two tones of the same colour, or to two different colours in a fixed proportion to the hank length.

Javelin
See **Curtain pole and rod**.

Jersey
See **Knitted fabric**.

Jute
A long bast fibre obtained from the bark of the plants *Chorus capsularis* and *C. olitorius* and used for **twines** and woven fabrics. It comes from Bengal particularly, and the name is derived from the Bengali *jhoto*, ultimately meaning 'braid of hair'. When woven, jute is commonly known as burlap or hessian and has had a number of uses in furnishings as well as wide applications outside of the home. Natural jute has a yellow to brown or grey colour, with a silky lustre. It consists of bundles of fibres held together by gummy substances. It is difficult to bleach completely, so many fabrics are bright, dark or natural brown in colour. Jute works well for bagging because it does not stretch and is somewhat rough and coarse. It has been widely used in the manufacture of backings for **linoleum** and **carpets**, or as a base fabric.

Jute was first introduced into Britain from India in the late eighteenth century and gradually found favour for a range of applications, including rope and **mat** making. In 1832, William Taylor discovered that jute could be softened with whale oil and this enabled large-scale spinning to be undertaken.

65. Jute union cloth used for covers in a 1930s' room setting (Private Collection)

Originally utilitarian and used for simple, cheap, often homemade furnishings, it was later adopted as a decorative fabric. The 1881 catalogue of American retailers, Lord and Taylor, offered ready-made **curtains** in 'printed jute' (Grier, 1988, p.239). In 1895, jute cloth was sold as furniture covering by Montgomery Ward.

In the 1930s, the British retailers, John Lewis, were selling printed jute fabric for curtaining. Immediately after World Ward II, British retailers sold piece-dyed or printed jute textiles as there was a shortage of other fibres. However, by 1955, it was no longer considered to be a suitable furnishing fabric, since it was too stiff to drape well.
See also **Arras cloth**, **Belgian tapestry**, **Burlap**, **Dundee tapestry**, **Dutch carpet**, **Gunny**, **Hessian**, **Jute carpet**, **Webbing**.

FURTHER READING

Atkinson, R.R. (1964). *Jute*, Temple Press: London.
Board of Trade (1948). *Working Party Report, Jute*, London: HMSO.
Woodhouse, T. (1921). *The Jute Industry from Seed to Finished Cloth*, London: Pitman.

Jute carpet
The use of jute as a **carpet** fibre was developed in the early nineteenth century and, in 1852, David Thomson received a patent for making a **Brussels**-type carpet from jute yarns. In the 1851 Exhibition, four pieces of jute stair carpeting were displayed (*The Art Journal Illustrated Catalogue of the Great Exhibition*, p.513).
See also **Dutch carpet**, **Jute**.

Jute tapestry
See **Dundee tapestry**.

Jute webbing
See **Webbing**.

Kalmuc
A **carpet** woven with a **woollen warp** that runs regularly over and under two **wefts**. An 1884 catalogue from London retailers, Maple and Co, described Kalmuc thus: 'thick, self-coloured material made in plain Indian red, sienna, olive, peacock, and like colourings, is also used for library or study floors, either as a covering by itself, or as a basis for rugs.' (1884, p.58). By 1950, it was still defined as a coarse woollen fabric used as a floorcovering (*The Mercury Dictionary of Textile Terms*).

Kamptulicon
Kamptulicon was a hard flooring which was invented as an improvement on **floorcloth**. It had similar properties to **linoleum** but was made from different ingredients. In 1844, Elijah Galloway added pulverised cork to unvulcanised rubber and produced a new material that he named Kamptulicon (Patent no.10054/1844). This material, which was produced about 0.2 of an inch (0.4 cm) thick, could be printed with oil paints using the same methods as for floorcloth, but it was intended to be stuck directly to the floor, rather than loose-laid. The nature of the material meant that it was applicable to heavy-duty situations.

In 1859, Thomas Dunn added stretched, woven **woollen** fabric into Galloway's recipe, to create his new version of Kamptulicon (Patent no.2926/1859). Kamptulicon must have had some degree of success as its qualities were being praised some 18 years after this first patent. The attractions can be gleaned from the following entry in Chambers' *Encyclopaedia* of 1862:

> The laying of lobbies and passages with encaustic tiles has lately led to the superseding of floorcloth in such situations, while ... [for the]

66. Kamptulicon design, c.1862 (Private Collection)

covering of floors in churches, reading rooms, and waiting rooms at railway stations [floorcloth has been] superseded by the newly invented material named Kamptulicon, or vulcanised rubber cloth. ... This material is made plain or figured to resemble painted floor cloth.

A report in the *Journal of the Society of Arts* says of this material, 'its qualities are noiselessness when trod on rendering it admirably suited for churches, banks nurseries, billiard rooms or any other place where quietness is desirable. Its resistance to wear and damp make it much more durable than floorcloth' (April 1862). The Kamptulicon material was exhibited at the London Industrial Exhibition of 1862 and, according to contemporary reports, was very well received. In the same year, *The Practical Mechanics Journal* noted that it 'had been used with success in the Houses of Parliament, that it was ideal for the cells of lunatics, and was of great service in lining the stalls of horse boxes, as its sound deadening properties helped to cure the horse of the habit of kicking' (August 1862, p.115). However, the enormous rise in the price of raw India rubber, due to Goodyear's discovery of the vulcanisation process, made the commercial production of Kamptulicon less attractive, so there were attempts to change its composition. In 1864, Kidd and Mather (Patent no.2340/1864) used linseed oil and rosin to provide the basis for a Kamptulicon-like material but without the rubber content.

Although it lost its popularity to linoleum, it still had some supporters. R.W. Shoppell, writing in *Modern Houses, Beautiful Homes* in 1887, described it as a 'soft warm floorcovering made of cork and India rubber', which he recommended for use around the perimeter of a bedroom similar to the use of linoleum (p.322). It was still listed in 1950 (*The Mercury Dictionary of Textile Terms*) but was obsolete by the 1960s.

Kapok (*Ceiba pentandra*)
The seed fibre or vegetable down of the ceiba tree and plant which is grown widely in Java and India, especially in the Calcutta region. It is processed like **cotton** by ginning, and has been used as **upholstery filling** since the eighteenth century. Rolt noted in 1761 that 'capoc' (kapok) was used for beds, **cushions** and **pillows**. By 1882, it was pointed out that 'kapok is employed to a limited degree in upholstery ... used for stuffing chairs and pillows' (Beck). It remains in use as a common loose filling for cushions and **quilts**, and a paper-backed version is used for upholstery **wadding**.

FURTHER READING

Zand, S. (1941). *Kapok, a Survey of its History, Cultivation and Uses*, New York: Lincoln.

Karastan
An American **Axminster**-type **carpet** with patterns resembling antique Oriental **rugs**, but without the stiff construction found in a standard Axminster. The **pile** patterns can be seen on the reverse and the carpet can be folded easily. They were often washed to give an antique look. The entrepreneur, Marshall Field, had a traditional Axminster weaving loom modified to create a machine-made rug, woven through to the back, just like a hand-made Oriental, featuring intricate designs and virtually unlimited colour variety. Karastan's rug mill was established in 1926, and the first Karastan rugs were sold in 1928.

Karvel
A non-woven **carpet** type, introduced into England from the USA in the 1930s. It was manufactured by bonding to a backing fabric a corrugated **pile** prepared from a carded web of fibres. The resulting carpet can be left with loops or prepared with a cut-pile. It has been widely used in the automobile industry (Robinson, 1966, p.146).

Kelim (aka Kilim)
A **rug** type woven in a variety of central Asian and Middle Eastern locations using a **tapestry** weave technique. It was particularly popular for so-called Turkish interiors during the late nineteenth and early twentieth centuries. 'Bagdad curtains can frequently be purchased very cheap, though the weave of the Kelim is more substantial and very much better in design and color. These hangings are not at all expensive, considering their great size. They should be provided at least for the divan or couch' (Coleman, 1899, p.79).

Kelims have been used for divan covers and **portières** in the twentieth century.
See also **Carpet upholstery**.

FURTHER READING

Huli, A. & Luczyc-Wyhowska, J. (2001). *Kilim, the Complete Guide*, London: Thames and Hudson.
Petsopulos, Y. (1979). *Kilims*, London: Thames and Hudson.

Kendal
A **woollen** cloth, either frizzed or plain, that was originally made in the town of Kendal in northwest England from the thirteenth century. Although widely known as a costume cloth, in 1697 a petition by quiltmakers makes reference to: 'there being great quantities of Norwich, Kidderminster, Kendal and other stuffs, used for the backsides of quilts' (Osler, 1987, p.88).

Kendal carpet
A **double cloth ingrain carpet** that takes its name from the locality of its manufacture. According to Nicholson's *Annals of Kendal* (1861, p.249):

> The manufacture of carpets was introduced in the year 1822 by Messrs Joseph and John Atkinson. Since which time, it has, by progressive steps, become an extensive and lucrative business. In 1828, Messrs Atkinson adopted some new machinery for weaving damask carpeting. Various descriptions are made here: Brussels, Kidderminster, Venetian and others. Most of these are for home use and sold chiefly in London. Some are exported... (Gilbert, Lomax & Wells-Cole, 1987, p.92.)

A Mr Whitwell, carpet manufacturer of Kendal, exhibited at the 1851 Great Exhibition a 'Kidderminster carpet of double cloth, not twilled in the warp, and the colouring produced by change of the shuttle' (*The Art Journal Illustrated Catalogue of the Great Exhibition*, 1851, p.248).
See also **Kidderminster carpet**.

Kenting
A fine, closely woven **linen** cloth, sometimes striped, used from the mid-seventeenth century for **curtains** and **bed furniture** and for napkins and **tablecloths**. An early mention of it is from 1657: 'Linen Cloth, as Canvas and Kentings' (Ligon, 1673, p.109, *OED*), but indications of its consumption are found in the *Boston Gazette* (29 May–5 June 1727) where were advertised 'linen cloth, diapers, kentines, chequered linen and Holland', which were 'lately imported from Glasgow'.

In the 1728 inventory of the shop of James Pilbeam, a mercer of Chiddingly, Sussex, there was listed 'One peece of kenting valued at £0 8s 6d', although it is not known to what use this was put. However, its use was clear in 1742, when John Little of Boston had '1 suit strip'd Kenting curtains and vallens' (Cummings, 1961, p.28). In 1793, the *Statistical Accounts of Scotland* recorded that 'Lawns, gauzes and linens called Kentings are exported to Ireland.' (Sir John Sinclair, VII, 175, *OED*).

Kersey (aka Carsey)
Thick **woollen** or **worsted** twill weave material, developed in the thirteenth century but occasionally used as a covering for **upholstery** in the seventeenth century. Its name varied depending upon the location of production (Devon kersey, Suffolk kersey, etc.). Its etymology is possibly from the village of Kersey in Suffolk, though evidence actually connecting the original manufacture of the cloth with that place has not been found.

In the sixteenth and seventeenth centuries, kerseys were frequently contrasted with cloths or **broadcloth**: the size of the latter was fixed by the statute of 1465 as 24 yards (22 metres) long by 2 yards (1.8 metres) wide, while a kersey was only 18 yards (16.5 metres) long and a yard and a nail (97 cm) in width. The Act of 1552 listed various kinds of kerseys as ordinary, sorting, Devonshire (called dozens), and **check** kerseys, and fixed their length at between 17 and 18 yards (15.5 and 16.5 metres); in 1557 this was reduced to between 16 and 17 yards (14.5 and 15.5 metres). In around 1618, three kersies were reckoned as equal to one cloth.

Although recognised as a clothing material, it was also used for upholstery. The 1601 Hardwick inventory listed 'eight stools of black and white carsey embroidered with needlework flowers' (Boynton, 1971, p.30). In 1603, an inventory of Hengrave Hall included a 'great foulding skreen of seven foulds with a skreen cloth upon it of green kersey' (Gloag, 1990, p.589). In 1626, Anne Wright of Ipswich had '2 chairs covered with green kersye' (Reed, 1981, p.103). By the mid-seventeenth century, it was also known in America. In a Cambridge, Mass., inventory of *c.*1640–50 there was:

> Philop and Cheny curtains in graine [green] with a deep silk fringe on the valance, and a smaller on the curtains, and a coverlet suitable to it, made of Red Kersie, and laced with a green lace, round [the sides and down] the middle. (Cummings, 1961, p.21.)

In 1666, a Boston inventory recorded 'pieces of Kersie wrought for chairs and stools' (Montgomery, 1984, p.273). By 1685, it was claimed by petitioners from the wool trade that 'Cloth, Serge, Perpetuanoes, Chamlets, Bays, Kersies, Norwich Chenies, and Kidderminster Prints' (Symonds, 1934, p.180) were widely used for upholstering in their argument against the development of cane seating.

*67. Kidderminster carpet design, Whitwell of Kendal (*The Art Journal Illustrated Catalogue of the Great Exhibition – London 1851*)*

Kerseymere
A soft, textured twilled **woollen** cloth, sometimes called cassimere. See **Cassimere**.

Kidderminster carpet
The distinctive name for a kind of ingrain **carpet**, originally manufactured in the Worcestershire town of Kidderminster, in which the pattern is formed by the intersection of two cloths of different colours so the designs are repeated on the back, but with the colours reversed. They are also known as two-ply carpets. The double cloth method allows two colours to be woven quickly and the various widths or quarters (Scottish ell, 37 inches, 94 cm) could quite easily be made up into larger carpets.

Burton, in his *A History of Kidderminster*, suggests that double cloths were first made in 1735 in Kidderminster, but there was a long tradition of weaving (see **Kidderminster stuff**), so this is not definitive. In 1751, Richard Pococke wrote of Kidderminster 'that the place is famous for carpets made without nap, like the Scotch, but now they make the same as Wilton, and it is said they are attempting to weave 'em in one piece' ('Travels of Richard Pococke' in Roth, 1967, p.30). Kidderminster carpet seems to have been a utilitarian product. In the 1795 inventory of the Grange, Northington, there is listed on the back stairs: 'Six yards and half of ½ yard Kidderminster stair carpeting … 45 yards of half ell Kidderminster on stairs and landing places (in several pieces) and 58 iron wires' (Gilbert, Lomax & Wells-Cole, 1987, p.89).

In 1812, Thomas Pardoe patented:

> a new method of working or making carpeting denominated Kidderminster or Scotch carpeting, in pieces of different width, exceeding eighteen inches wide, whereby a complete pattern, figure or flower is made to extend the whole width of the piece, and may be worked or made in a drop pattern or otherwise [offering] large, superior and more elegant designs than any that have been or can be produced. (Patent no.3604, 23 October 1812.)

Three months later, John Hanbury patented a method of weaving Scotch or Kidderminster carpets 'producing a finer texture and larger patterns than by methods hitherto known' (Patent no.3624, 19 December 1812).

A little later, Loudon commented that 'the kinds of carpet most suitable for cottages are chiefly the Scotch and Kidderminster on account of their cheapness' (1839, p.344). The mixed terminology used to describe these carpets is demonstrated by the following. In 1836, the *Penny Cyclopaedia* described them by saying that 'Kidderminster or Scotch carpets, or, as the Americans more descriptively term them, ingrain carpets, are wholly of worsted or woollen' (VI. 314/1).

The development of double cloth to a triple cloth involved an additional layer, which allowed a thicker cloth. Fewer striped or **checked** effects were found in the double cloth version. This method was patented by Thomas Lea of Kidderminster in 1812 when he devised a method of 'introducing three or more warps and shutes and three or more distinct and clear colours ... which is to be done by mounting the loom with a harness, divided into three or more distinct divisions' (Patent no.3613, 31 October 1812). Thomas Morton of Kilmarnock developed the triple cloth in the 1820s. In 1840, Hugh Graham patented a method of dyeing the **warp** in suitable colours to prevent the 'stripy appearance of the pattern' (Patent no.8740, 16 December). Advice about the various qualities was given in *Cassell's Household Guide,* 1870:

> Kidderminster carpets of a good quality are almost indestructible and having two surfaces, they are really double. They are soft to the touch being all wool; if hard, the wool is mixed with hemp or other harsh substance and will then quickly wear out... Some really good woven imitations of this kind of carpet in pattern and quality are to be met with in wide width for 3s 6d or 4s a yard. (vol.1, p.126.)

Some commentators were unimpressed. Writing in 1881, Mrs Haweis complained that Kidderminster 'is a good carpet for bedrooms and schoolrooms, but it is too thin to be as silent as luxury demands, or as warm as an English winter deserves. The flat visible threads always have a somewhat ascetic and "wrong-sided" look compared to deep delicious velvet-pile.' (1881, p 297–8.)

On the other hand, in 1884, the furnishing store, Maple and Co, was recommending Kidderminster as stair carpet because it was deemed to be 'very thick and durable. The ornamentation is Early English, the colours terra cotta, peacock, olive, bronze and other art shades.' (1884, p.70.) Lady Barker was apparently impressed with the fact that '[William] Morris has Kidderminster carpets for bedrooms, in pale pink, buff, and blue, etc., which are simply perfect in harmony of colour and design.' (1878, p.81.)

By 1904, the yarns used had changed: 'Kidder carpets resemble the two ply kind, except that instead of being all wool they have cotton warps and worsted wefts.' (*Chamber's Encyclopaedia*) Despite these changes, Kidderminster carpet was still considered a well-designed product. The carpet manufacturer, Brinton, has the following to say about carpeting:

> Owen Jones is again worth quoting in this connection, even if his strictures seem excessively severe. He says, 'I will say no more on the floral style, but to express a regret that, the more perfect the manufacturing process in carpets becomes, the more do they (the carpets) appear to lend themselves to evil. The modest Kidderminster carpet rarely goes wrong, because it cannot; it has to deal with but two colours, and consequently much mischief is beyond its reach. The Brussels carpet, which deals with five colours, is more mischievous. The Tapestry carpet, where the colours are still more numerous, are vicious in the extreme; whilst the recent invention of printed carpets, with no bounds to its ambition, has become positively criminal.' (Brinton, 1919, p.99.)

Production of Kidderminster-type carpets effectively ended in the 1920s in the United Kingdom.

See also **Art square**, **Barnard Castle**, **Double cloth**, **Ingrain**, **Kendal**, **Scotch carpeting**.

FURTHER READING

Bartlett, J.N. (1978). *Carpeting the Millions. The Growth of Britain's Carpet Industry*, Edinburgh: John Donald.

Smith, L.D. (1986). *Carpet Weavers and Carpet Masters: The Handloom Carpet Weavers of Kidderminster, 1780–1850*, Kidderminster: Tomkinson.

Thomson, M.R. (2002). *Woven in Kidderminster: An Illustrated History of the Carpet Industry in the Kidderminster Area Including Stourport, Bridgnorth, and Bewdley, 1735–2000*, Kidderminster: David Voice.

Kidderminster stuff

A coarse **worsted** material that was simply but often boldly patterned (i.e. diamonds or chevrons). It appears to have been used for a variety of furnishing needs and has been described as a **linsey-woolsey** with a **warp** of **linen** and a **weft** of **wool**, used for **table carpets**, bed hangings and **upholstery** work (Kerridge, p.87).

In 1634, the Countess of Leicester had '4 carpets of Kidderminster stuff' **double cloth** (Halliwell, 1854). In 1670, the Preamble to an Act of Parliament mentioned 'Abuses in the makeing of Stuffes called Kidderminster Stuffes.' (9, 22 & 23 Chas. II, c. 8.) During 1697, professional quilt-makers petitioned the Government against import restrictions on **calicoes**, and mentioned one of the roles of Kidderminster stuff:

> That depriving the quilt-makers of the liberty of using printed callicoe carpets will be a detriment to the Government, as to the customs and duties, and also the woollen manufacturers; there being great quantities of Norwich, Kidderminster, Kendal and other stuffs, used for the backsides of quilts... (Osler, 1987, p.88)

In the first half of the eighteenth century, Kidderminster was the 'seat of the moreen and damask manufacture and all sorts of bed furniture and hangings' (James, 1857, p.255). Daniel Defoe described how 'The Hangings, suppose them to be ordinary Linsey-Woolsey are made at Kidderminster, d'yd in the country, and painted or water'd at London.' (1727, vol.I, p.333.) Certainly *c.*1710, the third old nursery in Dyrham had the closet 'hung with Kidderminster stuff' (Walton, 1986, p.63). A little later, John Wood, in his *Description of Bath,* criticised its use, saying 'about the year 1727 [houses were furnished] with Kidderminster stuff, or at best with Cheyne' (Ayres, 1981, p.24).

Knitted carpet

Carpets were knitted on wooden needles from strips of cloth (rag) similar to woven **rag carpet**. It was made about 12 inches (30.5 cm) wide. It was especially established in Germany in the later nineteenth century.

In the 1880s, a description of knitted carpet explained that the rags were made up by knitting into blocks of 4½ inches (11.5 cm) and then joined so that they alternated in direction when made up into a large panel. A **border** was then knitted and fixed with mitred corners. The centre of the carpet was lined with bed **ticking**.

In 1950, knitted carpeting was described as 'a house industry practised in Germany and latterly introduced into America. The carpet is made from narrow strips of cotton or woollen cloth usually out of discarded clothing. The knitting is done by wooden needles in about 12 inch widths stitched together, very durable.' (*The Mercury Dictionary of Textile Terms*.)

FURTHER READING

Robinson, G. (1966). *Carpets* (Chapter 15 – 'Knitted carpets'), London: Pitman.

Knitted fabric

The use of knitted fabric in **upholstery** started with the use of knitted covers for furniture and car seats, developed in the late 1920s. These early fabrics used spun **rayon** and **cotton** and were not like the later 'stretch' knitted fabrics, so their success was limited. With the development of variously shaped plastic shells and tubular metal frames for chairs in the 1960s and 1970s, the demand for a stretch fabric was self-evident. **Weft**-knitted textiles, including jersey, double jersey and interlocked, all of which have good stretching properties, were employed as upholstery cloths for shaped frames. The designs included printed and woven effects, especially **moquette** and **linen unions**. These fabrics have been used as **top covers**, stretch (loose) covers and as switch covers that fit a range of basic shapes. In the 1960s, Raschel knit upholstery fabrics were developed allowing coarser yarns, especially bulked **nylon**, to be used.

FURTHER READING

Anon. (1967). 'The knitted stretch story', *Man-made Textiles*, March, p.44.

Darlington, K.D. (1970). 'Warp knit fabric developments', FIRA, *Upholstery Fabrics Study Conference*, November.

Knitted rug

See **Rug**.

Knotted fringe

See **Fringe: Knotted**.

Knotted work

Knots made in thread using a shuttle to make a form of decorative finish for furnishings. The resulting **fringe** work was used to decorate toilets, bed or window **curtains**. Alternatively, the knotted threads were sewn to a **linen** ground in a range of patterns. In the later seventeenth century, knotted threads were applied as decoration to chairs and covers in a similar fashion to **galloon**. The Hardwick inventory lists '5 curtains of blew cloth with black silk knottes' (Boynton, 1971, p.30). In the early eighteenth century, the work was applied to monochrome bed hangings and covers.

In the eighteenth century, knotting was a pastime for many women. Mrs Delany describes how she 'put on new white satin best covers on my chair, and the knotting furniture of my bedchamber, with window curtains of the same' (Clabburn, 1988, p.223). In 1735, Stephen Langley invoiced the Countess of Burlington for 'making 30 yards of fringe out of her Ladyship's knotted silk' (Beard, 1997, p.303). The French author, Saint-Aubin, in his *L'Art du Brodeur*, explained that:

> dresses and furniture are embroidered by sewing, with little stitches, the knots which ladies make with their shuttles to amuse themselves… There are few knots so sturdy. When the objects are rather large, one can space the knots as with silk thread… There are knots of different thicknesses; they are made in wool, in thread, or in silk (Saint-Aubin, trans. Scheuer, 1983, p.57).

68. Chair back of knotted wool on linen, late seventeenth century (Leeds Museums and Galleries, Temple Newsam House, Roger Warner Collection)

A similar use was described by Sophie von la Roche when she visited Windsor Castle in 1789 and noted that 'another chamber is entirely hung with knotted tapestry. The knotted threads are made by the women at Court here and a woman in Germany … thus the Court ladies are kept diligently employed' (cited in Clabburn, 1988, p.223). See also **Macramé**.

Kraft fibre rug

Kraft fibre rugs are made from twisted paper used as a yarn that is woven with **cotton** or cotton and **wool warps** to make a reversible rug. They may have stencilled designs on one side. The reason for their success is not difficult to understand. An article from an American home economics journal, published in 1918 explains:

> The cheapness of the paper fibre rugs is due to the simplicity of the manufacturing processes and because they are made from cheap and easily available material. There are three distinct varieties, cotton warp with paper filling [weft] threads, cotton or hemp warp with paper and wool filling and the rugs composed entirely of paper yarns. These are woven on a carpet loom, run through a size box containing the mixture for stiffening and setting colors, run over several steam calenders to dry and flatten and the finished rug is ready for the market. This type of floorcovering cleans easily, is sanitary, odorless and will wear well. In 1916 there were twenty-five factories in the United States making fibre

rugs, one with a daily output of twenty-five tons. (*Journal of Home Economics*, 1918, 10, 10, p.456.)

According to Bendure & Pfieffer, 'the rugs are woven in the plain, twill and Jacquard weaves, and in variations and combinations of these weaves. They may be all kraft fiber or kraft fiber combined with cotton, sisal or wool.' (1947, p.602.)
See also **Grass**, **Rug**.

Krinkle

A plain open-weave cloth embossed to give a crinkle effect to **Austrian shades** (Hunter, 1918, p.357).

Lace

(a) A sixteenth-century term for an ornamental braid. The terms derive from the early method of plaiting braid on long **cushions** in the manner of bobbin lace. It was fixed onto **upholstery** to break up large areas of cloth by banding or bordering (see also **Pane**). It could be of **silk**, gold or silver thread.

In the nineteenth century, American references to Coach or Broad lace refer to braids about 2 inches (5 cm) wide made from **worsted**, **wool** or **cotton** and **linen**, often with a **warp** patterned design. Mrs Harrison suggested that 'coach trimmings in dark, rich hues make an excellent finish to velvet or plush lambrequins' (1881) (see **Braid**).

(b) An openwork net textile often of linen, or sometimes metal threads, which was first made in Italy and Flanders. The origin of the name is from the Latin *lacqueus*, meaning 'noose'. The furnishing forms began in the fourteenth century using types such as **filet net**, **réseau**, embroidered **leno** and **cutwork**. Generally lace is either embroidered, **needlepoint**, bobbin (pillow) or machine lace.

69. Nottingham lace border woven on warp machine, c.1855–65 (Nottingham Castle Museum)

Embroidered lace is based on a number of techniques: cutwork, drawn and pulled threads, or from knotted nets (filet) and burato.

Needlepoint is made from a single thread and needle using the buttonhole **stitch**, and thus resembles **embroidery** work.

Bobbin or pillow lace is made from many threads wound on bobbins and twisted together in different ways whilst being held taught. The *Tudor Book of Rates* for 1582 listed: 'Lace called bone [bobbin] lace the dosen yards' (Willan, 1962, p.36).

Machine lace imitated hand-made lace and was developed in the later eighteenth and early nineteenth century. First was the warp frame machine in 1775, followed by the **bobbin net** machine devised by John Heathcote in 1808, and many subsequent developments in techniques ensued. For example, in 1809, the bobbin net machine produced a cotton twist-net suitable for furnishings, which were often hand embroidered. The **curtain** net machine was invented in the 1840s with the patent of John Livesey of Lenton in 1846. The machine produced a square mesh from tightly twisted warp threads from which loops were drawn out sideways to link the lines. The sideways links could be adjusted to make a wide range of effects and, when the jacquard was applied, the range of patterns was very wide indeed.

By the mid-nineteenth century, machine-woven lace, patterned by jacquard attachments, was being made in very large quantities, especially for curtains but also for a wide range of other furnishing decoration. By the 1860s, looms produced net up to 3½ yards wide. Brussels lace curtains were made by the application of hand-made bobbin lace motifs to machine-made netting but, by the 1870s, completely machine-made imitation Brussels was available. During the period 1860–80, the development of the Cornely and Schiffli embroidery machines that imitated techniques such as **appliqué**, run and tambour (as well as cut out effects) increased the range of options.

In the 1950s, the Raschel machine was re-developed on a warp-knitting process that produced curtains of synthetic yarns. Generally speaking, the use of lace in interiors was a late arrival, compared to its use in dress. The particular exploitation of French lace or *point de France* in the later seventeenth century encouraged its use, not only for fashionable dress, but also for interior decoration. The more delicate Argentan lace superseded the French during the eighteenth century.

Its use for upholstery **trimming** is well documented. In 1721, Blundell noted in his diary 'I Nailed the Lace on the Purple Chear, as I have lately Appolster'd' (Blundell, 1968-1972, entry for 20-12-1721). In 1730, in a *Treatise on Buggs*, Southall mentions that 'If for Ornament [for a bed] you use Lace, let it be sewed, not pasted on, for paste they [bugs] love much' (Boynton, 1965, p.18). During 1762, Queen Charlotte was supplied with a lace **counterpane** for a bed: Pricilla Maceune charged for 'a suit of superfine Flanders point lace to cover all over a crimson sattin counterpane with deep falls and a gathered head to Do. Also to trim the bolsters and four pillows £2,699.00'. She also supplied 'a suit of the like lace to cover a toilet table compleat' (Walton, 1975, p.113).

In *The Workwoman's Guide*, lace was recommended for bed decoration in conjunction with **fringes** as a **border** feature (Hale, 1840, p.193). The development of machine embroidery, which imitated **appliqué** and other hand techniques, as well as the army of domestic embroiderers, meant that lace became commonplace and lost its cachet.

Lace was particularly associated with **inner curtains** in the later nineteenth century. Various commentators made recommendations. Swiss or embroidered lace was championed by Charles Eastlake: 'infinitely superior to the ordinary muslin curtain for use as a summer curtain'

I. Toile de Jouy bed furniture, copper roller print, Antwerp, c.1802 (Courtesy of Musee de la Toile Jouy-en Josas)

II. Eighteenth-century cut velvet cloth example (Leeds Museums and Galleries, Temple Newsam House, Roger Warner Collection)

III. Axminster carpet (Private Collection)

IV. Wilton carpet with an Oriental rug design, c.1930s (HMSO)

V. Needlework carpet, 1990s, by Elizabeth Bradley

VI. Chair with pile on pile velvet and fringe. Northern Netherlands or France, c.1700–25 (Collectie Stichting Vrienden der Geldersche Kasteelen Arnhem)

VII. Cotton palampore, early eighteenth century (Rijksmuseum, Amsterdam)

VIII. Tapestry furnished room, Antony House, Cornwall (©NTPL/John Bethell)

IX. Chintz, pheasant and palm design, late eighteenth century (M. Percival, The Chintz Book, *1923)*

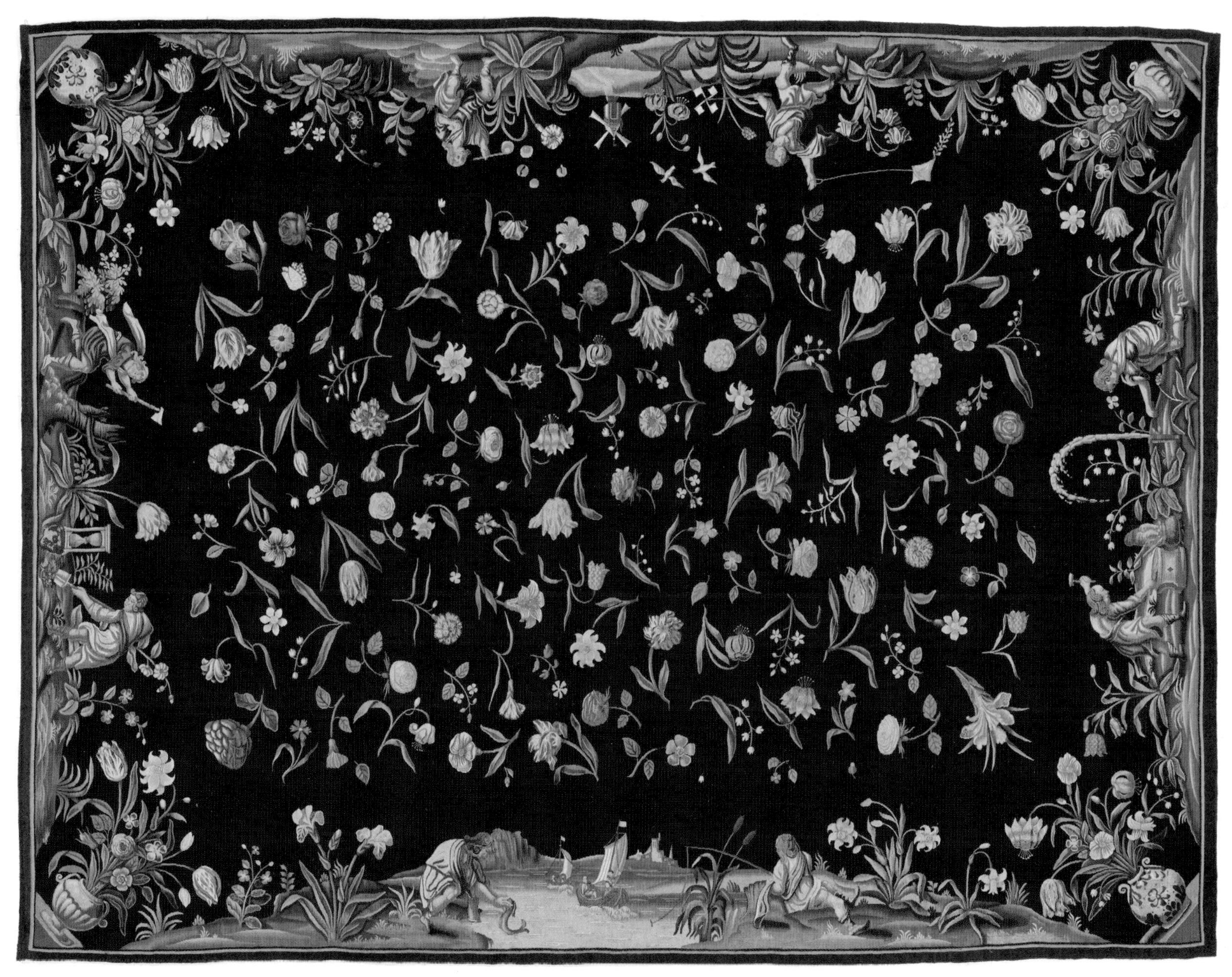

X. Tapestry table carpet, wool and silk, mid-seventeenth century. (Rijksmuseum, Amsterdam)

XI. Berlin wool-work on a prie-dieu chair, c.1840 (Courtesy of The Geffrye Museum)

XII. Tapestry carpet entitled 'The Betrayal', late nineteenth century, by Stoddard and Co

(1878, p.102). In the *Art of Decoration*, Mrs Haweis commented that 'some intelligent person has devised a thorough novelty in the shape of black lace curtains with patterns in old gold colour. They are very pretty, and ought to be durable… They are sold under the mysterious name of Cabul.' (1881, p.303)

Lace curtains were also discussed by Moreland: 'Laces are now sold so low that some kinds are within the means of almost everybody, and nothing freshens up the room so, or suggests to an outsider the refinement within, so much as a bit of lace in the window.' (*Practical Decorative Upholstery*, 1889, pp 158–60.)

Another view was expressed in 1904, when Hermann Muthesius commented upon lace curtains: 'Lace curtains still survive but only in the houses of the old-fashioned and people who cannot bring themselves to part with old knick-knacks' (1904, p.194). Despite this comment, lace as a curtain material certainly remained popular. An American author, writing on artistic furnishings, noted the range of lace available:

> Point Arabe lace has been a favourite for some years in high-class curtains, and its deep colour and cord effect suit the furnishings of handsome houses. The Marie Antoinette lace, in which a pattern is made with braid, is graceful and simple. Sometimes a mixture of the two styles is adopted. Cluny lace makes so durable and sensible a curtain that it has held its own through a series of changes in curtains. Brussels lace is the daintiest hanging for a drawing room and one of the oldest varieties. Irish Point is disappearing and many novelties are coming into vogue. (Kellogg, 1905, pp 151–2.)

Hunter noted the importance of made-up curtains, when he listed some of those available in the USA in 1918:

> French lace curtains: A general name for those made with real lace mounted on machine net or on silk or scrim as well as for the few that are made entirely of real lace.
>
> Nottingham lace curtains: A general name for those woven in one piece on the lace curtain machine, usually with an embroidered buttonhole edging added after weaving and sometimes with an appliqué cord, as in the once popular 'corded arabians'.

He noted that, in the USA, machine-woven 'Nottingham laces' were called craft lace, American lace or Scotch lace, as cheap mail order types debased the Nottingham name.

> Swiss lace curtains: A general name for those made by embroidering designs with the bonnaz sewing machine on machine net. The principle varieties are tambour, Brussels, appliqué, and Irish point. The tambours are so called from the embroidery frame; the Brussels have the field of figured filed in with bonnaz stitch of finer yarn. The appliqués have thin muslin appliqués filling the ground of the figures. The Irish points have openwork spiders in addition to the muslin appliqués.
>
> Novelty lace curtains: A general name for all kinds of effects produced without the use of real lace, by the application and insertion of Nottingham and other machine laces and braids on net, or scrim or muslin; sometimes but rarely now, with ruffled net or muslin or cretonne edging. (Hunter, 1918, p.105)

By the 1920s, Dyer explored what was available on the market. Although they were less fashionable, the range was still wide:

> The popularity of curtain materials, as of every other line of merchandise, depends on style. Lace curtains are not used so extensively as they were some years ago. They are much more elaborate and ornate than the materials mentioned above but less easy to wash and iron, and cost more if a good quality is purchased. For a sumptuously furnished room they are more suitable than inexpensive voile ... Some of the real laces usually found in a curtain department are: Irish point, a machine-made net on which a pattern is sewed or appliquéd. Often the foundation net under the pattern is cut away. This is one of the most beautiful lace curtains made. It is sometimes called Swiss because it was made originally in Switzerland. Saxony Brussels, Swiss Brussels (Swiss Tambour) Saxony Brussels is a machine-made net on which is worked by hand a pattern in a chain stitch, called Tambour. Double net is used in the pattern. In Swiss Brussels (Swiss Tambour), the embroidery in chain stitch is done by machine. The effect is more beautiful from a distance than close at hand. Saxony Brussels is much more difficult to make and therefore more expensive. Marie Antoinette a rather heavy net with cord appliqué sprays combined with tape bow-knots, flowers, and leaves appliquéd on to the net. Arabian a heavy net with patterns heavily corded or made of braids or tapes resembling Battenberg. Sometimes this is called Renaissance. Antique (also called Araneum or Spider Work) a coarse, open effect produced by darning. The darning is irregular and not made on a background. This is effective but not especially beautiful. Princesse a delicate and effective lace. Its pattern is made of separate braids which are sewed together or joined. (Dyer, *c.*1923, p.200.)

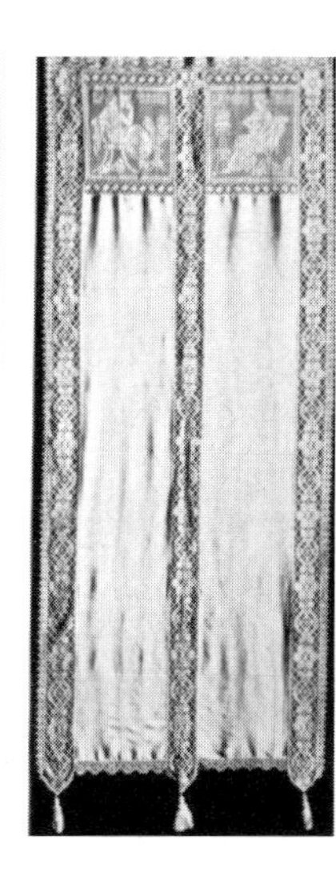

70. Lace door panel examples, USA, c.*1918 (G.L. Hunter,* Decorative Textiles, Coverings for Furniture etc., *1918)*

By the 1950s, the terms lace and net were used almost synonymously in the furnishing trade and distinctions were based on use. Thus, 'all-over net' described a patterned net designed for sale by the yard (91 cm), while a made-up article from precisely the same fabric was a 'lace curtain'. Again, a fabric with exactly the same construction designed to be hung over the lower half of the window only was a 'Brise-bise', and if it was a full-length panel to cover the entire window it became a 'store curtain' (Sheridan, 1953, p.264).

Lace has been in decline as a furnishing fabric since the mid-twentieth century. The warp-knitting Raschel machines that used synthetic yarns resurrected the market for a while but, as tastes changed towards other types of window furnishings, the lace (net) curtain lost favour.

Arabian (Arabe)

Ecru coloured piece lace corded in a darker tone.

Battenberg
Heavy coarse linen lace that has been popular as a **curtain lace** in the twentieth century.

Bobbin
A lace-making technique based on plaiting that uses bobbins to tension the threads in the making process. Though originally mainly flax, after the 1830s cotton threads were more common.

Brown
A reference to the state of machine-woven lace as it leaves the machine and before it is finished.

Bruges
Coarse types of lace used for curtains, bedcovers and cloths.

Nottingham
A particular mid-nineteenth century furnishing lace (not only from Nottingham) which was boldly patterned and heavily meshed. Nottingham lace curtains were manufactured to fit the larger paned, single glass windows, introduced to replace the divided windows of previous sash forms. One authority considered that 'the Swiss lace produced at Nottingham is very inexpensive and varies in width; it maybe had to suit the largest windows' (Caulfeild & Saward, 1887, p.467).

It was certainly a successful product. In 1908, the Sears Roebuck catalogue listed 'A strong, well-made Nottingham Lace Curtain, one of the most stylish and attractive drapes one could possibly desire for the parlor window'. Ten years later, the term Nottingham lace curtain was defined as: 'A general name for those woven in one piece on the lace curtain machine, usually with an embroidered buttonhole edging added after weaving and sometimes with an appliqué cord, as in the once popular "corded arabians"'. Hunter then noted that, in the USA, machine-woven Nottingham laces were called 'craft lace, American lace or Scotch lace as cheap mail order types debased the Nottingham name' (Hunter, 1918, p.101).

Swiss
A machine-made replication of sixteenth-century Swiss lace made from a coarse cotton yarn and widely used in the later nineteenth century for furnishing work. Charles Eastlake recommended Swiss lace 'made of stout thread-cotton, and worked in two or three small but well-defined patterns' for summer curtains, explaining that:

> It is apt to shrink a little in washing; but is otherwise faultless in a practical point of view; while in design it is infinitely superior to the ordinary muslin curtain, on which semi-naturalistic foliage and non-descript ornament is allowed to meander after an extravagant and meaningless fashion. (1878, p.102.)

Caulfeild & Saward discussed imitation Swiss lace and defined it:

> A machine-made textile employed in upholstery for window curtains, wallpaper preservers, behind washstands and for short blinds. Some new kinds have been produced in broad stripes, alternately coloured with designs, and white of the ordinary open work description. The Swiss lace produced at Nottingham is very inexpensive and varies in width; it maybe had to suit the largest windows. (1887, p.467)

See also **Bed lace**, **Brise-bise**, **Brussels curtain**, **Glass curtain**, **Net**, **Sectional panel curtain**, **Store curtains**.

FURTHER READING

Board of Trade (1947). *Working Party Report, Lace*, London: HMSO.
Earnshaw, P. (1980). *The Identification of Lace*, Prince's Risborough: Shire Publications.
Earnshaw, P. (1994). *A Dictionary of Lace*, 3rd edition, London: Batsford.
Earnshaw, P. (1986). *Lace Machines and Machine Lace*, London: Batsford.
Goldenberg, S.L. (1904). *Lace, its Origin and History*, New York: Brentano's.
Halls, Z. (1964). *Machine Made Lace in Nottingham in the 18th and 19th Century*, Nottingham: City Museum and Art Gallery.
Harding, K. (1952). *Lace-furnishing Manufacture*, London: Macmillan.
Levey, S. (1983). *Lace, A Visual History*, London: Victoria and Albert Museum.
Palliser, Mrs (1875). *A History of Lace*, London: Sampson, Low and Searle.
Sorber, F. (2001). 'Lace in the interior' in Mertens, W. (ed.), *Transitory Splendour: Interior Textiles in Western Europe 1600–1900*, Antwerp: Hessenhuis Museum, Stadsbestuur, pp 285–7.
Walton, K.-M. (1975). 'Queen Charlotte's dressing table', *Furniture History*, 11, pp 112–13.
Wardle, P. (1968). *Victorian Lace*, London: Herbert Jenkins.
Whitehouse, L. (1947). 'The lace furnishing industry: history, productions, prospects', *Journal of the Textile Institute Proceedings*, 38, pp 607–14.

Lacquered leather
Leather finished with a coloured lacquer or japanned finish, sometimes known as 'patent leather'. This process appears to have been first used in the later eighteenth century for leather intended for **upholstery**. In the later twentieth century, upholstery leathers were finished with a cellulose lacquer.
See also **Gilt leather**.

Ladder web (aka Ladder tape)
A narrow fabric that is woven to make two outer webs that are joined by two narrower staggered webs, each of these being woven alternately into each outer web. The intention is to support Venetian blind slats.

Up to about 1878, this web was made by hand from two broad tapes with a narrow one stitched between at the required intervals. In January 1869, a patent was granted to James Carr for his invention that allowed the weaving of the complete tape. It was commercially produced from 1874 and was improved upon in 1878 by Carl Vorwerk. By the 1930s, it was woven from yarn-dyed **cotton** for inside use, and **linen** for outside use, and in a range of sizes to suit the particular slats being used. The standard was 1½ to 2⅜ inches (3.8 to 6 cm).
See also **Ferret**, **Venetian binding**, **Venetian blind**.

Laid cord
An upholsterers' **twine** made by layers of **cord** twisted together, so as to avoid stretching. It is employed to lash **springs** into position when creating a fully hand-built sprung seat. The best quality is made from flax, the lesser quality from **hemp**.

Lambrequin
Originally, a **scarf** or piece of material that was worn over the helmet of a set of armour to act as a covering. In heraldry, it was represented with one end (which is cut or jagged) hanging down as a pendant. From the 1840s, this idea was transferred to the various-shaped cases designed to enclose the top of **curtains** and the fittings, as well as for mantelpieces, brackets and shelves. For windows, they were made from various mate-

rials including a face cloth to match the curtains, **lace**, **felt**, **macramé** etc. Often they were fitted with a scalloped edge, trimmed with **passementeries**. They were similar to a **valance**, though often with long extended sides, in some cases reaching to the floor. Although *The Workwoman's Guide* considered them to be 'very simple and may be formed to any shape according to the style of the room' (Hale, 1840, p.204), the term appears to have been used mainly in the USA.

In American usage, it refers to a cornice with a valance of pointed pieces, placed over a door or window; or a short curtain or piece of drapery (with the lower edge either scalloped or straight) suspended for ornament from a mantelshelf (see **Mantel drapery**). By the middle of the nineteenth century, lambrequins were a mainstay of window decorations. *Godey's Lady's Book* defined them as 'a fall of the same material as the curtain, edged with rich gimp and usually ornamented by heavy cords and tassels depending from the points of scallops' (October 1851, p.244). The Beecher sisters, in *The American Woman's Home*, suggested that 'the patterns of these can be varied according to fancy but the simple designs are usually the prettiest. A tassel at the lowest point improves appearance.' (1869, p.88.)

In 1882, Almon Varney said that lambrequins had been 'superseded by a valance which will shove aside with the curtains and the fact that they exclude the light from the top, whence it is most desirable, has served to make them unpopular'. However, he continued by pointing out that they were still made in rich material, cut in all manner of forms and trimmed with **fringe** and heavy **gimp** (1883, p.277). During 1898, Edith Wharton wrote, in *The Decoration of Houses*, that 'the modern use of the lambrequin as an ornamental finish to window curtains is another instance of misapplied decoration'. She goes on to say 'In old prints, lambrequins over windows are almost always seen in conjunction with Italian shades, and this is the only logical way of using them' (1897, p.71). By 1907, Sears Roebuck were selling ready-made lace lambrequins for the tops of windows.
See also **Cornice**, **Pelmet**.

Lamé
An effect achieved by weaving metal strips or threads into a cloth.

Lampas
There is some suggestion that this was originally a painted or dyed **silk** textile imported from the Coromandel Coast of India (Harmuth, 1924, p.92). It is a figured furnishing textile made from silk (and sometimes metallic threads) in a compound **satin** weave to create two-colour **damask** by the use of two sets of **warp** yarns to bind the figure **wefts** and ground wefts respectively. Probably originating in the Middle East, it was used for luxury vestments and **drapes**. In England, the weft-figured version is sometimes called 'tissue' while the warp-figured version is called 'liseré'. It was used in eighteenth-century **upholstery**.

The 1851 *The Art Journal Illustrated Catalogue of the Great Exhibition* (p.1262) shows a 'piece of figured lampas, in Algerian silk, crop of 1850, manufactured at Lyons'. Used mainly as an upholstery material, it was also woven with **wool** and **mohair**.

In 1951, it was noted that 'during the heyday of decorating in the twenties, it [lampas] reappeared and it may again' (Taylor, 1951, p.70).
See also **Damasquette**, **Liseré**, **Tissue**, **Weave: Lampas**.

Lampas broché
A French term for a **brocaded** cloth (made with the addition of **weft** threads).
See also **Lampas**.

Lamp rug
These were defined in 1841 as 'small square rugs, [designed] to prevent the feet of the lamps from marking the table. The cheapest are made of oil cloth, lined underneath with green baize and bordered with a very thick worsted fringe…' (Miss Leslie, 1841, p.184).

Lancaster cloth
A light, washable oilcloth intended for use on shelves, tables, around washbasins, etc. It was named after the town of Lancaster, a British centre of production throughout the nineteenth century and beyond. It was usually supplied in white, cream or other light colour background, with imitation marble veining or other printed design.
See also **Oilcloth**.

FURTHER READING

Christie, G. (1964). *Storeys of Lancaster,* 1848–1964, London: Collins.

Lappet cloth
A **muslin**-type fabric with a plain-weave ground and extra coloured threads woven by a special loom which inserts the threads in a zigzag motion to form the pattern. The lappet threads interlace with the ground fabric only at the edges of the figure. This creates the effect of a small embroidered pattern. The 1884 edition of the *Encyclopaedia Britannica* noted lappets as one of a range of cloths: 'For window curtains, hangings &c. there are manufactured harness and book muslins, lenos, sprigs, spots and lappets.' (XVII, 109/2.)

Lasting
A shiny, black **wool-cotton** fabric that resembled **calmanco**, usually used for coat linings and shoe tops. It was employed in the USA as an

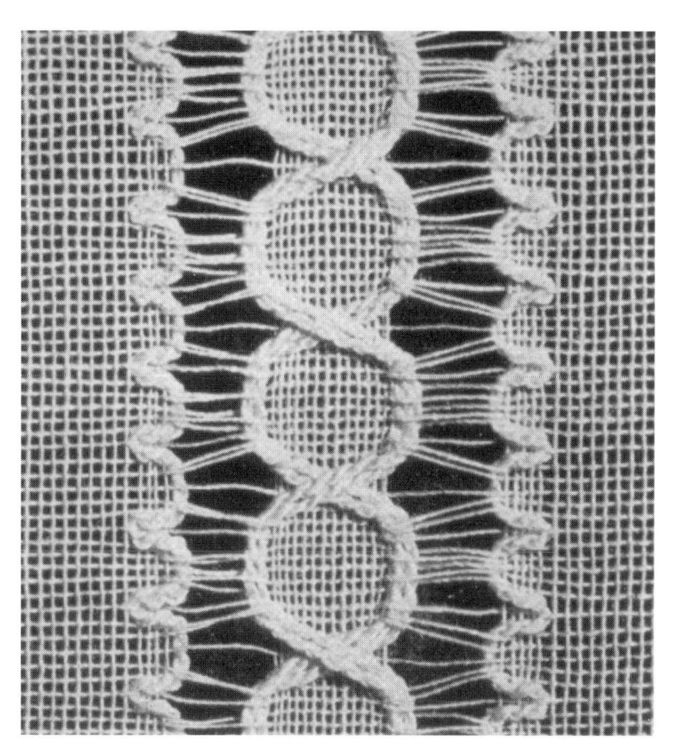

71. Lappet cloth (E. Ostick, The Draper's Encyclopaedia, *1955)*

upholstery cover during the 1870s as a substitute for **haircloth**, which it superficially resembled (Grier, 1988, p.222).
See also **Everlasting**.

Latex

Natural latex rubber is a plant exudation obtained from a variety of trees but especially from the rubber tree (*Hevea brasiliensis*). It was first brought to Europe in 1735 but was not developed commercially as rubber until the 1820s. It is naturally thermoplastic but a process called 'vulcanisation', i.e. the modification of rubber latex by sulphur and heat, overcomes this. The process was discovered in 1839 by Goodyear and patented in 1843 by Hancock and in again in 1844 by Goodyear. In 1929, the Dunlop Rubber Co patented latex foam or sponge rubber. Shortages caused by supply difficulties during World War II led to increased research and the subsequent production of synthetic latex by Pirelli and other companies.

Its main use in furnishings has been as an **upholstery** foam (developed in the late 1920s), and for rubber webbing systems. Experiments began at the Dunlop Co, where a food mixer was used to whisk liquid latex with additives, which was then 'cured' in an oven. The result was a flexible and resilient sponge material that returned to its original shape after being pressed. A typical process of making latex foam mixes the latex with chemicals such as sulphur, soaping agents and antioxidants. After maturing, the mix is foamed with air. The mix is then poured into moulds and steam-heated to vulcanise (cure) it. The later SP process uses a foam mixture to fill moulds partially; these are then closed, and a vacuum applied so that the material expands. After being frozen solid, CO2 is blown through to gel it. It is then cured at a higher temperature and finished. Initially, the moulding method, in which the cured latex shape was removed from a mould, meant that it was not reversible. The moulding process produced cavity-foam sheet material that needed to be 'walled' or built up into shapes.

Later developments include Pincore latex, a process in which the liquid mixture is baked in a mould with numerous thin pins penetrating it. This makes a reversible material with no mould limitations. The Pincore material is perforated with holes. The sheet material can be of various thicknesses and densities and the diameter of the holes may also be varied in order to change the 'softness'. This material does not need to be walled. Synthetic rubber-styrene butadiene rubber was often blended with natural latex to provide a variety of densities along with other features.

Dunlop's first commercial use of Dunlopillo was in 1929, when the company's latex cushioning was used in cockpit linings and, by 1930, cavity-moulded **cushions** were being supplied to the automobile industry. The contract markets (auditoria, office, hall and vehicle seating) accepted the new material well. However, most domestic furniture manufacturers were reluctant to change. In 1946, it was still referred to as a 'new' filling material.

As late as 1951, a British industry commentator thought that 'the potentialities of latex foam for upholstery and the influence it can exert on the design of chairs and seating units have not yet been fully realised' (Desbrow, 1951, p.2). Like many new materials, latex foam was clearly versatile enough to be used both as a substitute for existing materials, but also as the basis for completely new design possibilities. The benefits of latex cushioning were such that it gave the designer much more flexibility than the traditional methods. The costing of the cushion-making was much easier, due to the regular shape of the cushion, and it was the logical choice for contemporary furniture due to its shape-retaining capabilities. It was also promoted for hygienic **mattresses** and **pillows**. The development of plastic foams has had an impact on the role of latex since the late twentieth century.
See also **Foam**, **Rubber webbing, Webbing**.

FURTHER READING

Anon. (1954). 'Foam rubber and furnishing design', *Art and Industry*, 57, November, pp 172–3.
Desbrow, R. (1951). 'Latex foam in furniture design and manufacture', *Rubber Developments*, booklet, British Rubber Development Board.
Murphy, E. (1966). 'Some early adventures with latex', *Rubber Technology*, p.39.
Young, D. (1954). 'Freedom of design with latex foam', *Latex foam in Furniture*, report of a conference organised by the British Rubber Development Board, London, May, pp 35–47.

Lawn

A lightweight, soft and washable **cotton** or **linen** plain-weave cloth, usually fine and sheer, with a range of finishes which are then known by other names. It is usually white, but may be dyed or printed, and has a silky feel. When made with combed yarns with a soft feel and slight lustre it is called nainsook. The name may be derived from Laon, a city in France, where linen lawn was manufactured extensively.

Although noted as early as 1415 (*OED*), it was in 1588 that the Earl of Leicester's inventory listed 'a canopie of purple lawn, branched with sundry colours, lyned with crimson tinsel sarsnett and tasselled with silk and goulde'.

By 1947, it was defined as a:

> light weight sheer fine fabric made with fine carded or combed yarns woven in a high count… It is sized and calendered which results in a softly lustrous appearance. Lawn is similar to batiste, muslin and nainsook, three fabrics that are given different finishes from lawn. Used for curtains and bedspreads. (Bendure & Pfieffer, p.636.)

See also **Cambric**, **Muslin**, **Nainsook**.

Lea carpeting

Proprietary name for a **pile carpet** in which the pile is held in a backing by **adhesives** such as **latex** or rubber cement. It is also known as patent-back carpet. In the 1930s, the American *Journal of Home Economics* explained the benefits of 'recently developed forms of carpeting': 'Lea carpet, in which each pile fiber is held vertically in the rubber base, is made of unspun animal fibers by a high-speed process at a unit cost lower than woven carpets but durable and equal in appearance to high-grade velvet or Wilton' (*Journal of Home Economics*, 23, 8, August 1931, p.794).
See also **Patent-back carpet**.

FURTHER READING

Anon. (1931). 'Rubber-backed carpets', *India-Rubber Journal*, 81, 15, 11 April, pp 479–80.

Leather

Leather is a generic name given to hides prepared by a currier. Large animal hides and small **animal skins** from reptiles and birds provide leather. In the case of hides, the outer hair layer and the inner fleshy layer are removed, leaving the corium (with hair follicle grain marks) to be turned into leather by tanning. The basic techniques are (a) chamoising or treating with oils and fats; (b) tawing (soaking) with minerals such as alum and salt; and (c) tanning with vegetable matter, such as bark, sumach, etc. Traditionally, tanning was done with tree barks and roots. By the eighteenth century, the processes included tawing with alum and added fats, egg yolk and flour. Alum-tawed skin is not a true leather since it is untanned, but is given body by the addition of the ingredient above. Eighteenth-century down-filled **cushion** cases have been made from alum-tawed leather.

Modern methods now include the addition of chromium chemicals and alum tanning agents that speed up the process to a few hours. The tanning that uses mineral salts such as chrome sulphate completely tans the hides in 24 hours. This is in contrast to early techniques where skins could be kept in tannin for up to three years. Once tanning is complete, the hides may be split into layers and treated, to give a finer and more correctly balanced grain. The skins that result are then processed into **upholstery** leather, by dressing, shaving and **dyeing**. They are finally oiled and stretched, coated, polished and finished. The surface of plain leather may be embellished in a variety of ways to include polychroming, lacquering, gilding, staining, glazing, stamping, embossing, tooling, scorching or boarding – used alone or in combination, such as in the preparation of painted/gilt leather **screens** or **wall hangings**.

The versatility and durability of leather has made it a very popular furnishing material. Upholsterers have used leather for many tasks, both functional and decorative. These include jointing thongs, seat and upholstery covers, cushions and protective covers for cabinetwork, wall hangings and writing surfaces. It may be used for simple upholstery systems such as sling/**platform** or woven seats, chair backs or bed bases. Quilted leather is one of the earliest forms of layered upholstery. The structural use developed from an early age with the introduction of sling seats fitted to X-framed chairs. Details of other uses are commonly found in inventories.

Spanish leather seems to have been in demand for high-quality work. In 1423, Henry VI had Spanish leather covers for tables and, in 1534, Katherine of Aragon enjoyed cushions of 'lether, lyned withe yalowe cotton to the same' (R. Edwards, 1964, p338). The range of leathers that were available by the sixteenth century indicated an already sophisticated market. The *Tudor Book of Rates* for 1582 noted 'Skinnes for leather ... Basill, buffe for cushions, portingale [Portugal] red hides, roan, salt, Spanish, spruce and swan skinnes' (Willan, 1962, p.56). William France supplied six armchairs covered in 'Black Spanish leather bordered, welted, quilted and tufted and finished with burnished nails' in 1736 to Croome Court (Beard, 1997, p.307). In the eighteenth century, the range of upholsterers' leathers is indicated by the inventory of Samuel Norman. His stock included brown **damask** skins, white sheepskins, rone skins, bazil skins and gilt skins (Kirkham, 1969, p.509). Hepplewhite, in his *Cabinet Maker and Upholsterer's Guide*, recommended leather as a covering for dining room furniture, since it resisted food smells (1789).

By the nineteenth century, leather was chiefly used for upholstery work and tabletops. In 1839, Henry Brown took out a patent (Patent no.8193) for making veneer from the skins of animals to plate furniture. Its success is unknown but it anticipated later schemes where leather was used to cover hard furniture. Leather has been, and remains, an important upholstery and decorative finish for all sorts of furniture.

Calves' leather
A specific description of a particular hide derived from young bovine animals. An Essex inventory of 1691 specifies '5 calves leather chairs' (Steer, 1969, p.207).

Kid leather
Leather prepared from the skins of young goats. King George II had a travelling bed (*c.*1720), which had kidskin leather **ticking**.

Parchment and vellum
Parchment is generally from sheep, goat or calf skins that, rather than being tanned, are treated with lime and dried under tension. In this process, the bundles are aligned horizontally to form a flat opaque skin. Finishing processes may involve treatment with sodium carbonate, calcium carbonate or lime wash to degrease; dusting with pumice or magnesium silicate may follow this. Unlike tanned goods, parchment will dissolve in hot water. In furniture, it has been commonly used as a constituent material of elaborate **trimmings** (**passementerie**).

Rawhide
This is dried, untanned skin, usually a split cattle hide. When wet, it will putrefy, unlike tanned leather. Its tendency to shrink on drying has been exploited to make drum seats.

Upholstery leather
Split hides tanned to a soft, even feel, and dyed. Chrome-tanned upholstery hides are usually softer and stronger than those tanned with quebracho or bark. A full hide is up to a ¼ inch (7 mm) thick and can be split into three or four layers. The top split is called 'buffing', the second split is called 'deep buff', and the third is called 'No.2'. The remains are the slab and are not used for upholstery. The weight also describes the thickness of the leather, in the ratio 1 oz/ft^2 = 1/64 inch (0.4 mm). See also **Bazil**, **Damask leather**, **Gilt leather**, **Lacquered leather**, **Protective furnishing**, **Rawhide**, **Roan**, **Russia leather**, **Scorched leather**, **Sealskin**, **Spanish leather**.

FURTHER READING

Clouzot, H. (1925). *Cuirs décorées*, Paris: Librairie des Arts Décoratifs.
Davis, C.T. (1885). *Manufacture of Leather*, Philadelphia: H.C. Baird & Co.
Haines, B.M. (1985). 'Identification of leather' in Fogle, S. (ed.), *Recent Advances in Leather Conservation*, Washington, DC: AIC.
Muhlbacher, E. (1988). *Europaische Lederarbeiten*, Berlin: Staatliche Museen zu Berlin.
O'Flaherty, F., Roddy, W.T. & Loller, R.M. (eds) (1965). *The Chemistry and Technology of Leather*, 4 vols, New York: Reinhold.
Tanners' Council of America (1983). *Dictionary of Leather Terminology*, Washington, DC: Tanners' Council of America.
Trent, R. (1987) in Cooke, E.S. (ed.), *17th Century Upholstery in Massachusetts in Upholstery in America and Europe*, London and New York: Norton, pp 47–50.
Waterer, J. (1968). *Leather Craftsmanship*, London: G. Bell.
Waterer, J. (1971). *Spanish Leather: History of its Use from 800 to 1800 for Mural Hangings, Screens, Upholstery, Altar Frontals, Ecclesiastical Vestments, Footwear, Gloves, Pouches, and Caskets*, London: Faber and Faber.

Leather carpet
Although often used as a protection, **leather carpets** also seem to have been used as a floorcovering in their own right. As early as 1380, the Duke of Orleans had 'carpets of Aragon leather, to put on the floor in summer' (Hunter, 1918, p.431). In the 1641 Tart Hall inventory, there is listed a foot carpet of red leather, a carpet of yellow leather and others of white leather (Cust, 1911).

Leathercloth (aka Oilcloth)
See **Lancaster cloth**, **Oilcloth**.

Leather hanging
See **Gilt leather**.

Leno

(a) It is an openwork fabric often made from **silk**, **cotton** or **linen** etc, in which rows of gauze weave are interspersed or combined with areas of plain-weave. The **warp** threads are twisted in pairs before weaving; the pairs cross and re-cross each other between picks of **weft**. Leno was occasionally used for window **curtains** and **blinds** in the nineteenth century. In 1819, the London cabinet-maker and upholsterer, George Bullock, had in stock '7 pieces of figured leno, green stripe, figured buff and citron coloured leno.' (Levy, 1989, p.185.) In the mid-twentieth century, these cloths were made up into curtains and used as 'light filters'.

(b) As a weave, leno refers to a process where the warp threads are twisted round each other, as the weft is shot through to bind them.

See also **Gauze**, **Leno brocade**, **Marquisette**, **Muslin**, **Net**, **Weave: Gauze**.

Leno brocade

A **brocade cotton**, or cotton and **rayon** cloth, produced by a combination of ordinary brocade fabric with **gauze** or **leno** cross weaving. Nisbet pointed out that when manufactured from cotton, leno brocades were used for window **curtains**, summer dress material and fancy aprons (1919, p.272).

Levantine

A soft **silk serge** material first recorded in the early nineteenth century as a dress fabric. Porter, in his *Silk Manufacturing*, defined it as 'a stout, close made and twilled silk' (1831, p.298). It was later described in 1887 in *The Dictionary of Needlework* as 'a very rich-faced stout twilled black silk material, exceedingly soft, and of excellent wear. Its face and back show different shades; if the former be a blue-black, the latter will be a jet and vice versa.' (Caulfeild & Saward, p.324.)

Lignum

Hard flooring made of wood, ground with oil, and harder than cork-based **linoleum** with which it competed (Moreland, 1889, p.296).

Line

A particular cord intended to run over pulleys on a board, and then threaded through rings sewn to the back of the **curtain** to be raised. The tension was maintained by fixing the cord over a **cloak pin**. Line was often used in conjunction with **festoon window curtains**.

Line was also used in a decorative manner, combined with tassels, etc. Loudon explained:

> The description of line used should always be the plaited thread line… This patent thread line, as it is called, is manufactured of all sizes from that fit for a carriage window blind to one thick enough for a ships cable; and it should be used not only in curtains and blinds, but in hanging sashes, pictures, and in short in all cases requiring lines. (1839, p.342.)

See also **Cord**.

Linen

Linen is a name for the cellulosic fibres produced by retting the pulpy parts of the flax plant (*Linum usitatissimum*) stem. Its lack of resilience makes it easy to crease and it has a tendency to be brittle. However, linen fibres have been used in a wide range of fabrics, as it is very strong and lustrous. Originally a cheap yarn, the production of linen was well established by 1500, and it remained the major alternative to **wool** in the northern hemisphere until the later eighteenth century. The rise of **cotton** challenged its dominance and it gradually declined in importance.

Linen cloth has been employed for a range of uses in home furnishings. For example, Sewall's *Diary*, 10 January 1702, mentions how the ill Mrs Sewall 'gets on to the Pallat bed in her cloaths, and there keeps, while linen curtains are put within the serge, and is refreshed by it.' (Cummings, 1961, p.29.) One hundred and fifty years later, Miss Leslie discussed its use for **curtains**: 'Curtains of figured or damasked brown linen, though not handsome, are very lasting and economical; and may be set off with a bright coloured fringe or binding.' (1841, p.307.) Dyer discusses other uses: 'English linen: heavy linen, hand-blocked surface, desirable for its quaintness or beauty of color and design. More expensive than a cotton fabric. Used for scarfs, **drapes**, and cushion covers.' (*c*.1923, p.206.)

It was in the case of bed and **table linen** that it became most successful and gave its name to a generic product type. Domestic linen includes breakfast cloths, luncheon cloths, bridge cloths, dinner cloths, crumb cloths, buffet **runners**, tea-wagon cloths, **sheets** and cot sets.

See also **Abbot's cloth**, **Arras cloth**, **Art linen**, **Barrage**, **Barras**, **Batiste**, **Bed**, **Belgian tapestry**, **Blind holland**, **Buckram**, **Burlap**, **Brocatelle**, **Blind**, **Bird's-eye**, **Binding**, **Caffart damask**, **Calico**, **Cambric**, **Camlet**, **Canvas**, **Check**, **Crankey**, **Crash**, **Cretonne**, **Crumb cloth**, **Damask**, **Denant**, **Diaper**, **Dowlas**, **Duck**, **Forfar**, **Garlick**, **Harden**, **Hessian**, **Holland**, **Huckabuck**, **Kenting**, **Lawn**, **Linsey-woolsey**, **Lockram**, **Mockado**, **Momie cloth**, **Monk's cloth**, **Moquette**, **Osnaburg**, **Peruvian cloth**, **Plush**, **Raynes cloth**, **Russia cloth**, **Russian tapestry**, **Satin: Satin de Bridges (Bruges)**, **Seersucker**, **Siamoise**, **Silesia**, **Soultwitch**, **Southedge**, **Stair linen**, **Tablecloth**, **Tapestry**, **Toile**, **Ticking**, **Tow**, **Towel**, **Trellis cloth**, **Turkey work**, **Tweed**, **Union**, **Velour**, **Utrecht Velvet**, **Webbing**.

FURTHER READING

Bonneville, F. (1994). *The Book of Fine Linen*, Paris: Flammarion.

Burgers, C.A. (1987). 'Some notes on western European table linen from the 16th to the 18th centuries' in Cooke E.S. (ed.), *Upholstery in America and Europe From the Seventeenth Century to World War I*, London and New York: Norton, pp 149–62.

Gill, C. (1925). *The Rise of the Irish Linen Industry*, Oxford: Clarendon Press.

Mitchell, D.M. (1989). 'By your leave my masters: British taste in table linen in the fifteenth and sixteenth centuries', *Textile History*, 20, 1, pp 49–77.

Mitchell, D.M. (2001). 'Table linen in western Europe 1600–1900' in Mertens, W. (ed.), *Transitory Splendour: Interior Textiles in Western Europe 1600–1900*, Antwerp: Hessenhuis Museum, Stadsbestuur, pp 278–84.

Moore, A.S. (1914). *Linen from Raw Material to the Finished Product*, London: Pitman.

Swain, M. (1982). 'The linen supply of a Scottish household 1770–1810', *Textile History*, 13, 1, pp 77–89.

Warden, A. (1864). *The Linen Trade, Ancient and Modern*, London and Dundee, reprinted 1967, London: Frank Cass.

Linen damask

See **Damask: Linen**.

Lining

The practice of lining **curtains** was both an aspect of function and fashion. Whilst **blinds** controlled daylight, and the effect of sunlight on cloth was not a concern, linings were as much a fashion consideration as a functional one. When curtains were tied back or draped, the lining often showed a contrast. This was not a problem for 'reversible cloths', but for others it was, so a colourful lining was made into a decorative feature. For example, Hepplewhite noted that 'to furniture [hangings] of a dark pattern, green silk lining may be used to good effect' (1789, pp 17–18).

In the nineteenth century, James Arrowsmith commented upon 'a mode of trimming which has good effects, viz., turning over the lining upon the chintz to the breadth of an inch or more and cording the edge where they meet' (Thornton, 1984, p.225).

Later in the century, *The Workwoman's Guide* explained that white **dimity** was 'sometimes lined with coloured calico with turned up hems, sometimes merely coloured hems, at others finished with white fringe, or frill…' (Hale, 1840, p.193). Concerns about lining were not always directly about the hangings. *Cassell's Household Guide* pointed out that for bed curtain linings:

> care should be exercised in selecting a lining to chintz to have a tint that will contrast well with the complexion. A pale green will impart the cadaverous hue of sickness; a buff has no contrast with the skin. A pale pink or blue suits well, but strong dark colours should be avoided. (1870, vol.1, p.243.)

Sateen lining in white or ecru has been a standard feature of much twentieth-century curtaining, although fancy or decorative linings are still part of the decorator's repertoire.

See also **Aluminium coated lining**, **Chercanneys**, **Cotton rep**, **Drugget**, **Durance**, **Interlining**, **Muslin**, **Sateen**, **Satin**, **Self-lined curtain**, **Soultwitch**, **Southedge**, **Tammy**.

Linoleum

The person credited with the invention of linoleum is Frederick Walton (Patent no.109/1860). By 1863, Walton was applying for a patent concerned with 'Improvements in the manufacture of floorcloth and coverings, similar fabrics and in pavements'. This patent noted the recipe for the linoleum and also for the production process associated with it. Walton soon coined the name 'linoleum' to avoid confusion. It is simply the corruption of the Latin name for Linseed oil – *linum oleum*. Linoleum itself is manufactured from drying oils (especially linseed) and rosins to form linoleum cement, which is mixed and blended with wood flour, ground cork and whiting (chalk), and then coloured by pigments. This composition is granulated before being rolled into sheets and laminated to a **hessian** backing. The material is then cured in large ovens for completion of the process.

There were other attempts to emulate Walton's success. In 1865, the Patent Floorcloth Co of Bradford produced a material that covered both sides of a **linen** or similar fibre cloth with linoleum-type material so that it could be reversed. However, expense soon outweighed any advantages this cloth may have had and the business folded. By 1871, Corticine, or 'Taylor ware', was being produced. Caleb Taylor used Parnacott's patent process to produce a dark, highly elastic substance called 'Black oil' (William Parnacott, Patent no.2057/1871). This was produced from linseed oil with driers, which was heated to a high temperature, and at the same time had air streams passed through. The resultant rubbery substance was kneaded with cork and rolled onto a woven fabric base. *Cassell's Household Guide* (1870) noted that 'Corticine floorcovering is a new and much recommended material as a substitute for oilcloth' (vol.1, p.125).

The processes for linoleum printing were based on floorcloth manufacturing experience, and the early printed linoleum was block-printed by hand. Printing of linoleum by machine was considered impractical in 1884 but became part of factory practice by 1887 at least. The magazine *Engineering* discussed their visit to see the seven-colour linoleum machine at Barry, Ostlere & Co in Kirkcaldy, Scotland, which cleary impressed them (*Engineering*, 13 December 1889, p.685). The machine, which the magazine speculated was probably 'the largest printing machine in the world', comprised two drums each 26 feet 9 inches (*c*.8 metres) in diameter, which would take a piece of linoleum 2 yards (1.8 metres) wide by 25 yards (23 metres) long. The limitation of the machine was that the printing jets would only cover 1½ feet (45.7 cm) across the width at a time; therefore, it took four revolutions to complete the pattern across the width.

Although manufacturers promoted linoleum for every room in the house, nineteenth-century consumers seem to have had firm ideas about its place in the home. In the eighteenth century, distinct floorings for different areas were well established and were changed about. This distinction continued with the use of floorcloth and linoleum. By the mid-nineteenth century, it was *de rigeur* for floorcloth, **Kamptulicon**, etc. to be used in halls, lobbies and bathrooms, as well as in parts of dining rooms. Very pliant bordered linoleum was produced specially for secondary stairs in the 1880s.

In 1900, Davidson says that if encaustic tiles are not feasible, linoleum is very suitable for a hall and that either **oilcloth** or linoleum may be used as a **border** in bedrooms and is admirable for bathrooms, but such coverings would be too cold for an entire bedroom floor (1900, pp 112–3). The link between encaustic tiles in an entrance hall and linoleum design is obvious. If any range of linoleum produced before 1914 is inspected, it is clear that the encaustic designs were directly transferred to linoleum.

Lawrence Weaver wrote in 1910 that 'so far as linoleum is concerned there has been of late a distinct improvement … the plain coloured cork carpet … being very useful floorcoverings … [which] do not pretend to be other than they are… Linoleum then has a great future before it.' (Thornton, 1984, p.323.) In Germany, the idea of a Kultur product that was hygienic, practical and in touch with the spirit of the age was clearly successful.

72. Linoleum printed pattern, Germany, 1930s (Private Collection)

The marketing of linoleum has always been based on cleanliness and serviceability, and these attributes were inherent in the material. However, to stimulate the market, changes were needed periodically to remind the public or to introduce something 'new'. Often these changes in design and styling were cosmetic but, sometimes, technical processes could be combined with a sales message to create more interest. For example, in the late 1920s in the USA, two companies introduced new processes to seal the surface of linoleum. The Armstrong Co called it 'Accolac' and Congoleum-Nairn called it 'Sealex'. The technical aspects were subordinate to the sales message deriving from the improvement. In the case of Armstrong, their advertising copy for 1929 combined the benefits of 'artist designed' linoleum with the modern virtues of the material: 'the warmth, the absence of draughty cracks, the quietness and springy comfort so soothing to tired bodies' (Edwards, 1996, p.168). If that was not enough, they said that, due to the new sealing process, it was as though 'unseen hands helped to keep it beautiful'. Ten years later, the emphasis was even more on household management and efficiency. Phrases such as 'no floor scrubbing for me' and 'I want a safer place for baby to play' featured in Congoleum-Nairn's advertising during 1939 (*Ladies' Home Journal*, 1939).

Linoleum returned to favour in the later part of the twentieth century for custom installations, contract work and other applications.
See also **Felt-base**, **Felt-base linoleum**, **Floorcloth**.

FURTHER READING

Edwards, C. (1996). 'Floorcloth and linoleum: aspects of the history of oil-coated materials for floors', *Textile History*, 27, 2, pp 148–71.
Gooderson, P.J. (1996). *Lord Linoleum, Lord Ashton and the Rise of the British Oilcloth and Linoleum Industry*, Keele: Keele University Press.
Jones, M.W. (1918). 'The History and Manufacture of Floorcloth and Linoleum', a paper read before the Bristol section of the Society of the Chemical Industry at the University, Bristol, 21 November.
Kaldewei, G. (ed.) (2000). *Linoleum History, Design Architecture, 1882–2000*, Ostfilden: Hatje Cantz.
Lockhart, J.Y. (1939). *Kirkcaldy: A Century of Progress, 1838–1938; its Industries, the Pioneers of the Floorcloth and Linoleum Trade; its Benefactors, its Provosts*, Kirkcaldy: Allen Lithographic Co.
Mehler, W.A. (1987). *Let the Buyer Have Faith: The Story of Armstrong*, Lancaster, PA: Armstrong World Industries.
Simpson, P. (1997). 'Linoleum and lincrusta: the democratic coverings for floors and walls' in Adams, Annmarie & McMurry, Sally (eds), *Exploring Everyday Landscapes, Perspectives in Vernacular Architecture*, VII, Knoxville: University of Tennessee Press, pp 281–92.

Linsey-woolsey

A coarse cloth woven with a **linen warp** and a **woollen weft**, which appears to explain the name. Known since the fifteenth century (*OED*, 1483) and, although often used as a clothing fabric, hangings and other furnishings have been recorded as being made from this material.

An early English reference to its use as a **blanket** material is in the 1606 inventory of Jane Ward of Ipswich. This listed 'a pair of old blankets of lynceye wolsye' (Reed, 1981, p.66). There is an early American reference to its use as **curtaining** in the 1646 inventory of John Fairfield of Wenham, which listed 'Green lincye woolsie curtaynes' (Cummings, 1961, p.29). It was also used in England for bed curtains. Essex resident, Mary Willis (1681), had 'one great hutch with a set of striped linsey woolsey curtains and a vallance' listed in her inventory (Steer, 1969, p.165).

In 1698, Celia Fiennes noted, on a visit to the town of Kendall, that 'Kendall cotton [green woollen cloth] is used for blankets, and the Scott uses them for their plods and there is much made here and also linsi-woolseys' (1995, p.165).

In the eighteenth century, it appears to have been a relatively common material base for decoration. Daniel Defoe described the division of labour in their manufacture and identifies a significant trade: 'The Hangings, suppose them to be ordinary Linsey-Woolsey are made at Kidderminster d'yd in the country, and painted or water'd at London…' (1727, vol.I, p.333). In the 1728 inventory of the shop of James Pilbeam, a mercer of Chiddingly, Sussex, there was listed: 'Seventy six yards of linsey at 10d per yard, £3 3s 4d; Twenty four yards of linsey at ls per yard, £1 4s 0d; One hundred forty eight yards of linsey at 10d per yard, £6 3s 4d' (http://www.chiddingly.gov.uk/History/James%20Pilbeam.html). It was widely used for servants' **bed furniture** in the eighteenth century, and it remained as a dress fabric into the nineteenth century.
See also **Kidderminster stuff**.

Liseré

A **silk** fabric, usually ribbed, which was woven with **brocaded** flowers in a figured weave. Liseré also refers to a construction process using a supplementary **warp**. This warp can be used to 'brocade' or figure selected areas on the face of the fabric to create floats on the back. Striped liseré has often been used on wing-back chairs.
See also **Lampas**.

List

Architecturally, list is a synonym for a **fillet** or **band**. In the textile context, it refers to the edges or selvedges of cloth and is often connected to a carpet woven with lists. On occasion, it was used itself for particular purposes. The 1601 Hardwick Hall inventory had 'a quition [cushion] of lystes' (Boynton, 1971, p.33). In 1772, Mrs Delany noted in a letter that 'I have had list nailed round my doors, and stopping every crack and crevice that let in cold air [etc]' (*Letters*. series II. vol.I, p.401).
See also **List carpet**, **Rag rug**.

List carpet (aka Strip carpet or *Tapis de lizières*)

List generally refers to narrow strips of cloth or the selvedges of woven cloth. A list **carpet** is one that is made up from lists, rags or fabric strips in the **weft**, and **woollen cotton** or **linen** thread as the **warp**. It was usually woven 36 inches (91 cm) wide.

It appears to have been developed and become quite well known in the early to mid-eighteenth century. The turner, William Crompton, advertised in the *London Evening Post* of 29 January 1737 that he had devised 'a new invented machine, [to make] carpet of cloth list, which for beauty, strength and service far exceed anything of that kind hitherto made' (Thornton, 1984, p.101). Robert Campbell in his *London Tradesman* of 1747, again refers to the connection with the turner's trade: 'Those [carpets] mostly sold at the Turners shops are made of list, by people who do nothing else; it is but of late contrivance, and the work is mostly performed by women who earn five to eight shillings a week' (p.246).

Although it might be considered to be of an inferior quality due to its choice of raw materials, in the 1742 Dyrham Park inventory its use is recorded in 'Mr Blathwaytes Dressing Room – a list carpet' (Gilbert, Lomax & Wells-Cole, 1987, p.94). List carpet was exported to the USA from around the mid-eighteenth century and was certainly known there by 1761 when, on 29 January, the *Boston Gazette* published advertisements for imports from London and Bristol, including 'list carpeting for stairs' (Roth, 1967, p.46). The American trader, Samuel Rowland Fisher, visited Leeds in 1783 where he 'walked to see the carpet manufactory of the Scots kind' and he also called on a manufacturer of list carpeting (Hummel, 1975, p.67).

The comments made by Campbell in 1747 (see above) on the employment of women and children were reiterated 60 years later. According to the author of *A Book of English Trades,* written in 1807, list carpet was described as 'another sort of carpeting is made of narrow slips of list sewed together; these of course are very inferior ... but they employ many women and children' (Gilbert, Lomax & Wells-Cole, 1987, p.94). It seems clear that list carpets and **rugs** were also woven at home. An American reference states: 'the manufacture of carpet was not introduced into this country, with the exception of the home-made rag-carpet, until some time after the revolutionary war' (J.F. Watson 'Annals of Philadelphia' (1857), in Roth, 1967, p.46).

In the early nineteenth century, **Venetian carpeting** was superseding list carpeting, although list was still exhibited in the 1851 *Art Journal Illustrated Catalogue of the Great Exhibition* (p.1121).

As late as 1950, *The Mercury Dictionary of Textile Terms* defined list carpet as 'a factory-made carpet similar to rag rugs. A very strong thick cotton warp is used in combination with a weft of waste cuttings etc [especially in] USA.'
See also **Rag rug**.

Lithography
See **Printed textile**.

Lockram
A **linen** fabric of various qualities used for wearing apparel and household use, including **sheets**, napery and **tablecloths**. The name derives from Locronan, the name of a village in Brittany, France, where the fabric was formerly made. In 1520, Sir Thomas Elyot's will listed 'Lynnen cloth of canvas and lokeram for shetes and smockes and shirtes' (1883, I. App.A, 313, *OED*). It seems to have declined in use by the early nineteenth century.
See also **Dowlas**.

Longee (aka Lungi)
A **silk**, **cotton** or **grass** cloth that was made either **checked** or wrought with flowers. *The Merchant's Warehouse Laid Open* noted that the Longees Herba was 'proper only for slight use as linens of beds and for window curtains. They wear very slight and thin, being much stiffened, they feel pretty thick before they are worn or washed, but after either they are like a rag.' (J.F., 1696.) By 1887, Caulfeild & Saward defined loonghie as 'a mixed fabric composed of richly coloured silk and cotton' (1887). Thirty years later, it was considered to be made so that 'the body is of small blue and white checks, the selvedge is composed of various colored stripes and a narrow red stripe is running lengthwise in the middle' (Harmuth, 1915, p.97).

Looped-pile carpet
See **Brussels carpet**.

Loose cover
See **Protective furnishing**.

Lorrain (aka Lorine)
A lightweight **woollen** fabric. In 1787, the furniture-makers, Gillows, covered a sofa and three window stools with grey 'lorine' (Gillow Co Records).

Low warp tapestry
A tapestry weaving technique in which the **warp** thread rollers are organised horizontally and moved by treadles. It is usually cheaper and quicker than high warp tapestry. In this form of work, the cartoon is placed beneath the work, but the work is woven in reverse as the weaver is working from the back of the tapestry.
See **Tapestry**.

Lustring (aka Lutestring)
A lustrous **silk taffeta** fabric produced with a ribbed pattern. It was made from a taffeta that was stretched and covered with a syrupy gum (or beer) dressing, and dried in front of a fire to give a gloss finish. Alternatively, the yarns were so treated before weaving. They could be plain, striped, **changeable**, patterned or **brocaded**. A fairly lightweight fabric, it was used for **festoon window curtains**, **toilette**-table covers, **curtains** to night tables, **scarves** and sometimes linings to **chintz** bed hangings.

In around 1635, lustring was introduced into England from France and, in 1639, a patent was granted to Peter La Dorée for glossing plain and figured **satins** (see also **Grosgrain**). By the end of the century, it was an important fabric. In 1692, the Royal Lustring Co was established by charter to concentrate upon the making and selling of this fabric. An advertisement in the *London Gazette* in 1697 stated that 'their warehouse shall be opened every day to sell Allamodes, Renforces and Lustrings' (Edwards, 1964, p.342).

Lustring was also imported from France and Italy during the eighteenth century; so, it is not surprising to see that, in 1736, it was recorded as 'a glossy sort of French silk' (Baily, *Dictionarium Britannicum*). In that year, the Earl of Stanhope purchased 'Lutestring to back and make scarves to the 8 chairs and 2 settees: £3 16 8d' from William Bradshaw for use in the Tapestry Room at Chevening (Beard, 1997, p.304).

It remained a fashionable fabric through the eighteenth century. Lady Elizabeth Smithson, writing to her mother in August 1740, explained that: 'I must now speak of my bedchamber; my bed in cotton flowered with large natural flowers lined with grass green lutestring with fluted posts ... the window curtain, chairs, armchairs and *peche-mortel* and the hangings are all of the same' (Macquoid & Edwards, 1924, p.44). In 1752, Lady Leicester purchased 434 yards of crimson 'lutestring' for use at Holkham Hall at a cost of £190.6s.0d. (Beard, 1997, p.304) and, in 1790, the Earl Spencer employed John King at Althorp 'for making up a window curtain of stripe silk lutestring' (Macquoid & Edwards, 1924, p.291). In 1792, 'Three French grey lustring window curtains' were recorded at Newby Hall (Low, 1986, p.154).

Lustring was also used later in the century for **drapes**, to be hung over **French rods** at windows. It was still used as a furnishing fabric in the early nineteenth century. George Smith recommended lustring for elegant drawing rooms which should be 'of satin or lutestring, with under curtains of muslin, or superfine cassimere, [with] the fringe in contrast with the drapery' (1808, p.12). It was also recommended for **fire screens**, 'where the stands are wholly mahogany, the mounts may be covered with lustring in flutes with tassels to suit' (ibid. p.20). In 1809, Ackermann recommended that fashionable **bed curtains** were 'of blue satin lined with white lutestring and trimmed with a narrow gold edging' (*Repository of Arts etc.*, May 1809, p.331). Lustring was still being suggested in the 1840s for curtains in drawing rooms.

FURTHER READING

Great Britain, Parliament (1698). *An Act for the Better Encouragement of the Royal Lustring Company and the More Effectual Preventing of the Fraudulent Importation of Lustrings and Alamodes to London, The History and Proceedings of the House of Commons*, vol.4, http://www.british-history.ac.uk/source.asp?pubid=221

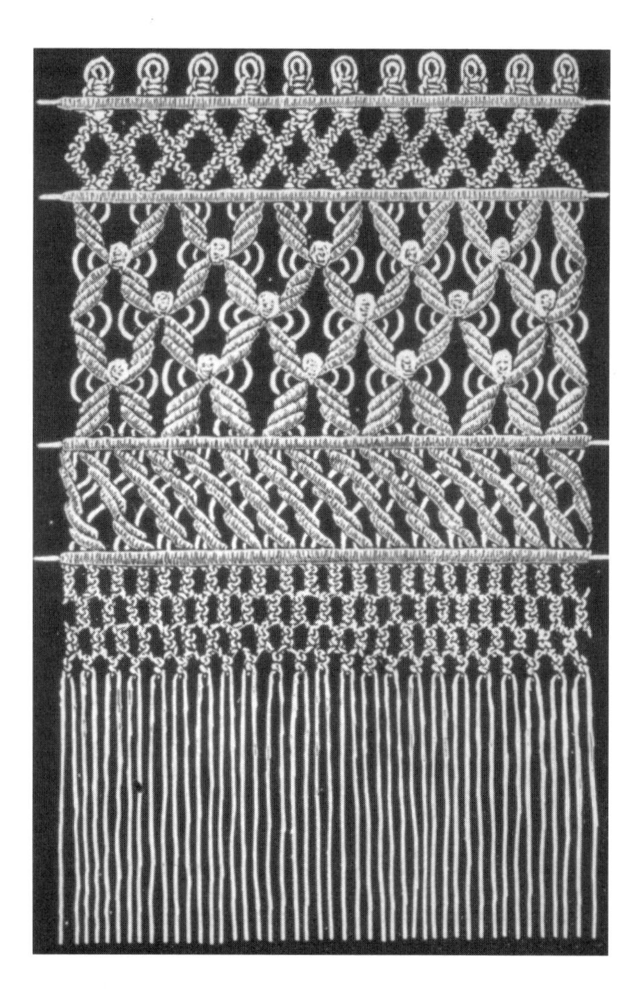

73. Macraméd fringe pattern (S. Caulfeild & B. Saward, The Dictionary of Needlework, *1887)*

Macramé

A knotted fringe or **trimming** using four or more elements that are knotted and looped into a design. Some authorities give the origin of the name as from the Turkish *maqrama*, meaning a 'towel', 'napkin' or 'handkerchief'. Others suggest it may be from the Arabic *miqramah*, meaning a 'striped cloth'. It is more likely to be from the Arabic *mucharram*, meaning 'lattice' or 'fringe'. Macramé also refers to the art of making this.

In 1869, it was explained that 'The art of macramé is principally applied to the ornamenting of Huckabuck towels [with] a long fringe of thread being left at each end, for the purpose of being knotted together in geometrical designs' (Palisser, *Lace*, vol.IV, p.65). By 1887, its repertoire had been extended. Caulfeild & Saward considered macramé to be 'celebrated for its durability and excellence … the coarser [kind] formed of ecru coloured or black Maltese thread and twine, make mantel and table borders, and other furniture trimmings' (1887, p.331). During the late nineteenth century, it was also used for shelf **lambrequins**.

Early in the twentieth century, an American author described the various furnishing uses of macramé:

> But the use of macramé is not confined to household linens. Porch cushions, hangings for the mountain bungalow, and a cover for the couch all of burlap, arras cloth, or monk's cloth, would be transformed from the commonplace into draperies with character by wide bands (at least five inches wide) of macramé made with jute. Use the three- or four-ply one-eighth-inch-thick jute and dye it either the same color or a color that is a pleasant contrast with that of the cloth.
>
> In a collection of old-time bell-pulls, among the many of tapestry were several knotted in macramé with heavy silk cord. And in old English houses the shades are still drawn at night by a long-looped band of macramé made an inch or more wide of fine linen cord. Some of them, instead of looping up, end in a large tassel fashioned out of knots. (Buchanan, 1917, p.66.)

Macramé underwent a revival in the 1970s for the creation of decorative **wall hangings**, plant holders and decorations.
See also **Fringe: knotted**, **Knotted work**.

Madapolam

A kind of cotton cloth that was intermediate between **calico** and **muslin**. It was originally manufactured at Madapolam (Madhavapalam), a suburb of Narsapur in the Madras region of India. Exported from India via the East India Co, Henry Yule quoted a reference from 1610: 'Madafunum is chequered, some-what fine and well requested in Pryaman' (1903, p.532). It was later imitated on British looms and exported back to India.

In 1858, the *Dictionary of Trade Products* explained that Madapolam was a kind of fine long cloth, shipped to the Eastern markets (Simmonds, 1858). A little later, *The Dictionary of Needlework's* definition of Madapolams went further, describing it as 'a coarse description of calico cloth, of a stiff, heavy make, originally of Indian manufacture, where it was employed for Quilts. Double widths are used for Curtains, Quilts, servants' aprons, etc' (Caulfeild & Saward, 1887, p.339).

By 1950, it was still defined as all-cotton, plain-weave, bleached and dyed with a soft dress finish (*The Mercury Dictionary of Textile Terms*).

Madras muslin

See **Muslin: Madras**.

Manchester

The city of Manchester was prominent by the mid-seventeenth century as a producer of a wide range of **cotton** and **linen** fabrics. Even earlier than this date, an Act mentioned 'All and every cotton called Manchester, Lancashire and Cheshire cottons, and all clothes called Manchester rugges otherwise Frices' (1552, Act 5 and 6 Edward VI, c.6).

Vermilion, **fustian** and **dimity** cloth were particularly associated with Manchester and its environs. Writing about Manchester's trades in 1641, Lewis Roberts noted that 'they buy cotton wool in London that comes from Cyprus and Smyrna, and work that same in to fustians, vermilions and dimities which they return to London where they are sold' (*Treasure of Traffic*, p.33).

In a description of Manchester and its surroundings in 1795, John Aikin reported on Manchester work saying that 'an application of the lighter open striped checks to bed hangings and window curtains forty years since, introduced the making of furniture checks, which have almost set aside the use of stuffs in upholstery' (Montgomery, 1984, p.197). A little later, the Earl of Breadalbane purchased furniture for a bedstead made from 28 yards (25.6 metres) of Manchester check from Newton and Son in 1812 (Ellwood, 1995, p.191).

See also **Corduroy**, **Frieze**, **Manchester quilt**, **Manchester stripe**, **Manchester velvet**, **Velour**.

Manchester cotton
A coarse **woollen** fabric similar to **frieze**, used in the sixteenth century.

Manchester quilt (aka Lancaster quilt)
'This quilt, so named from the town in England where it was originally made, is a cheap imitation of the Marseilles quilt. The figure is formed, as in damask, by the warp overlapping several threads of the woof. It is cheap in appearance and not very durable.' (Brown & Gates, 1872.) The 1771 Felbrigg inventory listed '2 white counterpanes Manchester' (Clabburn, 1988, p.248).
See **Bolton coverlet**, **Manchester**, **Marseilles**, **Quilting**.

Manchester stripe
Usually refers to a **cotton** fabric often woven with only two colours, used in the eighteenth century. It was mainly utilised for loose covers, **bed furniture** and window **curtains**. Manchester was known as the source of the supply of household textiles in the eighteenth century; hence, its name was often added to fabrics it supplied. In 1767–8, the American traveller, Samuel Rowland Fisher, noted the 'Checks, Stripes, Bed Ticks and Bunts, Fustians, Jeans, Thicksetts, Corded and Figured dimities, etc. are made all around the town to the distance of 12 or 15 miles' (Montgomery, 1984, p.287). It was clearly fashionable, as David Garrick's house in Hampton had 'green and white striped Manchester' in 1779 and, by 1793, Blickling Hall had many curtains of 'stript Manchester' (Clabburn, 1988, p.248). In 1794, Hepplewhite's *The Cabinet Marker and Upholsterer's Guide* noted that 'The Manchester stuffs have been wrought into Bed-furniture with good success' (p.17).

James Newton furnished the Duke of Buccleuch's house in London around 1813. Many of the bedrooms were supplied with Manchester stripe 'furnitures'. For example, the housekeeper's bedroom had a bed and its 'furniture of Manchester stripe complete with bases – the headcloth and tester lined' (Ellwood, 1995, p.193). In 1839, Loudon recommended Manchester stripes for the bed furnitures of cottages (p.337).
See also **Manchester**.

Manchester velvet
Manchester had produced fustians since the Middle Ages. In the latter half of the eighteenth century, it also produced **cotton velvet** and **velveteen**, the weaving of which had evolved from fustian making. These were known as Manchester velvets. They were popular from *c.*1760. Manchester was the centre of the cotton industry, and it was in 1641 that a pamphlet entitled *Treasure of Traffic* noted how Manchester bought in cotton **wool** from Cyprus and Smyrna 'and perfects it into fustian, vermilions, dimities and other such stuffs' (Roberts). Cotton velvet was made in the city and environs of Manchester during the eighteenth century. George Smith suggested that for a field bed 'the borders [might be] cut out in black Manchester velvet and sewed on' (1808, p.5). Ackermann, in his *Repository*, recommended 'Manchester coloured velvets used for furniture and curtains, produce a rich effect'.
See also **Fustian**, **Manchester**, **Velour**.

Mantel drapery
Mantel draperys were known during the seventeenth century especially in Dutch homes, which had large fireplaces with protruding shelves. The draperys were often made to match other drapes in a room. Initially, they were basically **chimney cloths** designed to channel smoke up the chimney and not into the room. In the second half of the nineteenth century, the application of **valances** or **lambrequins** as decoration was common in order to finish a mantelpiece. They were often embellished with **embroidery** and **passementerie**. Some advisors even suggested a set of curtains to hang in front of the fireplace to cover the grate when the fire was not in use (see **Fireplace curtain**).

74. Mantel drapery example (S. Caulfeild & B. Saward, The Dictionary of Needlework, *1887)*

In 1865, the Leeds upholsterers, Marsh and Jones, supplied Sir Titus Salt with mantelshelves for a bedroom in green **Utrecht velvet**, for the library in maroon **velvet**, and for the drawing room in brown silk, all **fringed** and brass nailed (Boynton, 1967, p.82). In 1870, *Cassell's Household Guide* makes the point that 'a good mantle-shelf is improved by a velvet hanging, and a bad one is rendered endurable'. It recommended that 'the mantle hanging always matches the window curtains'. It went on to recommend 'a shelf valance in point lace in deep vandykes mounted on silk edged with a narrow silk fringe, the colour of the furniture.' On each side hung curtains of fine **lace**, lined with coloured **tarlatan** or thin **silk**.

In 1889, Moreland considered that 'much of the mantel woodwork is now so elaborate that it requires no draping beyond a tasteful arrangement of scarves of silk'. Moreland recommended silk **plush** for **festoons**, or flat scarves that would be worked with **needlework**, **appliquéd** or hand-painted, whilst for bedrooms he recommended a matching **cretonne** or silk to the window curtains. Moreland described a complex treatment: a large rectangular false shelf, a plain scarf laid on top of this, and festoons of silk hung over a rod fixed to the board edge; the scarf was raised at the end to a smaller pole to give height. Curtains are fitted to a rod under the shelf to each side of the fireplace so they can be pulled back when a fire is lit. Plush or **velour** was the recommended fabric for this confection (p.270).

Mrs Haweis also commented on mantle drapery in her *Art of Decoration*:

> Festooned velvet is always dirty and not fit to be touched; lace, in my opinion, is unsuitable as aforesaid, because it looks like dress leavings, muslin most absurd of all. The sides of an ugly mantelpiece may be hidden by old bullion embroideries secured on thin wood with very good effect. (1881, p.339.)

For mantels that were not made from elaborate woodwork, the *Young Ladies' Treasure Book* recommended that:

> As mantel hangings, or valances have now become an accepted portion of household decoration … nothing is considered too costly a material upon which to paint or embroider a mantel valance, no pains ill-bestowed that serve to beautify these hangings, which are considered to constitute an elegant and highly acceptable bridal, Christmas

or birth-day gift. White velvet for example, decorated with a wreath of orange blossoms and leaves in oils, intermingled with fronds of that, most exquisite of ferns the maidenhair is a late bridal gift. (1884.)

A hint was published in the October 1883 edition of the American journal *Decorator and Furnisher*, which suggested that a drawing room mantel cover might be of 'Pompeian red plush, the square corners adorned with inset appliqués of Turkish embroidery, the finish a fringe of ecru cotton strands, edging an insertion of ecru lace, heavily worked with silks' (Burke et al, 1986, p.137).

Instructions as to how to make one's own mantle shelf were common in the later nineteenth century. This American example considers mantle drapery from a variety of points of view:

> When a drapery is a necessity, or when a householder thinks so, which amounts to the same thing, no law of arrangement can be laid down, although one positive statement can always be made. Nothing is so objectionable as a mantel-shelf to which an upholstered look has been given by pieces of cretonne or woollen stuff, fringed and draped, caught up at the corners with bows and rosettes, and made a general receptacle for dust. In some rooms a piece of heavy lace over a color is not so objectionable when nailed perfectly flat. A piece of stuff, a corduroy, or a velveteen with gimp, is admissible without gathers, nailed flat. A piece of stuff laid over the mantel-board and allowed to fall in natural folds is unpretentious, serves a certain purpose, and is therefore admissible. A piece of brocade in certain environments, or of embroidery when laid over a shelf with the obvious intention of introducing a note of color or of relieving an impression of bareness, is also at times most effective. But to employ any stuff or material over a mantel implies, in the very nature of things, that the mantel itself is ugly, and that the householder has been obliged to do something to relieve its unpleasantness. No exquisitely carved mantel could be so dishonored, certainly none of fine marble. (French, 1903, p.328.)

See also **Macramé**, **Scarf**.

FURTHER READING

Glaister, E. (1880). *Needlework*, London: Macmillan, pp 71–84.

Mantua

A thin, **silk**, plain-weave material, heavier than **taffeta** that was widely used in the eighteenth century as a dress textile. Although mainly used for clothing, mantua was occasionally employed for **curtains**, **toilette**-table coverings and linings. It was also used for **upholstery** as, in 1699, King William III was supplied with 'rich green mantua' to case chairs and stools at Kensington Palace (Beard, 1997, p.106). Over 100 years later, Thomas Jefferson used mantua for furnishings at Monticello. In 1808, he was sent: '4 window draperies… They are made of the best crimson mantua which I hope will give satisfaction' (Montgomery, 1984, p.289). They must have been agreeable as he later ordered a matching **coverlet**.

Marcella

See **Marseilles**.

Marocain

A twentieth-century, ribbed **crêpe cloth**, of **silk**, **wool** or **cotton**. It is similar in construction to **crêpe de Chine**, but heavier in weight, with the **weft** being woven in noticeable ribs across the fabric.

Marquisette

A fine net or **gauze** material made using the **leno** principle, producing a very lightweight, open, sheer, mesh fabric that wears and launders well. It has been available in white, solid colours and novelty effects. Sometimes it is woven with a swivel dot or clip spot. Originally, an **all-silk** dress fabric, it has been made with a variety of yarns, including **cotton**, **rayon** and synthetics. Since the mid-twentieth century, it has been used for window **curtains**, **mosquito netting** and the like.

American author, Elizabeth Dyer, said: 'Marquisette is a very open, dainty material, easily laundered, about the same price as voile, but more durable. Comes in very coarse as well as fine qualities.' (*c.*1923, p.199.) Whilst in England, Midgley described it as being more open than **voile** but not as large as **grenadine** (1931). By 1937, it was noted that 'a modern quality for use as curtains has fine, white cotton warp ands lustrous rayon weft in different colours. With silver and gold-coloured rayon wefts, for instance, the effect is very pleasing.' (French, 1937, p.140.)

In 1951, Taylor suggested that marquisette was used to replace **dotted Swiss** to a degree when it was made with dots. *The Draper's Encyclopaedia* refers to marquisette as 'a fine-set gauze fabric with two to three fold cotton yarns. It has more thread per inch than Madras.' (Ostick, 1955, p.370.)

See also **Net**.

Marseilles (aka French quilting)

A term for quilted work (also known as Marcella, etc.) that stitched two thicknesses of fabric together in such a way as to leave spaces in between, so that rovings of **cotton** were inserted in-between thus creating a padded effect. The name is derived from Marseilles, France. That city and the Provence region have been well known for quilting since the fifteenth century. From the seventeenth century, they not only had a high reputation but were also able to produce large quantities of quilt work for export.

In 1770, Saint-Aubin noted that: 'Tapestry workers have bestowed upon themselves the right to embroider bed coverings in this manner, an action that has led to some lawsuits' (1983, pp 56–7).

In England, in 1763, Robert Elsder and George Glasgow patented a machine for 'weaving and quilting in the loom' (Patent no.786). Its success was probably dubious as, in 1783, the London-based Society for the Encouragement of Arts, Manufactures and Commerce offered a premium 'to encourage the making in the loom, [of] an imitation of that species of needlework long known by the name of Marseilles quilting.'

> The manufacture is now so thoroughly established and so extensive, being wrought in all the different materials of linen, woollen, cotton, and silk, that there are few persons of any rank, condition or fix in the kingdom (and we may add, with the extent of British commerce, so greatly is it exported) who do not use it in some part of their clothing. (*Transactions*, p.36.)

Marseilles quilts were also fashionable for bedroom furnishings. The Felbrigg inventory of 1771 listed '1 counterpane Marcella quilting scarlet silk lined with green silk' (Clabburn, 1988, p.248). However, it was not only used for **counterpanes**. In the 1760s, Hopetoun House was supplied with a **petticoat** of 'some brocaded silk or crimson silk damask fringed at bottom, the top, covered with Marseilles or other fine quilting made to the shape' to fit a toilette (Coleridge, 1966, p.154). A similar example is from 1774, when Chippendale supplied 'a marcela quilted peticoat and cover' and a 'deal toylet table on castors' to Ninian Home, for Paxton House (Gilbert, 1978, p.274).

In the nineteenth century, Marseilles was also sold by the yard (91 cm) and used for making toilette covers, dressing table mats, etc. However, in 1841, Miss Leslie considered that 'Marseilles quilts keep clean much longer than the knotted white counterpanes. They are not however so durable, as the surface of a Marseilles quilt, being fine and thin, soon wears off. They may afterwards be covered with an outside of fine, white thick muslin, and quilted over again.' (p.311.)

Another definition explained that 'Massillian quilts or Marseilles quilts' are 'made in imitation of the old-fashioned quilting of old **blankets** between chintz and white linen, which were formerly so prized' (*Cassell's Household Guide,* 1870, p.285). This description was upstaged by *Scissors and Yardstick*, which defined the Marseilles quilt:

> This is the finest in appearance, and the most expensive counterpane, deriving its name from Marseilles, in France where it was first made. It has two distinct webs, which are incorporated into each other at one operation. Between these, and entirely concealed by them are coarse, loosely twisted threads, which are extended across the fabric raising the figures above the ground work. The surface web, which is woven plain, is very fine. The obverse web is also woven plain, but is much more sheer and the threads coarser. The figure which is usually elaborate, and fashioned in relief by means of the intermediate woof is surrounded and defined by a kind of quilted groundwork. (Brown & Gates, 1872.)

In 1887, *The Dictionary of Needlework* considered Marcella or Marsella as a 'description of cotton quilting or coarse piqué, for making toilet covers, dressing table mats, and other articles sold by the yard for making toilet covers, dressing table mats etc' (Caulfeild & Saward, p.341). In 1892, Cole noted that Marseilles quilts were woven of very fine yarns, with embossed figures.

By the early twentieth century, at least one commentator disapproved of Marseilles quilts:

> I am afraid that many of us fall short of our ideals in homemaking when we come to the beds. It is so easy to go to a department-store and get a ready-made Marseilles quilt, and we salve our conscience by telling ourselves that, after all, there is nothing like white on a bed. We do not honestly believe this, as is proved by the way women gush over decorative bedspreads made of colored materials that they see in the homes of their friends. (Priestman, 1910, p.157.)

Despite this, there was apparently a good business to be had in making and supplying the quilts. Thompson explains the production process:

> The marseilles counterpane, so called because first made in Marseilles, has a compound weave but the embossed pattern, usually a large design, appears on one side only. The yarn for the face is much finer than that used for the back and has twice the number of threads. Both of these are woven in continuous strips into from five hundred to one thousand counterpanes in a piece. After leaving the loom, the counterpanes are inspected. Knots and ends are removed and then they are passed over rollers into the bleaching vat, where they remain for about two hours in a solution of chlorine. After being rinsed, boiled and blued the long strip is dried over smooth, heated rollers. The counterpanes are then cut apart with sharp knives, hemmed, folded, ticketed, and shipped. (Thompson, 1917, p.131.)

By 1937, Marseilles quilting was described as a 'true reversible, heavier than toilet quilting usually, owing to having two complete fabrics one face and one back, with a heavier wadding weft. [It was] often bleached in piece form.' (French, 1937, p.140.)

See also **Bedspread**, **Bolton coverlet**, **Counterpane**, **Manchester quilt**, **Matelassé**, **Quilt**, **Quilting**, **Satin toilet bedspread**, **Toilette**.

FURTHER READING

Atkins, J.M. (2000). 'From lap to loom, Marseilles quilts, Marseilles style spreads and their white offspring', *Proceedings of the Textile History Forum*, 7–8 July 2000, Cooperstown, NY, pp 13–24.

Berenson, K. (1996). *Quilts of Provence: the Art and Craft of French Quiltmaking*, London: Thames and Hudson.

Marsh grass

See **Grass**.

Masulipatam

A very fine and highly finished **cotton** fabric of a chintz variety that was imported from India in the seventeenth century. It appears to have been very fashionable as, in 1682, the Masulipatam factory had an order for '45,000 Percallaes, the finest sorts, made into chintz 8 yards long, full yard broad, the ground to be green purple, red and some white, but the best paintings to be upon purple ground with variety of painting, curious and lively brisk colours' (Irwin & Schwartz, 1966, p.35). A few years later, Daniel Defoe wrote that at Windsor Castle, 'the late Queen Mary set up a rich Atlas and Chintz bed, which in those times was invaluable, the chintz being of Masulipatam on the coast of Coromandel, the finest that was ever seen before that time in England' (*A Tour Through the Whole Island of Great Britain*, vol.1, letter 3). Masulipatam was also imported into France from India during the eighteenth century.

In 1880, Birdwood, writing on Indian arts, still applauded 'the celebrated palampores, or bed-covers of Masulipatam which in point of art decoration are simply incomparable' (1880, vol.II, p.98).

See also **Chintz**, **Moree**, **Palampore**.

Matelassé

A thick dual weave fabric with a raised pattern, whose name is derived from the French term *matelasser*, meaning 'cushioned or padded'. The name refers to a **cotton**, **rayon** or **silk** 'double' fabric, woven with two sets of **warp** and **weft** threads, so that one set is the back, the other, the front. The two faces are interlaced at intervals where the pattern occurs. The patterns are like **quilting**, often of one colour, with a rich flowered design that only shows as a relief or embossed appearance. The pattern stands out and gives a 'pouch' or 'quilted' effect to the goods. **Wadding** threads may enhance this result. Matelassé has been woven in colours, novelty effects and sometimes with metallic yarns. Introduced in the late nineteenth century, it remained a furnishing fabric in the twentieth century. Some cotton matelassé has been used for **bedspreads**.

See also **Marseilles**.

Mat

Initially mats were made from **rush**, sedge, **straw**, etc. and used to clean footwear. Mats were often designated as being for small areas such as doorways or hearths, whilst matting was for larger floor areas or even wall-to-wall. Webster & Parkes's *An Encyclopeadia of Domestic Economy* suggested coarse mats such as coconut, straw or cornhusk for entrance halls and sheepskins, thick **woollen** mats or flat woven **grass** mats for use at room thresholds and for stairs to reduce the **wear** on carpets (1844, pp 255–7). By the early twentieth century, it seemed that perforated and otherwise prepared rubber, as well as wire-woven material, was also largely utilised for door and floor mats.

See also **Hearth rug**, **Matting**, **Rug**.

75. Matelassé cloth showing distinctive construction effect, c.1960 (Private Collection)

Matting

A general term embracing many coarse woven or plaited fibrous materials used for covering floors or furniture, for hanging as **screens**, or other purposes. More commonly, the term refers to a floorcovering that has been made from a range of natural or synthetic materials. Different kinds of matting are often known by their origins or make-up, e.g. Barbary, Canton, Chinese, Cornish, Dutch, India, Japanese, Portugal, **straw** and Tangier matting (see below).

From the Middle Ages, straw and rush was used to make plaited mats or matting. It was sold in rolls of about 18 inches (45 cm) wide and was then sewn together to make floorcoverings. In 1611, Robert Cecil purchased from his upholsterer '5 pieces of bulrush mats, 20 yd. piece, in all 100 yards and 13 pieces of bulrush mats 20 yd. a piece in all 260 yards all at 2½ d a yard' (Beard, 1997, p.285). In 1620, the *Household Book* of Lord Howard of Naworth recorded the purchase of 'vj bundles of mattes out of Norfolk containing six yards a peece' and a payment for 'sowing the mattes in Sir Francis his chamber viij.d' and for 'matting my Lady Phillips chamber vj.d' (Macquoid, 1924, vol.3, p.55).

Housekeeping problems relating to the cleanliness of matting were common. In the 1750s, it was recorded by Israel Acrelius, concerning American practice, that 'Straw carpets have lately been introduced in the towns, but the inconvenience of this is that they must soon be cleansed from fly spots, and a multitude of vermin, which harbour such things, and from the kitchen smoke, which is universal' (Roth, 1967, p.326).

American homes sometimes used 'straw carpet'. In 1760, the *Boston Gazette* listed an auction that included a handsome floor straw **carpet** for sale (ibid. p.27). In 1818, a Springfield, Mass. newspaper advertised '*c.*1,000 yards of straw carpeting for up to six quarters wide and at 28, 27, and 42 cents a yard.' Its use continued in the USA through most of the nineteenth century due to its inexpensive nature, although it was not considered hardwearing enough for heavy use. Grass matting had its problems and was not recommended on stairs as: 'It wears out very soon against the ledges of the steps, and is, besides, too slippery to be safe' (Miss Leslie, 1854, p.185). In 1869, the Beecher sisters wrote in their *American Woman's Home*:

> We humbly submit that it [matting] is precisely the thing for a parlor, which is reserved for the reception of friends, and for our own dressed leisure hours. Matting is not good economy in a dining room or a hard-worn sitting room; but such a parlour as we are describing is precisely the place where it answers to the best advantage. (1869, p.86.)

As in previous centuries, mattings were available in strips approximately 36 inches (91 cm) wide so they needed to be seamed up to fit a space. *The Workwoman's Guide* (Hale, 1840) suggested **bindings** of red or green **leather** to suit the room and Loudon recommended putting on binding with black or coloured ferreting if loose-laid, but having it nailed to the floor if close covered. Miss Leslie gave the same advice 16 years later when she suggested that strips were sewn together to make a large 'rug', which was to be then bound with **cotton** or **linen** tapes (1854, pp 184–5).

Trade names and varieties abounded. In 1884, the retailers, Maple and Co, offered 'Napier matting made from hemp twisted as twine sometimes known as String matting'. They also sold 'Manila Matting' and 'Jute Matting'. (Maple, 1884, p.66) By 1912, Maple and Co offered specialities including 'India mats to place in front of washstands in two sizes 54 x 27 inches from 1s 3d each and 66in x 36 in from 1s 9d each.' (Gilbert, 1987, p.98)

Although best known as a flooring material, matting has been used for walls and as insulation in winter for doors and windows in the Middle Ages and beyond. The use of these *paillassons* or straw mats continued for a long time. Around 1620, the Duke of Buckingham was charged for 'New Matting two chambers' and 'matting the walls under the hangings' (Gilbert, Lomax & Wells-Cole, 1987, p.96). In the nineteenth century, the idea was revived. Moreland pointed out that straw mattings 'are often used as dadoes (and why not for frieze and body as well?) using split bamboo for mouldings' (1889, p.200).

Africa

In 15 June 1666, Samuel Pepys was presented with 'a very fine African matt (to lay upon the ground under a bed of state) being the first fruits of our peace with Guyland' (Pepys, vol.7, p.167).

Barbary

Matting sourced from North Africa, particularly in the seventeenth century. The 1677 inventory of Temple Newsam listed 'one large Barbaza matt' in the bedchamber and, in 1685–6, Thomas Freeman supplied 'a fine barbary matt' for the King's bedchamber at Whitehall (Gilbert, Lomax & Wells-Cole, 1987, pp 96–7). Some time later, the *London Evening Advertiser* offered for sale 'Barbary, Dutch and English matting' (29 October 1741).

China

Matting was imported from China and was known as Chinese or Canton matting. It was woven with a manila **hemp warp** and a rush or rice-straw **weft**.

It was certainly used in America by the end of the eighteenth century. George Washington is known to have used China matting at Mount Vernon in 1789.

76. Matting made from maram grass (Museum of Welsh Life)

The American journal, *Carpet Trade*, commented that 'In selecting Chinese matting broad cross stripes should be avoided, as they never match, and the necessary stretching produce a curvature of the pattern which is disagreeable to the eye.' (June 1887.) Moreland was enthusiastic: 'Nothing is so nice for summer as the mattings of China and Japan. These are being made in colours to suit all occasions besides the old-fashioned checks and stripes, and also the whole web woven in one piece instead of joints at every two yards as formerly. Moreland recommended that matting be laid permanently and carpet fitted over in winter with an underlay between (1889, p.295).

Cornish

A locally produced English vernacular form of matting, in general use from at least Tudor times in royal residences, as well as lesser ones. In 1620, a charge was raised for 'New matting and mending with fine Cornish and bulrush mats [for] the King's bedchamber' at Greenwich (Gilbert, Lomax & Wells-Cole, 1987, p.96). In the Ingatestone inventory, taken in 1600, it was noted that 'the chamber is matted with Cornishe matte somewhat worne' (Thornton, 1978, p.358). In his *Survey of Cornwall*, published in 1602, Carew noted that:

> The women and children in the West of Cornwall, doe use to make mats of a small and fine kinde of bents there growing, which for their warme and well wearing, are carried by sea to London and other parts of the realme, and serve to cover floors and walls. These bents are grown in sandy fields, and are knit from over the head in narrow breadths after a strange fashion. (Ayres, 1981, p.118.)

Dutch (i.e. Dutch East India Co)

The importation into Europe of locally produced mats from Dutch trading posts was a successful business. They were clearly fashionable in the later seventeenth century as, in 1689, three rolls of Dutch mat were supplied to Nottingham House for the Queen's dressing room (Lord Chamberlain's Accounts, Public Records Office, LC/9). They were later used for applications that were more utilitarian. In 1718, Remy George was paid for '10 yds of chequered Dutch matt round ye clossett' for Temple Newsam House (Gilbert, Lomax & Wells-Cole, 1987, p.97). Fifty years later, in 1769, William Armitage announced in the *Leeds Mercury* that he sold 'Royal and Dutch matting for passages or wall', confirming the two main uses (ibid.).

By 1812, English imported goods included 'Rolls Dutch Matting. Matting is used by the Cabinet-makers for packing of goods' (Smyth, 1812, 154, 20). While in Virginia (USA), 'Holland rush carpets of different breadths and qualities' were advertised in 1818 (Thornton, 1985, p.155).

India

A particular matting woven from native grasses that were imported from India. Early references include 'a roll of Indian matts consisting of fourteen pieces' in the Tart Hall inventory of 1641. An interesting result of the taste for India matting was during the 1780s, when the Great Hall of Sir Richard Worsley's Appuldurcombe Park had 'a floor cloth painted in imitation of Indian Matting' (Boynton, 1965, p.44). India matting was apparently also used as an **underlay** for carpet. In 1795, the Harewood House inventory recorded 'One Brussels carpet with India Matting under it' (Gilbert, Lomax & Wells-Cole, 1987, p.98).

In the nineteenth century, Loudon suggested 'Indian matting, when bound with black or coloured ferreting, is a very neat article, and may be used either for walls or floors' (1839, p.347). Webster and Parkes were also impressed: 'Matting is used in some cases instead of carpet. The best are Indian mats, which are used to lay over carpets, particularly in summer, from their being cool. They are durable' (1844). Later on, the usefulness of Indian matting was still commented upon. *Cassell's Household Guide* noted that 'a piece of Indian matting, well bound at both ends is better than any carpet or thin oilcloth for laying down before the washstand' (1897, vol.1. p.184).

India matting was also used for dadoes and carpet surrounds. Following Robert Edis, who recommended India or Manila matting for dadoes (1881, p.65), Maple and Co suggested in 1884 that India matting was frequently used to form a dado for entrance halls, morning rooms or for smaller drawing rooms. In the 1880s, India matting was particularly recommended for carpet surrounds (Anon., *Artistic Homes*, 1880).

Early in the twentieth century, the *Encyclopaedia Britannica* praised Indian matting, and noted the range:

> Matting of various kinds is very extensively employed throughout India for floorcoverings, the bottoms of bedsteads, fans and fly-flaps, &c.; and a considerable export trade in such manufactures is carried on. The materials used are numerous; but the principle substances are straw, the bulrushes (*Typha elephantina* and *T. angustifolia*); leaves of the date palm (*Phoenix sylvestris*); of the dwarf palm (*Chamaerops ritchiana*); of the Palmyra palm (*Borassus fiabelliformis*); of the coco-nut palm (*Cocos nucifera*); of the screw pine (*Pandanus odoralissimus*) and the munja or munj grass (*Saccharum munja*); of which the well-known

Palghat mats of the Madras Presidency are made. Many of these Indian grass-mats are admirable examples of elegant design, and the colours in which they are woven are rich, harmonious and effective in the highest degree. (1911.)

Japan
A matting woven with a cotton warp and a rush weft that made it quite flexible and suitable for a range of applications. The American journal, *Carpet Trade*, noted that 'Japanese mattings are a lighter fabric, with a fragrance like prairie grass when fresh and new, and are very durable' (June 1887). In 1901, an alternative use was suggested 'where the top [of the table] is of wood covered with Japanese matting' (Hasluck, vol.III, p.48).

Portugal
Rush matting either made in or imported via Portugal. These mats were used in the Drawing Room of Kilkenny Castle in 1684 (Thornton, 1985, p.358). While in 1685, Mary Jackson supplied '3 yards of Portugal matt for St James's' (Gilbert, Lomax & Wells-Cole, 1987, p.97). The 1710 inventory of Dyrham House records 'a Portugal mat under the bed' in the Damask Bedchamber (Walton, 1986, p.58). In 1803, the American *Charleston Courier* advised its readers that 'a Lisbon floor matt' was available for sale (Thornton, 1984, p.155).

Rush
Initially made up in plaited strips to be fitted to a complete room floor surface. By the late seventeenth century, it was not fashionable but was used as a utilitarian floorcovering. It had later revivals.

Spanish
Matting made from Spanish rushes. In the 1767 Bailey's *Dictionarium*, mat-weed is defined as 'an herb or plant called feather grass, and Spanish rush of which mats ... are made' (Roth, 1967, p.28).

Straw
In the 1750s, in Philadelphia, Israel Acrelius noted that 'Straw carpets have lately been introduced to the towns, but the inconvenience of this is that they must soon be cleansed from fly spots, and a multitude of vermin, which harbour in such things, and from kitchen smoke, which is universal' (ibid. p.326).

In the nineteenth century, Loudon noted that:

> Matting is manufactured in many different manners, out of the straw of corn, rushes or other long, narrow, grassy or sedgy leaves... In Monmouthshire, easy chairs with hoods like porter's chairs in gentleman's halls are constructed of straw matting on a frame of wooden rods, or stout wire, and chairs are made entirely of straw in different parts of England in the same way as common beehives. (1839, pp 346–7.)

Domestic straw matting was introduced into the USA in the 1870s as a seamless manufactured product, made from straw with cotton chains, which made it stronger and smoother than the all-straw versions (Winkler & Moss, 1986, p.149).

Tangiers
A particular matting that was imported from North Africa. In 1684, 'A Tangier Mat [for] under the bed of the Duchess of Ormonde' was supplied to Kilkenny Castle (Thornton, 1984, p.25). In 1695, Mary Jackson supplied 'a fine large Tangier matt 8 yards long and 3 yards wide and for nayles, Galoons and laying the matt £5' (Gilbert, Lomax & Wells-Cole, 1987, p.97).

See **Bed mat**, **Coir fibre**, **Cocoa mat**, **Grass**, **Mat**, **Paillasson rug**, **Rush**.

FURTHER READING

Gilbert, C., Lomax, J. & Wells-Cole, A. (1987). *Country House Floors*, Leeds: Leeds City Art Galleries, pp 96–100.

Mattress

A term derived from the old French *materas*, modern word *matelas*; the origin being from the Arab *al-materali*, meaning a '**cushion**'. In simple terms, a mattress is a textile case that is stuffed full of soft and flexible material such as hair, **cotton** fibres, **feathers**, flock, leaves, millpuff, moss, pine hair, **seaweed**, **straw**, **tow** or other such suitable filling, and is primarily designed for sleeping on. The padded foundation of a bed is formed of **canvas** or other stout material stuffed with **wool**, hair, flock or straw. In the case of a straw mattress, it is properly known as a palliasse. The intention of a mattress was originally as a support for the top feather bed (see also **Palliasse**).

The filling materials usually determine the quality of a mattress, the best usually being wool or hair, followed by other materials as above. For example, Cardinal Wolsey owned 'eight mattresses, every one of them stuffed with 13 pounds of carded wool and covered with 12 ells of fine Holland cloth' (Edwards, 1964, p.35). Thomas Tryon, writing in 1683, was very explicit about the nature of mattresses:

> Now the certain means and way not only to prevent the generation of this vermin [bed-bugs] but also to preserve health and strength, is straw or rather chaff-beds, with ticks of canvas, and quilts made of wool or flocks to lay on them ... in every respect far beyond the softest feather beds on which, when a man lies down, he sinks into them, as into a hole, with banks rising on each side of him... [Feather mattresses also apparently] by their heat do powerfully dry up the *radical moisture*, causing a general *faintness* to attend the whole body. But on the contrary, hard, even beds that lye smooth are not only easy through custom ... but a man may turn freely both sleeping and waking' (*The Way to Health*, p.440).

In 1662, John Evelyn explained his recommendation of beech leaves for filling mattresses: they 'offered the best and easiest mattresses in the world to lay under our quilts instead of straw, because besides their tenderness and loose lying together, they continue sweet for seven or eight years long before which time straw becomes musty and hard' (1959, p.47). Beech leaves were still recommended in 1840, as 'they remain sweet and elastic for years' (*Daily Wants*). Even in the 1880s, 'Beech leaves are recommended for filling the beds of poor persons. They should be gathered on a dry day in the autumn and perfectly dried. It is said that the smell of them is pleasant and that they will not harbour vermin, they are also very springy' (Filp, 1882).

The use of a selection of different fillings in various mattresses to make something of a 'system' was considered by Sheraton:

> For delicate persons I offer my opinion how they should have their beds made: first to begin with a straw mattress, then a flock ditto, on which the feather bed is to be laid and lastly a hair mattress; but if it should feel too firm then a very thin flock mattress may be placed upon it. (1803, p.44.)

In the 1840s, *The Workwoman's Guide* recommended a similar mattress system. The first mattress onto the bed frame should be:

> of straw ... very thick and as hard as a board ... the second mattress

is made of horse hair or wool for large beds; and for children, of chaff, seaweed, beech leaves, cocoa nut fibre, paper, and many other things of that sort … for the poor, mattresses are often filled with mill-puff or flock, and for children, bran might be a good substitute (Hale, pp 198–9).

The range of fillings reflected price points and quality. Heal's bedding catalogue of 1853 lists in ascending price order the following mattress types, based on fillings: 'palliasse/Alva marina/bordered flock (under mattress for servants' beds)/coloured wool/white wool/upper white wool (to use over feather beds)/Best French (white wool and horsehair in twilled check cases)/Horse hair/spring mattresses (wooden frame)/ German spring mattresses/(no frame)'.

The American mail order company, Montgomery Ward, in their 1895 catalogue, provided a similar list:

> All excelsior/excelsior and white cotton/plain husk/plain husks and white cotton/plain palm leaves ('imported from Africa … a new material for mattresses used exclusively in Europe and said to make a healthy, pleasant durable bed')/Wool (various grades)/Sanitary Sea moss (possesses to a remarkable degree the properties of sea-water)/ Black moss/Cotton/Hair.

In about 1923, Elizabeth Dyer gave a comprehensive account of mattress fillings:

> The filling of mattresses is much more important than the covering. It may be corn husks, green grass or hay, cotton or wool, or short hair such as goat's hair or good horse hair; and the latter, which is commonly used in the better mattresses, may vary widely in quality. Corn husks, grass or hay, if clean, make a cheap mattress that will give service as long as it does not lump nor heap up in small pieces. The cotton-felt mattress, or the wool-and-cotton-felt, is cheap, comfortable and durable. If of good quality, these will give good wear, but the filling is not so suitable for re-making as are certain others, hair for instance. Silk floss is also used for filling, making a soft and very warm mattress. What has long been considered the standard mattress is that filled with horsehair. The white, if a natural color, is very expensive, but length is more important than color. Good hair costs about twice as much as cotton felt. Hair breaks and loses its spring unless properly taken care of. If the mattress is turned frequently, it keeps in better shape and wears more evenly. Mattresses with cotton tufting wear better than those with plain tufting. (p.214.)

The range of fillings was still current as late as 1949 (Bitmead, 1912, 5th impression, 1949). Bitmead recommended a palliasse or straw mattress for beds with lath bottoms. In addition, a mattress, stuffed with cotton (although animal hair was also widely used, as was wool or flock), coconut fibre or weeds and mosses, such as Alva marina.

Box spring
This form of mattress was probably developed soon after the adoption of springs for **upholstery**. Upholsterers were certainly making them in the 1860s. The mattress was built up on a wooden frame, using bedsprings, tied in a similar way to spring upholstery, using cord, canvas covering, stuffing materials and **top cover**. They were referred to as 'French' when made with a wooden side frame and therefore a 'firm edge', and 'German' when the springs came to the edge and were held in place by bamboo strips thus creating a 'sprung edge'. They were usually used in conjunction with a soft mattress or overlay, and a bedstead.

French
A mattress made up with half wool and half hair filling.

Spring
Interior sprung mattresses that have a built-in support system such as pocketed (nested) springs, coil springs or interlaced (woven) spring systems. They are usually upholstered with layers of fillings and covered with a final **ticking**.
See also **Alva marina**, **Bed**, **Bed furniture**, **Bed mat**, **Flock**, **Hair**, **Mattress-making**, **Millpuff**, **Moss**, **Springs**, **Wool**.

Mattress-making
Mattress-making was a specialist branch of **upholstery** work that was undertaken by mattress-makers who were trained in mattress stuffing. The principle of filling a mattress was based on either a '**stuffing**' or a 'layering' process. The first method entailed filling the mattress 'bag' with the required fillings from one open end, and the second method involved laying filling materials into an open case, and attaching the **top cover** when the whole case was filled. The manufacturing process originally used special mattress frames to ensure a rectangular shape and for ease of stuffing. Once the mattress-maker had filled the case, he temporarily slip-stitched the top in place so that he could insert the tufts. In better quality mattresses, the sides were also stitched, to create a regular shape. The side stitches were visible and could be up to three layers. Sewing through the fillings, close to the top and bottom sides,

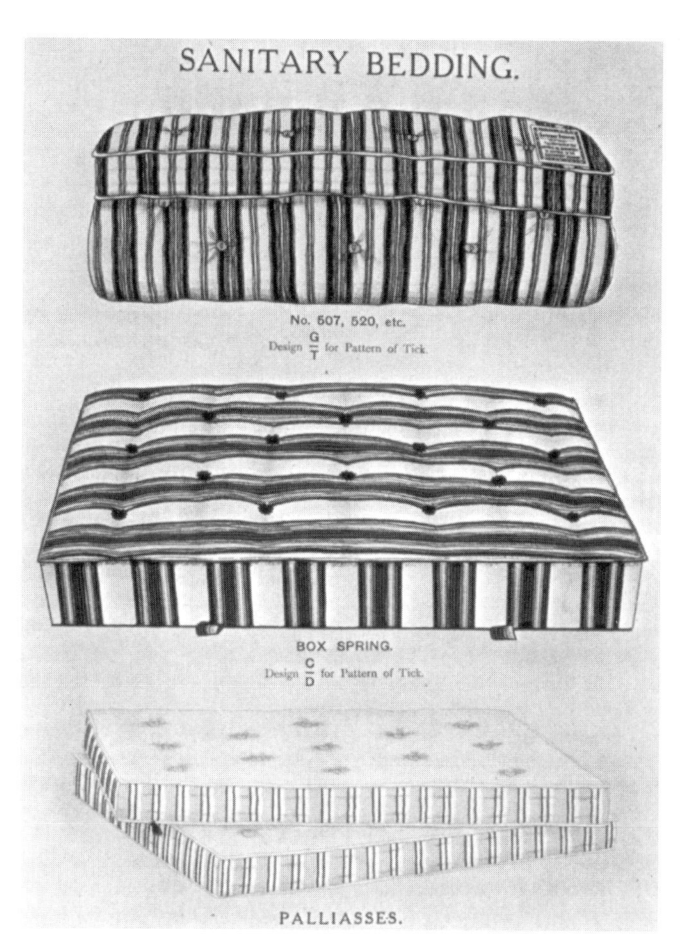

77. Mattress selection, late nineteenth/early twentieth century (Myers and Co)

might create a **rolled edge**. Then it was passed to an upholstress to seam up and bind the edges. The mattress-maker was 'only reckoned [to be] a third-rate hand, and the price paid for making [mattresses] is much lower than for other upholstery work' (Bitmead, 1912, p.23). The craft was gradually taken over by machine-assisted assembly processes of pre-fabricated parts after World War II, although some hand-made work is still produced.

In 1889, Moreland noted 'a regular full-size mattress is four feet six inches wide by six foot four inches long, and five inches thick, with thirty-five pounds of hair'. He noted two ways of making mattresses: one involved stuffing from an open end and the other by layering in to the fully open mattress case. Moreland also suggested making a mattress in two unequal sized parts so as to help its lasting properties. 'The larger part can be made square to the width of the bed frame and the small part made to fit the balance, thus the large part can be turned round bringing a fresh edge to the middle of the bed'.

See also **Mattress**, **Stitch**, **Wollen flock**.

FURTHER READING

Davies, V. & Doyal, S. (1990). 'Upholstered mattress construction and conservation', *SSCR Conservation of Furnishing Textiles*, postprints, Glasgow: Burrell Collection.

Ludlam, A.J. (1947). *The Craft of Mattress and Bedding Production*, London: Furniture Record.

Mattress pad

The protection of the bed **mattress** from soiling was a sensible precaution, as **tickings** were not easily washable. The following description from the early twentieth century explains the issues involved:

> Quilted pads are sold for covering the mattress. Placed under the sheets, they protect them from soil. Some housekeepers prefer to use an old blanket or quilt for this purpose. As a rule, the pad is more satisfactory, for it may be bought to fit the bed, it looks fresh and clean under the sheet and does not wrinkle easily. It greatly protects a mattress to be entirely covered with a stout material such as unbleached muslin. Such a cover can be bought ready-made or can be made at home. It should be changed occasionally. (Dyer, *c.*1923, p.214.)

Mercoolees

'A good plain white calico, woven in [north India], shipped to London in large quantities, and sometimes bought for transforming into chintz.' (Irwin & Schwartz, 1966, p.68.)

Merino

Merino sheep produce fine and prized **wool**, which has been spun into yarns to make various fabrics for furnishing purposes. Merino was particularly a name for a nineteenth-century fabric woven as **damask**, or printed, which had a finish similar to **cashmere**. It was used for hangings and as an **upholstery** cover. It was developed following the production of fine machine-spun **worsted** yarns.

In 1824, Ackermann's *Repository* published illustrations of furniture upholstered in merino damask. This damask cloth was recommended by George Smith for dining and drawing room hangings, where the **curtains** 'were continued over the piers of three windows in drawing rooms, with muslin glass curtains beneath', as it 'makes up beautifully, not requiring lining' (Smith, 1828). In the 1841 inventory of Queen Victoria's property at Frogmore, Windsor, there were 'printed merino curtains and drapery to the Venetian windows'. It remained fashionable. For example, it was particularly specified for upholstering bedroom furniture and hangings supplied to Sir Titus Salt, in 1866 (Boynton, 1967, pp 66–75).

See also **Damask: Merino**.

Mignonette (aka Minionet)

A thin, **lawn**-like, narrow pillow **lace**, which was a French speciality. It was used to trim clothing, **curtains** and **blinds**. In John Penn's 1788 inventory, there was listed 'minionet gauze' for a field bed (Montgomery, 1984, p.294). According to Caulfield & Seward's *Dictionary of Needlework*, mignonette netting was used for 'Curtains and window blinds, it being extremely easy, and worked with one mesh' (1887, p.361).

Millboard

Strong pasteboard rolled under high pressure into flexible panels. Millboard was used in **upholstery** work in Britain, especially during the Utility period (1940–50). It was an alternative to **hessian** for seat bottoms and also for lining up surfaces in unsprung work.

Milled drugget

An American term for 'a fabric lately introduced being painted in rich colours, and very thick and strong. It forms a very good substitute for carpets in small apartments. It is made up to two yards wide' (Webster & Parkes, 1844, p.256).

See also **Drugget**.

Millpuff

A very cheap **mattress** filling which used the ends, scraps and dusts from textile mills. For example, on 18 June 1833, an auction sale in Box, Wiltshire, included 'millpuff and flock beds' (*Devizes and Wilts Gazette*). It must have had some merit as a display in the 1851 Exhibition showed 'Specimens of mattress wools, woollen mill-puffs and flocks' (Great Exhibition, Cat. II, 496). In 1922, it was noted that **bolsters** were 'often filled with millpuff which is a product of the cotton plant' (Butterworth, 1922, p.73).

Mini blind

Window **blinds**, produced with very fine slats that can appear practically invisible when positioned horizontally, thus giving a clear view to the outside.

Mini portières

See **Fireplace curtain**, **Mantel drapery**.

Mitcheline (aka patent satin)

A special type of woven **quilting** fabric made with two **warps** and two fillings. The cloth was patented in 1868 by D. Mitchell and, in 1881, an improved texture of similar character was patented by T. Taylor and J. Warburton, and registered as 'patent satin'. In fact, there is no **satin** weave in the cloth. It is a compound reversible structure made by binding two plain cloths together so they form a compact texture. The figuring is achieved by causing the two plain cloths to interchange in order to conform to the outline of the design. Mitcheline was still being sold in the 1930s.

By the 1950s, patent satin or marcella was also a name for the **satin toilet bedspread**. It was described as 'a compound cloth of two plain-weaves with a raised figure on a plain ground, the figure being made from a coarse weft bound with a fine warp. Used in contract situations. The cloth was usually white.' (Ostick, 1955, p.355.)

Mixed damask
See **Damask: Mixed (half)**.

Mober banies
A **cotton** or **silk** striped **calico** sometimes used for **curtains**, and mentioned in *The Merchant's Warehouse Laid Open* (J.F., 1696).
See also **Calico**.

Mockado
The name for a **velvet**, woven from **wool** and **silk** or other fibres, with a short **pile**. The name may be derived from the Italian *mocaiardo*, meaning '**mohair**'. Mockado was one of the New Draperies, introduced in the later sixteenth century. In France, Mockado was called *moucade*, which was anglicised to 'mockado'. Mockado was woven in a variety of grades and patterns making it suitable for clothing, seat coverings or carpet. It was recorded in 1577 as being produced by Walloons in Norwich with a **linen warp** and a wool **weft**, which was then either embossed or left plain.

An early mention is in 1578: 'I will buy Velvet, Grograyne, Satten, Makadowe, Chambelot' (Florio, *1st Fruites*, 10, *OED*). Four years later, the *Tudor Book of Rates* for 1582 listed: 'Mockado of Flaunders making the peece' (Willan, 1962, p.41). In the 1590 inventory of Cassiobury, there were 'three chairs in mockado' in Lady Morison's chamber (Beard, 1997, p.31).

At Hardwick Hall, in the closet by the Pearl Bedchamber, there was recorded 'six pieces of hangings of red mockadowe' (Boynton, 1971, p.24). In 1601, Bess of Hardwick also paid 2s.8d. per yard for 27½ yards (25.14 metres) of 'stryped mockeadowe ... orrynge taweny and grene' (Levey, 1998, p.30).

In the eighteenth century, Savary des Bruslons (1750–65) related **mocade** to **moquette** and **peluche** (plush), and noted their use for **wall hangings**, chairs, **table covers**, **portières** and carriages (Montgomery, 1984, p.295).

By 1887, Henri Havard was linking *mocade* with moquette as (a) **Tapestry** with heaviest pile; (b) *Pied-court* woven in smaller patterns for seat furniture; (c) *Communes* woven in **checks** and stripes for **cushions** and benches; and (d) *Tripes* woven in a single colour or a stripe and sometimes stamped in imitation of **Utrecht velvets** (Montgomery, 1984, p.295).

Tuft mockado
A voided mockado with a pile of discreet tufts cut or uncut. In 1577, Harrison mentions 'Mockadoies tufted and plaine' (1577, p.132). Halliwell defined Tuft-mockado, as 'a mixed stuff made to imitate tufted taffeta, or velvet' (1847, p.78).
See also **Caffoy**, **Moquette**, **Moquette carpet**, **Plush**, **Tufting**, **Velour**, **Velvet: Panne**.

Mohair (aka Mocayare)
The term has three different meanings. It is a kind of fine **camlet** (which has sometimes been watered) made from the **hair** of the Angora goat. It is also a yarn made from this hair. In other usage, the name is often applied to a fabric made of **silk** or **worsted**. In the eighteenth century, this was wholly of silk, but has also been of worsted or of a mixture of **wool** and **cotton**. Early twentieth-century historians acknowledged this difference. Penderel-Brodhurst explained that mohair is 'a cloth sometimes used by the upholsterer, made from the hair of the Angora goat, or an imitation of it in silk, or in wool and cotton. In the eighteenth century the imitation was made of silk' (1925, p.110). Macquoid & Edwards also explained the distinctions:

> [Mohair is] a fabric occasionally used in the seventeenth and eighteenth centuries for upholstery and hangings. Originally, it was a fine camlet made from the hair of the Angora goat and introduced to Spain by the Moors. Later, the name was applied less accurately to a material entirely of silk. The word 'mohaoire' is mentioned by Purchas early in the seventeenth century among the 'new devised names for Stuffes' and the *Merchants' Map of Commerce* in 1638 alludes to 'mohairs of Angora' brought here [England] by the Turkey Company. (1924, vol.II, p.1.)

Kerridge explained that 'a mohair is a watered grosgrain... Both silk and goat's hair are well suited to making mohair cloth, but the name itself is nothing but a doublet of moiré [i.e. French for mohair]' (1985, p.54).
(a) Worsted mohair
While early sixteenth-century mohairs were woven from silk, worsted yarns were adopted in England, especially in Norwich, to make them. They were made from around 1594, and continued to be made for another 100 years (ibid. p.54).
(b) Silk mohair
In the sixteenth century, mohair was a name for a ribbed silk fabric that had been watered (moiré). In 1675, the Countess of Manchester had a room 'hung with six pieces of haire, called silk watered mohaire' (Cornforth & Fowler, 1974, p.132). Calendering two cloths together produced the particular watered effect, so that the ribs on one marked the face of the other. During 1688, the Duke of Hamilton purchased 'a crimson mohaire bed lined with green satin, fringe, with silk fringe and quilted mohaire cushing' and '80 yards of green morela mohare for the bed' (Beard, 1997, p.292).

In 1710, 'a strip'd mohair stuff' was used as a covering for a chair and stool in Dyrham Park. Whilst in the New Nursery at Dyrham, there was 'a mohair silk bed lined with green sarsenet' and 'four pieces of mohair stuff hangings' (Walton, 1986, p.61). The American newspaper, the *Boston Gazette* (17 October 1737), noted for sale: 'a yellow mohair bed lined with a persian of the same colour' (Cummings, 1961, p.30).

By the mid-eighteenth century, it was clearly described as:

> A kind of stuff, ordinarily of silk, both woof and warp, having its grain wove very close. There are two kinds, the one smooth and plain, the other watered like tabbies: the difference between the two only consists in this, that the latter is calendered, the other not. There are also mohairs both plain and watered whose woof is of wool, cotton or thread. (Chambers, 1728, p.566)

In 1763, William France supplied the Earl of Coventry with '79¾yd of fine yellow silk Mohair at 9/6 per yard' (Beard, 1997, p.306). Two years later, Benjamin Franklin wrote to his wife in 1765: 'the blue mohair stuff is for the curtains of the blue chamber. The fashion is to make one curtain only for each window. Hooks are sent to fix the rails by at top, so that they might be taken down on occasion' (Montgomery, 1984, p.297).
(c) Goat mohair
A term that refers both to a finished cloth as well as to the hair of the Angora goat. Mohair is the hair of a variety of goat originally inhabiting the regions of Asiatic Turkey of which Angora is the centre; hence the animal is known as the Angora goat. The fibres have rigidity, elasticity and a lack of felting ability, which helps keep them separate. The origin of the name is probably the Arabic *muizayyar*, meaning 'cloth of goats' hair'. The word probably came into English through the Italian *moccacaro* or French *mocayart*, although these names were applied earlier to textile fabrics of different material (see **Mockado**). In the seventeenth century, the

word, which before appears in such forms as mocayare or mokaire, became corrupted by connexion with 'hair' to mohair.

It was a highly prized fabric from the very late sixteenth century but, in Europe, it was woven with wool or silk mixed with the mohair yarns. Raw mohair was probably first exported from Turkey to England in the seventeenth century. The *Merchants' Map of Commerce* of 1638 (Macquoid & Edwards, 1924) alludes to 'mohairs of Angora'.

From about 1820 onwards, marked strides were made in its manufacture into useful yarns and fabrics. In the mid-nineteenth century, mohair yarn was made into:

> Many kinds of camblets, which when watered, exhibit a beauty and brilliance of surface unapproached by fabrics made from English wools. It [mohair yarn] is also manufactured into plush… Also large quantities of what is termed Utrecht velvet, suitable for hangings and furniture linings for carriages are made from it abroad. Recently this kind of velvet has begun to be made at Coventry, and it is fully anticipated that the English made article will successfully compete with the foreign one in every essential quality. (James, 1857, p.465.)

By 1884, it was also noted as a mohair cloth woven with mohair yarns. It was considered virtually indestructible and was widely used in public transport work. It was still used in the mid-twentieth century for its lustre and hardwearing properties.

Mohair comes in a variety of styles and fabrics with different trade names. It was used for **drapes** and, in heavy grades, for **upholstery**. It is expensive, durable and shiny, but may be wiry and slippery. It makes an attractive and serviceable cover (Dyer, *c.*1923, p.206).

See also **Allapeen**, **Astrakan**, **Casement cloth**, **Frisé**, **Lampas**, **Moiré**, **Palm beach**, **Utrecht velvet**, **Velvet**.

Mohair rug

A **hearth rug** developed in the twentieth century that, at one time, was hand-woven, but more recently was machine-woven. They are made from mohair yarns that have been 'curled' in a twisting machine and then set. This curl is a feature of the rug. The weaving process uses a **jute weft** and **cotton warp** to make a foundation. The **pile** is inserted, then mechanically raised, and may be looped or cut. The fabric is then cut to size as required by the rug-makers. The fitting of an interlining and sewing on of a backing completed the rug. Popular from the 1950s.

Moiré

Originally a term for a mohair fabric, it later referred to a **silk** fabric with a ribbed effect. Later still, the term referred to any 'watered' fabric. Henri Havard (1888) explains in his *Dictionaire de l'ameublement* entry:

> [At the end of the 17th century] we find the word moiré, mohaire, mohere, mouaire, used … to denote more especially fabrics all of silk, or grosgrain, very closely woven… The moirés, moreover, were of two kinds: smooth moiré … which was plain and without waves, and watered moiré, which had waves like tabbies… Soon it was this dressing, originally regarded as an accessory, that became the determining cause of the word, and the name moiré came to apply especially to watered stuffs having received this finish by being passed through the calender.

Moiré fabrics have a watermarked finish and a fairly stiff handle in most cases. By passing the fabric between engraved cylinders that press the design into the material, the required effect is produced, with the result that the crushed and uncrushed parts reflect the light differently. The

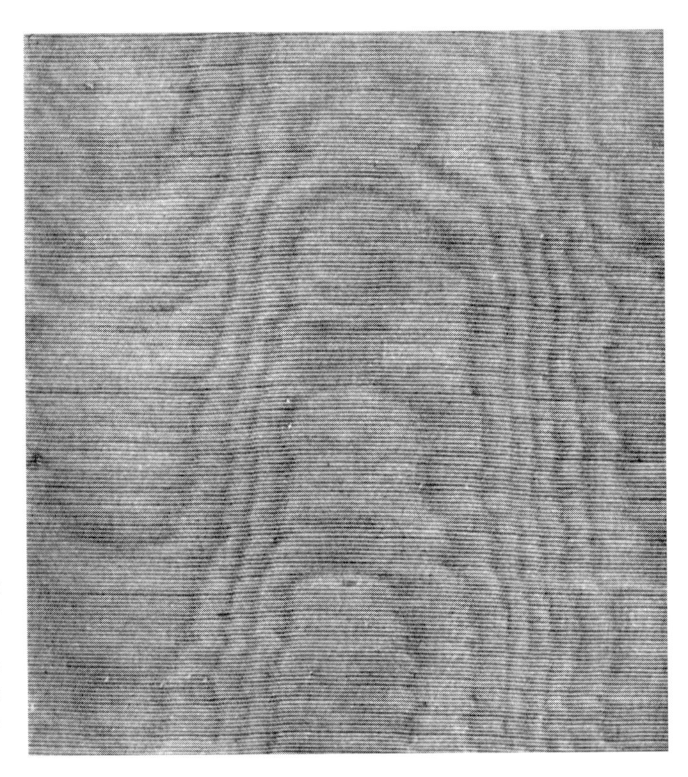

78. Moiré cloth showing distinctive 'watered' effect (T. French and Co, The Book of Soft Furnishing, *1937)*

pattern is not permanent, except on acetate **rayon**. By 1947, it was used for **drapes** and **bedspreads** (Bendure & Pfieffer, p.639), and, by 1955, it was noted that moiré furnishing fabrics were often used for period work (Ostick, p.374).

See also **Barracan**, **Faille**, **Grosgrain**, **Harrateen**, **Mohair**, **Moiré antique**, **Moreen**, **Tabbinet**.

Moiré antique

A variety of grosgrain **silk** that is both fine and heavy. Its 'watered appearance is produced by forcing moisture through the folds by means of a screw, or hydraulic press … width 22 to 36 inches' (Brown & Gates, 1872).

See also **Grosgrain**, **Moiré**.

Moleskin

Twill weave **cotton** fabric with fibres that are raised to form a nap. In 1803, it was defined as 'strong, soft, fine-piled cotton fustian the surface of which is shaved before dyeing' (*OED*). It was used for making up 'moleskin covers for kitchen table presses, &c. bound', in the Marsh and Jones account to Sir Titus Salt in 1866 (Boynton, 1967, p.83). In the mid-twentieth century, it was noted that exclusive decorators used moleskin occasionally for upholstered furnishings (French, 1947).

See also **Fustian**.

Momie cloth (aka Mummy cloth)

An unbleached **linen** and **cotton** or **woollen** fabric, although also known in **silk**, with a puckered surface appearance, similar to **crêpe cloth**. The designation has been used as a trade name for some modern fabrics that more or less resembled the material used for mummy cloths, i.e. the cloth in which ancient Egyptian mummies were wrapped. It was used for **curtains**, **embroidery** grounds and **towel** and dresser **runners** in the latter part of the nineteenth century. In 1881, American author, Constance Harrison noted the sale of 'raw silk momie cloth, for draperies, fifty inches wide, at $3.50. Cotton momie cloth in all the new shades for $1.10: Basket momie cloth, in woollen, costs $3' (1881, vol.I, p.46).

In England, Caulfeild & Saward described it as 'another fabric with a cotton warp and woollen weft, or else a silk warp and woollen weft [which] has the appearance of fine crape' (1887, p.350).

By the early twentieth century, in the USA, momie cloth was described as having 'an irregular weave, producing a pebbly surface similar to granite cloth in wool. Made in linen or cotton for towels and dresser runners and wider in white or colored for dress fabrics. Practically off the market.' (Denny, 1923, p.69.) Despite the comments above, it was apparently still available in mid-twentieth century America. In 1947, momie cloth was described as being 'Originally made from silk warp and wool weft and used for mourning dress due to its lustreless surface. Now [in 1947] used to simulate cloth with heavy crêped yarns. Used for tablecloths.' (Bendure & Pfieffer, 1947, p.640.)

Monk's cloth

Originally, a **worsted** fabric that was allegedly worn by monks in medieval England. It is a rough textured basket weave fabric woven from a variety of yarns, including **wool**, **cotton**, **linen**, **silk**, and later from **rayon** or synthetics. It has been used for **drapes**, all types of **upholstery** and house furnishings, particularly in the USA. The traditional brownish/oatmeal colour was used for draperies and slipcovers, both in the USA and England.

It is quite heavy, due to its construction, so it is difficult to sew or manipulate, the yarns having a tendency to slide, stretch and fray. It may sag in time, depending on the compactness of the weave. It is also known as Friar's cloth when woven in a 4 x 4 basket weave, and as Druid's cloth when in a 6 x 6 or 8 x 8 basket weave.

In 1936, Denny noted its use for 'hangings, couch covers and upholstery' (1936, p.45). While by 1947, it was described as being usually made of all cotton but sometimes flax, **jute** or **hemp** was used as filling yarns, and it was recommended for couch and furniture covers, draperies and the like (Bendure & Pfieffer, 1947, p.640). It was still in use in the 1970s.

See also **Abbot's cloth**, **Druid's cloth**, **Weave: Basket**.

Moorfields carpet

Thomas Moore founded a **carpet** factory at Chiswell Street, Moorfields, London, around 1756, where he produced hand-knotted carpets using a Turkish knot. He won a prize from the Royal Society of Arts 'for the best carpet in one breadth after the manner of turkey carpet' in 1757. Many of his carpets were made to the designs of Robert Adam and were supplied to Syon House, Osterley Park, Saltram and Harewood House. The factory closed for business in the 1790s. William Bingham's house in Philadelphia boasted a description from 1794: 'The carpet is one of Moore's most expensive patterns' (Montgomery, 1967, p.42).

FURTHER READING

Hefford, W. (1977). 'Thomas Moore of Moorfields', *Burlington Magazine*, 119, 897, December, pp 840–49.

Sherrill, S.B. (1996). *Carpets and Rugs of Europe and America*, New York: Abbeville, pp 152–87.

79. Moorfields hand-tufted and shaped carpet, designed by Adam Bros, c.1780 (C. Faraday, European and American Carpets and Rugs, *1929)*

Moquette

Originally, a lightweight narrow carpet strip fabric (see **Moquette carpet**), it was later used on **upholstery**. It was in the 1920s that its stiffness was transformed into a more suitable upholstery and **drapery** cloth, although its associations with railway and coach seating took a while to dispel.

The best qualities of modern moquettes have a **wool pile** on a **cotton** ground (known as all-wool face), but cotton and **rayon** piles were also introduced in the mid-twentieth century. It was amongst the most popular textiles for upholstery in post-war Britain. **Ramie** was also used as a pile yarn in the 1930s. Midgley described moquette as 'a double cloth with a warp pile of both cut and loop, or an all cut-pile. Cotton and wool mixes.' (Midgley, 1931.)

By 1955, *The Draper's Encyclopaedia* wrote that 'Moquette is one of the most popular fabrics for fixed covers. It is a pile fabric and may be cut, when it is known as velvet pile, or uncut, when it is called terry pile' (Ostick, 1955, p.378).

Moquettes are made in many forms, four of which are: (a) cut- or uncut-pile in self colours; (b) cut- or uncut-pile forming figures on a plain ground; (c) cut- or uncut-pile making a combined design; and (d) cut- or uncut-pile with a design in many colours.

See also **Caffoy**, **Mockado**, **Moquette tapestry**, **Plush**, **Velour**.

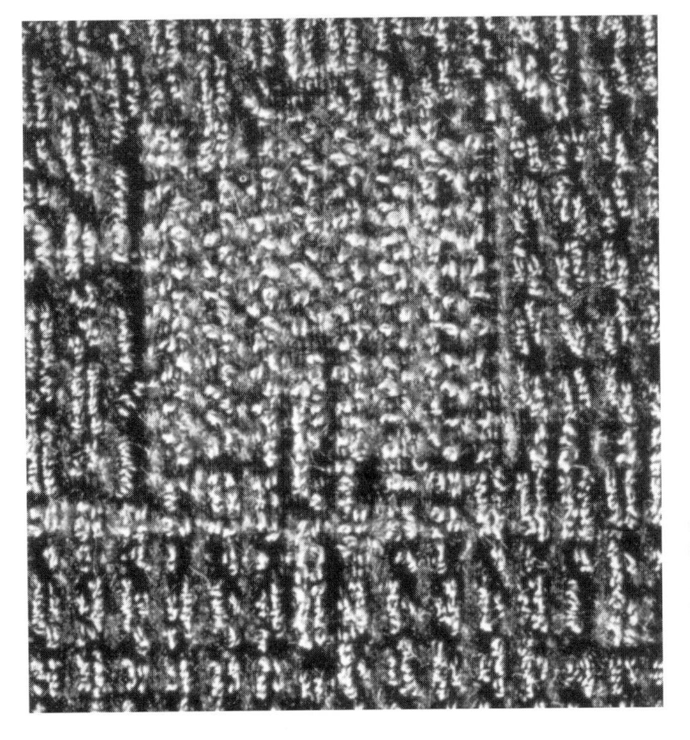

80. Moquette cloth detail showing loop effect (T. French and Co, The Book of Soft Furnishing, *1937)*

Moquette carpet

A thinnish fabric woven with a **pile** of cut or uncut loops, produced by a supplementary **warp**. It was originally used for **upholstery**, though later developed for floorcoverings This carpet was woven on a narrow loom and seamed together as required. Early references to the uses of moquette 'carpet' are found in a description of a mansion in Rheims, dated 1621, where there was a '*tapis de mocquette de couleur jaune et rouge fasson de Turqy*' and also a set of armchairs covered in '*moquette de diverse couleurs*' (Thornton, 1978, pp 221, 381).

In 1741, Ignatius Couran, a London merchant, John Barford, an upholder, and William Moody, a clothier, the latter two both of Wilton town, were granted a patent for a 'new invention of making carpets commonly called French carpeting or Moccadoes and in France moucades or mouquets' (Patent no.578, 18 July 1741). The development in England of a compound warp that removed the stripe effect of a supplementary warp created a cloth that was later known as 'Wilton', if the pile was cut, and 'Brussels', if left looped (see also **Ingrain carpet**).

Moquette carpet was also made in the USA from around 1849. In 1858, Simmonds' *Dictionary of Trade Products* defined moquette as 'a tapestry Brussels carpet of a fine quality; a species of Wilton carpet', while Tomlinson's *Cyclopaedia of Useful Arts* described it thus: 'Wilton carpet, called Moquette by the French, differs from the Brussels in the form of the wire [etc]' (1866, vol.II, p.867). In 1889, Moreland explained that moquette had a 'deep pile of soft wool fastened on a very thick cotton back as a groundwork, none of the wool showing through the back. The colours are usually soft and delicate, designs finely drawn and shaded and the fabric extremely durable; width always twenty-seven inches.' (1889.) A few years later, Cole described it as 'A variety of carpeting, with a soft velvety nap of wool and a warp of hemp or linen.' (1892.)

In the twentieth century, the American publication, *Dictionary of Textiles* (1924), went into some detail:

It is likely that moquette was introduced to Europe through Marseilles, France, perhaps during the XVI century but it was first manufactured in England although its production on a commercial scale became possible only after the invention of the Jacquard loom. The first moquettes made in Europe had two sets of warp, a coarser for the ground and a finer for the pile and two sets of filling, a coarser and a finer. The pile remained uncut; some grades were made by having a very coarse filling thread taking the place of the rods and by throwing the warp threads out, produce an imitation uncut-pile.

At the present the best grades in France come from Aubusson where in local parlance moquette means hand-woven cut-pile rugs made in strips; commercially the word moquette in France (outside of Aubusson) means rugs made in strips on power looms with cut warp pile.

The earliest mention of this word is found in France in an inventory of 1585 and another one of 1587, both from Marseilles, the spelling being 'mosquette' which gave rise to the assumption that it was derived from the word mosque and may have meant some sort of Oriental rug. (Harmuth, 1924, p.114, referring to Harvard's entry on Moquette.)

See also **Aubusson carpet**, **Axminster moquette**, **Brussels carpet**, **Mockado**, **Moquette**, **Moquette tapestry**, **Muskuetta**, **Wilton carpet**.

Moquette tapestry

In 1887, Caulfeild & Saward defined it thus: 'designed to imitate the genuine tapestry and much resembling Utrecht velvet. The fine kinds are employed for tablecloths, and the thick for carpets.' (p.473.)
See also **Mohair**, **Moquette**, **Moquette carpet**, **Utrecht velvet**.

Moree (aka Morea)

Originally, a South Indian **cotton** cloth, often used as a substitute for **linen** cloth and also for preparing **chintz**. Traditionally woven in **Masulipatam** but also later in the Madras area. It was specifically defined as 'a calico used for bed curtains and Linnen' by *The Merchant's Warehouse Laid Open* (J.F., 1695). Much later, Caulfeild & Saward (1887, p.350) defined morees rather differently as 'Manchester made muslins much employed for the African export trade.'
See also **Calico**.

Moreen (aka Morine)

A robust **wool** or wool and **cotton** material, either plain or watered, that often has a horizontal (**weft**) rib and stamped or watered effects in imitation of **moiré camlets**. It was used in the eighteenth and early nineteenth centuries for **drapery** and **upholstery**. According to Beck, 'the name of this stuff was formerly Moireen, which gives its origin more distinctly. It is an imitation of moiré in commoner materials for purposes of upholstery.' (Beck, 1882.) Hazel Cummin says 'watered mohair became moireen. The word mohair continued to be used … for fabrics of goats' hair, or of mixed hair and wool' (Cummin, 1940, p.286). The effect of watering 'with its silky texture, gave the name mouaire to eighteenth century silk moirés. Coarse qualities were sometimes watered, sometimes decorated with impressed designs. These were made of very common wools in great quantities in England, where they were given the name moreen.' (ibid. p.310.)

In the first half of the eighteenth century, 'Kidderminster was the seat of the moreen and damask manufacture and [of] all sorts of bed furniture and hangings.' (James, 1857, p.255.) Moreen was used widely in the eighteenth century. For example, in July 1768, John Morland, an upholsterer of unknown address, charged for 'making beds including 41¼ yds of Saxon blue Morine' (*DEFM*, p.627). In December 1764, William France, working at Moor Park, charged Sir Lawrence Dundas 'for making curtains of the above blue morine [24¾ at 2/3d a yard] &c to the 2 windows in the Blue Room, in the Attick, and putting up Do. Complete, long nails, Tax, &c' (Beard, 1997, p.307). Chippendale supplied Mersham in 1767 with '6 blue morine cases for cushions for cane seated chairs' (Gilbert, 1978, p.228). It was also used in America. Massachusetts' governor, Sir Francis Bernard, sold '1 mahogany four post bedstead with crimson moreen furniture' in 1770, through the *Boston News Letter* (Cummings, 1961, p.31).

By the nineteenth century, George Smith, in his *Household Furniture*, 1808, wrote of moreen, 'where expense is an object [in furnishing dining rooms] undressed morine of a fine quality will form a good substitute [for cassimere]'. In 1809, it was further noted that 'morone continues still in use, and the more so, where economy is requisite; which article also has experienced an improvement by being embossed in a variety of patterns. This process, however, renders it less appropriate for drapery, unless there should be sufficient extent to form it with boldness.' (Ackermann, vol.1, March 1809, p.188.) In an American publication of 1829, moreen was described as 'very serviceable [for bed hangings] being well suited to cold situations: it requires no lining, and therefore is less expensive than chintz, though not so pretty' (Mrs Parkes, pp 182–3). In 1833, British author, Perkins, in his *A Treatise on Haberdashery and Hosiery*, wrote of moreen:

> [They] are for furniture generally watered, and may be had figured [and] are 3/4ths wide. Lengths [are] from 28 yards and of all colours. This article verges on upholstery, in which trade these goods are to be met with in very superior makes advancing from the common material here named to the most costly and superb imitation of the original damask and recognised under a multitude of names.

Loudon suggested that if furniture was mahogany, 'the material of the curtains should be moreen or cloth; and the colour should be the same tone, and strong or dark' (1839, pp 1074–5). However, he said that moreen 'should never be used in cottages', rather:

> [It] used to be employed for the hangings of best beds and bedroom windows... [but] is now considered as apt to harbour moths and other vermin; and therefore in these economical times, it is much less used than formerly. It has, however, the advantage of not taking fire so readily as chintz or dimity. (ibid. p.1080.)

It was still recommended during the 1840s in the USA. Thomas Webster suggested that 'for eating rooms and libraries, a material of more substance is requisite than for drawing rooms; in these moreen is most usually employed' (1844, p.251). Andrew Downing agreed: 'For a better kind of curtain, moreens of single colors, browns, drabs, crimsons, or blues may be used, which, though more expensive, are more durable than cotton.' (1850, p.374.)

It was still used in the latter part of the nineteenth century in the USA. By 1872, moreen was described as 'a coarse all wool fabric woven plain. It is usually dyed in plain colours, heavily sized and pressed, or tabbied, to imitate watered goods. The colours are generally permanent, and the goods durable. It is used for covering **cushions** and furniture. Width 24 to 27 inches.' (Brown & Gates.) In 1887, Caulfeild & Saward talked of moreen in the past tense, and suggested that 'it resembled Tammie only less stiffened and watered or plain. Some rich qualities resembled **silk** damask and [these] were used for window curtains and some upholstery. It is 26 to 27 inches wide.' (p.350.)

See also **Cheney**, **Harrateen**, **Mohair**.

FURTHER READING

Cummin, H. (1940). 'Moreen – a forgotten fabric', *Antiques*, 38, December, pp 286–7.

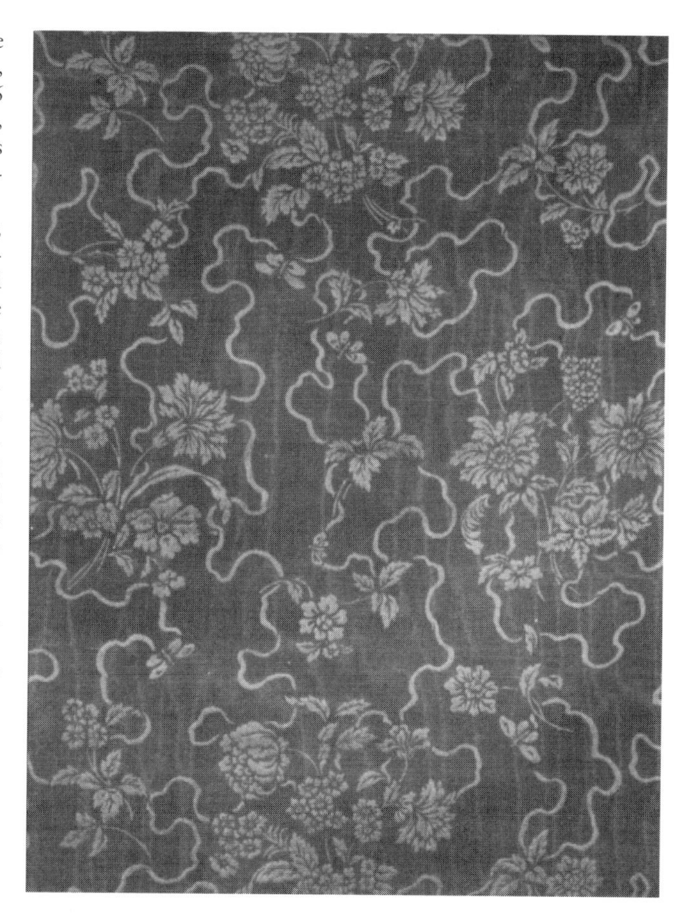

81. Moreen worsted, watered and stamped, c.*1750–85* (Classic Revivals)

Morella

A kind of material used in the seventeenth century for dresses, **curtains**, etc. that may be so named from the Italian for watered *marrezzo*. On 27 June 1674, Robert Bransby sold 'a rich colour morella bed made up complete ... six back chairs of walnut covered in morella silk' to the Countess of Kent of Wrest Park. (*DEFM*, p.63). The Ham House inventory of 1679 listed wall hangings in the Duchess' bedchamber: 'four pieces of hangings of morella mohair scarlet and black with embroidered borders' (Thornton & Tomlin, 1980, p.54). In 1702–3, 'Crimson morella mohair for the curtains' was supplied for use in Cambridge (Willis, 1886, vol.II, p.211).

Morocco cloth

A version of leathercloth introduced in the mid-nineteenth century and designed to replicate **morocco leather**. It was clearly considered a suitable material in the mid-nineteenth century:

> A most perfect imitation of morocco [leather] by the application of a preparation of caoutchouc, or gutta percha, to the surface of a plain-woven or twill cotton cloth. The surface is corrugated in imitation of morocco, and is coloured and varnished so as to present all the external appearance of that kind of leather. The elasticity is perfect, showing no tendency to crack, and so far as time has at present tested its durability, this appears to be satisfactory. Its cost is less that one-third that of morocco, and from the width of the cloth, it cuts to

much greater advantage in the covering of articles of furniture, for which, as well as carriage linings, particularly railway carriages, it is coming largely into use. (Wallis, 1854, p.23.)

See also **Oilcloth**.

Morocco leather (aka Maroquin)
Furnishing **leather** made from sumach-tanned goatskins. (Sumach is the reddish dried and ground leaves from trees of the *Rhus* genus.) This leather was originally from Morocco and the Barbary States and was invariably red. It was used in the eighteenth century for lining desk and tabletops as well as for covering chair seats and backs. Chippendale suggested that 'if the seats are covered with red morocco they will have a fine effect' (1762, Plate XV). The re-modelling of Weston Park occasioned '2 green morocco skins for a table in the study' to be supplied by Morel in 1805 (Rogers, 1987, p.28).

By the nineteenth century, morocco leather had acquired a name for quality and it was essentially used for dining, library and club chairs. It was considered to be 'by far the best leather used for covering purposes, its durability and the fastness of its colour being qualities not common to any other material' (Working Upholsterer, 1883, pp 5–6).

The 'Morocco leather suite' was the epitome of high-class **upholstery** in the early twentieth century. Although not quite as long lasting as Moroccos, cowhides became more popular for upholstery post 1914–18, as they were cheaper, larger and could be more easily obtained.
See also **Morocco cloth**, **Roan**.

'Morris' curtain
A late nineteenth-century American name for a single pair of **sheer curtains** hung at the lower portion of a sash window. Morris curtains were often used in conjunction with stained-glass top window lights. Also known as half-sash.

'Morris' rug
An American name for 'closely woven modern English rugs dyed with vegetable dyes and having simple floral, usually acanthus designs. Named after William Morris, its originator.' (Harmuth, 1924, p.112.)

Mortlake tapestry
In 1619, Sir Francis Crane established a tapestry factory in Mortlake, near London. The business was run by Flemish weavers who worked on both high and **low warp** looms, with **linen warps** and mixed **wefts** of **silk**, gold or silver thread **wool** or **worsted**. The factory was considered to be the most important tapestry works in England. It produced tapestry for the Court but suffered from declining fortunes until it closed at the end of the seventeenth century.
See also **Tapestry**.

FURTHER READING

Haynes, A. (1974). 'The Mortlake tapestry factory, 1619–1703', *History Today*, 24, p.32.
Marillier, H.C. (1930). *English Tapestries of the Eighteenth Century*, London: Medici Society.

Mosaic carpet
A type of **carpet** or **rug** that was first woven in 1850 by the firm Crossley and Co of Halifax, England. It appears to have been an early bonded type of non-woven carpet. The principle was to arrange a series of **worsted** yarns in a pre-determined pattern (not unlike the process of Tunbridge ware) within a frame, which was then tightened. The top of the block was fixed to a base cloth and then cut off to create a **pile**. The process was described in 1872:

> for the ground of this carpet a strong plain cloth is used. Upon this, a pile of warp threads is placed and cemented with Caoutchouc [rubber solution]. The warp is first arranged over and under parallel strips of metal, which are cut out leaving the ends like those of the velvet carpet. 27 inches wide. (Brown & Gates, 1872, p.174.)

It was probably out of use soon after this date.

FURTHER READING

Fairbairn, J.C. (1932). *The Crossley Mosaics*, Bankfield Museum Notes, 3rd series, no.2, Halifax: Bankfield Museum.
Innes, R.A. (1974). *Crossley Mosaics*, Halifax: Calderdale Museums.

Mosquito netting
Gnats and mosquitoes have plagued sleepers (and others) probably forever. The use of some form of netting over beds and to cover windows etc. was therefore considered essential in particular climes. In his 1519 work, Horman explains that: 'some have curteynes; some sparvers about the bedde to kepe away gnatties' (*Vulgaria*). Certainly, a form of **canvas** was used at Tart Hall in 1641 'for two beds to keep the gnats away' (Cust, 1911).

By the nineteenth century, especially in the USA, the problem was taken very seriously. The Beecher sisters wrote that 'close nets around a bed are the only sure protection at night' (1869, p.377). Caulfeild & Saward define mosquito netting as 'a coarse cotton net, employed for

82. Mosaic carpet design, 'The Smithy, after Landseer', mid-nineteenth century (Calderdale Museums)

bed curtains in warm countries where Mosquitos abound. It is likewise employed for purposes of embroidery.' (1887, p.351.)

It was, however also seen as a potentially decorative material. In June 1886, the American journal, *Decorator and Furnisher*, promoted the use of pink mosquito net over pictures or mirrors, looped back and fastened on each side with a bow of pin ribbon. This sort of treatment, it was said, furnished a 'pretty and inexpensive protection for gilded frames' (Burke, 1986, p.136). American author, Lillie French, explained how mosquito nets were practically important but could also be decorative:

> Our mosquito nets, in this country, by the way, are woefully ugly, a disfigurement to almost any room; in Cuba, on the other hand, they are so pretty that they become an agreeable feature of the bedroom. There the beds are always provided with upright posts at the four corners, supporting the tester. The netting is then stretched flat across the top, and falls as curtains around the bed, the edges of which are ruffled or trimmed with color. Malaria, and worse than all, as experiments in Cuba have proved, yellow fever itself, is produced by the bite of the mosquito, so that to the Cuban householder the netting is a necessity, and any trouble necessary to make it pretty is considered worth while. In some houses belonging to wealthy Cubans, the mosquito nettings are made of fine pineapple cloth, while in Spain a silk grenadine with a narrow stripe of blue is often used. (French, 1903, p.110.)

In 1936, mosquito netting was simply described as 'coarse cotton net, heavily sized and used for bed canopies and window screens' (Denny, 1936, p.69).

See also **Canopy**, **Grenadine**, **Marquisette**, **Net**.

Moss

Moss is the name for cryptogamous plants that are grown in clusters and sometimes used for the filling of mattresses. In 1792, Thomas Smith of Doncaster advertised a secret method of cultivating and harvesting moss especially for use in bedding (*Doncaster Journal,* 9 October).

In 1854, Miss Leslie suggested that 'A large, heavy, square foot-cushion of coarse **linen** stuffed hard and firmly with hair or with upholsterers' moss, and covered with carpeting, is a very usual and excellent accompaniment to a rocking chair.' (1854, p.177.) American retailers, Montgomery Ward, in their catalogue of 1895, sold mattresses upholstered with 'Sanitary Sea moss ([which] possesses to a remarkable degree the properties of sea-water) and Black moss', amongst others.

By the early twentieth century, it was noted that 'Other weeds and mosses, the products of Italy and America, are used for the same purpose, [i.e. filling mattresses] and are cheaper than horse-hair and wool.' (Bitmead, 1912, p.17.)

See also **Mattress**, **Spanish moss**.

Mottled tapestry

This was the name given to a 27 inch (68.6 cm) wide 'carpet with a pattern of all colours woven in at random from surplus wools of best Brussels [which] is also very useful for upper bedrooms' (Maple and Co, 1884, p.78).

Mullet fringe

See **Fringe: Mullet**.

Mummy cloth

See **Momie cloth**.

Muskuetta

Carpets imported from Anatolia that were probably named after the French term *mosquets*, which possibly refers to mosques and the prayer-rug style of these small carpets. In 1677, John Casbert supplied 'a fine Musketto carpet for our seat in Our Chapel' to King Charles (Beard, 1997, p.291). The *Daily Courant* (27 November 1711) carried an advertisement by Captain Parker's Warehouse for, amongst others: 'Twelve fine Moschet carpets proper for Ladies Chambers or Dressing Rooms' (Gilbert, Lomax & Wells-Cole, 1987, p.40).

See also **Moquette carpet**.

Muslin

An open-textured **cotton** cloth of plain-weave with a very fine spun yarn, varying in weight from semi-sheer to heavyweight **sheeting**. It is said to have come from Mosul in Mesopotamia. In 1573, it was noted that '…you have all sorts of Cotton-works, Handkerchiefs, long Fillets, Girdles … and other sorts, by the *Arabians* called Mossellini (after the Country *Mussoli*, from whence they are brought, which is situated in Mesopotamia), by us Muslin.' (Rauwolff, in Yule, 1903, p.84.)

Muslins were originally made in various parts of India, from where they were imported to England from the seventeenth century. With the invention of the spinning mule in 1779, they were later woven in England and especially in Scotland. The term originally referred to the yarn itself, and the name muslin often covers a number of fabrics, including **calicoes**, cambric, dimity and gingham.

Muslin was used for **curtains** during the seventeenth century and probably superseded cambric, **lawn** and **linen**. A very early reference to muslin is in 1695–6 when American settler, Margarita van Varick, had an inventory reference to 'a sett of white flowered muslin curtains' (Montgomery, 1984, p.304). Not long afterwards, in 1712, Celia Fiennes commented on 'the same fine flower'd muslin window curtains in the Queen's dressing room at Windsor Castle' (1949, p.359).

In the 1728 inventory of the shop of James Pilbeam, a mercer of Chiddingly, Sussex, there was listed: 'Forty-five yards of muslin at 2s 6d per yard, £5 12s 6d' (http://www.chiddingly.gov.uk/History/James%20Pilbeam.html). By 1752, Chambers defined muslin as 'a fine sort of cloth wholly cotton; so called, as not being bare, but having a downy knap on its surface resembling moss… There are various kinds of muslins brought from the East Indies; chiefly Bengal, betelles, tarnatans, mulmuls, tanjeebs, terrindams, doreas, &c.' (*Cyclopaedia*, 1752, p.609).

Muslin was also used for overskirts to toilettes, then again for window curtains. Later American references are found where muslin was a **lining**. Captain Staniford of Ipswich, Mass. had 'blue curtains with muslin linings, vallens, head cloth and tester' in his 1778 inventory (Cummings, 1961, p.33).

It was commonly used for **inner curtains** during the nineteenth century. In 1826, George Smith commented in his design book that 'muslin curtains are introduced in the present design as well as many preceding; they serve to break the light, without entirely secluding the cheering effect produced from the solar rays'. Loudon expressed a similar idea in 1839 when he said that the purpose of muslin **under curtains** was to: 'exclude insects, and in some degree soften the direct light of the sun' (1839, p.1075).

Muslin curtains, according to *The Workwoman's Guide*, were made 'with deep hems and rings at the top and so arranged to fall towards the inside of the window'. It went on to say that 'many persons take down their chintz curtains when they put up muslin ones' (Hale, 1840, p.205). In 1841, Miss Leslie noted in *The Lady's House Book* that muslin was used for blinds and dressing tables. For blinds 'for sitting rooms, chambers etc. the blinds generally in use are of white muslin. Those of plain

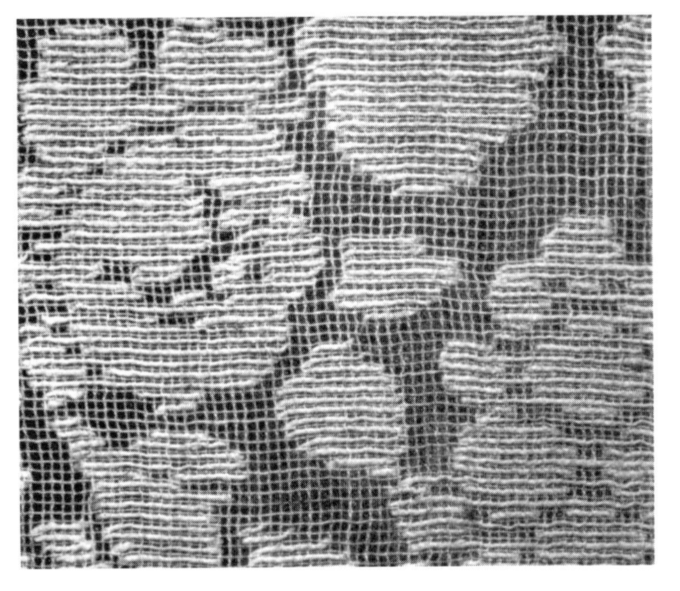

83. Muslin madras detail (T. French and Co, The Book of Soft Furnishing, *1937)*

unfigured Swiss or Scotch muslin look much the best, but are more easily seen through than when the muslin is striped or cross-barred' (p.191). In the case of dressing tables 'of plain unpainted wood, with white covers, and valances of muslin made full and deep and descending to the floor, are not yet quite out of use' (ibid. p.300).

Catherine Beecher, in *The American Woman's Home,* recommended muslin:

> The influence of white muslin curtain in giving an air of grace and elegance to a room is astonishing. White curtains really create a room out of nothing. No matter how coarse the muslin, so it be white and hang in graceful folds, there is a charm in it that supplies the want of a multitude of other things. (1869, p.88.)

On the other hand, the Garrett sisters were derogatory: 'The stiff white muslin curtains, so often seen in modern rooms, have neither beauty nor use enough to compensate for their ugliness' (1877, p.78). Twenty years later, Edith Wharton commented nearly as harshly in her *The Decoration of Houses*:

> Muslin window-curtain is a recent invention. Its purpose is to protect the interior of the room from the public view: a need not felt before the use of large sheets of glass... Under such circumstances muslin curtains are, of course, useful... Lingerie effects do not combine well with architecture, and the more architecturally a window is treated the less it needs to be dressed up in ruffles. (Wharton & Codman, 1897, p.72.)

She went on to say:

> Where muslin curtains are necessary, they should be a mere transparent screen hung against the glass. In town houses especially all outward show of richness should be avoided; the use of elaborate lace-figured curtains, besides obstructing the view, seems an attempt to protrude the luxury on the interior upon the street. It is needless to point out the futility of the second layer of muslin which, in some houses, hangs inside the sash-curtains. (ibid.)

In the early 1920s, in the USA it was fashionable to embroider muslin for bedspreads. One commentator was not totally convinced:

> Unbleached muslin. In the last few years, there has been a fad for embroidering unbleached muslin in gay colors and using it as a bedspread. It makes an inexpensive but often artistic and attractive covering, especially for simple bedrooms. It does seem, however, inconsistent to spend time embroidering such coarse, cheap material. It stays clean better than white, but owing to its embroidery it has to be washed carefully. For a change, unbleached muslin with cretonne appliquéd on it makes an inexpensive and attractive covering. These are fads. (Dyer, *c.*1923, pp 211–12.)

Muslin was recommended on occasion as the main curtaining fabric in the twentieth century. 'When employed in the decoration of bedrooms, boudoirs etc., they [muslin curtains] should always have a transparent [sic] of coloured silk or white satin placed underneath.' (Bitmead, 1912, p.35.) Muslin remained a staple for **sheer curtains** well into the mid-century. In the 1950s, it was used for inexpensive curtains for kitchen windows in England, and is still manufactured in Scotland.

The name muslin was also used to refer to early machine-spun, fine but strong cotton yarns or any cloth made from them, including those with woven details such as dimity.

Book

A reference to the way certain Indian calicoes were folded ready for sale. The term was certainly used from the early seventeenth century (Irwin & Schwartz, 1966, p.59). In 1769, the *Public Advertiser* listed '[a] Dozen Book and Jaconot Muslins and clear Lawns' (14 November, 3/3, 260).

Checked

White or semi-clear muslin with stripes of thicker texture or cords to form patterns in **checks** or stripes. They are employed for curtains and covers of furniture as well as for fashions.

Madras

A fine cotton fabric, with a **leno** ground structure often with extra **weft** figuring. It was originally exported from the Madras region of India. In the later part of the nineteenth century, muslin was recommended for curtains. In 1877, Mrs Orrinsmith suggested that:

> Instead of blinds [at windows] little curtains are suggested of delicate soft material such as white muslin, Tussore silk or madras muslin with tiny rings sewn on, to draw on slim brass rods, which should be fixed just above the top of the upper and on top of the lower part of sash or other windows. The Madras muslin being faintly coloured and patterned needs no embroidery. This muslin ... would be most suitable for festoon blinds, which draw up by means of many runners into graceful folds, and although they are not as heartily recommended as the dainty little hangings, [i.e. curtains] are a great improvement upon the old, stiff roller-blind. (1877, p.67.)

She went on to say that 'the delicately hued and patterned Madras muslin, delightful to look upon, and possessing gentle power of softening light and looking cool, may be suggested for summer curtains' (IBID. p.71). In 1887, *The Dictionary of Needlework* matter-of-factly described madras muslin as 'handsome but coarse make of muslin, produced in several varieties, some in cream colour, other with coloured designs of a bold character, and others again in uni-colour. They are all 72 inches wide.' (Caulfeild & Saward, p.339.) Two years later, Moreland, in his *Practical Decorative Upholstery,* suggested that 'Very pretty chamber draperies are made with cream madras or muslins, with light silk over-drapery; or the entire draping may be of muslin or cream madras over colours silesia.' (1889, pp 225 38.)

By the twentieth century, it was still a favourite for window curtains:

> Madras loose, open construction with a figure woven in with yarns much heavier than the background. The loose ends are on the right side, and help to make the figures stand out. Madras comes in many qualities, but the more expensive are much finer, better woven, and in more beautiful patterns. This material is especially useful where you want to obscure the view from the window. Because of the figures, it is more appropriately used in rooms that have plain wallpaper or plain overhangings. In buying any figured curtains, by the yard, allowance has to be made for matching figures. (Dyer, *c.*1923, p.199.)

Madras muslin was again confirmed as a highly suitable window curtain material in 1937: 'The lighter weights are used for window curtains, medium qualities are used for decorative purposes in the home and for hangings, as are the heavier and more expensive qualities which are often richly coloured and elaborately figured' (French, 1937, p.139).

By 1955, the quality of Madras muslin was judged on the amount of figuring weft used, which is called the cover of figure and was expressed as a percentage of figuring weft threads to grounds threads (Ostick, 1955, pp 368–9). The same source suggested that cloths of the Madras type are sometimes called **grenadine**.

Spotted

A muslin cloth 'spotted' with small motifs in a regular all-over pattern. Spotted muslins are made with extra warp of weft yarns with extra ends or picks cut away after weaving.

In the 1955 *Draper's Encyclopaedia* (Ostick), there are four methods of spotting muslin listed: (a) Book harness that resembles madras muslin except it is on a plain ground rather than a **gauze** ground; (b) Extra **warp** spots; (c) Extra weft spots; and (d) **Lappet** spots resembling **embroidery**.

Swiss

Fine sheer cotton material, which may be plain or patterned. Caulfeild & Saward defined it as a 'coarse description of buke or book muslin much used for curtains made with raised loose work in various patterns, and also plain' (1887, p.467).

In 1936, 'Curtain Swiss' was made either plain, dotted or figured (Denny, 1936, p.64). Contrasting coloured dots designs were used for kitchens, bathrooms and bedrooms on occasion. Swiss muslin was best used as a **tieback** curtain with **ruffle** or a cotton **ball fringe**.

See also **Abaca**, **Art Muslin**, **Bedspread**, **Blind**, **Cambric**, **Candlewick**, **Crete**, **Dimity**, **Dotted Swiss**, **Gingham**, **Glass curtain**, **Jaconet**, **Lace**, **Leno**, **Moree**, **Nainsook**, **Organdie**, **Tambour muslin**, **Tarlatan**, **Toilette**, **Scrim**, **Short blind**.

Nail

A measure of textiles that equates to 2¼ inches (6 cm). Four nails make a quarter, and four quarters make one yard (91 cm).

See also **Ell**.

Nainsook

A muslin-type cloth whose name derives from the Hindi *nainsukh*, meaning 'eye pleasure'. It is fine white plain-woven **cotton** muslin, both plain and vertically striped, that has been used for window shade foundations, **embroidery** bases and clothing. Imported from the early nineteenth century, nainsook was especially used for transparent **blinds** in the USA, later in the century. It is mainly a clothing fabric nowadays.

See also **Lawn**, **Muslin**.

Napt baize

See **Baize**.

Navajo rug

A product of the Navajo tribes of North America who initially wove **woollen** textiles for making up into wearing apparel. With the opening up of the West, there grew a demand for Navajo cloth, especially for bedcoverings, floorcoverings and clothing. As trade developed, the Navajo employed gaudy chemical **dyes**, and wove a loose cloth with an open **weft** and a **cotton warp** for commercial sales. Bordered, banded and specifically Navajo motifs were developed later and a return to natural materials was encouraged.

The **blankets** woven by the North American Navajo tribes were used as **wall coverings** or hangings as well as floorcoverings by designers working in an Arts and Crafts taste, especially in the USA. They were particularly popular in 'Craftsman' interiors in the 1890s, for being appropriate to their ethos. American commentators recognised their value early in the twentieth century:

> American Indian rugs, pottery and baskets, each offering a field rich in national and artistic interest. A Navajo blanket of bright colours when hung against the wall will look brilliant by artificial light; or it may be made of utilitarian value if thrown on a lounge for a cover, or laid on the floor as a rug. Some of the old Indian blankets, their gay colours subdued by time to a dull softness, are preserved as curiosities and valued at hundreds of dollars. (Kellogg, 1905, p.52.)

FURTHER READING

Amsden, C.A. (1934). *Navajo Weaving*, Santa Ana: Fine Arts Press.

Dedera, D. (1975). *Navajo Rugs: How to Find, Evaluate, Buy and Care for Them*, Flagstaff: Northland Press.

Kaufman, A. & Selser, C. (1985). *Navajo Weaving Tradition, 1650 to the Present*, New York: E.P. Dutton.

84. Navajo chief's rug/blanket (C. Faraday, European and American Carpets and Rugs, *1929)*

86. Lady's worktable for needlework (T. Sheraton, The Cabinet Maker and Upholsterer's Drawing Book, *1793)*

Needleloom carpet (aka Needle punch carpet)
Introduced in the 1960s, needleloom carpet is a non-woven **felted** floor-covering, whereby the webs of felted fibres are laid in a closely packed manner on a backing of **hessian**, which is then compacted into a thick layer. This is achieved by using penetrating barbed needles through a mat of fibres on either side of a backing layer of **scrim** or similar. The needles push and pull fibres very densely to create a tightly packed surface, which is then shorn level. The carpet is backed with **latex** or **foam** rubber. Wilson suggests that they would last five to seven years under average domestic conditions (1960).

Needlepoint
A generic term used in America for all types of **embroidery** worked on **canvas**.
See also **Lace**.

Needle punch carpet
See **Needleloom carpet**.

Needlework
The employment of needles and threads to decorate fabrics has a very long history. It is an ancient art that was developed in the Near East and later in China. Needlework is, simply, stitched patterns using threads of **cotton**, **wool**, **linen**, **silk** wire, etc. passed through a woven or **felt** fabric. However, this belies the enormous range of possibilities that lie within the remit of needlework. There are over 300 stitch types that fall into three main categories: flat stitches that lie on the surface without knots or loops, e.g. satin stitch, cross-stitch, herringbone stitch; linked or chain stitches that make a surface loop; buttonhole stitches and knot stitches that produce knots on the surface. The combination of these stitches with vast repertories of designs, as well as a wide range of materials to work with, shows the breadth of the topic.

Religious garments were embroidered in Europe from the tenth century and the practice was soon developed to decorate bed hangings, **wall hangings** and **upholstery**. It was from the fifteenth century that needlework became important for interiors and first manifested itself in the decoration of beds (see **Bed furniture**). Needlework or **canvas work** has been applied to and for the enrichment of beds, caskets, chairs, stools, mirrors, wall hangings, **cushions**, **valances** and upholstery covers. It has been used in panels as a substitute for tapestries, for woven carpets or **tablecloths**.

While the trade of embroiderer undertook professional work, it was often the amateurs, usually women, who took it upon themselves to decorate domestic furnishings. Roger North describes a visit to Beaufort in the seventeenth century and noted that 'the ordinary pastimes of the ladies was in a gallery on the other side where she [the Duchess] had divers gentlewomen commonly at work upon embroidery and fringe making for all the beds of state that were made and finished in the house' (Clabburn, 1976, p.208).

85. Embroiderers at work (D. Diderot, Encyclopédie, *1751–72)*

See also **Appliqué**, **Bargello**, **Beadwork**, **Berlin wool-work**, **Black work**, **Candlewicking**, **Chenille**, **Couching**, **Crewel and crewelwork**, **Embroidery**, **Knotted work**, **Needlepoint**, **Needlework carpet**, **Needlework seat**, **Pane**, **Patchwork**, **Petit-point**, **Purl**, **Quilting**, **Stitch**, **Stumpwork**, **Turkey work**.

FURTHER READING
Bridgeman, H. & Drury, E. (1978). *Needlework: An Illustrated History*, London: Paddington Press.
Clabburn, P. (1976). *Needleworker's Dictionary*, London: Macmillan.
Digby, G.W. (1963). *Elizabethan Embroidery*, London: Faber.
Dillmont, T. [1891]. *The Complete Encyclopaedia of Needlework*, Mulhouse: Dornach, reprinted 1978, Philadelphia: Running Press.
Glaister, E. (1880). *Needlework*, London: Macmillan.
Harbeson, G. (1938). *American Needlework. The History of Decorative Stitching and Embroidery*, New York: Coward-McCann.
Hughes, T. (1961). *English Domestic Needlework 1660–1860*, London: Lutterworth Press.
Jourdain, M. (1910). *English Secular Embroidery*, London: Paul Trench Trubner.
King, D. & Levey, S. (1993). *Embroidery in Britain from 1200–1750*, London: Victoria and Albert Museum Textile Collection.

Levey, S.M. (1998). *An Elizabethan Inheritance: The Hardwick Textiles*, London: National Trust.
Morris, B. (1962). *Victorian Embroidery*, London: Jenkins.
Staniland, K. (1991). *Medieval Craftsmen: Embroiderers*, London: British Museum.

Needlework carpet
A carpet with a **canvas** ground decorated with cross-stitch or tent stitch using **wool** yarns or, on occasion, **silks**. Usually an amateur product, the designs were based on Turkish carpets in the sixteenth and seventeenth centuries but, in the eighteenth century, floral designs were more popular.

The designs were often prepared and marked out on canvas, which was subsequently sold with the required woollen yarns to be made up at home. In 1543, the Earl of Rutland inventory listed 'five long table carpets of Turkey making … and two of needlework made for cupboards' (Clabburn, 1988, p.190). The 1588 Kenilworth Castle inventory listed 'a carpet of needlework of sundry coloured silks, the ground sad green, with a border of roses and sundry posies about it, the ground of the borders orange tawnie, six yards long, 1¾ wide' (Halliwell, 1854). Their use on tables was typical. The 1601 inventory of Hardwick Hall had 'another fayre long carpet for it [a long white table of white wood] of silk needlework with gold fringe lined with crimson taffetie sarcenet' (Boynton, 1971, p.24). The 1611 Hatfield inventory also listed 'One ritch needle worke carpet wrought with silk and silver lined with green taffata with green fringe' (Beard, 1997, p.286).

The Yorkshire retailers and furniture-makers, Wright and Elwick, advertised in 1748 that Mr Wright 'draws for all sorts of needle work for carpets, beds, chairs, fire screens etc, furnishes ladies with painted patterns and shades of silk, and worsted for such works in the best and cheapest manner' (Gilbert, 1976, p.46).

It is clear that women undertook the work at home on occasion. Mrs Delany wrote to her sister: 'My candlelight work is finishing a carpet in double cross stitch, on very coarse canvas, to go round my bed.' (III, p.176.)

Needlework **borders** were sometimes added to lesser quality carpeting and even **drugget**. Temple Newsam had 'a green serge carpet with a needle worked border lined' in the Picture Gallery (Gilbert, Lomax & Wells-Cole, 1987, p.48).

Berlin wool-work carpets using tent or cross-stitch with imported designs and yarns were introduced in the early Victorian era.
See also **Needlework**, **Stitch**.

FURTHER READING
Gilbert, C., Lomax, J. & Wells-Cole, A. (1987). *Country House Floors*, Leeds: Leeds City Art Galleries, pp 44–8.
Keyes, H.E. (1926). 'A note on embroidered carpets', *Antiques*, 26, June, pp 398–402.
Mayorcas, M.J. (1963). *English Needlework Carpets, 16th to 19th Centuries*, Leigh-on-Sea: F. Lewis.

Needlework seating
Embroidery is a term that refers to the processes and methods of applying decorative needlework to a textile ground or **animal skin** by an embroiderer. The range of threads, **stitches** and patterns is very wide and the processes have a 4,000-year history. Embroidery was initially used in furniture work for portable items such as **table covers**, **cushion** and **pillowcases**. As embroidery is an embellishing process, which increases the luxuriousness of the work, it is not surprising that it was highly valued, and when showing signs of wear would be reused in other situations. **Appliqué** was one of the early uses for re-working valuable embroidery.

87. Early eighteenth-century wing chair with needlework (Mallett and Co)

The 1547 Henry VIII's inventory of goods at Hampton Court included: 'One chair of wood covered with murray velvet all over embroidered with Venice gold having the King's armes crowned holded by his Majesties Beasts with back fringed with Venice gold and silk with pommels of silver and gilt' (Edwards, 1964, p.116).

In the sixteenth century, **black work** was popular but, by the beginning of the seventeenth century, **crewel** embroideries were most frequently encountered. An example from Hardwick Hall (1601) gives an indication of quality: 'a tester bed head and double vallans of black velvet imbrodered with silver gold and pearle with sivines and woodbines fringed with golde silver and black silk' (Boynton, 1971, p.24). The range of stitches used and types of work produced in the seventeenth century are indicated in the following lines:

> For Tente-worke, Rais'd-worke, Laid'-work, Frost-worke, Net-worke
> Most curious Purles, or rare Italian cutworke
> Fine Ferne-stitch, Finny-stitch, New-stitch and Chain stitch,
> Braue Bred-stitch, Fisher-stitch, Irish-stitch, and Queen stitch,
> The Spanish-stitch, Rosemary-stitch and Mowse-stitch,
> The smarting Whip-stitch. Back-stitch and the Crosse-stitch,
> All these are good and we must allow
> And these are everywhere in practice now.
> (John Taylor, *The Needle's Excellency*, 1631.)

By the seventeenth century, **wool** needlework on **canvas** had become the fashion and it was often seen as a woman's duty to supply needlework for chairs, either for upholstered seats and backs or for drop-in seats. During the eighteenth century, ready-made kits were available for this purpose. Saint-Aubin mentions that 'some merchants in shops selling chairs and sofas have canvas on hand on which shaded designs are already embroidered. Only the background remains to be filled in to amuse those who do not wish to expend much effort.' (Saint-Aubin, 1770.) In Bath, during 1727, for example, 'the Matrons of the City, their daughters and their maids [were] flowering the [coarse fustian] with Worsted, during the intervals between the Seasons to give the Beds a gaudy Look' (Ayres, 1981, p.24).

During the eighteenth century, embroidery and needlework were variously used for **upholstery** and bed hangings, including some imported embroidery from India and the Far East (e.g. the 1720 State bed, Erthig). Embroidering naturalistic flower motifs on plain **satin** grounds in the later eighteenth century was popular for **bed furniture**, or for occasional pieces such as pole **screens**. In the early nineteenth century, a taste for embroidery in satin stitch with coloured **silks** or metal thread for the backs of sofas and loose cushions was evident. The work was carried out on **velvet** or plain silk, often in classical motifs.

In the nineteenth century, **Berlin wool-work** was introduced and, from the mid-nineteenth century, revivals of traditional methods were encouraged. Embroidery returned to favour with a wide range of designs, methods and techniques being introduced or re-introduced as 'work for ladies', or as examples of Arts and Crafts' philosophy.
See also **Needlework**.

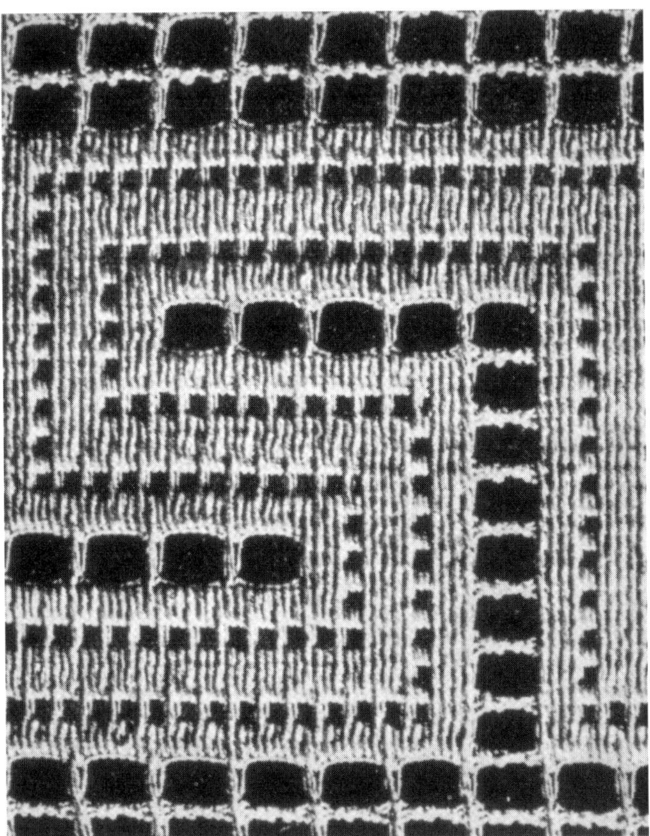

89. Detail of net construction (T. French and Co, The Book of Soft Furnishing, *1937)*

88. Fancy lace net examples (G.L. Hunter, Decorative Textiles, Coverings for Furniture etc., *1918)*

Net

A textile with an open weave made from thread, **twine**, yarn or **cord** of many fibres and yarns (including **silk**, **rayon**, **cotton**, synthetics and particularly **nylon**), but usually forming geometric-shaped meshes of different sizes and weights, which may be hand- or machine-made. The knotting technique is the basis of the product and net is characterised by being a simple mesh joined by knots. Net has been used as a curtain fabric, as a component in **bed furniture** and as a part of **trimmings**. It may be used to make various items such as veils and trimmings on clothing and furnishings, or for utilitarian purposes such as fishnets, insect repellent, etc. It forms the foundation for a great variety of **laces**, curtains, fancy **pillows** and trims. In cotton, some is used for **mosquito netting** and screening.

The 1611 Hatfield inventory has 'one old border of network to hang over the wainscot' (Beard, 1997, p.286). The 1641 Tart Hall inventory noted 'the curtaynes are lined with network and edged about with a silk and gold fringe, bottones and loopes' (Cust, 1911).

Net **fringes** were employed for curtains and **counterpanes** from early in the nineteenth century. Discussing **half curtains**, *The Workwoman's Guide* said 'curtains are sometimes knot [sic] of net of cotton; they look very neat and pretty, and are besides very durable' (Hale, 1840, p.205). Netting was also widely used for the tops of fringes in the early nineteenth century. In 1887, Caulfeild & Saward commented, 'Netting has always been practised for useful purposes, and sixty years [1820s] ago was much worked for curtains, window blinds, and drawing room covers either in darned or plain netting.' (p.356.)

During the 1930s, panel curtains were made from net with a lace **border** and/or insertions. These were made to fit each window exactly and were hung straight across without any fullness, so they remained fixed in this position.
See also **Bobbin net**, **Crepine**, **Filet net**, **Lace**, **Marquisette**, **Mosquito netting**.

Ninon
Originally, an early twentieth-century all-**silk**, plain, open mesh fabric, made of low denier raw silk that was fairly crisp, and heavier than **chiffon**. It has subsequently been made from synthetic fibre yarns. The **warp** yarns are often grouped in pairs. It is like **voile**, but has more body, and has been used as a 'sheer' for **curtains**. Smithells (1950) recommend it for curtains or bed and dressing table **trimmings**. In the USA, it was defined as generally a cellulose acetate **rayon** plain-weave cloth in a range of colours or self-patterned, but with variations. It was used as a **glass curtain** in place of silk **gauze**.

None-so-Pretty
A small figured **braid**, **tape** or ribbon used on **upholstery** in the eighteenth century. The London cabinet-maker, Samuel Norman, had in stock '12 pieces of nonsopretty' in 1764 (Kirkham, 1969, p.509). The colour matching of these tapes to furniture coverings was required in some cases. In 1772, an advertisement in the *Boston Evening Post* offered for sale 'blue and white, red and white, green and white furniture checks with None-so-Prettys to match' (Jackson in Cooke [ed.], 1987, pp 141–2). In an early nineteenth-century work, *Treatise on Haberdashery*, the following **binding** was listed: 'Diamond binding, otherwise None-so-Pretty' (Perkins, 1833).

Norman cloth
Cotton taffeta woven with tiny relief figures formed by floating the **wefts** (Hunter, 1918, p.357).

Norwich damask
See **Damask**.

Norwich stuff
A name for worsted cloths, and others, made in East Anglia and sold through the city of Norwich.
See also **Barracan**, **Bed cloth**, **Blanket**, **Bombasine**, **Brocatelle**, **Caffoy**, **Calimanco**, **Camlet**, **Challis**, **Cheney**, **Damask**, **Dornix**, **Fustian**, **Harrateen**, **Mockado**, **Mohair**, **Russell**, **Tammy**, **Worsted**.

FURTHER READING

Priestley, U. (*c.*1990). *The Fabric of Stuffs: the Norwich Textile Industry from 1565*, Norwich: University of East Anglia, Centre of East Anglian Studies.
Priestley, U. (1991). 'The marketing of Norwich stuffs, *c.*1660–1730' (with appendix), *Textile History*, 22, pp 193–209.

Norwich work
As English 'turkey work' was a speciality of Norwich, its name soon became a synonym of this type of work. In the 1588 Kenilworth inventory, there is a 'turquoy carpette of Norwiche work' (Halliwell, 1854, p.147). A little later, the 1611 Hatfield inventory had 'I longe Norwich carpet lined with buckrom' (Beard, 1997, p.285).
See also **Turkey work**.

Nottingham lace
See **Lace: Nottingham**.

Numdah rug
An Anglo-Indian name for a kind of **felted** or pounded goat **hair** or coarse **woollen** cloth that is decorated with **embroidery**. They seem to have been used from the 1870s as floor **rugs**. The name also refers to saddlecloths or pads made of this material. The name is derived from the Urdu *namda*, itself coming from the Persian *namad*, meaning '**carpet**' or 'rug'. They have been used for rugs in areas of light wear in Europe and the USA.

The 1907 catalogue of the London Army & Navy Stores listed for sale 'embroidered numdah rugs 4' 6" x 7'. Rutt considered that: 'Those with dark backgrounds may be used as floor rugs; those with light backgrounds make effective wall hangings. Because of their bold design and color, these rugs are likely to prove to be the center of interest in rooms where they are used' (1935). In 1936, Denny defined the numdah as a 'felt rug made in India of goat's hair and embroidered with coloured wool yarns in chain **stitch**. Commercial rugs lacked the artistic merit of fine old pieces.' (1936, p.49.) In 1955, the definition still reflected the early descriptions. The rugs were 'embroidered flat rugs, usually of goat hair, with an admixture of cotton. The designs, worked in worsted yarn, are hand-embroidered in Cashmire. The ground is usually a natural shade, but rugs are sometimes made with coloured grounds' (Sheridan, 1955, p.342). They were fashionable again in the 1960s and 1970s as part of 'ethnic' decorative schemes, as well as for general light use.

Nylon
At one time this was a major synthetic yarn utilised for **carpets** and **upholstery**. Used as filament or as staple yarn it is often blended to give strength to other yarns, especially **wool**. The famous 80 per cent/20 per cent wool-nylon mixture for carpets became something of a hallmark in the latter half of the twentieth century. Nylon was also used widely in fabrics. In 1946, the *Cabinet Maker* journal reported that 'today the [nylon] yarn is slowly being released for weaving into furnishing fabrics' (9 February, p.328).
See also **Net**.

O
An obsolete name for curtain rings. They were made from a variety of materials including horn and wood, but were mainly in brass. Many detailed eighteenth-century bills include 'Oes' listed amongst the sundries used in making up curtains, etc.
See also **Curtain ring**.

Oatmeal cloth
Textured **cotton**, **linen** or **wool** textile with a corrugated face, sometimes used as a foundation for **embroidery**. A thicker variety was used on **upholstery** (Caulfeild & Saward, 1887, p.371). Still found in the 1950s.

Oil baize
See **Oilcloth**.

Oilcloth (aka Leathercloth)
From the fourteenth century, cloth treated with oils was made to look like **leather** or similar. Linseed oil and clay fillers were applied and calendered to a base cloth and allowed to dry. The surface was levelled, dried in a heated oven and then rolled. The process was repeated several

times. Rollers applied three or four coats of enamel paint, and grain effects could be applied by the same means. In 1627, I. Wolfer obtained a patent in England for the production of oilcloth (Patent no.40).

The royal use of oilcloth is later recorded in 1677, when John Casbert supplied '4½ yards of green oyled cloth to make 4 curtains and a tester for the Queen's volary' (Beard, 1997, p.291).

In the early nineteenth century, Sheraton particularly noted in reference to protective covers for tables, etc. that 'lately they have introduced a new kind of painted canvas, varnished, and very elastic in its nature, and will probably answer better than leather' (Sheraton, 1803, p.336). This is probably a reference to a contemporary oilcloth.

In 1850, the British firm, Storeys of Lancaster, was making leathercloth for **upholstery** with linseed oil as the main ingredient, and the trade name 'Rexine' was introduced by the British Leathercloth Manufacturing Co. A cloth with a nitro-cellulose base was introduced in the 1850s as imitation leather. This was made from castor oil, cellulose nitrate and colouring matter. In 1856, four further patents were granted for improvements in leathercloth, including Rowley's, which was based on a mix of albumen, china clay and a coating of naphtha solution of gutta-percha (Patent no.1652). By 1884, Storeys of Lancaster manufactured leathercloth using a cellulose nitrate amyl acetate mixture which, when combined with castor oil, gave a degree of flexibility to the material. The American author, Miss Leslie, encouraged the use of oilcloth, as for kitchen floors 'there is no better covering than a coarse stout plain oilcloth, unfigured or all one colour ... as they keep the kitchen as dry and warm as it could be rendered by a woollen carpet; and they have the advantage of collecting and retaining no dust or grease.' (1854, p.183.)

George Cole (1892) described leathercloth as 'a name given in England to a cotton cloth prepared with a glazed and varnished surface to imitate Morocco leather, used for carriage trimming, known in the United States as enamelled or oilcloth'. In the late nineteenth century, it was part of the upholsterers' stock in trade and was widely used for covering dining room and library furniture, especially chairs, tables and desktops. For chair coverings, 'American cloth is treated in a manner similar to leather, and the same allowances for fullness will answer very well.' (*Working Upholsterer*, 1883, p.5.) The American authors, Williams and Jones, writing in *Beautiful Homes* (1878), considered 'the most appropriate chair for the hall... [was one with a] seat of leather, or the Leather Cloth, which Europeans call American Leather Cloth' (Adrosko, 1990, p.109). Caulfeild and Saward succinctly explained the benefits: 'it possesses much elasticity and is sold in black, sky-blue, white, and green, silver and gold' (1887, p.6).

During the early twentieth century, English manufacturers produced versions of 'American cloth' particularly, the trade names being Keratol and Rexine. Similar developments occurred elsewhere with Fabrikoid, by du Pont, becoming a famous American trade name. It has also been known as American cloth, wax cloth, toile cirée and **Lancaster cloth**. In 1928, leathercloth was recorded as 'a substitute for leather made by coating a cotton fabric with a nitro-cellulose preparation and embossing the surface to imitate leather'. Leathercloth was sold under the trade names of Pantasote, Leatherwove, Zapon, etc. By 1937, oil baize, American cloth or Lancaster cloth was popular for 'hangings, blinds, cushions and tablecloths not only in the kitchen, scullery and bathroom windows, but in many modern decorative schemes' (French, 1937, p.144).

Oilcloth was sometimes sold as 'Tablecloth baize', 'oil baize' and 'marble baize'. In 1946, these were all available in reproductions of grains, marbles and coloured effects such as jaspé, tiles and parquetry.

See also **Baize**, **Crumb cloth**, **Floorcloth**, **Morocco cloth**.

FURTHER READING

Brunn, M. (1990). 'Treatment of cellulose nitrate coated upholstery' in Williams, M.A. (ed.), *Upholstery Conservation*, preprints of a symposium held at Colonial Williamsburg, 2–4 February, American Conservation Consortium, East Kingston, NH, pp 449–55.

Christie, G. (1964). *Storeys of Lancaster, 1848–1964*, London: Collins.

Gooderson, P.J. (1996). *Lord Linoleum: Lord Ashton and the Rise of the British Oilcloth and Linoleum Industry*, Keele: Keele University Press.

Meikle, J.L. (1995). 'Presenting a new material: from imitation to innovation with Fabrikoid', *Decorative Arts Society Journal*, 19, pp 8–15.

Neuberger, R. (1934). 'History and development of the leathercloth industry', *Upholstery*, 1, 4, July.

Thorp, V. (1990). 'Imitation leather; structure composition and conservation', *Leather Conservation News*, 6, 2, Spring, pp 7–15.

Seymour, R.B. & Mark, H.F. (eds) (1989). *Organic Coatings: Their Origin and Development*, Proceedings of the International Symposium on the History of Organic Coatings, held 11–15 September 1989, in Miami Beach, Florida, New York: Elsevier.

Oil silk (aka Oiled silk)

A woven **silk** fabric treated with boiled linseed oil so that it may be partly transparent or opaque and waterproof. In 1887, it was apparently used for linings and surgical work. It was 'semi-transparent and may be had in a green or gold colour' (Caulfeild & Saward, p.371). By 1937, oil silk was produced in a wide range of colours, as well as in printed, sprayed stencilled and hand-painted designs. It was used as a hygienic **curtain** material in nurseries, children's playrooms, kitchens and bathrooms in the 1930s–40s (French, 1937, p.144). Thin silk treated with boiled linseed was suggested for shower curtains (Denny, 1942, p.50), but was soon replaced by synthetics.

Ombré

A fabric woven or dyed in a series of colour tones graduating from light to dark and usually producing a striped effect. The coloured or 'shaded' effect was produced in fabrics by laying in **wefts** of shades of the same colour or by the use of yarns printed before weaving. In 1895, ombré was described as 'a cheap grade of silk print' (*Funk's Standard Dictionary*, vol.II, 1227/2). In the 1920s, it was noted that shaded effects on hank **silk** could be obtained by binding the hanks firmly on rods, using only a small amount of dyestuff in the bath.

Organdie (aka Organdy)

A very fine and translucent kind of **silk** or **cotton** plain-weave **muslin** fabric, which is woven with tightly twisted fine yarns with a permanently stiff and crisp finish. The crispness is due to a finish with starch and calendering which washes out, or alternatively a permanent crispness obtained with chemicals (Heberlein process). It wrinkles badly unless given a wrinkle-free finish (Bellmanizing). It may be bleached, dyed, printed, frosted, **flocked**, embroidered or **plisséd**. Some have **lappet**, swivel or flocked designs. By the mid-twentieth century, organdie was recommended for short **curtains** and 'frilly' **trimmings** of all kinds (Smithells, 1950, p.229). It was also used for **bedspreads** and dressing table skirts.

Oriental blind

Exterior window **blinds** made with semi-circular tops but otherwise following the Florentine blind (Hasluck, 1907, pp 113–19).

See also **Florentine blind**.

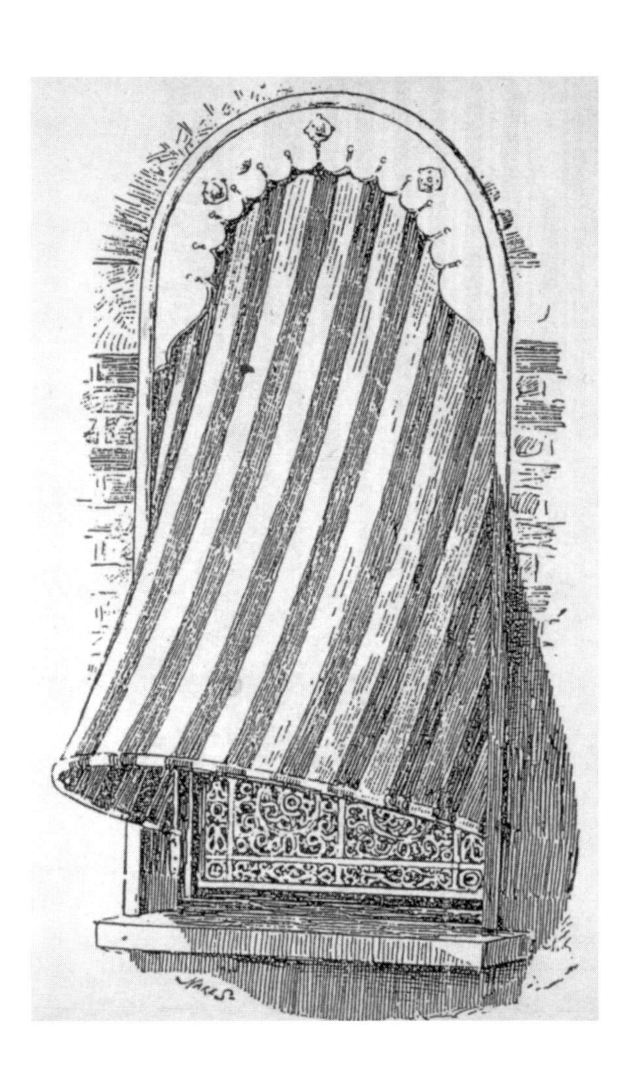

90. Oriental blind with distinctive semi-circular top (P. Hasluck, Window Blinds, *1907)*

Orris (Orrice)

A **braid** or **gimp trimming** that is woven from gold or silver threads in a variety of patterns. This was used in the late seventeenth and early eighteenth centuries for decorative trimmings. By the nineteenth century, it was a general term for all kinds of **galloons** used in **upholstery**. Orris is also a name given to lace of various patterns in gold and silver; or **embroidery** made of gold lace.

Celia Fiennes, writing in 1710, commented upon 'very fine orris hanging in which was much silk and gold and silver'. She also noted that the bed in the Chamber of State, Windsor, was of 'green velvet strip'd down very thick with gold orrice lace of my hands breadth, and round the bottom 3 such orrices and gold fringe all round it and gold tassels, so was the Cornish [cornice]' (1995, p.219).

In 1858, Simmonds defined orris as 'a peculiar pattern, in which gold and silver lace is worked. The edges are ornamented with conical figures placed at equal distances, with spots between them.' By 1882, Beck noted that the term now included a range of upholstery trimmings: 'Orris the name is still in use, but is given a wider application, so as to include nearly every description of upholstery galloons.'

See also **Lace**.

Ostrich feather
See **Feather**.

Osnaburg (aka Oznaburg)
Oznaburg was a coarse **linen** cloth woven in plain-weave in a medium to heavy weight that resembled crash. Its name derives from the town of Oznaburg in Hanover. Osnaburg was characterised by its strength and durability. It has also been used as a base for textile finishers to make up as cretonnes, chintz and crash.

The early use of osnaburg for domestic purposes is shown when, in 1554, 'ic yardes of Ossenbrydge [were supplied] for a towell to the hye tabyll…' (Willis, 1886, vol.III, p.363). By 1582, the *Book of Rates* listed imports of 'Ozenbridge, the c elles' (Willan, 1962, p.44).

More recently, it has been made from part waste **cotton** and may be used in the grey state for **mattress** coverings and base cloths for **linoleum** and artificial **leathers**. It was also used for **drapes** and **upholstery** in the OSA in the 1940s and 1950s (Denny, 1936, p.51). In 1947, it was suggested that the heavier weights could be used for **curtains**, mattress **tickings**, upholstery, **awnings**, etc. (Bendure & Pfieffer, p.643.) In 1950, Smithells still recommended it for curtains and drapes.
See also **Chintz**, **Cretonne**, **Crash**.

Ottoman
A later nineteenth-century furnishing fabric made with prominent transverse ribs. By the mid-twentieth century, it was usually woven with **cotton weft** and **silk** or **rayon warp**, dense enough to cover the weft. It was particularly used for **upholstery** (French, 1937). By the 1970s, it was woven from acetates, viscose or cotton, and was recommended for **curtains**.

Oxford cloth
A basket weave textile that is woven with two fine **warps** and one **weft** yarn, equal in size to the two warps. Coloured yarns may be used to form stripes. It has been used for **drapes**, spreads and dressing table skirts (Bendure & Pfieffer, 1947, p.644).
See also **Weave: Basket**.

Padua say (aka Padua serge)
Serge fabric, originally deemed to have been derived from Padua. It was woven in a twill-weave **wool** or **worsted**-mix cloth, and used for **drapes** and **upholstery** *c.*1670–1740.

Paduasoy (aka Pou de soie, Poudesoy)
Silk fabric woven with a closely corded effect and a **brocaded** decoration, which is usually used for dresses. The name appears to be a combination of Padua, the Italian city, and the French *soie*, meaning 'silk'. Padua has long been home to manufacturers of silk and other textiles. Another origin of the name may be the French for 'skin of silk'. It is a soft, **satin**-faced, good quality cloth, with a dull lustre. It has a grainy appearance, and fine close ribs run in the filling direction. With the best grades, the fabric can be used on either side. Lower qualities are finished on one side only. Because of the crosswise rib, the fabric is difficult to use. It is also sold as 'de-lustered satin'.

In 1694, John Chamberlayne noted that 'We yearly imported from France Silks, Sattins, Taffeta's, Stuffs, Armoysins, Poudesoy's' (*Magnae Brittainiae or the present state of England* vol.I, ch.VII, p.65, *OED*). In editions after 1716, it was spelt as Paduasoys. In 1765, Deborah Franklin wrote that she had seen dining chairs in Philadelphia covered in 'plain horsehair, and look as well as Paddozway' (Montgomery, 1984, p.255).

Poult-de-soie is the modern name for this fabric.

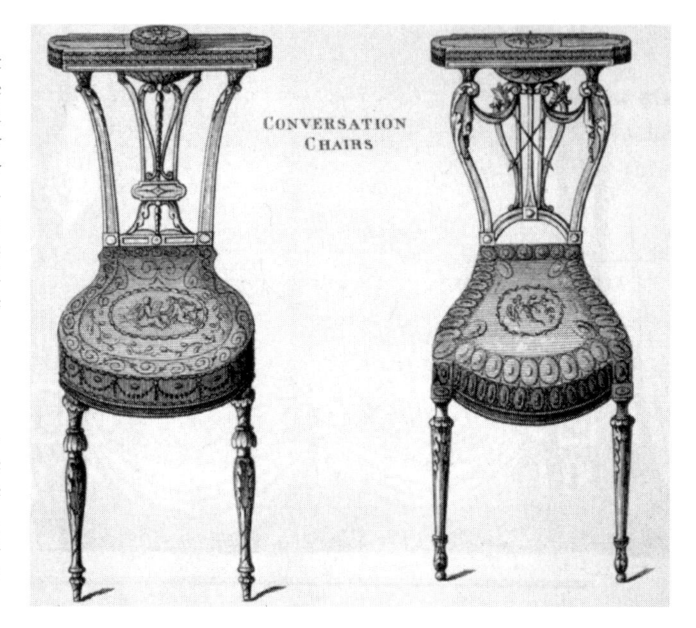

91. Design for a chair with painted silk panels (T. Sheraton, The Cabinet Maker and Upholsterer's Drawing Book, *1793)*

Padded brick

House bricks were an unlikely part of the furnishings of the interior but the author of *The Workwoman's Guide* employed them for forming the base of a hassock. She said 'This is made of two or four bricks tied firmly together, wrapped around with strong sacking, and then neatly covered with cloth and if not in good shape a little extra stuffing may be added.' (Hale, 1840, p.207.) Other uses included padding and covering them in a **wool** or **cotton** cloth, for doorstops. Catherine Beecher, in her *The Treatise on Domestic Economy*, suggested that 'blocks or bricks [covered] with carpeting like that of the room, [could be put] behind tables, doors etc. to preserve the wall from injury by knocking or by the dusting cloth (1846).

See also **Hassock**.

Paillasson rug

A sixteenth-century term for a **straw mat** or **rug** that provided insulation at doors and windows. In the nineteenth century, these mats were used by the French military as a base for bedding. In 1862, they were described as a 'straw mat, about six feet long and eighteen inches wide, narrower at the feet than the head' (Byrne, p.164). Later practice varied and the name was sometimes used as a general term for floorcoverings (*The Mercury Dictionary of Textile Terms*, 1950).

See also **Matting**.

Painted cloth

A relatively inexpensive product that imitated **tapestry** and was hung in a similar way. Members of the Painters' and Stainers' Company produced these painted decorations, working on a base of brown **hemp** cloth or **linen osnaburg**. They appear to have been relatively common in fifteenth- and sixteenth-century England. In 1558, a French visitor noted that 'The English make such use of tapestries of painted cloths [*tapisseries de toiles pinctes*] which are very well executed … for there are few houses you could enter without finding these tapestries' (Wells-Cole, 1997, pp 275–6). This comment seems to be confirmed by William Harrison, writing in 1577, who noted that 'the walls of our houses in the inner sides in like sort be either hanged with tapestry, arras work or painted cloths, wherein either diverse histories, or herbs, beasts, knots and suchlike are stained' (1577, p.197). They were also imported, as confirmed by the *Book of Rates* for 1582, 'painted clothes the dozen' (Willan, 1962, p.45). They appear to have been used for beds as well as for wall decoration. In 1590, Ipswich resident, John Cumberland, had 'I old posted bed with a testor of stayned work' (Reed, 1981, p.76).

The 1601 Hardwick Hall inventory of the High Great Chamber listed 'another sute of hangings for the same chamber being eight peeces of woollen cloth stayned [painted] with fret and storie and silk flowers' (Boynton, 1971, p.27). In the same year, it was commented that the 'painting of cloths is decayed and not a hundred yards of new painted cloth made in a years here [England] by reason of so much painted Flanders pieces brought from thence' (King in Edwards Ralph & Ramsey [eds], 1958, p.172).

See also **Canvas**, **Stained cloth**, **Wall covering and hanging**.

FURTHER READING

Baker, O. (1937). *In Shakespeare's Warwickshire*, Chapter 5, 'Stained Cloths', London: Simpkins Marshall.

Maunder, N. (1997). 'Painted cloths: history, craftsmen and techniques', *Textile History*, 28, pp 119–48.

Painted satin

See **Satin**.

Painted shades

See **Blind: Transparent/Painted**, **Roller blind**.

Painted silk

Originally an imported fabric used for furnishings, it was later an **upholstery** fabric, popular in England particularly between 1790 and 1810. In both cases, a delicate effect was achieved by using watercolour paints on a plain **silk** fabric. They were usually made into panels for chair seats and backs, or for small furniture items such as **fire screens**. An early example is a set of bed hangings from Raby Castle that appear to date from 1730.

Hepplewhite suggested that medallions of printed or painted silk might be used for circular-backed chairs (1794, p.3), and Sheraton noted painted silks in his *Cabinet Marker and Upholsterer's Drawing Book* (1791–4), particularly describing the 'printed and painted silks executed of late by Mr Eckhardt, at his manufactory in Chelsea'. Around 1793, Eckhardt and Co had established a 'Royal patent manufactory of painted silk, varnished linen cloth, paper, etc' in London and, in 1798, Francis and George Eckhardt patented various processes for this technique (Patent no.2208).

In 1825, William Trotter invoiced Lord Gray at Kinfauns Castle, Perthshire, for 'Cutting out and making a set of curtains of rich Chinese painted silk lined with green persian with outside cut out valens of same painted silk and inside valens of green sarcenet lined with buckram and green calico bound with Paris lace and finished with chintz fringe.' (Jones, 1997, p.248.)

Painted taffeta

Decorative designs were painted upon **taffeta** cloth and used for furnishings. The Duchess's dining room at Woburn had 'the chairs and sofas of painted taffeta' when Arthur Young visited in 1768 (Young, 1770, p.29). Chinese painted **silk** taffeta, known as pékin, was used in France during the eighteenth century. Mme de Pompadour's 'Bellevue' had furnishings of pékin in a range of colours.

See also **Pékin**, **Painted silk**, **Printed silk**.

Painted velvet

Painted velvet was a fashionable **upholstery** cover in the early nineteenth century. The practice of painting velvet has been called 'theorem painting', where the theorem is a stencil and the paint is made from watercolour and gum arabic. Ackermann illustrated a 'Dress Sofa' (January 1821, plate 9), which was designed to have a printed white velvet covering. A little later, Nathaniel Whittock considered 'the downy surface of the velvet and the brilliancy of the liquid colours used to produce fruit and flowers, [gave] it a decided superiority over any other kind of flower painting, for ornamenting bell ropes, ottomans &c' (Whittock, 1827).

It was evident that painting on velvet was very much a pastime for women to provide decoration for the home. *The Elegant Arts for Ladies* (*c.*1856) suggested that stencilled designs on velvet would 'look very handsome [on] music stools, the front of pianos, ottomans, banner screens, pole-screens and borders for tablecloths' (Hodges, 1989, p.23).

See also **Velvet**.

FURTHER READING

Whittock, N. (1829). *The Art of Drawing and Colouring Flowers Fruits and Shells ... Painting on Velvet*, London: Isaac Taylor Hinton.

Palampore

A palampore was a single panel of mordant-painted, resist-dyed Indian **cotton** (**chintz**). It was similar to pintado, but differing in respect of pintado being a length of fabric, and the palampore being generally used as a bedcover. The name has a confused derivation according to the *OED*. Yule (1903) says it is 'a kind of chintz bed-cover, sometimes made of beautiful patterns, formerly made at various places in India, especially at Sadras and Masulipatam, the importation of which into Europe has become quite obsolete, but under the greater appreciation of Indian manufactures has recently shown some tendency to revive'. He suggests an etymology as a corruption of hybrid Hindu and Persian to make *palangposh*, meaning 'bedcover'; which occurs as *palangapuze* in an Indo-Portuguese dictionary of 1727. However, Mr Pringle (*Madras Selections*, series IV, p.71, cited in Yule, 1903, p.663) suggests a derivation from Palanpur in Gujarat, which seems to have been an emporium for the manufacturers of north India.

Introduced to England in *c.*1614, and often made into **quilts**, palampores became increasingly popular during the seventeenth century. They were also used in America during the eighteenth century. Their success is seen in the letter of 1687, where the East India Co wrote to its officers in Bombay: 'Send no more quilts of any sort we have enough to last five or six years being put quite out of use by Palampores' (Irwin & Brett, 1970, p.27).

In 1880, Birdwood, writing on Indian arts, still applauded 'the celebrated palampores, or bed-covers of Masulipatam which in point of art decoration are simply incomparable' (1880, vol.II, p.98).

See also **Pencil**, **Pintado**.

FURTHER READING

Eaton, L. (2002). 'Winterthur's hand-painted Indian export cottons', *The Magazine Antiques*, 161, January, pp 170–75.

Palliasse

A mattress or bed support made from **straw**. The name is derived from the French *paille*, meaning 'straw'. The best palliasses were made from wheat straw. However, the term palliasse is often applied to an under mattress stuffed with substances other than straw. Whatever the filling, the palliasse was the base of a mattress system on which lay the **feather** bed and other bedding. Early references imply that the palliasse was not the most comfortable bedding. In 1577, William Harrison empathised with servants who did not have an under sheet on their bed 'to keep them from the pricking straws that ran oft through the canvas [of the palliasse] and raised their hardened hides' (p.201).

Bimont, who particularly noted the use of straw as a filling for palliasses, described their making, which might have alleviated some of the problems mentioned above. He said that the straw should be arranged evenly by hand, then compacted to create an edge, and finally stitched (1770, p.49). Indeed, this remained the basis of palliasse or straw mattress-making.

Sheraton noted that 'The palliasse is an inflexible mattress stuffed with drawn wheat straw, placed as the lower layer of bedding, for the purpose of raising it, and giving a more agreeable basis to the featherbed.' (1803.)

Instructions in an early twentieth-century manual reflect the eighteenth-century practices. To achieve a satisfactory product, a complicated process of making required that the straw was all running the same way in the mattress (see Bimont above). This required the palliasse **ticking** to be suspended in a frame so that the maker could ram straw into the case and pack it down. When this was finished, the case could be sewn and tufted in the manner of a mattress (Bitmead, 1912, p.23).

See also **Mattress, Mattress-making**.

Palm Beach

A fabric with **cotton warp** and **mohair weft**. It was used for men's tropical wears but also apparently made excellent **curtains** and covers (French, 1947).

Pane

A name for panes, widths or sections of fabric. The word is derived from the Latin *pannus*, meaning 'a piece of cloth'. Panes also refer to strips of cloth to be joined or **appliquéd** to other textiles. Thirdly, the word has been used as an abbreviation for **counterpane**.

In furnishing use, pane refers to widths of fabric of varying colours, and weaves joined together or applied over another cloth in such a way as to create a framed effect, often to fit walls, but also for **upholstery** coverings. The panes might be narrow pieces or strips of alternate or different colours (e.g. red and blue); or different materials (e.g. **velvet** and **cloth of gold**); or pieces of the same colour with **lace** or other **trimming** inserted in the seams, or (in later use) strips of the same cloth distinguished by colour or separated by lines of trimming, etc.

Early records note the use of panes on **curtains** and hangings. In the fourteenth century, a literary reference noted that 'her bedding was noble, of cortynes of clene sylk, wyth cler golde hemmez & couertorez ful curious, with comly panez.' (*Sir Gawain & The Green Knight*, line 855.)

The 1480 *Wardrobe Accounts of Edward IV* listed 'iiij costerings of wool paned rede and blue with rooses sonnes and crownes in every pane' (Nicolas, 1830, p.118). In 1509, Edmund Dudley had 'vij paynes of course tapstree werk' in the Great Chamber (Beard, 1997, p.282) and, in 1548, Henry VIII had 'another chamber [that] was hanged with green velvet in the middle of every pane or piece, was a fable of Ovid in Metamorphoses embroidered' (Hall, *Chronicle*, 207 b, *OED*).

Panes became particularly fashionable from the mid-seventeenth century. The inventory of Tart Hall in 1641 had the Great Chamber 'hanged with paned red and yellow damask hangings' (Cust, 1911). In 1679, the Yellow Bedchamber in Ham House had 'hangings of yellow damask fringed, and paned with blew mohair' (Thornton, 1978, p.361).

The term pane also refers to counterpanes for beds. In a 1459 inventory, there are listed 'Item, ij blankettys, j payre of schettys. Item, j rede pane furryd with connyngs' (*Paston Letters*, I, 484, *OED*). Whilst in 1495, there was recorded: 'iij ellis of scarlot to be a pane to the King's bed' (*Accounts Lord High Treasurer of Scotland*, I, 226, *OED*).

Panne velvet

See **Velvet: Panne**.

Pante

The base cloths or lower **valances** of a bed particularly found in the sixteenth and seventeenth centuries. In the 1601 Hardwick Hall inventory, there were 'pantes to go about the sides of the bed at the bottom of cloth of gold and crimson velvet, fringed with black and yellow silk fringe' (Boynton, 1971, p.23). In the 1653 inventory of Cardinal Mazarin's possessions, there was '*Un tapis de table de velours vert, tout uny àquatre pantes, garni de frange d'or et d'argent par le bas des pantes*' (*Inventaire de tous les meubles de Cardinal Mazarin*, 1861, London: Whittingham and Wilkins).

Paper carpet

The desire for an inexpensive but effective floorcovering that would imitate **floorcloth** was answered by the development of paper carpet. In this way, prepared, painted and varnished paper was introduced as a substitute for floorcloth.

In 1806 and 1810, American artist and inventor, Francis Guy of Baltimore, patented paper carpeting. A little later, in 1822, the *National Standard*, published in Middlebury, Vermont, explained that a substitute for floorcloth had been invented in Philadelphia:

> It is called "prepared varnished paper" and when finished has the appearance of the best and most elegant oilcloth. A pattern for an ordinary room which would take $50 worth of oil cloth may be covered by this material for $12.50 – and at the end of five years you can lay down a new pattern for the interest of the sum which the oilcloth cost. It is cool and very pleasant and will wear handsomely for five years at least. (Winkler & Moss, 1986, p.28.)

Although probably American in origin, the English author, Loudon, described a homemade version of paper carpet made by 'cutting out and sewing together pieces of linen, cotton, Scotch gauze, canvas, or any similar material &c', sizing it as necessary 'and carefully pasting it round the margins so as to keep it strained flat... When the cloth thus fixed is dry, lay on it two or more coats of strong paper, breaking joints, and finish with coloured or hanging paper, according to fancy.' (Loudon, 1839, pp 345–6.)

Fifty years later, a similar idea was advocated. Harriet Spofford, in her *Art Decoration*, recommended householders to build up their own paper carpet using layers of newspaper covered with a thick paste and finished with a layer of wallpaper. The whole carpet was then sized with glue and varnished (1878, p.173). In the same year, *Beautiful Homes* offered a different method that entailed fixing **muslin** on the floor and thoroughly pasting it, then applying layers of wallpaper in patterns as required. When dry, it was to be varnished with two coats of shellac followed by two coats of copal varnish (Williams & Jones, 1878, p.19).

Cole noted another version whereby the paper carpet was made from a product called 'hession' [sic] in which the paper pulp was subjected to the 'action of chloride of zinc and heavy pressure which made it hard and tough like leather' (1892, p.64).

Paper curtain

See **Wallpaper curtain**.

Paragon

From the French *barracan*, paragon is a **worsted** fabric, ribbed, printed or watered, used for hangings and **upholstery** from the seventeenth century to the mid-eighteenth century. It can also be described as a double camlet. It was well known by the early seventeenth century. In 1618, the Naworth Household Books recorded '74, xij yards of water paragon for my Lady at vs. viijd. 5 yards of French green paragon xxvs– xd' (*OED*). The *London Gazette* advertised 'hangings for a room of green paragon' in 1674 (no.852/4), and in a bill to Edward Sackville from Pat Barrett, submitted in 1675, there was an item: 'For one sute of hangings of French yellow paragon for your dining room printed with roman statuaries and other ornaments containing 46 yards of paragon at 4s per yd' (Beard, 1997, p.294). In 1684, 'his Grace's dressing room' in Dublin Castle had **curtains** of yellow paragon with **squab cushions** of yellow **damask** covered with paragon protective covers (Clabburn, 1988, p.251). Then in 1693, William Lash of Suffolk County (America) had 'Parragon curtains and vallaines and bedstead and curtain rods and testercloath' (Montgomery, 1984, p.317).

In 1703, a striped **velvet** and **silk**-lined bed in Dyrham Park had **case curtains** of worsted paragon to protect it. It was generally out of use by the mid-eighteenth century, being usurped by **harrateen**, **moreen** and damask.

See also **Barracan**, **Camlet**, **Wall covering and hanging**.

Passementerie (aka Passemaine)

The decorative **trimmings** associated with soft furnishings and **upholstery**, passementeries were originally formed from the tying off of **warp** ends of finished woven cloth. The fringes were knotted into patterns and it was soon clear that this decorative finish could be made to stand alone on its own heading. It also had practical applications as it could disguise joins in narrow fabric, creating a panelled effect.

The manufacture of passementeries was based on three stages: spinning, weaving and decorating. Spinning involves twisting yarns into stiff gimps or plied cords. The core of the trimming is made and then covered with coloured yarns. A large wheel works this process together with a tensioned bar which allows the threads to tighten and shorten as the wheel is turned. The weaving process can be simply a two-treadle loom. The warp forms the top of the fringe while the **weft** can be pulled out to the required length of fringe. The bullion fringe has an additional twist inserted by the spinner so that it plies up the warp. A cut fringe is

92. Passementerie: smoking the finished braids to lustre the gold content (D. Diderot, Encyclopédie, 1751–72)

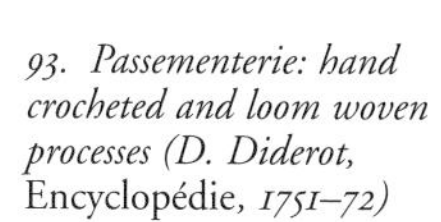

93. Passementerie: hand crocheted and loom woven processes (D. Diderot, Encyclopédie, *1751–72)*

made similarly, but without the extra twist. It is then cut following removal from the loom. Complicated designs can be made with 20 or more treadles for warp operation. Gimped braids have a metal rod parallel with the warps so that the gimp can be twisted round them to make projections at the sides. Any other decoration can then be sewn in.

Introduced into France from Italy where they had been used on hangings in the Renaissance, they soon became a speciality of French weavers. Its early use in upholstery work is confirmed by Elizabethan inventories that often list passamaine **lace** of gold. The choice was quite wide early on. For example, the *Tudor Book of Rates* for 1582 listed:

> Passemin lace of Cruell the dosen
> Passemin lace of golde or silver the pound containing twelve ounces
> Passemin lace of silk the groce containing twelve dosen
> Passemin lace of silk and thred the groce
> Passemin lace of thred called Cantlet of thred the groce [pearled?]
> Passemin lace look pomet lace. (Willan, 1962, p.45)

A fine example of passementerie is in the 1601 Hardwick inventory: 'Five curtains of black and white damask layde about with gold lace and gold fringe, and gold lace down the middle' (Boynton, 1971, p.24).

In the eighteenth century, specialist 'lace men' sold passementeries. The *London Tradesman* defined this trader as one who sold 'all sorts of gold and silver lace, gold and silver buttons, shapes for waistcoats, lace and networks for robeings and women's petticoats, fringes, bugles, spangles, plates for embroidery and orrice, and bone-lace weavers, gold and silver wire, purle, slesy, twist etc' (Campbell, 1747, p.147). Styles of passementeries followed the vagaries of fashion but remained an integral part of the upholsterers' and decorators' repertoire. However, it was commercially acknowledged as a speciality of France. Diderot's *Encyclopédie* (in Gillespie, 1959, pp 116–19) illustrates the special looms, including the various wheels and bobbins necessary.

In the early nineteenth century, trimmings were important but could be quite delicate and refined. By the mid-nineteenth century, there was an elaboration of trimmings for both **drapery** and upholstery, upon which some reformers voiced opinions. By the early twentieth century, trimmings were becoming more limited in use, and designs were generally simpler. By the late twentieth century, apart from period revivals and country house styles, trimmings were not generally employed.

See also **Bow and band**, **Braid**, **Cord**, **Fringe**, **Galloon**, **Gimp**, **Guard lace**, **Piping**, **Purl**, **Tape**, **Tassel**, **Tufting**.

FURTHER READING

Boudet, P. & Gomond, B. (1981). *Le passementerie*, Paris: Dessain and Tosca.

Donzel, C. & Sabine, M. (1992). *L'Art de passementerie, et sa contribution à l'historie de la mode et de la décoration*, Paris: Chêne.

Cornforth, J. & Fowler, J. (1974). *English Decoration in the Eighteenth Century*, London: Barrie and Jenkins.

Gasc, N. (1973). *Des dorelotiers aux passementiers*, exh. cat., Paris: Musée des Arts Décoratifs.

Heutte, R. (1972). *Le livre de la passementerie*, Paris: Dourdon.

Hogarth, S.D. (1997). 'Goldlace to girthwebs – the evolution of a trade in York', *Textile History*, 28, Autumn, pp 185–200.

Jackson, L.W. (1987). 'Beyond the fringe: ornamental upholstery trimmings in the 17th, 18th and early 19th centuries' in Cooke, E.S. (ed.), *Upholstery in America and Europe From the Seventeenth Century to World War I*, New York: Norton, pp 131–48.

Levey, S.M. (1983). *Lace, a Visual History*, London: Victoria and Albert Museum.

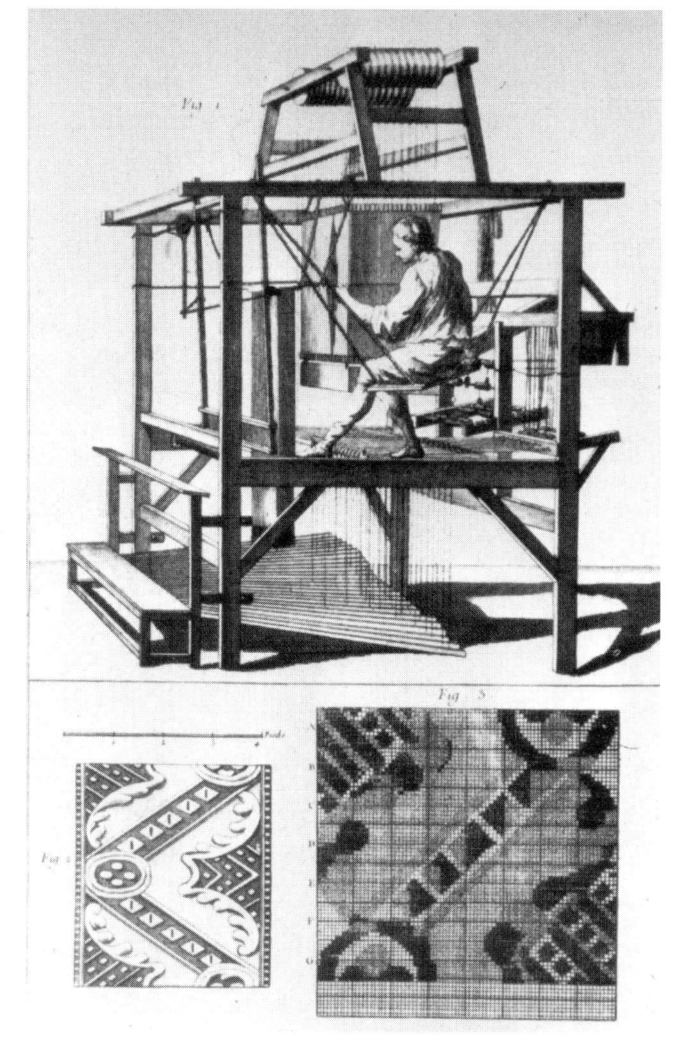

94. Passementerie loom and pattern (D. Diderot, Encyclopédie, *1751–72)*

Patch
Patch was another name for chintz-type cloth with 'a plain field of either white, red or blue or maroon, plain borders and wide cross borders' (Irwin & Schwartz, 1966). It was used for **curtains** and furniture coverings. Advertised as 'Indian patches' in 1736 in the *Boston News Letter* (Cummings, 1961, p.33), they are also found in nineteenth-century inventories. Patch was defined in an 1860 dictionary as a 'kind of printed and glazed cotton used for curtains, covering furniture etc' (Worcester, 1860).
See also **Chintz**.

Patchwork
A sewing technique which uses a large number of small shaped pieces of cloth that are stitched together to make patterns. It is used for covers, **cushions** and **quilts** and may be applied or pieced, but is particularly associated with bed quilts.

Patchwork is often associated with domestic sewing and economy. Although probably of early origin, patchwork developed in the eighteenth century. Swift, in his 'Directions to the Waiting Maid', said: 'Two accidents have happened to lessen the comforts and profit of your employment; First the execrable custom got among ladies of trucking their old clothes for china, or turning them to cover easy chairs, or making them into patchwork for screens, stools, cushions and the like' (Gloag, 1990, p.496).

In the eighteenth century, patchwork was often a version of **appliqué**, where cloth patches were sewn onto a base ground. In the nineteenth century, this was overtaken by pieced patchwork that sewed together geometric cut-out fabric pieces. The formal hexagon shape is typical. The crazy design is also characteristic of Victorian work: sewing a variety of scraps of textiles onto a backing cloth, such as **velvet**, and then stitching the outlines with feather stitch. This was used for **valances**, **tablecloths**, quilts and cushions.

Miss Leslie suggested that 'patchwork quilts of old calico are only seen in inferior chambers; but they are well worth making for servants' beds. The custom of buying new calico, to cut into various ingenious figures, for what was called handsome patchwork, has become obsolete' (1841, p.311). Indeed, in the 1870s, it was pointed out that pieces for patchwork, 'can generally be begged, but all good upholsterers' shops will sell, and even give, cuttings to good customers' (*Cassell's Household Guide*, vol.1, p.337). A little later, Caulfeild & Saward noted that 'Satin, silk and velvet patchwork is used for cushions, hand screens, fire screens ... cloth patchwork for carriage rugs, couvrepieds, and poor people's quilts; cretonne, twill and chintz for couvrepieds, curtains, quilts and blinds' (1887, p.379).

Patchwork returned to become a fashionable craft in the mid- to late twentieth century.
See also **Piecing**, **Quilting**, **Stitch: Feather**.

FURTHER READING

Bensasson-Janniáere, J. (1995). 'An important discovery of French patchwork', *The Magazine Antiques*, 148, December, pp 822–9.
Caulfeild, S.F.A. & Saward, B.C. (1887). *The Dictionary of Needlework*, London: Upton Gill.
Von Gwinner, S. (1988). *The History of the Patchwork Quilt*, West Chester, PA: Schiffer.

Patchwork carpet
A homemade **carpet** produced by using various remnants of cloth. Loudon (1839) suggested making substitutes for carpeting made from:

> remnants of cloth bought from the woollen draper, or taylor, and cut into any kind of geometrical shapes may be sewn together so as to form circles stars, or any other regular figures that may be desired; and when arranged with taste produce a very handsome and durable carpet at a trifling expense (p.345).

Patena
A top-quality French textile based on the indiennes but with blue and yellow colourings added to the standard black and red colours. When the blue and yellow printing overlapped, green shades were created.
See also **Indienne**.

Patent Axminster
See **Chenille Axminster**.

Patent-back carpet
Developed in the USA in the 1930–40s, it was woven on regular **carpet** looms with heavy **cotton** yarns for **warp**, **weft** and stuffers with **wool pile** yarn, which was woven through to the back. After finishing, the back was coated with a pyroxylin lacquer that binds the tufts securely, so the carpet could be cut in any direction without unravelling.

Another type was described in 1931:

> A woven carpet with a rubber back, manufactured only in 54-inch width in which the rubberized composition penetrates the pile and holds all the yarns so firmly in place that when cut it does not ravel; it can be joined invisibly; the back is waterproof and holds firmly to the floor; it suggests a Wilton weave in appearance and comes in a variety of colors. (*Journal of Home Economics*, 23, 8 August 1931, p.794.)

See also **Lea carpeting**.

Pavilion
A pavilion was a tent-like structure that was fixed above a bed, and appears to have originated in France, where it was referred to as a circular canopy. The Sackville inventory of goods of July 1624 included 'A chine blue silk damask pavilion for a bedde, with a wooden round block on top, gilt with gold, a deep silk and gold fringe about it, the pavilion edged with a silk and gold fringe round' (Beard, 1997, p.293). In 1697, the Duchess of Cleveland employed an upholsterer, Francis Lapierre, and he charged for the 'taking down [of] a flowered calico pavilion and putting up of a blue damask bed in the place' (Beard, 1997, p.298). The term also refers to small textile structures that were erected for special events by means of ropes and pulleys. Charles I's inventory listed:

> A pavillian or tent of printed callicoe blue with images and flowrs being in foure peeces for the lower part of it and on the topp of the said stuff with foure painted posts and Lyors to the same and all things fitting to sett it up and a Cover of blue and red callicoe for the same pavillian was presented to King James by the Russian Ambassador (Jervis, 1989, p.293).

It is not surprising to find the coat-of-arms of the Upholsterers' Company bearing pavilions as part of its design.
See also **Canopy**.

Peau de soie
See **Paduasoy**.

Pékin
A name for imported Chinese hand-painted or embroidered **taffeta silks** that were used in the eighteenth century for **upholstery** and hangings. The designs were copied by printing processes in France from the 1760s.
See also **Painted taffeta**.

Pelmet

A fabric (or other material, including wood or metal) strip designed to decorate and or disguise the **headings** of a window or bed **curtain** and the **tracks** that support it. It is usually fairly rigid. The name probably derives from *palmette* – a design on a cornice that appears to have been adopted as the name and was probably first used in the early nineteenth century. Pelmets generally differed from valances in that the latter were usually softer and sometimes had some fullness. Pelmets were important elements of a fashionable interior. An early twentieth-century historian noted that:

> Pelmet, a word used by upholsterers and sometimes by art dealers, who prefer the word 'palmette', to denote the horizontal stiff curtains or valance hiding the rod, rings and headings of the hanging curtain decorating a door, window, bed, etc… Although the word pelmet is now in very general use in England it has not found its way into many dictionaries; but a description of a throne in the Annual Register for 1821 shows that the word was used at that period. (Penderel-Brodhurst, 1925, p.123.)

During the twentieth century, various materials have been employed for pelmets, apart from fabrics. From the 1940s, mirror versions, stamped metal versions, wood and extending wood versions were available. In 1947, the aluminium 'Metapelmet', an extending anodised coloured pelmet system, was introduced (French, 1947). Easily painted plywood pelmets were available ready-made post-war, as were shaped fibreboard pelmets.
See also **Cornice**, **Lambrequin**, **Valance**.

Pelmet board

A wooden board designed to suit particular windows with boxwood pulleys inserted. Draw lines would run over the pulleys to raise or lower **curtains**. Later, the boards supported curtain **railway** systems.
See also **Pelmet**.

Pencil

The hand-painting of mordants or **dyes** onto cloth with a fine brush. The practice differed between India and Europe. Indian work on **palampores** and **calicoes** used a split bamboo with a wad of **hairs** or rag attached above the point, which could be pressed to release the liquid. European pencilling was undertaken by women using horsehair brushes and was chiefly used for additions to other printing methods. It was popular in the eighteenth century, but had generally disappeared by the early nineteenth century.

Pencil pleat

Curtain heading with narrow regular **pleats** usually formed by draw tapes.

Penistone

A heavily milled **woollen flannel** or **broadcloth** woven in the Penistone district of Yorkshire from the mid-sixteenth century. It appears to have been used for **upholstery** work on occasion. The Hardwick Hall inventory of 1601 lists 'two curtains of grene penistone for the windowes' of the low great chamber (Boynton, 1971, p.31). In April 1637, Ralph Grynder supplied penistone to Queen Henrietta Maria for use at her palace: 'For 48 yards of fine scarlet colour penistone to case 20 cushions at 3s a yard' (Beard, 1997, p.290). It seems to have become obsolete by the later eighteenth century.

Percale

The origin of the name is uncertain but modern usage (i.e. since the eighteenth century) is related to the French word, *percale*. Originally, percale was a plain-woven cloth made from **cotton** yarns, which was often a lighter weight than **chintz**. It was initially imported from south India where it was used as a ground cloth for chintz in the seventeenth and eighteenth centuries. It was made in England from around 1670.

In the twentieth century, it was considered as a sheeting fabric with a high thread count made from fine-combed cotton yarns, giving a **silk**-like feel. The fabric is singed during finishing to remove the nap, giving a smooth surface appearance to take the place of **linen** (French, 1937, p.145). In late twentieth century use, it was defined as a closely woven cotton fabric, originally of French manufacture, with higher finishing than **muslin**, and without gloss. It may be white or can be printed. Percale sheeting is the finest sheeting available, made of combed yarns and has a count of 200; carded percale sheeting has a count of 180. It has a soft, silk-like feel.
See also **Calico**, **Masulipatam**, **Sheet**.

Perpetuana

A **wool** twill fabric made from white **serge** (also called Perpetual). Introduced in the late sixteenth century, it was used widely in the seventeenth century for bed hangings and **upholstery**. The serge cloth was soaked and softened in oils and urine, then dried on tenterhooks. It was folded, placed on a coal-fired hot press and the upper plate was screwed down.

By 1638–9 Anne, Viscountess Dorchester, had a 'redd perpetuana bedd' in a nursery, as well as a 'French bed of green perpetuana' (Clabburn, 1988, p.251). A little later, Ham House also had a 'French bedstead hung with blew perpetuana leased with gilt leather, and a counterpoint of blew perpetuana' (Thornton & Tomlin, 1980, p.22). In 1698, Celia Fiennes recorded the process of preparing serges in Exeter in great detail (1995, pp 197–8).

The name perpetuana is similar to **durance**, **everlasting**, **lasting**, etc, in that the name implies long-lasting qualities.

Persian

A **silk** cloth used since the early eighteenth century for the lining of **chintz bed furniture** and for **curtains** behind glazed bookcase doors in the mid-eighteenth century. It was also occasionally used for window curtains and **toilettes**. In 1710, there was a Clouded Room in Dyrham Park with 'six pieces of clouded silk hangings, a clouded silk bed lined with yellow strip'd persian and a counterpane of the same' (Walton, 1986, p.62). In the 1728 inventory of the shop of James Pilbeam, a mercer of Chiddingly, Sussex, there was listed: 'One hundred sixty eight yards of persian at ls 3d per yard: Total: £10 10s 0d' (http://www.chiddingly.gov.uk/History/James%20Pilbeam.html).

Persian was also used in America for similar purposes. In 1736, Thomas Steel of Boston, Mass., had a 'yellow China sett of curtains and furniture lined with Persian' (Cummings, 1961, p.34) and, a year later, the *Boston Gazette*, 17 October 1737, noted 'a yellow mohair bed lined with a persian of the same colour' (ibid., p.30).

Its use as a lining continued into the nineteenth century. George Smith recommended that for a state bed 'the furniture should be of lilac silk, embroidered border and lining, with rose coloured Persian: the counterpane the same' (1808, p.6). While in 1825, William Trotter invoiced Lord Gray at Kinfauns Castle, Perthshire for 'Cutting out and making a set of curtains of rich Chinese painted silk lined with green persian' (Jones, 1997, p.248).

The nature of silks, including Persian, was discussed in 1842 by the *Penny Cyclopaedia*, which suggested that 'Persian, sarsenet, gros-de-Naples,

ducapes, satin and levantines are [all] plain silks, which vary from one another only in texture, quality, or softness.' (XXII, 12/1.) Towards the end of the century, *The Dictionary of Needlework* still noted that Persian was 'an inferior description of silk stuff, thin, and designed for linings of women's cloaks etc. It is soft, fine, almost transparent, and not durable.' (Caulfeild & Saward, 1887, p.389.)
See also **Bookcase curtain**.

Peruvian cloth
A fabric woven from heavy **linen** yarns, dyed in dark shades of red, brown, blue, etc. It was much used for **table covers** and may be embroidered (*The Mercury Dictionary of Textile Terms*, 1950).

Petit-point
Petit-point is a type of **embroidery** that is particularly used for upholstery work such as drop-in seats, chair backs and loose **cushions**. It produces a fine, closely worked and even surface that allows for detail in the pattern. It is worked on fine **canvas**, usually in a frame, and tent stitch (single stitches slanting upwards from left to right over one cross of canvas) is usually employed. The Gobelin stitch is sometimes employed for petit-point work. In this case, the stitches are over two threads in height and one in width (also known as Gros point). This creates a shaded effect that can be used in conjunction with the tent stitch. Fine **woollen** and sometimes **silk** yarns are used to create pictorial images, often against a dark background. From the Tudor period onward, it was used to make hangings, **table carpets**, and later for upholstery work.
See also **Stitch: Tent**.

95. Needlework chair cover (petit-point), c.*1720 (Mallett and Co)*

Petticoat
A toilet-table covering that was intended to reach down to the floor. A feature of many eighteenth-century bedrooms, they may have been tailored on site or purchased as 'ready-mades'. Chippendale shows two examples in his *The Gentleman and Cabinet Maker's Director*, noting that 'the drapery may be of silk damask, with gold fringes and tassels' (1762, Plate CXVIII). The basic toilet-table was cheap and made from deal or similar. Chippendale charged to make 'a petty coat for a toilet of your own tammy' at Nostell, and then, at Paxton House, for 'a marcela quilted petticoat and cover' (Gilbert, 1978, p.59).
The term was still in use in 1878 when Lady Barker, discussing toilette tables, mentioned that 'It is also an improvement, if instead of only a hideous crackle of calico beneath, [that] there be a full flounce or petticoat of batiste which would give colour and graceful folds together' (1878, p.78).
See also **Toilette**.

Philip and Cheney
See **Cheney**.

Piano cover (aka Scarves)
Covers for pianos and mantels were produced ready-made, or were homemade, in the later nineteenth century. They employed shawls, scarves or purpose-made covers that were hung as a front piece to an upright piano, as a key cover when the lid was open, or were draped over the body or back of a piano. In 1881, Constance Harrison noted in her *Women's Handiwork In Modern Homes* that:

> When, as is customary for the accommodation of singers, the upright piano is turned to face the room, a square, flat hanging, of a size to cover the fluted silk at the back may be made of Turk satin, sateen, serge, plush or linen, and embroidered, the ends fringed or trimmed with antique lace. (pp 176–7.)

The 1908 Sears Roebuck catalogue listed **silk** or **velour** covers with a knotted **tassel fringe** and draw **cords** that were suitable for either pianos or mantels. Similarly, in England, the Maple and Co furnishing company offered back covers specifically for pianos in their catalogues of 1908 and 1925. **Silkoline** was a trade name for a printed cloth, once given away with pianos in the form of a **lambrequin**, printed scarf or **throw** (Hunter, 1918).

The American decorator, Russell Herts, explained how piano covers should fit into a drawing room:

> Here we have a chamber essentially for the entertainment of the romantic and formal of both sexes, and here, if anywhere the woman decorator should find her sphere. Everything must be of the daintiest, from the light-toned rug, whether Oriental or slightly figured chenille, to the piano scarf of embroidery or brocade. (Herts, *c.*1922, p.58.)

Piano **drapery** rails were specialised hardware designed to facilitate the hanging of these covers.
See also **Scarf**, **Painted velvet**.

Piecing
Piecing is a **needlework** process that joins small cloth pieces together to create a patterned material.
See also **Patchwork**.

Pile
The raised pile surface of a fabric that projects from the cloth. Weaving

96. Piano drapery, c.1870s (Private Collection)

a supplementary **warp** or **weft** over a wire, which makes a loop, produces the pile. This may then be cut or left as a loop to create the pile.

Pillar
A furniture print designed to show a plain marble architectural pillar swathed in garlands of foliage, flowers or cereal plants.

Pillow
A particular soft **cushion** intended to support the head whilst sleeping. Known in Saxon times and referred to in *Beowulf*, they were often considered an effeminate luxury. Writing of earlier days, Harrison noted that 'Pillows were thought meet only for women in childbed.' (1577, p.201)

The usual filling for pillows has been **feather** and **down**, but more recently, **latex** rubber, rubber crumb, **acrylic** fibrefill, and **polyester** have been used.

Pillow bere (aka Pillow beer)
This is a medieval term for a pillowcase. The name occurs frequently in inventories. In the 1480 *Wardrobe Accounts of Edward IV*, there were 'Pillow beres of fustian unstuffed iiij' (Nicolas, 1830, p.131). While in a 1552 account of a christening, 'Pillows of fustian stuffed with down every each with beeres of raines' were commented upon (Edwards, 1964, p.46). The term was still used in the seventeenth century: 'Two pair of pillow beers' were listed in a 1681 inventory from Essex (Steer, 1969, p.165).

Pillowcase
A removable and washable sack-shaped covering, usually of white **linen** or **cotton** cloth, designed to fit over pillows. They often match **sheets** and accessories.
See also **Pillow**, **Pillow bere**.

Pillow fustian
This material was a kind of plain or common fustian that was woven with a narrow cord, and made of **cotton** in a manner similar to **velvet**. Mainly used for clothing in the eighteenth century, but in fine qualities it was made up for bed and pillow- or **bolster cases**.
See also **Bolster**, **Fustian**, **Pillow bere**, **Pillowcase**, **Pillow sham**.

Pillow sham (aka Pillow flap)
A textile covering which either encloses or is laid over pillows as a decorative finish. They are not the same as pillowcases, which enclose the pillow in a bag shape.

Webster explained that they are 'a covering usually of embroidered linen, laid over the pillow of a bed when it is not in use' (1879).
See also **Pillowcase**.

Pinch pleats
A **curtain** heading that is made from three folds of fabric of equal width. The pinch is sewn firmly in the centre in such a way as to pull the **pleats** together to create a pinched effect. A button may hide the sewing **stitches**. Proprietary brands of **curtain pins** with three prongs used with the appropriate tape have made the effect easy to obtain.

Pin cushion work
A specific form of **upholstery** technique that originated in the eighteenth century. It is used for making seats and back pads of delicate, often moulded, chair frames, so that the upholstery work appears as applied pads or 'pin cushions'. This work is usually carried out without a first **stuffing**, so the filling must be accurately laid to ensure evenness of line and appearance. The upholsterer, Sarah Lowey, supplied the House of Peers Lord Great Chamberlain's room with '12 pincushion seats for chairs' in 1739 (*DEFM*, p.558).

Pinoleum (aka Matchstick blind)
A later nineteenth-century name for sun-blinds. They are made up of very thin rods of pine wood, either stained or coated with oil-paint, which are then linked together close to each other so as to form a bendable sheet that can be rolled up to the top of a window.

They were used for interior and exterior work but were particularly associated with tropical use or effect. In 1905, the *Civil Service Supply Catalogue* offered 'Pinoleum or Tropical Sun Blinds, in a variety of new patterns' (p.432). Pinoleum blinds have had revivals during the twentieth century, especially as conservatory blinds.
See also **Rolleau**.

Pin and hook
The fittings designed to attach **curtains** etc. to rails or rings, including safety pin type, sew-in type, pin type, etc.

Pintado
In the sixteenth century, pintado (Portuguese for 'spotted') referred to a cheap Indian block-printed **cotton** cloth.

In the seventeenth century, pintadoes were resist-dyed mordant-**painted cloths**, similar to chintz. They were widely used for **quilts**,

curtains, **cupboard cloths**, etc. Pintadoes could be either painted or printed, and in some cases, they were both. Where the cloth was painted, it was done freehand, using **dyes** and painted mordants, and so was of a higher quality than those where the cloth was block-printed. In the first half of the seventeenth century, it was the expensive, painted cloths that were fashionable, being used for hangings for beds and walls. Pintadoes were sold as lengths of fabric measuring 13 yards (11.9 metres), and were cut up to fit the walls. The 'pintado quilt' was a stuffed quilt that was highly fashionable in the seventeenth century.

Early references occur in 1602 in the East India Co correspondence. One letter refers to 'ffardells of blewes and checkered stuffes, some fine Pinthadoes' (Birdwood, 1893, 34, p.60). In 1609, a letter from Surat to the East India Co headquarters noted that 'Pintadoes of all sorts, especially the finest, as it seemeth to me, should yield good profit, I mean such as are for quilts and for fine hangings… Quilts made both of white calicoes and of all sorts of painted stuffs are to be had in abundance' (Irwin & Brett, 1970, p.4).

Some different use was noted in 1638, when Sir Thomas Herbert commented that 'Upon the carpets were spread fine coloured pintado Table cloaths' (*Some Years Travels*, 2nd Ed., p.138). The multiple uses of pintadoes were confirmed in the 1641 Tart Hall inventory, which listed a 'suite of Hangings consisting of four Peeces of Indian Pintadoes, and Curtaynes of the same suite for the same room, and a canopye of the same suite with a valence thereunto. Also four little Pintadoe carpets for the same Room.' (Cust, 1911, p.235.) In 1657, an order was made for 'chintz or Pintadoes 1000 pieces … Pintadoes quilts that may match the works of ye chints 300' (Irwin & Brett, 1970, p.28).

Another use was recorded in 1660, when the *London Book of Rates* (in Beck, 1882) listed 'Pintadoes or Callecoe cubbard clothes.' A little later, Evelyn recorded how he 'supp'd at my Lady Mordaunt's at Ashley: here was a room hung with Pintado, full of figures great and small, prettily representing sundry trades and occupation of the Indians, with their habits &c: very extraordinary' (*Diary of John Eveyln*, 30 December 1665).

Their popularity was curtailed in 1720 when it became illegal to 'use [pintado] or wear in or about any bed, chair, cushion or other household furniture' (Irwin & Brett, 1970, p.5).
See also **Chintz**, **Palampore**.

Piped valance
See **Valance**.

Piping (aka Welting)
Piping is the process of **trimming** edges or seams by means of a fine **cord**, enclosed in a tube-like, bias-cut sewn fold. Piping cord is the basis for folded **tapes** over French seams, as well as cords stitched directly to the seam. The cord is made from **cotton** or compressed paper fibres that give a firmer edge. Used from the seventeenth century to accent the edge of **cushions** and **upholstery** seams, flat fabric or tape was wrapped around a cord, which was then sewn into the seam before fitting. It may be self-coloured or contrasting. In the early nineteenth century, references to the finishing off of raw edges of fabric bound with tape, often called **lace**, were also called piping.

Piqué
A nineteenth-century textile name derived from the French *piquer*, meaning 'to prick' or 'to quilt'. Piqué, or toilette welts, are a class of fabric characterised by cords or ribs in the plain-weave running either across the fabric in a **weft** direction or along in a **warp** direction. It is generally made of combed face yarns and carded stuffer yarns. Originally, it was a crosswise rib, but is now mostly a lengthwise rib and the same as **Bedford cord**. Ribs are often filled to give a more pronounced **wale** (cord weave), but it has been available in different patterns besides wales, including **bird's-eye** (small diamond), waffle (small squares) and **honeycomb** (like the design on honeycomb). It has been made from **cotton**, **rayon** and synthetics.

97. Piqué cloth detail (T. French and Co, The Book of Soft Furnishing, *1937)*

In 1887, toilet covers (**toilettes**) were described as 'small cloths, made for the covering of dressing tables, usually manufactured of marcella or piqué' (Caulfeild & Saward, 1887, p.496).

In 1947, piqué was recommend for **bedspreads**, **drapes**, slipcovers, table **runners**, etc. (Bendure & Pfieffer, p.645).

Placket
Although often associated with dressmaking, placket also refers to a **pleat** or slit in the side edge in a loose cover that allows for its easy removal. It is usually fitted with **hooks and eyes** or Velcro. The name is adopted from dress terminology.

Plaid (aka Plod)
Plaid is a striped and **checked** twilled **woollen** fabric, not unlike the modern tartan. Known by the early sixteenth century, its use for furnishings is demonstrated in 1641, when the Countess of Arundel had 'a couch bed, covered with scotch plad, thereon 4 little cushions of the same' (Cust, 1911, p.98). It has been used for **upholstery** and **curtain** work. The 1654 inventory of Ham House refers to 'hangings of plaides' for a closet (Thornton & Tomlin, 1980, p.27). Its association with Scotland was recorded early on. In 1695, the upholsterer, Francis Lapierre, was paid £11.14s.0d. for '3 pieces of skoch plad' by the Earl of Dorset (Beard, 1997, p.296).

It was still fashionable in 1710 when Dyrham Park had a 'Plod room' furnished with '5 pieces of Scots plod hangings, 2 window curtains and vallans of the same' and 'four chairs, 2 stools, couch and three cushions' all covered in the same (Walton, 1986, p.58). In 1712, Celia Fiennes noted in Lord Guildford's house at Epsom, an apartment furnished with 'pladd chamlet damaske neatly made up', and round the corner in Mr Ruth's house, there was 'a plad bed lined with Indian callicoe' (1995, pp 235–6).

It appears to have been out of fashion as a furnishing material by the early eighteenth century. However, Queen Victoria and Prince Albert revived the use of plaid as an essentially Scottish fabric during the 1850s at their residence, Balmoral Castle. They maintained the habit of furnishing rooms with plaids on the walls, and upholstery was often covered in the material. Lady Augusta Bruce commented on the Balmoral interiors:

> the carpets of Royal Stewart tartan and green Hunting Stewart, the curtains, the former lined with red, the same dress Stewart and a few chintz with thistle pattern, the chairs and sofas in the Drawing Room are Dress Stewart poplin. All highly characteristic and appropriate but not equally *flatteux* to the eye (Biddulph, 1988, p.49).

See also **Tartan**.

FURTHER READING

Biddulph, F. (1988). 'Tartanalia', *Traditional Interior Decoration*, 2, 4, February/March, pp 46–56.

98. Plaid cloth example c.*1900 (Waverely Fabrics Co.)*

Plastic chintz

As its name suggests, it is 'A printed cotton fabric given a glazed surface by means of an applied plastic. It looks like chintz, but can in fact be cleaned with a damp cloth.' (Smithells, 1950, p.229.)
See also **Chintz**.

Plastic webbing

See **Webbing**.

Platform

A platform is an **upholstery** suspension system that uses a one-piece elasticised diaphragm, flexolator or fab-web support to create the seat. Early experiments applied gutta-percha, using its elastic properties, to a form of platform springing. At the 1851 Exhibition, H. Pratt displayed a brass chaise-longue fitted with 'elastic' gutta-percha sacking (Class 26, Item 403). The real success came 100 years later when platform seating support was made from a resilient rubber diaphragm, designed for used in show-wood framed chairs and sofas. Introduced in the 1960s by the Pirelli Co, it was a useful way of supporting loose **cushions** on a tensioned supporting system that was simply held to the show-wood frame by four hooked bolts. Later, various textiles were used to create a flat suspension for cushions.
See **Four-point platform**, **Spring**, **Webbing**.

Pleater hook

A twentieth-century introduction to the soft furnishing trade, these are used in conjunction with pleater tapes to make stand-up **headings**, and similar effects, in **curtains**, without the need to sew them by hand.
See also **Hook**.

Pleat

A method of shaping fabrics into decorative effects by sewing or pressing them into a range of desired profiles. The material is stitched or pressed into even folds that double upon it. Widely used on **curtains**, loose covers and bed hangings. They vary in style and include box, French, **goblet**, inverted, knife, organ and **pencil pleats**, most of the names defining the resulting shape.

French pleats are triple pleats that are not pressed flat. Flat pressed pleats in triple use are **pinch pleats**. **Accordion pleats** are wide, sharply pressed pleats, evenly spaced and all facing in one direction; narrower versions are knife pleats. **Box pleats** are wide double pleats with material folded under at each side. **Inverted pleats** have the flat fold turned in, as opposed to being turned out. Cartridge (or organ) pleats are small cylindrical pleats representing a military cartridge belt.

The technique of pleating was also used for **wall coverings** and for stretched fabrics on furniture doors or frames, such as bookcases and workbaskets. Sheraton's *The Cabinet Marker and Upholsterer's Drawing Book* shows a sofa bed:

> It must also be observed, that the best kinds of these beds have behind what the upholsterers call a fluting, which is done by a slight frame of wood fastened to the wall, on which is strained, in straight puckers, some of the same stuff of which the curtains are made. (1804, p.379.)

The pleating technique was used for wall decoration in the mid-nineteenth century. The Boston dyers, Howe and Stevens, noted that: 'Instead of paper, paint or tapestry, [fabric] when used for this purpose it is not put on tight and flat like paper or tapestry but fluted and has a magnificent appearance.' (Montgomery, 1984, p.356.)
See also **Roman drapery**, **Tufting**.

Plissé

Plissé can be made from any fine material, e.g. **organdie**, **lawn**, etc. It is treated with a caustic soda solution that shrinks parts of the cloth all over, or in stripes, to give a blistered effect. It is similar to **seersucker** in appearance. Often it is called wrinkle **crêpe** and may be made with a wax/shrink process (the waxed parts remain free of shrinkage and cause the ripples). It has been used for **curtains**, **bedspreads** and bassinets.

> Casement cloth and plissé are being used widely in the place of blinds. Plissé has alternate stripes of crêpe and plain surface. It is heavier than the plissé used for clothing, and is frequently called Austrian shade cloth. Plissé shades are finished with a braid or fringe and are so arranged that they pull up and down by means of cords with tassels. Casement cloth, when used in place of curtains or shades, is usually hung on small rings, which are slipped over a brass rod. (Dyer, *c*.1923, p.207.)

See also **Austrian shade cloth**.

Plumbet

A small lead weight used in **curtains** and **drapes** to ensure correct hang or fall. The name is probably derived from the French *plomb*, meaning 'lead'. They have been in use since at least the seventeenth century. In 1677, John Casbert invoiced 'leaden plummets' to the Great Wardrobe (Beard, 1997, p.291). 'Plumbits' are also frequently mentioned in Chippendale accounts.

Plumes

See **Cup**, **Feather**.

Plush (Fr. *Peluche*)

A **pile** cloth woven from various yarns, often dependent upon the time of production, and widely used for **upholstery**. It may also be plain or embossed. Plush was less expensive than **velvet** but produced a similarly rich effect with a longer and less dense pile. The range of plushes included the mohair plush, which had a short stiff pile and an even close finish; **woollen** plush, which was sometimes stamped; and **silk** plush, which had a longer and less uniform pile.

Plush was a French speciality from the later seventeenth century (*pluche*) and remained an important upholstery fabric into the twentieth century. Chambers defined it in 1741 as being:

> a kind of stuff having a sort of velvet knap or shag on one side; composed regularly of a woof [weft] of a single woollen thread, and a double warp, the one wool of two threads twisted, the other goats-hair. Some plushes are made entirely of worsted and others composed wholly of hair.

An early furnishing reference is in 1639 when Anne, Viscountess of Dorchester, had '1 bed to lye on of purple plush … with a canapie, the outward vallance of purple plush laced with silver lace and silver fringe' (Clabburn, 1988, p.253). In 1710, Dyrham Park had various furniture items upholstered in 'striped plush' (Walton, 1986, p.59).

In the nineteenth century, plush was popular and was apparently made in a range of qualities. In his *Homestead Architecture,* Sloan commented that 'plush is made of goat's hair woven with the pile to stand erect like velvet, and is very durable. Common plush, for cheap furniture and coaches is made of wool; but time and little service show its worthlessness' (1861, p.323). Moreland also recommended mohair plush, or even better, silk plush. The latter offered an opportunity for flower painting as it receives paint well 'and a very dainty portière for a boudoir could be made in this manner'. Moreland also recommended silk plush for **festoons**, or for flat **scarves** that would be worked with **needlework**, **appliquéd** or hand-painted (1889). Mohair continued to be recommended as a pile fibre. In 1881, Alfred Spitzli said of mohair:

> [its] luster and elasticity peculiarly fit mohair for its chief use, the manufacture of Utrecht velvets, commonly called furniture plush, the finest qualities of which are composed principally of mohair, the pile being formed of mohair… The best mohair plushes are almost indestructible. They have been in constant use on certain railroads in this country for 20 years without wearing out (Grier, 1988, p.303).

Worsted plush was a cheaper version. According to Caulfeild & Saward, Banbury plush was a particular woollen plush, woven especially for upholstery (1887, p.400). In 1878, Clarence Cook wrote that 'probably the prettiest coverings for cushions are the stamped plushes which are now made in England, with patterns and colors that leave nothing to be desired' (1878, p.67).

During the twentieth century, it was noted that 'in the modern home, the portière curtain is almost as important as the door itself, and a variety of styles have been evolved… Brocatelles, damask velvet, plush, plain and figured are the most favoured fabrics for portière curtains.' (French, 1937.) In 1947, an American text considered plush to be an upholstery fabric that could have **brocade** designs upon it produced by burning the pile with rollers to form a lower background (Brady, 1947, p.520). By the mid-twentieth century, Taylor noted that plush was woven from **cotton**, mohair, silk and synthetics and it was used for upholstery and bedcovers (1951).

Some definitions say that any pile fabric with over 3mm (0.12 of an inch) pile length is generically a plush.

See also **Caffoy**, **Mohair**, **Shagg**, **Stamped plush**, **Utrecht velvet**.

FURTHER READING

Latour, A. (1953). 'Furniture plushes and moquette', *CIBA Review,* 96, February, pp 3438–63.

Point d'esprit

A dull surfaced net with various-sized holes woven in **cotton** or sometimes in **silk**, using **leno**, **gauze**, knotted or mesh construction. Probably first made in France in the 1830s, it has white or coloured dots individually spaced or in groups on the surface. It has been particularly used for **curtains** and bassinets. In 1951 *point d'esprit* was described as a 'variation of bobbinet in white cream or ecru. With tiny dots all over. Used over Venetian blinds. Better than bobbinet when hung straight as more substantial.' (Taylor, 1951.)

See also **Lace**, **Net**.

Polished cotton

An often inexpensive **cotton** fabric that has been calendered or chemically finished to give a polished effect. Used for **curtains** and loose covers in the twentieth century.

Polyester

A versatile synthetic fibre especially suited to **curtains** and **drapes**. First developed in the 1950s, especially under the trademarks Dacron and Terylene, it has been widely used in home furnishings, often in conjunction with **cotton**. Dacron in matted fibre form has been associated with a loose **cushion** filling, while Terylene was for a long time in the later twentieth century associated with net curtains.

See also **Fibre**, **Foam**, **Tufted carpet**, **Upholstery**, **Webbing**

Polypropylene
An olefin petrochemical fibre. It has a limited colour palette, but is very strong and has been widely used for **carpeting** and heavy-duty **upholstery** in the later twentieth century.
See also **Carpet tacking**, **Fibre**, **Tufted carpet**, **Webbing**.

Polyurethane coated fabric
An 'improved' plastic-coated **upholstery** fabric, which has inherent moisture permeability, and good resistance to abrasion, fatty materials and heat. Introduced in the 1960s, they were initially based on solid coated polyurethane on a woven fabric (Airskin and Lancina). They were developed with a **warp**-knitted **pile** backing cloth to improve stretch. **Weft**-knitted fabrics further improved stretch properties and gave better tear strength.
See also **Fibrefill**, **Foam**, **Underlay**.

Pongee
Once a lightweight, unbleached wild **silk** fabric from China, now any fabric of a similar weight made from a range of yarns, but especially **cotton**. It is available in its natural colour (ecru), or it may be dyed. Pongees were once called paunches: *An account of the trade in India* by Lockyer (*OED*) noted that 'wrought silks are cheap and good of innumerable sorts … damasks, sattins, taffeta paunches' (1711).

In the twentieth century, it has been used for **art embroidery**, dressmaking and for **curtains**. In 1947, it was specifically considered for curtain usage in the USA. Woven from irregular tussah or wild silk yarns, giving a broken cross-bar effect characteristic of pongee. If opacity was required for window curtains, pongee would often be selected (Bendure & Pfieffer, 1947, p.586). By the 1950s, it was suggested for **bedspreads** and curtains in England (Smithells).
See also **Dupion**, **Tussah**.

Poplin (Fr. *Papeline*)
A textile probably named from the French *papeline*. The name was used to describe this material because it was manufactured at Avignon (until 1791, a papal town). Papeline was an unwatered **camlet** with a **silk warp** and a **worsted weft**. As the weft is in the form of a stout cord, the fabric has a ridged structure like **rep**, which gives depth and softness to the lustre of the silky surface.

Poplins are used for dress purposes, and for rich **upholstery** work. The manufacture of poplin, brought to England by the Huguenots, has long been specifically associated with Ireland. In 1778, Thomas Campbell commented that 'Poplins, some of which, called tabinets, have all the richness of silk' (*Philosophical Survey of South of Ireland*, 201, *OED*). The French manufacturers distinguished between *popelines unies* or plain poplins, and *popelines a dispositions* or Ecossaises, equivalent to Scotch plads. The terms 'double poplin', or 'stiff poplin', in which the silk warp and the worsted weft are both very heavy, reflect quality. In 1887, the Irish connection was reaffirmed. Caulfeild & Saward noted poplin's use for **drapes**: 'The beautiful terry poplins that compose the draperies of Dublin Castle, Windsor Castle, Marlborough House, Osborne and Blenheim were produced by Dublin firms. Tabinet is a variety of the same description of textile as poplin and is employed for upholstery.' (1887, p.411.)

By 1937, poplins appear to have been less impressive: 'Poplins are suitable for the less important rooms. They hang well and give satisfactory service, particularly suitable for dress or draw curtains, and linings' (French, 1937, p.67). However, in 1950, Smithells comments that poplin was very useful for curtains etc.

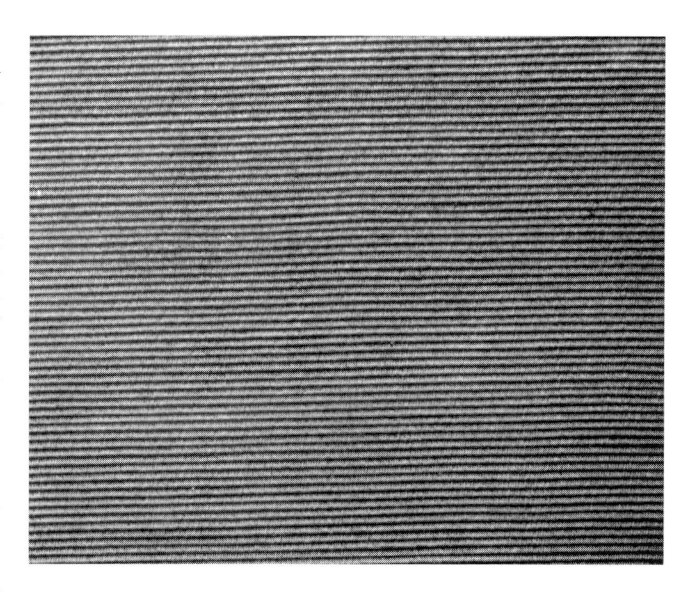

99. Poplin cloth detail (T. French and Co, The Book of Soft Furnishing, *1937)*

More recently, poplin refers to a **cotton** fabric, woven with a plain-weave construction with weft ribs, and a high warp sett. This produces a transverse rib. The filling is cylindrical and, as there are two or three times as many warps as wefts per inch, the prominence of the rib will reflect quality. It is mercerised and has quite a high lustre. It may be bleached, or **dyed** (usually vat dyes are used) or printed. Heavy poplin is given a water-repellent finish for outdoor use.
See also **Bengaline**, **Ducape**, **Rep**, **Tabbinet**.

Portière
The name for a door curtain that originates in the Latin word *portarius*, meaning 'to refer to a door or gate'. Portières have been used for a range of purposes including the covering of public doorways and double parlours. They have been used without doors to decorate openings. Portières have been made from window materials (to match) but also from shawls, **kilims**, **ingrain carpeting**, **embroidery** work or even recycled materials. In the latter cases, they were used as a point of display for the **needleworking** skills of the resident.

Portière curtains have their origins in medieval spaces as draught excluders, but they also imparted a luxurious textile effect to roomscapes. They were well known in Italian Renaissance interiors and were often an integral part of a furnishing scheme (Thornton, 1991). Renaissance furnishers used a range of fabrics including **tapestry**, **silk damask** or even **gilt leather**, as well as co-ordinated materials for bed hangings and door curtains.

Early references to their use in England occur in the Gage inventory of 1556, which listed a curtain of green **kersey**, 'with a curtain rod of iron which is to hang afore the door' and 'a great hook to put it up when it is not drawn' (Thornton, 1978, p.135). Fifty years later, the 1601 inventory of Hardwick noted that Bess's bedchamber had 'a coverlet to hang before the door' (Boynton, 1971, p.31). Kersey apparently remained a popular choice as, in 1603, Hengrave had 'at the great chamber door, one curtain of green kersey lined with southedge with a curtain rod of iron which is to hang afore the door with a great hook to put it up when it is not drawn' (Clabburn, 1988, p.132). Textiles were not the only materials used. In 1641, Tart Hall had 'eight anteportes to hang over doores of several sortes of lether gilt & red' (Cust, 1911). In 1698, Celia Fiennes visited Chippenham Park and was impressed by hangings with green

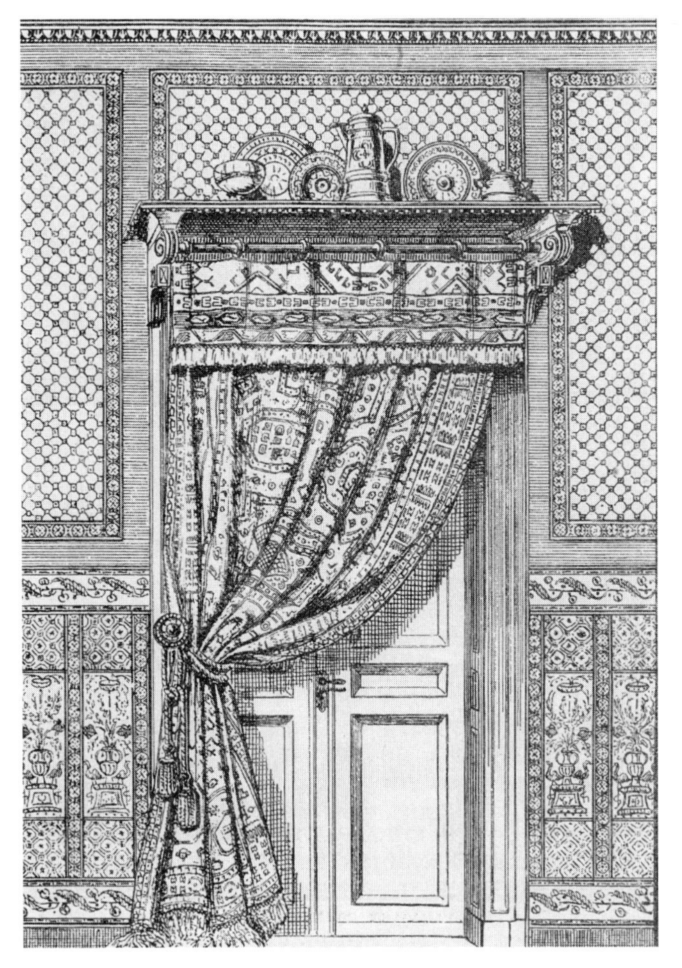

100. Portière curtain made from an Oriental carpet (Decorator and Furnisher, 1883. Courtesy The Winterthur Library: Printed Books and Periodical Collection)

damask borders, 'the window curtain the same green damask and doore curtains' (1949, p.153). Portières seem to have been out of favour in English interiors by the early eighteenth century, although they might still be used in areas that were more informal.

It was in the nineteenth century that portières became *de rigeur.* They followed the vagaries of fashion and reflected the various tastes for the Gothic, the Japanese, the Exotic or Eastern and the French styles. They were particularly important as vehicles of the demonstration of home skills in embroidery and needlework generally. Eastlake commended 'some very beautiful specimens of portière curtains ... composed of velvet and other stuffs, embroidered by hand and decorated with deep borders, consisting of alternate strips of velvet and common horse girths' (1878, p.101).

Portières became fashionable in the USA from around the 1870s. By 1883, Almon C. Varney was able to write: 'A beautiful room is far more beautiful when there is no square means of egress [i.e. a door] suggesting the unpleasant idea of departure' (1883, p.259). Varney went on to suggest **velveteen** or **plush** for portières and even ingrain carpet was recommended. He maintained that the ingrain carpet should be coloured olive or crimson as it faded 'handsomely'. The ingrain could also be decorated 'down one side of each breadth can be worked in Germantown wool, a pattern adopted from a Turkish rug' (ibid. p.263). Varney suggested that portière curtains should 'not repeat the curtains of the room, but they represent a separate idea, though in harmony with the room. They are frequently made double to correspond with rooms of different colours.' (ibid. p.259.)

Portières made from beads and bamboo strips were derided by the critics but were popular in the creation of a supposedly exotic atmosphere in the 1880s onward. One author did support these types of portière. Moreland expounded the benefits:

> for a hall or reception-room entrance, the Turkish or Arabian goods are very effective... They should be hung in a manner in keeping with their character. Use bamboo poles, or, better, suspend them from a rude spear or lance. The effect would be better if instead of being drawn apart, they were stationary at the top and were drawn up at the side with heavy drapery ropes. (1889, p.181.)

These bamboo and bead novelty portières were widely used, although in 1898 they were again roundly criticised in the journal *House Beautiful*: 'If there be any practical or decorative use to which one may put portières of beads or colored bamboo it has never been discovered.' (Winkler & Moss, 1986, p.220.)

In England, Mrs Orrinsmith suggested, in *The Drawing Room*, the use of needleworked portières, explaining that the 'heavy patterns worked upon Holland, cut out and sewn on serge and cloth, with an edging of filoselle or twisted silk make decorations suitable for portières' (1877, p.73).

In 1883, the American trade journal, *Carpet and Trade Review*, described some of the added advantages of portières. It suggested that portière curtains were useful as they 'cut off draughts much more effectively than doors', but they also acted as 'a strong preventative of bickering, backbiting and family jars, because sounds penetrated them easily'. The article then pointed out that 'apart from tapestry and rich embroidered velvet for the well-to-do, nearly all double-faced goods are used for portières, and at the present moment cashmeres, silk turcomans, double-faced jute and linen velours, chenille, and plush are the prevailing materials for the purpose' (Montgomery, 1984, p.89). Moreland also mentions a plain cloth, especially adapted for portières and manufactured from **jute** and flax, which was called single or double-faced **velour**. 'The single-faced velours are very suitable for appliqué work, and handsome portières can be made in that manner; good effects are also produced by inserting borders of figured velours, or by adding deep, heavy, netted fringe at the top or over the dado'. Finally, he recommended **mohair** plush or, even better, silk plush. The latter offered an opportunity for flower painting as it receives paint well 'and a very dainty portière for a boudoir could be made in this manner' (1889, p.180).

Despite all this, the critics were never far away from frowning upon not just extravagances in portière design, but also the very idea of them. Edith Wharton explains:

> The *portière* has always been used, as old prints and pictures show; but like the curtain, in earlier days it was simply intended to keep out currents of air, and was consequently seldom seen in well-built houses, where double sets of doors served far better to protect the room from draughts. In less luxurious rooms, where there were no double doors, and portières had to be used, these were made as scant and unobtrusive as possible. The device of draping stuffs about the doorway, thus substituting a textile architrave for one of wood or stone, originated with the modern upholsterer; and it is now not unusual to see a wide opening with no door in it, enclosed in yards and yards of draperies which cannot even be lowered at will.
>
> The *portière*, besides causing a break in architectural lines, has become one of the chief expenses in the decoration of the modern

room; indeed, the amount spent in buying yards of plush or damask, with the addition of silk cord, tassels, gimp and fringe, often makes it necessary to slight the essential features of the room; so that an ugly mantelpiece or ceiling is preserved because the money required to replace it has been used in the purchase of portières. These superfluous draperies are, in fact, more expensive than a well-made door with hinges and box-lock of chiselled bronze.

The general use of the *portière* has also caused the disappearance of the over-door. The lines of the opening being hidden under a mass of drapery, the need of connecting them with the cornice was no longer felt, and one more feature of the room passed out of the architect's hands into those of the upholsterer, or, as he might more fitly be called, the house-dressmaker. (Wharton & Codman, 1897, p.60.)

In the early twentieth century, tastes continued to change and there are delights such as the 'Mission' band portières that were made from 4 inch (10 cm) tapestry bands combined with velour cords. In addition, we can find **leather** strips hung in graduated sizes to create a portière effect. So popular were portières that ready-made portières in **chenille**, **armure** or tapestry, usually with dado pattern, large border or large non-repeating patterns, in standard lengths of nine feet (2.74 metres) (allowing for a self-fringe), were widely sold. In the case of chenille, for example, Sears Roebuck, in 1908, were selling chenille portières with a dado border and a **tassel** fringe. They also promoted rope portières.

Practicalities remained important, so it was recommended that 'every dining room and lounge should have a door curtain, and so should every bedroom which is intended to be draught-proof' (Martin, 1930). By 1937, portières were still considered important to a contemporary furnishing scheme:

In the modern home, the portière curtain is almost as important as the door itself, and a variety of styles have been evolved... Brocatelles, damask velvet, plush, plain and figured are the most favoured fabrics for portières curtains. These materials do not require lining unless they are found to be to light [but] all others do require to be lined. If price is not important, the best effect is obtained by an interlining of sateen, canton or shaker flannel. (French, 1937, p.61.)

See also **Antique textile**, **Appliqué**, **Archway curtain**, **Bead curtain**, **Chenille**, **Curtain**, **Dhurrie**, **Portière rod**, **Tapestry**.

FURTHER READING

Dornsife, S.J. (1975). 'Design sources for nineteenth century window hangings', *Winterthur Portfolio*, 10, pp 69–99.

Gibbs, J. (1994). *Curtains and Drapes: History, Design, Inspiration*, London: Cassell.

Winkler, G.C. & Moss, R. (1986). *Victorian Interior Decoration; American Interiors, 1830–1900*, New York: Holt.

Portière rod
A specially designed rod intended to suspend a **portière curtain** and often to have the facility to lift it slightly as the door was opened, thus avoiding snagging.

Portugal mat
See **Matting: Portugal**.

Pou de soie
See **Paduasoy**.

Powdering carpet
A floorcovering used in bedrooms and dressing rooms to save quality carpets from the fall of hair powder dust during the eighteenth century. The Lord Chamberlain's Accounts note payments in 1781 to a Mr J. Gilroy:

For 11 yds of strong Russia Duck 2s	£1 2s
For making above into a powdering carpet, with lead weights to the corners	(4s 6d)
For 2½ yds of Swanskin 2 ells wide for a carpet to cover ditto occasionally viz for Powdering	16s 3d

(Walton, 1980, p.279.)

See also **Swanskin**.

Prairie grass
See **Grass**, **Rug: Grass**.

Printed blind
A nineteenth-century material similar to glazed **chintz**, usually printed with a pattern that imitates **Venetian blinds**. They were made 36 to 100 inches (91 to 254 cm) wide in 2 inch (5 cm) increments (Caulfeild & Saward, 1887, p.412).
See also **Blind chintz**.

Printed carpet
See **Tapestry printed carpet**.

Printed cotton
Imported printed **cottons** from India were used in European furnishing schemes from the late sixteenth century. These were hand-printed cloths, finished with mordants (metallic oxides) that reacted with the **dye** to fix the colours in the fibres. Hepplewhite's *The Cabinet Maker and Upholsterer's Guide* explained that: 'Printed cottons and linens are also very suitable; the elegance and variety of patterns of which, afford as much scope for taste, elegance and simplicity, as the most lively fancy can wish' (1789, pp 17–18). A little later, Sheraton discussed cotton furnishings and pointed out that:

101. Calico printer's trade card, seventeenth century (M. Percival, The Chintz Book, *1923)*

> Printed cotton furniture or hangings for beds have been varied to almost an infinite number of patterns, and it is difficult to fix upon the most approved or fashionable ones. In the quality of printing, however, there is an essential difference, as some printed cottons will wash well, and others will not (1803, p.181).

In 1809, Rudolph Ackermann, discussing cotton prints, said: 'Should silk become objectionable from its expense, we strongly recommend the use of these new patterns [damask effect prints]. They need only be seen to become approved, and are particularly calculated for candlelight effect.' (*Repository of Arts etc.*, March, 1809, pp 188–9.)
See also **Blind chintz**, **Chintz**, **Cotton**, **Printed textile**, **Toile de Jouy**, **Washing furniture**.

Printed silk
These are plain **silk** fabrics that are overprinted with designs. It seems that it was an area of interest for inventors as, in January 1764, John Christian and Peter Browne received a patent for 'painting silks and satins in oil colours' (Patent no.804) and, in April 1779, Michael Braggini also received a patent for 'painting silk, tiffany, gauze and other goods in imitation of lace' (Patent no.1221). Sheraton recommended 'French printed silk or satin, sewed on to the stuffing with borders round them' or even pasting the silk onto a rebated top rail panel with a gold bead edging for drawing room chairs (1791–4, p.317).
See also **Gauze**, **Screen**, **Tiffany**.

FURTHER READING

Schoeser, M. (2001). 'Printed silk as an upholstery material' in Mertens, W. (ed.), *Transitory Splendour: Interior Textiles in Western Europe 1600–1900*, Antwerp: Hessenhuis Museum, Stadsbestuur, pp 320–22.

Printed textile
Although textiles printed with coloured designs in a variety of ways have been produced since early times, they remained relatively limited due to the lengthy hand processes involved. There are two primary processes:
(a) Direct printing, which treats the area to be coloured: these processes include block, rotary and screen printing.
(b) Indirect processes, which treat the area to remain clear. These processes include: mordant printing, where the mordant is applied to the cloth in the required pattern that is then revealed through a **dye** bath by removing surplus dyes from the unmordanted areas; resist printing that applies a barrier to parts of the cloth so a pattern is only produced on the unmarked parts; and discharge printing which creates a pattern by removing colour from an already dyed cloth.

Copperplate printing
A printing technique using flat, engraved copper plates. The incised areas take the colour, which is then transferred to the cloth under pressure in a rolling press. Early uses of copperplate or intaglio printing in relation to furnishing textiles seem to date from the mid to late seventeenth century. Philip Lea, a London printer, advertised *c.*1699: 'any of these [copperplate prints] ...may be printed on silk for a Sarsh [sic] window or to carry in the pocket in a little room as a handkerchief' (Schoeser, 2001, p.320).

The early prints were on squares of **silk** cloth, but from the mid-eighteenth century, the process was developed for continuous lengths of **cotton** or **linen**. This method was first established in Drumcondra, Ireland, by Francis Nixon and Theophilus Thompson in 1752, and later in England in 1756. In 1752, an advertisement in *Faulkner's Journal*,

102. Block print on linen/cotton cloth, multi-colour, c.1780 by G.P. & J. Baker

published in Dublin, was selling Drumcondra printed linens 'done from metal plates (a method never before practised) with all the advantages of light and shade, in the strongest and most lasting colours' (Longfield, 1972, pp 157–8). The printers used 36 inch (91 cm) square plates in combination with a press but, though limited to single colour prints, they had a long repeat pattern potential, ideal for **bed curtains** and **drapes**. Additional colours were occasionally added by a '**pencil**' technique or through the use of hand blocks, but the monochrome designs sold very well. On 19 February 1758, Benjamin Franklin purchased in London, '56 yards of cotton, printed curiously from copper plates, a new invention, to make bed and window curtains' (Cummings, 1961, p.23). From 1756, copperplate printing was a speciality of London. From 1770, the technique was taken to France by J.P. Oberkampf, who printed his famous 'Toiles de Jouy' at his works in Jouy-en-Josas. Incidentally, the French called the scenic copperplate prints *toiles d'Irelande* in recognition of the important developments that occurred there.

Designs were often floral. In 1767, a bedroom in William Cole's house in Bletchley, Bucks, referred to a bed of 'a most beautiful stained cotton of crimson and white by a copper plate, having parrots, & baskets of flowers etc. (Cornforth, 1989). Nevertheless, the technique is most commonly associated with scenic or narrative designs. In the 1790s, engraved copper cylinder rollers were developed to replace the flat plates.

Discharge printing
Two methods of discharge printing have been used. The first is to discharge the mordants before dyeing, as in madder work, and the second is to remove colours after the cloth is dyed. A cloth is piece-dyed to a ground colour after which a bleaching agent and another dye paste is applied to the design areas, so that the background colour is removed and the other colour added. Discharge cloths have a solid ground colour that is equal on the front and back of the fabric.

Hand block direct printing
The oldest method of printing textiles using a separate block for each colour in the design. The blocks have been of carved wood or have had strips of copper or brass inlaid to make a finer drawn design. The block is impressed upon the fabric by hand. It is a slow and costly process and has been superseded by powered methods in all but a very few cases. Products from this technique are slightly lacking in precision, which is often prized as a result of 'hand-work'. The guide points that are used on the blocks dot the cloth on the selvedge and other places and indicate a hand-blocked material. A major benefit of block printing is that the number of colours used is potentially unlimited.

Hand-produced block-printed (or other type) textiles have been used in the home for many centuries. In these cases, a design is carved into wood blocks, one for each colour of the pattern. Dye paste (colourant and thickening agent) is applied to the block and pressed onto the fabric. Early designs replicated the expensive woven textiles of silk and **velvet**.

The import of Indian cottons into the European home markets stimulated a demand for printed cloth from the early seventeenth century. The popularity of these 'new' cloths was such that imitations were soon being produced in Europe. It followed that technical changes would be developed to meet the growing demand. In the 1670s, English, French and Dutch manufacturers began to copy designs taken from Indian work and developed the process by using carved wooden blocks. In 1676, William Sherwin was granted a patent (no. 190/1676) for 'a new way for printing broad calicoe' in 'the only true way of East India printing and stayning such kind of goods' (Montgomery, 1970, p.16). These block-printed cottons were initially available in black, reds, purples and browns. By the 1750s, blue and yellow were added.

103. Plate print on linen/cotton cloth (detail) c. 1765–70 by G.P. & J. Baker

Heat transfer printing
A design is printed onto paper with disperse dye inks, which have an affinity with synthetic yarns. Using high pressure and temperature, the dye sublimates and then transfers from the paper to the cloth.

Ink jet printing
Dyes are injected over the fabric by many thousands of tiny jets whose operation is computer controlled. Used for **carpets** and **curtain** fabrics.

Resist
Similar to discharge printing which uses the idea that certain substances will destroy the affinity of a fabric for a particular dyestuff. By printing a design in a resist substance and dyeing the cloth, the design will resist the dyestuff and remain as printed. The resist process was initially associated with the preservation of areas of white cloth during the indigo-dyeing process.

Reversible printing
Prints whereby the dye is pushed through a cheap cloth are one example of this. Better qualities are the duplex prints, which have one side of the cloth printed, and then the other side is immediately printed.

Roller printing
Thomas Bell patented the important copper rotary-cylinder printing invention in 1785, but it was not until 30 years later, *c.*1810, that commercial production was significant in England. This resulted in faster printing, multi-colour results which, after 1830, took advantage of the new dyestuffs becoming available. The 'furniture print' intended for curtains, the filling, and the chair seat was especially popular in the early nineteenth century. This drove copperplate printing out of use.

From the early nineteenth century, England once again became the centre of printing, this time with the cylinder roller techniques. The advantages of roller printing, i.e. speed and multiple colour printing, were only partly limited by the small repeats that were possible. The development of mineral dyes, as opposed to vegetable, also gave the printer a palette that could produce brighter patterns. This revolution in technology ensured that the new market was catered for, as printed

104. Roller-printed furnishing fabric, purple on white, c.1825 by G.P. & J Baker

cottons became one of the norms for domestic furnishings. Stippling was a particular process that was combined with roller printing. Instead of sharp copper outlines being laid into the roller, small blunt points were fixed in to give a shaded and hazy effect to the print. This process was fashionable in the first quarter of the nineteenth century. Rollers with raised outlines or a 'surface' were developed, and became particularly important in twentieth-century trade.

Rotogravure printing
This process uses engraved steel cylinders and is used to print on non-cloth materials such as vinyl, and for paper patterns that will be used in 'heat transfer' printing.

Screen printing (resist)
Initially, a hand process that was half way between block prints and machine printing, and often used for relatively short runs of printing cloth. Although screen printing was known as early as the second half of the seventeenth century, it was not until the 1920s that commercial production was possible. This still remained a hand operation until the 1950s when the process was mechanised, and it is now the most economical method for printing cloth.

105. Screen print 1980s (Sue Timney Ltd)

The twentieth-century process uses open mesh frames that are partially covered according to the design, to create the blank spaces of patterns (like a stencil). The unblocked areas of the screen allow dyestuff to pass through the mesh creating the pattern on the cloth below. Overprinting of various colours using individual screens is possible. In rotary screen printing, the screens are rollers that have the design blocked out and the colour stuff passes through from the inside of the roller.

Warp printing
Originally developed in France in the eighteenth century, it was called chiné.
See also **Chiné**, **Chintz**, **Duplex**, **Dye**, **Pencilling**, **Printed cotton**, **Tapestry carpet**, **Toile de Jouy**.

FURTHER READING

Albeck, P. (1969). *Printed Textiles*, Oxford: Oxford University Press.
Bredif, J. (1989). *Classic Printed Textiles from France 1760–1843: Toiles de Jouy*, London, Thames and Hudson.
Chassange, S. (2003). 'Calico printing in Europe before 1780' in, Jenkins, D. (ed.), *The Cambridge History of Western Textiles*, Cambridge: Cambridge University Press, pp 513–27.
Clark, H. (1985). *Textile Printing*, Aylesbury: Shire.
Clayton, M. & Oakes, A. (1954). 'Early calico printers around London', *Burlington Magazine*, 96, May, pp 135–9.
Clouzot, H. & Morris, F. (1927). *Painted and Printed Fabrics*, New York: Metropolitan Museum of Art, reprinted 1974, New York: Arno Press.
Endrei, W. (1998). *The First Hundred Years of European Textile Printing*, Budapest: Akademiai Kiado.
Floud, P. (1957). 'Richard Overy and furniture printers', *Connoisseur*, 140, November, pp.92–6.
Floud, P. (1960). 'The origins of English calico printing', *Journal of the Society of Dyers and Colourists*, LXXXVI, May, pp 275–81.
King, D. (1962). 'Textiles and the origins of printing in Europe', *Pantheon*, XX, pp 23–30.
Longfield, A.K. (1937). 'History of the Irish linen and cotton printing industry in the 18th century', *Journal of the Royal Society of Antiquaries of Ireland*, 7, 7, pp 26–56.
Longfield, A.K. (1960). '18th century adverts and calico printers', *Burlington Magazine*, 102, March, pp 112–15.
Longfield, A.K. (1972). 'Early Irish printed fabric', *Country Life*, 7 December, p.157–8.
Montgomery, F. (1970). *Printed Textiles: English and American Cottons and Linen, 1700–1850*, London: Thames and Hudson.
Robinson, S. (1969). *A History of Printed Textiles: Block, Roller, Screen, Design, Dyes, Fibres, Discharge, Resist, Further Sources for Reseach* London: Studio Vista.
Standen, E. (1964). 'English washing furnitures', *Metropolitan Museum of Art Bulletin*, XXIII, 3, pp 109–24.
Turnbull, G. (1951). *History of the Calico Printing Industry of Great Britain*, Altrincham: J. Sherratt.

Priscilla curtain

An American term for criss-cross or cross-over curtains, which are sheer **ruffled curtains** hung on double rods – one curtain overlaps the other, always with ruffled **tiebacks**, and often with matching ruffled **valance**.

Protective furnishing

The necessity of protecting the expensive investment in fine furniture and textiles soon meant that protective covers were supplied for a whole range of furnishings. These were usually made from serviceable fabrics such as **leather**, **baize** or **flannel**.

The supply of fitted covers for globes and cases for cabinets, tabletops and triads began during the seventeenth century. The Tart Hall inventory lists amongst others: 'A long table of boardes sett upon tressells, thereon a long leather cover; A French drawing table of walnut tree with a leather carpet thereon; an oval table of wanscote with folding sides, thereon a cover of red leather bordered with blue gilt leather' (Cust, 1911).

Sometimes they made a dual contribution, being decorative in their own right. In 1688, Randle Holme recorded 'A Turkey table cover or carpet of cloth or leather printed' (XIV, p.15). In 1677, the marble dining room in Ham House had 'two oval cedar tables with two leather covers lined with clouded lutestring' (Thornton & Tomlin, 1980, p.45).

In 1710, Dyrham House had 'several large panalls of flannel for covering furniture (loosely)'. By the eighteenth century, these covers were common and were included in many invoices and inventories. For example, Chippendale supplied '2 Damask leather covers lin'd and bound with gilt leather' to the half-round sections of dining tables for Paxton (Berwick) in 1774 (Gilbert, 1978, p.274).

Protective covers continued to be used in the nineteenth century. In 1803, Sheraton explained how 'covers for pier tables [were] made of stamped leather and glazed, lined with flannel to save the varnish'. He goes on to say: 'Lately they have introduced a new kind of painted canvas, varnished and very elastic in its nature and will probably answer better than leather' (1803, p.336). In fact, it seems as if at least one maker specialised in the work: John Newbery of Upper Marylebone Street, London, listed his 1825 business as 'painted baize and leather cover maker' (*DEFM*, p.642).

Specific protection was afforded to particular objects. Globes and valuable furniture have been mentioned above. Other examples include protection of curtains, beds, walls and light fittings. Chippendale supplied Mersham in 1778 with '48 yards buff serge in bags to the window curtains' (Gilbert, 1978, p.232). While in 1830, the upholsterers, Morel and Seddon, supplied Stafford House with 'loose covers of fine brown holland for the window drapery and cornice with separate cases for the curtains' for a number of installations (Yorke, 1996, p.78).

Wall protection is demonstrated by the 1697 inventory of Kensington Palace, which lists 'white stuff curtains for before the hangings' (Cornforth & Fowler, 1974, p.257). And in 1830, Stafford House had 'large covers to suit for the whole of the walls loaded at bottom with shot, and fitted with brass eyes, ring plates etc. (Yorke, 1996, p.72).

Noetzli showed a design for a loose cover to protect chandeliers in a holland or **gauze** fabric with a wire frame fitted internally to avoid damage to the glasses (Noetzli, 1906, p.128). Even **tassels** had protection: William France supplied Moor Park with '4 baggs for tossels of your own blue serge'. Mrs Delany explained that 'if you cover [tassels] with a case of cloth, it may be slipped off when dirty to wash' (1861).

The desire to protect expensive furnishings continues with the use of **table felt**, loose covers and dustsheets.

Case cover (Slipcover)

There are distinctions between the semi-permanent covers employed to protect fine furnishings until used, and the decorative loose covers that are usually only removed for laundering (for the latter see *Loose cover* below). Loose or fitted covers for chairs and sofas, bookcases, table and commode tops and beds, intended to protect the finer materials underneath, were often made from leather, baize, **drugget**, **cotton check**, etc, and **linen** holland was popular in the nineteenth century for the making of protective and storage covers.

106. Slip case mid-eighteenth century (Courtesy The Winterthur Museum)

The commonplace and varied nature of protective covers can be seen in the household of Sir Richard Worsley. In *c.*1779, the housekeeper's storeroom had '8 crimson serge cases for gilt chairs in drawing room ... 2 damask leather covers for pier tables in Do ... 12 green serge covers for chairs in dining parlour ... green baize covers for pictures and glasses ... [and] 2 green and white stripe cases for sofas' (Boynton, 1965, p.51).

The range of protective furnishings for chairs was necessarily wide. Prior to 1535, Katherine of Aragon had iron chairs fitted in leather cases lined with yellow cotton (Clabburn, 1988, p.167). In 1588, Robert Dudley had a carved and embroidered walnut chair that was sufficiently important to have 'a case of buckerom to the same' (Beard, 1997, p.284). **Buckram** was used later in 1603 in the Great Chamber of Hengrave where there were 24 high joined stools 'covered with carpet work like the carpets, fringed with crewel; and yellow buckrams to over the stools with' (Clabburn, 1988, p.167). In 1637, Queen Henrietta Maria was supplied by Ralph Grynder with '25 yards of fine broad bayse to case 2 chairs 6 folding stools and a couch being cased down to the ground' (Beard, 1997, p.289). A little later, Samuel Pepys explained how he was 'alytering my chairs in my chamber, and set them above in the red room, they being turkeywork; and so put their green covers upon those that were above, not so handsome' (*The Diary of Samuel Pepys*, 11 October 1663).

In 1773, Chippendale advised Lady Knatchbull that 'serge is most commonly used [for covers] but ... you might choose some sort of callico' (Gilbert, 1978, p.57).

Sometimes the case covers were lined to protect delicate carvings, and they could often be removed for washing. The Gillow Co wrote to a client saying that: 'We presume [the chair] will require some sort of washing cover which requires a good deal of nicety to make them fit well to such sorts of chairs' (Gillow Company Records, Folio 22, p.202).

Sheraton described case covers and added a comment about the use of **oilcloth**:

> Covers for chairs &c. to keep them clean, and of any inferior stuff. Cases for covers or cushions, made to slip over and tie with tape. Covers for pier tables, made of stamped leather and glazed, lined with flannel to save the varnish of such table tops. Lately they have introduced a new kind of painted canvas, varnished, and very elastic in its nature, and will probably answer better than leather. (1803, p.336.)

The covers could be attractive in their own right. Stafford House was supplied in 1830 with 'loose covers of chamois leather bound with white ribband for the 2 elbow chairs', and loose covers 'of yellow striped printed furniture. Lined with fine white glazed calico, and bound with silk galloon' (Yorke, 1996, pp 69–70).

The particular use of linen holland for removable covers is shown in a representative example of housekeeping manuals of the nineteenth century. *The Workwoman's Guide* explained the whole process:

> When chairs are fitted up with damask, merino, stuff, horsehair, or other material that does not wash, they are generally covered with Holland, chintz, or glazed calico, which protects them from dust and dirt, and are easily removed, when required for company. Holland covers are the most durable, but too cold; chintz, unless very strong, should be lined with thin glazed calico. The cover should be made exactly to fit the chair or sofa, with or without piping at the edge, and with the loops sewed on three of the sides underneath, and a pair of strings on the fourth side; the cover is firmly fastened down by passing one of the strings through the three loops and making it tie. (Hale, 1840, p.206.)

In 1889, Moreland wrote that for case covers 'the very best material to use is plain brown linen, though they are made of striped and figured linen, dimity, French cottons and cretonnes etc' (pp 280–91).

In the twentieth century, American author, Elizabeth Dyer, described them:

> [Case covers] are used when furniture, which has delicate upholstery, is to be protected, or in summer when one prefers light, washable coverings because, they are cooler and more easily taken care of than the upholstery. There is material in both cotton and linen called furniture slip covering or Belgian linen, made especially for this purpose. Usually it is a tan or cream striped fabric in a herringbone weave, which will not show soil so badly as pure white, although pure white is often used. So also are lightweight canvas, denim, duck, drill, jean, cretonne and chintz, because they can be laundered. (*c.*1923, p.207.)

Loose cover

Fitted but removable decorative **top covers** for **upholstery** were also known as 'case' or 'slipcovers'. When called case covers this would usually refer to the role of protection of a quality material underneath. Occasionally this practice was reversed and the finer covers were fitted only when required. Loose covers were certainly known in the sixteenth century, and there are many examples of expensive furniture covers being protected by loose covers.

They were commonplace during the eighteenth century. During this time, side chairs often had covers made with a deep ruffle on the sides and sets of **tapes** to fix them to the chair legs. Hepplewhite's *Guide* illustrated a wing easy chair and noted that they may 'have a linen case to fit over the canvas stuffing as it is most usual and convenient' (1794, p.3). Sheraton described 'cushions stuffed with hair which are then quilted or tied down, and have loose cases into which they slip' (1803, p.186). Loudon described how:

> A very cheap yet tasteful loose sofa cover may be made of glazed self-coloured calico, with a narrow piece of different coloured calico or shawl bordering, laid on about a couple of inches from the edge. This kind of cover lasts clean much longer than one of common printed cotton; and when the bordering is carried round the covers of the cushions, bolster, etc., it has a pretty and even elegant effect. (1839, p.325.)

During the nineteenth century, there was a move towards using loose covers as the only finishing fabric. These would be fitted over **calico**-covered upholstery. The twentieth century saw the continued use of covers as decoration and for practicality. There was a practice of selling new upholstery with sets of loose covers that could be changed over at will. Loose covers remain a useful tool in the furnishers' repertoire.

See also **Bed protection**, **Carpet cover and protection**, **Holland**.

FURTHER READING

Balfour, D. & Gentle, N. (2001). 'A study of loose textile covers for seat furniture in England between 1670 and 1731' in Mertens, W. (ed.), *Transitory Splendour: Interior Textiles in Western Europe 1600–1900*, Antwerp: Hessenhuis Museum, Stadsbestuur, pp 295–9.

Baumgarten, L. (1990). 'Curtains, covers, and cases: upholstery documents at Colonial Williamsburg' in Williams, M.A. (ed.), *Upholstery Conservation*, preprints of a symposium held at Colonial Williamsburg, 2–4 February, American Conservation Consortium, East Kingston, NH pp 103–35.

Baumgarten, L. (1993). 'Protective covers for furniture and its contents', *American Furniture*, pp 3–14.

Clabburn, P. (1989). 'Case covers' in *The National Trust Book of Furnishing Textiles*, Harmondsworth: Penguin, pp 166–76.

Davies, M. (1982). *Tailored Loose Covers*, London: Stanley Paul.

Gill, K. (2001). 'Eighteenth-century close-fitting detachable covers preserved at Houghton Hall: a technical study' in Gill, K. & Eastop, D. (eds), *Upholstery Conservation: Principles and Practice*, Oxford: Butterworth-Heinemann, pp 133–42.

Montgomery, F. (1984). 'Case covers' in *Textiles in America 1650–1870*, New York: Norton, pp 123–7.

Swain. M, (1997). 'Loose covers or cases on British furniture', *Furniture History*, 33, pp 128–33.

Provençal print

In the later sixteenth century, printed and painted **calicoes** from India were imported into Marseilles and the local region (see **Indienne**). Local printers began to copy the designs using block prints, and had a flourishing trade. Although sales were later banned in France generally, sales in Marseilles and Avignon continued as they were under papal jurisdiction. In 1759, the ban was dropped and the fabrics became popular all over France. The prints are often characterised by small, stylised motifs that are repeated on a plain white or coloured background.

Pulley rod

From the beginning of the nineteenth century, rods or poles fitted with

pulleys allowed **curtains** to be drawn without touching the fabrics. They were a **cord** system for opening and closing curtains, recommended by Loudon (1839) and *The Workwoman's Guide* (Hale, 1840). However, even by 1844, Webster & Parkes could say that: 'a [cornice] pole with rings was still the general method at present, in the better sort of rooms' as opposed to the pulley rod system.
See also **Curtain pole and rod**, **French rod**.

Pulley and lath
See **French rod**, **Pulley rod**.

Pull-over edge
An **upholstery** term referring to the method of fitting a **top cover** by pulling the cloth over the leading edge and sides to create a convex shape and in which the seat and **borders** are one continuous piece of fabric.

Pull-up curtain
A form of **curtain** devised in France in the latter part of the seventeenth century. They usually hung in festoons, but they could be pulled up to the **cornice** to clear the window. Examples were purchased for Hampton Court Palace in 1699 (Thornton, 1978, p.363).
See also **Festoon**.

Purdah
The name is derived from the Urdu *pardah*, meaning a veil or **curtain**. Yule uses a reference from 1813 to explain: 'My travelling palankeen formed my bed, its purdoe or chintz covering my curtains' (1903). It was later defined in 1887 as 'an Indian cotton cloth having blue and white stripes used for curtains' (Caulfeild & Saward, p.386).

Purl
(a) A decorative **trimming** thread or **cord** made of hollow, twisted gold or silver wire, coiled round a thin rod and pushed off to form a flexible tube for use in **borders** and **embroidery**. It was especially used in the sixteenth and early seventeenth centuries. In 1887, Caulfeild & Saward described it: 'Pearl-purl is a gold cord of twisted wire, resembling a small row of beads strung closely together. Used for the edging of bullion embroidery.' (p.387.) **Silk** purl is worked in the same way as the gold. Flat gold wire is known by the name of 'plate'.
(b) Also a term to describe the minute loops or twists of which the edges of **lace**, **braid**, ribbon, etc. are decorated. In the machine-made lace trade, purls are a twisted loop on the edge or in the body of a piece of lace, **net** or braid. Thus, laces and braids categorised by such loops are known as purl laces, purl braids or, simply, purls.

PVC
Flexible PVC (polyvinyl chloride) eventually replaced leathercloth. Although the idea of a flexible surface applied to a backing cloth was not new (see **Oilcloth**), it was only with the introduction of PVC, used since the 1930s, that improved flexibility and a lesser chance of cracking made it truly popular as an **upholstery** cloth. By the 1940s, imitation **leather**, based on PVC, was a commercial proposition. Thermoplastic, low cost, flame resistant (because of chloride content), and rigid, though flexible in the presence of a plasticiser, PVC replaced earlier **coated fabrics** as it had fewer tendencies to crack. These flexible textured vinyl fabrics were very popular post-war for many kinds of upholstery work since they could be used 'traditionally' or through vacuum-forming processes. Developments in the science have consistently improved performance, and include advances in backing cloth, such as knitted backcloth, and the development of expanded PVC coatings to increase softness and handle.

In the mid-twentieth century, *The Draper's Encyclopaedia* said:

> PVC sheeting is an ideal material for bathroom curtains, table covers, etc. The sheeting may be opaque, translucent or transparent and may be dope-dyed in a wide range of colours. It can be embossed and may be printed in colours, which can be fast to abrasion… A few years ago PVC was unsatisfactory, it faded and had an unpleasant odour. It became stiff, cracked and was sometimes sticky… Now these materials are available and a great advance has been made in production, so they are now quite serviceable. (Ostick, 1955, p.365.)

Supported PVC-coated fabrics were more successful for upholstery as they had a strong woven or knitted base fabric (flexible enough to stretch slightly), upon which the coating was applied. Initially these fabrics were impermeable, but later developments allowed them to 'breathe' through vapour permeability. The plastic nature of the fabric enabled it to be welded by high frequency methods, thus avoiding stitching in some cases, and allowed for decorative effects to be employed by welding techniques. PVC has been used as a backing for soft covering material to improve cleaning ability and wear resistance.

Queen's stuff
A textile of which little seems to be known. It was used as a fashion fabric and for furnishings. In 1766, W. Gordon mentioned 'fine brocaded queens stuff' (*General Counting House and man of business*, 428, 16, *OED*). It was mentioned again, as yardage, in an 1866 invoice from furnishers Marsh and Jones to Sir Titus Salt (Boynton, 1967, p.78).
See also **Stuff**.

Quilt
A thick bedcover usually made from a sandwich of filling and two pieces of outer cover that is **stitched** through the three layers. In its earlier uses, the quilt was made to serve as a form of **mattress**. They were also used both above and below the sleeper as under quilts and upper quilts. The word came into English usage from the old French *cuilte*, or *coilte*, derived from the Latin *culcita*, meaning a 'stuffed mattress' or 'cushion'.

107. PVC cloth printed with 'contemporary' design (E. Ostick, The Draper's Encyclopaedia*, 1955)*

Although early references to quilts do occur, they are often ambiguous as to their meaning. The *OED* mentions a reference from 1290 that says 'Maketh a bed … of quoitene and of materasz' (see also **Twilt**).

An early reference that is quite explicit is from 1542. Andrew Boorde, in his *Compendyous Regyment or a Dietary of helth*, suggested:

> I do advertise you to cause to be made a good thick quilt of cotton, or else of pure flocks or of clean wool, and let the covering of it be of white fustian, and lay it on the featherbed that you do lie on; and in your bed lie not too hot nor too cold, but in temperance. (Fitzrandolph, 1955, p.83.)

By the sixteenth century, type names distinguished quilts. In the *Book of Rates* for 1582, there were listed: 'Quilts called French quilts the dosen/Quilts the peece/Quilts of satin or other silk for Beds, the Quilt' (Willan, 1962, p.49). Quilts appear to have been initially decorative if the instructions from 1595 to the Yeoman of the Wardrobe in the Montague Household are a guide. They were instructed 'to remove the quilts at night' and to have 'yrishe rugges lay'd in their places' in guests' rooms (Thornton, 1978, p.355). The decorative features were again to the fore in the Hardwick Hall inventory of 1601, which listed a quilt 'of yellow India stuff embroidered with birds and beasts and white silke fringe and tassells', and 'two quilts, whereof one linen, the other diaper' (Boynton, 1971, p.31).

In the seventeenth century, distinctions in quilt types were again noted. The 1611 inventory of Hatfield listed 'one olde turkie quilte of crimson silke' (Beard, 1997, p.286). A letter of 1619 to the East India Co also indicates the range of quilts: 'all of one kind of chintz', 'some of different chintzes, yet such as either side may be used', 'some to have borders only of different colours', 'excellent quilts of stained cloth, or of fresh coloured taffeta lined with their pintadoes' (Irwin, 1966, p.2). In 1635, the Duke of Buckingham's inventory had in the King's bedchamber: 'Three quilts, the first of Holland, the second of fustian, and the third of canvas.' (Jervis, 1997, p.59.) This mix of types is also evident in the bedding that the upholsterer, Jean Poictevin, sold to the Duke of Hamilton in 1688 that included: 'a thick lustieng [lustring] quilt and a checkered lining quilt and a finer Holland quilt and a fustineee [fustian] quilt to put between the other' for £10.5s.0d. (Beard, 1997, p.292.)

The decorated quilts had various uses. In 1679, Ham House records 'a blew stitched silk quilt with adders downe [eiderdown] in it' (Thornton & Tomlin, 1980, p.166). In a 1688 Whitehall inventory there are 'quilts for couches of crimson satin etc' (Edwards, 1964, p.420). Thirdly, a 'painted callicoe quilt' is recorded in the inventory of William Bird of Writtle on 16 May 1691 (Steer, 1969, p.207). The Dyrham Park inventory of 1710 again distinguishes 'under quilts' and 'upper quilts' of crimson **silk** and covering quilt of white fustian (Edwards, 1964, p.421).

In 1697, professional quilt-makers petitioned the Government against import restrictions on **calicoes**. This is revealing of a number of issues:

> I. That depriving the quilt-makers of the liberty of using printed callicoe carpets will be a detriment to the Government, as to the customs and duties, and also the woollen manufacturers; there being great quantities of Norwich, Kidderminster, Kendal and other stuffs, used for the backsides of quilts; besides abundance of ordinary wool, which must otherwise be thrown away; it being too short for spinning, and fit for no other use.
> II. That the calicoes used in making quilts, are cut into square pieces and printed in form of a carpet which renders then unfit for cloaths or garments of any kind: Neither can they be used in household furniture any otherways but in quilts, being only fit for that purpose.
> III. That linen cloths and woollens stuffs are not proper for quilts, the one being cold and heavy, and the woollen will harbour filth and dirt, and be much of the same kind as Rugs are: and not being capable of being clean'd so well as calico carpets, renders them altogether unfit for that purpose: For the whole design in having quilts for beds is to have them light and warm, and made of that which will clean often, and not harbour filth and dirt, as the rugs used to do. (Osler, 1987, p.88)

The nineteenth-century *Workwoman's Guide* mentions a range of quilts including Marseilles, Imperial, Summer, Toilet cover or Cradle quilts (Hale, 1840). In the late nineteenth century, paper quilts were made up for charitable purposes. Four inch (10 cm) squares of cloth were sewn together into bags that were then stuffed with shredded paper: each 'bag' was then sewn to another as in a patchwork to complete the 'quilt' (Caulfeild & Saward, 1887, p.415).

The twentieth century still offered the opportunity for hand-made quilts:

> A quilt is a bedcovering consisting of a soft layer of cotton or wool wadding covered with cloth on both sides, quilted or tacked together at regular intervals, and bound. The old-fashioned 'patchwork quilt' was made of small pieces of cotton or woollen cloth, made into 'blocks' of fanciful design. When the blocks were finished and sewed together, a piece of plain cloth was stretched on a wooden frame, sheets of wadding were placed on this cloth, and the patchwork piece laid on top. Then the three layers were tacked together for quilting. The frame consisted of wooden bars on four sides. The quilt was wound upon the two side bars, as the 'quilters' who sat in two rows at the sides of the frame stitched it together by hand. Modern quilts are usually covered with light cotton materials. (Thompson, 1917, p.129.)

In the 1950s, quilts were filled with either down, **kapok** or fleece. Widely used materials for covers were crêpe-backed **satins**, marocains, **chintzes** and **crêpes**. Decoration was varied but included ruching, which produced a raised or puckered effect to form a circular or oval pattern. **Embroidery** was used as well, including the cornely type, which resembled a chain stitch when worked from the front and a running stitch when worked from the back. Wide satin stitch was used for floral embroidery and was known as 'Irish embroidery'.

In 1950, *The Mercury Dictionary of Textile Terms* listed the following types:

> *Broché Quilts*: A **warp** faced fabric, often with elaborate designs in two colours.
> *Grecian Quilts*: Reversible cloth with fairly free-floating warps and **wefts**.
> *Honeycomb Quilts*: A cellular effect is created by the honeycomb weave, which is often shown off by bold designs.
> *Repp Quilts*: A heavy repp fabric made with large jacquard designs usually with white and one colour warp so the cloth is reversible.
> *Tapestry Quilts*: A substantial fabric, woven from dyed yarns, with the weft in two, three or more colours all woven to create patterns with coloured warps.
> *Toilet Quilts*: A non-reversible piqué fabric often with a third weft used as wadding.

Quilts and quilting remain a serious pastime, either as making or collecting, for wide-ranging sections of the community.

See also **Alhambra quilt**, **Caddow**, **Counterpoint**, **Down**, **Duree quilt**, **Duvet**, **Embroidered coverlet/quilt**, **Fustian**, **Honeycomb**, **Manchester quilt**, **Marseilles**, **Mitcheline**, **Patchwork**, **Pintado**, **Toilette**, **Quilt**.

FURTHER READING

Bishop, R. & Coblentz, P. (1975). *New Discoveries in American Quilts*, New York: E.P. Dutton.
Fitzrandolph, M. (1955). *Quilting. Traditional Methods and Designs*, Leicester: Dryad.

Glaister, E. (1880). *Needlework*, London: Macmillan, pp 96–107.
Houck, C. (1991). *The Quilt Encyclopaedia Illustrated*, New York: Harry Abrams and Museum of American Folk Art.
Lidz, M.R. (1998). 'The mystery of seventeenth century quilts', *The Magazine Antiques*, 6, December, pp 834–43.
Makowski, C.L. (1985). *Quilting 1915–1983*, an Annotated Bibliography, Metuchen, NJ: Scarecrow Press.
Orlofsky, P. & M. (1992). *Quilts in America*, New York: Abbeville.
Osler, D. (1987). *Traditional British Quilts*, London: Batsford.
Rae, J. (1987). *Quilts of the British Isles*, London: Constable.
Safford, C.L. & Bishop, R. (1972). *America's Quilts and Coverlets*, New York: E.P. Dutton.

Quilting
A sewing technique that **stitches** together two or more fabric layers and fillings to make padded or quilted panels for use on beds, walls or upholstery. The stitches often form a surface design or pattern. Initially used in saddlery and armoury for padded overlays, it was adapted to upholstery techniques during the seventeenth century. The connection with the origins of upholstery and the role of the saddler and carriage-maker is clear (see **Upholstery**). Quilting was also a well-known technique in the preparation of eighteenth and nineteenth century **bed furniture**. Campbell (1747) noted that specialists undertook quilting. Talking about quilted **petticoats**, Campbell goes on to say of the quilters: 'They quilt likewise quilts for beds for the upholders'.

Corded, **trapunto** or Italian quilting is a form of **embroidery** that gives high relief to the design where **cords** have been inserted under the surface of the material. It is a process that sews two parallel lines of stitching and then has a cord or heavy thread inserted to create a raised surface pattern.

False quilting
Flat or Queen Anne quilting is entirely unpadded and was originally worked on **linen**.

Shadow quilting
A variation of Italian quilting that uses a light coloured top fabric and a bright **cord** insert to create a shaded effect.

Stuffed quilting
See **Trapunto**.

Wall quilting
An associated practice linked to working with fabric-covered walls. Rather than having the fabric fitted flat or **pleated**, it has **wadding** fixed behind it and is then sewn or buttoned through to create a padded effect.
See also **Caddow**, **Couching**, **Marseilles**, **Matelassé**.

Quinze-seize
A thin taffeta, used in France in the eighteenth century, especially for windows. It was so-called because it was 15/16ths of a French **ell** wide.
See also **Taffeta**.

Rabbit down
Rabbit down was used as an **upholstery filling** material. Rabbit **hair** was referred to as an upholstery material (filling) on the trade card of James Marshall Jr of Leeds *c.*1766 (Banks Collection, British Museum).

Radnor
In 1936, radnor was described as an **upholstery** fabric woven in mercerised cotton of characteristic weaves; a **rep** with uneven **checks** in a corded pattern (Denny, 1936).

Rag carpet
A floorcovering, usually 36 inches (91 cm) wide, that was woven with a range of **warps** and a **weft** of cut fabric or rags. In the nineteenth century, in the USA, they were woven up to 15 feet (4.6 metres) wide in **carpet** mills but they were also produced on hand operated looms. In 1913, George Leland reported that there were 854 outlets in the USA, making rag carpet with a value of $1,714,480.
See also **List carpet**, **Rag rug**.

Rag flock
See **Woollen flock**.

Rag rug
A floor **rug** usually made at home using scraps of fabric, which was popular during the nineteenth and early twentieth centuries. Loudon explained the process:

> Another kind of cheap hearth rug may be made by the cottager's wife, of remnants of cloth cut into narrow strips about half an inch broad, and three or four inches long: these strips are doubled, and sewed at the bend in rows to a strong piece of cloth or knitted into a framework of pack thread. In either case the colours are disposed so as to form some kind of pattern; and the ends being left loose and cut even when the work is finished, with a large pair of scissors or shears, the whole presents a remarkably rich, warm, and massive appearance. (1839, p.346.)

Later in the nineteenth century, *Cassell's Household Guide* (1870) recommended that for 'upper bedroom doors', rag mats made from 'cloth cuttings, sewn onto canvas in innumerable loops as closely as possible', using cuttings of **felt carpet**, lists, or even old dress stuff, were appropriate.

Woven rag rugs or **carpeting** was also popular in the USA during the later nineteenth century. Almon Varney (1883) considered that a hand-loom set up in the home, using dyed **cotton warp** and a **weft** of rags cut into strips, would be able to make a reasonable floorcovering.
See also **Abnakee rug**, **Braided rug**, **List carpet**.

FURTHER READING

Steedman, C. (1999). 'What a rag rug means' in Bryden, I. & Floyd, J. (eds), *Domestic Space: Reading the Nineteenth Century Interior*, Manchester: Manchester University Press, pp 18–40.
Tennant, E. (1992). *Rag Rugs of England and America*, London: Walker.

Railroading
The practice of placing and sewing an **upholstery** fabric so that the **weft** is running vertically on the surface. Not all fabrics are suited to this.

Railway
A **curtain** suspension system that is based on extruded plastic, brass, aluminium or steel 'I' railway sections. These are fixed directly to a board or window frame and usually hidden behind a **pelmet** or **valance**. They can range from lightweight to extra heavy-duty types. They are equipped with wheeled runners that have rings fitted to hang the curtains.
See also **Curtain pole and rod**, **Pulley**.

Ramie cloth (aka China grass)
(a) A Chinese and East Indian plant of the nettle family, *Boehmeria nivea,* also called rhea and grass cloth plant. This plant is a native of the island of Sumatra, where it is cultivated for its bark, which has many fibres of very great strength and fineness in it.
(b) *Rami* is the Malay name for both the plant and the fibre of this plant, extensively employed in weaving. It is one of the strongest natural fibres and has lustre comparable to mercerised **cotton** or even **silk**. Before 1939, it was used in the finest grades of furnishing fabrics, especially those produced with a **pile**. Denny (1938, p.26) described grass cloth (Canton **linen**) as a fine translucent fabric made of ramie that looks like linen. It was used for **table linen** and dressmaking.

In the 1950s, it was recorded rather differently in a British publication, as a plain or twill weave cloth used for **tapestries**, furnishings and **towels** (*The Mercury Dictionary of Textile Terms*, 1950, p.418).
See also **Grass cloth**, **Moquette**.

FURTHER READING
Bally, W. (1957). 'Ramie', *CIBA Review*, 123, pp 2–30.

Rateen (aka Ratteen)
From the French *ratine* (1642), of unknown origin, it is a thick-twilled **kersey**-type **woollen** cloth with a friezed or curled nap.

Postlethwayt, writing in 1751–7, defined ratteen as 'a thick woollen stuff, quilled, woven on a loom with four treadles, like serges and other stuffs that have the whale or quilling-there are some prepared like cloths, others left simply in the hair, [not sheared] and others where the hair or nap is frized.' During the eighteenth century, rateen was used for **upholstery**, bed hangings and **curtains**. Its use for upholstery in Boston, USA, is shown by an inventory of Thomas Baxter, upholsterer, who, in 1751, had '65¾ yards of Ratteen at a total value of £121.18s.9d.' (Cummings, 1961, p.35.)

In the nineteenth century, it was chiefly used as a lining material. Sheraton (taking from Chambers' work) says that rateens are mostly made in France, Holland and Italy and are generally used in linings (*The Cabinet Dictionary*, 1803, p.294).

Rateen is also a generic name for coarse woollen stuffs, such as **baize**, **drugget** and **frieze**.

Ratiné
In 1947, ratiné was described as having a 'nubby surface texture acquired through ratiné yarns (with slubs) used in the warp'. It has been used for curtain materials (Bendure & Pfieffer, p.647).

Rattinet
A thin-twilled **woollen** material resembling **shalloon** but of a thinner substance than **rateen**. It has been used to line **curtains**, etc. Chippendale supplied Edward Knatchbull with '67 yards fine buff Rattinet to line curtains' in the late 1770s (Gilbert, 1978, I. p.233). In 1887, Caulfeild & Saward described it as 'a French cloth thinner than Rateen' (p.419).

Ravensduck
An eighteenth-century term for a coarse **canvas** or **sailcloth**, which appears to have been similar to **Russia duck**. Now a name for a heavy sailcloth 2/1 twill.
See also **Duck**.

Rawhide
A treated but untanned split cattle hide, preserved by a liming process that does not convert the skin to leather. As it dries, it shrinks, making it ideal for tight drum seats.
See also **Leather**.

Raynes cloth
Cloth of Raine(s), or raynes cloth, was a type of fine **linen** or **lawn** originally made at Rennes in Brittany. It was a superior quality linen that was used for **sheet** and **pillowcases**. Known in the fourteenth century in England, when Chaucer mentions it in *The Book of the Duchesse*:

> I will give him a feather-bed
> Rayed with gold and right well clad
> In fine black satin doutremere
> And many a pillow, and every bere
> Of cloth of Reynes, to sleep softe;
> Him thar not need to turned ofte. (Lines 251–6)

Its value is confirmed in a description of the bed made up for Lord of Gruthère by the wife of Edward IV: 'There was ordained a bed for himself of as good down as could be gotten, the sheets of raynes' (Macquoid, 1904, p.67). In a will of 1395, there was recorded 'a peyre schetes of Reynes' (*Early English Wills*, 1882, p.4).

Rayon
The first man-made fibre, it is processed from cellulosic materials, such as wood pulp, and was first developed as an alternative to **cotton**, as chemically, it performs very similarly. It is relatively inexpensive, light resistant and stable, so can be widely used as a **lining** or **drapery** fabric. It has a high lustre and yarn effects such as slubs can be created in it. Viscose rayon is the most common, but the cellulose acetate process produced a finer, more **silk**-like yarn. This processes the cellulosic material into a liquid that is then extruded as a continuous filament. With its high lustre, it often imitates silk. Also known as 'art silk' for this reason. Viscose rayon was patented in 1892 by Cross and Bevan, although it was not until the 1920–30s that the industry made an impact on furnishing fabrics as the prices fell in relation to the rising natural yarn prices.

American authors noted that: 'Soft cotton or rayon velveteen and rayon velvet make luxurious comfortables as do lustrous rayon satins and crisp taffetas' (Bendure & Pfieffer, 1947, p.581).
See also **Art silk**, **Artificial horsehair**.

FURTHER READING
Beer. E.J. (1962). *The Beginning of Rayon*, Paignton: Beer.

Reed
See **Grass**.

Reefed curtain
See **Festoon**.

Rep (aka Repp)
A furnishing textile, usually of **cotton**, **wool** or **silk**, with a fine **warp** and a thick **weft** that gave it a distinctive transverse, corded or ribbed effect. As an **upholstery** fabric, it was popular in the nineteenth century. It may also be woven with a warp rib and is then called **repette**. Sloan noted in his *Homestead Architecture* that:

> Wool reps [sic] is much used particularly for dining room furniture and drapery. Silk reps, plain, ribbed or striped in different colours are much used for dining rooms and parlours. The style of reps called cotelaine is very pretty, and no doubt will be a great favourite, as it has

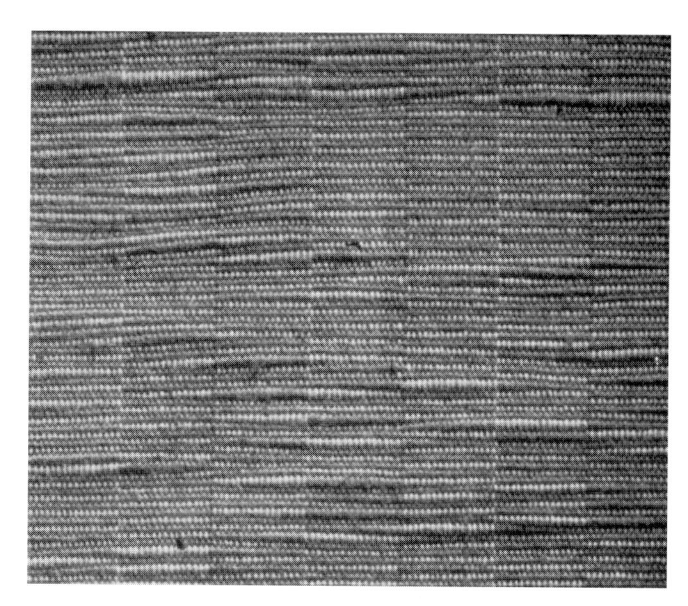

108. Rep cloth detail (T. French and Co, The Book of Soft Furnishing, *1937)*

all the beauty of brocatelle with the advantage of novelty and a greater durability. (1861, p.323.)

The American trade publication, *Scissors and Yardstick*, expanded the definition:

A heavy woollen fabric, used for covering furniture; for curtains, lambraques [sic] etc ... rep is formed by the coarse woof, which is composed of several threads twisted together and is covered and concealed by the warp. Both surfaces are exactly alike and about equally finished. In all except the very best qualities, the woof is cotton. Reps are made in all plain colours, but usually in colored stripes. (Brown & Gates, 1872.)

Tycoon rep, although usually described as a dress fabric, was used by 'DIY-ers' for upholstery as it was cheaper and gave a warm and soft effect in imitation of eastern designs. 'Tycoon' refers to the printed patterns, 'imitation of those of Eastern fabrics, as cashmere, which it resembles' (Brown & Gates, 1872). The authors of *Beautiful Homes* noted that tycoon rep was a 'really valuable material for persons of limited means ... is now used extensively for hangings and upholstering, and when lined hangs in rich soft folds that rival many a more costly fabric' (Williams & Jones, 1878, p.53). In contrast, the Garrett sisters commented that 'in the place of rep, which to within the last ten years was considered indispensable for the furnishing of a dining room ... we have now [many other fabrics]' (1877, p.76).

In the 1887 *Dictionary of Needlework,* there were three descriptions of rep noted: 'those composed of silk, those of silk and wool and those of wool only and which measure from 30 to 32 inches in width... Curtain rep averages 1½ yards in width... The quality made for upholstery is composed of wool only' (Caulfeild & Saward, p.421). In the late nineteenth century, 'furniture rep' referred to a flowered cotton fabric, whilst a 'worsted rep' was plain coloured and used for **curtains** and upholstery.

By the early twentieth century, cotton rep was also widely used. Denny explains that:

Rep has a heavier cord [than poplin] and is a wider fabric used for hangings and upholstering... Variations in effect are produced by dyeing warp one colour and filling another or by using an unevenly spun filling, which gives variety in texture as Shiki rep. When a jacquard figure is introduced on a rep background, it is called armure. (Denny, 1928, p.83)

By the 1930s, reps:

have gained an important place for draw curtains, used in place of window blinds, as they can be made to contribute very successfully to the adornment and colour scheme of a room ... Repps may be self-coloured piece-dyed materials in plain style; they may be made with slub weft and other fancy yarns, with geometrical all-over figuring, with elaborate jacquard-figured effects, with lustrous satin stripes in rayon on a cotton ground; or they may be cleverly printed in large design in attractive colours. (French, 1937, p.149.)

Gobelins or warp-printed rep
Introduced in France in the 1870s, it was produced to look like **tapestry** and was used for **drapery**.

Poplin rep
Used for hangings and curtains.
See **Cannelle rep**, **Casement rep**, **Coteline**, **Cotton rep**, **Royal rib**, **Shikii**, **Slub rep**.

Repette
A name sometimes used to describe a medium-weight fabric with ribs running in the direction of the **warp** (i.e. vertically).

Réseau
A sixteenth-century 'net' used for **curtains**, **valances** etc. If it had a pattern worked upon it, it was called 'lacis'. Later, the name réseau meant a plain net base for **bobbin lace**-making.

Reversible seat
A seat **cushion** that has a face cloth on both sides, and is designed so as to be used either way, thus making it serviceable on both sides. See **Seasonal furnishing** for Eckhardt's patent reversible seat.

Ring
See **Curtain ring**.

Ripping
Ripping is the process of stripping an upholstered chair of its outer covering, and sometimes the inner **stuffings**, in preparation for recovering or re-**upholstering**.

Roan
Roans are cured sheepskins that have been tanned with a sumach preparation. They have been used for **upholstery** purposes since the sixteenth century at least. An early reference is in the 1582 *Book of Rates*, which noted the importation of 'Skinnes for leather ... Basill, buffe for cushions, portingale [Portugal] red hides, roan, salt, Spanish, spruce and swan skinnes' (Willan, 1962, p.50).

In the eighteenth century, roan skins were included in the inventory of the London upholsterer, Samuel Norman. His stock included brown **damask** skins, white sheepskins, roan skins, **bazil** skins and gilt skins (Kirkham, 1969, p.509).

In the nineteenth century, roans were used in conjunction with **Morocco leather** to cover the outside chair backs when the seats and insides were upholstered in Morocco leather. The reason was clear: 'Some of the best roans, when quite new, so closely resemble morocco that an experienced man often finds it difficult to decide off-hand which is which. Roans are not so difficult to work as moroccos, being more elastic and supple' (Working Upholsterer, 1883, p.6).

Rod curtain
A **curtain** hemmed at the top and bottom and made to the size of the window with good fullness. The curtain is passed through rods at the top and the bottom so it fits the window frames exactly, and is then gathered up. They could be fitted top and bottom or side and side (Hale, *The Workwoman's Guide*, 1840, p.205).

Rod
See **Bed rod**, **Curtain pole and rod**, **French rod**.

Rolleau
A variety of window **blind** introduced in the latter half of the nineteenth century. Brown & Gates defined it as 'a variety of shade or more properly blind, made of coarse rushes, which are placed parallel and near each other and bound together by **cords** interwoven with them at regular intervals, passing from end to end of the shade. Different colours being used, a very pleasing effect is produced.' (1872, p.195.)
See also **Pinoleum**.

Rolled edge
The rolled edge was an **upholstery** technique favoured in the latter part of the nineteenth century. It consisted of a thick padded roll of filling material fixed to the leading edges of chairs and sofas. It was often covered in a contrasting material to the main body of the upholstery, and in some cases was bound with cord.
See also **Edge treatment**.

Roller blind (aka Window shade)
The seventeenth century had seen the use of blinds made of **straw** or **matting** to keep the sun out of rooms, as well as the occasional reference to roller blinds that protected paintings. The development of textile versions soon followed. Certainly, by the beginning of the eighteenth century, there were fabric blinds readily available. In 1726, John Brown advertised on his trade card that he supplied blinds 'the best painted of any in London' (Heal, 1953, p.15). A littler later, in 1741, a tradesman advertised: 'Spring curtains and blinds for windows … of a new invention, convenient to keep the sun off in summer or the cold winds from coming in between the sashes in winter, and particularly necessary in rooms upstairs in narrow streets where the opposite windows overlook each other' (Thornton, 1984, p.101).

In 1763, William France charged for '3 rowler curtains of brown Holland, gudgeons and staples and made to draw up with silk line and brass sliding pullies for the 3 windows' in the bedchamber and dressing room of Croome Court (Beard, 1997, p.306). A year later, France supplied Sir Lawrence Dundas with '3 spring barrels in frames with catches, green lustring curtains ferreted with silk ferret and every other particular…' (ibid. p.307).

Roller blinds became fashionable in the early nineteenth century and Sheraton gives an excellent description of how they worked:

> Spring rolling blinds for internal use are either with spring barrels made of tin, or turn on a plain oak stick of 1¼ inch diameter. Spring rolling blinds are charged by a worm spring made of wire, extending the whole length of the tin barrel or cylinder; but when the blind is drawn up to the top close to the cylinder, the spring is relieved, and the above-mentioned worm spring contracts in, but increases in diameter. Hence, if the power of this spring be not properly adjusted to the length of the canvas or in other words, to the height of the window, they are very liable to go wrong, and be spoiled. If a spring be over charged, then it has not sufficient room in the barrel, consequently the wire will twist out of form, and the spring is obstructed; but if it be not enough charged, then it is incapable of drawing up the canvas to the top. To remedy which, it must be taken out of the case by which it is screwed up to the window, and the charge must be increased by a few more turns round the roller, or barrel, before it is put up again. To remedy the defects of these spring blinds, Mr. Stubbs has invented a newly constructed spring, which, though confined to a small barrel, will draw up with ease any length of canvas, to 100 feet if required. And should a window be uncommonly narrow and high, his new spring is effectual in such a case, which upon the old plan always proved a matter of embarrassment.
>
> One peculiar advantage accompanying this new-invented spring blind is its not being subject to the disorders of the other kind. These blinds are intended to keep the sun from the room, not merely on account of heat, but to prevent the discharge of colours, and the injury which is done to furniture, where the heat of the sun is suffered to have uninterrupted access to any apartment which has elegant furniture. (ibid. p.57.)

He went on to say:

> Plain rolling blinds, without springs are most in use, being cheaper and answering the same end. These have either a wood or a brass pulley at each end. One with a channel to receive a line, and the other without any, to guard the canvas as it rolls up, which is effected by a line passing round in the above channel. Fixed to a brass rack, which contains a small pulley that receives the line, which, by being tight drawn down, the line draws up the blind to any height. (ibid. p.58.)

Loudon commented upon the ubiquitousness of roller blinds. He suggested that 'the roller blind, being much the cheapest, may be considered the most suitable for common cottages' (1839, p.341). With a growing market, it is not surprising to find a range of improvements to the basic roller mechanism. A spring roller blind patent was granted to John Gollop (11 January 1845). Pulley-operated versions with single **cord** rollers where the weight of the blind is on the lath and the cord runs in a flange were also developed. Others improvements included the check action roller that has a lever engaging in a cog. Similar were the Scotch fittings that have a friction action (usually top fixed and operated by a steel brake cup and ratchet movement whereby the blind is drawn up by the side cord and down by the centre cord or **tassel**). Wooden rollers were common but tin barrel rollers were used for very large windows, as they do not warp like wooden ones. Moreland discusses the actual rollers and defines the 'Hartshorn', or ratchet and spindle, and the Bray or Knapp whose weight opposes the tension of the springs (1889, p.168).

Roller blinds could clearly be made up at home. *The Workwoman's Guide* described the procedure:

> If possible, procure the materials of the exact breadth of the window, allowing for a good turning in, to herring down, as the blinds wear and set better without seams, and with the side herring boned. They should have tape loops or a case for the rod to slip in, and not be nailed on, as the blind is so apt to wear and tear when taken off for washing. Sometimes a small ring is fastened to the blind at the bottom of each side, through which a cord runs and is nailed tightly top

and bottom of the window, this contrivance always makes the blind draw up straight. A hem is made at the bottom, to admit the stick and a cord and tassel generally fastened to the middle, by which it may be drawn down. A cord moving round a pulley at the top, and window crank at the bottom, enable it to be drawn up and down at pleasure. (Hale, 1840, p.206.)

Later nineteenth-century reformers were not happy with roller blinds for various reasons. Mrs Orrinsmith considered that 'roller blinds have a stiff harsh look, and though sedate colours with modest stripes and better materials than white, have lately won favour amongst us, there is still the disadvantage of the absolute necessity to draw them up entirely if air is to be admitted effectually' (*The Drawing Room*, 1877, p.66). Aldam Heaton was much more dismissive. Writing in 1897, he said:

> Surely never was anything uglier bought into our houses than the ordinary roller blinds... No doubt they have been adhered to as being rather less cumbersome, and because their cords hurt the fingers less, than the terrible Venetian-blind; but in a well-furnished house they are totally inexcusable. I hope to live long enough to see roller-blinds entirely done away with, or relegated only to the kitchen and office. (*Beauty and Art*, 1897, p.122.)

In an interesting, but not surprising contrast, Hermann Muthesius, writing in his *Das Englische Haus*, noted that:

> Our [German] usual type with the endless cord has been totally abandoned in England in favour of an automatic spring device, which enables the blind to be pulled down to the desired point by means of a cord attached to the centre of the lower edge. The action of pulling down the blind locks a spring that allows the blind to jerk up again when the same cord is pulled with a slight forward tug. These roller blinds are used universally in England and are found in every house; they wear excellently and the mechanism never goes wrong. (1904, p.194.)

Despite this promising description, Muthesius finished by saying: 'Roller blinds are extremely useful contrivances but they have a certain unalterable air of impoverishment and are totally lacking in artistic quality' (ibid.).

Nevertheless, roller blinds remained practical and continued to be used on windows. Improvements were often in the nature of the fabric employed, rather than the mechanism. In 1947, Bendure & Pfieffer noted that window shades were being made of **coated fabrics**. **Muslin** and fine **cambric** was machine-coated with cellulose compounds such as pyroxylin, while for hand-made shades linseed oil was used. By the 1970s, 'picture style' roller blind were introduced with **PVC**-coated prints. The range of applications increased as they were used as room dividers and door replacements.

See also **Blind: Transparent/Painted**, **Silesia**, **Union**.

FURTHER READING

Lee, R. (1969). *Shades of History*, Chicago: Joanna Western Mills Co.

Roller-printed fabric

See **Printed textile**.

Roman blinds (aka Roman shade, Skyline shade)

Shades or **blinds**, generally of cloth, that pull up in wide horizontal **pleats**.

See also **Accordion shade**.

Roman drapery

A term used in the early nineteenth century to describe a **curtain** (or wall) treatment that consisted of widely-spaced conical **pleats**, which were brought upward, thus creating shallow curved shapes between them. Decorators working in the Empire style, including Percier and Fontaine and Thomas Hope, developed the fashion. George Smith, in 1808, published examples, describing the hangings as 'commonly called Roman drapery ... in fact taken from Roman standards' (1808, pl. 8). Others followed suit, including R. Ackermann and, a little later, J. Arrowsmith.

See also **Drape and drapery**, **Tenting**.

Romsley carpet

A **Kidderminster**-type reversible **carpet** that was based on the 'key' figuring principle. Two **wefts** are used for figure and one for binding.

Rose blanket

See **Blanket**.

Rosette

A finishing motif for **headings**, **swags** and **tiebacks**. It can be knife-pleated, **choux** or bow in shape.

Royal Axminster

See **Imperial Axminster**.

Royal rib (aka Royal rep)

Fabric with ribs running in the **warp** direction, obtained by using taped (or paired) ends. Royal ribs may be printed or dyed (Ostick, 1955, p.374).

See also **Rep**, **Repette**.

Rubber

See **Latex**, **Rubber cloth**, **Rubberised hair**, **Rubber webbing**, **Underlay**.

Rubber-backed carpet

A **carpet** with a built-in **underlay** or a rubber-coated backing for tuft retention. In 1937, it was noted that: 'Velvet and Axminster rugs and carpeting have recently reached the market in which the backing is impregnated with rubber' (Bennett, 1937, p.115). 'Rubber-backed' carpet has often been used as a pseudonym for tufted carpeting.

See also **Lea carpeting**, **Needleloom carpet**, **Patent-back carpet**, **Tufted carpet**.

Rubber cloth

The application of rubber to produce coated textiles provided them with a waterproof or inflationary capability. Coal-tar oil, which was a good solvent for rubber, produced a solution which, when pressed between two cloths, made a waterproof substance (see Patent no.11832, 1813). The use of rubber cloth in furniture included hydrostatic waterbeds, or inflatable chairs. In the 1851 Great Exhibition, Thomas Hancock, who worked with Charles Mackintosh, exhibited an inflatable bed chair in India rubber (Great Exhibition, Class 28, No.3).

Rubber-coated textiles were used to produce inflatable cushions (1813) and waterbeds (1832). The material was exploited for its waterproof properties in clothing (Macintosh) and carriage work, but its hardening during cold weather and softening in hot weather were disadvantages, which led to its being superseded by plasticised fabrics.

See also **Latex**.

Rubberised hair
New **latex** technology encouraged the use of rubberised hair, and the first use of this composite material appears to have been in cockpit seats during the 1920s. It is fabricated from curled hair that has been formed into a pad using either a natural or synthetic rubber binder. It may be moulded to particular shapes and has been used for a range of **upholstery** applications.

Rubber mat
Floor **mats** usually used at portals for wiping feet. Sir Titus Salt purchased 'an India rubber mat' in 1866 (Boynton, 1967, p.84). They have been widely used in domestic and commercial situations ever since.

Rubber webbing
An alternative support system for **upholstery** that did not need **springs**, as the webbing was elasticised and was fitted under tension. Auguste Fournier patented the earliest use of rubber for upholstery suspensions in England in July 1862 for 'webs of vulcanised rubber interlaced and fixed to framework' (Patent no.2080). In 1877, George Sims used vulcanised 'India rubber springs' in his Sybarite patented folding chairs. Apart from these isolated examples of use, elastic webs had to wait until the Pirelli Co developed the reinforced rubber webbing in 1948. In 1950, they set up a company called Arflex to develop **foam** rubber furniture. Marco Zanuso was commissioned to develop the potential of the conjunction of foam and rubber webbing in upholstery. The rubber webbing was designed for fixing to wood or metal frames, so it was versatile enough to be hidden within traditional seating, or it could be used as a revealed support in a minimal design. According to Zanuso, the exciting possibilities of the new materials were such that 'one could revolutionise not only the system of upholstery but also structural, manufacturing, and formal potential' (Bangert, 1988, p.33).

The combined advances of **latex cushions** and rubber webbing were related to the design developments of popular chairs and sofas in the 1950s onward. The show-wood frame that echoed an ideal of open-plan living, in which cabinets and upholstery were related in timber type, was extremely popular. Even if traditional style suites were required, the new materials meant that they could be produced at a lower cost and at a faster pace than the original built-up support system.
See also **Latex**, **Upholstery**, **Webbing**.

Ruche
A narrow **trimming** material with running stitches along its length which, when drawn up, produces a frilled or quilled effect. The name may be derived from the Latin *rusca*, meaning 'tree bark', but the French name for the plaits in a straw beehive are also called *ruches*: there is clearly a resemblance. When the centre threads of the trimming are pulled up, the ruched edges project in a double frill to create a 'furry' effect. This may be cut or uncut.
See also **Stitch: Running**.

Ruffle
Used as a trim for **curtains** or as an alternative to a valance. Moreland (1889) noted that 'for curtains of chintz, cretonne, dimity or similar goods, a ruffle of the same material is a pretty way to trim the work.' Gathered or **pleated** designs were popular.
See also **Base**, **Flounce**, **Priscilla curtain**, **Valance**.

Rufflette
See **Curtain tape**.

Ruffling
The decorative gathering of loosely **pleated** bands of fabric along the front edge, side and top of the seat back of tightly upholstered chairs. The technique was popular in the 1870s.

Rug
A name, possibly of Scandinavian origin, *rugga*, meaning 'a coarse coverlet' or 'a coarse woollen cloth', used as a bedcover. Bailey (1753) describes a rug as 'a shaggy coverlet for a bed' (see **Rugg**). This definition remained until the late eighteenth century. It later referred to a **mat** for the floor, or to a portable cover to keep one warm.

Anne Rutt noted the range of rugs available to the 1930s' American homemaker:

> Fiber rugs for indoor and outdoor porches can be procured in a wide range of prices. Plain and mixed effects are usually preferable to the decorated, although geometric designs, stripes, and plaids are very satisfactory. Large conventionalized flowers in stencil-like designs are particularly poor. If green is present it should be like the green of foliage and not a cold bluish acid green. Excellent rugs are made up of separate one-foot squares of rush fastened together to make any desired size. Jute rugs are inexpensive and often well designed. They make very good temporary rugs even for the living room for those who are waiting for the means to buy permanent ones. Chinese seaweed rugs are often excellent in design and color. (1935.)

In the twentieth century, the range of available rugs was very wide. Apart from woven rugs, these included:

Braided
A process of cutting fabrics into strips, braiding them by machine, and then stitching them together, is used to make these rugs. Another method is to braid heavy **cotton** yarns into wide and narrow strips, then stitching a wide and a narrow strip together with a criss-cross **stitch**. Rugs similar in appearance to braided rugs are produced by twisting strips of fabric and stitching them together with a criss-cross stitch.

Chenille
Shaggy or reversible effects can be made using chenille **weft** yarns for a variety of rugs.

Cotton
Cotton rugs are made from strong ply yarns or from thick rovings. The rugs may be woven flat in a plain, twill or **jacquard** weave, or in combinations of these weaves with thick soft dyed yarns.

Felted
Various fibres have been felted to make rugs. **Sisal** fibres may be blended with **jute** fibres and felted. Cotton or **wool** fibres may be felted: in either case, the fabric could be dyed and printed as required. Felting also applies to the process of making **needleloom carpeting**.

Grass
Rugs woven from tough prairie grasses were sometimes either left natural or printed on one side by stencilling or sprayed designs. Rugs woven from wiregrass were manufactured commercially by the early twentieth century in the USA. According to one authority:

> The grasses, particularly the swamp wire grasses, have come to have a very important commercial place in the production of grass rugs suited for dwellings and porches. They are especially adapted for sum-

mer uses. Grass rugs are neat, clean, and cool in appearance. No floor covering has so great future trade possibilities as grass rugs. A considerable amount of this class of goods is made in Wisconsin at Oshkosh, Superior, and Racine. (Nystrom, 1916, p.6.)

Bendure & Pfieffer considered: 'Grass rugs are attractive in the natural grass color or printed on one side by stencilling or by spraying. In addition, different coloured warp yarns may be introduced. These rugs are reversible. Most grass rugs are varnished for protection.' (1947, p.603.)

Hooked
These are made by inserting yarn and narrow strips of fabric through a heavy jute, **linen** or cotton fabric such as **canvas**, **burlap** or **monk's cloth**. The design is drawn on the back of the fabric, and the dyed strips of cotton or wool yarn are pushed through to the face according to the pattern. They may be left uncut or may be cut to form a cut-**pile** design.
See also **Hooked rug**.

Knitted
Knitted cotton rugs are made with dyed and heavy twisted yarns. The knitting machine is set to gauge the height of the pile. After knitting, the rug passes through a finishing process that sets the twist and gives a firm close body to the fabric.

Kraft fibre
Kraft fibre is obtained from a process of producing wood pulp that is then made into sheets known as 'kraft fibre'. The sheets are cut into strips, twisted into 'yarns' and woven in plain, twill or jacquard weaves. They may be all kraft fibre or combined with cotton, sisal or wool. They are called 'fibre rugs'.
See also **Kraft fibre rug**.

Linen
Rugs with a rough texture and a linen lustre, woven on plain or jacquard looms.

Sisal
Rugs woven in plain, twill or jacquard weaves. They are reversible and may be stencilled on one side.

Tufted cotton
Made by punching yarns into **duck** or canvas fabrics. Frequently two or more fabrics are stitched together to add strength and weight. A paper on which the design has been perforated is laid over the fabric, and a coloured powder or washable dye liquid is brushed over the perforations, tracing the design outline on the cloth. Then, with the use of punch work machines, the yarns are pushed through the back to form a pile on the face (Bendure & Pfieffer, 1947, pp 600–02).

The 'Crex' fibre rugs imitated the grass rug style and were woven using twisted paper around a wire core having a printed pattern on the surface. They were woven on the 'Lloyd loom' principle. Denny refers to their being available by the yard (91 cm) or in standard rug sizes (1942, p.33).

Rugs now range from limited edition fine art works to mass-produced short life products.

See also **Abnakee rug**, **Drugget rug**, **Grass**, **Hearth rug**, **Hooked rug**, **Kelim**, **Mohair rug**, **Morris rug**, **Navajo rug**, **Numdah rug**, **Rag rug**, **Rugg**, **Tufting**.

Rug fitting
To stop **rugs** moving about on polished floors, fittings were introduced to stabilise them. These included zinc rug corners to prevent turn up, 'Sultan rug fasteners' (Patent 18 June 1865), and 'eyes and sockets' to fit to hardwood floors.

Rugg
A type of rough **woollen** material often used as a bedcover, which was in common use in the sixteenth and seventeenth centuries. The name probably derived from a Norwegian dialect word *rugga*, meaning 'a coverlet' (often coarse). They have been made from a variety of techniques including flat or **pile** weaves, **tapestry**, or **needlework** (especially looped running **stitches**).

The process of 'cottoning' or friezing plain cloth into ruggs can cause confusion. In 1552, a statute listed 'All and every cottons called Manchester, Lancashire and Cheshire Cottons – and all cloth called Manchester rugges otherwise named Frices [Frieze]' (Acts 5 and 6, Edward VI). However, they do seem to have been a speciality of Ireland and Spain, as there are many references to ruggs with these origins. In 1592, it was recorded that 'English ruggs-none are made in England but Irish ruggs of divers sorts from 10s' (Kerridge, 1985, p.20). According to Kerridge, 'Six years later, the Salford area of northwest England was noted as a source of rugs made with 'hairy Irish wool' (ibid.). In 1561, the Ancaster accounts list payments 'For 54 yards of Irishe rugge for coverlettes for servants at 7d the yard' (Clabburn, 1998, p.122), whilst in 1594, under a definition of New Draperies, 'blankets called Spanish ruggs' were included (ibid. p.250). In the 1595 *Book of Household Rules*, Lord Montague at Cowdray demanded 'the better sorts of quiltes of beddes of any tyme of night taken off, and Yrish Rugges layd in their places' (Thornton, 1987, p.355). Hardwick had 'six Spanish blankets' in Lady Shrewsbury's chamber in 1601 (Boynton, 1971, p.31). Sometimes both would be listed in inventories. For example, the list of rugs at Kenilworth in 1583 included 'thirty-five white Spanish ruggs, one blew rugg, two green and two white Irish ruggs' (Clabburn, 1988, p.123).

Later on, the term 'rug' was used without geographical associations. In 1623, the King's Chamber of Standen Lordship House had 'One pair fine blancketts, whereof the one White Rugg and the other white cotton' (Clabburn, 1988, p.123). Pepys wrote: 'Mighty hot weather; I lying this night with only a rugg and a sheet upon me' (*The Diary of Samuel Pepys*, 13 July 1667). Changes in use are evident in the 1697 petition made by the **quilt**-makers, opposing the restrictions on the importation of **calico**. In the case they made, they pointed out the following observations upon bed rugs:

> That linen cloths and woollens stuffs are not proper for quilts, the one being cold and heavy, and the woollen will harbour filth and dirt, and be much of the same kind as Rugs are: and not being capable of being clean'd so well as calico carpets, renders them altogether unfit for that purpose: for the whole design in having quilts for beds is to have them light and warm, and made of that which will clean often, and not harbour filth and dirt, as the rugs used to do. (Osler, 1987, p.88)

The distinctions between a blanket and a rug were evident in the mid-eighteenth century. A Writtle cottage inventory from 1743 lists 'a sacking bottom bedstead with stuff curtains, 3 old blankets, one blue rugg' (Steer, 1969, p.269). A description of Wigan, in 1778, says that it was 'famous for the manufacture of coverlets, rugs, blankets, and other sorts of bedding' (*England's Gazetteer*, 2nd edition, *OED*).

The Wadsworth *Bed Ruggs* exhibition catalogue defines the modern meaning of a bed rug as 'a heavy needleworked bedcovering with a pile

or smooth face with or without shaped ends, worked in polychrome or rarely monochrome wools on a woven foundation' (1972, p.10).
See also **Blanket**, **Caddow**, **Fledge**, **Frieze**, **Fustian**, **Manchester**, **Rug**.

FURTHER READING

Callister, J. Herbert & Warren, W.L. (1972). *Bed Ruggs 1722–1833*, Hartford: Conn.: Wadsworth Athenaeum.

Rugging

Inexpensive **upholstery filling** made from **jute** rags and other materials, such as **carpet** and **hessian**. It has a tendency to pack down in time, but it has been used in cheap **mattresses**. According to the *Dictionary of Trade Products:* 'Rugging, [was] a coarse wrapping or blanket cloth' (Simmonds, 1858).

Runner

A textile designed to protect polished furniture surfaces. They were usually long, narrow and shorter than scarves. In the twentieth century, they were often used in conjunction with placemats.
See also **Bordecloth**, **Scarf**.

Rush

The harvested stems of reeds and rushes that are used in the production of simple seating systems, matting and flooring. The weaves may be plain or decorative and the surfaces may be painted, gilded or stained.

Rush has been used since ancient times in the Middle East (*c.*4000BC Egypt). Rush furnishings include products of the common bulrush (*Scirpus lacustrus*), marsh flag (*Juncus effusus*) and cat's-tail (or reed *Typha latifolia*). Fresh water and salt water ('Dutch') varieties are both used. A paper product, fibre rush, is made in imitation of these materials and has been available since World War I. The harvested stems of natural products are dried and bunched into 'bolts' for transport. The rushes are then moistened, laid end ('butt') to tip and twisted together to make an even coil for weaving. A simple but effective floor treatment was simply to strew rushes on the floor surface. Peter Brears discusses accounts of the custom of strewing rushes at Hampton Court in the sixteenth century:

> Writing to Wolsey's physician, Erasmus had described English floors as having accumulations of up to twenty years' rushes, stinking with the vilest mass of filth and rotting vegetable matter, but neither archaeology nor any contemporary evidence can confirm this. Nicola di Fare of the Venetian embassy more accurately observed: 'In England … every eight or ten days they put down a fresh layer; the cost of each layer being half a Venetian livre, more or less, according to the size of the house … the description of Queen Elizabeth's presence chamber strewn with rushes (which he mistook for straw) given by Paul Chintzier of Brandenburg … and Ben Johnson's 'ladies and gallants languishing upon the Rushes' show them to have been a clean and relatively high-status floorcovering. Certainly, a monarch as fastidious as Henry VIII would never have allowed masses of stinking rushes to lie about his palace. (Brears, 1999.)

The use of rush as flooring continued well into the nineteenth century in rural communities, and as a form of made-up matting has continued.
See also **Bed mat**, **Grass**, **Mat**, **Matting**.

FURTHER READING

Brown, M. (1984). *Cane and Rush Seating*, London: Batsford.
Holdstock, R. (1989). *Seat Weaving in Rush, Cane and Cord*, Lewes: The Guild of Master Craftsmen.

Russell

A **worsted satin** weave, **damask**-like textile, which was woven in Norwich from at least 1547. The name derives from Riesel, the Dutch name for Lille, from where the technology was taken. The cloth was hot pressed to create a 'satin-look' and was also called Norwich **satin** or Norwich **fustian**. In 1554, the manufacturers of Norwich petitioned Parliament saying that:

> Of late years Rustles, called russell satins and satin reverses, had been made abroad from wools in the county of Norfolk, and being brought into this kingdom were purchased and worn to the great detriment of the wool manufacturers at Norwich, which induced the inhabitants of that city to encourage certain foreign workmen to come to Norwich where they were set to work, and have instructed others; so that there are now made in this same city better russell satins and satin reverses and also fustians, in imitation of fustian of Naples, than had been received from abroad. (Cummin, 1941, p.184.)

Russell was widely used for clothing, as well as for bed and window **curtains** and upholstery, both in England and America. In Isaac Smith's 1787 inventory of his Boston, Mass., home, there was an 'easy chair in green russell, 6 mahogany chairs russell bottoms, 1 set green russell curtains' (Montgomery, 1984, p.337). In 1887, it was described as 'a woollen cloth [which] resembles baize, but with knots over the surface' (Caulfeild & Saward, p.429).

Russia cloth

A heavyweight coarse **linen** or **canvas** used for dust covers and similar applications. In the 1728 inventory of the shop of James Pilbeam, a mercer of Chiddingly, Sussex, there was listed 'Nine hundred and twenty seven ells of Rush Cloath at five pence per ell [total] £17 12s 11d' (http://www.chiddingly.gov.uk/History/James%20Pilbeam.html).
See also **Russia duck**.

Russia crash

See **Crash**.

Russia duck

A strong coarse **linen** jean material that originated in Russia but was manufactured in Dundee and the surrounding area in the later nineteenth century. The Lord Chamberlain's Accounts note an account to a Mr J. Gilroy in 1781:

For 11 yds of strong Russia Duck 2s	£1 2s
For making above into a powdering carpet, with lead weights to the corners.	4s 6d

(Walton, 1980, p.279.)
See also **Duck**.

Russia leather

A particular process of **leather** preparation that produced supple, sweet-smelling hides. The process involved steeping the hides in a variety of preliminary baths to remove hair by lime washing. After scraping, they were washed again in mixes that might be of flour and yeast, or dog and pigeon dung, depending on the recipe. They were put into a mix of oatmeal and water to undergo a slight fermentation, and then they were washed in running water. A steeping in a mix of birch (or possibly willow or poplar) bark and oil followed this. The visible cross-hatching scores are a result of the hammering process that left a distinctive **diaper** pattern. This was due to the use of textured wood blocks to agitate the skins while still moist, to allow the penetration of the oil and the partial breakdown of fibres. When tanned and dry, the skins were rubbed gently with birch oil and finished.

Russia leather was widely used for **upholstery** in the mid- to late seventeenth and all of the eighteenth century in England and America. In January 1660, John Spaceward of Writtle, Essex, had '4 Russia leather chairs' in his parlour (Steer, 1969, p.90). In 1689, the **woollen** manufacturers of England petitioned against the making of cane chairs and said that 'There was also at least 150 bales of Russia Leather yearly made up into chairs, which leather was the product of our cloth from Russia'. In 1703, the Capitol in Williamsburg was furnished with 'seven doz: of Russia leather chairs [for] furnishing the rooms above stairs' (Gloag, 1990, p.580).

In the nineteenth century, embossed Russia leather was still recommended by Loudon for library tabletops (1839, p.1055). According to Caulfeild & Saward, genuine Russia leather may be identified by 'dark blackish looking spots, which are not regarded as blemishes' (1887, p.429).

FURTHER READING

Garrett, G. & Skeleton, I. (1987). *The Wreck of the Metta Catharina*, Truro, Cornwall: New Pages Co, pp 23–8.

Russian cord

A **cord** cloth used for **curtaining**, made with two **warps**, a ground one and a fancy one, that created the particular cable appearance.

Russian tapestry

Caulfeild & Saward explained that this fabric was 'a material woven from hemp, designed for window curtains, having a decorative design and a border of fringe. It is a durable article and may be procured in various widths.' (1887, p.431.) This definition still stood in 1950. *The Mercury Dictionary of Textile Terms* stated that it was 'a stout linen or hemp fabric used for window **blinds**. It is usually embroidered with fancy designs with silk and cotton thread.'

Rya rug (aka Ryijy rug)

Knotted **pile rugs** made in Scandinavia since the Bronze Age. Used as bedcovers and cover cloths, they have a thin ground of **wool** or **linen** and a long woollen pile with several (10 to 20) **weft** shoots between each row: a space is therefore left between each line of knots. The long pile hides the unknotted parts. Some are plain but others have a range of designs incorporated. Often made by amateurs, the machine-made versions were introduced in the 1960s and were woven on **Axminster** looms.

FURTHER READING

Israelis, U.T. (1925). *The Hand-woven Rugs of Finland*, Helsinki: Government Printing Office.

Sabatos rug

The Sabatos **rug** was a product of Center Lovell, Maine. Mrs Douglas Volk of New York started production in 1900, employing a small number of local women. The designs were adapted from Native American Indian imagery, and were colourful in their final effect. They were intended to be hand-worked, from the spinning to final finish.

> The Sabatos rug is another form of pulled rug, and is made of native wool homespun yarn, giving opportunity to women in isolated regions, not only to make the rugs, but to weave the material from which they are made. The sheep are raised by the farmers, and their wives weave the material and dye the wool for the craft-workers who make the rugs. The foundation of the Sabatos rug is woven in a hand-loom from pure wool. It is then fastened securely into a wooden frame, and short pieces of the vegetable-dyed yarn are drawn through and separately knotted like those made in the Orient. This knotting of the yarn increases the durability of the rugs, but renders the making of them slow and laborious. (Priestman, 1910, p.161.)

Sackcloth (aka or Sacking)

A coarse textile of flax, **jute** or **hemp** often used to make sacks but also employed for **upholstery** purposes. The 'sacking' was a coarse bottoming cloth widely used for bases of beds often in conjunction with **cords** or slats. It was also used to bottom chairs and chaise-longues before caning was popular in the seventeenth century. Other furnishings also employed sackcloth. The Hardwick Hall inventory of 1601 listed 'green and yellow tufted sacking' as a **curtain** material (Boynton, 1971, p.23), while the 1611 inventory of Hatfield House listed 'fourteen shallow [window] curtains of sackcloth' (Beard, 1997, p.287). While in 1637, Ralph Grynder supplied Queen Henrietta Maria with 'double sackcloth and girth for three chairs and three folding stools' (ibid. p.290).

By 1764, the London cabinet-maker, Samuel Norman, had in stock '15 sacken bottoms of several sizes' (Kirkham, 1969, p.508). For beds, it was tacked to the rebate of the frame or fitted with a **canvas** edge and held in position by ropes. In the 1793 *The Cabinet-Makers' London Book of Prices*, cabinet-makers charged specifically for 'nailing in the sacking' of press beds (p.40). Sacking remained as a bed support well into the nineteenth century, but laths, **springs** and bed bases gradually replaced it.
See also **Bed cord**.

Sag

A term sometimes used to identify the fall of a **festoon** to indicate the shape and size of its lower edge.

Sailcloth

A firm, plain, strong and smooth woven fabric of **linen** or **cotton**, of a **canvas** type, that was used for **bottoming** upholstery work. Bottoming was often carried out with **sackcloth**, but the 1679 byelaws of the Upholders' Company demanded that 'all chairs, stools, couches and squabs whatsoever they be made of shall be cross girt in the bottom with new sail cloth' (Houston, 1993, p.58).

In the nineteenth century, it was also used in conjunction with **needlework**. In 1881, Harrison referred to its use as a needlework base fabric: 'Among other washing fabrics used in art needlework are crash, twilled cotton, duck, sail-cloth, [etc]' (1881, Vol I, p.48). Sailcloth was sometimes used for chair covers in the 1950s.
See also **Duck**.

Sameron

A medieval textile that may have been a finer version of harden, which was mainly used for **sheets**. Defined in 1684 as a Yorkshire dialect word meaning 'cloth between linen and hemp, not altogether so coarse as the one, nor fine as the other' (Leaf, 1934). References to sameron sheeting often occur in medieval inventories, e.g. 'I pair linthiaminum de lez sameron' (ibid.).
See also **Harden**.

Samite

A rich **silk** fabric used in the Middle Ages which was sometimes interwoven or embroidered with gold threads. It also refers to a garment or a **cushion** of this material. The Greek name, literally 'six-threaded', has been variously explained. Usually it has been supposed that the original 'samite' was woven of thread composed of six strands of silk, however, according to Middleton, it 'was so called because the weft threads were only caught and looped at every sixth thread of the warp, lying loosely on the intermediate part' (*Encyclopaedia Britannica*, XXIII, 210/1).

The thirteenth-century author, Ulrich von Lichtenstein, was taken by a bed upon which 'lay a fair mattress of samite whereon were two quilts of silk' (Mercer, 1969, p.27). In early seventeenth-century France, it was a name for a **satin** finish, **half-silk** fabric.

Sarcenet

A very fine, translucent and soft **silk** fabric made plain and twilled, in various colours. Originally, it was used for **curtains**, and this practice continued into the twentieth century. It was also used for **upholstery**, window **blinds** and bedcovers.

Sarcenet was introduced in the Middle Ages and possibly named after Saracen. In medieval Latin, *pannus saracenicus* meant 'Saracen cloth', so it is a possible source. Sarcenet was used in the fifteenth century for various **draperies**. For example, in the *Bury Wills* of 1463 (Camden Society, p.41) there is listed 'My tepet of black sarsenet'. A short while later, there is a reference to 'curteyns of white sarsenette' that were supplied to a bed made for Louis de Bruges in 1472 (*Archaelogia*, 26, pp 279–80). In the same year, a description of a bedroom made up for Lord of Gruthere by the wife of Edward IV recorded that: 'There was ordained a bed for him self … the curtains of white sarcenet, as for his head suite and pillows they were of the Queen's own ordinance' (Macquoid, *The Age of Oak*, 1904, p.67). Twenty years later, another listing included 'ij Curtens of Russet sarsynet fringed with sylke' (Leaf, 1934).

During the sixteenth century, sarcenet was still considered an important textile. In 1509, Edmund Dudley's Great Chamber had a range of **sparvers** stored: 'a great coffer with ii lyddes: wherin is a sparver of purpull velvytt with curteyns of blew sarsenett. A sparver of blew sarsenett… A sparver of red sarsnett, a sparver of crymsen cloth of gold and gren and crimson saten (Beard, 1997, p.282). In 1537, Katherine of Aragon had a set of purple sarcenet curtains as part of a sparver set (ibid.). Apart from sparvers, sarcenet was used for bed curtains. The Sir John Gage inventory of 1556 listed beds with curtains of **changeable** sarcenet, purple sarcenet, black and yellow sarcenet and crimson and yellow sarcenet (ibid. p.283). There were also various qualities or types as the *Tudor Book of Rates* explained: 'Sarcenet called Bolona sarcent the elle … Sarcenet of Florence making the elle … Sarcenet called Golde sarcenet the yarde' (Willan, 1962, p.51–2).

Its use in furnishings continued and, in 1600, the Ingatestone inventory notes a **coverlet** of 'taffeta sarcenet … embroidered all over with yellow twist, and lined with fine crimson woollen' (Thornton, 1978, p.370). This use as a bedcovering material is also found in the 1601 Hardwick Hall inventory that lists many **quilts** of sarcenet and a 'tester for a field bed of crimson taffetie sarcenet with red silk fringe and four curtains of crimson taffetie sarcenet to it' (Boynton, 1971, p.25). In the same inventory there were recorded 'curtains of Chaungeable taffety', and in another room 'a quilt of chaungeable taffetie sarcenet'. The selection of sarcenets was apparently growing, as the 1679 Ham House inventories list varieties including changeable, **clouded**, Florence, Persian and striped (Thornton & Tomlin, 1980, p.166). These were used for loose protective covers and blinds.

As sarcenet was transparent, it was an ideal material for making blinds. In 1687, John Smith, in his work *The Art of Painting in Oyl…*, described 'the manner of painting cloth or sarsnet sash-windows'. The material was 'wetted, strained onto the frame and when dry, varnished'. On the paper or silk fabric, you might 'paint upon then what fancy you please, but a landskip is most common and natural' (Smith, 1687). It seems to have come into its own in the early eighteenth century for this purpose. In 1729, John Brown, an upholsterer, advertised that he 'made and sold Window Blinds of all Sorts, Painted in Wire, Canvas, Cloth and Sassenet [Sarcenet], after the best and most lasting manner so that if ever so dull and dirty they will clean with sope and sand and be like new' (Heal, 1953).

In the eighteenth century, sarcenet seems to have been mainly used as a lining or as a covering. One example is the 1715 State Bed at Hampton Court: Thomas Phill charged for the 'quilting and making a pair of large white sarcenet blankets' (Beard, 1997, p.301). By the nineteenth century, sarcenet was still in use. In 1825, William Trotter invoiced Lord Gray at Kinfauns Castle, Perthshire, for 'cutting out and making a set of curtains of rich Chinese painted silk, lined with green persian with outside cut-out valens of same painted silk and inside valens of green sarcenet lined with buckram and green calico bound with Paris lace and finished with chintz fringe' (Jones, 1997, p.248).

In the early twentieth century it was still employed for chair backs, draperies, etc.

See also **Blind: Transparent/Painted**, **Persian**, **Scarf**.

Sash curtain

Curtains that fit next to the glass of a window are called sash or glass curtains. In his *Practical Decorative Upholstery*, Moreland (1889, p.158) noted that, 'they usually cover three quarters or the whole of the lower sash and should be made from silk, muslin or madras.'

See also **Glass curtain**, **Under curtain**.

Sateen

A soft **cotton** fabric made in sateen weave (**weft satin** weave) with a lustrous surface, achieved by mercerising and schreinering. Carded or combed yarns are often used to improve lustre. Some are only calendered to produce the sheen, which disappears with washing and is therefore not genuine sateen. Sateen can be either a strong **warp** faced sateen or a softer weft faced sateen. It may be bleached, dyed or printed.

Although generally used as a **lining** material for curtain and **drapery**, in the later nineteenth century it was used in American **upholstery** and bedroom furnishings, including **bedspreads** and slipcovers. One American commentator pointed out that: 'Plain sateen forms an inexpensive covering for the essential one armchair and a chaise-longue imparts an air of luxury that is worth an extra expenditure if the purse permits.' (Northend, 1921, p.238.)

From the 1940s onward, a variety of heavy sateen called 'Glosheen' was produced with multi-coloured flower prints or in plain colours, and was used in the 1960s for small chairs and loungers. By 1955, lining sateen was described as 'used mainly for lining fairly heavy curtains: it is usually dyed fawn and given a schreinered finish. Sometimes this cloth is called "Italian lining"' (Ostick, 1955, pp 373–4). It remains a curtain lining material.

See also **Weave: Satin**.

Satin

Satin is strictly speaking a weave term. However, it is also used to define a type of textile that has been widely used for furnishing practices. It can be defined as a silk (later with other yarns) fabric with a glossy surface on one side, produced by a method of weaving by which the threads of

109. Satin damask detail of construction (T. French and Co, The Book of Soft Furnishing, *1937)*

the **warp** are caught and looped by the **weft** at certain intervals. Satin usually has a characteristically lustrous surface and a dull back. Satin weaves are referred to as 'four-end', 'five-end' or 'eight-end satins' reflecting the number of threads lifted.

Satin as a fabric seems to have originated in China. It is likely that the name derives from the town of Zaytoun in China (now Canton), a port from which satins were exported during the Middle Ages. The terms 'atlas zaytuni' or 'satin of zaitum' refer. It became known in Europe during the twelfth and thirteenth centuries in Italy, and known in England probably by the thirteenth century. In 1366, Chaucer referred to satin cloth in his *Romance of the Rose*: 'The barres were of gold ful fyne, upon a tissu of satyne.' (line 1104.) A little later, in 1392, the Earl of Arundel's will included a reference to 'the bed of red and blue satin with half celour' (Eames, 1971, p.80).

It became a favourite for many applications because of its superb draping qualities and luxurious feel. An eighteenth-century definition confirms this. Chambers says that satin is 'a kind of silken stuff, very smooth, and shining, the warp whereof of very fine, and stands out; the woof coarser, and hid underneath; on which depends that gloss, and beauty that gives it its price' (Chambers, 1741).

Satin is well known as a base for embroidered decoration, and this has been so for centuries. In 1529, a will listed 'My bedde of grene tynsill and white satteyne embrotherid with blue velvit' (*Wills and inventories, illustrative of the history, manners, language, etc. of the northern counties of England*, 1908, p.93).

The *Tudor Book of Rates* for 1582 listed a variety of satin cloths including:

> Satten of Bridges the yard.
> Satten of Bridges counterfet tincell the yard.
> Satten of Cipers the peece.
> Sattin right crimson or purple in grainy the yard.
> Satten out of graine the yard.
> Sattin called tincel with golde the yard.
> Sattin called turkey satten the yard. (Willan, 1962, p.52)

A variation on this range was noted in 1603 when 'Sattins reverses, sattins of Cipres, and Spanish sattins' were listed (*OED*).

Satin continued to be used for **bed furniture** and hangings. In 1642, the upholsterer, Symondes, sent to Knole Park a bed, 'the valance of it white satin embroidered with crimson and white silk, and a deep fringe suitable ... tester of white satin suitable to the valance' (Edwards, 1964, p.35).

By the beginning of the eighteenth century, it was also painted. In 1710, a closet in Dyrham Park had 'a window curtain of painted sattin' and, in the Best Bed Chamber, there was a 'sattin counterpane flower'd with gold' (Walton, 1986, p.59). In 1733, John Legg of Boston, Mass., had 'I coach bed, camblet curtains, and vallens lin'd with thread satin and a satin coverlead' (Cummings, 1961, p.35). Hepplewhite recommended the use of satin bed hangings: 'where a high degree of elegance and grandeur are wanted' (1794, p.18). Satin was also used for **upholstery**. Lady Sussex wrote:

> My thanks to you for my satin it came very well, some of it I employ for the backes of chairs, the rest I intend for curtains, when the Chinese sofa come in, if you see any pretty ones remember me... I am very sorry I did not consider of the figured satin when I was at Chelsea for truly though the price be unreasonable, I had rather give it than buy any of the figured satins that are to be had here thirty shillings the yard, and the colours look like dirt to that I have. (Macquiod, 1904, p.177.)

Satin's popularity as an upholstery fabric continued in the nineteenth century. George Smith suggested that 'in elegant drawing rooms plain coloured satin ... assumes the first rank as well for use as richness' (1808, p.xii). At the end of the century, the description of satin in Cole's *Complete Dictionary of Dry Goods* confirmed that:

> The weft in ordinary qualities is cotton or linen, whilst the best goods, such as satin de Lyon, are all silk. When first taken out of the loom satin is somewhat flossy, and is dressed by being rolled in heated metal cylinders that ... impart ... a more brilliant luster and removes the floss. (1894)

It remains a furnishing fabric to this day. Particular satin types are noted below.

Antique satin
A satin weave fabric used for **drapery** that shows slubs yarns in the filling on the face side and has a satin effect on the reverse.

Crêpe satin
A satin woven with a **crêpe** weft, which gives a broken effect on the cloth's surface.

Cuttanee satin
An Indian textile variety mentioned in *The Dictionary of Needlework*, which defined it as 'a fine thick cotton backed satin, produced in stripes... It is 27 inches in width and is chiefly employed for upholstery.' (Caulfeild & Saward, 1887, p.434.)
See also **Cuttanee**.

Double-face satin
Yarn woven with two warps and one filling, to simulate a double satin construction. It has a satin surface on both sides. **Cotton** filling is often used in cheaper qualities.

Duchesse satin
A very soft, heavy kind of satin.

Furnishing satin
According to a trade publication of 1955:

> Furnishing satins are often made with a rayon warp and a cotton weft. In most attractive satins, the weave is a broken satin; the smooth surface is broken by irregular bindings, which gives a more decorative surface to the draping than a regularly spaced weave. Furnishing satin may have a warp face of rayon, mercerised cotton or two-fold spun rayon and are dyed in soft colours or printed. Generally speaking, they are not suitable for covers. (Ostick, 1955, p.373)

Paillette satin
A satin that is characterised by its changeable colours. It was originally woven from silk but is now made with man-made fibres.

Roman satin
A heavyweight satin, originally silk warp and **wool** weft, now applied to any fibre combination. In her *Art of Decoration*, Mrs Haweis discussed this material and pointed out that: 'The coarse threads have a pleasant "character" which does not offer comparison with one's gown … and I think there ought to be a distinction between furniture fabrics and the human garb' (1881, p.302).

Satin damask
Used for linen **table covers** and napkins in which the **jacquard** figuring is woven solid and not floated, thus making the cloth reversible.
See also **Linen**.

Satin de Bridges (Bruges)
A satin weave textile whose name is probably derived from Bruges, a city of Flanders. It was a smooth-faced cloth woven from a combination of silk warp and wool or **linen** weft, imported widely in the seventeenth century and initially popular for **linings**. In the 1556 inventory of Sir John Gage, there were **curtains** lined with satin of bridges as well as a **tester** made from black velvet and yellow 'satten of Bridges' (Beard, 1997, p.283).

The 1601 Hardwick Hall inventory recorded 'a table carpet of tissue and purple wrought velvet, lined with crimson sattin bridges' (Boynton, 1971, p.24). Hardwick Hall had 'four cushions of green damask lined with russet satten bridges'. It was also used for upholstery: 'One old chair of yellow sateen of bridges' (ibid.).

It was still identified as a furnishing fabric in the late nineteenth century. Caulfeild & Saward noted it as being designed for upholstery and state that 'Satin de Bruges is made of silk and wool, and is used for furniture purposes' (1887, p.435).

Satin de laine
Plain or printed all-wool satin, that can sometimes imitate woven patterns if printed. Used for curtains and upholstery in the nineteenth century. French satin de laine was 'approved' for use in mid-nineteenth century American dining rooms, libraries and parlours (*Godey's Lady's Book,* 1859, vol.58, p.554).

Slub satin
A satin cloth with a **slub** weft that creates an uneven surface texture.

Venetian satin
Usually a satin cloth woven with cotton or rayon, that is lighter than Roman satin.
See also **Atlas**, **Bedspread**, **Brocade**, **Brocatelle**, **Caffoy**, **Calimanco**, **Cuttance**, **Damask**, **Duchesse toilet cover**, **Everlasting**, **Lampas**, **Mitcheline**, **Paduasoy**, **Printed silk**, **Quilt**, **Rayon**, **Russell**, **Sateen**, **Seating**, **Silk**, **Tabaret**, **Ticking**, **Tinsel**, **Velvet**, **Venetian cloth, Weave**.

Satin toilet bedspread
In 1955, these were described as a particular kind of bedspread, which, oddly, has no **satin** weave in it:

> Counterpane also known as patent satin and marcella. Satin is not part of the weave as the cloth is a compound structure of two plain-weaves. The cloth consists of a raised figure on a plain ground, the figure being made with a coarse weft bound with a fine warp. They are usually woven white but may have a coloured weft. They were used widely for public services such as railways, ships and hospitals. (Ostick, 1955, p.355.)

See also **Marseilles**, **Mitcheline**.

Savonnerie
A name that was originally for **carpets** made at the Savonnerie workshops but is now the generic name for French-made **pile** carpets. The pile was hand-knotted over sharp-edged iron rods which, when withdrawn from the loom, would cut the pile.

Founded in 1627 in an old Parisian soap works, the Savonnerie factory specialised in weaving floor carpets, but also made covers for **upholstery**, **screens** and **wall hangings**. As the production was under the control of the King (by 1673), the products were always specially commissioned for particular locations and had little impact on the wider markets. The business declined and then revived its fortunes with the early nineteenth-century Empire style and finally amalgamated with the **Gobelins** tapestry factory in 1826.
See also **Brussels carpet**, **Fulham carpet**.

FURTHER READING

Jarry, M. (1966). *The Carpets of the Manufactory de la Savonnerie*, Leigh-on-Sea: F. Lewis.
Jarry, M. (1969). 'Savonnerie panels and furnishing materials of the seventeenth and eighteenth centuries', *Connoisseur*, 170, April, pp 211–19.
Sherrill, S.B. (1996). *Carpets and Rugs of Europe and America*, New York: Abbeville, pp 60–106.
Verlet, P. (1982). *The Savonnerie: Its History*, London: National Trust.

Saxony
Strictly speaking, this is a high-quality fabric made from **worsted wool**. In **carpet** terms, it is a construction having a level cut-**pile**, less dense and longer than in velvet pile carpet, in which each tuft is clearly defined. It may also refer to the wool used in making carpets.

In 1910, Humphries noted that 'Saxony Pile Carpets are made in precisely the same way as the Brussels variety' (*Oriental Carpets*, Vol. IV, p.300). According to Hunter, 'Saxony Brussels and Saxony Wilton differ from the others in texture, being coarser and less velvety in appearance, but more durable in use, because of the thread employed' (1918, p.165). In 1933, London retailers, Heal & Son, were advertising 'Carpet; seamless Saxony, in various colours.' (1972.)

The term was revived in the later twentieth century for broadloom carpet of similar effect.
See **Brussels carpet**, **Saxony velvet**, **Velvet carpet**.

Saxony Brussels
The Mercury Dictionary of Textile Terms (1950) explains that these are 'Curtains having a net ground with designs formed by laying another thickness of mesh, tambouring the outline by hand and cutting away the loose outer parts'.
See also **Brussels curtain**.

Saxony velvet
A name used from the 1950s for long-**pile velvet carpets**.
See also **Saxony**.

Say (aka Saye)
A lightweight, fine textured part-**silk** material of twill weave described as 'a sort of thin woollen-stuff or serge' (Bailey, 1736). Later it was an all-**wool** cloth. The name may derive from *saai* being the Dutch for 'woollen cloth'. Often used for linings, says were also woven into 'beds'. These 'beds' were specially woven says of coarser yarns up to four yards (3.7 metres) wide and were intended for bed hangings.

It appears to have been used as a furnishing fabric from quite early on (*OED*, 1297). In 1488, Robert Morton had a 'bed, celure, tester, three curtains, three hangings and a riddle of green say' (Clabburn, 1988, p.105) and, in 1509, Edmund Dudley had green say 'hanging in the windows' of his London house (ibid. p.131). Say seems to have been quite common in sixteenth-century inventories. In 1514, Joseph Borel of Great Yarmouth had 'two bed cloths of say; one green and one black' (ibid. p.254). Then, in 1551, Henry Parker of Norwich had a 'trussing bed with a tester and valance of red and greene saye, panyd, three curtains of the same' (Hall, 1901, pp 150–1) and, in 1553, a will listed 'One seller & tester of reede and greene seye wth curtens of the same' (*Lancashire and Chester Wills*, I. 105, *OED*). The *Tudor Book of Rates* for 1582 also listed 'sayes the peece/Sayes look in silk sayes' (Willan, 1962, p.51).

It was still used as a furnishing fabric in the seventeenth century and, in some cases, says were also being decorated. In 1601, in Hardwick Hall there was a 'cupboard carpet of saye stained red and white' and a 'canopy of yellow saye stayned with birds and Antikes' (Boynton, 1971, p.25). In the 1605 Hengrave Hall inventory, there were listed 'blue and yellow say hangings in the chamber where yet musicians play' (Clabburn, 1998, p.93). In America, say was also used for **bed furniture**. In 1655, Frances Lawes of Salem left his daughter Mary his 'best bed' and the 'greene say curtains and vallens' that went with it (Cummings, 1961, p.35).

Say was later mainly used for clothing. In 1728, Chamber's *Cyclopaedia* defined it thus: 'Say, or Saye, a kind of serge, a very light crossed stuff, all wool; much used abroad for linings, and by the religious for shirts; and with us, by the Quakers, for aprons, for which purpose it is usually dyed green.' By 1858, it was defined as 'an old name for serge or bunting' (Simmonds, 1858).
See also **Bed cloth**, **Bunting**, **Serge, Shalloon, Wall covering and hanging**.

Scalloped heading
A **curtain heading** featuring scallop-shaped cutouts that have the points sewn to rings, which run on rods. They are often associated with café curtains. Scallop effects may also be found on **pelmets**, mantle **scarves**, etc.
See also **Café curtain**.

Scarf
Originally, a scarf was a precursor to the **antimacassar** of the nineteenth century, designed to protect **upholstery** from the dust from powdered wigs, etc., by the use of a flap of material brought over the back and draped on the upholstery surface. In 1735, the bills for Temple Newsam showed an entry for '19 yards of crimson ingrain sarsnitt to make scarves for the backs of chairs and settees' (Gilbert, 1967, p.18). A year later, in 1736, William Bradshaw invoiced the Earl of Stanhope for 'Lutestring to back and make scarves to the 8 chairs and 2 settees £3 16 8d' in the Tapestry Room at Chevening (Beard, 1997, p.304). The term also described dressing table **drapery**. In 1768, Chippendale supplied Hopetoun House with a toilette and scarf drapes:

> The Scarf over the Glass should be twice as long as the length from the Top of the Glass as it Stands in its place from the Table to the ground & half a yard more & when the scarf is double the middle half yard makes the hood… (Coleridge, 1966, p 154.)

By the nineteenth century, scarf drapery referred to uncut fabrics, used to form freehand ornamental drapings over furniture, chairs, etc. There were scarves for bureaux, dressers, pianos, tables and washstands. Mantel drapery was also achieved with scarves. In 1889, Moreland considered that 'much of the mantel woodwork is now so elaborate that it requires no draping beyond a tasteful arrangement of scarves of silk' (1889, p.270). Moreland recommended **silk plush** for **festoons**, or for flat scarves that would be worked with **needlework**, **appliquéd** or hand-painted, whilst for bedrooms he recommended matching **cretonne** or silk to the window **curtains**.

In the last decades of the nineteenth century, scarf draperies were a particular fashion. One example from 1890 described the French arrangement of a fireplace with 'a combination of dark green plush, set off with old pink silk, which is embroidered with floss silk in delicate shades of green, pink and gold, edged with long tassels in variegated chenille. Ball fringe in gold gimp around the mantel board, and the side scarf end.' (Grier, 1988, p.171.) In 1895, the American company, Montgomery Ward, sold by mail order 'embroidered felt scarves for mantles, stands and decorating'.

Scarf can also refer to the loose drapery hanging as part of a toilette, washstand, dresser or bureau.
See also **Lustring**, **Mantel drapery**, **Piano cover**, **Runner**, **Table scarf**, **Toilette**.

Scarlet
A high-quality carded **woollen** cloth, usually dyed scarlet red but sometimes available in other colours. The 1495 *Accounts of Lord High Treasurer* listed 'iij ellis of scarlot to be a pane to the King's bed' (Scot. I. 226, *OED*). In 1516, the same accounts listed 'ij elne iij quartaris Inglis scarlet to be ane pane for the King's bed in the schip' (ibid. III. 50). In 1591, the Countess of Shrewsbury bought for Hardwick Hall small pieces of scarlet at 40s. and 50s. per yard. This was very expensive in comparison to other contemporary cloths (Levey, 2001, p.30).

Scorched leather
Reddish-brown **leather** that had a pattern branded onto it (often a damask pattern) with the use of a hot plate and a mould postioned

underneath. It was favoured in the seventeenth century for protective cases for furniture items.
See also **Damask leather**, **Protective furnishing**.

Scotch carpeting

An eighteenth-century term referring to **pile**-less double weave **carpets**, that were woven in a variety of places including Kidderminster (Worcestershire), Kilmarnock (Scotland) and Yorkshire. The name 'Scotch' seems to relate to the carpet type and has no particular meaning, other than becoming a generic label for ingrain carpet.

There are many references to Scotch carpeting from the eighteenth century, but an earlier inventory listing is noted in 1619, when John Herne of Ipswich had in his hall 'a skottish carpet' (Reed, 1981, p.100) and, in 1660, the *London Book of Rates* listed 'carpets of Scotland' as an import (Kraak, 1996).

The making of Scotch carpeting began to flourish in the eighteenth century. In 1751, Richard Pococke wrote of Kidderminster: 'that the place is famous for carpets made without nap, like the Scotch, but now they make the same as Wilton, and it is said they are attempting to weave 'em in one piece' (Roth, 1967, p.30). The American traveller, Samuel Rowland Fisher, viewed 'Scotch carpets the same as Wilton and very neat' in Edinburgh in 1767 (Hummel, 1975). Scotch carpet was clearly used in a range of situations. In 1769, Lord Monson purchased from cabinet-maker and upholsterer, John Cobb, '10 Scotch bedside carpets at 4s 6d' and later purchased '19 yards of Best scotch carpet for the Billiard Room at 4s' from a Thomas Preston (Gilbert, Lomax & Wells-Cole, 1987, p.89).

However, it was later considered to be low-grade and was denigrated by Sheraton who, in his *Cabinet Dictionary*, considered 'Scots carpet [to be] one of the most inferior kind' (1803, p.132). Another commentator also considered Scotch carpets to be 'inferior to Kidderminster… [as] they are greasy and smell bad' (Gilbert, Lomax & Wells-Cole, 1987, p.72). Loudon was more pragmatic. He suggested that 'the kinds of carpet most suitable for cottages are chiefly the Scotch and Kidderminster on account of their cheapness' (1839, p.344). By 1854, the distinctions were still in the name. Tomlinson's *Cyclopaedia of Useful Arts* described Scotch carpeting as 'the same as Kidderminster but included a three ply or triple ingrain version'.

In 1879, further distinctions were made: 'A real Scotch carpet is all wool, but fabrics similar in appearance are made with cotton warps and worsted wefts, in which case they are called "unions" (*Cassell's Technical Educator*, vol.IV, 387/2).
See also **Barnard Castle carpet**, **Imperial**, **Ingrain carpet**, **Kidderminster carpet**, **Yorkshire carpeting**.

FURTHER READING
Anon. (1843). 'A day at a Scotch carpet factory', *The Penny Magazine*, August, pp 329–6.
Habib, V. (1997). 'Scotch carpets in the eighteenth and early nineteenth centuries', *Textile History*, 28, pp 161–75.
Habib, V. (2000). 'Scotch carpeting at Stirling: Thomas Gilfillan's cash book and ledger 1764–1770', *Proceedings of the Society of Antiquaries of Scotland*, 130, Part 1, pp 795–807.
Hefford, W. (1987). 'Patents for strip carpeting 1741–1851', *Furniture History*, 23, pp 1–7.
Roth, R. (1967). *Floorcoverings in 18th-Century America*, Smithsonian Papers, Washington, DC: Smithsonian Institution, pp 29–35.
Swain, M. (1978). 'A note on Scotch carpets', *Furniture History*, 14, pp 61–?

110. Scotch carpet, wool, c.1790–1810 (National Trust for Scotland)

Scotch cloth

Plain-woven **cotton** cloth finished with starch or sizing, that resembled **lawn**, but was cheaper. It was once made from nettle fibres. An early reference from 1675 noted that 'Hemp is nothing else but the Sap-Vessels of the Barque of the Plant so called. And Scotch-Cloath, is only the Housewifery of the same Parts of the Barque of Nettle' (*OED*).

The use of Scotch cloth in home furnishings was recorded in 1677, when the Duchess's dressing room in Ham House had 'one curtain over the door of white scots stuffe' (Thornton & Tomlin, 1980, p.89). A little later, it was clearly defined: 'Scotch Cloth is a sort of white Sleasie Soft-Cloth, and since Callico hath been dear, is much used for Linnens for Beds and for Window Curtains' (J.F. 1696, p.37).

In the 1728 inventory of the shop of James Pilbeam, a mercer of Chiddingly, Sussex, there was listed 'Twenty-three ells of scotch cloath at lld per ell, £1 1s 1d' (http://www.chiddingly.gov.uk/History/James%20Pilbeam.html). In 1768, upholsterer, John Morland, supplied 'scotch cloth to back line the outside vallans' of a bed (*DEFM*, p.627).

Scottish work

A particular form of **needlework** that seems to have been popular in Ipswich. Richard Smart, a gentleman of Ipswich, in 1608 had 'one chair covered with Scottish work' (Reed, 1981, p.71). In 1619, John Herne had 'viii joined stools covered with skottishe work' (ibid. p.100). Anne Wright, in 1626, had 'a skottishe work coverlet' (ibid. 1981).

Screen

Small, fixed or folding furnishing items used to shield the user from draughts (*paravent*), heat (*écran*), or merely to give privacy. Early screens that were intended to protect against heat were made of wicker. Hardwick Hall has several examples, and the 1641 inventory of Tart Hall listed a 'round screen of wicker', a 'long square wicker screen' and a 'long plain wicker screen' (Cust, 1911). Screens that were employed to keep off draughts and cold were often covered in textiles. In 1603, Hengrave Hall had 'a great folding screen of seven folds, with a screen cloth upon it of green kersey' (Macquoid & Edwards, 1924, vol.III, p.67).

Fire screens were developed either into the horse (cheval) style, where the panel was either fixed or slid up and down in a frame, or into the pole screen, which had a smaller panel sliding on a pole, set upon a tripod or base. Screens were often supplied en suite with **upholstery**. **Tapestry** was popular as a filling, as was **needlework**, although plain or **fluted silk**, and later painted and **printed silks**, were also used.

A particular version was developed in the nineteenth century, which was called a banner screen. *The Workwoman's Guide* suggested that: 'These may be made by merely hemming a piece of rich silk at the top, through which a rod is passed, which is secured to the pole of the screen. The bottom of this silk is hemmed neatly and has a deep fringe set on' (Hale, 1840, p.207).

See also **Chair screen**.

Screen cloth

A protective cloth intended to fit over screens. The 1601 inventory of the Gallery at Hardwick Hall listed 'a screen with a cover for it of carnations velvet imbrodered with gold and a gold fringe' (Boynton, 1601, p.29), while in one of the chambers there was 'a wood screen [and] a cover for it of grene cloth' (ibid. p.31).

See also **Screen**.

Screen printing

See **Printed textile**.

Scrim

Thin, open-weave, lightweight but durable fabric. Originally made of **linen**, and later of **cotton** or mixes, it is a **muslin**-like material that has been used to line or bottom chairs, to give stability to glued wooden panels, and for **curtaining**, etc. The name is of obscure origin but is recorded in the 1792 *Statistical Account of Scotland*, which referred to 'a few yard-wides called Scrims' (VI. 514, *OED*).

In the twentieth century, it was defined as: 'a fabric with a coarse, open construction made of much heavier yarn than voile; inexpensive, and very durable, but not so beautiful as voile or marquisette' (Dyer, *c.*1923, p.200). White, cream or ecru were the usual colours although a taste for scrim, woven with coloured stripes and intended for curtains and **drapery** was noted in the mid-twentieth century. The employment of scrim is explained by an American commentator: 'Another variety of cheap curtains is heavy cream scrim with straps (for looping back) and valance of chintz. These come cheaper than all chintz curtains and are very effective, suggesting the now popular and expensive combination of plain toned taffetas combined with chintz.' (Wood, 1917, p.233.)

Later on in America, Taylor specified scrim to be used as a **glass curtain** fabric, noting that it was rather fuzzy in effect (which was caused by loosely twisted threads), so it was only recommended for less formal settings. She recommended that it hung best in straight folds or was French headed (1951). British attitudes were less gracious: '[Scrim] is used for dusters and other humble purposes, but can make quite passable small curtains' (Smithells, 1950).

Seagrass

See **Grass**, **Seagrass**.

Sealskin (aka Soyle)

A hair-hide type of **leather** made from sealskins that were cured by drying on frames and having alum worked into the surface. In 1737, Samuel Grant of Boston, Mass., bought '9 red sile skins [for] making 25 seats' (Jobe in Cooke [ed.], 1987, p.88). They have been used for sling seat covers and for covering trunks and cases.

See also **Sealskin cloth**.

Sealskin cloth

Caulfeild & Saward noted: 'the yarn used for this kind of cloth is the finest kind of Mohair', while silk sealskin, 'is a very beautiful patent textile, composed of Tussar Silk, and made in imitation of Sealskin Fur' (1887, pp 442, 450).

See also **Sealskin**.

Seasonal furnishing

The intention of having differing **upholstery** covers for the particular season of the year, i.e. the French practice of, for example, **silk damask** hangings for the winter, and **printed cotton** for the summer. This need was met by various sets of **drapes** and covers that could be changed at will, or less commonly by the use of slip seats (drop in) and reversible or loose back **cushions** and removable arm pads. These were sometimes known as *à chassis*. An ingenious chair design was patented in 1798 by Anthony Eckhardt (Patent no.2208), which was based on a seat pad fixed on swivel pegs to the frame, so that it could be turned through 180 degrees to even out wear, or change the **top cover** instantly. The design included a model that allowed the back and seat to exchange places.

See also **Protective furnishing**.

FURTHER READING

Gill, K. (2001). 'Eighteenth-century close-fitting detachable covers preserved at Houghton Hall: a technical study' in Gill, K. & Eastop, D. (eds), *Upholstery Conservation: Principles and Practice*, Oxford: Butterworth-Heinemann, pp 133–42.

Seating

Another name for haircloth. Seating was defined as: 'A textile made of hair, of satin make, designed for upholstering purposes, such as the seats of chairs, sofas, and cushions.' (Caulfeild & Saward, 1887, p.443.)

See **Haircloth**.

Seaweed

An aquatic alga found on the shores. Processed seaweed was used as an **upholstery** and bedding filling during the nineteenth century. Lady Barker mentions 'a seaweed mattress in an Irish hotel, in which I should imagine many curious specimens of marine zoology had been entombed by mistake' (1878, p.34).

See also **Alva marina**, **Grass: Sea wrack**, **Mattress**.

Sectional panel curtain

A lace curtain made in various widths designed to suit assorted window sizes. The lace is produced in panels that run across the width of the fabric. The panels are usually 9 or 12 inches (22.9 or 31 cm) wide, there being an openwork seam between each panel which, when cut, will not fray, so each length cut is ready for use (Ostick, 1955, p.367).

See also **Lace**.

Sedge

See **Grass: Sedge**.

III. Seersucker cloth c.1955 (Private Collection)

Seersucker

Originally, a striped fabric of mixed **silk** and **cotton** from northeast India. The name appears to be derived from the Persian *shirushaker*, a kind of striped cloth, literally meaning 'milk and sugar'. It has a crimped or puckered surface (**crêpe**-stripe effect) caused by looser tensioned cotton **warps**. Also (and now chiefly) applied to imitations made elsewhere. Some seersucker may be produced by pressing or by using chemicals, which are unlikely to be permanent; they are then often called plissé.

Since the end of the seventeenth century, it has been used for **curtains** and hangings. A 'pair of searsucker curtains and vallens' was listed for Thomas Hunt of Boston, Mass. in 1734 (Cummings, 1961, p.36).

In 1947, the use of seersucker for curtains, **bedspreads** and slipcovers in American interiors was noted (Bendure & Pfieffer, p.650) and, in 1950, Smithells considered it to be excellent for bedspreads.

See also **Austrian shade cloth**, **Plissé**.

FURTHER READING

Cummin, H. (1940). 'Early seersucker', *Antiques*, 38, July, pp 231–2.

Segovienne

According to Havard, segovienne was a hairy, twilled **flannel** used for **upholstery**. It was particular popular from the fourteenth century to the seventeenth century.

Self-lined curtain

A fabric introduced in the latter part of the twentieth century which produced acetate **warp**-knitted **curtain linings**, foam-bonded to the curtain material. This was usually of a warp-knitted brushed **nylon** fabric, which gave a **velvet** effect.

See also **Foam-backed curtain**.

Sempiternum

A twilled **woollen** cloth similar to **serge**, with a name related to its supposed lasting qualities. In 1633, the *Naworth Household Books* (Surtees, 295, *OED*) listed an entry 'for one yearde and a halfe of Sempiternum iiij. Vjd.'. In the 1647 inventory of William Clarke, of Salem, Mass., sempiternum is recorded as the fabric used for a 'cubbord cloth with silke fringe' (Montgomery, 1984, p.344).

Sendal

A thin but rich silk material, sendal has been known since at least the thirteenth century, and was certainly used for **bed furniture**. In 1395, a will bequeathed 'a keuerlet [coverlet] of red sendel ypouthered with Cheuerons' (*Early English Wills*, 1882, p.4). A little later, Robert de Roos had two beds: the first '*de viridi sandal*', and the second '*de glauco sandal, poudred cum mollett*' (*Testamenta Ebor.*, vol.I, pp 95–6). Thirdly, Edmund Earl of March mentions in his will: '*un lit blank de sandale poudres des roses rouges sur le chambre entiere*' (Leaf, 1934).

Sendal is also a name for a fine **linen lawn**, which was obsolete by the early seventeenth century.

Serge

A twill (diagonal ribbed) weave cloth, with a **silk**, or later of **worsted**, **warp** face and **woollen weft**. Serge was used from the twelfth century for **upholstery** and clothing. The nature of serge has probably differed considerably at various periods: the name appears to have been derived from the Latin *serica* and later the Italian *sergea*, meaning 'wool mixed with silk'. Later versions used **cotton**. Certain imported varieties were formerly known by French designations indicating the place of manufacture: *serge de Ghent, serge de Nimes* (later, cotton denim), *serge de Ro(h)an*, and *serge de Châlons* (shalloon).

From the fifteenth century, serge was used as a chair covering material as well as for **curtains**, **valances** and **protective furnishings**. In 1491, 'coverings of beddis of sarge, price x li.' were listed (*Acta Dominorium Concillii*, (1839) 228/2, xxij, *OED*). In 1585, an interesting reference to serge as **blankets** is recorded: 'Some peece of a white sarge or blanket' (T. Washington (tr.), *Nicholay's Navigations into Turkie*, vol.I. ch.viii. p.8, *OED*). Like saye, serges were sometimes called 'beds' on account of their use and width.

In the seventeenth century, it was popular for all furnishing requirements in both England and North America. In 1660, William Paine's estate in America listed 'one bedstead, curtains and vallens of red searge' (Montgomery, 1984, p.344). In the same year, Samuel Pepys recorded how: 'this morning my dining room was finished with green serge hangings and gilt leather which is very handsome' (vol.I, p.269). The material seemed to be popular at all levels of society. In 1684, the Duke of Ormonde had bed **case curtains** of grey serge, covers for chairs in red serge, and window curtains of both white and yellow serge (Clabburn, 1988, p.254). In 1691, the yeoman, William Bird of Essex, had a 'gray serge quilt, the like curtains and valans, curtain rodds, bedstead and six serge chairs' (Steer, 1969, p.207).

In 1728, Chambers defined serge as 'a woollen [twilled] stuff, manufactured on a loom with four treddles, after the manner of ratteens, and other cross'd stuffs that have the whale' (*Cyclopaedia*). Serge was widely used in the eighteenth century for loose cases and case curtains, backing materials for chairs and for protective covers to other furnishings. In 1773, Chippendale advised Lady Knatchbull that 'serge is most commonly used [for covers] but … you might choose some sort of callico' (Gilbert, 1978, p.57). In 1778, Thomas Chippendale supplied Sir Edward Knatchbull with '48 yards Buff Serge in bags to the window curtains' (Boynton, 1968, p.103), probably to protect the curtains. The commonplace nature of serge protective covers can be seen in the household of Sir Richard Worsley. In 1779, the housekeeper's storeroom had '8 crimson serge cases for gilt chairs' (Boynton, 1965, p.51).

One particular use for serge was as a floorcovering protection. Sir Gilbert Heathcote paid Chippendale in 1778 for 'thread and piecing out the Serge Carpet in the Breakfast room to fit the floor, making eyeholes in do and laying down with studs compleat' (Gilbert, 1978, p.251). In 1789, fashion considerations affected the choice of protection. Ninian Home wrote to Chippendale: 'there must be a covering for it [a new carpet] of green serge. Perhaps that may not be fit for a drawing room, or that now some other sort of stuff is used for capes. Make them of what you think is right.' (Gilbert, 1978, p 51.) In the end, he was supplied with baize, as the house inventory taken in 1820 lists 'a green baize floor cloth 37 feet 3in by 19 feet 3in nearly worn out' (Gilbert, Lomax & Wells-Cole, 1987, p.107).

During the nineteenth century, serge continued to be an appreciated fabric for furnishings and other uses. In 1877, Mrs Orrinsmith wrote in her book, *The Drawing Room*, that 'Portières look well made of serge or serge cloth in soft greens or peacock blues' (1877, p.77). She also suggested that 'heavy patterns worked upon Holland, cut out and sewn on serge and cloth, with an edging of filoselle or twisted silk make decorations suitable for portières' (ibid. p.73). Ten years later, Caulfeild & Saward noted that 'there are a great many varieties of cloth known as Serge, viz. French Flannel Serge; the Serge de Berri, Witney Serges, and Pompadour Flannel Serges. The coarse and heavy kinds employed for upholstery are of double width whether of wool or silk.' (1887, p.443.)

By the mid-twentieth century, it was noted that 'the only type now handled is Art Serge; 50 and 72 inches wide. An inexpensive curtain in art colours, wool and cotton loosely woven, much less popular now, its place being taken by the "folk weave" type cloths' (French, 1947).

See also **Art serge**, **Caddis**, **Carpet cover and protection**, **Curtain serge**, **Denim**, **Furnishing serge**, **Leventine**, **Paduasoy**, **Perpetuana**, **Say**, **Sempiternum**, **Shalloon**.

Set work

A seventeenth-century term for turkey work. Theophilus Eaton, Governor of New Haven Colony, who died in 1657, had in his hall 'two high chairs with sett work 20s. 4d. each'. In 1689, a petition for the 'Encouragement of the woollen manufacture of England' noted that 'there has been a very great consumption of wool used in making Set-work cushions of chairs, couches etc' (Symonds, 1951a, pp 13–14).

See also **Turkey work**.

Shadow cretonne

A variety of cretonne in which the **warp** is printed prior to weaving, which then interweaves with an uncoloured **weft** to produce shadow cretonnes or shadow **tissues**. 'The warp is printed before weaving and when woven with a white or neutral coloured weft the printed warp colours are reduced to delicate half tones.' (Ostick, 1955, p.378) The finished effect is therefore shadowy and toned down with a lack of sharpness to the design. This fabric was particularly popular in the 1930s and was often used to imitate **ikats**.

See also **Cretonne: Warp-printed**.

Shag carpet

Rugs or fitted **carpets** with a long shaggy **pile**. They were tufted with fewer tufts per square inch (square centimetre) than short pile carpets and were developed in the 1960s.

See also **Tufted carpet**.

Shagg

A **worsted** or **silk** textile woven with a long nap creating a shaggy effect. Probably derived from the Old Norse word, *skegg*, meaning 'beard'.

(a) A heavy worsted material with a long nap. There are references to it in the sixteenth century, and it was certainly in use for **upholstery** by the eighteenth century. In 1710, Dyrham had 'three pieces of red shagg hangings', and 'two Dutch chairs with shagg cushions' (Walton, 1986, pp 58, 62). The worsted connection was noted in 1805, when Luccock discussed 'the [manufacture] of worsted shaggs at Banbury' (Luccock, p.277). Eighty years later, considering **Utrecht velvet**, Caulfeild & Saward said: 'There is an imitation made, which is woven in wool, and is called Banbury plush' (1887, p.507).

(b) A cloth made from silk waste, which was teased to create a nap. During 1671, Edmond Booth developed the manufacture of a rich silk shagg, using silk waste (Warner, 1921, p.400). In 1701, the *London Gazette* advertised that 'All sorts of Mercery Goods, viz. Bristol Stuffs, Toys, Shalloons, Silk Shags, Chenies will be sold by Auction.' (No.3701/4.)

Shalloon

An inexpensive twill **worsted** fine-yarn **say** or **serge**-type cloth, used for lining clothes and occasionally for **upholstery** and furnishings. Although there are earlier references it was developed in the seventeenth century (*OED*, 1678). The name appears to derive from the French *chalon*. Shalloon fabric was sometimes glazed and hot pressed. In 1684, Kilkenny Castle had bed and chair cases made from red shalloon (Clabburn, 1988, p.254).

A similar usage was in 1710, when Dyrham Park had **case curtains** 'to ye bed of blew shalloon' (Walton, 1986, p.58). The 1727 inventory of

112. Shadow cretonne showing detail of yarns (T. French and Co, The Book of Soft Furnishing, *1937)*

Mary Saunders of Boston had 'a suit of red shalloon curtains' (Cummings, 1961, p.36). There are later sporadic references to its use as a **bed curtain**. In the 1728 inventory of the shop of James Pilbeam, a mercer of Chiddingly, Sussex, there was listed 'Two hundred sixty and one yards and a half of shalloon at ls 2d per yard, £14 8s 5d' (http://www.chiddingly.gov.uk/History/James%20Pilbeam.html).

In 1793, cabinet-makers charged specifically for 'putting on the tammy or shalloon with braid on each side of each pannel' of a folding **fire screen** (*The Cabinet-Makers' London Book of Prices*, p.211).
See also **Chalon**, **Rattinet**.

Shantung

A late nineteenth-century introduction to the furnishers' repertoire. It was a rough textured, plain-woven **silk** cloth made from Chinese wild silk that was sometimes used for light furnishings. It was heavier and bumpier than **pongee**.

Shantung was described in 1947 as being made from 'elongated slub filling yarns creating an irregular surface texture [that was] used for curtains and apparel' (Bendure & Pfieffer, p.650). **Rayon** and **cotton** versions have been made in imitation of the silk fabric.
See also **Dupion**.

Shawl bordering

A decorative trim used from the early nineteenth century for accenting slipcovers or window **curtains**. When used for curtains, these borders often came in pairs with a narrower one designed for the top border and a broader one for the bottom. Grecian key patterns or Indian designs were popular. Loudon recommended slipcovers fitted 'with a narrow piece of different coloured calico or shawl bordering laid on about a couple of inches from the edge'. He also praised curtains of 'muslins, cottons and lenos of different colours, sometimes accompanied by shawl bordering sewed upon the cottons' (Loudon, 1839, p.338). Bordering has been used in curtain work on occasion ever since.
See also **Border**.

Shawling

Mainly known as a dress material, woven from a **silk warp** and a **worsted weft**. Although it was usually intended to replicate Indian shawls, in the eighteenth century it was apparently used for furnishings as well. 'Shawl counterpanes' are known at Blickling Hall (Clabburn, 1988, p.77).
See also **Cashmere**.

Sheer curtain

Curtains made of any transparent or very lightweight material (e.g. **chiffon**, **georgette crêpe**, **voile**, sheer **crêpe cloth**): they are often open-weave, plain white and commonly used as **under curtains**. Sheers are often plain but could be produced using various weaves. Triple sheers are heavier and flatter than normal sheers, and are almost opaque.
See also **Glass curtain**, **Lace**, **Net**.

Sheet

A **cotton**, **linen**, **hemp** or other fibre, woven into sheeting material and usually intended for bedding use. Many textiles have been converted into or used as sheeting, including barras, Bolton sheeting, cambric, dowlas, Forfar, Garlick, harden, holland, lockram, percale, raynes cloth, **silk** and towen.

Sheets were important parts of the bedding ensemble. In 1587, a will bequeathed 'A pare of sheets, a covering, a tester, curtaynes and valances' (*Wills & Inventories, illustrative of the history, manners, language, etc. of the northern counties of England,* Surtees Society, 1860, p.317). Three examples of sheeting from the seventeenth century give an idea of qualities. In 1664, Mary Mitchell of Roxwell, Essex, owned just two pairs of **canvas** sheets (Steer, 1969, p.100). William Garret of Writtle in 1689 owned 'I pair of flaxen sheets, I pair of calico sheets (ibid. p.202), while in 1672, the yeoman, Abraham Brecknock of Writtle, owned 'a paire of holland sheets, sixe pair of flaxen sheets, 18 pair of towing sheets' (ibid. p.123).

The variety and choice widened in the nineteenth century. In 1887, Caulfeild & Saward noted a great variety of sheeting including:

> Those of linen are named Scotch and Barnsley bleached, loom dowlas and loom scotch the widths of which are known distinctively by the number of inches they measure. Also the Irish, union Irish, which is mixed with cotton; Lancashire linen, union Lancashire, Russia and imitiation Russia. The strongest coarse sheeting is the Russia… Bolton sheeting otherwise called Workhouse sheeting is of calico… (p.446.)

By the 1920s, the choice was, if anything, greater. American author, Elizabeth Dyer, explained:

> There are many grades of sheeting; the lowest is unbleached sheeting, and the best is percale. The latter is of smooth, fine texture, and closely resembles linen sheeting. It gives some people the same kind of pleasure to possess real linen sheets as it does to own sterling silver or real pearls, but few can afford them as they are very expensive and for most of us would be unnecessary extravagance, because the finer grades of cotton are almost as beautiful, wear well, and do not wrinkle so badly. Linen is cooler, more durable, and very smooth, but wrinkles easily.

The exposition on the topic of sheets then went on to discuss the distinctions between made-up sheets and torn:

> Sheets may be purchased by the yard or already made. As a rule, it is not much cheaper to buy the sheeting by the yard, but sometimes better qualities can be purchased in that way. Frequently, you see 'torn sheets' advertised. That means that the muslin was torn before hemming rather than cut, thus making a straighter sheet, which will not pull crooked in laundering. This holds true only if it has been done carefully and with muslin that tears straight. The best way is to pull a thread and cut by that.

Finally, the distinctions between qualities were laid out:

> There are on the market many reliable brands of medium-priced sheeting, which wear well. The cheaper sheeting is very coarse, and is often sized, or if not sized, it feels rough to the touch. It is heavy to wash and hard to iron. Percale sheetings are very durable, white, and fine, but expensive. Sheets and pillow-cases come either hemmed, hemstitched or embroidered (scalloped). For hard, everyday wear, the plain hems are most serviceable. (Dyer, *c.*1923, p.208.)

In the 1950s, similar comments were made about quality. Linen sheets were most highly recommended but, if these were not affordable, cotton was suggested: 'Cotton sheets vary in quality from the finest weaves to the thick type, made from condenser yarns which has a soft, almost woolly handle. The latter have always been much in favour in industrial areas.' (Sheridan, 1955, p.292.) In 1955, bed linen for a basic trousseau was recommended as eight pairs of sheets and twelve pairs of **pillowcases**.

When sheets and bedding became more of a fashion item, they were printed to co-ordinate with **duvet** covers, **curtains** and the like. The

first non-iron sheets were produced in 1966 and other developments included 'fitted' sheets. Sheeting has also been promoted for non-bedding uses such as for **tablecloths**, **coverlets**, slipcovers, etc.
See also **Barras**, **Bedclothes**, **Bolton sheeting**, **Cambric**, **Dowlas**, **Forfar**, **Garlick**, **Harden**, **Holland**, **Lockram**, **Percale**, **Raynes cloth**, **Towen**, **Workhouse sheeting**.

Shelf lambrequin
See **Lambrequin**, **Mantel drapery**.

Shikii
A type of **rep** that uses an unevenly spun filling, which gives variety in texture known as Shiki rep (Denny, 1928). It is also a name for a particular thin **silk** cloth woven in plain-weave with uneven **weft** threads that texture the surface (Taylor, 1951).

Shirred curtain
A **curtain** that is gathered or shirred in close parallel fold. It is often fixed at the top and bottom and is not opened.
See also **Store marquise**.

Shoddy
A woven product, originating in the nineteenth century, made from reclaimed **wool**. Simmonds explains: 'worsted yarn from old stockings, tailors clippings and old woollen rags, torn up, fibre by fibre, in a devil (as it is technically termed) and re-spun into yarn with the addition of a little fresh wool. Shoddy is made into an inferior cloth, into druggets, padding etc' (Simmonds, 1858).
See also **Comfort**, **Tweed**.

Short blind
Fixed **curtains** introduced in the first half of the nineteenth century, which were intended to cover the lower half of a window, were known as short blinds. They were hemmed at the top and bottom, and were fixed onto **brass rods**, or threaded onto string or wire and hooked up against the window. Typical fabrics that were used for short blinds included **muslin**, **gauze**, **chintz** or **leno**. They were intended to prevent people looking into rooms from the street and to prevent the occupant being seen by neighbours. The *Lady's House Book* firstly suggested fabric choices and, subsequently, how to make them: 'For sitting rooms, chambers, etc., the blinds generally in use are of white muslin. Those of plain unfigured Swiss or Scotch muslin look much the best, but are more easily seen through than when the muslin is striped or cross barred' (Leslie, 1854, pp 191–2). The author, Miss Leslie went on to say:

> Two yards of [54'] muslin will generally be sufficient for a pair of blinds. They should reach to the top of the lower sash and descend to the windowsill. Hem the bottom of each blind, and make a case in the top, through which runs a tape … and leaving long ends of tape to wrap tightly round the nails, which fasten the blind on each side of the window frame. There should be two sets of blinds as they will frequently require washing. It is well always to starch them a little. (ibid.)

By 1904, Hermann Muthesius, the German author of *The English House*, wrote approvingly of English short blinds:

> Beside the heavy curtains, English windows have smaller ones hung against the actual lights, which they call short blinds. Often, as, for example, in round bays with continuous strips of windows, from which main curtains are automatically precluded, they are the only curtains. They will then be made of thicker materials so they really shut out the light, and there will be a series of smaller curtains for the upper lights as for the lower. (p.194.)

See also **Blind**, **Casement blind**, **Glass curtain**, **Lace**.

Shutter blind
In Renaissance Italy, these were a form of blind, used in conjunction with shutters, called *fenestre impannate*. This was a wooden frame with oiled white cloth stretched over it to make the surface translucent. These frames were fitted in the window opening in place of glass (Thornton, 1991, pp 28–9). Although the materials had changed over centuries, the idea remained the same.

In the early nineteenth century, Sheraton noted:

> The sort [of shutter blinds] most commonly used are of mahogany, either to fold in two or one leaf, with green stuff of some kind strained into a rabbet in the frame. The more fashionable blinds are all of wood, painted green except the frame that is of mahogany. The blind part is either composed of upright or horizontal narrow laths, an eighth of an inch thick, painted a bright green, which move by means of a level to any position for admitting more or less light. (1803, p.58.)

Shutter blinds were still recommended for interiors and for exterior use in the nineteenth century.
See also **Blind**.

Siamoise
A group of materials of various yarns, including **silk warp** and **cotton weft**, sometimes with other yarns. They were apparently woven to imitate the multiple striped or **checked** cloths of the Siamese ambassadors to Louis XIV's court in the 1680s. Siamoise was manufactured in Rouen in large quantities from *c.*1700. One variety was thin (silk warp and cotton weft), and later **linen** was used more than silk. Another variety woven with linen warp and cotton weft (which resembled striped **camlet**) was produced and widely use for furnishing requisites. Bimont confirms that siamoise was suitable for all furnishing purposes except **upholstery**. He also said these fabrics should be fitted with **cord**-pulls to avoid tearing. They were used for summer slipcovers, bedcovers, hangings, etc. '*Siamoises pour meubles*' were advertised by a Parisian upholsterer in 1790 (Montgomery, 1984, p.348). Siamoise continued to be available into the nineteenth century.

Silence cloth
A heavy twill weave cloth called silence cloth or **table felt**. It is a strong, close material, heavily napped on both sides, which was usually sold unbleached or white. It was used to protect dining tables or ironing-boards (Denny, 1923, p.44).

A later definition described it as a usually napped, fairly heavy cloth cover for use under a white cloth. It was 54–64 inches (1.37–1.63 metres) wide and 60 to 240 inches (1.52–6.10 metres) long, made in **damask** designs, reversible, and made from coarse cotton yarns (*The Mercury Dictionary of Textile Terms*, 1950).
See also **Table felt**.

Silesia
A fine **linen** furnishing fabric originally made in Hamburg and sometimes called 'sleazy'. It has been used for a range of household purposes, including window **blinds**. 'Sleasie' holland was defined in 1670 as only 'properly [referring to] Sleasie or Silesia Linen cloth, which is made in [and] comes from the Country Silesia in Germany' (Blount, 3rd edition). By 1696, another careful definition stated that Sleasie Lawn was

'a very useful Linen here with us, it takes its name from a town called Slesia in Hamborough, and not for its wearing Sleasie, as a great many do imagine' (J.F., 1696, p.36).

Silesia was used from the mid-eighteenth century for lining furnishings. Cabinet-makers, William Vile and John Cobb, invoiced the Earl of Coventry for work at Croome Court in 1757 for '52.5 yards of Silesia to line your cotton for a furniture to the 2 bedsteads' (Beard, 1997, p.305). It appears that silesia was also printed. In 1764, the *Annual Register* (*OED*, p.107) advertised 'Fine printed linens of all sorts, Cambricks, Britannias, Silesias'.

In the early nineteenth century, it was specially woven as a coarse **cotton** cloth in a range of widths to make blinds to suit various-sized window frames. In 1813, Thomas Martin wrote, in his *Circle of Mechanical Arts*, that:

> White Silesia is to be obtained of any width from 2'3" to 4'6" or wider ... it is absolutely necessary to have them exactly the width of the window, in order that the selvedges may be retained, as hemming would otherwise render the widths too thick to roll close about the cylinder. (p.228)

The Dictionary of Needlework confirms this. The authors noted that silesia was 'a fine brown Holland originally made in the German province of Silesia, and now produced in England. For roller blinds, it is glazed and may be had in various widths from 28 to 90 inches.' (1887, p.449.) It was not only used for blinds. Moreland recommended its use for linings for chamber **drapes**: 'the entire draping may be of muslin or cream madras over colored silesia' (1889, p.238).

In the twentieth century, Smithells (1950) defined silesia as twill weave cotton fabric with a close, highly calendered surface, mainly used for linings.

See also **Holland**.

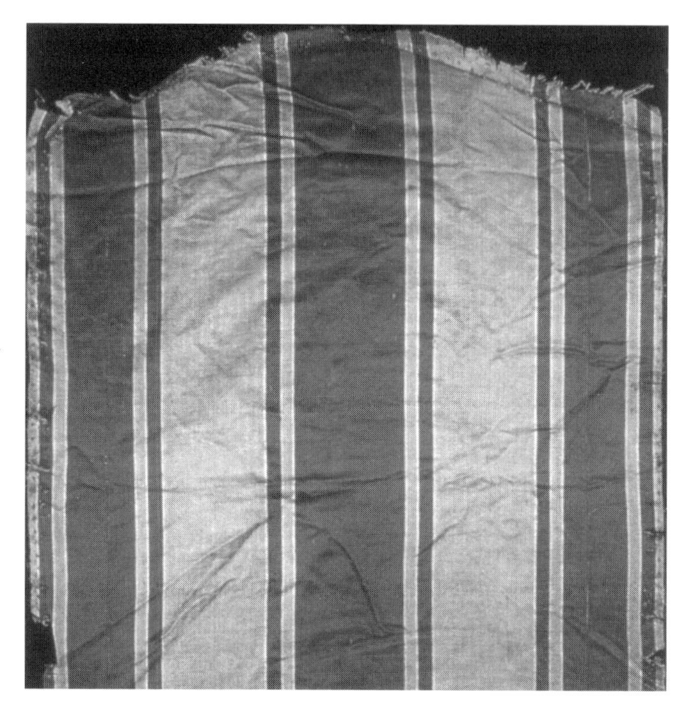

113. Furnishing silk stripe, late eighteenth century (Leeds Museums and Galleries, Temple Newsam House, Roger Warner Collection)

Silk

A generic name given to the fibres and the cloth woven from the product of the cocoon of the mulberry silk moth (especially *Bombyx mori*). Other varieties of moth cocoons that are used for silk are the undomesticated tussah (*Antheraea paphia*) which is light brown and rather coarse, and the *Bombyx croesi* which produces full yellow, uneven textured wild silk.

Silk is very strong, with a natural lustre, and is easily dyed. Filament bundles direct from the cocoon produce the best silk, while spun silk from the remainder is made into a more heavy-duty fabric. Raw silk still has a gummy exudence upon it. Silk's inherent qualities of strength and resistance to wear, as well as its fineness and absorbency of dyestuffs, made it a perfect furnishing fabric.

Of Chinese origin, silk weaving has been known for 4–5,000 years. Introduced into Europe as a cloth as early as 200BC, sericulture was developed by the ninth century in Spain and a little later in Venice and Genoa. By the twelfth century, Sicilian weavers were producing silk cloth and, by the fourteenth century, the main industry had moved north to Lucca and Venice. In Lucca, velvets, **brocatelles**, damask, lampas and plain and brocaded silks were manufactured for interior use. At that time, Italy was the largest producer and exporter of silk textiles in the West and dominated the trade until the early seventeenth century. However, Genoa remained supreme in the manufacture of furnishing silks until the late seventeenth century, although by the seventeenth century other centres had been established in France and England. Indeed, from the seventeenth century onwards, French silk textiles, particularly those made in Lyon, have played a very important role in furnishings. The French supremacy was due in no small part to the state support that the industry received, as well as its emphasis on technical innovation and design.

In 1831, Dionysus Lardner discussed silk in his *Cabinet Cyclopedia*:

> The plainest mode of silk weaving takes the name of Persian, sarsenet, Gros-de-Naples, Ducape etc. varying only in the thickness of the fabric, or the quality of the materials of which it is composed, and not at all differing in the arrangement of its interlacings. The quality first mentioned is exceedingly flimsy in its texture, and has of late nearly gone out of use, its place being taken by the description next in quality, sarsenet... Gros de Naples is made of stouter and harder thrown organzine silk and is put together with more care and labour, containing a greater number of threads, both warp and shoot in a given surface. Ducapes are likewise plain-wove stout silks, but of softer texture than the last. (1831, p.296.)

Silk continues to be a luxury furnishing fabric, although rayon and other synthetic fibres with silk-like effects have often replaced it for furnishing fabrics in the twentieth century.

Clouded

The use of **warp** yarns dyed in a particular manner before weaving created a decorative, shaded, cloud-like pattern in the cloth. Ham House used a 'clouded lutestring' lining to the leather table covers in 1677 (Thornton & Tomlin, 1980, p.45) and, in 1710, there was a Clouded Room in Dyrham Park with 'six pieces of clouded silk hangings, a clouded silk bed lined with yellow strip'd persian and a counterpane of the same' (Walton, 1986, p.62).

See also **Clouded**.

Damask

See **Damask: Silk**.

Gauze
Simply described as a thin translucent silk of plain-weave, gauze has been widely used as **glass curtain** material when **net** has not been chosen. In deep windows, it was used in conjunction with nets and over **drapes** as an intermediate **curtain**.

Painted
See **Painted silk**.

Silk: Printed
See **Printed silk**.

See also **Armazine**, **Art silk**, **Atlas**, **Belzamine**, **Bolting cloth**, **Baudekin**, **Brocade**, **Bourette**, **Caffa**, **Carde**, **China silk**, **Damask**, **Ducape**, **Dupion**, **Durance**, **Gorgoran**, **Grosgrain**, **Habutai**, **Lampas**, **Levantine**, **Liseré**, **Lustring**, **Mantua**, **Matelassé**, **Mohair**, **Ninon**, **Paduasoy**, **Painted silk**, **Passementerie**, **Persian**, **Printed silk**, **Rayon**, **Rep**, **Samite**, **Sarcenet**, **Satin**, **Say**, **Sendal**, **Shantung**, **Tabaret**, **Tabby**, **Tabbinet**, **Taffeta**, **Tiffany**, **Tulle**, **Tussah**, **Velvet**.

FURTHER READING

Anquetil, J. (1996). *Silk*, Paris: Flammarion.
Banham, J. (ed.) (1997). *Encyclopaedia of Interior Design*, Chicago: Fitzroy Dearborn, entries on silks, pp 1171–80.
Cheney Brothers (1915). *A Glossary of Silk Terms*, South Manchester, Conn.: The Company.
Darby, W.D. (1922). *Silk: the Queen of Fabrics. A Survey of the Broad Silk Industry From the Raw Material to the Finished Product, Including Descriptions of Manufacturing and Marketing Methods, a Chapter on Imitations of Silk, and a Dictionary of Silk Fabrics*, New York: Dry Goods Economist.
Falke, O. von (1922). *Decorative Silks*, New York: Helburn.
Gow, I. (1997). 'Robert Adam's silk at Audley End', *Furniture History*, 33, pp 163–71.
King, B. (2005). *Silk and Empire*, Manchester: Manchester University Press.
Muthesius, A. (2003). 'Silk in the medieval world' in Jenkins, D. (ed.), *The Cambridge History of Western Textiles*, Cambridge: Cambridge University Press, pp 325–55.
Rothstein, N, (1990). *Silk Designs of the Eighteenth Century in the Collection of the Victoria and Albert Museum*, London: Victoria and Albert Museum.
Rothstein, N. (2003). 'Silk in the early modern period, *c*.1500–1780' in Jenkins, D. (ed.), *The Cambridge History of Western Textiles*, Cambridge: Cambridge University Press, pp 528–61.
Rothstein, N. (2003). 'Silk: the Industrial Revolution and after' in, Jenkins, D. (ed), ibid. pp 795–808.
Scott, P. (1993). *The Book of Silk*, London: Thames and Hudson.
Slomann, V. (1953). *Bizarre Designs in Silk*, Copenhagen: Murkgaard.
Thornton, P. (1965). *Baroque and Rococo Silks*, London: Faber and Faber.
Varron, A. (1938). 'The early history of silk', *CIBA Review*, 11, pp 350–85.
Warner, F. (1921). *The Silk Industry of the United Kingdom, Its Origins and Development*, London: Drane.

Silkoline

A mercerised **cotton** cloth that was popular in the early twentieth century for **drapery** and **bedspreads**. In 1902, the *Toronto Evening News* featured 'a girl's dainty den' in which the 'mantle drapery consisted of fancy silkoline to correspond with the general color scheme' (16 January 1902). **Cushions** were made to match in the same material. It was also appreciated for windows: 'Silkoline, when a good shade can be had, does very well, if economy has to be considered. I have known yellow silkoline, that cost but ten cents a yard, to hang in a sunny window for several years without fading, and to be laundered in the meantime too' (French, 1903, p.281).

Silkoline was also used for bedcovers: 'A down spread is the lightest and warmest, but cotton-filled spreads with a cover of silkoline or cheesecloth are ordinarily selected' (Kellogg, 1905, p.170). A guide to department stores noted that 'The coverings for comfortables may be of Cheese-cloth, Silkoline, Challis, Sateen, Chintz, Silk, Batiste' (Thompson, 1917, p.129). It was out of fashion by the mid-twentieth century.

Silkoline was also a trade name for a printed cloth once given away with pianos, in the form of **lambrequin**, printed **scarf** or **throw** (Hunter, 1918). See also **Piano cover**.

Sisal

Named after a port in Yucatan, sisal is a fibre obtained from the agave plant. It is a little softer than **coir** but with similar properties. It was used in the USA prior to the 1930s as a filling for **mattresses** and **cushions**, and as an inexpensive **stuffing**, sometimes in a rubberised version. It has also been made into pads for use over arm and **spring** units. Sisal was used for **matting** and floorcoverings from the 1950s onward. The fibre is spun, doubled and woven in plain or twill weaves.
See also **Rug**.

Skiver

The top grain split of a sheepskin (tanned in sumach) often used to line desktops or writing slides. Varying from paper-thin to *c*.1 mm (0.039 inch), it is available in a wide variety of colours, finishes and effects, often copying superior **leathers**.

Slipcover

See **Protective furnishing**.

Slub rep

Rep fabric in which the slub yarns have been used in the **weft** to create the particular 'knobbly' effect common in slub yarns.
See also **Rep**.

Smocked heading

A particular hand-made **curtain** heading technique that imitates smocking, where the **pleats** are alternately linked to create a **honeycomb** effect.

Smoothedge

A later twentieth-century proprietary name for a 'tackless' **carpet fitting** system, which uses pre-nailed plywood strips nailed around the perimeter of the room. The carpet is stretched over the angled nails and held firm. The system avoids unsightly nail indentations around the edge of a fitted carpet.

Smyrna rug

Smyrna in Turkey (now called Izmir) gave its name to floorcoverings associated in the West with the Orient. Seamless **rugs**, woven with a **cotton warp**, **jute** filler and a double-faced chenille weft, thus making them reversible in use, are known as Smyrna rugs. They were made in sizes up to 12 feet by 18 feet (3.66 by 5.49 metres). Initially, these rugs were apparently, by-products of the chenille carpets first produced by Scottish manufacturers, Templeton and Co, but they were soon mainly associated with the USA. From the waste chenille, they made what was initially called an Afghan rug with a double face. According to Cornelius Faraday:

> Smyrna carpet takes its name from the city of Smyrna, in Turkey, or rather the Oriental carpets made there. Its method of manufacture is similar to the process used for chenille, except that the strips of 'fur' are not steamed into the V-shape. When woven into fabric, one set of cut-ends appears on the top and the other set appears on the bottom or underside of the carpet, thus making a rather loosely woven cut-pile fabric the same on both sides. (1929, p.438.)

In 1881, Constance Harrison wrote, comparing Philadelphia productions with Near Eastern originals: '[The American rugs are] as admirable in colour and design and they are sold at a smaller price, [they also] have the additional advantage of being reversible, and are expected to wear as well' (1881, p.138). Their apparent artistic qualities endeared them to Leland Hunter, who recommended Smyrna rugs for 'use in rooms where Mission furniture is suitable, and in rustic and modern homes, where extreme delicacy of tone and texture graduation is not desired' (1918, p.160).

However, it seems that their demise came soon after this endorsement. Cornelius Faraday noted in 1929 that 'Smyrna carpets and rugs have been rapidly on the decline for several years' (p.438). A 1940s' commentary on the rugs confirmed this:

> A particular US reversible patterned carpet cloth woven from door mat size to 15 feet wide, called Smyrna, which was claimed to be a distinctive American weave, whereby the chenille wefts were twisted to provide a pile surface on both sides of the cloth. Patterns included florals, and geometrics but also animals and birds. By 1920s the vogue had passed. (Cole & Williamson, 1941.)

Smyrna **art squares** were machine-woven versions of the same merchandise produced in the later nineteenth century, especially in the USA.
See also **Chenille**, **Smyrna rug work**.

Smyrna rug work
According to Caulfeild & Saward, nineteenth century **Smyrna rug** work was a form of knitting to make rugs, small carpets and mats at home. (1887, p.453)
See also **Smyrna rug**.

Sofa rug
A **rug** intended to be draped over **upholstery**. These rugs were popular in the later nineteenth century. Williams & Jones noted that:

> Every sofa and lounge should be furnished with its soft, warm rug or Afghan, for not only are these articles of great comfort and convenience to a person resting … but they add a peculiar aspect of luxuriousness to the apartment, especially if made of bright oriental-looking woollen stuffs, whether of richly crocheted stripes, or some woollen strip or figure covered with curious Turkish designs. (1878, p.284.)

See also **Scarf**, **Throw**.

Soho tapestry
A generic name for English tapestries following the demise of Mortlake as a weaving centre. Joshua Morris was associated with a tapestry workshop in Soho from the early eighteenth century. The workshop was subsequently taken over by William Bradshaw who was connected with important tapestry commissions (Beard, 1997, pp 153–4).
See also **Mortlake tapestry**, **Tapestry**.

FURTHER READING
Marillier, H.C. (1930). *English Tapestries of the Eighteenth Century,* London: Medici Society.

Soultwitch
A **linen** cloth that possibly originated from Salzwedel in Germany. The 1556 inventory of Sir John Gage noted four **curtains** for windows that had **linings** of soultwich (Beard, 1997, p.283). The 1582 *Tudor Book of Rates* listed 'Soultwitch the c elles' (Willan, 1962, p.56). Also known as **southedge**.

Southedge
A **linen** textile used for **linings** and **blinds** in the seventeenth century. The Hengrave inventory of 1603 listed 'two great southedge curtyones for ye great window' (Thornton, 1978, p.358). Also known as **soultwitch**.

Sowetage
A coarse fabric used for lining **upholstery** from the sixteenth century onward.

Spandex
Developed in the second half of the twentieth century, spandex is a generic fibre category that has elastomeric properties similar to rubber, but is harder wearing and more resistant to deterioration. It is used in flexible fabrics, especially on sculptural forms of **upholstery** where the cloth has to follow contours.

Spanish blind
A later nineteenth-century window **blind** made from **linen** cloth fixed upon a roller terminating at the bottom end in a hood shape. The top was fixed into a case and the whole was operated with a roller and irons from the gusset at the bottom of the blind. It was adjustable in height (Hasluck, 1907, pp 92–102).

Spanish leather
Decorative **leather** finished with gilding, used for **wall coverings** and chair covers during the seventeenth century. Chippendale notes how a 'slider [should be] covered with green cloth or Spanish leather for writing upon' (1762, Plate CXXVI). Spanish leather also refers to hides that have been tanned in strong quebracho liquor, which gives a slightly wrinkled appearance. This version has been used for **upholstery** in the USA during the twentieth century.
See also **Gilt leather**.

FURTHER READING
Waterer, J. (1971). *Spanish Leather,* London: Faber and Faber.

Spanish matting
See **Matting: Spanish**.

Spanish moss (*Tillandsia usneoides*)
A type of vegetable matter (epiphyte) growing on other plants, especially trees, in the swampy areas and on the coast of the Gulf States of America, especially Louisiana and Florida, as well as in South Carolina. It grows in trees and hangs down like a beard (also known as Spanish beard, *barba Hispanica*).

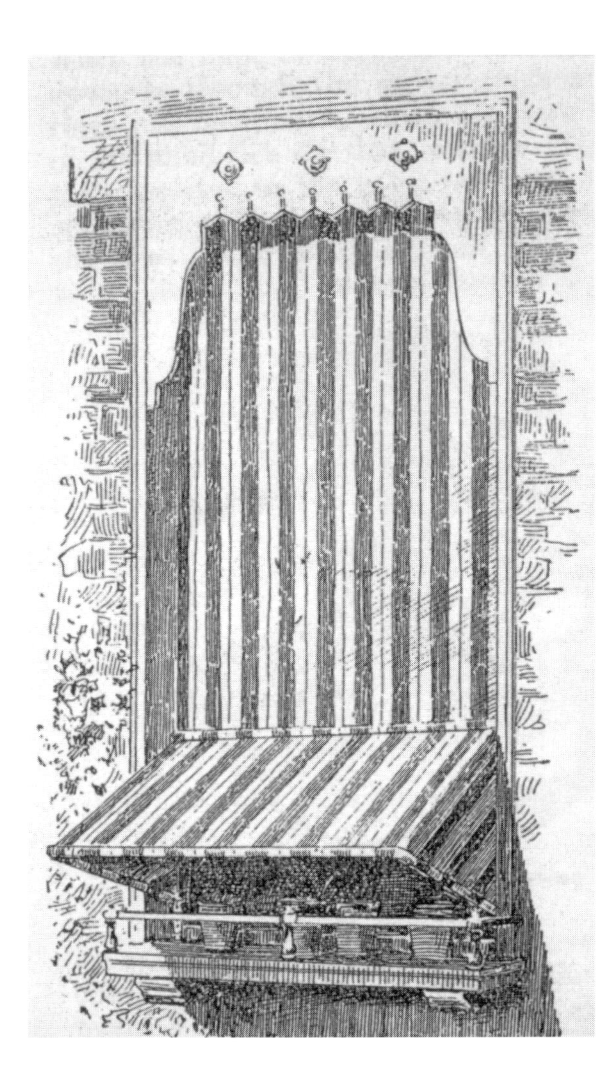

114. Spanish blind designed for outside use and to be rolled up when not required (P. Hasluck, Window Blinds, *1907)*

The removal of the tough outer skin leaves black fibres that are similar in appearance to curled **hair**. When dried, it is very resilient and has been widely used as an **upholstery stuffing**, being equivalent to medium quality hair.

In 1810, a visitor commented on the preparation that included 'burying it underground until the niterbark of the fibre that is soft and damp rots away, and when it is taken up and washed, it has exactly the resemblance of horsehair and makes a very comfortable mattress' (Michie, 1985, p.96). Certainly used commercially by the early 1800s and was considered by some in the 1930s as second only to hair. It was still used in the USA during the 1940s for cheap upholstery.

See also **Moss**.

Spanish rug

See **Blanket**, **Rugg**.

Sparver

A suspended cover over a bed, hanging from **cords** fixed to hooks in the ceiling. From the French *espervier*, meaning 'sparrowhawk', a sparver is a term used for a tent-like hanging or **canopy bed curtain**; or it may refer to the bed itself. Medieval beds were sometimes fitted with a conical bowl, or tent-shaped canopy, suspended over the head half of the bed. Sparvers are made from tapering strips of fabric formed in a bell shape, and fitted to a disc. They should be distinguished from celures and testers.

During the fifteenth century, they appear to have been used in conjunction with curtains of some sort. A 1444 reference lists a 'sparver with covering of linen cloth' (*Testamenta Ebor.*, vol.II. p.112). In 1480, Edward IV had a 'sparver of red damask with curtyns of sarsynett' (Nicolas, 1830, p.129).

By the sixteenth century, sparvers were made from a range of textiles. In 1501, a will recorded 'a sperver of sylke' (*Bury Wills*, Camden Society, p.91) and also 'vj payre shetes wyth the sparver curtanys of dornykes' (ibid. p.135). By 1509, Edmund Dudley's Great Chamber had a range of sparvers stored: there was 'a great coffer with ii lyddes: wherin is a sparver of purpull velvytt with curteyns of blew sarsenett. A sparver of blew sarsenett... A sparver of red sarsnett a sparver of crymsen cloth of gold and gren and crimson saten.' (Beard, 1997, p.282.) A little later, Horman noted a distinction between those who had beds with curtains and those who used sparvers, as well as commenting upon their function: 'Some have curteynes: some sparvers about the bedde to keep away gnattis' (*Vulgaria*, 1519, p.167h). Towards the end of the century, they were still important. Henry VIII's inventory listed: 'one sparver of red torque silk striped lined with buckram' (Macquoid & Edwards, 1924, III, p.482). As late as 1641, the Countess of Arundel possessed 'a greate Sparver round about over the Bed of the like stuff, [yellow taffeta] tied up with yellow strings' (Cust, 1911, p.100).

See also **Celure**, **Sarcenet**, **Tester**, **Train**, **Valance: Bed**.

Spikes

Protruding rods that were fitted to the tops of bedposts so as to locate the **tester** firmly on the frame. They might also support 'flying testers'.

Splint

Splints are strips of wood split from green saplings including white oak, hickory and ash. The strips are used to produce woven seats and backs in North American country or rustic furniture. The frames used are of the dowel rail type.

Sponge

One of the most unlikely materials for **upholstery** work was natural sea sponge. Around 1868, the American Patent Sponge Co offered for sale patent sponge as a substitute for curled **horsehair**. Natural sea sponge was mixed with water and glycerine, which was then evaporated to leave a stable product. The company produced an upholstery **stuffing** that was inexpensive, easy to use and germ free. The products of **latex** extract are sometimes referred to as sponge rubber or sorbo. Whether this forerunner of **foam** was successful is not known.

See also **Latex**.

Spool Axminster

See **Axminster carpet**.

Spotted muslin

See **Muslin: Spotted**.

Spring

A resilient device used as support for upholstery and bedding work. Although the coil spring is the most well known (see below), many versions and varieties have been employed in upholstery work.

Centripetal
The centripetal spring mechanism for a chair had four hoops of spring steel radiating from a central pivot point. The arrangement, patented by Thomas Warren in 1849 (US Patent no.6740), was initially adapted from railway coach seating by the American Chair Co and was used on mid-nineteenth century American rocker chairs. The principle was based on the leaf spring but, in this case, the leaves were not straight, but inverted back on themselves to form an ellipse or semi-circle. Chairs with this springing were exhibited at the 1851 London Exhibition and were very well received: 'The springs are connected to another centrepiece, which sustains the seat of the chair on a vertical pin; on this the chair seat revolves while at the same time the springs sustaining the seat from the under frame give it an agreeable elasticity in every direction.' (*The Illustrated Exhibitor.*)

Coil
These springs, originating in the requirements for carriage suspension, probably found their first upholstery use in the eighteenth century for chamber or exercising horses. The 1793 *The Cabinet-Makers' London Book of Prices* charges for making chamber-horses included: 'springs each ... and for fixing the springs and girth webbing each [and included charge for] turning of the springs' (1793, p.208). **Mattresses** were also made with interior springs but it is difficult to show whether they preceded upholstered chairs or vice-versa. It has been suggested that true sprung upholstery was a Biedermeier invention and that it was Georg Junigl, a Viennese upholsterer, who was first granted a patent in 1822 for upholstery springs. This patent was 'for his improvement on contemporary methods of furniture upholstery, which, by means of a special preparation of hemp, and with the assistance of iron springs, he renders so elastic that it is not inferior to horsehair upholstery' (Himmelheber, 1974, pp 89–90). However, this probably was a codification of previous practice and not a major advance. The phrase 'improvement on contemporary methods' would suggest that this is so.

In England, the acceptance of upholstery springs seems to have grown rapidly. Timothy Terrey, a London upholder, received payment from George IV's accounts for making a library chair: 'recently invented, by being constructed on metallic springs, handsomely carved' (*DEFM*, p.881). Soon after, in 1826, Samuel Pratt took out a patent (Patent no.5418) for 'improvements in the application of springs to beds, couches and seats to be used on ship-board for the prevention of sea sickness'. This consisted of wire springs, twisted into circular or angular coils in the shape of an hourglass, which were attached to webbing inside the upholstered seat. In 1828, Pratt developed the spring further and his new patent (Patent no.5668) was for 'elastic beds, cushions seats, and other articles of that kind'. This latter development was applied to sprung **cushions** and simple spring units for upholstery rather than for seasickness prevention. Pratt's patent defined the 'spring unit' in such a way as to indicate that it had the advantages that would be its selling points for many years. These included the sprung edge, the advantages of reversibility and the fact that they could either be built into furniture or be fitted to a removable cushion.

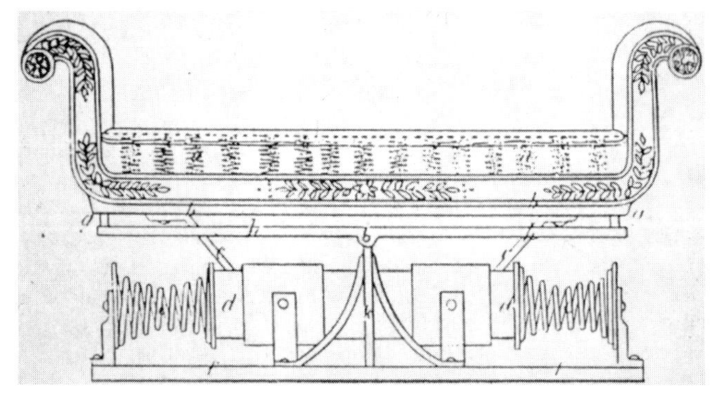

115. Drawing of a patent elastic spring, 1826 (Samuel Pratt, Patent no.5418)

Although the use of springs in upholstery has been traced to at least the mid-eighteenth century (see above), it can be assumed that spring upholstery for general domestic use was not widely introduced into the furniture trade until the 1830s. However, in 1834, it seemed that there were few workmen who had a sound knowledge of spring upholstery: 'They [the upholsterers] will be found pretending to know, rather than [being] really and truly acquainted with the art; the necessary result of which has been that the public have been dissatisfied with the spring-stuffed sofas, and they have, consequently, grown into disuse.' (Crofton, 1834, p.47.) This implies that spring seats were available generally before 1834, but upholsterers had little idea as to their correct application. Crofton hoped his publication would enable young upholsterers to learn, so that: 'the art of spring stuffing may then be reinstated in its original perfection' (ibid. p.60).

In 1839, Loudon confirmed that the use of 'spiral springs as stuffing has long been known to men of science; but so little to upholsterers, that a patent for using them was taken out some years ago, as a new invention. Beds and seats of this description are now, however, made by upholsterers generally'. Loudon went on to say that 'springs may be had from Birmingham by the hundredweight' (1839, p.336). His statement indicates the very few years' delay before the trade wholeheartedly embraced the idea of springs.

Although springs were available commercially, furniture-makers continued to produce their own. Sheraton recorded the making process and the reason for cone shaped springs: 'strong wire [is] twisted round a block in regular gradation, so that when the wire is compressed by the weight of those who exercise each turn of it may clear itself and fall within the other' (Sheraton, 1791, Plate 22 Appendix). In 1835, John Hancock of Philadelphia had '2 blocks for making springs' and '6 stone of iron wire' in his stock-in-trade sale (Conradsen, 1993, p.53).

The earliest attempts at securing springs were to the solid boards as used in chamber-horses, with the result that they did not have the same degree of resilience that came with the later use of webbing. Some early nineteenth-century American sofas exist with iron coil springs stapled directly to board or slatted bottoms, in the manner of the chamber-horses of the eighteenth century. This method of fixing bed bases was in fact patented in 1831 by Josiah French of Ware, Mass. (Grier, 1988, p.227). The resultant upholstery was inevitably heavier and less resilient than the conventional methods of using webbing, but it enabled spring upholstery to become available to another level of the market.

Various techniques were invented to assist in the making of upholstered chairs. The first was simplifying the setting of springs in the interior seat. In 1853, James Finnemore patented a method of fixing springs in upholstery and mattresses (Patent no.1652). His method used springs with loops formed at the top and bottom. The springs were held in place by straps that passed through the loops on the spring. A simple solution to the seat-springing problem was to make a spring unit that just had to be inserted into the frame. Louis Durrieu patented an important process in 1864 (Patent no.1054). This patent consisted of a set of springs connected at top and bottom using the continued wire of the springs that allowed them to make their own frame. The obvious advantages of this process over individual hand knot-tying resulted in

116. Rheiocline bedstead and spring by E. Cottam, c.1851 (Private Collection)

not only a consistent product, but also the possibility that the unit could be developed so as to fit onto chair backs and sides, as well as into loose cushions.

The manufacture of springs remained a manually controlled operation for most of the century. In 1871, *The House Furnisher* could say that this was not for want of machines but rather for the 'want of uniformity in the wire' (May, p.42). The problem was that soft spots in the spring wire needed to be removed before they could be made up into springs. This could be done manually because the maker could see the flaws. Machine processes however, could not develop until reliable supplies of wire became available. These problems were reflected in consumer complaints. In 1877, the Garrett sisters complained that iron springs were 'always out of order and cannot have their anatomy readjusted without the intervention of the manufacturer, by whom alone the complexity of their internal structure is understood' (Grier, 1988, p.117). Even later, in 1889, complaints were still being voiced about the poor quality of English springs, especially in comparison to French ones. A report on upholstery from the Mansion House Committee, visiting the Paris Universal Exhibition in 1889, complained that all this was even more annoying as the cost of springs was a nominal part of the cost of an upholstered job (Mansion House Committee, 1889, p.658).

Attempts to speed up the springing process also included the continuing development of the fitting of springs without webbing support. These methods used in England and the USA included wooden battens to which springs were nailed; a platform of intertwined coiled wires, called a 'lace web', to which springs were clipped; and metal laths with springs pre-fitted by the manufacturer. In 1878, it was reported that a Paul Roth of New York was exhibiting machinery that would produce a **stitched** edge, pack the **hair** into a seat and tie the springs (*Furniture Gazette*, 23 February, p.106).

By the mid-twentieth century, traditional methods of springing were being challenged. In the same way that **foams** revolutionised the filling of cushions and the padding process of upholstery, changes in spring technology allowed a move away from the coil-sprung platform that was the mainstay of upholstery prior to World War II. The hourglass-shaped coil spring had remained the same since its invention, with a range of sizes for particular applications: 5 inch (12.7 cm) for couch scrolls, 6 inch (15.2 cm) for the seats of small chairs, and 7–10 inch (17.8–25.4 cm) for the seats of easy chairs, couches and backs.

Fish-mouth

A serpentine spring with the addition of a small section of spring metal to the leading edge, designed to create a 'sprung edge'. When fixed in situ the resultant effect resembles the mouth of a fish.

No-sag

A patented form of serpentine springing for upholstery that is based on a zigzag-shaped length of spring steel, fixed under convex tension from one side of a frame to the opposite side.

See *Serpentine.*

Pocket

A straight-sided coil spring enclosed in a **calico** pocket or sleeve. Each pocket was sewn or clipped together in such a way as to create a mattress with a degree of independent operation for each spring. Patented in 1901 by Vi-spring and mainly used in mattresses.

Serpentine (Sinuous)

A type of upholstery support based on zigzag-shaped lengths of spring wire that are fitted in convex tension between rails. These springs enable upholsterers to fit a support system into a deep profile chair or sofa, without the skills involved in traditional upholstering.

Sinuous springs

See *Fish-mouth, Serpentine.*

Spring unit

In the very late nineteenth century, the newly invented assembled spring unit was made up from a number of coil springs fastened together with clips and surrounded with a bent wire frame. The developments were encouraged by the burgeoning motorcar industry. These factory-made spring units had steel spring bars as a substitute for webbing; the conical springs were clipped on as handwork was, and steel wire was used to clamp and secure the springs in a grid instead of the lashing process. The whole spring unit was then covered with **canvas** and upholstered as required. The types included single, double and triple layers of springs (all riveted to steel base laths). The cheapest was made from two diagonal laths having five springs fitted in a cross; a better quality was made with three laths each way, having nine springs. All were fitted with a wire mesh top. These were a useful innovation for speeding up the process of laying springs into a frame for a fully upholstered chair. Further developments included interior-sprung seat cushions that were often used in conjunction with the spring units.

Tension

In 1841, John Wilkie, an upholsterer, and Charles Schiewso, a musical instrument maker, patented an early form of tension spring, which used the principle of expansion and contraction of small springs mounted on straps (Patent no.8861). This was an important development as it avoided the need to have a deep seat to accommodate the original hourglass-shaped coil springs. This concept was developed further when, in 1856, George and William Hooper patented 'improvements in springs for carriages, and for the cushions of carriages, chairs, mattresses, beds and similar articles' (Patent no.282). This patent relied on the idea of compensating springs made from rings or strips of vulcanised India rubber. Yet another example and a precursor of the modern tension spring was invented by William Searby in 1857 (Patent no.2939). This consisted of a piece of elastic metal, wood or bone compressed into a curved form. Each end was attached to a buckle and strap, fixed to the frame of the furniture, and used lateral tension to create a spring. Arched metal laths fixed under tension were also used in France for outdoor chairs and later for railway carriage seating. In the twentieth century, the introduction of the tube-shaped tension spring, sometimes encased in cloth, allowed chairs to have the spring benefits without the deep frame profiles that were needed to accommodate full coil springing. This was particularly useful for fireside and wing chairs. The development of this type of tension spring is credited to Willy Knoll, who patented his method in 1928 (Patent no.322638). It was a success and formed the basis of the famous Parker-Knoll range of tension-sprung chairs, from the 1930s onward.

Wood springs

Thin laminated strips of timber were occasionally fitted to beds in a convex shape, to act as a firm suspension for mattresses. The idea appears to have originated in Switzerland.

See also **Four-point platform**, **Mattress**, **Upholstery**, **Webbing**.

FURTHER READING

Grier, K. (1988). *Culture and Comfort, People, Parlours and Upholstery, 1850–1930*, New York: Strong Museum.

Holley, D. (1981). 'Upholstery springs', *Furniture History*, 17, pp 64–7.

Thomas, D.G. (1976). *A. Howard and Sons, Upholsterers' Spring Makers, A Short Record of the Firm's History*, London: Greater London Industrial Archaeological Society.

Spring barrel blind

See **Roller blind**.

Spring mattress

See **Mattress: Spring**.

Squab

This refers to two completely different items. One is a type of sofa; the other a loose **cushion**.

(a) A sofa, ottoman or couch. An early use of the word is in 1664: 'For a drawing-rome I should have 2 squobs, & 6 turned wooden chars of the haith of the longe seates' (Macquoid, 1905, p.211). The Upholders' Company Byelaws of 1679 refer to the fact that 'all chaires, stoles, cowches and squabb whatsoever they be made of, shall be cross girt'. A reference from 1788 defines a squab as 'a couch, common in most farmhouses' (Marshall, II, 355, *OED*). A little later, Sheraton illustrates a more luxurious Grecian-style couch, which he still calls a squab and defines as 'a kind of seat' (1803, p.247).

(b) A small cushion for use with wood or **rush**-seated chairs that might be fitted with ties or laid loose. Early squabs developed in the seventeenth century were filled firmly and sometimes were boxed and buttoned. In 1689, the *London Gazette* advertised 'The Covering of a large Squab, the upper side of Cloth of silver, the Ground white and toward a Filamot' (No.2495/4). In 1706, Phillips defined a squab as 'a soft stuffed Cushion or Stool' (*New World of Words*). They were particularly used on cane-seated chairs and often had ties to hold them on. The term is still used on occasion for a small cushion, especially for a chair. See also **Cushion**.

Stafford cloth

A heavy **cotton** fabric woven as plain or rep and used for **curtains** (*The Mercury Dictionary of Textile Terms*, 1950, p.477).

Stained cloth

Textile wall and **curtain** hangings that were decorated with stained patterns using watercolour pigments. They have an ancient origin, as Aldhelm speaks of 'the hangings or curtains being stained with purples and other colours and ornamented with images' in the seventh century (Wright, 1851, p.49). An early London guild called the 'mistery of steynours' existed from at least 1268. Various disputes with the painters occurred, so by mutual consent the London Company of Stainers amalgamated with the Painter's Company in 1502 and subsumed themselves into that organisation. The painters eclipsed the stainers and the craft of staining appears to have died out in England by the end of the sixteenth century.

Stained cloths appear to have been used in a variety of furnishing situations. In 1522, Agas Herte of Bury St Edmunds left 'a covering of arras, and a second coverlit, a celour and a tester stained with flowers, and three curtains and the stained cloths hanging about the floor behind the chimney' (Baker, 1937, p.129).

By the end of the sixteenth century, there were concerns about the craft of stained cloth working. In 1579, Richard Hakluyt organised an expedition to Persia to learn the craft of staining as 'it hath been an old trade in England, whereof some excellent cloths yet remain, but the art is now lost and not to be found in the realm' (Baker, 1937, p.126). In 1598, Stow confirmed the demise: 'On Trinity lane … is the Painter Stainers hall, for so of old time were they called, but now that workmanship of staining is departed and out of use in England' (p.317). This demise was commented upon in 1601 when it was reported to Parliament that the 'painting of cloths is decayed and not a hundred yards of new painted cloth made in a year here, by reason of so much painted Flanders pieces being brought from thence' (Baker, 1937, p.126). See also **Painted cloth, Wall covering and hanging**.

FURTHER READING

Ayres, J. (2003). *Domestic Interiors, the British Tradition 1500–1850*, New Haven and London: Yale University Press.

Baker, O. (1937). *In Shakespeare's Warwickshire*, Chapter 5, 'Stained Cloths', London: Simpkins Marshall.

Stair button

Ornamentally headed screws finished in brass, copper or nickel for fixing **carpet** on stairs from the late nineteenth century. They were screwed to the riser at the inner bottom.

Stair carpet

See **Axminster**, **Dutch**, **Kidderminster**, **Venetian, Wilton carpets**.

Stair clip

See **Stair rod**.

Stair corner

Brass, copper or nickel devices used to pin into the right angle of a stair to avoid a dust trap. These appear to have been developed in the late nineteenth century and were patented.

Stair covering

See **Carpet**, **Drugget**, **Oilcloth**, **Stair linen**.

Stair linen (aka Stair damask)

A cloth intended to be used as a protective covering for quality **stair carpets**. It was defined in 1872 as:

A coarse heavy twilled linen fabric used for covering stair carpets. A coloured stripe is usually printed near each edge. Sometimes it is printed in other plain patterns. A superior quality of stair linen is made resembling damask in pattern. It is not bleached, but the natural colour of the material. This is usually wider than the cheaper grades. (Brown & Gates, 1872, p.175.)

See also **Drugget**.

Stair rod
A fixing method intended to hold carpet tight against a stairway. An assortment of types has been devised which are usually based on variations of clips or rods. Stair clips hold the carpet at the edges, operating on a spring and ratchet principle that allows the clip to be swivelled down onto the carpet. The other version is a grip, which has a back plate screwed to the stairs, which then has the top plate slotted onto it after the carpet is laid. Rods are fixed by eyes screwed to the stair, close to the width of the carpet. Hinged eyes have been used to make fitting easier. In the 1950s, plastic rods and plastic-covered expanding wire rods were also used. However, the main materials were wood, brass and metal, the last being plated in a range of finishes with innumerable designs.

In 1855, *Godey's Lady's Book* suggested **velvet** or **tapestry carpet** for stairs that were fitted with 'flat stair rods, from one to three inches in width, of brass or silver plate' (Winkler and Moss, 1986, p.89).

In the latter half of the twentieth century, hidden gripper rod fixings have become common, although decorative rods may still be used.
See also **Carpet fitting and planning**, **Smoothedge**.

Stammet
See **Tammy**.

Stamped plush
A strip of fabric of about 4 to 5 inches (10 to 12.7 cm) in width, used for **borders** to **curtains** and other **upholstery** (Caulfeild & Saward, 1887, p.459).
See also **Plush**.

Stamped velvet
See **Utrecht velvet**, **Velvet: Embossed**.

Steel webbing
See **Webbing**.

Stencil printing
Stencilled fabrics were widely promoted in the early twentieth century and their importance was such that they led to screen printing processes after World War I.

Candace Wheeler discussed the use of stencilling on **muslin** as a wall decoration (1903, p.209). Stencilling on **cheese cloth**, **scrim**, aurora cloth, **pongee**, **linen** and **velour** has also been used for **curtains** and **portières**.
See also **Burlap**, **Fortuny print**, **Printed textile**.

Stitches and stitching
Needlework techniques are based on passing a needle and thread through a cloth in a particular way to create the desired effect. Stitches fall into four basic categories: flat stitches (including satin, cross and herringbone); linked or chain stitches, which provide loops on the surface; buttonhole stitches; and knot stitches.

Baste tack
A flat stitch that holds materials together temporarily with long loose stitches. Technically, baste stitches mark out designs on one surface only; tacking is sewing through two or more fabrics.

Blanket
A stitch of interlocking loops used as an edging stitch to cover a turned-over raw edge of cloth or to make a decorative **border**.

Blind
An **upholstery** technique with the intention of stitching in a manner that pulls fillings towards edges to firm and solidify them. The vertical edges are indented as a result.
See **Mattress**.

Cross
Counted threads worked diagonally from left to right and crossed back right to left. Also known as gros point.

Double stuff
In seventeenth-century upholstery, the technique of double stuff stitching, usually in the centre of the seat, was intended to hold the sandwich of **stuffing**, **sackcloth** and **webbing** into a firm and integral whole. The stitching may be in an oval or rectangular form, the former being favoured in American examples, and the latter in European chairs.

Feather
An upholstery stitch that has been used to give sharp definition to the edges of upholstered work. Made in conjunction with the first stuffing of show-wood or gilt-framed upholstery. A row of stitching is placed crosswise around the edge of the seat and is in a herringbone shape. The feather stitch is applied to the top row to compress the edge into a sharp line of stuffing. In addition, it is an **embroidery** stitch of loop stitches in a zigzag pattern.

Flame
This is the name for both a stitch and a pattern. As a stitch, it refers to the long and short stitch work on **canvas** that is also called Florentine, **Bargello**, Irish or Hungary (point d'Hongrie) work. As a pattern, it refers to the graded, shaded design that resembles flames. Fine open canvas is worked with stranded, not twisted, threads and six shades of the same colour are used. These are sewn in short and long stitches in strict order. The outline of each row is then made in gold, black or other contrast to define it.

Running
A flat stitch that runs the thread in and out of the material in even spaces. It is used especially for gathering material.

Tent
A flat stitch slanting diagonally and parallel over one thread of the canvas to form a solid background of even lines. Counted thread type.
See also **Petit-point**.

Stitch bonded fabric
Warp yarns and filling yarns are **stitched** together by a third yarn creating a **bonded fabric** that is often ribbed in appearance. It was used for **curtains**, chair covers and **bedspreads** in the 1970–80s.

117. Store curtain, embellished net, c.1948 (HMSO)

Store curtain

A **lace curtain** usually hung flat against a whole window. Each curtain was made as a single unit between 30 and 60 inches (76.2 and 152.4 cm) wide and 2½ and 3 yards (2.29 and 2.74 metres) long. They were usually decorated with a single large design with narrow **borders** having a heavy **fringe** on the bottom to assist hanging (Ostick, 1955, p.367).

In *The English House,* Hermann Muthesius noted 'the stores [curtains] of which we Germans are so fond are unknown in England, nor is the name English. The word which we use for curtains comes from the French and means in France the little roller blinds on carriage windows' (1904, p.194).
See **Store marquisé**.

Store marquisé

An eighteenth-century French window **blind** of slightly gathered material. It now generally refers to **shirred curtains** or **festoon** blinds.

Straw (aka Chaff)

The dried stalks of corn, wheat and other cereals after harvesting. It has been used as a furniture-making material for centuries in a variety of forms, including **upholstery stuffing**, for decoration, as a constructional material or for flooring. For centuries, straw was particularly used for stuffing **mattresses** (especially **Palliasses**) and bedding. In 1577, William Harrison empathised with servants who did not have an under sheet on their bed 'to keep them from the pricking straws that ran oft through the canvas [of the palliasse] and raised their hardened hides' (Harrison, 1577, p.201). In the early seventeenth century, a farmer, Henry Best, sent 'our foreman about sunset to make ready their bedstead and to get straw laid into it, and give him a mattress to lie next the straw'. Rye or oat straw was used since 'it is the toughest and will last the longest in beds' (Woodward, 1998, p.66).

For interior upholstery filling work, Bimont in 1770 recommended the use of straw, particularly for the backs of chairs, as 'it did not collapse upon the seat' (1770, p.48). A little later, in the 1780s, the prestigious Gillows firm was ordering quality straw in lieu of hair, which was then in short supply (Gillow Co Records, Memo Books, p.37).

In the nineteenth century, straw was still used as an inexpensive upholstery and bedding filler. Loudon (1839, p.336) noted the use of oat chaff in mattresses in Scotland, and maize chaff in Italy. Straw chaff was still used for children's cot mattresses in the 1940s, as it was cheaper and could be easily renewed when soiled (Kaye, 1940, p.200).

Straw was also used to make complete chairs and to bottom wooden-framed ones. In seventeenth-century turned chairs, straw was twisted together to make a **twine**, then plaited and finally woven into chair seat bottoms. In construction, lipp work was an ancient vernacular process of making chairs, cradles, etc. which were either built upon an ash framework, to which a straw shell was threaded up, or made from coiled straw rope (the lipp), which was lashed together with strips of bark or other vegetation. The constructional tradition continued into the nineteenth century when Loudon noted:

> Matting is manufactured in many different manners, out of the straw of corn, rushes or other long, narrow, grassy or sedgy leaves... In Monmouthshire, easy chairs with hoods like porters' chairs in gentleman's halls are constructed of straw matting on a frame of wooden rods, or stout wire, and chairs are made entirely of straw in different parts of England in the same way as common beehives. (1839, pp 346–7.)

See also **Matting**, **Paillasson rug**, **Rush**, **Underlay**.

Stretch cover

Stretch covers were developed around the 1950s onward to act either as replacement covers for existing **upholstery** or as new fitted covers for the organically shaped and often plastic-shelled furniture of the period. They were made from single and double jersey **knitted fabric**, using **nylon** yarns sometimes back-coated with **polyester foam**.

FURTHER READING

Anon. (1969). 'Stretch covers', *Draper's Record,* 27 September, pp 41–56.

Strip carpeting

A general term for any woven **carpet** made 3/4 (27 inches, 68.6 cm) or 4/4 (36 inches, 91 cm) wide. This distinguishes it from **broadloom**. The traditional measurement was in quarters.
See **Body**, **Ingrain**, **Kidderminster**, **List, Scotch carpets**.

Striped rug

A flat woven **rug** or **carpet** that was produced in **warp** length stripes using heavy **homespun wools** in widths suitable for stair covering or for seaming up into larger carpets. Particularly associated with early nineteenth-century America.

Stuff

Stuff is a general term for fabrics that were woven from **worsted** yarns but did not have a nap or **pile**. The term was in use from around 1643 (*OED*). Stuffs were defined in *The Dictionary of Needlework* (1887) and included **calimancoes**, **camlets**, **lustrings**, **merinos**, **moreens**, **plaids**, **shalloon** and **tammies** (Caulfeild & Saward).
See also **Kidderminster stuff**, **Norwich stuff**.

Stuffing

One of the major procedures that is undertaken in full upholstery work. The 'first stuffing' refers to the process of laying and fixing padding materials over the prepared base of webs, **springs** and **hessian**. The 'second stuffing' refers to a range of methods of fixing fillings, laid over the first stuffing. This second stuffing is usually another layer of padding, over which a **calico** cover is fitted. The work is then finished with a **top cover**. Various types of stuffing methods are identified by name. Pillow stuffing is that in which the first and second stuffings are tufted to control the filling. Round stuffing is loose, while French stuffing was the same as 'pillow' but with added **quilting** rows, close to the edges, to produce a defined edge. Pin cushion stuffing describes how upholstery work appears when applied as pads or 'pin cushions' on wooden-framed chairs.
See also **Pin cushion work**, **Stuffing pad**, **Tufting**, **Upholstery**, **Upholstery filling**.

Stuffing material

See **Upholstery filling**.

Stuffing pad

A pre-fabricated **upholstery** material made, for example, from **hair**, **coir** or **sisal**, etc., attached onto a **hessian** back by a needle process. It is used as a speedy way of fixing padding to upholstery frames in factory work.
See also **Stuffing**, **Wadding**.

Stumpwork (aka raised work)

A **needlework** effect that results in raised and decorated reliefs standing proud of the surface. Stumpwork was popular in the mid-seventeenth century when it was ingenious in its use of materials, including wood or parchment moulds covered in **silk**, wire, **lace**, sequins, pearls, etc. As it was prone to wear and tear, it was mostly applied to areas such as mirror frames or box tops.

FURTHER READING

Baker, M. (1978). *Stumpwork: The Art of Raised Embroidery*, London: Bell and Hyman.

Best, M. (1990). *Stumpwork: Historical and Contemporary Raised Embroidery*, London: B.T. Batsford.

Sub curtain

See **Under curtain**.

Suede

A **wool** or wool mix cloth with a short nap, finished to look like suede **leather**. Sometimes used for **upholstery** in the twentieth century.

Sufis

The Merchant's Warehouse Laid Open defined sufis in 1696 as: 'A sort of stuff made of half silk and half cotton and is adorned with very delightful colours … the greatest and most general use in this Kingdom are for Linnen and bed and window curtains for which they are extraordinarily pretty, because they are usually light colours and cheap.' (J.F., 1696.)

Summer spread

Lightweight bedcovers that are intended for warm weather use. They may be similar to the top layer of **quilts** but have bound edges and finished seams to make them tidy.

Sun curtain

An outside **curtain** designed to protect exterior woodwork (especially doors) from fading. 'Strong striped ticking is the most usual material, and rings are attached with tape loops to give special strength against wind' (Sheridan, 2nd edition, 1955, p.415).
See also **Casement cloth**.

Superfine

See **Cassimere**.

Surface roller

See **Printed textile**.

Swag

Swags are made from material suspended from the top of a window frame and often replace **pelmets** or **cornices**. They were particularly developed in the later neo-classical period and have remained in and out of fashion ever since. Webster & Parkes explained that:

> Valances are sometimes made in the form of festoons, and are then, by upholsterers, termed draperies; the festoon itself is called a swag, and the end that hangs down is termed the tail… These are frequently ornamented with fringes, tassels and cords in various ways. This, which is the former French style, was introduced some years ago, as being richer and more elegant than ours at present [1844] it is less used. (1844, p.251.)

Noetzli shows swags for stair railings external to the banisters fitted 18 inches (45.7 cm) up the rails. The idea was to give some discreet protection to ladies as they walked up and down, and also to decorate the board. In addition, he shows spiral tails for fixed pendants, which hide lighting wires, etc. (Noetzli, 1906, pp.105 and 166)
See also **Drape and drapery**, **Festoon window curtain**, **Tail**.

Swanskin

A fine, thick kind of closely woven twill **flannel** material with lamb's **wool wefts** that was used for **blankets** in the seventeenth century, and also for **powdering carpets** in the eighteenth century. Ben Jonson mentions one use in his play *The Alchemist:* 'the swan-skin coverlid, and cambrick sheets' (1610, Act III, Scene III). A similar reference to bedding is found in Bailey's work, which defined swanskin as 'a sort of thick flannel, so named by reason of its extraordinary whiteness, and imitating for warmth the down of the swan' (1755). At the 1777 sale of the goods of Sir Thomas Robinson, there was included 'a swan skin blanket, two others' (Yorke, 1994, p.171).

The alternative use of swanskin as a **carpet cover** is referred to in the Lord Chamberlain's Accounts that noted payments 'for 2½ yds of Swanskin 2 ells wide for a carpet to cover ditto occasionally, viz for Powdering 6s.6d.' (Walton, 1980, p.279)

By the nineteenth century, swanskin was defined as 'a calico stuff one side napped and resembling feathers. Also a thick, closely woven wool cloth' (Caulfeild & Saward, 1887, p.465).

Swiss lace

See **Lace: Swiss**.

Swiss muslin
See **Dotted Swiss**, **Muslin: Swiss**.

Tabaret (aka Tabouret, Tabourette, Tabaray)
At one time this was a name for a **worsted** striped cloth, which apparently had the effect of **brocaded silk**. By the end of the eighteenth century, it was a medium to heavy silk fabric used for **upholstery**, characterised by **warp**-figured alternate stripes of plain and **satin** surface, generally in different colours and sometimes watered.

In the eighteenth century, tabaret was used for **curtains**, hangings and upholstery. Green tabaret with coloured **trimmings** appears to have been popular. In 1779, Sir Richard Worsley's Dining Parlour had '3 pea-green festoon tabaray window curtains fringed at bottom' (Boynton, 1965, p.42). A little later, Hepplewhite suggested that for window stools: 'the covering should be of taberray or morine, of a pea-green, or other light colour' (1794, p.4).

By the early nineteenth century, George Smith considered that tabarets were not highly valued: 'In elegant Drawing Rooms, plain coloured satin or figured damask assumes the first rank, as well as for use as for richness; lustring and tabarays the next; the latter, however, makes but indifferent drapery.' (1808, p.xii.) Nevertheless, it seemed to be fine for upholstery. Ackermann showed a 'beautiful French scroll sofa adapted for the drawing room, which may be made of rosewood, with gold ornaments, and covered with rich chintz or silk tabouret, corresponding with other parts of the furniture' (*Repository*, August 1812, p.113). Tabaret was also used in the 1825 estimate submitted to Sir Duncan Campbell by William Trotter for the drawing room: '2 window curtains of tabouret lined with durant with full pleated valens and angled dreep [drape] betwixt windows bound with silk lace and finished with silk plummet fringe.' (Gow, 1983, p.131.)

Tabaret appeared to have a renaissance in the 1840s with the products of Louis Schwabe of Manchester who was praised for 'the flowers wrought in his silks and satins [which] appear more like the work of the best painter than the weaver' (Edwards & Ramsey [eds], 1968, p.1456). Towards the end of the century, *The Dictionary of Needlework* praised tabaret as being 'a stout satin-striped silk, employed for furniture hangings and much resembling tabbinet, but is superior in quality. It has broad alternate stripes of satin and watered material differing from each other respectively in colour: blue, crimson, or green satin stripes are often successively divided by cream-coloured tabby ones' (Caulfeild & Saward, 1887, p.467).

118. Tabaret stripe showing satin and plain weave effects (E. Ostick, The Draper's Encyclopaedia, *1955)*

Tabaret was also popular in the mid-nineteenth century in the USA for **drapery** and upholstery, as well as for lining walls. Writing for the dye trade in 1864, Howe and Stevens pointed out that:

> [It] is never used for any other purpose than for bed and window curtains, and for covering sofas, chairs, ottomans and coach linings. It is very much used for drawing room and sitting room walls... [and] curtains are always lined with tammy. (Montgomery, 1984, p.356.)

By 1950, it was still being recommended as suitable for upholstery, wall panels and **screens**. The trade press continued to use the term in 1955 when tabaret was described as a:

> Well-made furnishing fabric with satin stripes on a poplin ground... The plain-weave ground makes very firm poplin, which may be given a moiré finish if desired. It is necessary to have a firm rib across the cloth to produce the moiré effect. The satin stripes are not affected. (Ostick, 1955, p.374.)

Tabbinet
An arbitrary trade term perhaps derived from **tabby**, or possibly a diminutive form of tabine. It is an **upholstery** fabric made of a **silk warp** and **wool**, or **linen**, **weft**, like poplin, with a watered or tabbied surface, sometimes with figures woven on the watered ground. Its production has been chiefly associated with Ireland. In 1778, it was commented that Irish 'Poplins, some of which [are] called tabinets, have all the richness of silk' (*Philosophical Survey of South Ireland*, 201, *OED*).

In 1864, an American company described tabbinet's use for **drapery** and upholstery and, in particular, for wall decoration: 'It is very much used for drawing room and sitting room walls. Instead of paper, paint or tapestry, and when used for this purpose it is not put on tight and flat like paper or tapestry but fluted and has a magnificent appearance.' (Montgomery, 1984, p.356.) Caulfeild & Saward noted that 'Tabinet is a variety of the same description of textile as poplin', and 'is chiefly used for window curtains and upholstery purposes' (1887, pp 411, 467).
See also **Poplin**.

Tabby
Tabby is a name for both a weave type and a fabric. The name may derive from '*al-attabiya*', the quarter of Baghdad in which it was probably once made.
(a) Also known as plain-weave, tabby is the simplest and most common weave type with an alternate **warp** and **weft**. When the warp and weft are equal, they are called 'linen weave', when there are more warps it is called 'warp faced', and when more wefts it is called 'tapestry weave'.
(b) A rich, ribbed, **silk taffeta**-type cloth with either a plain or a watered surface. Tabbying was a name given to the process of watering or waving as a finish. The Huguenots manufactured it in England after the Restoration (1660). It was occasionally produced with a small pattern, when it was known as *tabis à fleurs*. The 1677 Ham inventory noted a room with 'hangings of white morello [morella] mohair bordered with spotted tabbie with silver fringe' (Thornton & Tomlin, 1980, p.78).

In the 1728 inventory of the shop of James Pilbeam, a mercer of Chiddingly, Sussex, there was listed 'Ten ells of tabby att 5s per ell £2 10s 0d' (http://www.chiddingly.gov.uk/History/James%20Pilbeam.html). A little later, Chambers defined tabby as:

> A kind of coarse taffety watered. It is manufactured like the common taffety, excepting that it is stronger and thicker both in the woof and

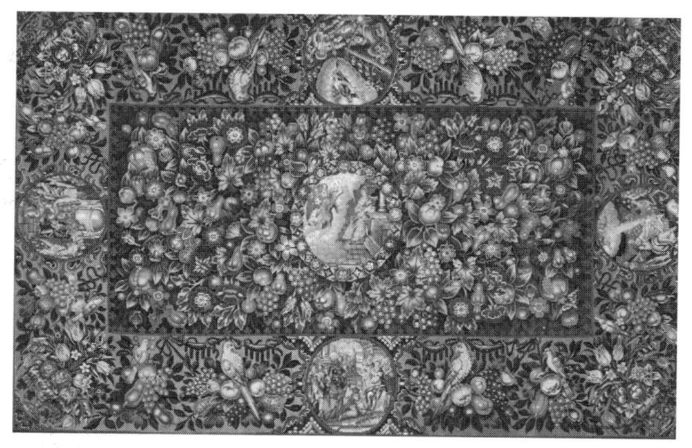

FAR LEFT
119. Tabby weave furnishing cotton, nineteenth century (Leeds Museums and Galleries, Temple Newsam House, Roger Warner Collection)

LEFT
120. Table carpet depicting scenes from the life of Christ. Linen, wool, and silk, slit and double interlocking tapestry weave, two selvedges present, Northern Netherlands, 1600–50 (Ada Turnbull Hertle Endowment, 1978.58, The Art Institute of Chicago. Photography ©The Art Institute of Chicago)

> in warp… The watering is given it by means of a calender, the rolls whereof are of iron or copper, variously engraven, which bearing unequally on the stuff render the surface thereof unequal, so as to reflect the rays of light differently. (1741.)

A guide to Windsor Castle noted that the Queen's bedchamber had **curtains** and valances of a 'rich green corded tabby' in 1785 (Edwards, 1964, p.513).

Sheraton described tabby as a 'kind of rich silk, which has undergone the operation of tabbying which is performed by an engraved roller, which presses it into uneven surfaces, and these reflecting the rays of light differently, makes it appear wavey' (1803, p.315).

In the later nineteenth century, Caulfeild & Saward defined tabby as 'a coarse kind of taffeta, thick, glossy, and watered by pressure between the rollers of a cylinder, and the application of heat and acidulous liquor… The beautiful description of silk called Moiré is a tabby; and worsted stuffs such as moreen are likewise tabbies.' (1887, pp 467–8.) As late as 1915, Harmuth defined tabby as 'the British equivalent of moire'.

See also **Camaca**, **Changeable**, **Moiré**.

Table carpet

Heavy knotted **pile**, **tapestry**, **needlework** or other material **table covers** often trimmed with a **fringe** and used to decorate table surfaces. The nature of the table cover reflected the owner's wealth. Oriental cloths were amongst the most sought after; **turkey work** and pile fabrics were next in line. In the 1543 Earl of Rutland's inventory, there were 'five long table carpets of Turkey making, one foot carpet, thirteen cupboard carpets and two of needlework made for cupboards' (Clabburn, 1988, p.190). In the Lumley inventory of 1590, there were 'carpets of velvet for tables and windows' (Cust, 1918, p.28).

Some table carpets were important enough to have their own protection. In the 1635 inventory of the Duke of Buckingham, there was 'One livery table and one rich carpet wrought with gold and a leather carpet to cover the same' (Jervis, 1997, p.60). In contrast was the 1641 inventory of Tart Hall, which had 'a round table of wanscote with falling leaves, thereon being a green clothe carpet, four yards long and seven quarters broade' (Cust, 1911).

By the eighteenth century, even though in general they had gone out of fashion as new furniture finishes were introduced, they were still noted. In 1728, Chambers' *Cyclopaedia* still defined carpet as 'a sort of covering to be spread on a table, trunk, an astarde [platform] or even a passage or floor'.

See also **Gilt leather**, **Needlework carpet**, **Toilette**.

Tablecloth

(a) A cloth, usually of white linen, spread upon a table in preparation for a meal, and upon which the dishes, plates, etc. are placed.

In the 1950s, there were a number of alternatives:

Crash cloths: these are usually made of flax tow yarns in plain-weave with coloured borders.
Printed tablecloths: spun rayon cloth woven in a plain-weave and screen-printed in a tablecloth design including a border. Linen, cotton and hemp are also used for printed cloths.
Dice tablecloths: much used in cafés and restaurants and made both in cotton and linen. The design is woven on a dobby loom and is, consequently, cheaper than a damask.
Damask tablecloths: these are woven from linen, cotton or rayon or any combination. Like other damasks, the floating of the warp and weft yarns creates the pattern and, as they are at right angles to one another, one reflects the light more than the other, according to the viewpoint. The weaving systems for tablecloths include the full harness, where each thread in a repeat of the design is controlled separately by a hook

121. Tablecloth linen c.1955 (Private Collection)

and needle, and the binding of the satin weaves is done in the design and the card cutting. Alternatively, there is the common harness, where a needle controls two or three hooks and two or three adjacent threads in a repeat of the design. Although called 'common', this system is used for the finest double damasks. It is used for large designs. Double damask usually implies a much finer setting of the threads (Ostick, 1955, pp 357–8).

There are two types of damask tablecloths: (1) single damask: woven with approximately equal yarns in **warp** and **weft**; (2) double damask: a **satin** construction usually with twice as many filling weft yarns as warp yarns. This makes the pattern much more distinct.

There were clearly issues of etiquette associated with table linen. In 1575, Cambridge colleges decreed that 'If either fellowe or pensioner do wipe his hande or finger of the tableclothe he shall pay for every time jd.' (Willis, 1886, vol.III, p.363.)

(b) A cloth, often of **woollen** material and with an ornamental design, used to cover a table permanently or when not in use for meals. According to Elizabeth Glaister:

> a soft woollen material that is not very rough and will hang well, is best. Line and Flaxen materials never look well; they slip uneasily about and stick out instead of hanging down. The decoration of little tables in drawing rooms, with white cloths suggestive of crumbs and a promiscuous repast, bordered with many-coloured flowers in crewels that are not suggestive of ready washing is one of the outrages that have been committed under the name of Art Needlework. (*Needlework*, 1880, pp 80–1.)

Chenille was common in the first half of the twentieth century.

See also **Broadcloth**, **Damask**, **Diaper**, **Dorrock**, **Gravy-proof cloth**, **Linen**, **Oilcloth**, **Rayon**, **Table cover**, **Table felt**, **Table linen**, **Tabling**.

Table cover

A covering used to protect a table permanently or when not in use for meals. Common materials used for table covers included **oilcloth**, **printed cotton**, **tapestry**, **serge**, **chenille** and **velvet**. The variety available in the mid-nineteenth century is demonstrated by Simmonds in 1858: 'Table covers for ornament are also made of other materials, as printed embossed or plain cloth, velvet pile, French silk damask, cotton or worsted damask, Turkey-red checkers, etc. (Simmonds, 1858). In 1872, American table covers were defined as:

> A woollen fabric, the pattern of which is usually printed or embossed but sometimes woven like damask. There are four varieties: broadcloth, felt, plain-woven and damask-woven. The plain-woven are usually printed, but sometimes embossed. The felts are embossed, and the broadcloth embroidered, with coloured silk. Small sizes are made for stand covers and extra sizes for pianos. (Brown & Gates, 1872.)

See also **Broadcloth**, **Damasclene**, **Table carpet**, **Toilenette**.

Table felt (aka table pads)

A fitted pad or cloth designed to protect table surfaces. Often made of **flannel** or **felt**, table pads are used under a **tablecloth** on a dining table to protect the surface and to deaden noise. They are often made with a quite thick felt and finished with a plastic or **oilcloth** coating to the surface. American author, Elizabeth Dyer, gives a full description:

> The purpose of the table pad is to protect the table from hot dishes and to serve as a silence cloth. Four kinds most frequently used are heavy, double-faced outing flannel, asbestos pads, felt and quilted padding. The asbestos pads protect the table better but are hard to keep clean. They can be purchased in sections that are easy to handle, and can also be ordered in special sizes. Muslin or cotton flannel covers for these pads may be made to order. The outing flannel, while heavy to handle, can be laundered. The pad should fit the table. If ends have to be turned under, they should not be allowed to show ridgy under the tablecloth. The quilted padding protects the table better than the felt or flannel, but is more expensive. (*c.*1923, p.218.)

See also **Silence cloth**, **Underlay**.

Table linen

This general title covers a range of domestic linen including **tablecloths**, damask slips, five o'clock tea cloths, doilies, tray cloths, servants' hall cloths, men's servants' thumb waiting napkins, pastry napkins, fish napkins, breakfast napkins, dinner napkins, etc. (Caulfeild & Saward, 1887, p.468).

See also **Damask**, **Linen**.

Table scarf

A nineteenth-century name for a cloth **runner**, sometimes embroidered, which ran the length of a table, overhanging the edges in some cases.

Tabling

An American name for various cloths used to cover tables.

See also **Crankey**, **Tablecloth**, **Table cover**.

Tacks

Upholsterers used tacks to fix covers to frames and to fit up a range of textile furnishings. Generally speaking, the larger tacks and staples are used to hold **webbing**; the smallest and finest are used to hold the **top cover**. Metals used include iron, steel and copper alloys.

Eighteenth-century tacks have hand-forged iron shanks and hammered heads (sometimes referred to as 'rose head', though this term is also used to describe some machine-made types and should therefore be avoided to prevent confusion). By the late eighteenth century, the process had developed – shanks were machine-cut but the heads were still hammered by hand. It was not until the early nineteenth century that the heads were machine-stamped. 'Jovial tacks, white tacks and tin-n'd tacks' are listed in the bills of London upholsterers, Mayhew and Ince (Beard, 1997, p.309).

Today, **upholstery** tacks are generally 'blued' cut steel and of two types, 'fine' and 'improved', the latter being slightly heavier with a larger head. They have a small spur of metal used for temporary tacking and can be used with a magnetic tack hammer: sterilised tacks are kept in the mouth, spat out onto the magnetic head, temporarily placed and then driven home with the hammer head. Clout tacks have burred shanks to increase the anchoring into the wood.

See also **Tacking**.

Tacking

The process of affixing fabrics, **leather**, etc. to a chair frame or wall studding. Blind tacking is a method which can disguise the **tack** line on outside panels by layering the fabrics face down, so that they are tacked and pulled over a 'tacking strip' (card or metal) that allows a straight edge to be seen. The other edge is, of course, normally tacked inside the frame. **Tapes**, **gimps** and **borders** are also used to hide tack tops.

See also **Back tacking**, **Tack**.

Taffeta

A name that has been applied at different times to different fabrics. The name ultimately comes from the Persian *taftah*, meaning 'a silken cloth'. It was initially a plain-woven glossy **silk** (of any colour); it was sometimes stiffened with extra **weft** threads. More recently, it was a thin, light but lustrous silk or **union** material. In furnishings, it was often used for **cushion** covers, **bed furniture** and **drapes** from the fifteenth century onward. In 1485, there is a reference to 'the dosers alle of camaca, [and] the bankers alle of taffeta' (*EE Misc.*, 1855, p.4). While in 1537, a description of 'two curteynes of taffata paned white and red' refers to the decoration of beds in the household of Katherine of Aragon (Beard, 1997, p.282).

In the sixteenth century, there was also a growing range of names for various types of taffeta based on production centres. The *Book of Rates* noted: 'Taffata the yard'/'Taffata called Levant taffata the yard'/'Taffata narrow called Spanish taffata the yard'/'Taffata called towers Taffata the yard'. Mention is also made of 'linen taffety' (Willan, 1962, pp.59–60).

By the seventeenth century, taffeta was an important furnishing fabric. The 1601 Hardwick Hall inventory lists 'a long cushion of cloth of gold and black striped tuffaffetie' and a bed with 'five curtains of carnation taffety' (Boynton, 1971, p.24). In 1611, the Hatfield inventory records '1 window curtain of changeable taffata' (Beard, 1997, p.285). Clouded taffata was also used at this time: 'Nine streamed Taffeta curtains hanging at the windows without any lining.' (Thornton, 1978, p.140). In 1642, Knole Park had a bed with 'five curtains of crimson and white taffeta, the valance of it white satin embroidered with crimson and white silk' (Edwards, 1964, p.35) and, 50 years later, Dyrham Park's 'Little Red Room' had 'a scarlet taffeta silk bed' (Walton, 1986, p.63). The 1699 estimate for beds for Hampton Court includes '50 yards of persian taffety to line the bed and make a quilt', making a direct link to Persia (Beard, 1997, p.299).

In the first quarter of the eighteenth century, the encyclopedist, Savary des Bruslons, explained that taffeta was fashionable for dress and for furnishings:

> Taffetas are made in all colours. Some are glossy, some changeable, some striped, with silk, gold or silver; others are flamed, checked, flowered, or with patterns called point de la chine and de Hongrie… Most taffetas are used for women's summer dresses, for linings, scarves, headdresses, canopies for beds or easy chairs, window curtains, bedspreads and other furnishings. (1723.)

Eighty years later, Sheraton followed these remarks closely when he said in his *Cabinet Dictionary* that 'taffety was remarkably glossy', and was 'made in all colours, some plain, and others striped with gold, silver etc – some are chequered, others flowered' (1803, pp 315–6).

Webster & Parkes commented on the glossy nature of taffeta and noted that taffetas 'usually have a remarkable wavy lustre, imparted by pressure and heat, with the application of an acidulous fluid to produce the effect called watering' (1844, p.969).

In the 1930s, thin taffetas were used as light filter cloths for window drapes. By this time, taffeta was also woven from silk, **wool**, **rayon**, **cotton** and unions of these. It was used for **curtains**, **bedspreads**, **cushions**, **eiderdown** covers, etc. (French, 1937, p.152). By 1947, it was still woven from rayon, silk or wool and was recommended for bedspreads, curtains, draperies, dressing table skirts, etc. It was particularly noted that taffeta had 'a cross rib effect, as weft yarns are larger than the warps. Chiffon taffeta has good draping qualities; changeable taffeta has warp and weft of varying colours.' (Bendure & Pfieffer, 1947, p.651.) In 1950, it was recommended in a heavy weight for curtains and bedspreads, and in lighter weights for cushions and lampshades.

In recent times, the name has been misapplied to various mixtures of silk and wool, and even cotton and **jute**, thin, fine woollen material, etc.

Antique taffeta

Plain-weave fabric, often woven with unevenly spun filament yarns, which resembles eighteenth-century taffeta.

Changeable taffeta

A taffeta with the **warp** of one colour and the weft of another. The Easton inventory of 1637 listed 'one crimson velvet canapie … with two rich taffeta changeable trayned curtaynes to it' (Thornton, 1978, p.367).

China taffeta

In 1614, Henry Howard recorded ownership of 'one tester with head and double valance fringed, and seven curtains whereof foure are made up and three unmade, the stuff of China taffeta white embroidered with birds and flowers' (Clabburn, 1976, p.60).

Crackle taffeta

A taffeta with some threads more tightly strung on looms, creating a slight crinkly effect.

Florence taffeta

Savary des Bruslons (1723) describes it as 'made in Lyon … very narrow and of a mediocre quality'.

See also **Armazine**, **Coverlet**, **Diaphane**, **Lustring**, **Norman cloth**, **Painted silk**, **Painted taffeta**, **Pékin**, **Quinze-seize**, **Sarcenet**, **Tabby**.

Tail

Tails are used as part of a decorative design for the top of a **curtain** scheme. The tail is the section that hangs down on either side of a window in conjunction with swags or **drapes**.
See also **Swag**.

Tambour muslin

Embroidered muslin made using a small frame called a 'tambour'. It was used for **curtains** in the later nineteenth century (Caulfeild & Saward, 1887, p.470).
See also **Muslin**.

Tammy

Although the derivation of the name tammy is not fully clear, it is likely that it probably originated from the French *etamine* for **worsted** yarn, itself from the Italian *stame*, meaning a 'worsted yarn' or 'warp'. Tammy is usually defined as a fine worsted cloth of good quality, often produced with a glazed finish.

Tammy was woven in Norwich since *c.*1605 and was in use during the seventeenth and eighteenth centuries for **drapes**, bed hangings and **curtains**, as well as for lining **fire screens**. In 1634, Lady Leicester had hangings on her best bed of tammy (Thornton, 1978, p.115). It was used for **lining** curtains in the mid-eighteenth century. For example, in the 1770s, Chippendale supplied Edward Knatchbull with '3 spring curtains of green tammy complete' and '166 yards of fine tammy lining' (Boynton, 1968, pp 99–100). Tammy was also used for the backs of **upholstered** items by Chippendale and his contemporaries.

A specific use for tammy was noted in the nineteenth century when *The Cabinet-Makers' London Book of Prices...* listed a charge for 'putting on the tammy with braid each side' for fire screens (1793). By the mid-nineteenth century, tammy was described as 'a commercial name formerly given to Scotch camlets; a worsted fabric resembling bunting, but closer and finer' (Simmonds, 1858). In 1877, it was observed that 'Tammies are now made of wool with a cotton warp. They are highly glazed and dyed in bright colours, and are still favourite fabrics.' (Archer, 1877, p.46.)

Towards the end of the nineteenth century, tammies were described as being composed of 'a union of cotton and worsted, the warp being like buntings, made of worsted; yet unlike the latter, they are plain, highly glazed, and chiefly used for upholstery [mainly curtains and window blinds]. They are a kind of Scotch camlet, and are otherwise called Durants.' (Caulfeild & Saward, 1887, p.471.)
See also **Bunting**, **Camlet**, **Durance**.

FURTHER READING

Cummin, H. (1941). 'Tammies and durants', *Antiques*, 40, September, pp 153–4.

Tangiers matting

See **Matting: Tangiers**.

Tape

Tapes are both utilitarian and decorative and have been widely used in furnishings. Plain tapes were used for ties and **binding** work, using either factory-made or home-woven tapes. Factory-woven **honeycomb** weave tape was more impressive, and was used to trim bed hangings and printed **curtain** fabrics. Tapes were also used to cover seams or define shapes on **upholstery** to create a piped effect when they were folded over. A ⅜ inch (95 mm) wide plain tape sewn into a loop was used in conjunction with rings to hold curtains onto rods.
See also **Braid**, **Galloon**, **None-so-Pretty**, **Trimming**.

Tapestry

Generally a plain-weave **weft** face textile fabric, with discontinuous weft patterning. They are decorated with designs of ornament or pictorial subjects, painted, embroidered, or woven in colours, used for **wall hangings**, **portières**, **curtains**, seat and **cushion** coverings, and to hang from windows or balconies on festive occasions, etc. Tapestry specifically refers to a textile in which a weft containing ornamental designs in coloured **wool** or **silk**, gold or silver thread, etc. is worked with bobbins or broaches, and pressed close with a comb, on a **warp** of **hemp** or flax stretched in a frame. The name is often loosely applied to imitative textile fabrics, but is not a generic term for a wall hanging.

The Latin *tapesium*, from which our word 'tapestry' is derived, implied a covering to furniture and floors, as well as curtains or wall hangings. The decorations on Greek and Roman coverings were effected by painting, printing, **embroidery** or a method of weaving with coloured threads; specimens and other conclusive evidence show that early Egyptians, Babylonians, Chinese, Indians, Greeks and Romans employed at least some of the tapestry weavers' skills.

Tapestry is woven on either a high or a low loom. In the case of the high warp loom, the workers sit up to their work; in the case of the low warp loom, they bend over it. In the low warp, the loom is horizontal and the weaver works with the cartoon of the design (drawn in reverse) laid under the loom, whilst working the rear of the tapestry. In the high warp system, the loom is vertical and the weaver again works from the rear of the tapestry. The worker can inspect the work as it progresses via mirrors reflecting the front side. In each case, they are supplied with the design according to which they weave and, regardless of the different positions, the method of weaving is the same. The thread-supply of each separate colour required in the design is wound upon its appointed peg or bobbin, which is a simpler implement or tool than a loom weaver's shuttle.

The *Dictionarium Polygraphicum* defined tapestry as:

> A curious kind of manufacture, serving to adorn a chamber or other apartment by hanging or covering the walls thereof. It is a kind of woven hangings; of wool and silk, frequently raised and inriched with gold and silver, representing figures of men animals and landscapes, histories etc. (1758.)

The European tapestry industry was developed around the eleventh century, and initially tapestries were used for wall hangings and door curtains. Early tapestries were woven in northern France and the Low Countries. Initially, Arras was the centre of high-quality tapestry production and this led to the use of the name as an alternative to tapestry (see also **Arras**). They were useful in medieval interiors as they were relatively portable and could be easily fitted up and removed. They also provided much needed insulation and decoration for bare-walled rooms, as well as providing examples of status and wealth.

By the fifteenth century, there were attempts to co-ordinate wall hangings with loose furnishings and cushions, which were woven to match and were called 'chambers'. Later, tapestries were made to fit specific rooms' spaces or architectural features, but there are many instances of tapestries being 'adapted' to new spaces without thought for the design.

The fortunes of Arras declined in the mid-fifteenth century and **Tournai** took the centre stage. Soon after, Brussels and Bruges also developed tapestry production centres and, by the end of the fifteenth century, Brussels was the most important centre of tapestry weaving. Flanders remained important until developments in other parts of Europe, especially England and France, challenged them (see **Aubusson tapestry**, **Beauvais tapestry**, **Gobelins tapestry**, **Mortlake tapestry**).

122. Tapestry carpet/rug, early eighteenth century (C. Faraday, European and American Carpets and Rugs, *1929)*

In Ireland, the taste for tapestry was evidenced by a manufactory at Kilkenny of 'tapestry, Turkey carpets and diapers' (*Encyclopedia Britannica*), founded early in the sixteenth century at the instance of Piers, 8th Earl of Ormond and his lady, Margaret FitzGerald, which gave employment to workmen introduced by him from Flanders.

William Sheldon established tapestry works at Weston and Barcheston in Warwickshire in the mid-sixteenth century. A few Flemings were probably brought over by him and set to work at Barcheston. In his will of 1569, Sheldon referred to his employee, Richard Hickes, somewhat erroneously perhaps as 'the only auter and beginner of tapestry and Arras within this realm' (*Encyclopedia Britannica*). About 1640, his son, Francis Hickes, had some tapestry maps woven, which have since been called the 'Sheldon maps'.

James I encouraged the establishment of the Mortlake tapestry works, where several foreign workmen were employed under the direction of Sir Francis Crane. Both James I and Charles I supplied considerable sums of money for the Mortlake works: the tapestries made there were as fine as any available from Paris or Brussels. After the execution of Charles I, Mortlake declined, and new life was infused into the industry at Paris under the influence of Colbert, who encouraged the establishment and organisation, in 1667, of the Hotel des Gobelins under the leadership of the painter Charles Le Brun. This was known as the Manufacture Royale des Meubles de la Couronne, which became the premier tapestry weaving centre in Europe for large hangings (see **Gobelins tapestry**). Three years previously, Colbert had initiated a similar manufactory, chiefly with low warp frames, at Beauvais, which was noted for sofa and chair seats and backs, **screens** and small panels (see **Beauvais tapestry**).

The consumption of tapestries was prodigious. For example, included in the list of the 'cloths of Arras and of Tapestre work' of Sir John Fastolf (*d.*1459) are:

1 new banker of arras
1 tester of arras with a lady crowns and a great rolle about her head...
1 cover for a bed of new arras
1 cloth for the nether hall of arras with a giant in the middle bearing a leg of a bear in his hand
1 cloth of arras for the dais in the same halle
1 tester of blue tapestry work with eight branches
Etc.
(*Archaelogia*, 21, pp 257–9.)

In 1577, William Harrison, in his *Description of England*, wrote confirming the widespread use:

> Certes in noble men's houses it is not rare to see abundance of Arras, rich hangings of tapestries... Like wise, in the house of knights, gentlemen, merchantmen, and some other wealthy citizens ... great provision of tapestry, Turkey work, pewter, brass, fine linen... Inferior artificers and many farmers ... garnish their cupboards with plate, their joined beds with tapestries and silk hangings, and their tables with carpets... (p.200.)

The *Tudor Book of Rates* for 1582 lists a range of tapestry types including:

Tapestry with Caddas the elle Flemish
Tapestry with gold called Arras the Flemish elle
Tapestry with silk the Flemish elle
Tapestry of Heare course the Flemish elle
Tapestry with wul or Verdure the Flemish elle (Willan, 1962, p.60.)

These imports confirm the comments made in 1583 by Philip Stubbes, in his *The Anatomie of Abuses* (p.72), who endorsed the use of tapestries to demonstrate conspicuous consumption:

> Cloth of gold, Arase, Tapestrie and such other rich ornaments, pendices, and hangings in a house of estate serve not only to manual uses and servile occupations, but also to decore, to beautifie and adorn the house, and to shew the riche estate and glorie of the owner.

The importance of the collections of tapestries made by Cardinal Wolsey and Henry VIII, who both possessed enormous quantities of the best Flemish tapestries of their time and earlier, must be considered as a lead in taste. The king had in his service not only agents in Brussels to buy hangings, but also a considerable staff of Arras-makers.

Changes in the religious and political landscape affected the location of tapestry weaving centres in Europe during the later sixteenth and seventeenth centuries. Weavers left the Netherlands and moved to France and England, amongst other places. Flemish guilds attempted to prevent further migration of weavers by decree and this meant that Brussels again dominated the market for standard quality tapestries. The French factories of Gobelins produced the best quality tapestries of the time, while the works at Aubusson and Beauvais met the demand of the middle market.

By the second half of the eighteenth century, there was a fashion for covering chairs with tapestry made to fit their frames exactly and to match wall hangings. This fashion had been led by Beauvais.

The late eighteenth century saw a decline in fashion for tapestry as other wall decorations featured more prominently. Sheraton is brief. He defined tapestry as 'a kind of cloth made of wool, and silk adorned with figures of different animals and formerly used for lining walls of rooms' (1803, p.317).

Mrs Haweis, writing in her *Art of Decoration*, said:

> Nothing looks better as a portière than a tapestry of moderately conventional design; nothing wears better… For my own part I would not even line them, to hide the honest-looking back, full of ends of wool, and the large folds in which they would hang would be suited to any dining room or study where solid splendour seems in place. (1881 p.300.)

The Arts and Crafts revival encouraged English tapestry work, and those woven after 1878 at the Merton works, from designs by William Morris as well as Sir Edward Burne-Jones and Walter Crane, were of high quality.

By the early twentieth century, tapestries were still considered valuable. According to Richard Bitmead:

> Tapestry is, in fact, generally speaking, only employed by the upholsterer to give variety to the furniture when the house to be furnished consists of more than the usual number of rooms. Among the varieties of this furnishing material, the tapestries of the Gobelins and the Savonnerie hold the first rank but not being articles of commerce, are rarely to be met with except in royal residences. There are however, some excellent imitations of these materials, the tapestries of Beauvais and Aubusson among the number, but they are expensive and are only employed in the manufacture of first-class upholstery. (1912, p.33.)

Occasional examples of modern interpretation of the technique occur. In the 1920s, the French furniture designer, Pierre Chareau, worked with Jean Lurcat to design and produce tapestries in a modern idiom for **upholstery** covers. Tapestry production continues in Scotland, in the USA and elsewhere.

See also **Alentours**, **Appliqué**, **Arras**, **Aubusson tapestry**, **Beauvais tapestry**, **Berlin wool-work**, **Brussels tapestry**, **Cluny tapestry**, **Dundee tapestry**, **Fulham tapestry**, **Gobelins tapestry**, **Kelim**, **Low warp tapestry**, **Mortlake tapestry**, **Navajo rug**, **Savonnerie carpet**, **Soho tapestry**, **Verdure**.

Cluny tapestry

In 1892, Cole described Cluny tapestry as 'a strong thick cloth made of wool and silk, especially for hangings and curtains, the manufactures of which was introduced into England in 1875' (Cole, 1892).

Imitation tapestry

Mrs Haweis discussed imitation tapestry: 'such as canvas painted or stamped in oils, look very well on the wall, but the oil colour is apt to stiffen fabric to make the fold ungainly, to crack off white and to smell a little in summer' (1881, p.300).

Moquette tapestry

The Dictionary of Needlework defined **moquette tapestry** as 'of recent date. It is of wool, designed to imitate the genuine Tapestry, and much resembling Utrecht velvet. The fine kinds are employed for table-cloths, and the thick for carpets.' (Caulfeild & Saward, 1887, p.472.)

Neuilly or Jacquard tapestry

A cloth woven on a **jacquard** loom in imitation of the Gobelins tapestries, with up to 24 colours in the wefts (Cole, 1892).

Tapestry Brussels

See **Tapestry carpet**.

Tapisséries de Bergame

Coarse woollen tapestry with **hemp** warps, used for wall hangings and upholstery, especially in the seventeenth century. These tapestries often had large patterns woven into them, but they were generally second-rate products imitating high-style tapestries.

See **Bergamo**.

123. Tapestry printed velvet carpet, c.1860 by Crossley and Co

FURTHER READING

Barnard, E.A.B. & Wace, A. (1928). 'The Sheldon weavers and their work', *Archaeologica*, LXXVIII.

Campbell, T. (1995–6). 'Tapestry quality in Tudor England: problems of terminology', *Studies in the Decorative Arts*, 3, 1, pp 29–50.

Dossie, R. (1764). *Handmaid to the Arts*, London: J. Nourse, pp 479–502.

Hartkamp-Jonxis, E. (2001). 'Flowers on the table, Dutch tapestry carpets in the seventeenth century' in, Mertens, W. (ed.), *Transitory Splendour: Interior Textiles in Western Europe 1600–1900*, Antwerp: Hessenhuis Museum, Stadsbestuur, pp 272–8.

Hunter, G.L. (1925). *Tapestries, Their Origin, History and Renaissance,* New York: John Lane.
Hunter, G.L. (1925). *The Practical Book of Tapestries,* Philadelphia: J.B. Lippincott.
Phillips, B. (1994). *Tapestry, A History,* London: Phaidon.
McKendrick, S. (1995). 'Tapestries from the Low Countries in England during the fifteenth century' in Barron, C. & Saul, N. (eds), *England and the Low Countries in the Late Middle Ages,* Stroud: Sutton Publishing, pp 43–60.
Mertens, W. (2001). 'The steady rise in the use of tapestry as an established upholstery textile in seventeenth century Western Europe' in Mertens, W. (ed.), *Transitory Splendour: Interior Textiles in Western Europe 1600–1900,* Antwerp: Hessenhuis Museum, Stadsbestuur, pp 288–95.
Shaw, C.A., 'Tapestry, A Guide to Information Sources', http://www.sil.si.edu/silpublications/tapestry-bibliography/Tapestry-Bibliography-Shaw.pdf
Stack, L. (ed.) (1993). *Conservation Research: Studies of Fifteenth to Nineteenth Century Tapestry,* Washington, DC: National Gallery of Art.
Standen, E.A. (1981). 'Tapestries in use: indoors', *Apollo,* 114, July, pp 6–15.
Thomson, W.G. (1906). *A History of Tapestry,* London: Hodder and Stoughton, reprinted 1973, Wakefield: E.P. Publishing.
Thornton, P. (1960). 'Tapisséries de Bergame', *Pantheon,* VI, XVIII, Jahrgang, March.
Turner, H.L. (2002). 'Finding the Sheldon weavers', *Textile History,* 33, 2, pp 137–61.
Various authors (1987). *The Conservation of Tapestries and Embroideries: Proceedings of Meetings at the Institute Royal du Patrimoine Artistique,* 21–24 September, Brussels: Getty Conservation Institute.
Weigert, R.A. (1962). *French Tapestry,* London: Faber and Faber.

Tapestry carpet

A loop-**pile** carpet where the pile **warp** is printed in the appropriate designs and colours before weaving. It is similar in appearance to **Brussels carpet**, but in this case all the pile yarn is on the surface, so filling and stuffer yarns are required to give body, and the pile yarns do not show on the back. It was used for **upholstery** in cheaper grades from the 1850s, and sometimes it was custom-woven to fit particular chair backs and seats. The 1858 *Dictionary of Trade Products* explained: 'Tapestry-carpets, the name generally given to a two-ply or ingrain carpet, the warp or weft being printed before weaving, so as to produce the figure in the cloth.' (Simmonds, *OED.*)

Richard Whytock experimented in 1831–2 with large drums on which were wound pre-printed warps for the entire length of a piece (Patent no.6307, 8 September 1832). This technique ensured that 'all the intricate machinery of the Brussels and Wilton looms, with their expensive harness, is superseded … there is scarcely any limit to the number of colours or shades that may be introduced, with scarcely any additional expense' (Hefford, 1987, p.2). This carpet was variously called tapestry, tapestry Brussels or tapestry velvet dependent upon the style.

The intention was to avoid the burying of thread when not part of the design. There was only one frame, the threads of which were printed with the patterns before weaving, but with the pattern elongated, so that the looping up in the weaving restores it to normal shape. It is characteristic of tapestry Brussels for the colours to run into each other and blur slightly. Pattern and pile were formed at the same time. Enormous colour varieties were available due to the pre-printing process, but plain colours have also been made.

In the 1940s, designs were printed on the pile warp by drum printing or by roller printing on the woven material. Drums were about 39 feet (11.9 metres) in circumference and wide enough to accommodate a continuous strand of yarn wound 330 times around the drum. The design was elongated by about three times the length to produce the finished tuft. The colour was printed in a stripe across the width of the drum, thus printing each strand of the yarn. When all was printed, the drum was partially collapsed to remove the yarns. It was then set in ovens. Finally, it was wound onto a beam in the correct order and then woven on a plain loom over wires, whereby the warps supply the surface yarns that are lifted over pile wires to leave uncut loops, as in a Brussels carpet. Tapestry carpet survived until the 1950s. In 1955, it was still being offered, although the caveat was added that it 'is almost impossible to produce the clearly defined colour effects of a fine Wilton, but for those who like plenty of colour the tapestry carpet has much to commend it' (Ostick, pp 342–4). Although still referred to in a 1960s textbook (Wilson, 1960), it was in very limited production and ceased to be made soon afterwards.
See also **Velvet carpet**, **Wilton carpet**.

Tapestry cloth

As well as describing a plain weave weft face fabric, tapestry is also a term for a machine-woven cloth in which all or nearly all the colours are found in the **warp** yarns. Many fabrics have been woven or printed to simulate tapestry, often on **cotton** cloths, but other yarns have been used. They have been used for **upholstery**, **cushion** covers, table **runners**, **curtains**, etc. These imitation tapestries were woven on the **jacquard** loom from the 1830s. The Neuilly or jacquard tapestry was a later nineteenth-century imitation of **Gobelins tapestry**, where the **weft** creates the design with up to 24 weft colours. All-cotton versions were woven in France, Belgium and Philadelphia from around 1890, and were considered expensive. Hand block-printed coarse **rep** could also produce a tapestry-like effect, which was preferred by some as being more like the real thing, as opposed to the jacquard tapestry that resembled **needlework**. The so-called Cluny tapestry was a strong, thick

124. Tapestry cloth detail (T. French and Co, The Book of Soft Furnishing, *1937)*

cloth made of **wool** and **silk**, especially for hangings and curtains, and was introduced into England around 1875 (Cole, 1892).

Its heyday appears to have been during the nineteenth and twentieth centuries. Mrs Haweis discussed: 'The ordinary cloth or tapestry curtain usually sold for dining rooms, is fairly worth the money; it is wool mixed with silk, often in really fine conventional patterns, but the silk is apt to fade away from the wool.' (1881, p.301.) A different description is found in Caulfeild & Saward who defined it as a 'Rep made of linen and unbleached; it measures 28 inches in width and is employed as a foundation for painting in the style of tapestry' (1887, p.474).

Tapestry cloth was particularly popular in the early twentieth century. Nisbet noted that tapestry fabrics were woven with particular end uses in mind, especially for 'window curtains or hangings, door-hangings, furniture upholstering, wall coverings, table covers and counterpanes' (1919, p.471). Hunter considered that:

> The all-cotton ones [jacquard tapestries] are *inexpensive*, even those with landscape and figures in addition to verdure... Other imitation tapestries are those block-printed by hand, like 'hand-blocked' chintzes and wall papers, but on a coarse horizontal rep in simulation of real tapestry texture. The general effect is much more tapestry-like than that of the jacquards, all but the simplest of which resemble petit point needlework, having a square point with lines running both ways instead of strongly marked ribs. (1918, p.228.)

A few years later, tapestry cloth was being praised as a furnishing fabric in the USA:

> A heavy, substantial material either all-wool, wool-and-silk, wool-and-wool with silk patterns is very beautiful and expensive, the cotton is least expensive but less durable. In the wool, the colors are especially rich and soft. Used for upholstery and covers, sometimes draperies, but it is very stiff, and if used as a hanging must be considered a wall decoration. Probably the most desirable of any fabric for durable upholstery. (Dyer, *c.*1923, p.205.)

The English author, Helen Gloag, explained one use for another type of tapestry cloth: 'If there is not sufficient needlework to cover the chair entirely, the back and the outside of the arms can be covered in tapestry cloth, a plain material that will be in keeping with the needlework that covers the seat, back, front and inside of the arms.' (1921, p.62.)

By the 1950s, the description was matter-of-fact:

> Machine made tapestries have a compound structure with two or more figuring warps and two or more figuring wefts. In addition, there may be a fine black binding warp and a fine black binding weft. The materials used in the yarns are usually cotton for the warp and binding weft, and the coarse figuring wefts may be wool or cotton... The figures produced in the figure resemble the fine petit-point of hand-made tapestry, and the ground, the gros-point or vice versa. (Ostick, 1955, p.376.)

See also **Appliqué**, **Arras**, **Aubusson caarpet**, **Berlin wool-work**, **Tapestry**.

Tapestry embroidery work

A name now frequently applied to pieces of **canvas embroidery**, executed typically with **wool** in tent stitch. In 1887, it was said that, 'Tapestry worked by the needle differs but slightly from Embroidery. The stitches are made to lie close together, so that no portion of the foundation is visible' (Caulfeild & Saward, p.473).

Pamela Clabburn has pointed out possible confusions in terminology:

> Nowadays in Britain, any piece of canvas work, large or small, is called tapestry work, which is a misnomer, while America, although not falling into that particular trap, calls canvas work needlepoint, which is also confusing as that word should apply to lace made with a needle. (1976, p.263.)

125. Tapestry upholstery 'mille fleur', USA (G.L. Hunter, Decorative Textiles, Coverings for Furniture etc., *1918)*

See also **Stitch: Tent**.

Tapestry filler

In 1951, Taylor described **tapestry** fillers as plain tapestry weaves with no pattern. It was used as filler for **upholstery** in conjunction with woven patterned cloth.

See also **Tapestry cloth**.

Tapestry printed carpet

A carpet woven with undyed or base colour only yarns, which was then overprinted. In 1891, James Dunlap of Philadelphia patented a system that used deeply incised rollers designed to trap the **pile** and **dye** it according to a pattern. The English carpet manufacturer, Brinton, was vehement in his opposition to both tapestry and tapestry printed carpets:

> Owen Jones is again worth quoting in this connection, even if his strictures seem excessively severe. He says: 'I will say no more on the floral style, but to express a regret that, the more perfect the manufacturing process in carpets becomes, the more do they (the carpets) appear to lend themselves to evil... The Tapestry carpets, where the colours are still more numerous, are vicious in the extreme; whilst the recent invention of printed carpets, with no bounds to its ambition, has become positively criminal'. (Brinton, 1919, p.99.)

See also **Tapestry carpet**.

FURTHER READING

Bartlett, J.N. (1978). *Carpeting the Millions, The Growth of Britain's Carpet Industry*, Edinburgh: John Donald.

Burch, J. (1856). 'On the printing of fabrics with special reference to shawls and carpets', *Journal of the Society of Arts*, 4, 1809, pp 401–08.

White, G. (1895). 'The making of tapestry and Brussels carpets. A visit to Dean Clough Mills, Halifax', *Art Journal*, New Series, pp 237–42.

Tapestry quilt

A quilted bedcovering material that is woven on the **jacquard** loom. It can have a variety of pattern repeats and colours but it is always woven with **tapestry** motifs.

Tapestry velvet carpet
See **Tapestry carpet**.

Tarlatan
A thin, open, muslin-type of fabric, probably of Indian origin. It was explained in 1727 that 'there are various kinds of muslins brought from the East Indies; chiefly Bengal; betelles, tarnatans, mulmuls [etc]' (Chambers, *Cyclopaedia*, 1841).

By the mid-nineteenth century, tarlatan was woven in the United Kingdom: 'Tarlatan, a kind of book muslin principally made in Scotland' (Simmonds, 1858).

In one case, tarlatan was recommended for lining a **fireplace curtain**: 'On each side [of the fireplace] hung curtains of fine lace, lined with coloured tarlatan or thin silk' (*Cassell's Household Guide*, 1870). Caulfeild & Saward defined tarlatan as 'A thin gauze like muslin, much stiffened, and so called from the chief centre of the manufacture Tarare in France… Originally an Indian manufacture which was copied in Europe.' (1887, p.475.)

An early twentieth-century definition concurred, describing tarlatan as 'a very loosely constructed cotton cloth, heavily sized, used most extensively for fancy-dress costumes and decorative purposes, and sometimes for inexpensive window screening' (Dyer, *c*.1923, p.314). A later American definition confirmed the thin gauze-like description: 'Thin open cotton fabric, highly sized. [It is] about as coarse as cheese-cloth, only very stiff and transparent. Used for bed canopies instead of mosquito netting.' (Denny, 1936, p.67.) In 1947, tarlatan was defined again as: 'a lightweight open-weave fabric either white or dyed. Has been used for curtains. When glazed on one side it is called Argentine cloth.' (Bendure & Pfieffer, p.652.)
See also **Gauze**, **Muslin**.

Tarpaulin
A heavy plain-weave of **jute** and **cotton**, waterproofed with a composition substance. It was sometimes used in the twentieth century for **curtains** for summer houses and verandas, and stencilled with designs.

Tartan
A twilled plaid **linsey-woolsey** type cloth, called *tiretaine* in French and *tartein* in the Netherlands, that is particularly associated with Scotland. The word became Anglicised as 'tartan'.
See also **Plaid**.

FURTHER READING
Biddulph, F. (1988). 'Tartanalia', *Traditional Interior Decoration*, 2, 4, February/March, pp 46–56.

Tartarin
A rich **silk** material whose name may derive from Tartary (in China). The 1397 inventory of goods belonging to the Duke of Gloucester included 'a large bed of cloth of gold and 3 curtains of tartarin "beaten" to match' (Eames, 1971, p.43). Henry VI clearly enjoyed tartarin as he possessed 'two curtains of red tartarin; 3 curtains of green tartarin', and one 'travers with seven green tartarin curtains' (Leaf, 1934).

Tassel
A form of **passementerie** that is distinguished by its particular pendant shape and threaded appearance. Tassels were often used in conjunction with other passementeries or **trimmings**. Simple tassels are made from looped threads, which are wrapped with **cord**. The loop top may be fitted with other material or stuffed. The laid threads are covered with mesh, straps or **gimps** as required. This is joined at the junction to a cord by a process called 'snailing', using thread worked with a needle. There may also be a tufted **pile** 'ruff' around the ends of the shaped piece. The fringe of a tassel, called a 'skirt', is made up from many yarns such as loose cord fringe, hangers of other smaller moulds, bows, etc. or combinations thereof. The tassel may be fixed directly to a cord or with a separate rosette. Large tassels are formed over wood or plastic moulds and can be very decorative with the addition of other components such as ruffs, bands, etc.

Tassels have been widely used in window treatments, to hold back bed **curtains**, as finishes to **cushions**, for **blinds**, and to decorate **pelmets**. Tart Hall had 'a green damask [table] carpet fringed about with silk and gold and four tassels at each corner' (Cust, 1911, p.100). Special weighted tassels were made for **fire screen** balances. Sheraton described their uses:

> The drawing lines of festoon curtains have tassels at their ends. And opposite to this side, there should be a false line and a tassel to it, to match the right side of the window; and also for balance screens; the weight of the screen must be ascertained, and then a lead tassel is formed of equal weight, with a hole through the centre to take a line, which is then covered and worked as any other tassel. (1803, p.317.)

See also **Fringe**.

FURTHER READING
Welch, N. (1999). 'Tassels: universal decoration', *Piecework*, 7, 1, January/February, pp 45–9.

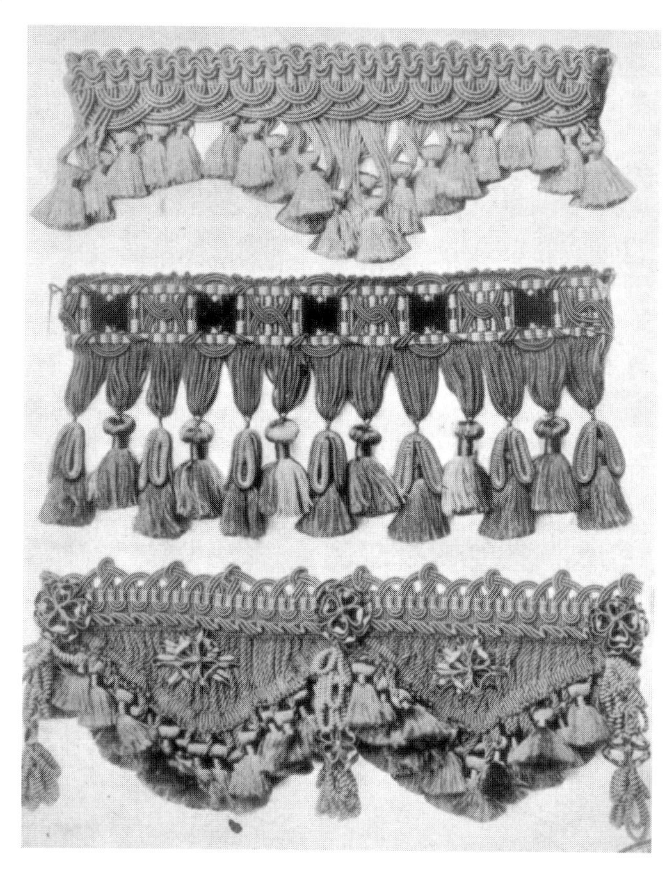

126. Tassel examples (G.L. Hunter, Decorative Textiles, Coverings for Furniture etc., *1918)*

Welch, N. (2001). 'Tassels through time', *Shuttle Spindle and Dyepot*, 32, 2, Spring, pp 48–53.

Tassel hook

A two-pronged **cleat hook** intended to have the **cords** of **blinds** lashed to it to support them when drawn up.

Tent

A sixteenth- to eighteenth-century name for a **hemp**, **jute** or **linen** plain-woven cloth. Its useful grid structure made it very suitable for counted **canvas work**.

Tent **stitch** is an alternative name for **petit-point**.

Tenting

Fitting out rooms with **drapes** that imitate tents. Draping walls and ceilings mainly created the effect with fabrics in particular designs to reflect military or Near Eastern imagery. The effect was particularly popular in the Regency and Empire periods of the early nineteenth century. The decorators, Percier and Fontaine, were especially renowned for this style.

Terry

A textile of uncertain origin. If 'terry' was an adjective, the name may have been a corruption of the French word *tire*, meaning 'drawn'. In the nineteenth century, terry was a horizontally ribbed, **warp** faced fabric often with a **wool** face and a **cotton weft**. **Silk** was also used for terry weaves with a worsted weft and silk warp that was sometimes woven to create a **damask** effect. It is similar in appearance to **rep** and was used for **upholstery**.

Brown & Gates explained that terry was a combination of wool and cotton yarns that resembled rep. It was woven with wool for the warp face, with a cotton weft for the reverse and for the heavy wefts that form the ribs. They went on to say:

> Terries are used for the same purposes generally as reps. A superior article is made, having a worsted woof [weft] and a silk warp. It is woven in the same manner as the wool terry, and is called 'silk terry'. It sometimes bears upon its surface raised figures of flowers etc., which are formed like those of damask. This variety is much more durable and expensive than the ordinary wool terry. (1872, p.208.)

In 1879, Irish terries were illustrated in Yapp's *Art Industry*. Yapp pointed out that this silk and worsted cloth has 'a peculiar richness and metallic lustre which renders it admirably fitted for upholstering purposes, and it is considerably cheaper than stuffs composed of silk alone' (1879, Plate 73).

From the mid-nineteenth century, terry was the technical name for loop-**pile** textures known as 'towelling'. In 1906, Nisbet explained: 'Terry fabrics produced by means of terry motions are exemplified in so-called Turkish towels. The majority of these goods are produced entirely from cotton, although terry towels are sometimes produced either entirely or in part from linen.' (vol.VIII, p.163.)

Towelling may be woven either with all-over loops on both sides of the fabric, or patterned loops on both sides. These loops were formed with an extra warp yarn. When the pile is only on one side, it is called 'Turkish towelling'. Terry varies in quality, with the better qualities having a close, firm, under weave, with very close loops.

Terry also refers to pile fabrics having the loops that form the pile left uncut, as in terry pile, terry velvet.

See also **Towel**, **Velvet**.

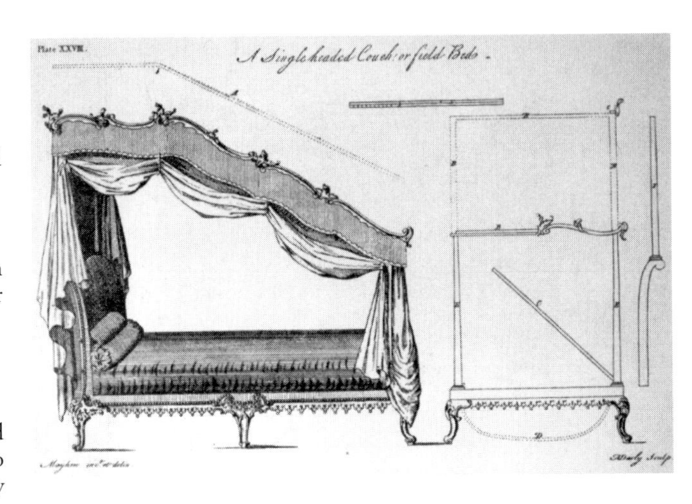

127. Tester example from a couch or field bed, c.1762 (Ince and Mayhew Universal System of Household Furniture)

Terry carpet

Terry carpet was woven in a similar manner to an **ingrain carpet** but produced in plain or solid colours. It was particularly used for carpet surrounds in American homes in the late nineteenth century.

Tester

In the later medieval period, a tester referred to the vertical head end of a bed while the **celure** was the top 'roof' of the bed. In 1440, a line in *The Romance of Sir Degrevant* stated 'Hur bede was off aszure, with testur and celure' (*OED*). Later, the name referred to a roof-like or canopy component supported above the bed by posts and covering the whole area of the bed. The fabric used may be shirred, radiating from a central star, or stretched taut. There are distinctions between tester and tester cloth in some definitions, but these are not regular. In 1546, 'A bed stok with cortins of dornix, and testerne of the same' was recorded in Cambridge University (Willis, 1886, vol.III. p.351). The range of distinct bed **drapes** is shown in the Lumley inventory of 1590, which lists in summary 'testers 12, Sparvers 3, pavilions 3, canopies 6' (Cust, 1918).

Flying testers are roof-like components of a bed that are usually cantilevered from the **headboard**, and extend out over the whole bed. In the last quarter of the seventeenth century, a fashion for flying testers, with complex cresting, **valances** and drapery, was found in some circles (also known as *lit d'ange*). Half-testers are similar to flying testers. They usually extend over the head half of the bed.

See also **Canopy**, **Dome**, **Throw over**, **Valance**.

Thread

A continuous strand, either single or multiple, to make a filament suitable for weaving. The types are many and various but include **bouclé** yarns, cabled yarns, **chenille** and **crêpe**. It is a term that also refers to **linen** thread particularly. It remained until the early twentieth century. **Cotton** threads were called 'cottons' to distinguish them from the linen. Thread is usually considered to be finer, more highly finished and more tightly twisted than yarn.

See also **Yarn**.

Three-ply carpet

See **Double cloth carpet**, **Ingrain carpet**, **Kidderminster carpet**.

Throw

A portion of fabric, plain or decorated, intended to be thrown over a sofa in a casual manner. They were popular in the later nineteenth century. The 1895 Montgomery Ward retail catalogue listed: 'Drapery Silk', 'suitable for throws, sash curtains, mantel drapes, etc'. The throw was revived in the later twentieth century.

Throw over

A name for the combined **tester** and **curtains** designed to be 'thrown over' the frame of a field or tent bed to save time and complicated fitting up. Chippendale supplied a field bed for Paxton in 1774, which had 'a blue and white check thro over furniture' (Gilbert, 1978, p.275). Throw overs were sometimes weighted to keep them in place.

Thrum

Thrums are the ends of the **warp** threads left unwoven and remaining attached to the textile when the web is cut. They create a **fringe**, in effect. In 1519, Horman quoted this passage: 'The baudy thrummys of the carpettis toke me faste by the feete' (*Vulgaria*, p.167 b). Another reference, which uses the word in a slightly different manner, is from 1645 where: 'The wrong side of a Turky carpet, which useth to be full of thrums and knots, and nothing so even as the right side' (Howell, 1650, vol.III. p.33, *OED*).

According to *The Workwoman's Guide*, 'Carpets should always be mended with a loose kind of untwisted worsted called thrums' (Hale, 1840, p.202).

See also **Sofa rug**.

Tick

The case or outer cover for forming a **mattress** (filled with **stuffing** materials) to be used as part of a bed.

See also **Ticking**.

Ticking

A **linen**, and later **cotton**, herringbone twill weave material, specially suited to **mattress** covering. Later twentieth-century bed tickings have been made from decorative damasks. It is often very tightly woven with more **warps** than filling yarns. Types include **flock** tick at 5½ ounces (156 grams), **feather** tick at 7½ ounces (212.6 grams) and hair tick at 8+ ounces (226+ grams) per square yard (0.84 square metres). The designations refer to the appropriate cover for mattress fillings. The traditional ticking has white and coloured stripes (traditionally of blue and white or pink and white), but there have been many patterned (floral) styles available. Ticking can be made water-repellent, germ-resistant and feather-proof. Originally, to ensure feather-proofing, it was the custom to rub the underside of the cloth with beeswax or a gum made from a mix of turpentine and rosin before filling with **stuffings**.

Ticking has certainly been known since at least the early sixteenth century for enclosing feathers, etc. The *Tudor Book of Rates* for 1582 listed 'ticks called Brussels ticks, the Tick/Ticks called Turney ticks for beds, the dozen' (Willan, 1962, p.61). In 1683, Thomas Tryon mentions that 'You may have Flock-Beds, with Canvas-Tickings' (*The Way to Health*, p.595).

Although ticking has been mainly used for bedding, in 1637 Ralph Grynder supplied Henrietta Maria with '8 baggs of tyke for the 2 chairs and 6 stools' as protective covering and '1 lardg bagg of fine stript tyke for the seat of a couch bedd' (Beard, 1997, p.289).

During the eighteenth century, retailers sold ticking by the yard. In the 1728 inventory of the shop of James Pilbeam, a mercer of

128. Ticking with retail label c. (Leeds Museums and Galleries, Temple Newsam House, Roger Warner Collection)

Chiddingly, Sussex, there was listed 'Forty-one yards of bed tick at ls 8d per yard = £3 8s 4d' (http://www.chiddingly.gov.uk/History/James%20 Pilbeam.html). While in his London shop, between 1768 and 1777, Nathaniel Hewitt offered both 'Flanders and English ticking' (Heal, 1953, p.84).

In the nineteenth century, George Wallis commented upon the use of cotton for ticking in his 1854 report on the New York Industrial Exhibition. He said 'It is scarcely possible to conceive a firmer or better made article, and the traditional notion that really good tickings can only be manufactured from flax receives a severe shock when such cotton goods as these are presented for examination.' (1854, p.13.)

In 1887, *The Dictionary of Needlework* stated that 'it is also used for window and door blinds, and for this purpose can be procured in other stripes of fancy colour. Ticking is of Jean make or basket woven.' (Caulfeild & Saward, p.491.)

The feather-proofing of ticks changed in the nineteenth century. *Cassell's Household Guide*, 1870, lamented the fact that the beeswax has given way to another method whereby 'even the ticking of a good bed is painted over on the inside with whitening and size or some equivalent; the result is that when it is quite dry, the dust comes through' (vol.1, p.156). This seemed to remain an issue, as mid-twentieth century remarks about ticking also emphasised that an indication of quality is dependent upon the quantity of filling that the cloth contains. *The Furnisher's Encyclopaedia* pointed out that 'the addition of filling is quite unnecessary in a good ticking and has moreover a definite disadvantage, since it may well tend to absorb an unduly high percentage of moisture and thus make the bed damp' (Sheridan, revised edition 1955, p.131).

Belgian

A nineteenth-century, **satin**-faced linen-cotton fabric woven 64 inches (162.6 cm) wide. It was produced in a range of colours and patterns and used especially for **upholstery** and bedding (Caulfeild & Saward, 1887, p.26). It was still listed in 1923 (Dyer).

Bohemian

This ticking has a plain-weave, a very high texture, and is feather-proof. It is of a lighter weight than regular ticking. It is patterned with narrow coloured stripes on a white background, or it may have a **chambray** effect by using a white or unbleached warp with a blue or red filling.

See also **Art ticking**, **Bolzas**, **Chambray**, **Crankey**, **Damask**, **Sun curtain**.

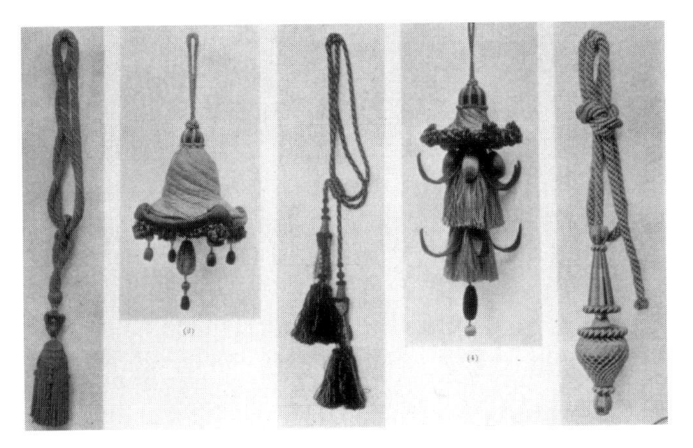

129. Examples of tiebacks with tassels (G.L. Hunter, Decorative Textiles, Coverings for Furniture etc., *1918)*

Tidy
See **Antimacassar**.

Tieback (aka Holdback)
Decorative holders for **curtains** and **drapes** that are usually fixed to either side of the window to hold back the curtains when opened. They have been made from a range of materials including fabric, metal and wood.

An early reference is from the Ham House inventory of 1679 that recorded some black and gold **damask** curtains held back by 'silk strings with tassells' fixed to 'four guilded [sic] hooks' (Thornton & Tomlin, 1980, p.63).

Almost 200 years later, the American publication, *Godey's Lady's Book*, discussed tiebacks and pointed out that:

> One method is by a long loop of silk or worsted cord, with or without a tassel, suspended from a hook three or four feet above the floor, which is the usual height. Bands of bronze or brass, too, are much used, fixed either upright or horizontally, as may be tasteful and convenient. The upright bands are generally most suitable for small rooms. (June, 1860, p.507.)

They have also been made in the same fabric as the curtains in a variety of shapes and patterns.

Tieback is also a name for a curtain that is closed at the top of the drop and almost fully open at the point of tie back.
See also **Bow and band**, **Cleat hook**.

Tiffany
Thin, transparent **silk gauze** material that was mainly used for clothes, but on occasion was used for napery. It was originated by Walloon weavers in the early seventeenth century. Beck cites a 1771 reference to a 'tablecloth and napkins which were all of tiffany, embroidered in silk and gold in the finest manner, in natural flowers. It was with the utmost regret that I made use of these costly embroidered napkins. You may be quite sure they were quite spotted before dinner was over.' (Montgomery, 1984, p.366). *The Dictionary of Needlework* still defined tiffany as 'a semi-transparent silk textile resembling gauze' (Caulfeild & Saward, 1887, p.495).

Timbuctoo
A nineteenth-century **curtain** material. *Cassell's Household Guide* (1870) discusses a textile called timbuctoo: 'an excellent stout kind of curtain, very general in Paris, has lately been introduced. It wears well, looks well, and needs no trimming. It is striped horizontally in white, scarlet, black and yellow, on a green, red or blue ground.'
See also **Algerian**.

Tinsell
A rich material woven from **silk** or **woollen** yarns interwoven with gold or silver strips. The name may be derived from the French *étincelle*, meaning 'sparkling'. It may well have been produced by brocading with these strips, or by overlaying with a thin coating of gold or silver. It has also been defined as 'a thin net or gauze thus made, or ornamented with thin plates of metal' (*OED*). It appears to have been particularly used for bed hangings.

The 1526 inventory of the goods of Duke of Richmond recorded 'A testour, payned with clothe of gold, grene tynsell, and crymsen velwet.' (Camden Society, *Camden Miscellany*, 1855, vol.III, p.18.) Later, in 1601, the Hardwick Hall wardrobe had a 'double vallans of tinsill and black wrought velvet' (Boynton, p.25). During 1638, the Lady Dorchester had a bed with summer hangings of 'white tinsel wrought with flowers of several colours of silke' (Thornton, 1978, p.357).

In 1656, Blount stated that 'Tincel signifies with us a stuff or cloth made partly of silk, and partly of copper; so called, because it glisters or sparkles like stars or fire.' (*Glossographia*.) Hence, in 1730, Bailey could define it as 'a glittering Stuff made of Silk and Copper'.
See also **Baudekin**, **Tissue**.

Tissue
A class of textiles that are woven on a draw loom with a system of two **warps** and two **wefts**. The **satin** ground had a second weft of loosely twisted yarns to create a figure in the weft, which was often made from gold or, particularly, silver threads. Tissues could also be **brocaded**.

Tissue was an important material in the sixteenth century for hangings and **upholstery**. In 1509, Stephen Hawes noted how 'With cloth of tyssue in the rychest manner the walles were hanged' (*Pastime of Pleasure*, xvi, Percy Society, 61, *OED*). In 1537, the Wardrobe of Katherine of Aragon had 'a riche cloth of assate of crymsene clothe of tissue enbrowed with the armes of Englande and Spayne' (Camden Society, *Camden Miscellany*, 1855, vol.III). A little later, in 1559, John Grene invoiced Elizabeth I 'for covering of the [Coronation] chair with clothe of tisshewe with gilt nails for the garnishing of the same (Beard, 1997, p.283). The Hardwick Hall inventory of 1601 lists a variety of uses: 'seven pieces of embroidered cloth of gold, and silver cloth of tissue, a carpet for a court cupboard of cloth of tissue, a chair of cloth of gold and cloth of tissue, a bed head and vallens of cloth of tissue' (Boynton, 1971, p.24).

Tissue was also used for bed hangings. A bed in the Ingatestone inventory of 1600 had furnishings of 'tysshew layde with crimson silke and goulde lace' (Thornton, 1978, p.357). In 1603, Drayton mentioned a bed 'on which a Tissue counterpoyne was cast' (*The Baron's wares in the reign of Edward II*, VI, XLI, *OED*). The 1679 Ham inventory of the White Closet listed 'four pieces of a rich clothe of tissue green and gold' (Thornton & Tomlin, 1980, p.80).

Over 100 years later, Smith discussed the manufacturing method of tissue and said that the patterns were 'commonly drawn with large ornamental flowers and leafs … the ground work is frequently filled up with mosaick work of one sort or another' (*The Laboratory or School of Arts*, 1799).

A twentieth-century definition describes tissues as being lightweight fabrics similar to **muslin** with a plain-weave ground. *The Book of Soft Furnishing* explains:

The cloth is ornamented with extra weft in large overall design by a jacquard. The extra weft is suitably bound by the fine ground ends where the figuring is required, but is floated bodily over the intervening spaces when it is not required for figure forming. The unwanted weft is cut away after weaving, leaving the design clear but with a ragged edge like Madras muslin. (French, 1937, p.156.)

Tissue in English usage may also refer to a cloth with an extra colouring weft.
See also **Brocatelle**, **Lampas**.

FURTHER READING

Monnas, L. (1998). 'Tissue in England during the 15th and 16th centuries', *CIETA Bulletin,* 75, pp 63–80.

Tobine
A range of mainly dress materials woven from **silk**, silk mixtures, **linen** and **cotton unions** that have **warp** float patterns of small flowers or dots. In 1799, G. Smith pointed out that: 'There are likewise lutestring tobines, which commonly are striped with flowers in the warp, and sometimes between the tobine stripes, with brocaded sprigs.' (*The Laboratory or School of Arts,* vol.II. p.45.) It was apparently used for **upholstery** work on occasion. In 1740, John Boydell, of Boston, USA, had 'I field bedstead lin'd with Tabine stuff curtains' (Cummings, 1961, p.37).
See also **Cannellé**.

Toile
A generic name for the scenic, copperplate-printed designs produced on an all-**cotton** cloth, including those influenced by the productions of Christophe Philippe Oberkampf at Jouy-en-Josas.
See also **Calencas**, **Printed textile**, **Toile de Jouy**, **Toile de Nantes**, **Toilette**.

Toile cirée
See **Oilcloth**.

Toile de Jouy
A name for a monochrome copperplate-printed, usually **cotton** furnishing fabric with the design in red, blue or black on a pale ground, particularly produced at Jouy-en-Josas, in France. Christophe Philippe Oberkampf first made the fabric from around 1770, although the printing works in the town of Jouy-en-Josas had been established since 1760. Oberkampf used the copperplate printing techniques, and later (after 1797) the roller printing technique to produce **printed cottons** with repeats of up to 39 inches (1 metre). Block prints were also produced here. The particular attractiveness of the fabrics from Jouy was based on the pictorial representations they offered, which were often designed by well-known artists. The designs are typically associated with representations of contemporary life, classical antiquity, politics, the Orient and country living. They were antidotes to the formality of some courtly influenced interiors. Toiles were used as summer furnishings to replace heavier winter hangings in more exclusive interiors, but their popularity meant that they were soon available for all sorts of interior work.

Modern screen printing methods and finishes, as well as an increase in the variety of patterns and colourways, have meant that this fabric continues to meet a particular taste, including the co-ordination of fabrics and wallpapers.
See also **Printed textile**, **Toile**.

FURTHER READING

Bredif, J. (1989). *Classic Printed Textiles from France 1760–1843: Toiles de Jouy,* London: Thames and Hudson.
Chapman, S.D. & Chassagne, S. (1981). *European Textile Printers in the Eighteenth Century: A Study of Peel and Oberkampf,* London: Heinemann.
Clouzet, H. (1928). *Histoire de la Manufacture de Jouy et de la Toile Imprimée en France,* 2 vols, Paris: Van Oest.
Riffel, M. & Rouart, S. (2003). *Toile de Jouy, Printed Textiles in the French Style,* London: Thames and Hudson.

Toile de Nantes
The copperplate printing process that produced toile similar to that from Jouy was, by 1780, adopted in Nantes, hence the name. Block prints were also produced here.
See also **Printed textile**, **Toile**.

130. Toile de Jouy-type panel design inspired by Jean Baptiste Pillement (French, 1728–1808), panel, linen, plain weave, copperplate-printed, two selvedges present, Jouy-en-Josas or Nantes, France, c.1786 (Gift of Robert Allerton, 1924.499, The Art Institute of Chicago. Photography ©The Art Institute of Chicago)

FURTHER READING

Musée de L'Impression sur Etoffes (1978), *Toiles de Nantes, des XVIIIe et XIX siècles,* exh. cat., Mulhouse: Musée de L'Impression sur Etoffes.

Toile de Reims
See **Toile peinte**.

Toilenette
A name of uncertain origin that was applied to a number of different fabrics, which were used for dresses and waistcoats as well as for furnishings during the nineteenth century. One definition explains that it is a name for a heavy **cotton** fabric that was specifically used for **table covers**. Brown & Gates said that 'it is of two varieties, one of which is two colours only; usually red and white. The other variety is always woven like a **rep** in coloured stripes. This variety of toilenette is not as heavy as the former, but so much finer and softer.' (1872.) In 1858, Simmonds, described toilinet, as a 'kind of German quilting; silk and cotton warp with woollen weft' (*Dictionary of Trade Products*).

Toile peinte
Large panels of heavy **linen** (or similar) upon which designs were painted for use as **tapestry** cartoons. They were sometimes hung as if they were tapestries. In the eighteenth century in France, a copperplate printing process was used to create designs in this tradition. Also known as Toile de Reims.
See also **Printed textile**, **Toile**.

FURTHER READING

Geijer, A. (1979). *A History of Textile Art: A Selective Account,* London: Pasold Research Fund in association with Sotheby Parke Bernet.

Sartor, M. (1909). *Descriptive Catalogue of the Collections of the Musée de Reims: Paintings, Toile Peinte, Pastels, Gouaches, Watercolours and Miniatures,* Paris: Petit.

Toilet cloth
A term applied to a number of fabrics such as bed **quilts** or **counterpanes**, or dressing table covers, where the face cloth is **stitched** down according to a pre-arranged design by means of a tightly woven binding **warp**. This causes the figure to stand out in relief, and it is enhanced when a **wadding weft** is used. Nisbet noted that there might be some confusion over the name:

> Although the term 'toilet' fabric is the general description of all kinds of cotton fabrics that are used for toilet purposes, such as, for example, counterpanes or bedcovers, dressing table covers, and mats, quite irrespective of the particular class or type of fabric to which they belong, [it is] also employed as a technical term descriptive of a particularly well-known type of cotton fabric known as toilet-quilting. (1919, p.436.)

A handbook for salespersons published in 1937 says that the term 'toilet' applies to:

> a number of fabrics such as beds, quilts or counterpanes, dressing table covers, mats etc. and connotes a distinctive type of fabric the chief feature of which is a fine lace in the plain-weave, stitched down according to a pre-arranged design by means of a tightly woven binding warp. A further feature of good quality toilets is the use of a wadding weft, which causes the figure to stand out in relief, aided by the tightness of the figuring warp threads. (French, 1937, p.156.)

See also **Toilette**.

Toilette (aka Toilet, Toylet)
A dressing table cover that was originally made of a rich fabric, but later could be made from many materials according to taste. Later references are usually called a 'toilet cover'. Developed in the early seventeenth century as a protection for the **table carpet** used on dressing tables, it evolved in the eighteenth century into a tabletop cover with a **valance** or frilled edge and a gathered petticoat that hung to the floor. A mirror cover or **drape** was often included. An early reference of 1696, from the *New World of English Words,* explains: 'Toilet, a kind of Table-cloth, or Carpet of Silk, Sattins, Velvet or Tissue, spread upon a Table in a Bed-chamber.' (Phillips, p.96.)

In 1683, the *London Gazette* advertised a notice: 'Stolen the 20th instant, a Toilet of blew Velvet, with a Gold and Silver Fringe' (no.1811/4). The use of fine fabrics explains the following combination from a 1705 French inventory: 'a small dressing table of firwood with its toilette comprising an underlay of silk material with an overlay of muslin with furbelows' (Thornton, 1984, p.382).

By the mid-eighteenth century, toilettes were apparently more extravagant. In 1761, Rolt described a 'toilet' as:

> A fine cloth of linen, silk or tapestry spread over the table in a bed-chamber or dressing room, to undress and dress upon. They are now made of satin, velvet, brocade, and point de France: but anciently

131. Toilet table design (T. Chippendale, The Gentleman and Cabinet Maker's Director, *1762)*

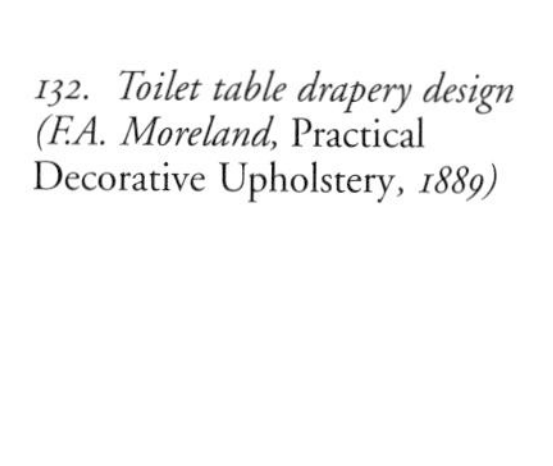

132. Toilet table drapery design (F.A. Moreland, Practical Decorative Upholstery, *1889)*

> were much plainer whence the name, which is, formed from the French, toilette a diminutive of toile, any thin stuff.

This taste was demonstrated in 1762, when Queen Charlotte was supplied with a **lace counterpane** for a bed and a matching toilette set. Priscilla Maceune charged for 'a suit of superfine Flanders point lace to cover all over a crimson sattin counterpane with deep falls and a gathered head to Do. Also to trim the bolsters and four pillows £2,699.00'. She also supplied 'a suit of the like lace to cover a toilet table compleat' (Walton, 1975, p.113).

The range of fabrics used is demonstrated by the following accounts. Chippendale shows two examples of toilettes in his *The Gentleman and Cabinet Maker's Director*, stating that 'the drapery may be silk damask, with gold fringes or tassels' (Plate cxviii). Chippendale also supplied Nostell with a 'petty coat for a toilet of your own tammy', and at Paxton he supplied 'a marcela quilted petticoat and cover' (Gilbert, 1978, p.59). The use of **Marseilles** quilting was also part of the commission undertaken by James Cullen for Hopetoun House. In 1768, he supplied a toilette with a petticoat of 'some brocaded silk or crimson silk damask fringed at the bottom, the top, covered with Marseils or other fine quilting made to the shape'. The description continues:

> The shade and outside petticoat is generally the finest sheer muslin (striped) or wrought & edged with flounced or puckered lace in which they mix narrow and broad Ribbons according to the fancy of the owner or performer. The Scarf over the Glass should be twice as long as the length from the Top of the Glass as it Stands in its place from the Table to the ground & half a yard more & when the scarf is double the middle half yard makes the hood… (Coleridge, 1966, p.154.)

Toilettes seem to have been made at home as well as professionally. In 1767, Mrs Delany wrote 'Your fancy about taking a gimp round the flowers on the toilet would be pretty, but too much work.' (*OED*)

By 1840, it appears that for some, at least, the toilette was simplified in its design. *The Workwoman's Guide* noted that:

> These are of various kinds; sometimes merely a piece of diaper of the proper size is used, at others a kind of Marseilles quilting made on purpose, and muslin or dimity trimmed with fringe or frills. Much depends on the shape of the toilet table; some have merely the cover laid on the top, others are bordered along the sides and fronts with frills or work. Some persons have merely a piece of oilcloth, the proper size, and bound with ribbon round the edge, upon their dressing tables and washing stands they look very neat and are very durable. (1840, p.182.)

While in 1854, the American author, Miss Leslie, suggested that:

> For a common bedroom, a toilet cover of fine buff-dyed cotton cloth, with a frill at the top to conceal the place where it is nailed on to the table, and set off with a purple or dark brown binding, looks infinitely better than might be supposed: and will appear clean much longer than one of white muslin. (1854, p.300.)

These less complicated designs for toilettes were not apparently universal. In 1878, Charles Eastlake protested,

> against the practice, which exists of encircling toilet-tables with a sort of muslin petticoat, generally stiffened by a crinoline of pink or blue calico. Something of the same kind may be occasionally seen twisted round the frame of the toilet-glass. They represent a milliner's notion of the 'pretty' and nothing more. (1878, p.212.)

In the same year that Eastlake was complaining, the opposite point of view was being expressed in the USA. Williams and Jones considered that a toilette-table 'is one of those tasteful additions to a lady's bedchamber or dressing room which is perhaps, more characteristic than any other portion of the furniture'. They suggested **dimity** for the top, and **cretonne**, Swiss or lace over coloured, glazed muslin for the skirt (1878, pp 95–103). Harriet Spofford went further by pointing out that 'muslin curtains, suspended from a pretty ornament close beneath the ceiling, falling and parting over the toilet table … have been in use for hundreds of years', because 'they save the glass from dust and specks, and are drawn before it, according to ancient usage, on occasion of a death in the family' (1878, p.208). In the same year, the British author, Lady Barker, suggested the use of **batiste** in conjunction with muslin as appropriate for summer **quilts**, toilette-tables, and **screen** material (1878, p.22).

However, they remained popular, as in 1887 toilette covers were described as 'small cloths, made for the covering of dressing tables, usually manufactured of marcella or piqué. They are also to be had in damask, of various dimensions, finished with common fringe and also by the better kinds of fringes, which are knotted' (Caulfeild & Saward, 1887, p.496).

In 1889, Moreland suggested that 'the dressing table can be made a very convenient and attractive addition to the furnishing of a chamber especially in a summer house, as its usual light and airy dressing is in keeping with the general treatment of the room for the season.' (1889, p.201.) Moreland further recommended 'plain or figured silks, cretonnes, chintz, printed sateen, cream or ecru madras trimmed with coloured ribbons or muslin with box pleated silk ribbon or soft ball fringe'. Moreland also noted that some women have suggested that dressing tables might be made from old packing cases or discarded tables, but thought that it was quite as economical for a carpenter to make a frame.

The taste for dressing table toilettes continued in the twentieth century, but there were some caveats about servicing them. Smithells, writing in 1950, suggested using a frilled valance and a **top cover** as well as drapes over the triple mirror, 'but as the drapes of the bed head and the dressing table will catch dust and need frequent washing, [they] should only be adopted by those who really think the frilliness worth the extra trouble' (p.162). According to the *Furnisher's Encyclopaedia* (Sheridan, 1955, p.433), 'Kidney shaped dressing tables with soft flowing skirts never go out of fashion'. It went on to warn against supplying quilted material for dressing table skirts, as it did not hang very well, and if made from glazed **chintz**, was not capable of being re-glazed.
See also **Muslin**, **Petticoat**, **Piqué**, **Toilet cloth**.

FURTHER READING

Leben, U. (2002). 'The toilette in the eighteenth century', *The Magazine Antiques,* 162, 3, pp 84–91.
Walton, K.-M. (1975). 'Queen Charlotte's dressing table', *Furniture History,* 11, pp 112–13.

Top cover
The name for the final material covers on upholstered work.

Tour de cheminée
A **pelmet**-like cloth used in seventeenth-century France, the Netherlands, and probably England, to hang from the edge of the chimney opening in order to deflect smoke.
See also **Chimney cloth**, **Valance**

Tour de lit
French term given to protective case **curtains** for an important bed.
See also **Bed protection**.

Tournai (aka Tournay)
Tournay (or in Flemish, Doornik) in Belgium has had a long association with textile production (see **Dornix**). In 1858, Simmonds applied the name 'Tournay' to 'a printed worsted material used for furniture' (*Dictionary of Trade Products*). Richard Munns, upholsterer and cabinet-maker of Oxford Street, London, had an advertisement for 'arabesque tournays' in October 1840 (*DEFM*, p.636).
See also **Tournai carpet**, **Tournay velvet carpet**.

Tournai carpet
Hand-knotted **pile** carpets, similar to the products of the **Savonnerie** in Paris, were produced in Tournai from the mid-eighteenth century, although there had been a weaving tradition there since at least the fourteenth century. By the late eighteenth century, there was an established business that sold high-quality carpets to wealthy clients across Europe. Napoleon particularly patronised the industry, which was dominated by the Lefebvre firm.

An English reference to Tournai carpet is made by Benjamin Mildmay, Earl Fitzwalter, who purchased 'a Tournay carpet sufficient to go round two beds' in January 1731 (Hefford, 1987, p.1).
See also **Tournai**, **Tournay velvet carpet**.

FURTHER READING

Sherrill, S. (2001). 'Carpets of Tournai' in Mertens, W. (ed.), *Transitory Splendour: Interior Textiles in Western Europe 1600–1900,* Antwerp: Hessenhuis Museum, Stadsbestuur, pp 323–32.

Tournay velvet carpet
A term for a **velvet carpet** 'with a pile of 3/16 inch … long' (Wingate, 1979, p.625). It was described as **plush** carpet in an American lawsuit of 1895 (USA Supreme Court, Beuttel v. Magone, 1895).
See also **Tournai**, **Tournai carpet**.

Tow
Tow is the shorter fibres of flax or **hemp**. After the heckling process in **linen** production, the line and tow are separated. The line is spun into linen yarn and the tow is used as a foundation in **upholstery** work, chiefly on seats and arms. It is a dense filling material that has poor resilience. It has been used for roll edges, first **stuffings** and for a skimmer in upholstery work. A 1735 bill to Temple Newsam included an item 'tow to make the rowls' (Gilbert, 1967, p.18).

Its reputation was acknowledged in the mid-nineteenth century. Sloan's *Homestead Architecture* noted that 'tow is also used in connection with hair in medium class goods, and is used alone in stuffing what is called Eastern or Yankee furniture' (1861, p.322).

In the later twentieth century, it was still used for upholstery foundations in the USA.

Tow is also the name for a bundle of untwisted man-made or natural fibres.
See also **Crash**, **Cretonne**, **Hemp**, **Towen**.

Towel
A cloth, usually of **linen**, **cotton** or **hemp**, for wiping something dry, especially for wiping the hands, face or person after washing or bathing. It also formerly included references to a table napkin or other cloth used at meals. Towel is often used with a prefix indicating its particular use: hand-towel, dish-towel, glass-towel, razor-towel, bath-towel, face-towel and kitchen-towel. The weaving process might also be indicated: for example, terry-towel, linen cotton **union**, plain-woven, twill, huckabuck, **honeycomb** or **diaper**. The lettered kind, which need a small **jacquard** or similar, have lettering in the cloth which might include the words kitchen, glass, teacloth, basin, lavatory or razor.
See also **Crash**, **Forfar**, **Glass towelling**, **Harden**, **Huckabuck**, **Macramé**, **Momie cloth**, **Ramie cloth**, **Terry**.

Towen
A term to describe a quality of seventeenth-century sheeting, woven from **tow**. William Coleman's 1635 inventory records 'fower pair of towen sheets xvjs' (Steer, 1969, p.71). The name was still in use during the eighteenth century.
See also **Sheet**.

Track
A generic term used to describe **curtain** suspensions.
See also **Railway**.

Train
The name given to the seventeenth-century **curtains** that hung from the bowl of a canopy bed. They were called 'trains' as they had to drag (French *trainer*) on the floor in order to have enough cloth to enclose the bed. The 1626 Cockesden inventory noted '2 longe traynes of green taffety sarcenet … [are] belonging to the canopy', while the Easton inventory of 1637, listed 'one crimson velvet canapie … with two rich

taffeta changeable trayned curtaynes to it' (Thornton, 1978, p.367). See also **Canopy**.

Transom curtain

A specially designed **curtain** intended to cover fanlights either in shirred, folded or radiating designs.

Transparent blind

See **Blind: Transparent/Painted**.

Trapunto

A term probably of Sicilian origin, from the Italian for 'quilting', that refers to a sewing/design method that only quilts in particular areas of the product. A raised or quilted effect is obtained, first by lining a fabric, and then by making running **stitches** with a double outline dependent upon the thickness of the **cord** to be inserted to create the raised effect. The cord is let into the back of the material and held in place by small stitches. The cord should fit tightly into its slot to create the raised effect on the surface of the material.

An alternative involves sections of **stuffing** pushed through the backing fabric between the threads or using cording threaded on a needle and pushed through the backing.

Baker says that 'A variation known as cording (also known as Italian, English, or Portuguese quilting) became popular… A single or double strand of cord or yarn is drawn through two parallel lines of quilting to produce the raised design.' (Baker, 1995, p.62)
See also **Quilting**.

FURTHER READING

Baker, M. (1995). 'Trapunto – a gift of light and shadow', *Piecework*, January/February, pp 60–65.

Traverse curtain

A medieval term for a **curtain** or **screen** that was placed crosswise or drawn across a room, hall or other space with the intention of dividing it for a range of uses. A reference from 1589 explains how 'the floor had in it sundry little divisions by curtains as traverses to serve for several rooms where they might change their garments' (Puttenham, *The Art of English Poesie, OED*).

Henry VIII possessed quantities of traverses, including one of 'redde and yellow satten lined with buckram being four yards square very worn and stayned' (Edwards, 1964, p.619). In 1601, Hardwick Hall had 'a travice like a screen covered with violet-coloured cloth layde about with black lace' (Boynton, 1971, p.31). In 1609, the Lumley inventory listed 'one large traverse of purple taffetie' (Cust, 1918, p.40).

The name 'traverse' has been used in the twentieth century in North America to describe hanging curtains and the rods they hang upon (**traverse rods**).

Traverse pole

See **Cornice pole**.

Traverse rod

A **curtain** suspension method that uses metal rods and integrated pull **cords**. The name is particularly associated with the USA. Webster & Parkes described traverse rods: 'this curtain rod and pulleys may be made of hard wood instead of brass. It is to be observed that each curtain must be large enough to lap over the other some inches in the centre to exclude the draught.' (1844, p.251.)
See also **French rod**.

Trellis cloth

A stout or coarse kind of cloth that in later use was often synonymous with **buckram** or **sackcloth**. In 1706, Phillips defined trellis, as 'also Cloth, otherwise call'd Buckram' (*New World of English Words*). Simmonds gave a different definition in 1858, in his *Dictionary of Trade Products:* 'Trellis, a kind of coarse quilted linen, imported into France'.

Trellis fringe

See **Fringe: Trellis**.

Trimming

Since ancient times, textile trimmings and metal fasteners have been used to decorative effect on furniture. Trimmings were at the height of opulent development in the seventeenth century, particularly in France (**passementerie**). These very elaborate and costly trimmings often completely concealed the furniture framework. The perfected hand-executed techniques of the seventeenth century have been copied in the following centuries, but the costs are prohibitive as the hand finishing is very labour intensive. In the eighteenth century, tastes were simpler: flat braid and dome-headed nails predominated as complements to elaborately carved furniture or to the clean lines of neo-classical furnishing types. In the nineteenth century, industrial developments made elaborate textile trimmings more widely available as some processes were mechanised; however, their popularity declined with the loss of status of elaborate trims.

Trimmings can evolve for practical reasons: for example, a fringe formed of knotted-off **warps**, which prevent a textile from unravelling. Trimmings have been used to conceal details of construction (seams, raw edges, **tack** lines); to hold back **curtains** or hangings (**tiebacks**); to secure loose fillings in buttoned or tufted seats, **cushions** or **mattresses**; and as fastenings joining one piece to another (corners of **valances** or **table covers**).

Trimmings are also used to accentuate the lines of furniture or room hangings. Cord or decorative nails may be used to draw the eye or simply to embellish and enrich the appearance. In the seventeenth century, nails were often of several sizes and might be clustered to decorative effect. In the eighteenth century, close nailing might be used in multiple or shaped lines within the depth of a rail. During the nineteenth century, items such as **shawl bordering**, which was a ready-made printed border, were applied to curtains and covers. In the later twentieth century, ready-woven **borders** were applied in a similar way.

Trimmings are known by names which vary by country, shape, function, scale and materials type. However, they can be described generically: (a) flat tapes/braids; (b) cords (includes piping/welt); (c) fringes; (d) tassels (parts known as mould and skirt); (e) tufts (includes buttons and rosettes); and (f) metal trims (includes decorative nails, mouldings, bosses).

Materials and techniques found in trimmings are diverse and are used singularly or in combinations. Lustrous threads may be worked over metal wire, wood moulds or skin bases. Metal threads, glass beads or gelatine sequins may be included. **Top cover** materials may be worked around lead mouldings with integral nails; these are bent to shape and tapped into position. Top covering materials may also be used over cord to form piping or welting. Button moulds may be covered in the same way.

The techniques employed in making trimmings include weaving, braiding, **lace** (includes needle-made, bobbin-made, and crochet), knotting, knitting and embroidery, which includes **appliqué** and **cutwork**.

For particular trimming types, see **Braid**, **Cord**, **Fringe**, **Passementerie**, **Piping**, **Ruche**, **Tape**, **Tassel**, **Tufting**.

FURTHER READING
Posselt, E.A. (1916). *Manufacture of Narrow Woven Fabrics: Ribbons, Trimmings, Edgings, etc,* Philadelphia and London: Sampson, Low, Marston.

Trucking cloth
A material used for **blankets**, **bed curtains** and **coverlets** in seventeenth-century inventories, especially in America. Also known as duffields or shag. Trucking refers to trading, as this material was often used as a bartering cloth in North America.

Tufted carpet
The basis of the tufted **carpet** is the needling of yarns into a foundation cloth, which are then anchored in some particular way. The **candlewick bedspread** making process was an inspiration for the later carpet work. Early attempts at producing tufted-type carpets by Hodgam and Wyckoff were patented in the USA on 1 May 1849:

> By our invention a plush napped or tufted surface is superimposed upon and attached to a plain surface or base of plain cloth with the aid of a glue or cement composed of Indian rubber, gutta-percha or ... other gums and resins producing rugs, carpeting, mats ... having a plush napped or tufted surface. (US Patent no.6412.)

The real origins of commercial tufted carpets were found in the USA during the 1930s, where the first mechanised tufting machine was developed for the production of bedspreads. The single-needle commercial sewing machine was adapted so that it would tuft thick yarns into unbleached **muslin** without tearing the fabric, and an attached knife would cut the loop. Machines quickly developed with four, then eight, twenty-four and more needles to make the parallel rows of tufting for bedspreads. The same process, with **cotton** yarns and fabric, was used to create **mats** and **rugs**. The development of the tufted carpet was immensely aided by developments post-World War II. These included the development of **broadlooms**, continuous filament yarns and technical developments in dyeing, printing and processing.

Introduced in 1947, **nylon** yarns grew steadily to dominate the market for tufted carpets for some time. **Polyester** was first used in 1965 and was soon followed by **polypropylene** yarns. Other yarn types have since been used. In 1950, only 10 per cent of all carpet and rug products were tufted, and 90 per cent were woven. By the end of the twentieth century, tufted products accounted for more than 90 per cent of the total made.

Tufted carpet was initially limited to plain yarn effects but, gradually, printing white carpet improved so that by 1995 fully patterned tufted carpets were being produced in England by Ryalux Carpets.

FURTHER READING
Attfield, J. (1994). 'The tufted carpet in Britain: its rise from the bottom of the pile 1952–70', *Journal of Design History*, 7, 3, pp 205–16.
Ward, D. (1969). *Tufting*, Manchester: Textile Business Press.

Tufted cotton rug
See **Rug**.

Tufted sacking
The 1601 Hardwick inventory lists window **curtains** that were made from 'tufted sacking' (Boynton, 1971, p.23).

Tufting
A method used by upholsterers to ensure that the fillings of **cushions** and **mattresses** remain level. **Cords** were inserted through the thickness of the pad and held by a bunch of threads that stopped the cord being pulled through the pad. This technique was introduced in England and America in the mid-eighteenth century, and it suited the flatter, squarer design of their chairs, rather than the more fashionable domed seats favoured in France. Sometimes the process was worked under the **top cover**, although **buttoning** might mark this. In the later nineteenth century, the diamond tufting method was developed (see below).

Loudon's *Encyclopaedia* discusses mahogany dining chairs with **leather** seats which 'are quilted, but, instead of tufts, small rings are used, covered with the same leather as the chair; these rings being found to look as, and wear better than, tufts of silk; at the same time, they do not harbour dust' (1839, p.1049).

Biscuit tufting
The tufting technique that demonstrates a square arrangement of buttons on the surface of the upholstered object is called 'biscuit tufting'.

Diamond tufting
A tufting technique that creates a regular decorative diamond-shaped design, usually on the backs and seats of **upholstery**. The 'extra' cloth used was often sewn into **pleats**.

Jiffy tufting
A ready-made tuft and cord, which can simply and speedily be inserted through a mattress or cushion by using a specially adapted needle to make the insertions. It was widely used on mattresses and cushions in the twentieth century.

Looped tufting
A form of fixing intended to retain **upholstery fillings**. Introduced in the seventeenth century, it was simply a loop of thread that held a tuft of fabric or **linen**, to even the strain on the surface fabric. It was later superseded by buttoning in upholstery, but remained a feature of mattresses.

Machine tufting
The demand for buttoned furniture ensured that a development in devising templates (tufting boards) would further extend into tufting machines. For furniture use, these machines or presses were generally designed to clamp together the top material and filling, and then button it through with pins and washers. This built-up 'blanket' of backing, **stuffing** and material top cover could then be applied to a sprung frame with much more speed and ease than the traditional hand-layering process. Naturally, this encouraged the division of labour and a consequent reduction in the skill required for upholstering chairs and sofas. Machine processes for tufting were developed in the USA in the 1890s. The Novelty Tufting Machine by the Freschl Co, which mechanically tufted backs and seats of upholstery jobs, was apparently operated by boys, and was alleged to have taken the place of 25 skilled workers. In the USA, these machines were nicknamed 'hay-balers'.

Mattress tufting
A method of firmly holding fillings in a mattress using prepared tufts. It is simply done by passing a needle and strong thread through the thickness of the mattress, catching little tufts of **worsted** yarns or circles of red leather, then returning it, and tying off the end firmly. The spacing is maintained by letting the **stitches** fall opposite the middle of the previous row of stitches. Once fitted, the tufts hide the stitch and ornament the surface.

Pleated tufting
A version of diamond tufting.
See also **Candlewick**.

Tulle
A term that, in England, refers to a fine **bobbin net** of **silk** used for veils, scarves and millinery purposes. The French use the term to mean all machine-made **lace**, which is based on the intertwisted **net** made from the bobbin-net machine. The word appears to be derived from the town of Tulle in France.

Turkey leather
A seventeenth-century term for inlaid gilded **leather**, originally of Turkish or north African origin. Evelyn recorded seeing 'a cabinet of Maroquin or Turkey leather so curiously inlaid with other leathers, and gilding, that the workman demanded for it 800 livres' (*Diary of John Evelyn*, 25 May 1651). In 1669, turkey leather was used to cover some chairs in Oxford and, in 1682, the Cowdray inventory listed a dozen chairs in turkey leather (Thornton, 1978, p.359). Turkey leather also refers to leather tawed (softened) with oil before the hair side is removed.
See also **Gilt leather**, **Leather**, **Morocco**.

Turkey work
A cloth that is made as **carpet** with a **pile** composed of knotted **wool** yarns using a turkey knot on a single **linen warp** and double linen weft. Once the weaving process was completed, the cloth was removed from the loom, the edges were finished, the pile clipped tidy and the whole was washed to soften the cloth. It has been widely used for **upholstery**.

Early references to turkey work (as carpet) occur in the sixteenth century. In the 1509 inventory of Edmund Dudley, there are '23 cussins of carpett work' and '3 coverings for cussins of carpet worke' (*Archaeologia*, LXXI, 1921, p.40). In the 1588 Kenilworth inventory there is a reference to 'turquoy carpette of Norwiche work' (Halliwell, 1854, p.147). The Hardwick Hall 1601 inventory lists a 'foote carpet of turkeywork in the withdrawing chamber', and a 'carpet of fine turkey work for a square table cover'. Turkey work was distinguished from carpets from Turkey. In 1602, the Countess of Bedford mentions 'one turkey carpet of English making' and 'two window turkey carpets of my own making' (Boynton, 1971, pp 27, 29). In the dining chamber at Cockesden in 1610, there was 'a side table with thereupon a very good Turkey carpet large' (Thornton, 1978, p.381). It was not long, however, before they were used on the floor, as the Easton Lodge inventory lists 'little turkey carpitts for foote carpets or sideboards' (ibid.). While in 1614, the Earl of Northampton inventoried a 'wallnuttree cupboard with a Turkie cupboard clothe' (Beard, 1997, p.287).

The height of fashion for turkey work appears to have been the latter half of the seventeenth century. Randle Holme wrote regarding the furnishing of a dining room: 'a turkey table cover or carpet of cloth or leather printed. Chaires and stooles of turkeywork, Russia or calves leather, cloth or stuffe or of needlework.' (1688, Book III, Chapter XIV, p.15.) In 1667, Pepys fell out with Mrs Martin over 'her expensefulness, having bought turkeywork chairs' (*The Diary of Sameul Pepys*, 14 April 1667). However, she was clearly fashionable in her taste. The inventory taken upon the death of retailer, William Ridges, in 1670 lists '10 doz of Turkeywork back seats for chayres' made to a standard size and '1 doz and ½ of fine Turkeywork chayres' in his shop stock (Beard, 1997, p.16).

During 1683, it was claimed by the woollen industry that 'there were yearly made and vended in this Kingdom above five thousand dozen of Sett-work chairs (commonly called turkeywork chairs, though made in England) … and great quantities of these chairs were also vended and sent yearly beyond the seas' (Symonds, 1934, p.180). Following this claim, in 1689 a petition for the encouragement of the woollen manufacturers of England noted that 'there has been a very great consumption of wool used in making Set-work cushions of chairs, couches, carpets called Turky-work made in Yorkshire'. This referred to a petition against cane seat chair-makers, who were seen to be stealing the trade enjoyed by English wool-workers. The cane chair-makers retorted by pointing out the problems of cloth upholstery, including 'the dust, worms and moths, which inseparably attend turkeywork, Serge and other stuff-chairs and Couches…' (Symonds, 1951a, pp 13–14). Turkey work continued to be used into the early eighteenth century. For example, chairs purchased between 1704 and 1733 for the House of Commons included over 150 with turkey work covers. By the 1730s, however, it had begun to lose its popularity although, in 1751, Samuel Johnson noted how 'a large screen, which I had undertaken to adorn with turkey-work against winter, made very slow advances' (*The Rambler*, no.84, 8, *OED*).

It is noteworthy that chair frames were often made to fit previously prepared turkey work covers and there is evidence that the covers were exported widely.
See also **Norwich work**, **Set work**.

FURTHER READING

Hughes, G.B. (1965). 'The Englishness of turkeywork', *Country Life*, 11 February, p.309.
Swain, M. (1987). 'The turkeywork chairs of Holyrood House' in Cooke, E.S. (ed.), *Upholstery in America and Europe From the Seventeenth Century to World War I*, New York: Norton, pp 51–64.
Symonds, R.W. (1934). 'Turkeywork, beech and japanned chairs', *Connoisseur*, 393, April, pp 221–7.
Symonds, R.W. (1951). 'English cane chairs', *Connoisseur*, 127, March, pp 8–15.

Tussah (aka Tussore)
A coarse, browny wild silk produced by the larvae of *Antheraea paphia* and other species of wild silkworm found in and imported from India. The name is derived from the Hindu (and Urdu) *tasar*, meaning 'shuttle'. Wild silk is distinguished from domesticated versions in that it needs to be spun to produce a filament, as the larvae break the threads when they hatch.

An early reference from 1619 mentions tussah as 'a kind of Bengal stuff of silke called tessar' (Foster, 1906, p.112). By 1620 at least, it was used in furnishings: **quilts** of Sutgonge were noted as being 'lined partly with taffeta and partly with tessur' (ibid. p.198).

In the later nineteenth century, 'the silks now generally recognized as tussahs, are a description of wild silk [etc]' (Cobb, 'Silk' in, Bevan (ed.), 1876, vol.V, p.171). The material appears to have been mainly used as a dress fabric but this did not stop Mrs Orrinsmith recommending in her book, *The Drawing Room*, that: 'Indian Tussore, the silken fabric used for dresses, makes exceedingly pretty curtains, and when slightly lined is an effective ground for embroidery' (1877, p.71). In the Paris Exposition of 1878, Thomas Wardle promoted the printing of 'tasar' silk, where the waste was demonstrated as being eminently suitable for spinning into yarns for clothing, **rugs**, **upholstery** and **trimmings**. In 1887, *The Dictionary of Needlework* explained that tusah silks 'are of Indian manufacture and all are wild or raw silks, plain made, and without any cord or woven patterns, although some are stamped or printed in England from Indian blocks' (Caulfeild & Saward, 1887, p.504).

Although Caulfeild & Saward did not refer to furnishing use, it was utilised in the early twentieth century for **curtains**.

By 1923, tussah was defined as 'silk, [with a] dull luster, slightly stiff, lightweight, easy to clean, excellent for moderate-priced draperies' (Dyer, *c*.1923, p.202).
See also **Gingham**, **Pongee**, **Silk**.

Tweed
A twilled woollen cloth of rather rough surface, and of great variety of texture, originally made in the south of Scotland (usually with two or more colours combined in the same yarn); inferior kinds are made of **wool** with a mixture of **shoddy** or **cotton**. Tweed is the Scottish name for twill and is sometimes known as 'tweel'. In 1847, McCulloch noted that 'Narrow cloths, of various kinds, known by the name of Tweeds, are extensively produced at Galashiels and Jedburgh, but especially at the former. They also used to be produced in considerable quantities at Hawick.' (*A descriptive and statistical account of the British Empire,* 3rd edition, I, p.667, *OED.*) In 1887, *The Dictionary of Needlework* described tweed as a 'woollen cloth woven of short lengths of wool, and lightly felted and milled, the yarn being dyed before woven. It is soft, durable, and flexible being unmixed with either shoddy or cotton.' (Caulfeild & Saward, 1887, p.505.)

Tweed is a similar cloth to the **homespun** Cheviot and Shetland. They are the same in texture, yarn, weight, feel and use. Originally, tweed was made only from different-coloured stock-dyed fibres, producing various colour effects. There are also some closely woven, smoother, softer yarn fabrics, and many monotone tweeds. Tweed may be woven in **plaid**, **check**, stripe or other patterns. On occasion, tweed may be used for upholstery.

The Book of Soft Furnishing said that tweeds 'have been discovered to suit admirably the clear simple lines of modern furniture' (French, 1937, p.138).
See also **Furnishing tweed**, **Harris tweed**.

Twill
See **Weaving**.

Twilt
Twilt is a term for a quilt or bedcover. An early reference is from a will of 1538 in which the deceased wrote 'I wyll the bed, and the twylt couerlyt be solde' (*Bury Wills,* Camden Society, p.134). In 1556, a Durham merchant, William Dalton, had 'a feather bed, a twilt, a happing [coverlet] and a bolster' (Wright, 1871, p.480). Later, in 1641, the Countess of Arundel in Tart Hall listed 'Twilt carpets (whereof one very fine) and … an Indian crimson silk twilt lined with yellow sarcenet with curtains and double vallance to the same'. She also had 'a folding bedstead of wood standing upon a leather carpet, thereon two large course flocke twilts' (Cust, 1911, pp 99–100). The name twilt was still current into the early twentieth century in northeast England but is now obsolete.
See also **Quilt**.

Twine
A form of **cord** made from flax or **hemp** used for **upholstery** work. Twines are characterised by being composed of two or more yarns. Various types of twine used include fine twine for **buttoning**, **stitching** twine, and **laid cord** for lashing.

Tycoon rep
Brown & Gates explain that it was 'a cotton and wool dress fabric. [The name Tycoon] applies to the gay-colored patterns … imitations of those of Eastern fabrics such as cashmere, which it resembles… Its manufacture was introduced into the United States from England … about 1840' (1872, p.210).

Although generally seen as a dress fabric in the nineteenth century, American authors, Williams and Jones considered it,

> [a] really valuable material for persons of limited means. This material comes in rich colors and … beautiful patterns, some of which possess a truly Oriental character in design … and soft warmth in appearance. It is now used extensively for hangings and upholstering, and when lined hangs in rich soft folds that rival many a more costly fabric. (1878, pp 14 and 53.)

See also **Rep**.

Umbrello
A sunshade fixed above an external window. Known in the seventeenth century, it was defined in 1706 as 'a Wooden Frame cover'd with Cloth or Stuff, to keep off the Sun from a Window' (Phillips, *The New World of Words*). Upholsterers supplied these shades as part of their furnishing services. In 1736, William Bradshaw supplied the Earl of Stanhope with '2 spring umbrellows and rod' for £2.10s.0d. (Beard, 1997, p.289.) They were still in demand in the later eighteenth century.

Undercover
An undercover is a generic term for an **upholstery** foundation material such as **linen**, **muslin** or **sackcloth** that is used under the finishing **top cover**.

Under curtain (aka glass curtain or sub curtain)
A set of slight, thin, often sheer **curtains** used under the main curtains to soften light. From early in the nineteenth century, under curtains were used to soften the main **drapes** of a window treatment and assist in creating the layered effect (especially in the **French drapery** style). In 1808, George Smith suggested that drawing room draperies should have 'under curtains of muslin or superfine cassimere' (1808, p.1). He later explained that they were intended to 'break the strength of the light, without entirely secluding the cheering effect produced from the solar rays' (1826). They were shirred onto a rod and hung straight to the floor or, if intended to be looped back, were longer so that the fabric touched the floor during the open periods and bunched onto the floor when closed. Muslins or laces, either plain or embroidered, were common fabrics for this treatment. These curtains were superseded by half-length under curtains from around 1850 onwards.
See also **Glass curtain**, **Lace**, **Muslin**, **Sash curtain**, **Sheer curtain**.

Underfelt
A specific form of underlay that uses a felted product to act as a support beneath a **carpet** or, on occasion, under a **tablecloth**. During 1865, Marsh and Jones supplied '257 square yards of grey felt to go under carpets', for Sir Titus Salt (Boynton, 1967, p.82). In 1895, Harrods, the London store, advertised 'Paper and felt for laying under carpets: Underfelt 0/10 and 1/1 per yard.' (*Harrods Catalogue,* p.1487.)

However, these underfelts were more like felt textiles rather than the thick sandwich of **jute** web into which is needled quantities of **hair** and **wool shoddy**, etc. They were comparatively easy to lay, and relatively inexpensive. Felt underlays were also recommended for use with seamed-up **body carpet**, as the seams bedded into the felt. Also known as needlefelt.
See also **Felt**, **Underlay**.

Underlay (aka Lining)

Underlays are essentially sheets of material laid beneath a carpet or other main floorcovering, for the protection and support. They may also be used in conjunction with **spring** bed bases and **mattresses**.

The range of materials used for flooring underlays has varied widely over the centuries and has included **straw**, **drugget**, **felt**, rubber, paper and **grass**. Underlay is used to lengthen the life of a carpet, as it absorbs pressure from furniture and footsteps; it also acts as a sound absorber and insulator for the rooms in which it is used.

Straw was probably the earliest and easiest to acquire and lay. In 1795, Harewood House inventory listed a 'Brussels Carpet with India Matting under it' in the Great Hall. In 1846, it was still being used. In her *Treatise on Domestic Economy,* Catherine Beecher recommended that instead of using straw for a carpet underlay, which made the carpet 'wear out in spots', straw matting should be used since it made carpets 'last much longer, as it is smooth and even and the dust sifts through it'. Further evidence of the use of straw underlay is found in the following declaration: 'It is cheap to lay down an undressed floor, covering the joints with slips of brown paper, and then spreading old newspapers, instead of straw, under the carpet' (Dwyer, 1856, p.50). As late as 1878, in the American publication, *Beautiful Homes,* a range of carpet underlays was discussed, including paper, straw and grass:

> In this country, clean straw, smoothly spread, or even sweet well-dried grass will be found a most pleasant strata, upon which to spread the carpet and it is astonishing how very greatly these linings add to the apparent depth, heaviness and richness of the carpet. (Williams & Jones, 1878, p.49.)

Paper was considered appropriate for underlay and it appears that there were a number of varieties. *Ward & Lock's Home Book* suggested 'Taplow Mills Brown paper' as a carpet underlay. In the 1880s in England, the choice of paper underlays included 'drab felt called underfelt', 'coarse hessian', 'Glenpatrick or wadded brown paper', 'Boulinikon, a thick soft paper', and 'ordinary stout brown paper' (Maple and Co, 1884). The trade name of Cedar Felt was used for an improved paper felt underlay, designed especially for carpets in the early twentieth century.

The American authors, Williams & Jones, also discussed what appears to have been a new underlay type: 'The sponge carpet linings, chemically prepared to prevent moths, produce a delightful elastic softness … but where unavailable, felting paper or even several thicknesses of newspapers will answer the purpose' (1878, p.49). In their catalogue of 1895, the American retailers, Montgomery Ward, sold 35 inch (89 cm) wide **carpet lining** made from **jute** or **cotton** fibres that were sewn between outer covers of paper.

One early twentieth-century type was made chiefly of cow hair with an inner layer of **burlap**. After the 1930s, this hair was mixed with rubberised jute. In the USA, synthetic carpet underlay is made by needle punching off-grade carpet fibres.

After World War II, natural rubber or styrene and butadiene rubber underlay was developed as a suitable product for rubber manufacturers to divert their capacity. The underlay that was produced was a cellular, sponge-like cushioning material. The rubber manufacturers also used recycled rubber crumb to make an underlay. Developments that are more recent include **polyurethane** foams, either as the prime material or bonded to a substrate. The bonded process uses off-cuts and waste from the prime uses of polyurethane foams and recycles them into floor underlay or as a cushioning.

Bed underlay

Underlays were also used as soft pads, designed to cover the wire support and protect the filled mattress. The 1907 Army & Navy Stores catalogue offered for sale 'Moth proof Cotton underlay to go between wire bottom of bed and mattress' (275/2). These are still produced and are now used to protect mattresses from the rubbing effects of wooden-slatted bed frames.

See also **Bed mat**, **Felt**, **Foam-backed carpet**, **Rubber-backed carpet**, **Tufted carpet**, **Underfelt**.

Union

Union textiles are woven from a combination of **linen** and **cotton** yarns, or from cotton and some other yarns such as **wool**, **silk** or **jute**. The term appears to have been introduced in the nineteenth century. In 1844, George Dodd noted that 'a mixture of flax and cotton [is] called union' (British Manufactures. The *Textile Manufactures of Great Briain,* vol.V, p.167). Its quality was seen as inferior to pure linen. According to Henry Mayhew 'then we had an Irish linen, an imitation, you know, a kind of Union, which we call double twist. Linen of good quality used to be extensively hawked, but from 1820 to 1825, or later the hawkers got to deal in an inferior quality, unions.' (1861–2, vol.I, p.378; also vol.II, p.376.)

In 1887, *The Dictionary of Needlework* described unions as being particularly suitable for **blinds**:

> Much dressed and stiffened and chiefly used for linings and window blinds. The width is regulated by inches and the size required to fit the various widths of window frames are always to be had. In procuring union cloths for window blinds, it is advisable to purchase inferior kinds, well glazed; as they do not bear washing satisfactorily, and when soiled should be replaced with new ones. (Caulfeild & Saward, 1887, p.507.)

In the twentieth century, printed union cloths have been widely used for loose covers.

See also **Crewel and crewelwork**, **Taffeta**.

Upholstery

The work and materials used in the covering and stuffing of furniture, the fitting up of soft furnishings, **drapery**, bed hangings, etc. in a home.

All seat upholstery consists of four basic elements: the frame, the supporting system, the padding or cushioning, and the outer cover. Although textiles and various fillings had been used to make **cushions** and **squabs** since the Middle Ages, it was not until the sixteenth century that anything like true upholstered furniture was made, as the peripatetic nature of life among the upper classes was not conducive to fixed furnishings. When they had established a more sedentary way of life, the demand for comfort grew rapidly and a range of upholstered articles began to meet their needs. Chair backs and seats were covered with fabric and some examples had the whole frame covered with cloth. Sir John Harrington noted:

> Would it not become the state of the chamber to have easy quilted and lyned forms and stooles for the lords and ladies to sit on which fashion is now taken up in every merchant's hall as great plank forms that two yeomen can scant remove out of their places, and waynscot stools so hard that since great breeches were layd aside, men can skant endewr to sitt upon. (Jourdain, 1924, p.194.)

Upholstery was a combination of the long-established wooden-framed chairs; the girth webbing derived from animal harnessing; the quilted

133. Upholstery showing pleated wall fabric and built-in Turkey work (T. Sheraton, The Cabinet Maker and Upholsterer's Drawing Book, *1793)*

padding used by armourers for protection within suits of armour; and applied decorative textiles. The techniques of upholstery, and the four basic elements, were well known by 1588. The reference in a steward's account to the making up of stools with '2 dussen of gyrthwebe for 3s., 700 garnishing nails for 1s 9d, four pounds of deer hair at 1s 4d., nine skins, and fringe at 11s.' indicated this well (Clabburn, 1988, p.148). Less than 100 years later, Randle Holme explained the process of making a chair fully:

> Girth it, is to bottom it with girth webb, stret drawn and crossed.
> Canvice it, is to nail the canvice on the top of the stool or chair frame, over the girth webb.
> Rowle it, is to put rowls on the top edges.
> Stuffing, is to stuff it with hay, wool, flocks or feathers.
> Fringing, is to nail the fringe about the stool seat at the sides.
> The seat is that place sitten on.
> Backing is to nail the back on a chair suitable to the seat.
> Garnishing is the finishing with brass nails.
> (1688, 1, Book 3, p.97.)

The early techniques of upholstering were simple but workmanlike. Webbing, **canvas** and a variety of stuffing materials were employed to make up the seat or back. By the Restoration, most fashionable families were employing upholsterers to supply comfortable seating and other furnishings, often decorated with elaborate **trimmings**. During the mid-eighteenth century, the upholstery procedures followed a similar pattern. Webbing was stretched to form an interlaced support over which was fixed **hessian**. Curled hair was laid onto this, and stitched through to the webbing to prevent excessive movement. A roll edge was made by fixing a tube of stuffing material to the front rail to maintain the shape at this wear point. A layer of **linen** was fixed over the hair, and then the final **top cover** was close fitted. In these systems, the filling quality was all-important. Hay, **wool** and hair were common, but there were also various attempts to develop alternative fillings. The ideas ranged from feather cushions to pigs' bladders filled with air. Tufting, a technical development that was originally meant to stabilise the fillings, soon turned into a design feature.

Loose seats and backs were also introduced because the often-elaborate mouldings made it impossible to fix covers tightly. In addition, it meant that seats could be re-upholstered, or removable covers could be used for the various seasons.

Springs, originating in the requirements for carriage suspension, found their first use in chamber or exercising horses. Some nineteenth-century American sofas exist with iron coil springs stapled directly to the board or slatted bottoms in this manner. The resultant upholstery work was inevitably heavier and less resilient than the conventional methods of using webbing, but it enabled spring upholstery to become available to a lower level of the market.

Whatever processes were devised to simplify the methods of spring stuffing, the problem for chair manufacturers still remained: the full upholstering of an easy chair or sofa was a skilled trade that successfully resisted mechanisation for a long time. The most difficult parts consisted of the tying of the spring bed and the processes of even stuffing and tufting. However, techniques were invented to assist in the making of upholstered chairs. The first was simplifying the setting of springs in the interior seat. A simple solution to the seat-springing problem was to make a spring unit, which just had to be inserted into the frame. The sewing of covers was aided by the use of the industrial sewing machine, but otherwise it seemed that the mechanical assistance that became available in other parts of furniture-making was not possible with upholstery.

There was also an attempt to mechanise other parts of the upholstery process. In 1878, it was reported that a Paul Roth of New York was exhibiting machinery that would produce a stitched edge, pack the hair into a seat and tie the springs. This was not always appreciated: 'The modern upholsterer pads and puffs his seats as though they were to form the furniture of a lunatic's cell.' (Wharton & Codman, 1897, p.128.)

It is clear that the internal spring revolutionised upholstery practice and design in the nineteenth century. During the twentieth century, the natures of all of these elements have changed in varying degrees. Perhaps the most significant change has been the gradual use of ready-made parts such as spring units, needled and layered fillings on paper backings, foam and polyether cushioning all cut to size, as well as ready-made frame sections and the pneumatic staple gun, all of which meant that the skills of an upholsterer changed.

The technical changes in upholstery have been related to both the internal structure and the external coverings. At the beginning of the century, the spiral spring was supreme but, in the 1930s, tension springs were introduced into Germany and England. This released the designer from having to create a deep section to a chair to accommodate the spiral springs: he could produce a more elegant easy chair whilst retaining the benefits of metal springing. In 1929, Dunlop patented the development of **latex** rubber cushioning. When made up into cushions, this became an ideal partner to the tension-sprung chair. Post-war developments included the four-point suspension (one-piece rubber **platform**) and the introduction of **rubber webbing** by Pirelli. Both these processes hastened the demise of the traditional spring until the introduction of serpentine metal springs, which enabled manufacturers to produce a traditional-looking upholstery range without the cost of a fully sprung interior. Metals were also utilised by designers like Ernest Race, who created new lightweight organic-shaped chair and sofa frames from metal rods.

Plastics also earned a place in post-war upholstery with the introduction of polyether and **polyester** foams for cushions and padding. Developments continued with substitutes for most traditional materials, e.g. man-made **fibrefill** in place of **cotton**-fibre wrap. External coverings have been revolutionised by the use of **PVC**-coated fabrics

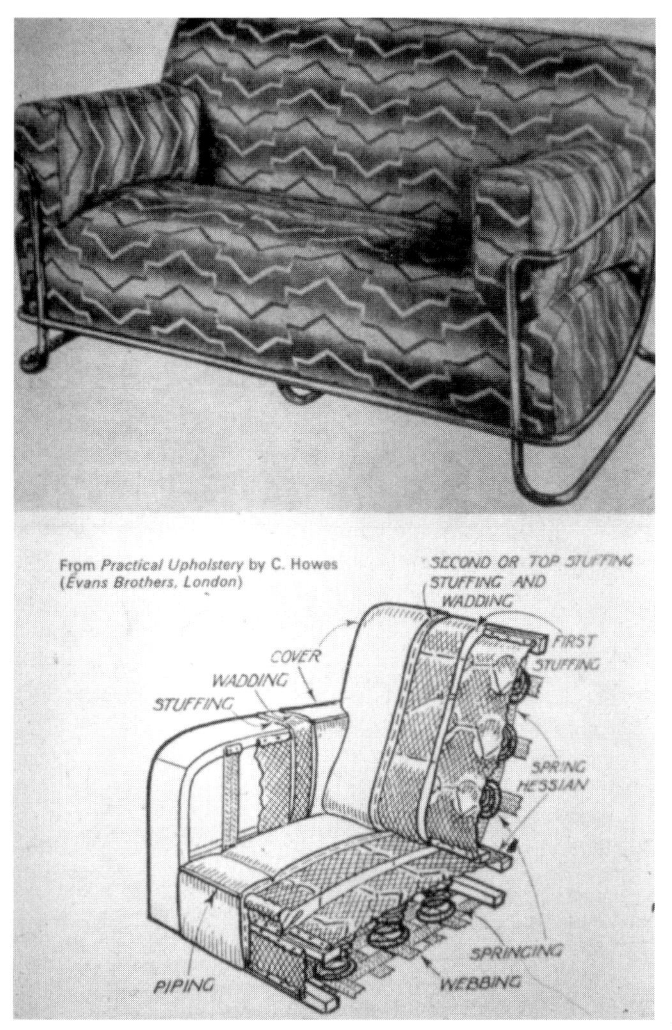

134. Upholstery process, c.*1950 (C. Howes,* Practical Upholstery*)*

that were themselves a substitute for the earlier **oilcloths**. Although upholstery design for the high street market has remained stubbornly traditional, a variety of innovations has been introduced in the manufacturing processes. These include frames made from particleboard or plywood, pre-formed plastic arm, wing and leg sections, and even complete plastic frames for 'Queen Anne' chairs.

See also **Buttoning**, **Carpet upholstery**, **Edge treatment**, **Foam**, **Four-point platform**, **Hair**, **Mattress**, **Pane**, **Pull-over edge**, **Rolled edge**, **Rubber webbing**, **Spring**, **Stitch**, **Stuffing**, **Tufting**, **Upholstery filling**, **Upholstery fixing**, **Upholstery technique**, **Van Dyke**, **Webbing**.

FURTHER READING

Anderson, M. & Trent, R. (1993). 'A catalogue of American easy chairs', *American Furniture,* pp 213–34.

Bast, H. (1947). *New Essentials of Upholstery,* New York: Bruce.

Beard, G. (1997). *Upholsterers and Interior Furnishing in England 1530–1840,* London: Yale.

Bimont, J.-F. (1770). *Principes de l'art du tapissier,* Paris: Lotte L'Aîné.

Bitmead, R. (1876). *Practical Upholsterer and Cutter-out,* London: C. Lockwood and Sons, and other editions.

Bland, S. (1995). *Take a Seat, the Story of Parker-Knoll 1834–1994,* Whittlebury: Baron Birch for Quotes Ltd.

Cooke, E.S. (ed.) (1987). *Upholstery in America and Europe From the Seventeenth Century to World War I,* New York: Norton.

Crofton, J.S. (1834). *The London Upholsterer's Companion,* London: The Author.

Garnier-Audiger, A. (1830). *Manuel du tapissier, decorateur, etc,* Paris: Roret.

Grier, K. (1988). *Culture and Comfort, People, Parlours and Upholstery,* New York: Strong Museum.

Houston, J.F. (1993). *Featherbedds and Flock Bedds, Notes on the History of the Worshipful Company of Upholders,* Sandy: Three Tents Press.

Michie, A.H. (1985). 'Upholstery in all its branches: Charleston, 1725–1820', *Journal of Early Southern Decorative Arts,* XI, 2.

Nothelfer, K. (1942). *Das Sitzmöbel. Ein Fachbuch für Polsterer, Shulbauer,* Ravensburg: Otto Maier Verlag.

Ossut, C. (1994). *Le siège et sa garniture,* Paris: Vial.

Passeri, A., Trent, R. & Jobe, B. (1987). 'The Wheelwright and Maerklin inventories and the history of the upholsterers' trade in America 1750–1900', *Old Time New England,* 72, pp 312–54.

Symonds, R.W. (1956). 'Crafts of the upholsterer', *Antique Collector,* June, pp 103–108.

Tierney, W.F. (1965). *Modern Upholstering Methods,* Bloomington: McKnight.

Walton, K.M. (1973). *English Furniture Upholstery 1660–1840,* Leeds: Leeds City Art Galleries.

Walton, K.M. (1973). 'The Worshipful Company of Upholders of the City of London', *Furniture History,* 9, pp 41–79.

Williams, M.A. (ed.) (1990). *Upholstery Conservation,* preprints of a symposium held at Colonial Williamsburg, 2–4 February, American Conservation Consortium, East Kingston, NH.

Working Upholsterer. (1883). *Practical Upholstery,* London: Wyman and Sons.

Upholstery filling

For upholstery fillings, anything from pigs' hair to seaweed has been considered as a possible contender.

See **Algerian fibre**, **Alva marina**, **Caranday fibre**, **Coir**, **Cotton flock**, **Down**, **Excelsior**, **Feather**, **Felt**, **Fibrefill**, **Foam**, **Grass**, **Hair**, **Hemp**, **Kapok**, **Latex**, **Mattress**, **Millpuff**, **Moss**, **Rabbit down**, **Rubberised hair**, **Rugging**, **Seaweed**, **Sisal**, **Spanish moss**, **Sponge**, **Straw**, **Wadding**, **Wool**, **Woollen flock**.

Upholstery fixing

See **Bible front**, **Buttoning**, **Cord**, **Fly**, **Laid cord**, **Quilting**, **Spring**, **Tack**, **Tufting**, **Twine**, **Webbing**.

Upholstery techniques

See **Back tacking**, **Binding**, **Buttoning**, **Capitonné**, **Couching**, **Knotted work**, **Mattress-making**, **Pane**, **Stitch**, **Stuffing**, **Tack**, **Tacking**, **Tufting**, **Upholstery**, **Van Dyke**.

Utrecht velvet

A confusing term for a variety of plush velvet. The name appears to be a corruption of the French term for a figured version of velvet woven on a draw loom, *velours de trek* (drawn). According to Thornton, it seems unlikely that they were actually woven in Utrecht (1978, p.112).

Generally, it is a tightly woven velvet-type cloth made of **silk** or goats' **hair** with a **linen warp**. It was sometimes pressed and crimped to produce a raised effect. Today, both **mohair** and silk are used. The name was also applied to a strong, thick kind of plush (furniture plush), made of **worsted**, mohair or mohair and **cotton**, with a cotton back used in upholstering furniture, carriages, etc. Bimont described Utrecht velvets as being 'woven from linen and goat hair and should be used for upholstery, as it was cheaper than damask' (1770).

In 1840, Richard Munns, an upholsterer of Oxford Street, London, advertised a range of **upholstery** fabrics including 'velours d'Utrecht' (*DEFM*, p.636). By 1857, John James wrote that:

> large quantities of what is termed Utrecht velvet, suitable for hangings and furniture, linings for carriages, are made from it [mohair] abroad. Recently this kind of velvet has begun to be manufactured at Coventry, and it is fully anticipated that the English made article will successfully compete with the foreign one in every essential quality. (1857, p.465.)

According to a contemporary technical manual of 1881: 'The best mohair plushes [Utrecht velvets] are almost indestructible. They have been in constant use on certain railroads for twenty years without wearing out.' (Grier, 1988, p.43.)

Utrecht velvet was used on good-quality furniture for much of the nineteenth century due to its lustre as well as being hardwearing and dirt-repelling. Although *Cassell's Household Guide* (1870) said that 'it has never been made popular in England by furniture makers', *The Dictionary of Needlework* described it as:

> A very strong and thick material composed of worsted, but of velvet make, having a raised deep pile, and sometimes a cotton back. It may be had in all colours, and is used by upholsterers and coach-builders. There is an imitation made, which is woven in wool, and is called Banbury plush. (Caulfeild & Saward, 1887, p.507.)

Utrecht velvet was also embossed with designs. Sir Henry Bessemer, of steel-making fame, described how he was employed to devise an embossing method and machinery specifically for Utrecht velvet, by the decorators, Pratt of Bond Street (Sir Henry Bessemer, [1905]. *An Autobiography*, London: The Offices of 'Engineering', ch.IV).
See also **Alpaca**, **Moquette tapestry**, **Plush**, **Velvet**.

Valance
A term of obscure origin for a short piece of **drapery** fitted above a window curtain, around a bedstead or divan, on a shelf that hangs down to hide fittings, around architectural details, or simply to give a finish to a window or bed. The name may be derived from the old French *avaler*, meaning 'to descend'. At various times it has been taken to be particular to windows, beds and shelves, and has been designated as such (see types below).

An early reference to the valance is found in 1494 when a domestic etiquette book explained: 'The ninth question; whether in the same feast, the Queen's cloth of Estate shall hang as high as the King's or not? Answer thereunto; the Queens shall hang lower by the vallance' (*Household Ordinances*, Society of Antiquaries, 1790). By the seventeenth century, valances were used to finish off a room at the top of the **wall hangings**. In the 1603 inventory of Hengrave, there were wall 'hangings of grey flannel complete, with a valance indented, with lace and bells' (Clabburn, 1988, p.245). Tart Hall also had a 'long valance for a room' in 1641 and, at the end of the century, Daniel Marot included valances in his plans for rooms (Thornton, 1978, p.133).

Valances were best known as finishes for bed and curtain treatments. Nicholson, writing in 1826, defined the valance as a 'narrow drapery hanging around the cornices, testers, steads [bed bases] and curtains of beds, and also accompanying window-curtains to give them a fullness and completion' (Nicholson, 1826).

Bed valance
Borders of drapery hanging round the **canopy** of a bed that were usually lined. In high-quality work, there were two valances, an inner and an outer, the inner valance hiding the mechanism of the curtains for the occupier. In 1773, Samuel Johnson described a valance as 'the fringes or drapery hanging round the tester and stead of a bed' (*Dictionary*). This simple description belies a host of various effects that have been made.

Clearly, valances were an integral part of bed furnishings from medieval times. In 1450, the *Boke of Curtasye* explained: 'For lords two beds shall be made so the valance on the celour shall hang with wyn [in?], iij curteyns straight drawn with-in' (Furnivall, 1868, p.447). The valance's importance was underlined by the *Wardrobe Accounts of Edward IV* for 1480 which included 'A sperver, containing tester, celour, and valances lined with busk' (Nicolas, 1830, p.132).

It is not surprising to find valances featuring in many other examples. In 1601, Hardwick Hall had a 'single vallans of blewe cloth sticht with white with blewe and white silk fringe' (Boynton, 1971, p.33) and, in 1679, the *London Gazette* advertised 'The Curtains and double Vallence of a red Damask Bed' (No.1434/4). The fixing of the valance was mentioned in 1730: 'The Tester-Cloth, to which the Head-cloth, and inside and outside Vallens are to be fixed' (Southall, *A Treatise on Buggs*, p.40). Near the end of the century, Hepplewhite explained that 'the valance to elegant beds should always be gathered full, which is called a petticoat valance' (1794, p.18).

In the nineteenth century, attitudes to **bed furniture** changed and the valance was not universally accepted. In 1861, Florence Nightingale specified 'An iron bedstead, (no vallance, of course), and hair mattress' (*Nursing*, 2nd edition, p.56, *OED*). The advent of the half-tester also reduced the size of the valance.

In later use, a bed valance referred to a short curtain around the lower frame of a bedstead, etc., serving to screen the space underneath.

Curtain valance
With the introduction of **pull-up curtains**, and the use of **pulleys** and **cords**, it was soon found that a disguise would be appropriate to cover the fittings. Therefore, a pelmet or valance was added, unless a **cornice** was already in place. Thornton cites a French reference of 1673, which describes curtains '*avec les petites pentes du haut*' (1978, p.138).

The distinction between a curtain pelmet and a valance can be obscure, but generally pelmets tend to be solid structures and valances are more like short curtains. In 1877, Knight defined a valance as 'a lambrequin, or drooping curtain hiding the curtain-rods of a window' (2688).

135. Bed valance with appliqué and cord work, France, c.1580 (Mallett and Co)

By the nineteenth century, Loudon, citing Pugin, suggested that a 'boxing of wood' be fitted above the curtains 'in front of which a valance is suspended to exclude air'. The effect of this would be to keep draughts out more effectively (1839, p.1274). The simplest valance was a flat piece of material, cut or decorated in various ways, and fitted to the box. In 1833, Thomas King, in his *Upholsterer's Accelerator*, described these as straight, plain or geometric.

A further design known as the piped valance was hung from rings or cornices in such a way that the fabric fell in folds. The range of finishes for valances varied according to fashion and included the use of straight, crocheted, **fringed**, plain **pleated**, **pinch pleated** and **Van dyke** effects, as well as alternative materials, **trimmings**, etc. Valances, which were made completely of fringe or **tassels** were also introduced.

Webster & Parkes explained their use in the mid-nineteenth century:

> Besides the rod on which the curtain slides, there is generally a piece of the same material with the curtain, called a valance, suspended before it, to conceal the rod... This valance gives great richness and finish to the window; but when the rooms are low, they should not be deep, as they hide much of the light; on the contrary, when the windows are very lofty, they are often useful in moderating the too great glare of light.
>
> Valances are sometimes made in the form of festoons, and are then, by upholsterers, termed draperies; the festoon itself is called a swag, and the end that hangs down is termed the tail... These are frequently ornamented with fringes, tassels and cords in various ways. This, which is the former French style, was introduced some years ago, as being richer and more elegant than ours at present [1844] is less used. (1844, p.251.)

During the twentieth century, the valance continued to be used as a vehicle for decorative finishes. An example from the 1908 Sears Roebuck catalogue offered 'Rope valances' on sale made from velour, rope or **chenille** cord.

Valances in the twentieth century could be shaped in a range of ways. A simple selection included valance frills, gather frills, pleated valances or fall-over valances.

Flop- or fall-over valance

A treatment whereby the curtain is made longer than the required finished length (or joined if non-reversible), so that the top portion can flop over and become a valance integral to the curtain. Almon Varney wrote about these valances in 1882 suggesting that they had superseded pelmets or lambrequins as a fashionable finish (1883, p.263).

The fall-over valance was still being recommended in the mid-twentieth century:

> [The] fallover valance takes the form of a top heading folded over the right side and cut long enough to fall as a valance frill below this heading. This is a good top finish for dress curtains, portières or windows so near the ceiling that a pelmet cannot be hung. (Sheridan, 1953, p.411.)

Piped valance

A nineteenth-century term, common from the 1840s, for a pleated pelmet or valance that hung from rings or a cornice.

Other valances

Valance also refers to pendant borders or edgings of **velvet**, **leather** or other material fitted to shelves, hangings, mantelpieces, etc. In 1603, Hengrave Hall had 'hangings of green flannelle complete, with a valance indented and fringed with lace and bells' (Clabburn, 1988, pp 93–4). Later in the century, John Evelyn commented on the library of the Duke of Orleans, where he saw 'the valans of the shelves being of green velvet fring'd with gold' (*Diary of John Evelyn*, 1 April 1644).

By the nineteenth century, *The Young Ladies' Treasure Book* commented that: 'As mantel hangings, or valances have now become an accepted portion of household decoration ... nothing is considered too costly a material upon which it paint or embroider a mantel valance...' (1884).

See also **Base**, **Bed furniture**, **Brindley valance**, **Cloth of estate**, **Curtain**, **Dust ruffle**, **Feather work**, **French drapery**, **Fringe**, **Lambrequin**, **Mantel drapery**, **Pante**, **Pelmet**, **Tester**, **Toilette**.

Valance shelf

A board mounted above a window at right angles to accommodate rails, **track**, **cornices**, **valance**, **swags**, etc.

Van dyke

A term for diamond or triangular shapes that have been cut into cloth for practical or decorative reasons. The term relates to the particular shape of the beard, popular in the portraits painted by Van Dyke (1599–1641).

Rudolf Ackermann comments upon a sofa draped with 'a Chinese palampone with [a] handsome Vandyke border, tassels &c.' (*Repository of Arts etc.*, Plate 6, July 1809).

Ackermann later refers to 'Vandyke muslin', which has a zigzag edging applied to the **curtain** (*Repository*, Plate 30, August 1811).

Van dyking also refers to a method of cutting out fabric for buttoned-back **upholstery** work, especially in **leather**. The term refers to the serrated edge of the fabric pattern when cut. The zigzag edge (V-shaped) has diamond-shaped pieces fitted to it in such a way that the joins follow the creases of the **buttoning** pattern and ensure a good match of hides or other material.

Velour

The French name for **velvet**, (*velours*) has been used to describe a variety of fabrics. Velour is recognised now as a plain or figured cut-**pile** all-**cotton** fabric, in which the pile is usually made from additional **warp** yarns that are raised over rods to create loops, which can either be cut or left uncut. It has a thick, **plush** pile, with a plain or **satin** ground. Sixteenth-century references refer mainly to its use as clothing.

In 1858, the *Dictionary of Trade Products* defined velour as 'a kind of velvet or plush for furniture, carpets, etc. manufactured in Prussia, partly of linen and partly of double cotton warps with mohair yarn weft' (Simmonds, 1858).

The pile is sometimes characterised by uneven lengths (usually two), which give it a rough look. The two lengths of pile create lighter and shaded areas on the surface and produce a rather pebbled effect. This type of velour was invented and made in Lyons, France, in 1844. In 1892, Cole recorded that velour was 'a cotton fabric, woven with a coarse stiff pile on the terry cloth principle, alike on both sides and dyed in solid colours' (*A Complete Dictionary of Dry Goods*, 1892).

By 1951, it was described as a 'Mercerized cotton pile and plain back. It had a slight effect of horizontal lines running across it and the pile tends to lie down rather than stand up. Used for sofas and chairs of Victorian type' (Taylor).

136. Velvet: figured with cut- and uncut-pile, c.1960 (Private Collection)

Velours de Gêne
See **Velvet: Genoa**.

Velvet
The name velvet is ultimately derived from the Latin *villus*, meaning 'shaggy hair'. It is an extra **warp**-woven **pile** fabric, having a short, dense, and smooth-piled surface woven over wires or 'face to face'. Originally from **silk**, velvet has been woven from **rayon**, **cotton**, synthetics, **acrylic**, **mohair**, or **wool** and **worsted**. It is mostly woven with a plain back but some have twill. Some are made with a silk pile and a rayon or cotton back. It is woven in a selection of finishes and a range of weights from dress to heavy **upholstery**. The velvet weave technique can also make **corduroy**, which is woven with a **weft** yarn, long-floated between each ground weft in such a way that ridged effects are made. When the pile is uncut to make looped-pile effects, these create cloths such as **terry**, **Brussels** or **moquette**. Various special effects may be applied to velvet as other fabrics. Stamping the silk face with irons applied under pressure to create a raised pattern and a ground effect pattern was not uncommon. Other special effects, either applied or woven-in, can create fabrics such as: 'antique' velvet; broderie (the cut-pile is the same height or lower than the uncut); *cisèle* (the cut-pile is higher than the uncut); pile on pile (the pattern is made from pile of two or more heights); terry (looped-pile); voided (also known as Genoa) with free areas left; terry velvet with uncut-pile; and velveteen. Stencilled, embossed and cut velvets are also used for upholstery.

Velvet was introduced into Europe (especially Italy) from the early thirteenth century and was used for furnishings. The 1509 inventory of Edmund Dudley describes both clothing and furnishings made from velvet, including **sparvers** (**curtain** or **canopy**) and **cushions** (Beard, 1997, p.282). Amongst the best early velvets were those from Lucca, Florence and Genoa. These were figured furnishing velvets with a **satin** ground and a multi-coloured pile, which could be cut, or left uncut, or even made with a mixture of both. The cut- and uncut-pile was sometimes called *cisèle*. The large patterns and bold colours made them popular in the late seventeenth century and through much of the eighteenth century. Little velvet appears to have been manufactured in England until the immigration of the Huguenots, from 1685.

In 1741, Chambers defined velvet as:

> A rich kind of stuff, all silk, covered on the outside with close, short, fine soft shag; the other side being a very strong, close tissue… The nap or shag called the velveting, of this stuff, is formed of part of the threads of the warp, which the workman puts on a long narrow channelled ruler, or needle; and which he afterwards cuts, by drawing a sharp steel tool along the channel of the needle, to the ends of the warp. (*Cyclopaedia*.)

Although originally silk, velvet fabrics with a cotton pile were introduced in the mid-eighteenth century. These were known as Manchester velvets. They were popular after 1760 and are now known as velours. George Smith suggested that for a field bed 'the borders [might be] cut out in black Manchester velvet and sewed on' (1808, p.5).

By 1955, *The Draper's Encyclopaedia* observed that:

> Furnishing velvets should be cut warp pile fabrics. They should not have a weft pile as in velveteen. The most popular furnishing velvet is all cotton and is sometimes called furnishing velour or warp-pile velvet. Cotton furnishing velvets are ideal for curtains, good qualities can be used for covers. Mohair is still satisfactory for public service, Rayon pile more lustrous than cotton especially when given a crushed finish. (Ostick, 1955, p.376.)

Cisèle velvet
A velvet cloth so designed that the pile is formed from a mix of cut and uncut yarns, thus creating the pattern. *Velours cisèle* have the cut-pile higher than the uncut, whilst *velours broderie* have the cut- and uncut-pile the same height.

Cotton velvet
See **Manchester velvet**.

Crushed rayon velvet
Market leader in the USA in the 1970s for fixed upholstery.

Cut velvet
Chambers simply says that it 'is that wherein the ground is a kind of taffety, or gros de tours and the figures velvet' (1741).

Embossed velvet
'A process not as popular today as in 1901 when embossed velvet was the usual type of upholstery material for all except the least expensive furniture.' (French, 1947.)

Faconne velvet
Patterned velvet made by the **burn-out** print process. The design is produced by the velvet pile left after the chemical treatment has removed part of the surface within a plain background.

Genoa velvet
There are frequent references to Genoa velvets in bills. Genoese velvet weavers specialised in pile on pile velvets. When combined with voiding techniques, the *velours de Gêne* (Genoa velvet) was developed. Genoa also specialised in the *velluti a giardino* that was used for hangings and upholstery. These featured multi-coloured cut and uncut velvet on a voided white or cream ground.
See also **Velvet: Cisèle**.

Lyons velvet
Stiff, thick pile velvet that has been used for hats, coat collars, suits, coats and dresses, when thick velvets were fashionable.

Manchester velvet
See **Manchester velvet**.

Nacre velvet
The back is of one colour and the pile of another, so that it gives a changeable, pearly appearance.

Panne velvet
This version has a longer or higher pile than normal velvet, but is shorter than plush. It is pressed flat and has a high lustre made possible by a tremendous roller-press treatment, given to the material in finishing. Known since the Middle Ages, this was a speciality of Italy initially, and then later of France. In 1723, Savary des Bruslons listed '*velours, trippes de velours, pannes, pluches*' as manufactured in Paris (Thornton, 1978, p.355) and defined '*pannes de laine*' as '*tripes* or *moquette*'.

A definition from 1877, in Knight's *The Practical Dictionary of Mechanics,* suggests that panne is worsted plush of French manufacture. A similar definition from 1898 says that 'among the new materials is that called panne, a very silky make of cloth, almost resembling velvet in softness of surface' (*Daily News,* 10 December, 6/3).

Mid-twentieth century definitions concur: the 1940 Chamber's *Technical Dictionary* explains: 'Panne velvet, warp pile fabrics with silk pile; used for dresses and furnishings' (611/2).

Plush
Velvet or velveteen where the pile is ⅛ of an inch (3 mm) thick or more, e.g. cotton velour, hat velour, plush 'fake furs'.
See also **Plush**.

Stamped velvet
See **Velvet: Embossed**.

Transparent velvet (Chiffon velvet)
Lightweight, very soft, draping velvet made with a silk or rayon back and a rayon pile.

Utrecht velvet
See **Utrecht velvet**.

Velvet satin
A **satin** weave is used as the base for this luxurious figured silk, made with a cut-pile effect.

Woollen velvet
See **Caffoy**, **Plush**, **Shagg**.
See also **Painted velvet**, **Velour**, **Velveteen**.

FURTHER READING

Cooke, J.H. (1922). *The Velvet and Corduroy Industry: A Brief Account of the Various Processes Connected With the Manufacture of Cotton Pile Goods*, London, New York: Sir I. Pitman & Sons, Ltd.

De Marinas, F. (1993). *Velvet: History, Techniques, Fashions,* London: Thames and Hudson.

Latour, A. (1953). 'Velvet', *CIBA Review,* 96, February, pp 3441–63.

Velvet carpet
A cut-**pile carpeting** that imitated **Wilton carpet** but did not have any yarns buried beneath the surface, as did a true Wilton weave.

> Velvet is really the Wilton weave made with the colours printed on the worsted patterned warps and woven without the aid of a jacquard attachment [as in Wilton]. In other words, when tapestry carpet is woven over wires with a knife-fitted end and this knife cuts the pile open as it is withdrawn, a carpet known as velvet is produced. Velvet needs the addition of jute as a stuffer to give the necessary body. Velvet carpets are gaining in popularity and are now made in broadloom widths, up to 15 feet. (Faraday, 1929, p.428.)

The need for less **wool warps** made this a cheaper version of Wilton.
See also **Tapestry carpet**, **Tournai carpet**, **Saxony**, **Velvet**.

Velveteen
Fabric that is woven in such a way as to create a very short **pile**, but still has the appearance and surface effect of **velvet**. Velveteen has an **extra-weft** pile, with either a plain or twill back (twill back is the best), as opposed to the **warp** pile in velvet. In the twentieth century, it has sometimes been made from **rayon** yarn, in place of **cotton** or **silk**. It was once widely used for loose, soft seat **cushions** on hide-upholstered suites of furniture.

An early reference is from 1776, when Woolstenholme was granted a patent for 'his new kind of goods called velvateans, being an improvement on velveretts' (Patent no.1123).

By 1887, *The Dictionary of Needlework* defined velveteen as 'a description of fustian, made of twilled cotton, and having a raised pile, and of finer cotton, and better finish than the latter.' (Caulfeild & Saward, 1887, p.511.) It was widely used for garments at that time. It remained popular into the twentieth century, where it was used for chairs, hangings, **portières** and spreads (Taylor, 1951).
See also **Fustian**.

Venetian binding
According to *The Dictionary of Needlework*, 'Venetians [bindings] are used for several purposes in upholstery. Their chief use, however, is at present for Venetian blinds … they are dyed ingrain, and are green, blue, yellow, white; they are now sometimes used for embroidery.' (Caulfeild & Saward, 1887, p.35.)
See also **Binding**, **Ladder web**.

Venetian blind
Venetian blinds for both interior and exterior use were introduced in Europe some time in the sixteenth century, and have remained in fashion on and off to the present day. Their wooden slats were linked with cloth tape, and raised with a pulley **cord**; a **valance** or **swag** above the blind could disguise the mechanism. As with louvred shutters, a rod controlled the tilt of the slats. Initially in Italy, these adjustable blinds were often suspended between the pillars of a veranda, as protection

137. Venetian blind advertisement, c.1770 (Courtesy The Winterthur Library: Joseph Downs Collection of Manuscripts and Printed Ephemera)

against the sun's rays entering a room. By the mid-eighteenth century, they had become commercially successful for interior use.

In 1757, the cabinet-makers and upholsterers, Vile and Cobb, billed the Earl of Coventry for 'Italian window blinds painted green for your drawing room' at Croome Court (Beard, 1997, p.305). In *c.*1766, London cabinet-maker, Robert Adamson, produced a trade card illustrating a Venetian blind that gave 'three different sights by pulling a line, draws up as a **curtain**, obstructs the troublesome rays of the sun in hot weather, and greatly improves the furniture, prevents being overlooked, and may be taken down or put up in a minute' (Gilbert, 1978, p.59).

The American market was also interested in Venetian blinds. In the *Pennsylvania Chronicle* (3 December 1767), John Webster, an upholsterer from London, offered blinds similar to Adamson's:

> The best and newest invented Venetian sun-blinds for windows on the best principles, stained to any colour, moves to any position so as to give different lights, screens from the scorching rays of the sun, draws a cool air in hot weather, draws up as a curtain, and preventing being overlooked, and is the greatest preserver of furniture of the kind ever invented. (French, 1937, p.99.)

In 1769, Edward Bevan, a carpenter of Air Street, London, advertised that he made 'Venetian Window Blinds' (*Public Advertiser,* 25 May 3/2) and later in the year he was granted a patent for his method (11 December 1769, Patent no.945). In the same year, Diderot referred to a distinction between *jalousies à la persienne* for the taped and corded versions, and *jalousie* for exterior shutters with louvres. The popularity of Venetian blinds may be judged by the comment, in 1794, of W. Felton, who noted that 'the Venetian blind [is] frequently used as a substitute for the common shutter and spring curtain.' (*Carriages* I., 148 (*OED*).)

According to Sheraton, Venetian blinds were 'drawn up by pulleys fixed in a lath 1 inch thick, the same as a festoon window curtain'. He went on to note that:

> The more fashionable blinds are all of wood, painted green, except the frame, which is of mahogany. The blind part is either composed of upright or horizontal narrow laths, an eighth part of an inch thick, painted a bright green, and which move, by means of a lever, to any position, for admitting more or less light. Those most approved of at present are with upright laths, and move by turning a brass knob at the upper side of the frame. The latest improvement of these is by Mr. Stubbs, of Oxford Street, who caps the ends of the laths with brass, so that the ends are secure from splitting by the wire put in to move them by. At each end of the laths are two of these wires, which by holes communicate with two brass slips let into the top and bottom of the mahogany frame. These brass slips slide past each other in the manner of a parallel ruler, for the laths fixed to the brass, and with them in the same manner as the brass joints to the sides of these sort of rulers… (Sheraton, 1803, pp 56–9.)

For exterior use, Sheraton noted:

> There are other external blinds for first floor windows, which draw up under a cornice fixed to the outside of the head frame of the window. But these being of canvas are not so proper for outside blinds as those of the Venetian kind, with brass chains, instead of the usual way of hanging the laths in green tape. These last mentioned have been introduced by Mr. Stubbs as above, and bid fair for answering the intended purpose as external window blinds. The Venetian part is enclosed under a cornice; when drawn up is guarded by a frame, so that the wind cannot blow them aside. (ibid.)

Loudon concurs with this description, adding that 'Outside blinds are generally painted a stone or cream colour in the country; and green in towns' (1839, p.270). Loudon also mentions a strange arrangement for a Venetian blind whereby the slats are made from iron, and copper chains take the place of tapes. He goes on to say 'These bullet-proof blinds, as they are called, are manufactured by Bramah of Pimlico, and have been employed by the Duke of Wellington, at Apsley House to protect his windows from the mob'. (ibid.)

Although the blind slats were commonly painted wood, it was inevitable that the desire for something different and more interesting would occur. In 1844, Venetian blinds with glass slats were produced and, in 1851, blinds with silvered metal lath slats were displayed. However, older methods continued in use. The brass chain arrangement that was detailed by Sheraton (above) was still being recommended by Webster & Parkes for blinds intended for outside use in 1844.

Another development that was a pre-cursor to the aluminium blinds of the twentieth century was noted in *Cassell's Household Guide,* 1870, which recorded:

> Lately iron Venetian blinds have been introduced and patented. One of their merits is stated to be greater lightness, being made of metal

not thicker than ordinary note-paper. The laths too never break or splinter. Being japanned in place of being painted, they are brighter, more easily cleaned, and the expense of repainting is avoided. They go into less than half the space when drawn up than wooden lath blinds, thus allowing more light to penetrate into the room. (vol.1, p.176.)

Not all commentators were happy about the benefits of Venetian blinds. Miss Leslie suggested that 'it is not necessary that Venetian blinds should, like curtains, have a conspicuous effect in the room. On the contrary, it is better that their colour should as nearly as possible match that of the wall.' (1854, p.190.) The American Garrett sisters, writing in their *Suggestions for House Decoration*, complained of the 'everlasting drab or yellow Venetian blinds, which are constantly out of order, and always drawn up crooked [and] invariably used in modern rooms' (1877, p.70). In the same year, Mrs Orrinsmith, in *The Drawing Room,* wrote that although ventilation was necessary, Venetian blinds 'are heavy and ugly, and constantly out of order'. She went on to recommend exterior **jalousies** as seen in France and Italy, as 'they are most furnishing in their outside effect upon a new or bare looking house' (1877, p.66).

Particular efforts were made to personalise blinds as well. The Lux patent Venetian blind, which was decorated with selected patterns, was said to be 'the lightest, cheapest, most artistic and perfect blind in the world. This is the only Venetian blind that can be made to harmonise with the decoration of the apartment' (Patent Venetian Blind Co of Birmingham advertisement in *The House,* April 1897).

By the early twentieth century, timber slats found favour and particular timbers were selected as appropriate. Yellow pine or basswood was recommended for laths, completed in a plain varnish, with a flatted appearance using water stain and a medium, or by painting green, fawn, pale blue or drab (Hasluck, 1907).

Mrs Humphrey complained in her *Book of the Home* that 'the craze for cheapness had led to the manufacture of a wretched article, the slats of common spruce roughly painted, with cotton ladders and jute cord' (1909, p.228). Despite these comments, Venetian blinds seem to have remained popular.

In their *Practical Book of Interior Decoration,* published in 1919, Eberlein, McLure & Holloway reiterated the advice given by Miss Leslie 50 years previously: 'the good old Venetian blind is unsurpassed ... it may be painted any tint to agree with its surroundings'. Twenty years later, the taste for wooden slats was again commented upon:

In England, the best quality Venetian blinds are usually made of St. John spruce, and Columbian pine wood is used for those of the second grade quality. In America Port Orford Cedar is considered the best for the purpose, but unfortunately the supply of such timber is limited; manufacturers use bass wood and magnolia as good substitutes. (French, 1937, p.98.)

The introduction of aluminium slats in the late 1930s gave them a modern, streamlined image: the 'House of Tomorrow' at the 1933 Chicago World's Fair had Venetian blinds, and Bauhaus expatriates, Walter Gropius and Marcel Breuer, used them for their Massachusetts homes in 1938–9. Aluminium Venetian blinds were inexpensive and sold in a wide range of colours and sizes.

An American commentator explained the taste for the use of Venetian blinds in the 1930s:

Venetian blinds have been revived lately, and are rightly popular. They function especially well because they admit air and light while giving privacy. They are fairly inconspicuous when painted like the walls or wood trim, as in conventional usage. In the modern and in the Empire styles they are often boldly contrasted with the wall color. They can be used without curtains if the effect is not too severe for the room. Le Corbusier often omits curtains entirely from his modern rooms and uses indoor shutters instead. (Rutt, 1935, p.375.)

In the late 1970s, high-tech design relied heavily on Venetian blinds as space dividers and for large-scale window treatments. Various features distinguish the newer versions: thin **mini-blind** slats (almost invisible when opened); wood or vinyl instead of aluminium; and safety cords that pull apart under pressure (an innovation that prevents children from strangling themselves on the cords). Nevertheless, they still have one major failing: they collect dust. To address this problem, vertical blinds were designed in 1948. Although they were initially used for commercial spaces, by the later 1970s they were popular in domestic interiors. Now available with metal, plastic or fabric slats, these have gradually come into use for wide expanses of glass in residential interiors.

Dwarf Venetian blind

A blind-making system used in the early twentieth century, which used vertical laths measuring ⅞ of an inch by 3⁄16 of an inch (22.2 by 4.7 mm) fitted in a frame, which was usually of mahogany. The frame was then fixed between the beads of the window sash frame. A brass sliding mechanism operated it.

Fixed Venetian blind

A fixed blind used for curved or semi-circular windows to complement the movable blinds.

See also **Awning**, **Blind**, **Venetian binding**, **Vertical blind**.

FURTHER READING

French, T. and Co (1941). *Venetian Blinds,* Manchester: The Company.
Garrett, E.D. (1971). 'The American home: venetian shutters and blinds', *The Magazine Antiques,* 128, August, pp 258–65.

Venetian carpet

A striped, flat-weave, single-ply **carpet**, woven with a **worsted warp** that completely hides the **weft**. The stripes run the length of the carpet warps. Venetian carpet was probably introduced in the late eighteenth century, but was most popular throughout the nineteenth century. It was generally a utilitarian floorcovering for areas of light wear.

The origin of the name is in dispute. Sheraton, in his *Cabinet Dictionary,* suggests that Venetian carpet was 'generally striped' and was one of the 'sorts, which have their names from the places where they are manufactured' (1803, p.132). On the other hand, Webster & Parkes suggested that 'it is not known that what we call Venetian carpeting was ever made in Venice' (1844, p.255).

It was clearly established by the early nineteenth century. In 1805, Weston Park was furnished with '40 yards of neat pattern Venetian carpet for bed and dressing rooms' (Rogers, 1987, p.29). In 1813, the Duke of Buccleuch's London house was supplied with '12 Bedside carpets of Venetian for young ladies' and nursery room' (Ellwood, 1995, p.197). The 1827, the Attingham sale included for the southwest end dressing room, 'a striped green-ground Venetian carpet, planned to the floor and cut to fireplace, 6¾ yards by 4½ yards' (Gilbert, Lomax & Wells-Cole, 1987, p.94).

By 1836, it was available in a range of finishes and intended for a variety of uses:

Venetian carpets – here the warp or chain which is of worsted, and generally arranged in stripes of different colours, is alone visible, the

138. Venetian carpet fragment, cotton warp, woollen weft, c.1830 (Photograph courtesy of Peabody Essex Museum)

> shoot which is of a dark colour and usually black, is concealed between the upper and under surface. By using shoots of different sizes, these carpets are sometimes made to assume the appearance of plaids or checks, and by the arrangement of the treadles, a twilled or dotted appearance is at other times given to them. Venetians are generally used for staircase carpets, but the plaid kinds are occasionally used for rooms. Although the dots, waves, small figures and plaids, are sometimes introduced, the general character of Venetian carpets is a simple stripe throughout. (*Penny Cyclopaedia*, 1836.)

Although it was generally utilitarian carpeting, it still attracted attention from inventors. In May 1827, Thomas Clarke, a Leicestershire carpet manufacturer, patented a method of improving figured Venetian carpet which used the **jacquard** in conjunction with **double cloth** weaving, whilst in 1851, John Crossley, Halifax carpet-maker, patented a method of weaving Venetians 'to present two similar corded surfaces, showing the same pattern on both sides of the cloth … similar … to that fabric commonly known by the name of Venetian carpets only that in place of being in stripes it is figured by means of the warp being printed' (Patent no.13474, 28 January 1851). In 1840, *The Workwoman's Guide* mentions Danish Venetian but without further description (Hale, p.201). By 1862, the *Cyclopaedia of Useful Arts* discussed 'a variety of carpet called British or Venetian Damask' and described it as 'a kind of mixture of Venetian and Kidderminster Damask' (Tomlinson, 1862). A little later, another dictionary noted that 'Figured Venetian carpets are woven in the two-ply Kidderminster looms' (Ure, 1867).

American usage was similar to English practice. Webster says of Venetian carpets that they are of:

> the simplest kind, the texture of which is plain: a striped woollen warp on a thick woof of thread made of hemp, cotton, or woollen; and the warp is so thick as to cover entirely the woof. Venetian carpeting is used chiefly for bedrooms and stair-carpets, the dust adhering less to them than to others. (Webster & Parkes, 1844, p.255.)

The utilitarian nature of the carpet was never far from any description. *The Workwoman's Guide* (Hale, 1840) considered common Venetian carpet as good for servants' rooms and home schoolrooms, whilst the American author, Miss Leslie, writing in 1854, noted that Venetian carpet was 'rarely used, except for stairs and passages' (p.173). Forty years later, *The Dictionary of Needlework* considered the same qualities and noted that the pattern was necessarily a simple 'diced' one, and the carpets were durable as well as thick and therefore they were recommended for bedrooms and nurseries (Caulfeild & Saward, 1887, p.512).

However, its popularity was declining in the last quarter of the nineteenth century. In 1870, *Cassell's Household Guide* noted that for stair carpeting 'the real Venetian is best, but it is now rarely to be obtained.' (vol.1, p.125.) Nevertheless, in 1884, retailers Maple and Co described 'Venetian Twill' carpeting, as 'another most durable carpet, very soft to the treads, and much used in old country mansions'. They went on to say: 'It usually has a crimson, oak or green centre with a self or contrasting border.' They also pointed out that it is sold for bedrooms 'though now only in limited quantities' (Maple and Co, 1884, p.77).

In the USA, Montgomery Ward, the American mail order company, published in their catalogue of 1895 images of Venetian carpet and described it as being woven of heavy **cotton** warp and **jute** filling. By 1900, the demise of Venetian carpet was clear. Cole noted it as:

> A low-grade floorcovering of simple structure… The fabric is ornamented with stripes of various colours and widths, and is used as a cheap covering for halls, stairways and bedrooms. For many years the production of Venetian was an extensive and profitable branch of Philadelphia manufacture, but of recent years it has largely been supplanted by the lower grades of ingrain carpet. (Cole, 1900, revised edition, p.87.)

See also **Damask carpet**, **Dutch carpet**.

Venetian cloth

Originally, Venetian cloth was a closely woven fabric with a fine twilled surface, which was used as a dress or suiting material. In 1710, the *London Gazette* advertised 'For Sale, Venitions, Tabbies and other Stuffs' (No. 4706/4). By 1786, 'A method of manufacturing Silk and Mohair, with materials which have never before been combined or manufactured together [as wood, reed, cane, straw, etc], and which is called (by the Specifier) Venetian Sattin' was advertised (*OED*).

An American description from 1947 explained that it was a smooth **warp** faced satin weave cloth, often made from **cotton** or **wool**. The cotton version was similar to **sateen** but heavier; it was used for dresses, **drapes** and soft furnishings (Bendure & Pfieffer, 1947, p.656). In the United Kingdom, it was defined slightly differently. Smithells described it as 'twill woven cotton used for plain curtains and for linings of all kinds' (Smithells, 1950, p.232).

See also **Fortuny print**, **Satin: Venetian**.

Venetian curtain

A simple **pull-up curtain** that hung flat (or with fullness in gathers) when let down, and was gathered at the top when pulled up. It was raised on **cords** like **Venetian blinds**, and looked similar to the later Austrian or festoon blinds.

In around 1780, William Shreve advertised that he was 'the only inventor and maker of Venetian curtains for common windows to hand in the same form as ye right Venetian curtains' (Heal, 1953, p.167).

By the nineteenth century, *The Workwoman's Guide* described Venetian curtains as 'old-fashioned simple curtains still in use in churches, small houses and for housekeepers' rooms' (Hale, 1840, p.205). Old-fashioned or not, Loudon took pains to describe their making up:

> [Take] a piece of dimity or other material ... [nailed] to a flat piece of wood, in one end of which are inserted two pullies; whilst two others are let into it, one in the middle and the other at the opposite extremity. Three pieces of tape are sewed down the curtain one on each side and one in the middle, to which are affixed small rings, at regular distances: through these rings are passed three pieces of cord, which afterward go over the pullies and being fastened together on one side are kept tight by means of a pulley rack. (1839, p.341.)

By the last decades of the nineteenth century, these pull-up curtains were again recommended, although they were known as Austrian blinds.
See also **Austrian shade**, **Festoon window curtain**.

Verdure

A rich **tapestry**-type cloth, ornamented with dense representations of trees, foliage or other green vegetation, which was hung on walls or sometimes fitted to specific spaces. It was also used for bedcovers and **cushions**. The name originates from the French *vert*, meaning 'green'. Verdures were widely produced in northern Europe from the Middle Ages through to the eighteenth century.

In 1470, payment was made in the royal accounts of England to 'Rauf Underwood, wyre drawer, for iij and a quart'on of weyre for to hang verdours against the great window in the Queen's old chamber' (Beck, 1882).

In 1513, 'a counterpoynt of paly verdure, [and] an old counterpoint of redde verdures' were listed in the papers of Henry VIII (MS. Papers 5 Henry VIII, no.4101, Public Records Office). The verdures were apparently distinguished from tapestry. The 1586 *Rates of Custom Duty* listed 'Tappistry with wul or Verdure the Flemish elle, xii. d' (*OED*). In the 1601 Hardwick inventory, verdures are distinguished from tapestries with designs of persons or of stories, as they listed ' five pieces of tapestry hangings of forest work, nine foot deep' (Boynton, 1971, p.33) in Mr William Cavendish's chamber. In 1660, reference was made to 'bankers of verdure, the dozen pieces, ivl' (1660, Act 12, Chas. II, iv. Schedule).
See also **Arras**, **Tapestry**.

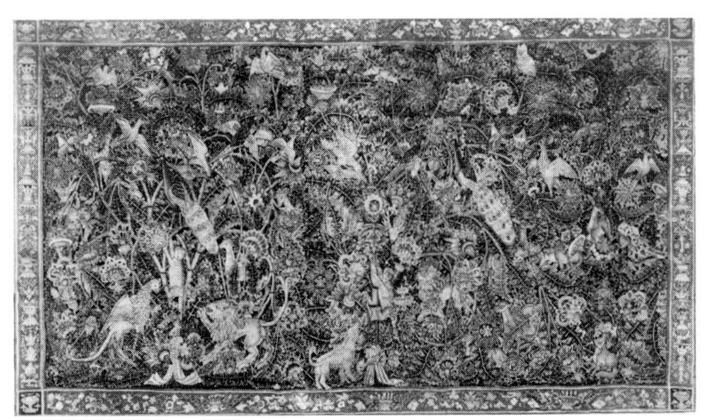

139. Hanging of a type known as 'Verdure de Bocages et de Bêtes Sauvages', wool, slit, single dovetail, and interlocking tapestry weave, Netherlandish, Hainault, Tournai, first half of sixteenth century (Gift of the Antiquarian Society of The Art Institute of Chicago through the Jessie Landon Fund, 1934.4, The Art Institute of Chicago. Photography ©The Art Institute of Chicago)

FURTHER READING

Sternberg, C. (1983). *Verdure Tapestry*, London: Vigo-Sternberg Galleries.

Vermilion

A **cotton** cloth, often dyed red, and particularly associated with **Manchester** and the surrounds. Writing about Manchester's trades in 1641, Lewis Roberts noted that 'they buy cotton wool in London that comes from Cyprus and Smyrna, and work that same in to fustians, vermilions and dimities which they return to London where they are sold' (*Treasure of Traffic*, p.33). Vermilion is referred to in the 1654 Ham House inventory. In a chamber there were 'hangings of white vermilion all wrought in colours', and in addition there was a 'French bedstead with curtains, valance, counterpoint and all furniture belonging to it of the same' as well as 'two chairs, eight stools, two carpets all of white vermilion' (Thornton & Tomlin, 1980, p.28). The authors define vermilion in this instance as a **worsted** textile. In the eighteenth century, vermilion was mainly used for bedding and for coverings of components.

Vertical blind

Window **blinds** with overlapping vertical slats or vanes that can be opened or closed, adjusted to control light or pulled to one side to reveal the window. Sheraton seems to be talking about these:

> There are other blinds now in use for shop windows, made in light frames strained with canvas, which being hinged to an outer frame made to receive these, some-times three, or more in number, move all at one time to any convenient angle, so as to keep out the sun. The means by which they move all at one time, is by a small lath screwed to each frame, so that when one is moved, the other necessarily follows in a parallel direction, on the same principle that the parlour blinds, with upright laths move, for the screw having play at the head, the frames will fall down of themselves, so that they must be kept to their appointed position by a line fixed to the upper frame, and passing through a pulley at the upper end of the outer frame, which is tied to a hook. These sorts of blinds are made to take off when they are not wanted. (1803, pp 56–9.)

In 1907, Paul Hasluck discussed dwarf Venetian blinds that had vertical slats fitted to a frame of mahogany: 'the whole which was then fitted between the beads of a sash window frame' (Hasluck, 1907, p.66).

Vertical blinds made from fabric and hinged on **track** with movable suspenders were developed in the 1940s. They generally remained as office furnishings until the 1970s. Today, they are widely used in domestic window furnishings. Translucent textile laminates have been used for the vanes from the 1970s onward.
See also **Blind**, **Venetian blind**.

Vestibule curtain

Curtains designed to cover glass-panelled doors. The curtain was stretched between two rods that could draw it tightly down the glass in **pleats**. In some cases, fullness was allowed that let the curtains be tied at the centre to create a diamond effect (Moreland, 1889).

Vinyl

See **PVC**.

Viscose

See **Rayon**.

Voile

A transparent, plain-weave, loosely woven, lightweight, sheer **cotton** or **wool** fabric that drapes and gathers very well. The name appears to be derived from the French for 'veil'. It is usually woven from cylindrical combed cotton yarns, but it may also be made from wool. In the latter case, it may be called '*voile de laine*'. To obtain a top-quality fabric, very highly twisted yarns are used. The clear surface is obtained by singeing away any fuzzy yarns. A feature of voile is that all **warp** ends and picks should appear singly in the cloth; that is, with a tiny space separating every thread from adjacent ones. It has been available in plain white, piece-dyed or printed, and has been used for **drapes**, **bedspreads** and lampshades.

An American author commented that:

> In cream color with plain hemstitched hems, it is suitable for any unpretentious room. Voile is easily washed and ironed and falls in long, graceful folds. It comes in many qualities, the more expensive having a clear, open-mesh effect and being evenly woven. Imported voiles are as a rule finer in texture than domestic. (Dyer, *c.*1923, p.199.)

From the 1950s, synthetic fibres were widely used in voile manufacture. See also **Dotted Swiss**, **Marquisette**, **Ninon**, **Muslin**, **Scrim**.

Wadding

Sheets of carded fibres that are needled, bonded or **felted** onto a textile backing for **stuffing** and wrapping purposes in **upholstery** work. It has been used to prevent **hair** fillings from protruding through the **top covers** of upholstery work. Wadding can be made from **cotton**, **wool** or synthetic fibres (**polyester**). In 1841, Christopher Nickels patented an early English 'felting machine', devised to prepare ready-made stuffings covered with **hessian** (Patent no.9012). The process of 'wadding' the edge of a **curtain**, i.e. to place wadding material about 2 inches (5 cm) or so in the hems of curtains, was used to soften and round the hard edge as well as improving the appearance (Martin, 1930).
See also **Comfort**, **Cotton flock**, **Fibrefill**, **Interlining**, **Kapok**, **Quilt**, **Upholstery**, **Upholstery filling**.

Wadmal (aka Homespun)

A kind of coarse **woollen** cloth used principally for covering horse-collars and for other rough purposes. The name appears to be derived from *vadmel*, Danish for '**homespun**'. In 1404, the following was recorded: '*Item j pannus de wadmale pro rebus cariandis*' (*Extracts for the account rolls of the Abbey of Durham*, Surtees, 395, *OED*).

In the sixteenth and seventeenth centuries, it was mentioned as being manufactured in Wales and at Witney (Oxfordshire). It was thick enough to be used, unlined, for hangings in unimportant rooms. In 1645, the inventory of the Earl of Dorset included '1 ould woodmeal cover for the tester [of a bed]' (Beard, 1997, p.293).

Wale

A term that defines one of the ribs or ridges (consisting of a thread or threads) that occur on a woven fabric such as **corduroy**.

Wall coverings (aka Hanging and Halling)

Covering walls with suspended, or later, 'fitted', textiles, which were stretched, **pleated**, padded or otherwise hung, has been part of the repertoire of interiors since the Middle Ages at least. Although tapestries and gilt leather hangings were amongst the most important wall coverings, textiles such as **silk velvet**, **damask**, **worsted** damask and **camlet** were all finding favour by the seventeenth century. **Chintz**, tapisséries de Bergame, **perpetuana**, camlet, **dornix** and **paragon** were often used in the more important rooms and, in less important rooms, worsted materials would be used.

An early example from York demonstrated the importance of prepared wall coverings as part of a furnishing scheme. In the hall of the cleric William Duffield (*d.*1452), there was a complete set of blue say halling cloths. There was also 'a matching dorser thirteen yards long by four yards deep, two costers nine yards long by two and a half yards deep each one; a banker eight yards long and twenty-seven inches deep, with ten matching feather filled pillows'. In addition, the hall cupboard had its own blue say cupboard cloth (Kightly, 2001, pp 4–6).

Over 100 years later, William Harrison particularly commented upon the use of hangings: 'The walls of our houses on the inner sides in like sort be either hanged with tapestrie, arras work, or painted cloths wherein diverse histories or herbs, beasts, knots and such like are stained' (1577, p.197). The splendid examples from the 1601 Hardwick Hall inventory demonstrated this varied taste:

> Six pieces of gilt leather hangings/ six pieces of hangings imbrodered upon white damask murry velvet and other stuff/ four pieces of tapestry hangings with personages/ six pieces of hangings of red mokcadow/ seven pieces of hangings of embroidery of cloth of gold and silver, cloth of tissue, velvet of sundry colours and needlework twelve foot deep/ six pieces of hangings of yellow, blue and other coloured damask and satin wrought with gold flowers and trees and lined with canvas. (Boynton, 1971.)

A delightful description from 1603 of Hengrave Hall's blue and yellow say hangings in the 'chamber where the musicians play' and also 'hangings of green flannelle complete, with a valance indented and fringed with lace and bells' gives an indication of their use and application (Clabburn, 1988, pp 93–4).

During the first half of the seventeenth century, patents were taken out specifically for wall hangings. In 1636, Richard and Edward Greenbury had a patent granted for 'Painting with oil colours upon woollen cloth kerseys and stuff for hangings, also silk for windows' (Patent no.99).

In the seventeenth century, hangings were made to fit a wall by using lengths of fabric of matching or differing colours, **bordered**, and sometimes paned. The hanging of alternate widths of fabric as **panes** was popular in the Renaissance and was adopted in England during the second half of the seventeenth century. The inventory of the Wardrobe of Ham House in 1683 lists a number of sets of hangings 'impaned and bordered' in damask, **brocade**, **morella mohair** and 'fine plading' (Thornton & Tomlin, 1980, p.172). Dornix was also used for wall hangings as was brocade, damask, **taffeta** and **frieze**: the latter was used especially for replacement winter hangings. In the 1641 Tart Hall inventory: 'My Lordes room is hanged with yellow and green taffeta consisting of 49 breadths. A suite of freeze hangings also belongeth to this roome' (Cust, 1911, p.100). In 1675, Pat Barrett supplied Edward Sackville with 'one suit of hangings of persian taffety printed with roman statuaries, and satin pillars and borders lined with callicoe' (Beard, 1997, p.294). In 1698, Celia Fiennes visited Chippenham Park and saw 'in the best drawing room was a very rich hanging gold and silver and a littler scarlet; mostly tissue and brocade of gold and silver and border of green damask round it' (Morris [ed.], 1985, p.140).

Printed cloth was popular for hangings. On 5 September 1663, Pepys recorded that 'Creed, my wife and I to Cornhill and after many trials bought my wife a chinke; that is a painted Indian calico for to line her new study, which is very pretty' (*The Diary of Samuel Pepys*). Thirty years later, William Bayly patented 'Glazed printed hangings made of cotton, worsted, or woollen yarn of all sorts of curious figures and landscapes, which for beauty of colours, exactness of figures, strength and gloss is hard to be distinguished from the finest silk tapestry hangings brought from foreign parts' (1692, Patent no.296, 22 April).

The method of fixing wall coverings comprised a lining of the walls with **scrim** or **canvas**. This was then covered with a lining paper and the top material was fitted over this. The intention was to keep the dust from the surface of fabrics. (More recently, the use of domette or **bump** has been used in addition to **linen**-backed paper to even out the differences in temperature due to central heating.) This process was achieved with the assistance of '42½ yds of strong stout Tick to assist in straining the hangings' and '19 yards of stout brown cloth to assist as the tick' (Beard, 1997, p.307). Additional expense was often incurred. A 1764 reference in an invoice from upholsterer, William France, to Sir Lawrence Dundas at Moor Park showed the costs involved. 'For making hangings of your own crimson damask, to fit the 2 large rooms compleat, and putting up the whole and moving trussels and scaffolding, as the business required without which assistant rooms so large and high, could not be hung without the greatest difficulty and expense' (Beard, 1997, p.307).

In addition to the fabric and hanging costs, there was the matter of finishing off. One example demonstrates the process. In *c.*1780, the drawing room of Sir Richard Worsley's Appuldurcombe Park was 'hung with white watered tabby, [and finished with] a moulding all round the hangings, carved and gilt in burnished gold' (Boynton, 1965, p.44).

By the early eighteenth century, Daniel Defoe described the division of labour in their manufacture and identifies a significant trade in painted hangings: 'The Hangings, suppose them to be ordinary Linsey-Woolsey are made at Kidderminster d'yd in the country, and painted or water'd at London' (*Complete English Tradesman*, 1727, I, p.333). The reference to painting was echoed faintly in the *Boston Gazette* (15 September 1760):

> Hangings for rooms – Jane Savell acquaints her customers that since the fire she is removed to a chamber at the upper end of Milk Street near the Fourth Meeting House where she has got several pieces of beautiful painted canvas hangings for rooms, some stone pickled pots and jugs; a quantity of pickled cucumbers and mangoes.

At the other end of the century, English inventor, Francis Eckhardt, received a patent for a:

> method of preparing linen and cotton cloth, with a paste to give it a smooth surface and a pliable quality, for receiving a coat of water-size colours, and afterwards printing ornaments on the same, in silver and gold or colours, in patterns to resemble damask, lace, and other silk stuffs, for hangings and other furniture for rooms. (1793, Patent no.1954.)

The nineteenth century still saw a taste for wall hangings. For example, in 1830 Nicholas Morel charged for:

> hangings for the walls of (purple & deleted) gold colour figured tissue, framed into panels with wide mouldings of rosettes, husk &c with internal and external members, and large shell scroll & foliage ornament in the angles gilt in the best manner in mat and burnished gold, including canvas hangings and paper to prepare the walls for the silk. (Yorke, 1996, p.69.)

If this extravagant scheme was out of reach, Loudon, in his 1833 *Encyclopaedia*, commented that drawing rooms could be:

> hung with a buff colour, watered, or having satin or watered stripes alternately... Where silk or velvet is used for the furniture of a room, a papered wall generally has a poor effect except perhaps a plain flock paper, which has the appearance of cloth, or a paper printed in imitation of striped or watered silk. (1839, p.797.)

Towards the end of the century, tastes had changed but the principle was the same. Mrs Orrinsmith suggested a scheme for *The Drawing Room*:

> If the wall hangings are of silk, they may be tightly stretched without pleats or folds; if of wool and silk, wool or cotton they must have groups of pleats with intervals of about twelve inches between. Hooks should be fixed at the junction of the wall and ceiling, and rings upon the hangings, which may be edged with a more or less elaborate fringe, and hang loosely down to the skirting or surbase.' (1877, p.23.)

She added that, if silk or **wool** fabrics were too expensive, 'cotton damasks with woven patterns, printed cottons and Bolton sheetings' were suitable.

Moreland discussed the particular benefits of covering walls in textiles. He said that they tend to soften the decorative effect, which is particularly useful for 'picture galleries or other rooms where many paintings are to be displayed, as softness and depth of tone is obtained by the use of velours or similar goods in suitable colors that would be impossible by other means' (1889, p.194). He then included descriptions of possible wall hanging schemes including 'furring the walls, stretch fitting, pleating as you go or cut and fitted as strips'. Alternatively, 'Cretonnes may be glued on with paste direct but silk or woollen need tacking'. Thirdly, to cover 'walls and ceiling with tufted work use a frame covered with burlap covered with curled hair (best), but tow, moss or cotton could be used. When the top cover is marked out to match marks in burlap, pleat it down, remove from frame and fit to wall.' (ibid. pp 194–200.)

In the 1970s, new techniques of suspending and tensioning fabrics between rail systems known as 'suspended fabric systems' were introduced.

See also **Arras**, **Bergamo**, **Bolton sheeting**, **Caffoy**, **Carpet**, **Dhurrie**, **Fluted silk**, **Fortuny print**, **Gauze**, **Gilt leather**, **Painted cloth**, **Palampore**, **Pane**, **Pintado**, **Savonnerie**, **Say**, **Stained cloth**, **Tapestry**.

FURTHER READING

Kightly, C. (2001). 'The hangings about the hall: an overview of textile wall hangings in late medieval York', *Medieval Textiles*, 28, June, p.306.

Wall hanging

See **Wall covering and hanging**.

Wallpaper curtain

The use of printed-paper for **wall coverings** and **blinds**, intended to replicate fabric, is well known. However, there was a practice of using printed-paper for making window **curtains**. References to 'head papers' consisting of wallpaper backed with newspaper and fitted with **binding** to make **valances** occur in the USA in 1780 (Cummings, 1961, p.33). Draped curtains were also made from textured, pliable paper in the mid- to later nineteenth century. The London firm of Jeffrey and Co is known to have made them.

In 1872, wallpaper curtains were displayed in the International Exhibition. Manufactured by Pavy Pretto and Co of London, they were made from a special paper-like material printed by wallpaper mills, banded, sewn and lined like ordinary curtains. How successful they were is difficult to tell, but it is evident that one critic did not appreciate them. Lady Barker commented in her book, *The Bedroom and the Boudoir*, that: 'The curtains made of it [wallpaper] are not only a sham, but they are generally of very ugly patterns, and hang in stiff ungraceful folds, crackling and rustling with every breath of air, besides being very inflammable.' (1878, p.10.)

Warp

The warp is the name for the yarns that run longitudinally along a woven fabric. Individual strands are known as ends. A binding warp is a secondary warp that binds **weft** yarns. In woven textiles with more than one weft, the binding warp is used to bind the pattern or brocading weft. A pattern, or flushing warp, is used supplementary to the main warp creating a pattern in flats above the ground of the textile. **Wadding** warps (also stuffer yarns) are thick warps inserted into fabrics to give relief to the surface and weight to the cloth.
See also **Brocade: Warp**, **Cretonne: warp printed**, **Printed textile: warp**, **Rep**, **Weave**.

Warp-printed

See **Clouded**, **Cretonne: warp printed**, **Tapestry carpet**.

Washing furniture

A term used to describe printed cottons, chintzes, **calicoes** and the like, particularly in reference to the eighteenth century. The ability to wash one's furnishings, especially in the case of bed **drapery**, was important in the age of bed bugs. Mrs Purefoy asked of her mercer: 'I suppose you will warrant [the chintz] standing the colour when it is washed.' (Eland, 1931, p.104) One upholsterer specifically listed the product: James Woodruffe (1761) sold 'Bedsteads with damask, Harrateen, Chenys, Linceys and Washing Furnitures' (*DEFM*, p.1000). A little later, the Gillow Co wrote to a client saying that: 'We presume [the chair] will require some sort of washing cover which requires a good deal of nicety to make them fit well to such sorts of chairs.' (*Gillow Co Records,* Folio 22, p.202.) The Harewood House inventory of 1795 listed '24 Painted Chairs with cane bottoms, Cushions & washing covers'.
See also **Chintz**, **Printed cotton**.

FURTHER READING

Standen, E. (1964). 'English washing furnitures', *Metropolitan Museum of Art Bulletin*, vol.XXIII, 3, pp 109–24.

Washstand mat

Mats for the washstand were an essential accoutrement for the Victorian bedroom. They were intended to protect the surface of the table. Embroidered **linen** cloths lined with **baize**, or **oilcloth** squares trimmed with **embroidery**, were often used.
See also **Toilette**.

Waxing

A method of feather-proofing a cloth with a wax compound.
See also **Calico (Down-proof)**, **Ticking**.

Weave

There are a number of basic weave structures in fabrics:

Basket weave

Versions of plain-weave where two **wefts** cross two **warps**. The result is a basket weave, such as **hopsack**.
See also **Abbot's cloth**, **Druid's cloth**, **Huckabuck**, **Monk's cloth**, **Oxford cloth**.

Damask weave

An effect usually created by a **satin** weave where a glossy warp face contrasts with the matt weft producing a play of light and shadow. Simple versions are reversible, e.g. **linen** damask **tablecloths**.
See also **Damask**.

Dobby weave

Dobby weaves are produced using a mechanism that controls the harnesses that operate the warps to produce cloths with small-scale geometric designs.
See also **Bark cloth**, **Bird's-eye**, **Huckabuck**, **Tablecloth**.

Gauze weave

A weave that uses the principle of two different types of warp: one that is controlled by a normal shaft; the other (a doup warp) is controlled by a shaft that can move sideways on the loom. This means that the threads can cross the normal warp and are helped by the weft. The diaphanous fabrics created were popular for applied work such as **embroidery** or **brocaded stitching**.
See also **Gauze**, **Grenadine**, **Leno**.

Lampas weave

A compound-weave type with additional warps and/or wefts.
See also **Brocatelle**, **Camaca**, **Lampas**, **Tissue**.

Satin weave

In a satin weave, more warp yarns run over the weft and are interlinked at widely spaced intervals to create a smooth unbroken surface effect. **Sateen** is woven in the opposite manner, with more weft yarns running over the warp, but creating a similar effect. Satin weave was widely used for **silk** and linen but less so for **cottons** until mercerisation was developed.
See also **Brocade**, **Brocatelle**, **Cuttanee**, **Damask**, **Everlasting**, **Lampas**, **Russell**, **Satin**, **Velvet Satin**, **Venetian cloth**.

Simple or plain-weave

Plain-weave is the simplest weave system where every individual warp thread interlaces with every weft thread. It is widely used for materials, from the finest silks to **gauze** and print grounds. A variation on plain-weave is basket weave, in which several warp and weft yarns are respectively grouped together and woven as one. Many plain-weave fabrics rely on a denser warp or weft yarn, or even groups of yarns to create a ribbed-effect fabric. In the case of **kilims** and **Navajo rugs**, many more weft yarns are employed on a scant warp, for example.
See also **Buckram**, **Cambric**, **Camlet**, **Casement cloth**, **Check**, **Cheese cloth**, **Chintz**, **Cretonne**, **Crash**, **Dimity**, **Gingham**, **Grosgrain**, **Lawn**, **Muslin**, **Tabby**, **Tapestry**, **Voile**, **Webbing**.

Tapestry weave

See **Tapestry**.

Twill weave

In twill weave, the wefts run over one or more warp yarns in offset progression to create the effect of diagonal lines, or they may create zigzag, **bird's-eye**, or **diapering** effects. The process uses three or more shafts so quite complicated patterns can be woven relatively simply. Twill was

also used for the ground effects of elaborate patterned fabrics and is often associated with **table linen**. **Serge** is a typical twill weave.
See also **Bolton sheeting**, **Bomber cloth**, **Covert**, **Denim**, **Kersey**, **Moleskin**, **Say**, **Silesia**, **Ticking**, **Webbing**.

Velvet weave
A two-warp system that has the second warp raised over wires or rods to create loops that may be cut or uncut.
See also **Velvet**.

FURTHER READING
Emery, I. (1966). *Primary Structures of Fabrics*, Washington, DC: Textile Museum.

Webbing (aka Girth web)
A closely woven narrow fabric used in the foundation of **upholstery** and beds. The webbing may be used to give shape and support to a chair or sofa frame, seat or back. It may also be used to support a **spring** platform, or it may be tensioned to support loose **cushions** or to build up a drop-in seat. The principle of webbing is that it should be resilient and not be stretched too tightly. Its application may be either by the so-called French webbing method, using 4 inch (10 cm) wide web, which is close fitted and completely covers the base; or the English method, using 2 inch (5 cm) wide web, which is used to create a more open criss-cross mesh. Both these methods are used worldwide.

The earliest webbing was known as girth web, the term coming from the girth straps that were used to hold saddles etc. onto an animal or to fit round a barrel. Girth weavers wove this webbing, which was a branch of narrow weaving (see the Randle Holme quotation in **Upholstery**).

An early record of the use of webbing is from 1381–2, 'in girth webbys capistris flokkys' (Durham MS. Hostill. Roll, *OED*). Two hundred years later, in 1571, it was being sold 'in ye great shoppe ij groce of gyrthwebe and xv peces at vijs. ijd. ye groce' (*Wills and inventories, illustrative of the history, manners, language, etc. of the northern counties of England*, Surtees Society, 1835, 36). Its use in beds is recorded in Ralph Blakestone's will in 1548, which included 'a trussing bed with gyrthes' (Edwards, 1964, p.321). Its use for bed supports was later recorded in 1634, when Sir Thomas Herbert noted that 'The better sort sleep upon cots or beds two foot high, matted or done with girth web' (*Some Years Travels*, p.149).

Since the sixteenth century, the supporting system for upholstery has been based on varieties of webbing laid across the seat cavity of a chair or sofa frame. Its use in chair-work was noted in 1582, when Thomas Grene, a cofferer, was paid for 'bottoming double girth webb and work' (Beard, 1997, p.284). Nearly 100 years later, the process was regularised. The Upholders' Company Byelaws of 1679 refer to the fact that 'all chaires, stoles, cowches and squabb whatsoever they be made of shall be cross girt in the bottome with new sailcloth being made to be put on sale by any person using the trade of an Upholder' (Houston, 1993, p.58). This decree was apparently effective as a 1698 petition to Parliament mentioned that seat furniture was using 'great quantities' of girth web 'all of our own growth and manufacture' (Symonds, 1934, pp 221–2).

Webbing can made be made from natural materials, including **linen**, **jute** or **cotton**, or, in the twentieth century, from synthetics such as reinforced rubber or **polypropylene**. The nature of the yarns used in making the web is often a useful indicator of age and history of some upholstered furniture. For example, fibre analysis would indicate that if the yarn were of cotton, it was made in the twentieth century, if of jute, the web would be post-1830, and if of either flax or **hemp**, it is likely to be prior to that date. The method of weaving is also an indicator. Initially, before 1700, webbing was made in a plain-weave, which was fairly open and irregular. By 1800, the texture was denser. From the beginning of the nineteenth century, a twill weave was introduced, as plain-weave was being derided as cheap. Varieties changed over time. In the late eighteenth century, the types of webbing included common, brown, strong brown, blue and **diaper** web. *The Dictionary of Needlework* described the various webs as **Manchester**, Holland, black or red, and stay tapes (Caulfeild & Saward, 1887, p.517).

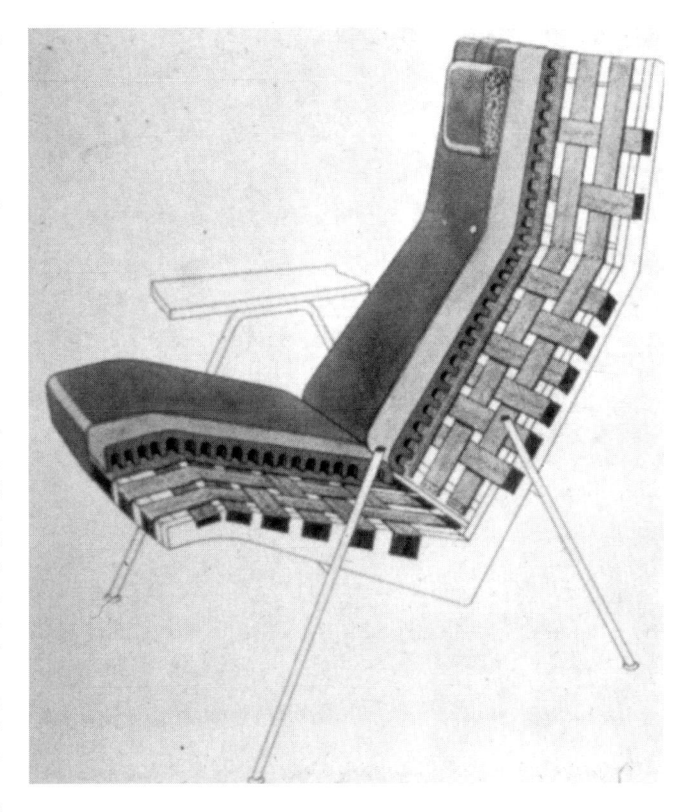

140. Example of webbing on a chair with a latex cushion, c.1955 (Private Collection)

A distinction also existed in the twentieth century between English and Scotch webbing (superior) and Belgian or Continental (for use in less strained areas, such as backs and arms of work). The term 'best black and white' is a reference to the black and white herringbone patterns that are a feature of high-grade webbing.

Jute webbing
A less expensive, but more resilient form of webbing that was introduced in the nineteenth century and specifically designed for upholstery.

Plastic webbing
The use of 'webbing' made from **polypropylene** or similar yarns (Fabweb) was adopted in the latter half of the twentieth century for hammock-shaped chairs and chairs designed for outdoor use.

Steel webbing
This was a ¾ inch (2 cm) wide steel strap that was plain, perforated or corrugated and punched so that springs could be easily fitted onto it.

142. Wilton manufacture detail showing rods and blades to cut looped pile, c.1960 (Private Collection)

Cheaper upholstered furniture of the twentieth century used this webbing method.
See also **Rubber webbing**, **Spring**.

FURTHER READING
Milne, E.C. (1983). *History of the Development of Furniture Webbing*, Leeds: Private print.
Milne, E.C. (1984). 'Development of English webbing', *Antique Collecting*, May, pp 8–12.

Weft
The weft or stuffer yarns are the transverse strands of a fabric woven through the **warp**. Individual weft threads are known as picks. A brocading weft does not cross the full width of the cloth but is limited to where it is needed for the pattern. A pattern weft is supplementary to the main weft and runs the width of the fabric to create a pattern or enhance a design. A weft **pile** may also be created using a supplementary weft or filling, whilst a **wadding** or stuffer weft produces relief effects and adds weight to a cloth.
See also **Weave**.

White damask
See **Linen**.

Whitework
A term for white decoration of white cloth used for clothing and domestic situations, especially for bedding and window **curtains**. From the later eighteenth century, white **muslin** was often elaborated with **lace** insertions, needle-run designs or **appliqué**. **Coverlets** using supplementary **weft** loops or long floats of white yarns in **damask** or geometric designs were produced from early in the eighteenth century.
See also **Bolton coverlet**.

Wilton carpet
A particular **carpet** weave, whose name is derived from Wilton, a town in the south of Wiltshire, noted since the reign of Queen Elizabeth I for the manufacture of carpets. The term is applied to a **worsted warp** faced carpet, woven in factories at a range of sites, using handlooms with a **jacquard** until the 1850s, when the process was mechanised. It is a similar weave to Brussels carpet but with a thicker **pile** and a **velvet** finish caused by cutting the pile. The pile threads run continuously into the carpet and are integral to the weaving process. Because of this, the range of colours used is limited (the number of frames indicates the number of colours), although extra colours can be 'planted'.

141. Wilton carpet loom showing jacquard cards overhead, c.1960 (Private Collection)

The traditional Wilton loom incorporates a jacquard selector. The weave is made up of standard **linen** or **jute** warp, a chain warp and stuffer yarns. Between each warp were additional threads that made colour and pattern arranged in spools behind the loom. Each spool contained enough yarn for the carpet's length, but was only raised to the surface as the pattern required. Therefore, the excess yarn ran beneath the surface until required. Wires temporarily woven into the carpet formed the pile. When removed, those wires fitted with a blade cut the pile as Wilton; those without a blade made loops as Brussels carpet. Six blades represented a cheaper quality whilst twelve represented a better-quality manufacture.

Traditionally, Wilton carpet was woven at 27 inches (68.6 cm) wide (a Flemish **ell**) on a handloom. Bishop Pococke, writing in 1754, noted that 'Wilton is famous for a manufacture of carpets, like those of Turkey, but narrow – about three quarters of a yard wide, which is in the hands of three people.' (Sherrill, 1996, p.222.) Wilton carpet was mainly used for floorcoverings, although examples exist of its use for **upholstery**. In 1769, James Beekman wrote to Thomas Harris in London and requested that he 'send me as much fine wilton carpeting as will cover 7 chair bottoms, [with] small figure and bright-colours' (Roth, 1967, p.38).
See also **Bed carpet**, **Brussels carpet**, **Cinema pile carpet**, **Carpet fitting and planning**, **Moquette carpet**, **Tapestry carpet**, **Velvet carpet**.

FURTHER READING
Bartlett, J.N. (1978). *Carpeting the Millions, The Growth of Britain's Carpet Industry*, Edinburgh: John Donald.

Window carpet
Simply, a woven carpet-like textile used for hanging at windows. In 1602, the Countess of Bedford mentions 'two window turkey carpets of my own making' (Boynton, 1971, pp 27, 29). In 1624, the Sackville family purchased 'a window carpet of ye same [wrought velvet] of crimson trimmed

with gold lace and fringe' (Beard, 1997, p.293). In 1658, Lady Sussex commented that: 'Concerning the choice of a small carpet, if it will not serve for a window it will serve for a foot carpet' (Macquoid, 1904, p.177).

Window cloth

A textile fitted into a window frame or embrasure to protect the interior from the elements. Some were made from **arras** or **verdure** and would hang across the window opening. At Henham in 1602, there were 'two window cloths of tapestry work'. Other references seem to confirm that these were generally of **tapestry** (Thornton, 1978, p.362).
See also **Curtain**.

Window curtain

See **Curtain**.

Window shade fabric

See **Austrian shade cloth**, **Blind holland**, **Blind**.

Windowsill cover

A later nineteenth-century covering for a windowsill, complete with a fitted **lambrequin** or **pelmet**. They were fitted with pockets hidden under the lambrequin and were often made at home.

Wire blind

See **Blind: Wire**.

Wood carpet

A later nineteenth-century, mainly American, substitute for parquet flooring that used strips of wood about a ¼ of an inch (6.4 mm) thick, glued to **muslin** or **drill** backing and produced on a roll, which was then laid over the original wooden floor. Popular in the last quarter of the nineteenth century, it was priced to compete with **carpeting**. The designs ranged from simple strips and pre-planned **borders** to complex bordered and panel designs that could be made up to fit a room.

In September 1894, *Household News* noted that 'wood carpeting is more and more coming into vogue as housekeepers understand its advantages in the matter of cleanliness and beauty' (Winkler & Moss, 1986, p.197). A similar description was published ten years later, which seemed to identify wood carpet as a parquet-type process:

> Hard wood is now almost universally provided in the building of a new house; but where an old floor is impossible to use, the wood carpet may be adopted. This was originally made in France, and it can be procured in two different thicknesses, in squares or diagonal pieces that are nailed down over the old floors, the brads then being puttied over to match the colour of the wood. Wide borders of various coloured woods, or simply straight lines, of a darker colour than that of the body of the room, are used to finish the edge of the wood carpets. (Kellogg, 1905, p.136.)

Wool

(a) The scoured and washed virgin sheep's wool which has been used as an **upholstery** and bedding filling. It may be used pure or as an ingredient in woollen flock and its varieties.
(b) Animal wool (protein fibre) that has been spun into yarn: the two main distinctions are between wool and worsted. Woollen cloths are woven from carded short staple fibres. The cloth is often fulled or shrunk to make it denser. Worsted cloths are tightly spun from long staple fibres, ensuring a parallel arrangement in the yarn to create a finer cloth. Wool is generally a resilient fibre that is durable, shape-regaining and flexible.
See **Algerian**, **Art serge**, **Baize**, **Barracan**, **Berlin wool-works**, **Billiard cloth**, **Blanket**, **Bocking**, **Broadcloth**, **Bunting**, **Caddow**, **Calimanco**, **Camlet**, **Camleteen**, **Cassimere**, **Cheney cloth**, **Crewel and crewel-work**, **Drugget**, **Everlasting**, **Felt**, **Fledge**, **Flannel**, **Frieze**, **Harrateen**, **Kendal**, **Kidderminster stuff**, **Merino**, **Mockado**, **Moreen**, **Paragon**, **Perpetuana**, **Plaid**, **Plush**, **Rateen**, **Rattinet**, **Rep**, **Rugg**, **Russell**, **Saxony**, **Say**, **Scarlet**, **Sempiternum**, **Serge**, **Shoddy**, **Suede**, **Tweed**, **Wadmal**, **Woollen flock**, **Worsted**.

FURTHER READING

Bischoff, J. (1842). *A Comprehensive History of the Woollen and Worsted Manufactures,* London: Smith Elder.
Latour, A. (1948). 'Names and kinds of woollen fabrics of 17th and 18th century France', *CIBA Review*, 67, pp 2473–5.

Woollen flock

A woollen filling material used by upholsterers and mattress-makers and once considered a superior filling material. As early as 1474, the Mystery of Upholders petitioned the Lord Mayor of London against the use of 'imitation flock' by complaining about 'mattresses stuffed with hair and flocks and sold for flocks … cushions stuffed with hair and sold for flocks which have been deceivably made to the hurt of the King's liege people' (Houston, 1993, p.5). Its prestige may be reflected in the example of Ralph Grynder who, in 1637, used '4 baggs of flox for the backe of 2 french chairs and 2 couch heads' for Henrietta Maria's works at Greenwich (Beard, 1997, p.289).

In 1744, George Bowes was supplied with a 'Holland quilt filled with the best carded blanket flocks and tufted with silk tufts' (Medlam, 1990, p.151). Much later, its popularity as a filling material was still recorded by Thomas Sheraton, who noted flock as 'a kind of wool used by upholsterers for mattresses' (1803, p.210).

Its reputation appears to have declined during the twentieth century. In 1949, it was noted that there are 'various graduations, ending in the veriest rubbish, composed of old woollen cloths, rugging, and rags of different kinds which are torn to pieces and cleaned by powerful machinery, and rendered fit for the purpose of stuffing' (Bitmead, 1949, p.16).

Nevertheless, it was a very common **stuffing** material. Later twentieth century regulations deemed that it should be not less than 70 per cent wool obtained from the finishing processes of newly woven, **felted** or knitted woollen textiles. 'Washed flock' contains not less than 50 per cent wool, either old or new. 'Washed woollen mixture' contains 70 per cent animal fibre, whether old or new. Flock can use recycled, shredded wool cloth that is often matted into a felt.

In mattress-making, a layer of wool is often placed over a hair pad to prevent the hair penetrating the **tick**, and to give a softer finish. The process is called topping. Woollen flock is also known as rag flock, black flock or linsey wool.
See also **Flock**, **Mattress-making**, **Upholstery**, **Wool**.

Wool-work

See **Berlin wool-work**, **Needlework**.

Worcester carpet

A horsehair-faced **carpet** that was apparently very hardwearing. In 1884, the furnishing store, Maple and Co, sold it, but rather disparagingly said: 'While the wear-resisting capabilities cannot be disputed, yet, from their tendency to so quickly look shabby, they are not very much in favour.' (*Concerning Carpets*, 1884, p.70.)

Workhouse sheeting
Coarse twilled and unbleached cloth used for **sheets** and bedroom **curtains**. It was often embroidered with Turkey red, and much used as a base for **embroidery** purposes in the later nineteenth century. Lady Barker commented upon this material: 'I know a whole wing of "bachelors' quarters" papered by fluted Japanese curtains, and they are exceedingly pretty. The curtains of these rooms are of workhouse sheeting lined and bordered with Turkey red, and leave nothing to be desired for quaint simplicity and brightness' (*The Bedroom and Boudoir,* Barker, 1878, p.10).
See also **Bolton sheeting**, **Sheet**.

Worsted
The designation probably derived from the name of a parish in Norfolk, north of Norwich. The term can refer to both the fibre and the cloth woven from it. The cloth is defined as a **woollen** fabric or **stuff** made from well-twisted yarn, spun of long staple wool combed to lay the fibres parallel. From a furnishing point of view, it has been used for many centuries. An early reference from 1307 discussing worsted mentions that '*en la ville de Norwiz en la count de Norfolk draps q home appele worth tedes*' (Leaf, 1934). Arnold Monteny's inventory of 1386 had a quantity of worsted cloth:

> one great chamber [amongst others] striped in white and red of worsted, that is to say 1 coverlet, 1 tester, 1 bed-ceiling, 3 curtains, 6 hangings of 5 yards in length, and 2 and a half in width, 2 tapestries for forms, each of four yards in length and 6 cushions… (Steer, 1958, p.155.)

In 1411, a will again noted worsted being specified in bed hangings: 'bequeath to Robert, my eldest son, a reed bedde of worsteyd.' (*Early English Wills,* 1882, p.19), while in 1465 there was reference to a bed and the 'coverlyte of whyte werstede longyng therto' (*Paston Letters*, 1904, IV. 201, *OED*).

Embroidered work in worsteds (often called crewels) was a particular use of the yarns. When visiting Windsor Castle in 1702, Celia Fiennes commented upon the beds, where she saw: 'One with a half bedstead as the new mode, dimity with fine shades of worsted works well made up.' (1947, p.277.)

Worsted yarns have been used in the weaving of a range of upholstery cloths.
See also **Amens**, **Bed cloth**, **Bombazet**, **Caddis**, **Calimanco**, **Camlet**, **Carpet worsted**, **Challis**, **Cheney**, **Crape**, **Crewel and crewelwork**, **Damask**, **Fringe: Worsted**, **Harrateen**, **Lasting**, **Merino**, **Mohair**, **Monk's cloth**, **Moreen**, **Paragon**, **Plaid**, **Plush**, **Poplin**, **Rateen**, **Saxony**, **Serge**, **Shagg**, **Shalloon**, **Stuff**, **Tammy**, **Terry**, **Velvet**, **Wool**, **Worsted binding**.

FURTHER READING

James, J. (1857). *History of the Worsted Manufacture in England…*, London: Longman, reprinted 1968, London: Frank Cass.
Kerridge, E. (1985). *Textile Manufactures in Early Modern England,* Manchester: Manchester University Press.

Worsted binding
A fine binding made from **worsted** yarns. In 1887, *The Dictionary of Needlework* noted that upholsterers and saddlers employed these bindings (Caulfeild & Saward, 1887, p.524).
See also **Binding**, **Carpet binding**.

Worsted damask
See **Damask: Worsted**.

Worsted fringe
See **Fringe: Worsted**.

Woven tape
See **Braid**, **Curtain tape**, **Galloon**, **Tape**.

Yarn
A broad term for less highly-processed single or plied structures, which are often associated with weaving and knitting, as opposed to thread, which is often associated with sewing. Yarns may be described in many ways to reflect their structure, texture, spinning, etc.
See also **Thread**, **Weave**.

Yorkshire carpeting
A term for ingrain or Scotch carpeting produced in the county of Yorkshire. Yorkshire carpet was certainly known early in the eighteenth century. In 1783, the American trader, Samuel Rowland Fisher, visited Leeds (Yorkshire) where he 'walked to see the carpet manufactory of the Scots kind' and he also called on a manufacturer of list carpeting (Hummel, 1975, p.67). In 1795, half-yard (45.7 cm) wide Yorkshire stair carpet was for sale second-hand from one of the apartments of Hampton Court (Hefford, 1987, p.4).

It was not always considered highly. In February 1822, Henry Lace opened a business in Liverpool and advertised his new enterprise, explaining that he did *not* stock Yorkshire carpets! (*DEFM*, p.521.) Yorkshire carpeting was also mentioned in the patent granted to Adam Eve, the inventor of Prince's Patent Union Carpet. The patent taken out in 1825 discussed the manufacture of carpets: 'The manner in which Kidderminster, Yorkshire or Scotch carpeting have always been wove' (Patent no.5254).
See also **Ingrain carpet**, **List carpet**, **Scotch carpeting**.

Abbreviations Used

DEFM	*Dictionary of English Furniture Makers*
EE Misc.	*Early English Miscellanies in prose and verse*, 1856
OED	*Oxford English Dictionary*
Rot. Parl.	*Rotuli Parliamentorum* (1783)
Testamenta Ebor.	*Testamenta Eboracensia*

Bibliography

Ackermann R. (1809–1828), *The Repository of Arts etc.* (3rd series), London: R. Ackermann.

Adburgham, A. (1973). *Liberty's: A Biography of a Shop,* London: George Allen and Unwin.

Addy, J. (1976). *The Textile Revolution,* London: Longman.

Adrosko, R. (1990). 'Identifying late 19th-century upholstery fabrics' in Williams, M.A. (ed.), *Upholstery Conservation,* preprints of a symposium held at Colonial Williamsburg, 2–4 February, American Conservation Consortium, East Kingston, NH, pp 2–4.

Adrosko, R. (1998). *A Checklist of Carpet Patent Models in the Textile Collection,* Washington, DC: National Museum of American History, Smithsonian Institution.

Agius, P. (1984). *Ackermann's Regency Furniture and Interiors,* Marlborough: Crowood Press.

Albrecht-Mathey, E. (1968). *The Fabrics of Mulhouse and Alsace 1750–1850,* Leigh-on-Sea: F. Lewis.

American Fashion and Fabrics (various dates). *AF Encyclopaedia of Textiles,* Eaglewood Cliffs: Prentice Hall.

Anon. (1880). *Artistic Homes or How to Furnish with Taste: a handbook for all housekeepers,* London: Ward Lock.

Anon. (1949). 'Early American textiles', *CIBA Review,* 76, May, Basle, Switzerland: CIBA, pp 2773–98.

Anon. (1958). 'Curtains and coverings for upholstered furniture', *CIBA Review,* 126, May, pp 26–32.

Anon. (1961). 'Machine made carpets', *CIBA Review,* 4.

Anon. (1986). *Rideaux et tentures: fenetres et portes, lits, passementerie, tentures de tissus et de papier peint, garniture de sieges depuis le Moyen Age,* Paris: Baschet.

Anquetil, J. (1996). *Silk*, Paris: Flammarion.

Archer, T.C. (1877). 'Wool & its applications' in Bevan, G.P. (ed.), *British Manufacturing Industries,* 2nd edition, London: Edward Stanford.

Arnolde, R. (1502). *The Customs of London Otherwise Called Arnold's Chronicle,* London, reprinted 1811, London: F.C. and J. Rivington.

Arrowsmith, J. (1819). *An Analysis of Drapery or the Upholsterer's Assistant, Illustrated with Twenty Plates to Which is Annexed a Table, Showing the Proportions for Cutting One Hundred and Thirty Various-sized Festoons,* London: M. Bell, reprinted 1993, New York: Acanthus.

Art Journal, (1851). *The Art Journal Illustrated Catalogue of the Great Exhibition – London 1851,* London.

Autour du Fil, (1991). *Encyclopédie des arts textiles,* 20 vols, Editions Fogtdal: Paris.

Ayres, J. (1981). *The Shell Book of the Home in Britain,* London: Faber and Faber.

Ayres, J. (2003). *Domestic Interiors, the British Tradition 1500–1850,* New Haven and London: Yale.

Baersen, R. (1988). *Courts and Colonies, The William and Mary Style in Holland, England and America,* New York: Cooper Hewitt Museum.

Bagnall, W.R. (1893). *The Textile Industries of the United States,* Cambridge, Mass.: Riverside Press.

Bailey, N. (1730 and later editions). *Dictionarium Britannicum,* London: T. Cox.

Baker, G.P. & J. (1984). *From East to West, Textiles from G.P. and J. Baker,* exh. cat., London: Victoria and Albert Museum, 9 May–14 October 1984.

Bangert, A. (1988). *Italian furniture design: ideas, styles, movements,* Munich: Bangert Verlag.

Barker, Lady (1878). *The Bedroom and the Boudoir,* London: Macmillan.

Barron, J. (1814). *Modern and Elegant Designs of Cabinet and Upholstery Furniture,* London: W.M. Thiselton.

Barrow, L. (1758). *Dictionarium Polygraphicum: Or, the Whole Body of Arts Regularly Digested,* (second edition, corrected, etc.), London: C. Hitch and L. Hawes.

Bartlett, J.N. (1978). *Carpeting the Millions, The Growth of Britain's Carpet Industry,* Edinburgh: John Donald.

Baumgarten, L. (1975). 'The textile trade in Boston 1650–1700' in Quimby, Ian (ed.), *Arts of the Anglo-American Community in the Seventeenth Century,* Charlottesville: University Press of Virginia, pp 219–73.

Baumgarten, L. (1990). 'Curtains, covers and cases: upholstery documents at Colonial Williamsburg' in Williams, M.A. (ed.), *Upholstery Conservation,* preprints of a symposium held at Colonial Williamsburg, 2–4 February, American Conservation Consortium, East Kingston, NH, pp 103–35.

Baumgarten, L. (1993). 'Protective covers for furniture and its contents', *American Furniture,* pp 3–14.

Beard, G. (1993). 'Decorators and Furniture makers at Croome Court', *Furniture History,* XXIX, pp88–114.

Beard, G. (1994). 'Some eighteenth century English seats and covers re-examined', *The Magazine Antiques,* 146, June, pp 842–9.

Beard, G. (1997). *Upholsterers and Interior Furnishing in England 1530–1840,* London and New Haven: Yale.

Beard G. & Westman A. (1993). 'A French upholsterer in England, Francis Lapiere 1653–1714', *Burlington Magazine,* 135, August, pp 515–24.

Beawes, W. (1752 and later editions). *Lex Mercatoria Rediviva; or The Merchant's Directory,* 4th edition enlarged by Thomas Mortimer, London: J. Rivington and Sons.

Beck, S.W. (1882). *The Draper's Dictionary: a Manual of Textile Fabrics: Their History and Application,* London: The Warehousemen & Drapers' Journal Office.

Beecher, C.E. (1846). *The Treatise on Domestic Economy for the Use of Young Ladies…,* New York: Harper Bros.

Beecher, C.E. & Stowe, H.B. (1869). *The American Woman's Home,* New York: J.B. Ford.

Beecher, Mrs H.W. (1879). *All Around the House, or How to Make Homes Happy,* New York: Appleton and Co.

Beer, A.B. (1970). *Trade Goods. A Study of Indian Chintz in the Collection of the Cooper-Hewitt Museum of Decorative Arts and Design,* Washington, DC: Smithsonian Institution Press.

Bendure, Z. & Pfieffer, G. (1947). *America's Fabrics,* New York: Macmillan.

Bennett, H. (1937). *More for Your Money,* London: Spon, and New York: Chemical Publishing Co.

Bentley, M.M. (*c.*1924). *Good Housekeeping's Book on the Business of Housekeeping: a Manual of Method,* New York: Good Housekeeping.

Bertram, J. (1968). *The Story of British Carpets,* London: Carpet Review.

Best, M. (1990). *Stumpwork: Historical and Contemporary Raised Embroidery,* London: B.T. Batsford.

Bevan, G.P. (ed.) (1876). *British Manufacturing Industries,* London: Edward Stanford.

Beyer, R. (1958). 'Furnishing fabrics in present-day interior decorating', *CIBA Review,* 11, May, pp 2–7.

Bigelow-Hartford Carpet Co (1925). *A Century of Carpet and Rug Making in America,* New York.

Bimont, J.-F. (1770). *Principes de L'Art du Tapissier,* Paris: Lottin l'Aîné.

Birdwood, G.C.M. (1880). *Industrial Arts of India,* Piccadilly, London: Chapman and Hall.

Birdwood, G.C.M. (1893, reprinted in 1893). *The Register of Letter of the Governour and Company of Merchants of London Trading into the East Indies, 1600–1619,* edited by Sir George Birdwood, assisted by William Foster, London: Quaritch.

Bitmead, R. (1912 and later edition). *The Practical Upholsterer and Cutter Out,* London: Technical Press.

Blackshaw, H. & Brightman R. (1961). *Dictionary of Dyeing and Textile Printing,* London: George Newnes.

Blount, T. (1656 and later editions). *Glossographia,* reprinted 1972, Hildesheim: G. Olms.

Blundell, N. (1968-1972). *The Great Diurnal of Nicholas Blundell of Little Crosby, Lancashire, 1702-1728,* in 3 vols, Frank Tyrer (ed.), Liverpool: Lancashire and Cheshire Record Society.

Board of Trade (1947). *Carpet Industry Working Party Report,* London: HMSO.

Boudet, P. & Gomond, B. (1981). *Le Passementerie,* Paris: Dessain and Tosca.

Bowden, P.J. (1962). *The Wool Trade in Tudor and Stuart England,* London: Macmillan.

Bower, H. (2000). *Textiles at Temple Newsam, The Roger Warner Collection,* Leeds: Leeds Art Collection Fund.

Boynton, L. (1965). 'Sir Richard Worsley's furniture at Appuldurcombe Park', *Furniture History,* 1, pp 39–59.

Boynton, L. (1967). 'High Victorian furniture: the example of Marsh and Jones', *Furniture History,* 3, pp 54–91.

Boynton L. (1968). 'Thomas Chippendale at Merstham-le-Hatch', *Furniture History,* 4, pp 81–104.

Boynton, L. (ed.) (1971). *The Hardwick Hall Inventories of 1601,* London: Furniture History Society.

Boynton, L. & Goodison, N. (1968). 'Thomas Chippendale at Nostell Priory', *Furniture History,* 4, pp 10–61.

Bradbury, F. (1904). *Carpet Manufacture,* Belfast: Municipal Technical Institute.

Brande, W.T. (1842). *Dictionary of Science, Literature and Art,* London: Longman.

Brady, G. (1947). *Materials Handbook,* New York: McGraw-Hill Book Co.

Braun-Ronsdorf, M. (1958). 'Curtains and coverings for upholstered furniture', *CIBA Review,* 11, May, pp 26–33.

Braun-Ronsdorf, M. (1958). 'French furnishing fabrics', *CIBA Review,* 11, May, pp 17–25.

Braun-Ronsdorf, M. (1958). 'Furnishing fabrics of the Middle Ages and Renaissance', *CIBA Review,* 11, May, pp 8–16.

Braun-Ronsdorf, M. (1960). 'Mixed fabrics of later times', *CIBA Review,* 12, pp 16–28.
Brears, P. (1999). *All the Kings Cooks: The Tudor Kitchens of Henry VIII at Hampton Court,* London: Souvenir Press.
Bredif, J. (1989). *Classic Printed Textiles from France 1760–1843: Toiles de Jouy,* London: Thames and Hudson.
Bremner, D. (1869). *The Industries of Scotland,* Edinburgh: A. and C. Black.
Bridgeman, H. & Drury, E. (1978). *Needlework: An Illustrated History,* London: Paddington Press.
Brightman, A. (1964). 'Woollen window curtains – luxury in Colonial Boston and Salem', *Antiques,* 97, December, pp 184–7.
Brightman, A. (1972). *Window Treatments for Historic Houses 1700–1850,* Washington, DC: National Trust for Historic Preservation.
Brinton, R.S. (1919). *Carpets,* London: Pitman.
Brown C.M. & Gates, C.L. (1872). *Scissors and Yardstick; or All About Dry Goods,* Hartford, Conn.: C.M. Brown and F.W. Jaqua.
Brown, R. (1822). *The Rudiments of Drawing Cabinet and Upholstery Furniture,* 2nd edition, London: J. Taylor.
Brunn, M. (1990). 'Treatment of cellulose nitrate coated upholstery' in Williams, M.A. (ed.), *Upholstery Conservation,* preprints of a symposium held at Colonial Williamsburg, 2–4 February, American Conservation Consortium, East Kingston, NH, pp 449–55.
Buchanan, F. (1917). *Home Crafts of Today and Yesterday,* New York: Harper and Bros.
Burbank, E. (1922). *Be Your Own Decorator,* New York: Dodd Mead.
Burke, D.B. et al. (1986). *In Pursuit of Beauty: Americans and the Aesthetic Movement,* New York: Metropolitan Musuem of Art.
Burnham, D.K. (1980). *Warp and Weft – a Dictionary of Textile Terms,* Toronto: Royal Ontario Museum.
Burnham, H. & D. (1972). *Keep Me Warm One Night, Early Hand Weaving in Eastern Canada,* Toronto: University of Toronto Press in cooperation with the Royal Ontario Museum.
Burton, J.R. (1890). *A History of Kidderminster,* London: Eliot Stock.
Bury, H. (1981). *A Choice of Design 1850–1980, Fabrics by Warner and Sons Ltd, Braintree,* Essex: Warner and Sons.
Bury St. Edmund's. (1850). *Commissary of Wills and Inventories from the Registers of the Commissary of Bury St. Edmund's and the Archdeacon of Sudbury,* London: printed for The Camden Society.
Butterworth, A. (1922). *Manual of Household Work and Management,* London: Longman.
Byrne, J.C. (1862). *Red, White and Blue Sketches of Military Life,* vol.2, London: Hurst and Brackett.

Camden Society. (1855). *Camden Miscellany,* vol.III. London:
Campbell, R. (1747, reprinted in 1969). *The London Tradesman,* Newton Abbot: David and Charles.
Candee, H.C. (1930). *Weaves and Draperies, Classic and Modern,* New York: Stokes and Co.
Carlano, M. & Salmon, L. (1985). *French Textiles From the Middle Ages to the Empire,* Hartford, Ct.: Wadsworth Athenaeum.
Carpenter, F.G. (*c.*1911). *How the World is Housed,* New York: American Book Co.
Cassell's Household Guide (1870 and various later editions). *Cassell's Household Guide: Being a Complete Encyclopaedia of Domestic and Social Economy,* 4 vols, London: Cassell.
Cassell's Technical Educator (1875). London: Cassell.
Caulfeild, S.F.A. & Saward, B.C. (1887). *The Dictionary of Needlework,* London: Upton Gill.
Centre International d'etude des Textiles Anciens (CIETA) (1959, and other editions). *Fabrics: A Vocabulary of Technical Terms,* Lyon: CIETA.
Chambers, E. (1728 and later editions). *Cyclopaedia or a Universal Dictionary of Arts and Sciences,* London: D. Midwinter et al.
Chapman, S. (1997). *The Textile Industries,* edited by Stanley Chapman, 4 vs, London: I.B. Tauris.
Chapman, S.D. & Chassagne, S. (1981). *European Textile Printers in the Eighteenth Century: A Study of Peel and Oberkampf,* London: Heinemann.
Charles, R. (1874). *Three Hundred Designs for Window-draperies, Fringes and Mantel Board Decorations,* London: R. Charles.
Charles, R. (1877). *For Upholsterers, Decorator Cabinetmakers: Designs for Various Styles of Fringes and Draperies for Windows, Beds and Mantel Boards…,* London: R. Charles.
Chattopadhyaya, K. (1969). *Carpets and Floorcoverings of India,* Bombay: D.B. Taraporevala Sons and Co.
Chippendale, T. (1754). *The Gentleman and Cabinet Maker's Director,* 3rd edition 1762, London: T. Chippendale.
Chisholm, H. (1911, 11th ed.). *Encyclopaedia Britannica: A Dictionary of arts, sciences, literature and general information.* Cambridge: Cambridge University Press.
Christie, G. (1964). *Storeys of Lancaster, 1848–1964,* London: Collins.
Church, E.R. (1883). *How to Furnish a Home,* New York: D. Appleton.
Clabburn, P. (1976). *Needleworkers' Dictionary,* London: Macmillan.
Clabburn, P. (1988). *The National Trust Book of Furnishing Textiles,* London: Viking.
Clark, H. (1985). *Textile Printing,* Aylesbury: Shire.
Clay, J.W. (ed) (1902). *Testamenta Eboracensia,* Durham: Surtees Society
Clayton, M. & Oakes, A. (1954). 'Early calico printers around London', *Burlington Magazine,* 96, 614, May, pp 135–9.
Clouzot, H. & Morris, F. (1927). *Painted and Printed Fabrics,* New York: Metropolitan Museum of Art, reprinted 1974, New York: Arno Press.
Cole, G. (1892, 1900). *A Complete Dictionary of Dry Goods,* Chicago: J.B. Herring.
Cole, A. & Williamson, H. (1941). *The American Carpet Manufactures: a History and Analysis,* Cambridge, Mass.: Harvard University Press.
Coleman, O. (1899). *Successful Houses,* Chicago: Herbert Stone and Co.
Coleridge, A. (1966). 'James Cullen cabinet-maker at Hopetoun House', *Connoisseur,* 163, no.657, November, pp 154–9, no.658 December, pp 231–4.
Coleridge, A. (1967). 'Sir Lawrence Dundas and Chippendale', *Apollo,* 86, 67, September, pp 168–225.
Collard, F. (1985). *Regency Furniture,* Woodbridge: Antique Collectors' Club.
Conradsen, D. (1993). 'The stock-in trade of John Hancock and Company', *American Furniture,* pp 39–54.
Cook, C. (1878). *The House Beautiful, Essays on Beds, Tables, Stools and Candlesticks,* New York: Scribner Armstrong.
Cooke, E.S. (ed.) (1987). *Upholstery in America and Europe From the Seventeenth Century to World War I,* New York: Norton.
Cooper, G.R. (1971). 'The Copp family textiles', *Smithsonian Studies In History and Technology,* Washington, DC: Smithsonian Institute Press.
Cornforth, J. (1978). *English Interiors 1790–1848: The Quest for Comfort,* London: Barrie and Jenkins.

Cornforth, J. (1986). 'British state beds', *The Magazine Antiques*, 29, February, pp 392–401.

Cornforth, J. (1989). 'A Georgian patchwork' in Jackson Stops, G.J., Schochet, L., Orlin, C. & MacDougall, E.B. (eds), *The Fashioning and Functioning of the British Country House*, Washington, DC: National Gallery of Art.

Cornforth, J. (2005). *Early Eighteenth Century Interiors*, New Haven and London: Yale.

Cornforth, J. and Fowler, J. (1974). *English Decoration in the Eighteenth Century*, London: Barrie and Jenkins.

Cotgrave, R. (1611). *A Dictionarie of the French and English Tongues*, London, various editions, reprinted 1968, Menston, Yorks.: Scolar Press.

Courtaulds Ltd. (1964). *Courtauld's Vocabulary of Textile Terms*, 2nd edition, London: Courtauld Institute.

Crofton, J. (1834). *The London Upholsterer's Companion*, London: The Author.

Cummin, H. (1940). 'Early seersucker', *Antiques*, 38, July, pp 231–2.

Cummin, H. (1940). 'Moreen – a forgotten fabric', *Antiques*, 38, July, pp 286–7.

Cummin, H. (1940) 'What was dimity in 1790', *Antiques*, 38, July, pp 23–5.

Cummin, H. (1941). 'Calamanco', *Antiques*, 39, April, pp 182–4.

Cummin, H. (1942). 'Camlet', *Antiques*, 42, December, pp 309–12.

Cummings, A.L. (1961). *Bed Hangings, A Treatise on Fabrics and Styles in the Curtaining of Beds 1650–1850*, Boston: SPNEA.

Cummings, A.L. (1964). *Rural Household Inventories: Establishing the Names, Uses and Furnishings of Rooms in the Colonial New England Home 1675–1775*, Boston: SPNEA.

Curtis, H.P. (1921). *Glossary of Textile Terms*, Manchester: Marsden and Co.

Cust, L. (1911). 'Notes on the collection formed by Thomas Howard, Earl of Arundel and Surrey', *Burlington Magazine*, 20, November, pp 97–100, 233–6, 341–3.

Cust, L., Walpole Society (1918). *The Lumley Inventories*, vol.VI, Oxford: Oxford University Press.

Davidson, H.C. (1900). *The Book of the Home*, London: Gresham Pub. Co.

Defoe, D. (1725). *A New Voyage Round the World*, London, various printings, reprinted 1895, London: Dent.

Defoe, D. (1727). *A Tour Through the Whole Island of Great Britain*, 2 vols, London: Printed for Peter Davies.

Defoe, D. (1727). *The Complete English Tradesman*, London: Charles Rivington, reprinted 1987, Gloucester: Sutton.

Delany, Mrs (1861). *Autobiography and Correspondence of Mary Granville*, edited by Lady Llanover, London: Richard Bentley.

De Marinas, F. (1993). *Velvet: History, Techniques, Fashions*, London: Thames and Hudson.

Denny, G.G. (1923). *Fabrics and How to Know Them: Definitions of Fabrics, Practical Textile Tests, Classification of Fabrics*, Philadelphia and London: J.B. Lippincott Company (later editions 1928, 1936, 1942).

Deville, J. (1878–80). *Dictionnaire du tapissier critique et historique de l'ameublement francais*, Paris: C. Claesen.

Dickinson, S.N. (1840). *Boston Almanac.* Boston: B.B. Mussey and Thomas Groom.

Dietz, B. (1972). *The Port and Trade of Early Elizabethan London: Documents*, Leicester: London Record Society.

Dodd, G. (1844–5). *British Manufactures. The Textile Manufactures of Great Britain*, 5 vols, London: Charles Knight.

Donzel, C. & Sabine, M. (1992). *L'Art de passementerie, et sa contribution à l'historie de la mode et de la décoration*, Paris: Chêne.

Dornsife, S.J. (1975). 'Design sources for nineteenth century window hangings', *Winterthur Portfolio*, 10, pp 69–99.

Dornsife, S.J. (1981). 'Timetable of carpet technology', *Nineteenth Century*, 7, Autumn, pp 38–41.

Dossie, R. (1764). *Handmaid to the Arts*, London: printed for J. Nourse, pp 479–502.

Downing A.J. (1850). *The Architecture of Country Houses*, New York: Appleton.

Dresser, C. (1873). *Principles of Decorative Design*, London: Cassell, Petter & Galpin.

Dubois, M.J. (1967). *Curtains and Draperies. A Survey of the Classic Periods*, New York: Viking.

Dwyer, C.P. (1856). *The Economic Cottage Builder*, Buffalo: Wanzer, McKim and Co.

Dyer, C. (1989). *Standards of Living in the Later Middle Ages*, Cambridge: Cambridge University Press.

Dyer, E. (*c*.1923). *Textile Fabrics*, Boston: Houghton, Mifflin Co.

Eames, P. (1971). 'Documentary evidence concerning the character and use of domestic furnishings in the fourteenth and fifteenth centuries, *Furniture History*, 7, pp 41–60.

Earnshaw, P. (1986). *Lace Machines and Machine Lace*, London: Batsford.

Eastlake, C. (1868, 1872, 1878). *Hints on Household Taste*, London: Longman.

Eberlein, H.D., McLure, A. & Holloway, E.S. (1919). *Practical Book of Interior Decoration*, Philadelphia: Lippincott.

Edis, R. (1881). *Decoration and Furnishing of Town Houses*, London: Kegan Paul.

Edwards, C. (1991). 'Furnishing a home at the turn of the century: the use of estimates from 1875 to 1910', *Journal of Design History*, 4, 4, pp 233–9.

Edwards, C. (1996). 'Floorcloth and linoleum: aspects of the history of oil-coated materials for floors', *Textile History*, 27, 2, Autumn, pp 148–71.

Edwards, F. (1870). *Our Domestic Fireplaces*, London: Longman Green.

Edwards, J. (1975). *Crewel Embroidery in England*, London: Batsford.

Edwards, R. (1964). *The Shorter Dictionary of English Furniture*, London: Country Life.

Eland, G. (ed.) (1931). *Purefoy Letters 1735–1753*, London: Sidgwick and Jackson.

Eland, G. (ed.) (1947). *Shardeloes Papers of the Seventeenth and Eighteenth Centuries*, Oxford: Oxford University Press.

Ellison, T. & Ramsden, G.W. (1929). *The Cooperative Apprentice: Dry Goods Departments, Textbook for Co-operative Apprentices in Drapery, Boot and Shoe, Furnishing and Allied Depts…*, Manchester: Cooperative Union Ltd.

Ellwood, G. (1995). 'James Newton', *Furniture History*, 31, pp 129–205.

Elyot, Sir T. (1531). *The Boke Named the Gouvenour*, London: Thomas Berthelet, reprinted 1970, Menston: Scolar Press.

Emery, I. (1966 and later edition). *The Primary Structure of Fabrics*, Washington, DC: Textile Museum.

Emmison, F.G. (introduction) (1954). *Ingatestone Hall in 1600: An Inventory*, Chelmsford: Essex Record Office.

Evelyn, J. (1959). *Diary of John Evelyn*, edited by E.S. De Beer, Oxford: Oxford University Press.

Fairclough, O.L. (1981). *Textiles by William Morris and Morris & Co., 1861–1940*, London: Thames and Hudson.

Faraday, C. (1929). *European and American Carpets and Rugs*, Grand Rapids: Dean Hicks, reprinted 1990, Woodbridge: Antique Collectors' Club.

Farnam, A. (1985). 'Household textiles in the Essex Institute Salem Mass.', *The Magazine Antiques*, 127, April, pp 888–95.

Fell, S. (1920). *The Household Account Book of Sarah Fell of Swarthmoor Hall*, ed. Norman Penney, Cambridge: Cambridge University Press.

Fenning, D. (1768). *The Royal English Dictionary*, London: R. Baldwin.

Fiennes, C. (1949, 1995). *The Illustrated Journeys of Celia Fiennes*, edited by C. Morris, Stroud: Alan Sutton.

Filp, R.K. (1882). *Enquire Within Upon Everything*, London: Houlston and Sons.

Fiske, P. (ed.) (1975). *Imported and Domestic Textiles in Eighteenth Century America*, Proceedings of the 1975 Irene Emery Round Table on Museum Textiles, Washington, DC: Textile Museum.

Fleming, E. (1997). 'Staples for genteel living: the importation of London household furnishings into Charleston during the 1780s', *American Furniture*, pp 335–58.

Fleming. E.R. (1927). *An Encyclopaedia of Textiles From Earliest Times to the Beginning of the 19th Century*, New York: E. Wehye.

Fletcher, B. (1910). *The English Home*, New York: C. Scribner's Sons.

Florio, J. (1578). *Firste Fruites, Also a Perfect Induction to the Italian and English Tongues*, London: Thomas Dawson.

Foster, A. (1917). *Interior Decoration for Modern Needs*. New York: Frederick Stokes.

Foster, W. (1906). *English Factories in India*, Oxford: Clarendon Press.

Frankl, P. (1954). *American Textiles*, Leigh-on-Sea: F. Lewis.

French, A. (ed.) (1990). *Conservation of Furnishing Textiles*, post-prints of a conference held at the Burrell Collection, Glasgow, March, Scottish Society for Conservation and Restoration.

French, L.H. (1903). *Homes and Their Decoration*, New York: Dodd, Mead and Co.

French, T. and Co. (1937). *The Book of Soft Furnishing*, Manchester: The Company.

French, T. and Co. (1947). *Soft Furnishing Workroom Manual*, Manchester: The Company.

Frohne, H. (1937). *Decorative Draperies*, Garden City, New York: Funk and Wagnall Co.

Fryer, J. (1698, reprinted 1909). *A New Account of East India & Persia*, 3 vols, London: Hakylut Society.

Funk, I.K. & Wagnall, A.W. (1895). *Practical Standard Dictionary*, New York: Funk and Wagnall Co.

Furnivall, F.J. (ed.) (1868). *The Babees Book … The bokes of Nurture of Hugh Rhodes and John Russell, Wynkyn de Worde's Boke of Keruynge, The Books of Demeanor, The Boke of Curtasye, Seager's Schoole of Vertue, &c. &c., With Some French & Latin Poems on Like Subjects, and Some Fore Words on Education in Early England*, London: EETS.

Furnivall, F.J. (ed.) (1882, reprint 1964). *The Fifty Earliest English Wills in the Court of Probate, 1387-1439*. Early English Text Society (Original Series no. 78). Reprint Woodbridge: Boydell and Brewer.

Garnier-Audiger, A. (1869). *Nouveau Manuel Complet du Tapissier, Décorateur et Marchand de Meubles*, Paris: Roret.

Garrett, E.D. (1985). 'The American home', *The Magazine Antiques*, Part V, 128, pp 259–654.

Garrett, R. & A., (1877). *Suggestions for House Decoration in Painting, Woodwork and Furniture*, Philadelphia: Porter and Coates.

Gauldie, E. (ed.) (1969). *The Dundee Textile Industry, 1790–1885: from the papers of Peter Carmichael of Arthurstone*, vol.6, 4th series, Edinburgh: Scottish History Society.

Gentle, N. (2001). 'A study of the late seventeenth century state bed from Melville House', *Furniture History*, 37, pp 1–16.

Gibbs, C. (1914). *Household Textiles*, Boston: Mass.: Whitcomb and Barrows.

Gibbs, J. (1994). *Curtains and Drapes: History, Design, Inspiration*, London: Cassell.

Gilbert, C. (1967). 'The Temple Newsam furniture bills', *Furniture History*, 3, pp 16–28.

Gilbert, C. (1976). 'Wright and Elwick of Wakefield 1748–1824, a study in provincial patronage', *Furniture History*, 12, pp 34–5.

Gilbert, C. (1978). *The Life and Work of Thomas Chippendale*, London: Studio Vista/Christies.

Gilbert, C. & Beard, G. (1986). *Dictionary of English Furniture Makers 1660-1840*. London: Furniture History Society.

Gilbert, C., Lomax, J. & Wells-Cole, A. (1987). *Country House Floors*, Leeds: Leeds City Art Galleries.

Gill, K. & Eastop, D. (eds) (2001). *Upholstery Conservation: Principles and Practice*, Oxford: Butterworth-Heinemann.

Gillispie, C. C. (1959). *A Diderot pictorial encyclopedia of trades and industry manufacturing and the technical arts in plates selected from "L'Encyclopédie, ou Dictionnaire raisonné des sciences, des arts et des métiers"*, New York: Dover.

Gilroy, C.G. (1845). *The History of Silk, Cotton, Linen, Wool, and Other Fibrous Substance*, New York: Harper & Brothers.

Ginsburg, M. (1991). *The Illustrated History of Textiles*, London: Studio Editions.

Glaister, E. (1880). *Needlework*, London: Macmillan.

Glazier, R. (1923). *Historic Textile Fabrics*, London: Batsford.

Gloag, H. (1921). *Simple Furnishing and Arrangement*, London: Duckworth.

Gloag, J. (1990). *Dictionary of Furniture*, London: Unwin Hyman.

Goldsmith, O. (1774). *A History of the Earth and Animated Nature*, London: J. Nourse, reprinted 1990, London: Studio Edition.

Goodale, E. (1954). 'Furnishing fabrics of the past two hundred years', *Journal of the Royal Society of Arts*, February, pp 195–216.

Goodale, E. (1971). *Weaving and the Warners, 1870–1970*, Leigh-on-Sea: F. Lewis.

Gooderson, P.J. (1996). *Lord Linoleum, Lord Ashton and the Rise of the British Oilcloth and Linoleum Industry*, Keele: Keele University Press.

Gordon, B. (1978). *Domestic American Textiles: a Bibliographic Source Book*, Pittsburgh: Pittsburgh Centre for the History of American Needlework.

Gow, I. (1983). 'William Trotter's Estimate for Furnishing No. 3 Moray Place Edinburgh *c.*1825', in *Furniture History*, XIX, 1983.

Grayson, M. (1984). *Encyclopaedia of Textiles, Fibres and Non-woven Fabrics*, New York: John Wiley.

Great Britain, Public Record Office (*c.*1999). *A Brief History of Textiles in England: Introduction to Archival Materials*, Richmond: Public Record Office.

Great Exhibition. (1851). *The Illustrated Exhibitor, A Tribute to the World's Industrial Jubilee: Comprising Sketches, by Pen and Pencil, of the Principal Objects in the Great Exhibition of the Industry of all Nations*, London: Cassell.

Great Exhibition. (1851-1852). *Official descriptive and illustrated catalogue by authority of the Royal Commission*, London: Spicer Brothers.
Grier, K. (1988). *Culture and Comfort, People, Parlours and Upholstery, 1850–1930*, New York: Strong Museum.

Hale, S. (1840). *The Workwoman's Guide*, London: Simpkin Marshall and Co.
Hall, H. (1901). *Society in the Elizabethan Age*, London: Swan Sonnenschein.
Halliwell, J.O. (1847). *Dictionary of Archaic and Provincial Words*, London: J.R. Smith.
Halliwell, J.O. (1854). *Ancient Inventories of Furniture Pictures etc.*, London: private circulation.
Halliwell, J.O. (ed.) (1856). *Early English Miscellanies ... from an inedited manuscript of the fifteenth century.* London: Warton Club.
Hannan, W.I. (1902). *The Textile Fibres of Commerce: A Handbook*, London: C. Griffiths.
Hardouin-Fugier, E. et al. (1994). *Les Etoffes Dictionnaire Historique*, Paris: Editions de L'amateur.
Harmuth, L. (1915, 1924). *Dictionary of Textiles*, New York: Fairchild Publications
Harrison, C.C. (1881). *Women's Handiwork in Modern Homes*, New York: Charles Scribner's Sons.
Harrison, W. (1577). *The Description of England*, edited by George Edelen, 1968, Ithaca, New York: Folger Shakespeare Library, Cornell University Press.
Harte, N.B. (1997). *The New Draperies in the Low Countries and England, 1300–1800*, Oxford: Oxford University Press.
Harte, N.B. & Ponting, K.G. (eds) (1973). *Textile History and Economic History: Essays in Honour of Miss Julia de Lacy Mann*, Manchester: Manchester University Press.
Hasluck, P. (1901). *Bamboo Work*, London: Cassell.
Hasluck, P. (1907). *Window Blinds*, London: Cassell.
Hassall, W.O. (1962). *How They Lived, An Anthology of Original Accounts Written Before 1485*, Oxford: Blackwell.
Havard, H. (1887–90). *Dictionnaire de l'ameublement et de la decoration depuis le XIIIe siècle jusqu'à nos jours*, Paris: Ancienne Maison Quantin, Librairies-imprimeries Réunies, May & Motteroz.
Haweis, Mrs (1881, and later edition 1889). *Art of Decoration*, London: Chatto and Windus.
Hawes, S. (1509). *Pastime of Pleasure*, ch.xvi, London: Percy Society.
Hayward, H. & Kirkham, P. (1980). *William and John Linnell, Eighteenth Century London Furniture Makers*, London: Studio Vista.
Heal, Sir A. (1953). *The London Furniture Makers*, London: Batsford.
Heal Ltd (1972). *Catalogues 1853–1934 Middle-class Furnishing*, Newton Abbott: David and Charles.
Heaton, A. (1897). *Beauty and Art*, London: Heinemann.
Hefford, W. (1987). 'Patents for strip carpeting 1741–1851', *Furniture History*, 23, pp 1–7.
Hefford, W. (1992). *Designs for Printed Textiles in England 1750–1850*, London: Victoria and Albert Museum.
Hepplewhite, G. (1789). *The Cabinet Maker and Upholsterer's Guide*, London: I. and J. Taylor.
Hepplewhite, G. (1794 and later editions). *The Cabinet Maker and Upholsterer's Guide; or, Repository of designs for every article of household furniture ... From drawings by A. Hepplewhite and Co ... The Third Edition, improved*, London: I. and J. Taylor.
Herbert, T. (1664). *Some Years Travels into Divers Parts of Africa and Asia the Great*, various editions, London: A. Crook, reprinted 1971, Amsterdam: Theatrum Orbis Terrarum; New York: Da Capo Press.
Herts, B. Russell (*c.*1922). *The Art and Business of Interior Decoration*, Boston: Small Maynard.
Heutte, R. (1972). *Le livre de la passementerie*, Paris: Dourdon.
Heutte, R. (1980). *Les etoffes d'ameublement*, Dourdan: H. Vial.
Higgin, L. (1880). *Handbook of Embroidery*, London: Sampson Low.
Hills, R.L. (*c.*1970). *Power in the Industrial Revolution*, Manchester: Manchester University Press.
Himmelheber, G. (1974). *Biedermeier Furniture*, trans. S. Jervis, London: Faber.
Hodges, F. (1989). *Period Pastimes*, London: Weidenfeld and Nicolson.
Hodgson, F.T. (1891). *The Practical Upholsterer*, New York: Industrial Publication Co.
Hoffman, E. (1974). *Fairchild's Dictionary of Home Furnishings*, New York: Fairchild Publications.
Holly, H.H. (1878). *Modern Dwellings in Town and Country...*, New York: Harper and Bros.
Holme, R. (1688). *The Academy of Armory or A Display of Heraldry*, reprinted 1972, Menston: Scolar Press.
Holmes, Jr, U.T. (1952). *Daily Living in the Twelfth Century, Based on the Observations of Alexander Neckam*, Madison, WI: University of Wisconsin.
Horman, W. (1519). *Vulgaria*, London: R. Pynson, reprinted 1975, Amsterdam: Theatrum Orbis Terrarum.
House Beautiful Furnishing Annual (1926). Boston: The Atlantic Monthly Company.
Household conveniences... (1884). New York: Orange Judd and Co.
Houston, J.F. (1993). *Featherbedds and Flock Bedds, Notes on the History of the Worshipful Company of Upholders*, Sandy: Three Tents Press.
Hummel, C.F. (1975). *Proceedings of the 1975 Irene Emery Round Table on Museum Textiles*, Washington, DC: Textile Museum.
Humphrey, Mrs (1909). *Book of the Home*, London: Gresham.
Humphries, S. (1910). *Oriental Carpets, Runners and Rugs, and Some Jacquard Reproductions*, London: A. and C. Black.
Hunter, G.L. (1913). *Home Furnishing, Facts and Figures About Furniture, Carpets and Rugs...*, New York: John Lane.
Hunter, G.L. (1918). *Decorative Textiles, Coverings for Furniture etc.*, Philadelphia: Lippincott.

Impey, O. (1989). 'Eastern trade and the furnishing of the British country house', *Studies in the History of Art*, 25, pp 177–92.
International Looms Inc. (1938). *The Fabric Encyclopaedia*, New York.
Irwin, J. & Brett, K.B. (1970). *Origins of Chintz*, London: Victoria and Albert Museum.
Irwin J. & Schwartz, P.R. (1966). *Studies in Indo-European Textile History*, Ahmedabad: Calico Museum of Textiles.

J.F. (1695). *The Merchant's Warehouse Laid Open; or the Plain Dealing Linen Draper*, London.
Jackson-Stops, G. (1994). 'A Baroque house and its furnishings: the Hanbury Hall inventory of 1721', *Apollo*, 139, 387, May, pp 10–19.
Jacobs, B. (1957, 1970). *Axminster Carpets, 1755–1957*, Leigh-on-Sea: F. Lewis,
Jacobs, B. (1968). *The Story of British carpets*, London: Carpet Review.
Jacobs, N.W. (1890). *Practical Handbook on Cutting Draperies*, Minneapolis: Harrison and Smith.
James, E. (1880). *Indian Industries*, London: Allen.

James. J. (1857). *History of the Worsted Manufacture in England...*, London: Longman, Brown, Green, reprinted 1968, London: Frank Cass.

Jameson, C. (1987). *Pictorial Treasury of Curtains and Drapery Design 1750–1950*, Thirsk: Potterton Books.

Jarry, M. (1966). *The Carpets of the Manufactory de la Savonnerie*, Leigh-on-Sea: F. Lewis.

Jarry, M. (1969). *The Carpets of Aubusson*, Leigh-on-Sea: F. Lewis.

Jeered, J. (1992). *Encyclopaedia of Textiles*, New York and Oxford: Facts on File.

Jenkins, D.T. (ed.) (1982). *The British Wool Textile Industry 1770–1914*, London: Heinemann Educational.

Jenkins. D.T. (ed.) (1994). *The Textile Industries*, Oxford: Blackwell.

Jenkins, D.T. (ed). (2003). *The Cambridge History of Western Textiles*, 2 vols, Cambridge: Cambridge University Press.

Jenkins, S. (1998). 'The Duke of Chandos and the upholstered rooms at Cannons: how fine fabrics furnished rooms in the early 18th century', *Apollo*, 147, 431, January, pp 10–12.

Jeremy, D.J. (1973). 'Innovation in American textile technology during the early 19th century.' *Technology and Culture*, 14, 1, pp 40–76.

Jervis, S. (1989). 'Blazon of the bed' in 'Les Blazons Domestiques by Giles Corrozet', *Furniture History*, 25, pp 5–35.

Jervis, S. (1997). 'Furniture for the first Duke of Buckingham', *Furniture History*, 33, pp 48–74.

Jobe, B. (1974). 'The Boston furniture industry 1720–1740' in Whitehall, W.M. (ed.), *Boston Furniture of the Eighteenth Century*, Charlottesville, VA: University of Virginia Press, pp 3–48.

Johnson, S. (1756 and later editions). *Dictionary of the English Language*, London: J & P Knapton.

Johnston, D. (1961). 'Surveys of industry, no.5, furnishing fabrics', *Design*, 153, September, pp 42–58.

Johnston, J.A. (2000). 'Furniture and furnishing in seventeenth century Lincoln', *Lincolnshire History and Archaeology*, 35, pp 7–20.

Jones, D. (1997). 'William Trotter's furniture for Kinfauns Castle', *Furniture History*, 33, pp 240–52.

Jourdain, M. (1924). *English Decoration and Furniture of the Early Renaissance*, London: Batsford.

Jourdain, M. (*c*.1910). *The Morant Collection of Old Velvets, Damask, Brocades Etc.*, London: Virtue and Co.

Jourdain, M. (1946). 'Window curtains of the Eighteenth century', *Country Life*, 99, 12 April, pp 668–9.

Joyce, C. (1997). *Textile Design: the Complete Guide to Printed Textiles for Apparel and Home*, New York: Watson-Guptill.

Kaye, A. (1940). *A Students Guide to Housewifery*, London: Dent.

Kellogg, A.M. (1905). *Home Furnishing, Practical and Artistic*, New York: F.A. Stokes.

Kendrick, A.F. (1919). 'British carpets', *Journal of the Royal Society of Arts*, 67, 24 January, pp 136–45.

Kendrick, A.F. & Tattershall, C.E.C. (1922). *Hand-woven Carpets, Oriental and European*, 2 vols, London: Benn, reprinted 1973, New York: Dover.

Kennedy, P.A. (1962). *Nottinghamshire Household Inventories*, Nottingham: Thoroton Society.

Kerridge, E. (1985). *Textile Manufactures in Early Modern England*, Manchester: Manchester University Press.

Kightly, C. (2001). 'The hangings about the hall: an overview of textile wall hangings in late medieval York', *Medieval Textiles*, 28, June, p.306.

Kimball, M. (1929). 'Thomas Jefferson's French furniture', *Antiques*, 15, February, pp 123–8.

Kimball, F. & M. (1947). 'Jefferson's curtains at Monticello', *Antiques*, 52, October, pp 266–8.

King, C. (1721). *British Merchant or Commerce Preserved*, London: J. Darby, reprinted 1968, New York: Kelley.

King, D. (1958). '"Textiles" in the Tudor period, 1500–1603; "Textiles" in the Stuart period, 1603–1714; "Textiles" in the early Georgian period, 1714–1760; "Textiles" in the late Georgian period, 1760–1810, in Edwards, Ralph and Ramsey, L.G.G. (eds), *Connoisseur Period Guides*, London: The Connoisseur.

King, D. (1962). 'Textiles and the origins of printing in Europe', *Pantheon*, XX, pp 23–30.

King, D. (1989). 'Textile furnishing' in McGregor, A. (ed.), *The Late King's Goods*, Oxford: Oxford University Press, pp 307–21.

King, D. & Levey, S. (1993). *Embroidery in Britain from 1200–1750*, London: Victoria and Albert Museum Textile Collection.

King, T. (n.d.). *Fashionable Bedsteads with Hangings, Consisting of Original Designs*, London: T. King.

King, T. (1833). *The Upholsterer's Accelerator, Being Rules for Cutting and Forming Draperies, Valances etc.*, London: Architectural and Scientific Library.

King, T. (1839). *The Upholsterer's Sketchbook of Original Designs for Fashionable Draperies*, London: T. King.

King, T. (1848). *The Upholsterer's Guide; Rules for Cutting and Forming Draperies, Valances etc.*, London: T. King.

Kinne, H. (*c*.1913). *Shelter and Clothing: a Textbook of the Household Arts*, New York: Macmillan and Co.

Kirk, J.T. (1981). 'Tradition of English painted furniture', *Antiques*, 119, January, pp 184–97.

Kirkham, P. (1969). 'Samuel Norman. A study of an eighteenth century craftsman', *Burlington Magazine*, 111, August, pp 500–11.

Kirkham, P. (1974). 'The partnership of William Ince and John Mayhew 1759–1804', *Furniture History*, 10, pp 56–67.

Kirsch Co (1976). *Window Treatments Through the Ages*, Sturgis, Michigan: Kirsch Co.

Kirsch, C.W. (1930). *How to Drape your Windows*, Sturgis, Michigan: Kirsch Co.

Knight, C. (ed.) (*c*.1833–43). *The Penny Magazine of the Society for the Diffusion of Useful Knowledge*, London: Charles Knight.

Knight, E.H. (1877). *The Practical Dictionary of Mechanics*, 4 vols, London: Cassell.

Kraak, D.E. (1996). 'Ingrain carpets', *The Magazine Antiques*, 149, January, pp 182–91.

Landrau, A. (1976). *America Underfoot: A History of Floorcoverings From Colonial Times to the Present*, Washington, DC: Smithsonian Press.

Lardner, D. (1831). *The Cabinet Cyclopedia*, London: Longman Rees.

Lee, R. (1969). *Shades of History*, Chicago: Joanna Western Mills Co.

Leech, P. (1999). '"Who says Manchester says cotton". Textile terminology in the Oxford English Dictionary (1000–1960)' http://www.intralinea.it/intra/vol2/leech/default.htm

Legg, P. (1994). 'The Bastards of Blandford', *Furniture History*, 30, pp 15–42.

Lemire, B. (2003) 'Domesticating the exotic: floral culture and the East India calico trade with England, *c*.1600–1800', *Textile: The Journal of Cloth and Culture*, 1, March, pp 64–85.

Lenoir, G.F. (1890). *Practical and Theoretical Treatise on Decorative Hanging or Guide to Upholstery;* Brussels: Lyon-Clausen.

Lenygon, F.H., (1909). *The Decoration and Furniture of English Mansions During the Seventeenth & Eighteenth Centuries,* London: T.W. Laurie.

Leslie, E. (1841). *The House Book or a Manual of Domestic Economy,* Philadelphia: Carey and Hart.

Leslie, E. (1854). *The Lady's House Book,* Philadelphia: Parery and Macmillan.

Levy, M. (1989). 'George Bullock's partnership with Charles Fraser 1813–1818. and the stock-in-trade sale, 1819', *Furniture History,* 25, pp.145–213.

Levey, S.M. (1983). *Lace, A Visual History,* London: Victoria and Albert Museum.

Levey, S.M. (1998). *An Elizabethan Inheritance: The Hardwick Hall Textiles,* London: National Trust.

Levey, S.M. (2001). *Of Household Stuff: the 1601 Inventories of Bess of Hardwick,* London: National Trust.

Lewis, F. (1935). *English Chintz. From the Earliest Times to the Present Day,* Benfleet: F. Lewis.

Lindley, J. (ed.) (1866). *The Treasury of Botany,* London: Longman Green.

Little, F. (1931). *Early American Textiles,* New York: Century Co.

Little, N.F. (1967). *Floorcoverings in New England Before 1850,* Sturbridge, Mass.: Old Sturbridge Village.

Little, N.F. (1975). 'Floorcoverings', *American Art Journal,* 7, May, pp 107–117.

London Society of Cabinet Makers. (1793). *The Cabinet-Makers' London book of prices, and designs of cabinet work, calculated for the convenience of cabinet makers in general ... The second edition, with additions.* London: printed by W. Brown & A. O'Neil.

Long, H. (1993). *The Edwardian House,* Manchester: Manchester University Press.

Loudon, J.C. (1833, revised 1839). *An Encyclopaedia of Cottage Farm and Villa Architecture and Furniture,* London: Longman.

Low, J. (1986). 'Newby Hall: Two Late Eighteenth Century Inventories', *Furniture History,* 135–75.

Lubell, C. (1976–7). *Textile Collections of the World,* 3 vols, London: Studio Vista.

Luccock, J. (1805). *The Nature and Properties of Wool,* Leeds: E. Baines.

Lynn, C.W. (1980). *Wallpaper in America, from the Seventeenth Century to World War II,* New York: W.W. Norton.

Macke, J.H. (1891). *The Carpet-dealer's Guide…,* Cincinnati: Cranston, Stowe.

Macquoid, P. (1904). *The Age of Oak,* London: Lawrence Bullen.

Macquoid, P. (1905). *Age of Walnut,* London: Lawrence Bullen.

Macquoid, P. & Edwards, R. (1924–7). *The Dictionary of English Furniture from the Middle Ages to the Late Georgian Period,* 3 vols, London: Country Life.

Macquoid, P. & Edwards, R. (1954). *Shorter Dictionary of English Furniture,* London: Country Life.

Malton, T. (1778). *A Complete Treatise on perspective in theory and practise; On the True Principles of Dr. Brook Taylor. Made Clear, in Theory, by Various Moveable Schemes, and Diagrams; and Reduced to Practice, in the Most Familiar and Intelligent Manner.* London: Printed for the Author.

Malynes, G. (1622). *Consuetudo del lex Mercatoria, or the Ancient Law Merchant,* London: Adam Islip.

Mansion House Committee (1889). *Reports of Artisans Selected by the Mansion house Committee to visit Paris Universal Exhibtion.* London: C.F. Roworth

Maple and Co (1884). *Concerning Carpets – The Art Decoration of Floors,* London: The Company.

Markham, G. (1615 and later editions). *English Housewife,* London: J. Harison, reprinted 1986, Kingston: McGill-Queens University Press.

Marsden, J. (2000). 'The Chastleton inventory of 1633', *Furniture History,* 36, pp 23–42.

Marshall, W.H. (1788). *The Rural Economy of Yorkshire,* London: T. Cadell.

Martin, T. (1813). *Circle of Mechanical Arts,* London: R. Rees.

Martin, W.A. (1930). *The Furnishing Soft Goods Department: a Handbook and Guide,* London: E. Benn Ltd.

Mayhew, H. (1861–2). *London Labour and London Poor,* London: Griffin, Bohn and Co, reprinted 1968, New York: Dover.

McIntyre, M.C. & Daniels, P.N. (1991). *Textile Terms and Definitions,* Textile Institute Textile Terms and Definitions Committee, 9th edition, Manchester: The Institute.

Medlam, S. (1990). 'William Greer at Gibside', *Furniture History,* 26, pp 142–56.

Meikle J.L. (1995). 'Presenting a new material: from imitation to innovation with Fabrikoid', *Decorative Arts Society Journal,* 19, pp 8–15.

Mercer, E. (1969). *Furniture 700–1700,* London: Weidenfeld and Nicolson.

Mertens, W. (ed.) (2001). *Transitory Splendour: Interior Textiles in Western Europe 1600–1900,* Antwerp: Hessenhuis Museum, Stadsbestuur, December 2001–March 2002.

Metz, K., Mossinger, I. & Poser, W. (1999). *European Textile Design of the 1920s,* Zurich: Kunstsammlungen Chemnitz and Stemmle.

Mèuntz, E. (1885). *A Short History of Tapestry: From the Earliest Times to the End of the 18th Century,* London: Cassell & Co.

Michie, A.H. (1982). 'The fashion for carpets in South Carolina, 1736–1820', *Journal of Early Southern Decorative Arts,* May, pp 24–48.

Michie, A.H. (1985). 'Upholstery in all its branches: Charleston, 1725–1820', *Journal of Early Southern Decorative Arts,* XI, 2.

Microulis, L. (1988). 'Charles Hindley and Sons, London house furnishers of the nineteenth century: a paradigm of the middle range market', *Studies in the Decorative Arts,* 5, Spring and Summer, pp 69–96.

Midgley, E. (1931). *Technical Terms in the Textile Trade: a Dictionary of Yarns, Cloths, Makes, Weaves and Terms for Spinners, Manufacturers, Merchants, Distributors, etc,* Manchester: Emmott & Co Ltd.

Miles, L.J. (ed.) (1927). *The Textile Educator. A Comprehensive Practical and Authoritative Guide to Fibre, Yarns and Fabrics in Every Branch of Textile Manufacture,* 8 vols, London: Gresham.

Millar, A. (1908). 'The making of carpets', *Art Journal,* January, April, July, October.

Miller, N.J., Schofield-Tomschin, S. & Kim, S. (1998). 'Consumer's apparel and home furnishings in shopping behaviour in rural communities', *Clothing & Textile Research Journal,* vol.16, 4.

Mitchell, D.M. (1998). 'Coverpanes; Their Nature and Use in Tudor England', *Bulletin de CIETA,* 75, pp 81–96.

Montgomery, C. (1967). *American Furniture, The Federal Period,* London: Thames and Hudson.

Montgomery, F. (1960). 'English textile swatches of the mid eighteenth century', *Burlington Magazine,* 114, 828, June, pp 182–3.

Montgomery, F. (1970). *Printed Textiles: English and American Cottons and Linens 1700–1850,* London: Thames and Hudson.

Montgomery, F. (1984). *Textiles in America 1650–1870: a Dictionary Based on Original Documents, Prints and Paintings, Commercial Records, American Merchants' Papers, Shopkeepers' Advertisements, and Pattern Books With Original Swatches of Cloth,* New York and London: Norton.

Montgomery Ward. (1895, reprinted 1969). *Catalogue and Buyer's Guide*, no.57, Spring/Summer.

Moore, G. (1847). *Extracts from the Journal and Account book of the Rev. Giles Moore, rector of Horstead Keynes, Sussex, from the year 1655 to 1679.* Edited by Robert Willis Blencowe, Sussex Archaeological Collection, vol.I, pp.65-127.

Moore, Revd T. (1829–31). *History of Devonshire From Earliest Times to the Present,* 2 vols, London: R. Jennings.

Moreland, F.A. (1889). *Practical Decorative Upholstery,* Boston: Lee and Shepard, reprinted 1979, as *The Curtain Maker's Handbook,* New York: E.P. Dutton.

Morris, B. (1958). '"Textiles" in the Regency period, 1810–1830; "Textiles" in the early Victorian period, 1830–1860' in Edwards, Ralph & Ramsey, L.G.G. (eds), *Connoisseur Period Guides,* London: The Connoisseur.

Morris, B. (1962). *Victorian Embroidery,* London: Herbert Jenkins.

Morris, C. (ed.) (1949). *Journeys of Celia Fiennes.* London: Cresset Press.

Murphy, W.S. (1910). *The Textile Industries,* 8 vols, London: Gresham.

Murphy, W.S. (1914). *Modern Drapery and Allied Trades,* London: Gresham.

Murray, James. (1888–1928). *A New English Dictionary on Historical Principles,* Oxford: Clarendon Press

Muthesius, H. (1904–5). *The English House,* condensed and translated by Dennis Sharp, London: Crosby Lockwood and Staple.

Neuberger, R. (1934). 'History and development of the leather cloth industry', *Upholstery,* 1, 4, July.

Nichols, J. (1780). *A collection of all the wills, now known to be extant, of the kings and queens of England, to that of Henry VII exclusive,* Reprint: Union, New Jersey. (1999), Law Book Exchange.

Nicholson, P.& M. (1826). *Practical Cabinet Making,* London: Fisher and Jackson.

Nicolas, Sir Harris (1830). *Wardrobe Accounts of Edward IV,* facsimile edition, 1972, London: F. Muller.

Nicolas, Sir Harris (1830). *Privy Purse Expenses.* London: W. Pickering.

Nielson, K.J. (1989). *Understanding Fabrics: a Definitive Guidebook to Fabrics for Interior Design and Decoration,* North Palm Beach: Clark Publishing Co.

Nisbet, H. (1906, 1919, 1927). *Grammar of Textile Design,* London: Scott.

Noetzli, E. (1906). *Practical Drapery and Cutting,* London: Batsford.

Northend, M.H. (1921). *The Art of Home Decoration,* New York: Dodd, Mead.

Nylander, J.C. (1983). *Fabrics for Historic Buildings,* Washington, DC: Preservation Press.

Nystrom, P.H. (1916). *Textiles,* New York: D. Appleton.

Oetzmann and Co (n.d.). *Hints on House Furnishing and Decoration.* London: The Company.

O'Leary, I. (1916). *Department Store Occupations,* Cleveland, Ohio: Survey Committee of the Cleveland Foundation.

O'Neill, C. (1862). *Dictionary of Calico Printing and Dyeing: Containing a Brief Account of All the Substances and Processes in Use in the Arts of Printing and Dyeing Textile Fabrics; with Practical Receipts and Scientific Information,* London: Simpkin, Marshall & Co.

Orme, E. (1807). *An Essay on Transparent Prints, and on Transparencies in General,* London: The Author.

Orrinsmith, Mrs. (1877). *The Drawing Room, Its Decorations and Furniture,* Art At Home Series, London: Macmillan.

O'Shea, M. (1981). *Interior Furnishings: a Critical Appreciation of Recent Developments, Textile Progress,* vol.II, no.I, Manchester: Textile Institute.

Osler, D. (1987). *Traditional British Quilts,* London: Batsford.

Ossut, C. (1996). *Tapisseire d'ameublement,* Paris, H. Vial.

Ostick, E. (ed.) (1955). *The Draper's Encyclopaedia,* London: London Trade Press.

Paine, M. (1990). *Textile Classics: a Complete Guide to Furnishing Fabrics and Their Uses,* London: Mitchell Beazley.

Palisser, Mrs, (1869). *Lace,* London: Sampson Low, reprinted 1984, New York: Dover.

Pallot, B. (1989). *The Art of the Chair in Eighteenth Century France,* Paris: ACR-Gismondi.

Palmer, F. (1921). *Practical Upholstery and Cutting Out of Loose Covers,* London: Benn.

Parisot, Peter (1753). *An Account of the New Manufactory of Tapestry After the Manner of That at the Gobelins; and of Carpets After the Manner of That at Chaillot, &c., Now Undertaken at Fulham,* London: Dodsley.

Parissien, S. (1992). *Curtains and Blinds,* London: The Georgian Group.

Parker, J.H. (1861). *Our English Home, Its Early History and Progress, With Notes on the Interpretation of Domestic Inventions,* Oxford: J.H. Parker.

Parkes, Mrs (1829). *Domestic Duties, or Instructions to Young Married Ladies, on the Management of Their Households…,* London: Longman.

Parry, L. (1983). *William Morris Textiles,* London: Weidenfeld and Nicolson.

Parry, L. (1988). *Textiles of the Arts and Crafts Movement,* London: Thames and Hudson.

Parry, L. (1993). *British Textiles from 1850–1900,* London: Victoria and Albert Museum.

Peel, D.C. (1898). *The New Home: Treating of the Arrangement Decoration and Furnishing of a House of Medium Size to be Maintained by a Moderate Income,* Westminster: A. Constable and Co.

Penderel-Brodhurst, J. (1925). *Glossary of English Furniture of the Historic Periods,* London: John Murray.

Pennant, T. (1768–70). *British Zoology,* 4 vols, London: Chester.

Pepys, S. (1970). *The Diary of Samuel Pepys: a New and Complete Transcription,* edited by Robert Latham and William Matthews, London: Bell.

Perkins, E.E. (1833). *A Treatise on Haberdashery and Hosiery,* London: T. Hurst.

Pettit, F.H. (1970). *America's Printed & Painted Fabrics, 1600–1900,* New York: Hastings House.

Phillips, B. (1994). *Tapestry, A History,* London: Phaidon.

Phillips E. (ed.), Kersey, J. (1658 and later editions). *New World of Words, or Universal English Dictionary,* London: R. Bentley.

Phillips, H. (1912). *Old English Chintzes and Printed Linens: Reproduced in Most Cases from Original Examples of the Georgian Period and from the Original Wood Blocks,* Hitchin: F.W. Phillips.

Ponting, K.G. (1981). *Discovering Textile History and Design,* Aylesbury: Shire.

Porter, G.R. (1831). *A Treatise on the Origin Progressive Import and Present State of the Silk Manufactures,* London: Longman Rees.

Postlethwayt, M. (1751–7). *The Universal Dictionary of Trade Commerce Translated from the French of the Celebrated Monsieur Savary,* 2 vols, London: J. and P. Knapton.

Praz, M. (1964). *An Illustrated History of Furnishing from the Renaissance to the Twentieth Century,* London: Thames and Hudson.
Priestman, M.T. (1910). *Art and Economy in Home Decoration,* New York: J. Lane.
Proctor, M.G. (1972). *Victorian Canvas Work,* London: Batsford.
Pryke, S. (1989). 'A study of the Edinburgh furnishing trade taken from contemporary press notices 1708–1790', *Regional Furniture,* 3, pp 52–67.
Pugin, A.W.N. (1841). *The True Principles of Pointed or Christian Architecture,* London: Weale.

Quimby, I. (ed.) (1974). *Arts of the Anglo-American Community in the Seventeenth Century,* Winterthur Conference Report, Charlottesville: University Press of Virginia.
Quinn, M.J. (*c.*1914). *Planning and Furnishing the Home, Practical and Economical Suggestions for the Homemaker,* New York and London: Harper Bros.

Raine, J. (1835). *Wills and inventories, illustrative of the history, manners, language, etc. of the northern counties of England,* Durham: Surtees Society
Raine, J. (1853). *Richmond, Wills and inventories from the registry of the archdeaconry of Richmond,* Durham: Surtees Society.
Ratzki-Kraatz, A. (1986). 'French Lit-de-parade, "A la duchesse" 1670–1715', *J. Paul Getty Museum Journal,* 14, pp 81–104.
Reed, M. (ed.) (1981). *The Ipswich Probate Inventories 1583–1631,* Woodbridge: Boydell Press for the Suffolk Record Society.
Rees, A. (1810–24). *The Cyclopedia or Universal Dictionary of Arts, Sciences, and Literature,* 41 vols, London: Longman, Hurst.
Reynolds, H. (1812). *Directions for House and Ship Painting,* New Haven: Eli Hudson, reprinted 1978, Worcester, Mass.: American Antiquarian Society.
Roberts, L. (1641). *Treasure of Traffic or a Discourse of Foreign Trade,* London: printed by EP for Nicholas Bourne.
Robertson, L. (1917). *The Healthful House,* Battle Creek, Mich.: Good Health Publishing.
Robinson, G. (1966). *Carpets,* London: Pitman.
Robinson, S. (1969). *A History of Printed Textiles: Block, Roller, Screen, Design, Dyes, Fibres, Discharge, Resist, Further Sources for Research,* London: Studio Vista.
Roche, S. von la (1786). *Sophie in London,* translated by C. Williams, 1933, London: Cape.
Rock, D. (1876). *Textile Fabrics,* London: Chapman and Hall.
Rogers, P. (1987). 'A Regency interior: the remodelling of Weston Park', *Furniture History,* 23, pp 12–34.
Rolt, R. (1756 and later editions). *A New Dictionary of Trade and Commerce,* London: T. Osborne.
Rose, M.B. (1996). *The Lancashire Cotton Industry: A History Since 1700,* Preston: Lancashire County Books.
Rosoman, T. (1986). 'The Chiswick House inventory', *Furniture History,* 22, pp 81–106.
Roth, R. (1967). *Floorcoverings in 18th-Century America,* Smithsonian Papers, Washington, DC: Smithsonian Institution.
Rothstein, N. (1990). *Silk Designs of the Eighteenth Century in the Collection of the Victoria and Albert Museum,* London: Victoria and Albert Museum.
Rowe, A.P. (1973). 'Crewel embroidered bed hangings in Old and New England', *Bulletin,* Museum of Fine Arts, Boston, 71, pp 102–66.
Royal Commission on Historical Manuscripts (1990). *Records of British Business and Industry 1760–1914, Textiles and Leather,* London: HMSO.
Rutt, A. (1935). *Home Furnishing,* London: Chapman and Hall.
Rymarczick, G.R. (1903). *The American Weaver and Catalogue of Woolen and Worsted Fabrics: With Names and Descriptions of the Many Cloths of All Wool, Commercially All Wool, Worsteds, Union Woolens, Cotton Worsteds, Angoras, etc., etc.: Tests for the Discovery of Adulterants in Woolen and Worsted Fabrics, and Ready Reference for Merchant and Salesman,* Boston: Boston Printing Co.

Saint-Aubin, C.G. de (1770). *L'Art du Brodeur,* Paris, translated by N. Scheuer, 1983, Los Angeles: Los Angeles Museum.
Saumarez-Smith, C. (1993). *Eighteenth Century Decoration: Design and the Domestic Interior in England,* London: Weidenfeld and Nicolson.
Savery des Bruslons, J. (1723). *Dictionnaire universal de commerce,* Paris: Jacques Estienne.
Schoelwer, S. P. (1979). 'Form function and meaning in the use of fabric furnishings: a Philadelphia case study 1700–1775', *Winterthur Portfolio,* 14, Spring, pp.25–40.
Schoeser. M. (2003). 'Furnishing and industrial textiles, 1914–2000' in Jenkins, D. (ed.), *The Cambridge History of Western Textiles,* Cambridge: Cambridge University Press, pp 1075–1100.
Schoeser. M. (2003). *World Textiles: A Concise History,* London: Thames and Hudson.
Schoeser, M. & Dejardin, K. (1991). *French Textiles From 1760 to the Present,* London: Thames and Hudson.
Schoeser, M. & Rufey, C. (1989). *English and American Textiles: From 1790 to the Present,* London: Thames and Hudson.
Schopenhauer, J. (1988). *A Lady Travels,* London: Routledge.
Schumacher, F. & Co (1924). *The Development of Various Decorative and Upholstery Fabrics,* New York: The Company.
Schwartz, P.R. & Irwin, J. (1966). *Studies in Indo-European Textile History,* Ahmedabad: Calico Museum of Textiles,
Seal, E.D. (1924). *Furnishing the Little House,* New York and London: Century Publishing.
Sears Roebuck And Company. (1969). *1908 Catalogue No 117: the great price maker,* Chicago: Follett Publishing Company.
Seiler-Baldinger, A. (1994). *Textiles: a Classification of Techniques,* Washington, DC: Smithsonian Institution Press.
Sennex, J. (1721). *A New General Atlas, containing a Geographical and Historical Account of all the Empires, Kingdoms and other Dominions of the World ...,* London: D. Brown
Seymour, R.B. & Mark, H.F. (eds) (1989). *Organic Coatings: Their Origin and Development,* Proceedings of the International Symposium on the History of Organic Coatings, 11–15 September 1989, in Miami Beach, Florida, USA, New York: Elsevier
Sheraton T. (1793 and later editions). *The Cabinet Maker and Upholsterer's Drawing Book,* various editions, London: T. Sheraton.
Sheraton, T. (1803). *The Cabinet Dictionary,* London: W. Smith.
Sheraton, T. (1804–7). *The Cabinet Maker and Artists Encyclopaedia,* London: T. Bensley.
Sheridan, C.M. (1987). 'Textile manufacturing in American history: a bibliography', *Textile History,* 18, 1, pp 59–86.
Sheridan, M. (1953, revised 1955). *The Furnisher's Encyclopaedia,* London: National Trade Press.
Sherrill, S.B. (1976). 'Oriental carpets in seventeenth and eighteenth century America', *The Magazine Antiques,* 109, January, pp 142–67.
Sherrill, S.B. (1996). *Carpets and Rugs of Europe and America,* New York: Abbeville.
Shoolbred and Co (n.d.). *Practical Methods of House Furnishing,* London: The Company.

Shoppell, R.W. (*c*.1887). *Modern houses, Beautiful homes*, New York: Co-operative Building Plan Association.

Siddons, G. (1830). *The Cabinet Maker's Guide*, 5th edition, London: printed for Sherwood Gilbert and Piper.

Silber & Fleming (1885). *Illustrated Pattern Book of Furniture, Carpets, Rugs etc*, London: J.S. Virtue.

Simmonds, P.L. (1858). *Dictionary of Trade Products*, London: Routledge.

Simpson, J. and Weiner, E. (1989). *Oxford English Dictionary*, 2nd edition, Oxford: Oxford university Press.

Sloan, S. (1861). *Homestead Architecture*, Philadelphia: Lippincott.

Smail, J. (1999). *Merchants Markets and Manufacture: The English Wool Textile Industry in the 18th Century*, Basingstoke: Macmillan.

Small, C. P. (*c*.1925). *How to Know Textiles*, Boston: Ginn and Co.

Smee & Son (n.d). *Designs for Window Curtains and Beds*, London: The Company.

Smith, A. (1952). *Soft Furnishing for Craftsmen and Salesmen*, London: Pitman.

Smith, G. (1756 and later editions). *The Laboratory or School of Arts*, London: printed for James Hodges.

Smith, G. (1808). *A Collection of Designs for Household Furniture and Interior Decoration*, London: J. Taylor, reprinted 1970, New York: Praeger.

Smith, G. (1812). *Collection of Ornamental Designs*, London: J Taylor.

Smith, G. (1826). *The Cabinet Maker and Upholsterer's Guide*, London: Jones.

Smith, J. (1687). *The Art of Painting in Oyl...*, London: printed for Samuel Crouch.

Smithells, R. (1948). *Make Yourself at Home, Ways and Means of Furnishing Today*, London: Royle Publications.

Smithells, R. (1950). *Fabrics in the Home: Their Place in the Furnishing Scheme*, London: Jenkins.

Smithells, R. & Woods, S.J. (1936). *The Modern Home: its Furnishing and Equipment*, Benfleet: F. Lewis.

Smyth, J. (1812). *The Practice of the Customs in the Entry, Examination and Delivery of Goods etc*, London: printed for John Richardson.

Society for the Diffusion of Useful Knowledge. (1833–58). *The Penny Cyclopaedia of the Society for the Diffusion of Useful Knowledge*, 30 vols, London.

Society for the Encouragement of Arts, Manufactures and Commerce. (1783). *Transactions of the Society for the Encouragement of Arts, Manufactures and Commerce for 1783*, London: Society of Arts.

Society of Antiquaries of London. (1790). *Household ordinances (A collection of ordinances and regulations for the government of the Royal Household, Edward III to King William and Mary; also receipts in ancient cookery)*. London: John Nichols.

Southall, J. (1730). *A Treatise of Buggs*, London: J. Roberts.

Southey, R., (1807). *Letters from England*: by Don Manuel Alvarez Espriella, (pseud). Translated from the Spanish, 3 vols. London: Longman.

Spofford, H. (1878). *Art Decoration Applied to Furniture*, New York: Harper.

Spufford, M. (1984). *The Great Reclothing of Rural England*, London: Hambeldon Press.

Standage, A. (1865). *Practical Illustrations of Upholstery Work*, London: Atchley & Co.

Stavenow-Hidemark, E. (1990). *18th Century Textiles: the Anders Berch Collection at the Nordiska Museet*, Stockholm: Nordiska Museet Forlag.

Steer, F.W. (1958). 'Smaller houses and their furnishings in the seventeenth and eighteenth centuries', *Journal of the British Archaeological Association*, 3rd series, vols 20–1, pp 140–59.

Steer, F.W. (1969). *Farm and Cottage Inventories of Mid-Essex, 1635–1749*, 2nd edition, London: Phillimore.

Stephenson, J.W. (1926, 1934). *Drapery Cutting and Making: a Practical Handbook for Drapery Workers, Upholsterer, and Interior Decorators*, New York: Clifton and Lawton.

St George, R.B. (ed.), (1988). *Material Life in America 1660–1860*, Boston: North Eastern University Press.

Stokes, J. (1829). *The Complete Cabinet Maker and Upholsterers Guide*, London.

Stow, J. (1598). *Survey of London*, London, reprinted 1971, Oxford: Clarendon Press.

Strachey, J. et al. (eds.). (1767–77). *Rotuli Parliamentorum*. London: Record Commission.

Streitenfeld, A. & L. (1892). *The Practical Decorator: A Collection of Practical and Plain Designs of Window, Bed, and Door Curtains, for Upholsterers and Decorators*, New York: Hessling and Spielmeyer.

Stubbes, P. (1583). *The Anatomie of Abuses*, London: J.R. Jones, reprinted 2002, Tempe, Ariz.: Arizona Center for Medieval and Renaissance Studies in conjunction with Renaissance English Text Society.

Sullivan, O.S. (1953). 'Woven furnishing textiles', *Architectural Review*, 114, October pp 265–8.

Swain, M. (1970). *Historical Needlework*, London: Barrie and Jenkins.

Swain, M. (1991). 'Covered with care', *Country Life*, 185, 11, 14 March, pp 50–53.

Swain, M. (1992). 'Furniture for the Comte D'Artois at Holyrood, 1796', *Furniture History*, 28, pp 98–128.

Symonds, R.W. (1934). 'Turkeywork, beech and japanned chairs', *Connoisseur*, 392, 93, April, pp 221–7.

Symonds, R.W. (1951a). 'English cane chairs', *Connoisseur*, 127, March, pp 8–15.

Symonds, R.W. (1951b). 'Domestic comfort in the medieval home, an illusion dispelled', *Connoisseur*, 130, June, pp 40–47.

Symonds, R.W. & Whineray, B. (1962). *Victorian Furniture*, London: Country Life.

Symonds, W.E. & Furniture Industry Research Association (1981). *A Concise Guide to Upholstery Fabrics*, Stevenage: Furniture Industry Research Association.

Tattershall, C. & Reed, S. (1934, 1966). *A History of British Carpets*, Benfleet: F. Lewis.

Taylor, A. (1874). *History of Carpet Trades*, Heckmondwike: J. Ellis.

Taylor, I. (1836). *Scenes of Commerce or Where Do We Get It From*, London: John Harris.

Taylor, J. (n.d.). *Original and Novel Designs for Decorative Household Furniture Particularly for the Department Connected with Upholstery*, London.

Taylor, J. (1631). *The Praise of the Needle* in Epstein, K. (ed.) (1995), Austin: Curious Works Press.

Taylor, L. (1951). *Know Your Fabrics: Standard Decorative Textiles and Their Uses*, New York: Wiley.

Templeton, J. & J.S. (1880). *Curtains and Portières*, Glasgow: C. and W. Griggs.

Textile Mercury (1950). *The Mercury Dictionary of Textile Terms*, compiled by the staff of Textile Mercury, Manchester: Textile Mercury Ltd.

Thompson, E. (ed.). (1998). *The American Home*, Delaware: Winterthur Museum.

Thompson, E.B. (1917). *The Cotton and Linen Departments*, New York: Ronald Press.

Thomson, W.G. (1973). *A History of Tapestry,* 3rd edition, London: E.P. Publishing.

Thorne, E. & Frohne, H. (1929). *Decorative Draperies and Upholstery,* Grand Rapids: Deane-Hicks.

Thornton, P. (1960). 'Tapisséries de Bergame', *Pantheon,* VI, XVIII, Jahrgang, March.

Thornton, P. (1965). *Baroque and Rococo Silks,* London: Faber and Faber.

Thornton, P. (1974). 'French beds', *Apollo,* 99, 145, March, pp 182–7.

Thornton, P. (1978). *Seventeenth-Century Interior Decoration in England, France and Holland,* London: Yale University Press.

Thornton, P. (1984). *Authentic Décor: The Domestic Interior 1620–1920,* London: Weidenfeld and Nicolson.

Thornton, P. (1991). *The Italian Renaissance Interior, 1400–1600,* London: Weidenfeld and Nicolson.

Thornton, P. & Tomlin, M. (1980). *The Furnishing And Decoration of Ham House,* London: Furniture History Society.

Thorp, V. (1990). 'Imitation leather; structure composition and conservation', *Leather Conservation News,* Spring, 6, 2, pp 7–15.

Throop, L.A. (1912). *Furnishing the Home of Good Taste: a Brief Sketch of the Period Styles in Interior Decoration,* New York: McBride, Nast & Co.

Thurstan, V. (1934). *A Short History of Decorative Textiles and Tapestries,* Ditchling and London: Pepler & Sewell.

Times Furnishing Co (*c.*1936). *Better Furniture,* London: The Company.

Times Furnishing Co (n.d.). *The Times Furnishing Company,* London: The Company.

Tomlinson. C. (1866). *Cyclopaedia of Useful Arts,* 2 vols, London: Virtue.

Tortora, P.G. & Merkel, R.S. (1996). *Fairchild's Dictionary of Textiles,* 7th edition, New York: Fairchild.

Trent, L. (ed.) (2000). *Materials and Techniques in the Decorative Arts: An Illustrated Dictionary,* London: John Murray.

Tryon, T. (1683). *The Way to Health,* London: printed for Andrew Sowle.

Tubbs, M.C. & Daniels, P.N. (eds) (1991). *Textile Terms and Definitions,* Manchester: Textile Institute.

Tuchscherer, J.-M. (1972). *The Fabrics of Mulhouse and Alsace 1801–1850,* Leigh-on-Sea: F. Lewis.

Turner, T. (1894). *Some Account of Domestic Architecture in England...,* Oxford: Parker.

Tweene, C.F. and Hughes, L.E.C. (1940) *Chamber's Technical Dictionary,* London: Chambers W & R.

Ulrich, L. (2001). *The Age of Homespun: Objects and Stories in the Creation of an American Myth,* New York: Knopf.

Ure, A. (1839 and later editions). *Dictionary of Arts, Manufactures and Mines,* London: Longman Orme.

Varney, A. (1883). *Our Homes and Their Adornments,* Detroit: J.C. Chilton.

Various authors (1975). *Identification of Textile Materials,* 7th edition, Manchester: Textile Institute.

Ville de Nantes, *Inventaire Sommaire des Archives communals anterieuries a 1790.* Section HH. (http://www.archives.nantes.fr/PAGES/RESSOURCES/inventaires/fichierspdf/serie_HH.pdf)

Vincent, M. (1988). *The Ladies' Worktable: Domestic Needlework in Nineteenth Century America,* Allentown, PA: Allentown Art Museum.

Von Rosenstiel, H. (1978). *American Rugs and Carpets, Seventeenth Century to Modern Times,* New York: William Morrow and Co.

Wadsworth, A.P. & Mann, J. (1931). *The Cotton Trade and Industrial Lancashire 1600–1780,* Manchester: Manchester University Press.

Wallis, G. (1854). *Special Report, New York Industrial Exhibition, General Report of the British Commissioners,* London: printed by Harrison and Son.

Walton, A. (1935). 'Furnishing textiles', *Royal Society of Arts Journal,* 83, January, pp 168–76.

Walton, K.M. (1973). *The Golden Age of English Furniture Upholstery 1660–1840,* exh. cat., 15 August–15 September, Temple Newsam House: Leeds City Art Galleries.

Walton, K.M. (1986). 'An Inventory of 1710 from Dyrham Park', *Furniture History,* 22, pp 25–80.

Ward & Lock (1880). *Ward & Lock's Home Book, A Domestic Encyclopaedia,* London: Ward & Lock.

Ware, I. (1756). *Complete Body of Architecture,* London: T. Osbourne & J. Shipton.

Warner, F. (1921). *The Silk Industry of the United Kingdom, Its Origins and Development,* London: Drane.

Waterer, J. (1968). *Leather Craftsmanship,* London: G. Bell.

Waterer, J. (1971). *Spanish Leather: History of its Use From 800 to 1800 for Mural Hangings, Screens, Upholstery, Altar Frontals, Ecclesiastical Vestments, Footwear, Gloves, Pouches and Caskets,* London: Faber and Faber.

Watson, Mrs R. (1897). *The Art of the House,* London: George Bell and Sons.

Webster, T. (1828 and later editions). *An American Dictionary of the English Language,* New York: S. Converse.

Webster, T. & Parkes, Mrs W. (1844). *An Encyclopaedia of Domestic Economy,* London: Longman.

Weibel, A.C. (1952). *Two Thousand Years of Textiles: the Figured Textiles of Europe and the Near East,* New York: Pantheon Books.

Weigert, R.A. (1962). *French Tapestry,* London: Faber and Faber.

Wells-Cole, A. (1997). *Art and Decoration in Elizabethan and Jacobean England,* London and New Haven: Yale.

Wescher, H. (1948). 'Textile art in sixteenth century France', *CIBA Review,* 69, July, pp 2514–52.

West, J. (1962). *Village Records,* London: Macmillan.

Westman, A. (1990). 'English window curtains in the eighteenth century', *The Magazine Antiques,* CXXXVII, 6, June, pp 1406–17.

Westman, A. (1993) 'Festoon window curtains in Neo-classical England: An analysis and comparison', *Furniture History,* pp80–7

Westman, A. (1994). 'Francis Lapiere's household inventory of 1715', *Furniture History,* 30, pp 1–14.

Westman, A. (1994). 'Splendours of state, the textile furnishings of the King's apartments', *Apollo,* 390, August, pp 39–45.

Wharton, E. & Codman, O. (1897). *The Decoration of Houses,* New York: Charles Scribner's Sons.

Wheeler, C. (1903). *Principles of Home Decoration,* New York: Doubleday.

White, L. (1988). 'The furnishing of interiors during the time of William and Mary', *The Magazine Antiques,* 134, December, pp 1362–9.

Whittock, N. (1827). *Decorative Painters' and Glaziers' Guide,* London: T. Hinton.

Whytock, A. (1856). 'Recent improvements in carpet manufacture, their use and abuse; with a word on beauty and deformity in carpet design', *Journal of the Society of Arts,* 22 February, pp 240–53.

Willan, T.S. (1962). *A Tudor Book of Rates (1582),* Manchester: Manchester University Press.

Williams, M.A. (ed.) (1990). *Upholstery Conservation,* preprints of a symposium held at Colonial Williamsburg, 2–4 February, American Conservation Consortium, East Kingston, NH.
Williams, H.T. & Jones, Mrs C.S. (1878). *Beautiful Homes or Hints in House Furnishing,* New York: H.T. Williams.
Williamson & Cole Co (1912). *The Home Beautiful,* London: Victoria and Albert Museum.
Willis, R. (1886). *The Architectural History of the University of Cambridge ... Brought Up to the Present Time by J.W. Clark,* 4 vols, Cambridge: University Press.
Wilson, L.L. (1911). *Handbook of Domestic Science and Household Arts for Use in Elementary Schools,* New York: Macmillan.
Wilson, J. (1960). *Decoration and Furnishing, Materials and Practice,* London: Batsford.
Wilson, M. (1838). *The Workwoman's Guide,* 2nd edition 1840, London: Simpkin Marshall.
Wingate, I. (1949). *Textile Fabrics and Their Selection,* New York: Prentice Hall.
Wingate, I. (1979). *Fairchild's Dictionary of Textiles,* New York: Fairchild Books.
Winkler, G.C. (1994). 'Capricious fancy – curtains and drapery 1790–1930', *The Magazine Antiques,* CXLV, January, pp 154–65.
Winkler, G.C. & Moss, R. (1986). *Victorian Interior Decoration; American Interiors, 1830–1900,* New York: Holt.
Wolfe, E. de (1913). *The House in Good Taste,* New York: Century Co.
Wood, D. (2000). *The Practical Encyclopaedia of Soft Furnishings,* London: Lorenz.
Wood, G. (1917). *The Art of Interior Decoration.* New York: Dodd, Mead.
Woodward, D. (1998). 'Straw, bracken and the Wicklow whale', *Past and Present,* 159, May, pp 43–76.
Woolman, M.S. (1913). *Textiles: a Handbook for the Student and the Consumer,* New York: Macmillan.
Worcester, J. (1860). *An Elementary Dictionary of English Language,* London: Lippincott & Co.
Working Upholsterer (1883). *Practical Upholstery,* London: Wyman and Sons.
Wright, A.F. (1917). *Interior Decoration for Modern Needs,* New York: F.A. Stokes Co.
Wright, E. & Broadbent, J. (1995). *Soft Furnishings 1830–1930,* Glebe, NSW: Historic Houses Trust.
Wright, L. (1962). *Warm and Snug,* London: Routledge.
Wright, T. (1851, 1862). *A History of Domestic Manners and Sentiments of the Middle Ages,* London: Chapman and Hall.
Wright, T. (1871). *The Homes of Other Days,* London: Trubner and Co.

Yapp, G.W. (1879). *Art Industry: Furniture, Upholstery and House Decoration,* London: J.S. Virtue and Co, reprinted 1972, Farnborough: Gregg.
Yorke, J. (1994). 'The very valuable household furniture ... and other effects of Sir Thomas Robinson Bart, Dec.', *Furniture History,* 30, pp 150–82.
Yorke, J. (1996). 'The furnishing of Stafford house by Nicolas Morel 1828–1830', *Furniture History,* 32, pp 46–80.
Young, A. (1770). *A Six Month Tour Through the North of England,* London: W. Strahan.
Young, F.H. (1944). *A Century of Carpet-making 1839–1939,* Glasgow: Jones Templeton and Co.
Young Ladies Treasure Book (1884). London: Ward Lock.
Yule, Sir Henry (1903). *Hobson-Jobson: A Glossary of Colloquial Anglo-Indian Words and Phrases, and of Kindred Terms, Etymological, Historical, Geographical and Discursive,* new edition edited by William Crooke, London: J. Murray.

UNPUBLISHED

Collings, C. (1972–3). 'A history of furnishing fabrics with particular reference to printed upholstery', unpublished MPhil thesis, University of Leeds.
Gillow Company Records, City of Westminster Library, London.
Leaf, M. (1934). 'A glossary of textile fabrics used in England prior to AD1500: their history and application', unpublished MA thesis, University of Leeds (School of History).
Mitchell, D.M. (1998). 'Fine table linen in England 1450–1750, the supply ownership and use of a luxury commodity', unpublished PhD thesis, University of London.
Powell, C. (1987). 'A research tool for reference work on late eighteenth century and early nineteenth century upholstered furniture...', unpublished typescript, Winterthur Museum and Library.
Rogers, K.W. (1994). 'The Art and Mystery of Upholstery', unpublished MA thesis, Royal College of Art.
Speirs, Judi Sarah (1996). 'A tale of two houses: the consumption of luxury soft furnishings 1790–1825', unpublished MA thesis, University of Southampton.
Tilson, Helen (1977). 'From flock to feather and harden to Holland. The beds of Nottingham, 1688–1757', unpublished MA thesis, University of Nottingham.
Walton, K.-M. (1980). 'Eighteenth century upholstery in England with particular reference to the period 1754–1803: The work and status of the upholsterer', unpublished MPhil thesis, University of Leeds.